Windows 10

the missing manual®

The book that should have been in the box®

Windows 10

the missing manual®
The book that should have been in the box®

David Pogue

O'REILLY®

Beijing | Cambridge | Farnham | Köln | Sebastopol | Tokyo

Windows 10: The Missing Manual

by David Pogue

Copyright © 2015 David Pogue. All rights reserved.
Printed in the United States of America.

Published by O'Reilly Media, Inc., 1005 Gravenstein Highway North,
Sebastopol, CA 95472.

O'Reilly Media books may be purchased for educational, business, or sales
promotional use. Online editions are also available for most titles: *safari.oreilly.
com*. For more information, contact our corporate/institutional sales department:
800-998-9938 or *corporate@oreilly.com*.

September 2015:   First Edition.
October 2015:   Second Printing.

ISBN: 978-1-491-94717-3
[LSI]

Table of Contents

The Missing Credits .... **XV**

Introduction **1**
    What's New in Windows 10 1
    About This Book 8
    The Very Basics 11
    About MissingManuals.com 16

Part One: The Windows Desktop

Chapter 1: Desktop & Start Menu **19**
    The Lock Screen 19
    The Login Screen 20
    The Desktop 22
    Meet the Start Menu 22
    Start Menu: The Left Side 24
    Start Menu: The Right Side 31
    Shutting Down 38
    Navigating the Start Menu by Keyboard 41
    Jump Lists in the Start Menu 42
    The Secret Start Menu 43

Chapter 2: File Explorer, Taskbar & Action Center **45**
    Universal Window Controls 45
    Window Management 48
    The Ribbon 56
    File Explorer Window Controls 63
    Optional Window Panes 67
    Libraries 72
    Tags, Metadata, and Properties 77
    Window Views 80
    Sorting, Grouping, and Filtering 83
    The "Folder Options" Options 86
    Taskbar 2.0 92
    Jump Lists in the Taskbar 98
    The System Tray (Notification Center) 102
    Three Ways to Get the Taskbar Out of Your Hair 106

Taskbar Toolbars..108

Notifications..111

The Action Center..113

Chapter 3: Organizing & Finding Your Files.................................. **119**

The Search Box...119

File Explorer Window Searches..124

The Search Index..130

Customizing Search..133

The Folders of Windows 10..137

Selecting Icons...142

Life with Icons...145

Shortcut Icons..151

Copying and Moving Folders and Files...154

The Recycle Bin..157

OneDrive..161

Compressing Files and Folders...167

Burning CDs and DVDs from the Desktop...171

ISO Disk Images...171

Chapter 4: Redesigning the Desktop **173**

Wallpaper, Color, and Themes..173

Screensavers..183

Turning Off the New Look..185

Monitor Settings..187

Multiple Monitors..190

Virtual Screens...193

Chapter 5: Cortana, Your Voice Assistant...................................... **195**

Setting Up Cortana...196

How to Use Cortana...198

What to Say to Cortana...199

Cortana's Personality...211

Cortana's Cards—and the Notebook 216

Cortana Settings..219

Part Two: The Programs of Windows 10

Chapter 6: Programs & Documents.. **223**

Opening Programs..223

An (Unfortunately) Necessary Word on Windows 8 Apps....................................224

The App Switcher: Alt+Tab...226

Task View: The New Alt+Tab..226

Exiting Programs..228

When Programs Die: The Task Manager..228

Saving Documents.. 232
Closing Documents 235
The Open Dialog Box.. 236
Moving Data Between Documents 236
Speech Recognition.. 239
Filename Extensions and File Associations... 240
Choosing Your Default Apps... 247
Installing New Apps 248
Uninstalling Software... 252
Program Compatibility Modes 253

Chapter 7: Settings & Control Panel 257

The Settings App.. 257
System.. 259
Devices... 262
Network & Internet 264
Personalization 265
Accounts 265
Time & Language.. 265
Ease of Access 266
Privacy.. 269
Update & Security 269
The Control Panel... 270
The Control Panel, Applet by Applet 274

Chapter 8: The Windows Starter Apps 291

The New, Unified Design of Apps 291
3D Builder 293
Alarms & Clock 293
Calculator 296
Calendar 297
Camera 303
Character Map 304
Command Prompt 305
Contact Support... 306
Cortana 307
Games... 307
Get Office, Get Skype... 307
Get Started 307
Groove Music... 308
Magnifier 312
Mail.. 314
Maps... 314
Math Input Panel 320

Microsoft Edge 321

Microsoft Solitaire Collection.. 321

Money 322

Movies & TV 323

Music 325

Narrator 325

News 326

Notepad 328

On-Screen Keyboard 329

OneDrive 329

OneNote 329

Paint 331

People 332

Phone Companion 337

Photos 337

Remote Desktop Connection 346

Run 346

Settings 346

Skype 346

Snipping Tool 346

Sports 349

Steps Recorder 349

Sticky Notes 350

Store 351

Voice Recorder 351

Weather 353

Windows Defender 355

Windows Fax and Scan 355

Windows Journal 355

Windows Media Player 358

Windows PowerShell 358

Windows Speech Recognition 358

WordPad 358

Xbox 360

XPS Viewer 364

Part Three: Windows Online

Chapter 9: Getting Online **369**

Connecting to a WiFi Hotspot 370

Wired Connections 373

Tethering and Cellular Modems 374

Dial-Up Connections 375

Connection Management 375

WiFi Sense 376

Chapter 10: The Edge Browser 381

The Start Page 382
The Address/Search Bar 384
Tabbed Browsing 387
Favorites (Bookmarks) 388
History List 390
Cortana Meets Edge 390
Mark Up Your Web Pages 391
Tips for Better Surfing 393
The Keyboard Shortcut Master List 397

Chapter 11: Mail 399

Setting Up 400
The Amazing Expand-O-Window 402
Checking Email 403
What to Do with a Message 404
Account Options 411

Chapter 12: Security & Privacy 415

Windows Defender 417
Action Center 420
Windows Firewall 420
Windows SmartScreen 423
Privacy and Cookies 425
History: Erasing Your Tracks 426
The Pop-Up Blocker 427
InPrivate Browsing 428
Do Not Track 429
Hotspot Security 430
Protect Your Home Wireless Network 431
Family Safety (Parental Controls) 432
Privacy from Your Apps 436

Part Four: Hardware and Peripherals

Chapter 13: Tablets, Laptops & Hybrids 439

Battery Saver 441
For Hybrid PCs Only: Tablet Mode (Continuum) 443
The Onscreen Keyboard 445
Handwriting Recognition 449
Mobility Center 452
Offline Files and Sync Center 453
Windows To Go 454
Dialing In from the Road 455

Chapter 14: Printing, Fonts & PDFs..**467**

Installing a Printer 467

Printing... 470

Controlling Printouts... 473

Fancy Printer Tricks 474

Printer Troubleshooting... 477

Fonts.. 477

PDF Files 479

Faxing.. 480

Scanning Documents.. 480

Chapter 15: Hardware & Drivers...**483**

External Gadgets... 484

Troubleshooting Newly Installed Gear 485

Driver Signing 487

The Device Manager 487

Part Five: PC Health

Chapter 16: Maintenance, Speed & Troubleshooting.........................**495**

The Action Center... 495

Windows Update.. 495

Task Scheduler 502

Two Speed Boosts 505

Resetting (Erasing) Your Computer 508

Windows Recovery Environment (WinRE) 510

Troubleshooting Tools 514

Startup Items Revealed... 516

Chapter 17: Backups & File History..**517**

System Images... 518

System Restore 521

File History 526

The USB Recovery Drive 531

Chapter 18: The Disk Chapter..**533**

Storage View 534

Disk Cleanup... 536

Disk Defragmenter 537

Hard Drive Checkups.. 539

Disk Management 540

Storage Spaces.. 545

Dynamic Disks 546

Encrypting Files and Folders... 546

BitLocker Drive Encryption 549

Part Six: The Windows Network

Chapter 19: Accounts (and Logging On) 553
Local Accounts vs. Microsoft Accounts.. 554
Accounts Central 555
Adding an Account.. 558
Editing an Account 562
Seven Ways to Log In... 566
After You've Logged On.. 574
The Forgotten Password Disk 575
Deleting Accounts... 576
Disabling Accounts... 577
The Guest Account 577
Fast User Switching 579
Authenticate Yourself: User Account Control... 580
Three Advanced Features Worth Mentioning (Maybe) 582

Chapter 20: Setting Up a Small Network 585
Kinds of Networks.. 586
The Network and Sharing Center 591

Chapter 21: Sharing Files on the Network 595
Two Ways to Share Files... 596
HomeGroups.. 597
Sharing Any Folder... 604
Accessing Shared Folders... 608
Mapping Shares to Drive Letters... 611
Sharing a DVD Drive.. 614
Corporate Networks 616

Part Seven: Appendixes

Appendix A: Installing & Upgrading to Windows 10 623
Before You Begin... 623
How to Upgrade to Windows 10... 624
The Clean Install 631
Jobs Number 1, 2, 3 634

Appendix B: Where'd It Go? 635

Appendix C: Master List of Keyboard Shortcuts & Gestures 641

Index 651

The Missing Credits

About the Author

David Pogue (author, illustrator) wrote the weekly tech column for *The New York Times* for 13 years. In late 2013, he joined Yahoo to launch a new consumer tech site for non-techies: *yahootech.com*.

He's also a monthly columnist for *Scientific American*, a three-time Emmy-winning correspondent for *CBS News Sunday Morning*, the host of four *NOVA* miniseries on PBS, and the creator of the Missing Manual series. He's written or cowritten over 80 books, including 38 in this series, six in the *For Dummies* line (including *Macs, Magic, Opera,* and *Classical Music*), two novels (one for middle-schoolers), and *The World According to Twitter*. In his other life, David is a former Broadway show conductor, a magician, and a funny public speaker. He lives in Connecticut with his wife, Nicki, and three awesome children.

Links to his columns and videos await at *www.davidpogue.com*. He welcomes feedback about his books by email at *david@poguemun.com*.

About the Creative Team

Julie Van Keuren (editor, indexer, layout) quit her newspaper job in 2006 to move to Montana and live the freelancing dream. She and her husband, M.H.—who's living the novel-writing dream—have two teenage sons, Dexter and Michael. Email: *little_media@yahoo.com*.

Phil Simpson (design and layout) runs his graphic design business from Southbury, Connecticut. His work includes corporate branding, publication design, communications support, and advertising. In his free time, he is a homebrewer, ice cream maker, wannabe woodworker, and is on a few tasting panels. He lives with his wife and four great felines. Email: *phil.simpson@pmsgraphics.com*.

Acknowledgments

The Missing Manual series is a joint venture between the dream team introduced on these pages and O'Reilly Media. I'm grateful to all of them, and also to a few people who did massive favors for this book.

First of all, I discovered the hard way that Windows 10 is a brand-new operating system; there's very little up-to-date, accurate information about it. My bacon was saved by Waggener Edstrom's Greg Chiemingo and his team, who patiently helped dig up answers to the tweakiest questions. The Microsoft team members he corralled to assist included Marcus Ash and Mohammed Samji, and I wouldn't have known what I was talking about without them.

I also owe a debt of thanks to O'Reilly's Nan Barber, who accommodated my nightmarish schedule with grace; and proofreaders/helpers Kellee Katagi, Judy Le, Gretchen Tipps, and Nancy Young.

In previous editions of this book, I relied on the talents of several guest authors and editors; some of their prose and expertise lives on in this edition. They include Mike Halsey, Brian Jepson, Joli Ballew, C.A. Callahan, Preston Gralla, John Pierce, and Adam Ornstein.

Finally, a special nod of thanks to my squadron of meticulous, expert volunteer beta readers who responded to my invitation via Twitter: Robin Chattopadhyay, Justin Higgins, Nora Buckley, Carlos Cordera, Rev. Robert J. Kelley, Lim Thye Chean, Jerry Peek, Joel Taylor, Kasim Hassan, Ann Hyatt Logan, Chris Rauchle, Thomas Kerber, Devin Sijan, Lou Fonolleras, Jon Colt, Cori Culp, Pete Morey, Thabo Zijlstra, Jiayan Xiang, Bob Myrick, Shaun Orpen, Jeff Franklin, and Ralph Sanchez. They're the superstars of crowdsourcing, selfless and eagle-eyed, and they made the book a lot better.

Thanks to David Rogelberg for believing in the idea. Thanks, above all, to Nicki, my muse and my love, and the three Poguelets: Kelly, Tia, and Jeffrey. They make these books—and everything else—possible.

—David Pogue

Introduction

Even Microsoft admits it now: Windows 8 was a huge mistake. It was, in essence, two radically different operating systems, superimposed (see Figure I-1). There was the regular desktop, which worked a lot like the popular Windows 7. And then, lying over it, there was a new, colorful world of tiles and modern typography—I called it "TileWorld," since Microsoft didn't have a name for it—that was designed for the new world of touchscreen tablets and laptops.

Unfortunately, the result was two Web browsers, two Control Panels, two mail programs, two ways of doing everything. And, in general, people couldn't *stand* it.

In hopes of getting as far away from Windows 8 as possible, Microsoft skipped Windows 9 entirely; there never was a Windows 9. But now there's Windows 10.

In this new operating system, Microsoft achieved something rather brilliant: It eliminated the split personality of Windows 8 but managed to retain the touch-friendly features. Just in case, you know, the world moves to touchscreen computers after all.

If you're a PC veteran, then you'll recognize Windows 10: It's pretty much Windows 7 with a few new features and nicer typography.

And if you're relatively new to all this, then get down on your knees beside your bed tonight and thank whatever you believe in that you were spared the emotional and mental whiplash of Microsoft's changing its mind.

What's New in Windows 10

The most radical new feature of Windows 10 is that Microsoft doesn't consider it *a* version of Windows. Instead, it's going to be a work in progress—a continuously im-

---

proved, living blob of software. The age of service packs—megalithic annual chunks of updates and patches—is over. Instead, Microsoft intends to fix bugs (there are plenty) and add features continuously via quiet, automatic software releases.

That should make life interesting for you, and miserable for people who write computer books.

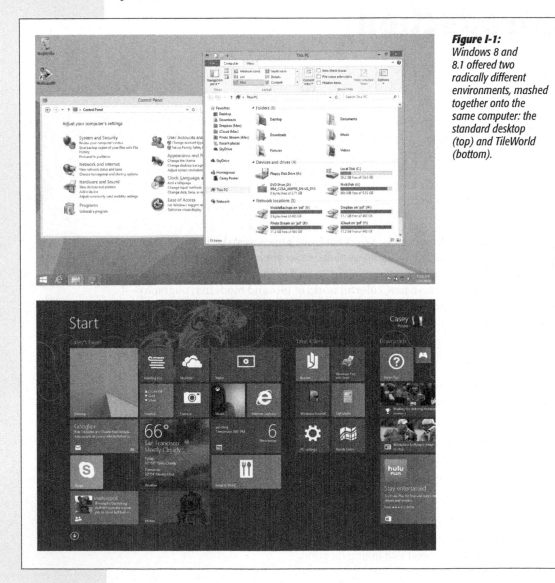

Figure I-1:
Windows 8 and 8.1 offered two radically different environments, mashed together onto the same computer: the standard desktop (top) and TileWorld (bottom).

But you have to start somewhere. So here's the list of new features that came with the *first* download of Windows 10:

- **The Start menu.** It may have taken four years, but Microsoft finally realized the foolishness and incoherence of the Start *screen* that, in Windows 8, replaced the Start *menu*.

  In Windows 10, the Start menu is back, and it works pretty much just as it always has—but the Windows 10 *tiles* are still here, attached to the right side of the menu (Figure I-2).

Figure I-2:
In Windows 10, the right side of the Start menu offers what Microsoft calls live tiles; many of them display useful information without your even having to click, like the weather, news, the latest Twitter tweets and email, and your next calendar appointment.

The main thing is this: The Windows 10 Start menu doesn't take over your entire screen, interrupting what you were doing, like the Windows 8 Start screen did. It behaves, in other words, like a *menu*.

Note: Meanwhile, a lot of conventions from the Windows 8 era are gone now. All that business about swiping in from the sides of the screen? Gone. (Mostly.) Charms bar? Gone. App bar? Gone.

- **All apps work alike.** In Windows 8, there were two kinds of programs: the traditional Windows programs like Word, Excel, and Photoshop, and then a new kind designed for touchscreens. These TileWorld apps had no menus. They had no windows, either—each one filled the entire screen. They were available exclusively from Microsoft's online Windows Store. They tended to be simple in design and function. They were, basically, tablet apps.

They also meant that you had two different kinds of programs to learn.

In Windows 10, those tablet apps are still around. But they behave just like Windows apps, in that they now float in their own windows. They still look a little different, and there's still no good name for them. But they're a lot less confusing now. Some people may never even realize they're using a different class of app.

- **Cortana.** You know Siri, the voice-activated "assistant" on the iPhone? Or Google Now on Android phones? Well, Microsoft now has Cortana. Same exact idea, except it's not just on your phone—it's on your *PC*, which takes its usefulness to a whole new level. (Cortana is *also* available on your phone—Windows phones, of course, but even iPhone or Android phones.)

- **The Edge browser.** Microsoft has retired the wrinkly old Internet Explorer browser and replaced it with an all-new, bare-bones one called Edge. It's designed to eat up very little screen space with *controls*, so that the Web pages you're reading get as much room as possible. (Internet Explorer is still available.) See Chapter 10.

- **Task view.** With one click on this new taskbar button, all your open windows shrink into index cards (Figure I-3), so you can see them all at once—a great way to find a program in a haystack.

Figure I-3:
In the new Task view, every app is represented by a card—and they don't overlap. This way, you can't lose a window you need.

- **Virtual screens.** You can now set up multiple "virtual monitors," each with a certain set of windows open. Maybe you like your email on screen 1, Facebook and Twitter on screen 2, and graphics apps on screen 3. With a simple keystroke (■+arrow keys), you can bounce from one simulated monitor to another.

- **New Settings app.** In Windows 8, you had a minimal page of often-used settings for your PC called Settings. And you also had the time-honored Control Panel, where you could change *all* your settings.

  In Windows 10, that logic has been flipped. The newly designed Settings app offers *almost* every switch and slider you'll ever need, in a clean, well-organized app. The old Control Panel is still around, filed in a junk drawer somewhere, for the rare occasions when you need an obscure option.

- **Action Center.** This is a panel that pops out from the right side of the screen, listing all recent notifications up top and, at the bottom, one-click buttons for on/off switches like Bluetooth, WiFi, Battery Saver, and Airplane Mode. If you've used a Windows phone, or a Mac, you've seen this effect before.

- **Snap four apps at once.** *Snapping* a window, in Windows, means dragging it to the right or left side of your screen, whereupon it snaps there as though magnetically, occupying exactly half the screen. You can then snap a second app in the empty half of the screen.

  In Windows 10, you can snap *four* windows. As a bonus, each time you snap an app, the remaining apps shrink to index cards in the empty space, making it very easy to specify which one you want to snap next.

- **Universal apps.** Windows 10 is designed to look and work the same on every gadget that can run Windows: PCs, tablets, and even phones. In fact, software companies can, if they wish, write their apps in such a way that the *same exact program* runs on all three kinds of devices. You see the same controls and the same features, auto-squished to whatever screen size you're using. Word, Excel, and Outlook are all universal apps.

- **Windows Hello (face or fingerprint login).** Instead of typing a password every time you wake your machine, you can just *look* at it. Windows Hello recognizes your face and logs you in, without your ever having to touch the computer.

  This feature works only on machines equipped with an Intel RealSense camera, which rules out any pre-2015 computers. But Windows can also log you in with your fingerprint, if your machine has a fingerprint reader. Or even your eyeball iris, once someone sells a computer with an iris scanner.

- **Continuum (Tablet mode).** If you own a *convertible* tablet—one with a detachable keyboard, like one of Microsoft's Surface tablets—then Windows 10 can do something very useful indeed. When you take away the physical keyboard, Windows enters Tablet mode, in which everything is bigger and more finger-friendly, each app fills the entire screen, and an onscreen keyboard pops up automatically. More on Tablet mode in Chapter 13.

- **Xbox streaming.** If you have an Xbox game console—downstairs in your living room, for example—you can now play its games anywhere else in the house on your tablet or laptop. The game's audio and video are streamed from the console to you, wirelessly. The rest of the family can watch TV in peace, completely unaware that you're blissing out on Halo up in your office.

- **Rejiggered File Explorer.** The basic desktop folder window—once called Windows Explorer, now called File Explorer—has had a makeover. The list at the left side now displays frequently accessed disks, folders, and files. The sharing controls on the Ribbon at the top have been cleaned up, too.

- **A whole lotta misc.** The taskbar at the bottom of your screen comes with newly designed app icons, and the system tray at the far right comes set to hide all but the most important icons.

You can now resize the command-prompt window and use keyboard shortcuts in it for Copy and Paste. When Windows downloads an update that requires you to restart the PC, you can now specify when you want that restart to happen. Windows 10 comes with DirectX 12, Microsoft's graphics software, which can speed up games and professional graphics programs that are rewritten to exploit it. There's a new Phone Companion app that lets you sync photos and music between your phone (even an iPhone or Android phone) and your PC.

What Else Is New

If you're used to Windows 7 or something even earlier, then it's probably worth reading about all the *good* things Microsoft added in Windows 8—which still rear their lovely heads in Windows 10:

- **Smartphone features.** Some of Windows' features are adapted from smartphones, like a Lock screen that shows your battery level and the time, a Refresh command that resets Windows to its factory-fresh condition without disturbing any of your files, and a Reset command that erases it completely (great when you're about to sell your PC to someone).

And there's an app store that's modeled on the iPhone App Store, for ease of downloading new apps that Microsoft has approved and certified to be virus-free.

- **It's touchscreen friendly.** Microsoft strongly believes that, someday soon, all computers will have touchscreens—not just tablets, but laptops and desktop computers, too. So Windows is filled with touchscreen gestures that work as they do on phones. Tap to click. Pinch or spread two fingers on a photo to zoom in or out. Log in by drawing lines over a photo you've chosen instead of typing a password.

- **It's cloudy.** Your login account can now be stored online—"in the cloud," as the marketers like to say. Why? Because now you can sit down at any Windows 8 or 10 computer anywhere, log in, and find all your settings just the way you left them at home: your address book, calendar, desktop wallpaper, Web bookmarks, email accounts, and so on.

- **It's beribboned.** The mishmash of menus and toolbars in desktop windows (called File Explorer) has been replaced by the Ribbon: a big, fat toolbar atop each window that displays buttons for every possible thing you can do in that window, without hunting.

- **It comes with free virus software.** You read that right. Antivirus software is now free and built-in.

- **File History** lets you rewind any file to a time before it was deleted, damaged, or edited beyond recognition.

- **BitLocker to Go** can put a password on a flash drive—great for corporate data that shouldn't get loose.

- **Windows To Go** (available in the Enterprise version) lets you put an entire PC world—Windows, drivers, programs, documents—on a flash drive. You can plug it into any PC anywhere and find yourself at home—or, rather, at work. And you can use your own laptop without your overlords worrying that you might be corrupting their precious network with outside evilware.

- **New multiple monitor features.** Now your taskbars and desktop pictures can span multiple monitors. You can have TileWorld on one screen and the desktop on another.

- **Narrator,** a weird, sad, old feature that would read your error messages to you out loud, has been transformed into a full-blown screen reader for people with impaired vision. It can describe every item on the screen. It can describe the layout of a Web page, and it makes little sounds to confirm that you've performed touchscreen gestures correctly.

- **Storage Spaces** lets you trick Windows into thinking that several hard drives are one big drive, or vice versa, and simultaneously gives you the incredible data safety of a corporate RAID system.

- **New apps.** All-new apps include Alarms & Clock, Calculator, Voice Recorder, Maps, Movies & TV, Sports—and Reading List, which lets you round up Web articles and other materials onto a single, handsome, magazine-style layout.

  On the other hand, a few Windows 8 apps have been eliminated on the way to Windows 10, including Food & Drink, Health & Fitness, and Xbox Music (it's now called Groove).

- **Customization.** You can dress up your desktop, Start screen, and Lock screen in more ways now. Your Lock screen can be a slideshow, for example.

- **OneDrive integration.** When you save a new document, Windows offers you a choice of location: either your computer or your OneDrive (a free, 15-gigabyte online "hard drive"). (OneDrive used to be called SkyDrive.)

- **Miracast.** You send video from your PC to TV sets that have Miracast wireless features—great for streaming movies or YouTube videos to your TV.

- **Miscellaneous overhauls.** The Task Manager has been beautifully redesigned. Parental controls have blossomed into a flexible, powerful tool called Family Safety, offering everything from Web protection to daily time limits for youngsters. The Recovery Environment—the screens you use to troubleshoot at startup time—have been beautified, simplified, and reorganized.

The Editions of Windows 10

There are no longer 17,278 different versions of Windows, praise Microsoft. No more Starter, Home, Home Premium, Superduper, Ultimate, Existential, and so on.

Only two versions are for sale to the public: Home and Pro. The differences are minor. The Pro version adds high-end features like these:

- Accepts incoming Remote Desktop connections.

- Can join a corporate network (a Windows Server domain).

- Offers the Encrypting File System (lets you encrypt files at the desktop).

- Includes BitLocker and BitLocker To Go encryption systems.

Note: There are two other versions that *aren't* available to the public: Enterprise, available only to corporate buyers, and Education, available only to schools.

About This Book

Despite the many improvements in Windows over the years, one feature hasn't improved a bit: Microsoft's documentation. Not only does Windows 10 come with no printed user guide at all, but, for the first time, it doesn't even come with a built-in Help system!

When you do find online help, you'll quickly discover that it's tersely written, offers very little technical depth, and lacks examples. You can't mark your place, underline things, or read it in the bathroom. Some of the help screens are actually on Microsoft's Web site; you can't even see them without an Internet connection. Too bad if you're on a plane somewhere with your laptop.

The purpose of this book, then, is to serve as the manual that should have accompanied Windows. In these pages, you'll find step-by-step instructions for using almost every Windows feature, including those you may not have understood, let alone mastered.

Incredibly, Microsoft intends for Windows 10 to run pretty much the same on desktop PCs *and* laptops *and* tablets *and* phones. This book covers desktops, laptops, and tablets; the Windows 10 version that runs on phones is just a wee bit too different.

System Requirements for Your Brain

Windows 10: The Missing Manual is designed to accommodate readers at every technical level (except system administrators, who will be happier with a very different sort of book).

The primary discussions are written for advanced-beginner or intermediate PC users. But if you're using Windows for the first time, special sidebar articles called "Up to Speed" provide all the introductory information you need. If you're fairly advanced, on the other hand, keep your eye out for similar shaded boxes called "Power Users' Clinic." They offer more technical tips, tricks, and shortcuts for the veteran PC fan.

Also, to keep the book under that 3,000-page threshold that consumers seem to care about, a number of the most technical features of Windows 10 are no longer printed here. Instead, they're now free downloadable chapters at *www.missingmanuals.com*.

About the Outline

This book is divided into seven parts, each containing several chapters:

- **Part One, The Windows Desktop,** is really *book* one. These five chapters offer a complete course in the new (old) desktop-based world of Windows 10. Here's all you need to know about the Start menu, icons and folders, taskbar, Recycle Bin, shortcuts, shortcut menus, Cortana, the Action Center, and other elements of the new world.

- **Part Two, The Programs of Windows 10,** is dedicated to the proposition that an operating system is a launchpad for *programs*. Chapter 6, for example, describes how to work with applications and documents in Windows—how to open them, switch among them, swap data between them, use them to create and open files, and so on.

  This part also offers an item-by-item discussion of the individual software nuggets that make up this operating system. These include not just the items in Settings (the new Control Panel), but also the long list of free programs Microsoft threw in: Windows Media Player, WordPad, Speech Recognition, and so on.

- **Part Three, Windows Online,** covers all the special Internet-related features of Windows, including setting up your Internet account, Windows Edge (for Web browsing), and Mail (for email). Chapter 12 covers Windows' dozens of Internet fortification features: the firewall, antispyware software, parental controls, and on and on.

- **Part Four, Hardware & Peripherals,** describes the operating system's relationship with equipment you can attach to your PC—scanners, cameras, disks, printers, and so on. Fonts, printing, and faxing are here, too. So is Windows 10's new ability to play Xbox games even when you're not in the same room with your Xbox.

- **Part Five, PC Health,** explores Windows 10's beefed-up backup and troubleshooting tools. It also describes some advanced hard drive formatting tricks and offers tips for making your PC run faster and better.

- **Part Six, The Windows Network,** is for the millions of households and offices that contain more than one PC. If you work at home or in a small office, these chapters show you how to build your own network; if you work in a corporation where some highly paid professional network geek is on hand to do the troubleshooting, these chapters show you how to exploit Windows' considerable networking prowess. File sharing, accounts and passwords, remote access, and the HomeGroups insta-networking feature are here, too.

• **At the end of the book, four appendixes** provide a guide to installing or upgrading to Windows 10, a master list of Windows keyboard shortcuts, and the "Where'd It Go?" dictionary, which lists every feature Microsoft moved or deleted on the way to Windows 10.

About→These→Arrows

Throughout this book, and throughout the Missing Manual series, you'll find sentences like this: "Open the Computer→Local Disk (C:)→Windows folder." That's shorthand for a much longer instruction that directs you to open three nested icons in sequence, like this: "Inside the Computer window is a disk icon labeled Local Disk (C:); double-click it to open it. Inside *that* window is yet *another* icon called Windows. Double-click to open it, too."

Similarly, this kind of arrow shorthand helps to simplify the business of choosing commands in menus. See Figure I-4.

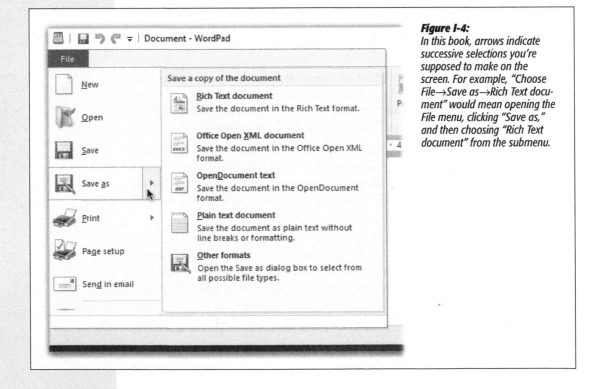

Figure I-4:
In this book, arrows indicate successive selections you're supposed to make on the screen. For example, "Choose File→Save as→Rich Text document" would mean opening the File menu, clicking "Save as," and then choosing "Rich Text document" from the submenu.

The Very Basics

To get the most out of Windows with the least frustration, it helps to be familiar with the following concepts and terms. If you're new to Windows, be prepared to encounter these words and phrases over and over again—in the built-in Windows Help, in computer magazines, and in this book.

Windows Defined

Windows is an *operating system*, the software that controls your computer. It's designed to serve you in several ways:

- **It's a launching bay.** At its heart, Windows is a home base for the various software programs (*apps*, or *applications*) that you use to do work or to kill time. When you get right down to it, programs are the real reason you bought a PC.

  Windows is a well-stocked software pantry unto itself; for example, it comes with such basic programs as a Web browser, a simple word processor, and a calculator.

  If you were stranded on a desert island, the built-in Windows programs could suffice for everyday operations. But if you're like most people, sooner or later, you'll buy and install more software. That's one of the luxuries of using Windows: You can choose from a staggering number of add-on programs. Whether you're a left-handed beekeeper or a German-speaking nun, some company somewhere is selling Windows software designed just for you, its target audience.

- **It's a file cabinet.** Every application on your machine, as well as every document you create, is represented on the screen by an *icon*, a little picture that symbolizes the underlying file or container. You can organize these icons into onscreen file folders. You can make backups (safety copies) by dragging file icons onto a flash drive or a blank CD, or you can send files to people by email. You can also trash icons you no longer need by dragging them onto the Recycle Bin icon.

- **It's your equipment headquarters.** What you can actually see of Windows is only the tip of the iceberg. An enormous chunk of Windows is behind-the-scenes plumbing that controls the various functions of your computer—its modem, screen, keyboard, printer, and so on.

The Right Mouse Button Is King

One of the most important features of Windows isn't on the screen—it's in your hand. The standard mouse or trackpad has two mouse buttons. You use the left one to click buttons, to highlight text, and to drag things around the screen.

When you click the right button, however, a *shortcut menu* appears onscreen. Get into the habit of *right-clicking* things—icons, folders, disks, text inside a paragraph, buttons on your menu bar, pictures on a Web page, and so on. The commands that appear on the shortcut menu will make you much more productive and lead you to discover handy functions you never knew existed.

Tip: On a touchscreen, you "right-click" something by holding your finger down on it for a second or so.

This is a big deal: Microsoft's research suggests that nearly 75 percent of Windows users don't use the right mouse button and therefore miss hundreds of timesaving shortcuts.

Tip: Microsoft doesn't discriminate against left-handers…much. You can swap the functions of the right and left mouse buttons easily enough.

From the ⊞ menu, choose Settings→Devices→"Mouse & touchpad." Where it says "Select your primary button," choose Right. Windows now assumes that you want to use the left mouse button as the one that produces shortcut menus.

There's More Than One Way to Do Everything

No matter what setting you want to adjust, no matter what program you want to open, Microsoft has provided four or five different ways to do it. For example, here are the various ways to delete a file: Press the Delete key; choose File→Delete; drag the file icon onto the Recycle Bin; or right-click the filename and choose Delete from the shortcut menu.

Pessimists grumble that there are too many paths to every destination, making it much more difficult to learn Windows. Optimists point out that this abundance of approaches means that almost everyone will find, and settle on, a satisfying method for each task. Whenever you find a task irksome, remember that you have other options.

(This book generally offers the one or two *shortest* ways to accomplish a task. Life's too short to read about all of them.)

You Can Use the Keyboard for Everything

In earlier versions of Windows, underlined letters appeared in the names of menus and dialog boxes. These underlines were clues for people who found it faster to do something by pressing keys than by using the mouse.

The underlines are hidden in Windows 10, at least in disk and folder windows. (They may still appear in your individual software programs.) If you miss them, you can make them reappear by pressing the Alt key, the Tab key, or an arrow key whenever the menu bar is visible. (When you're operating menus, you can release the Alt key immediately after pressing it.) In this book, in help screens, and in computer magazines, you'll see key combinations indicated like this: Alt+S (or Alt+ whatever the letter key is).

Note: In some Windows programs, in fact, the entire menu bar is gone until you press Alt (or F10).

Once the underlines are visible, you can open a menu by pressing the underlined letter (F for the File menu, for example). Once the menu is open, press the underlined letter key that corresponds to the menu command you want. Or press Esc to close the menu without doing anything. (In Windows, the Esc key always means *cancel* or *stop*.)

If choosing a menu command opens a dialog box, you can trigger its options by pressing Alt along with the underlined letters. (Within dialog boxes, you can't press and release Alt; you have to hold it down while typing the underlined letter.)

Don't miss Appendix C, which lists all the important keyboard shortcuts.

The Search Box Is Fastest

If you have a keyboard, the fastest way to almost anything in Windows is the search box at the left end of the taskbar, where it says either "Ask me anything" or "Search the web and Windows."

Used to be, this search box was at the bottom of the Start menu. But in Windows 10, it's *always* available; it's part of the taskbar now. This is also the Cortana box, where you can pose questions like "What's the weather this weekend?" and "How many feet in 50 kilometers?"

But most of the time you'll use this box to *find and open things*.

For example, to open Outlook, you can click there and type *outlook*. To get to the password-changing screen, you can type *password*. To adjust your network settings, *network*. And so on. *Display. Speakers. Keyboard. BitLocker. Excel. Photo Gallery. Firefox.* Whatever.

Each time, Windows does an uncanny job of figuring out what you want and highlighting it in the results list, usually right at the top.

Here's the thing, though: You don't need the mouse to click into this box. You can just tap the ⊞ key or button. The Start menu opens *and* your cursor blinks inside the search box.

You also don't need to type the whole search query. If you want the Sticky Notes program, *sti* is usually all you have to type. In other words, without ever lifting your hands from the keyboard, you can hit ⊞, type *sti*, confirm that Windows has highlighted the correct program's name, hit Enter—and you've opened Sticky Notes. Really, really fast.

Now, there is almost always a manual, mouse-clickable way to get at the same function in Windows. Here, for example, is how you might open Narrator, a program that reads everything on the screen. First, the mouse way:

1. **At the desktop, open the Start menu (press ⊞); click Settings.**

   The Settings app opens, teeming with options.

2. **Click Ease of Access.**

   Now another Settings screen appears, filled with options having to do with accessibility. Narrator is highlighted.

3. **Turn Narrator on.**

   Narrator begins reading what's on the screen.

OK, then. Here, by contrast, is how you'd get to exactly the same place using the search method:

1. **Press ⊞ to put your cursor in the search box. Type enough of *narrator* to make Narrator appear in the results list; press Enter.**

There you go. One step instead of three.

Now, you're forgiven for exclaiming, "What?! Get to things by typing? I thought the whole idea behind the Windows revolution was to eliminate the DOS-age practice of typing commands!"

Well, not exactly. Typing has always offered a faster, more efficient way to getting to places and doing things; what everyone hated was the *memorizing* of commands to type.

But the search box requires no memorization; that's the beauty of it. You can be vague. You can take a guess. And, almost every time, it knows what you want and offers it in the list.

For that reason, this book usually provides the most direct route to a certain program or function: the one that involves the search box. There's always a longer, slower, mousier alternative, but hey: This book is plenty fat already, and those rainforests aren't getting any bigger.

About Shift-Clicking

Here's another bit of shorthand you'll find in this book (and others): instructions to *Shift-click* something. That means you should hold down the Shift key and then click before releasing the key. If you understand that much, then the meaning of instructions like "Ctrl-click" and "Alt-click" should be clear.

You Could Spend a Lifetime Changing Properties

You can't write an operating system that's all things to all people, but Microsoft has certainly tried. You can change almost every aspect of the way Windows looks and works. You can replace the gray backdrop of the screen (the *wallpaper*) with your favorite photograph, change the typeface used for the names of your icons, or set up a particular program to launch automatically every time you turn on the PC.

When you want to change some *general* behavior of your PC, like how it connects to the Internet, how soon the screen goes black to save power, or how quickly a letter repeats when you hold down a key, you use the Settings app (described in Chapter 7).

Many other times, however, you may want to adjust the settings of only one particular element of the machine, such as the hard drive, the Recycle Bin, or a particular application. In those cases, *right-click* the corresponding icon. In the shortcut menu, you'll often find a command called Properties, which offers settings about that object.

Tip: As a shortcut to the Properties command, just highlight an icon and then press Alt+Enter.

Every Piece of Hardware Requires Software

When computer geeks talk about their *drivers*, they're not talking about their chauffeurs (unless they're Bill Gates); they're talking about the controlling software required by every hardware component of a PC.

The driver is the translator for your PC and the equipment attached to it: mouse, microphone, screen, printer, scanner, and so on. Without driver software, the gear doesn't work.

When you buy one of these gadgets, you receive a CD containing the driver software, or a download link for it. If that driver software works fine, then you're all set. If your gadget acts up, however, remember that equipment manufacturers regularly release improved (read: less buggy) versions of these software chunks. You generally find such updates on the manufacturers' Web sites.

Fortunately, Windows 10 comes with drivers for over 15,000 components, saving you the trouble of scavenging for them. Most popular gizmos from brand-name companies work automatically when you plug them in—no CD required (see Chapter 15).

It's Not Meant to Be Overwhelming

Windows has a staggering array of features. You can burrow six levels down, dialog box through dialog box, and still not come to the end of it.

Microsoft's programmers created Windows in modules—the digital-photography team here, the networking team there—for different audiences. The idea, of course, was to make sure that no subset of potential customers would find a feature lacking.

But if *you* don't have a digital camera, a network, or whatever, there's nothing wrong with ignoring everything you encounter on the screen that isn't relevant to your setup and work routine. Not even Microsoft's CEO uses every single feature of Windows.

GEM IN THE ROUGH

The Touchscreen Verb Challenge

Microsoft intends for Windows 10 to work just as well on touchscreen tablets as it does on PCs with keyboard and mouse (or trackpad). That presents something of a challenge to people writing books about it.

Thousands of times in this book, instructions direct you to activate something on the screen: a button, checkbox, icon, or tile. But what's the right verb here? If you have a touchscreen, telling you to *click* something doesn't sound quite right. And if you have a mouse, it'd be weird telling you to *tap* something on the screen.

So in the spirit of peace and understanding, in this book, you're generally instructed to *hit, select,* and *choose* things on the screen. Those are equal-opportunity verbs that should offend neither touch people nor mouse people.

About MissingManuals.com

To get the most out of this book, visit *www.missingmanuals.com*. Click the "Missing CD-ROM" link—and then this book's title—to reveal a tidy, chapter-by-chapter list of the shareware and freeware mentioned in this book.

The Web site also offers corrections and updates. (To see them, click the book's title, and then click View/Submit Errata.) In fact, please submit such corrections yourself! In an effort to keep the book as up to date as possible, each time O'Reilly prints more copies of this book, I'll make any confirmed corrections you've suggested. I'll also note such changes on the Web site so that you can mark important corrections into your own copy of the book, if you like.

Part One:
The Windows Desktop

Chapter 1: Desktop & Start Menu

Chapter 2: File Explorer, Taskbar & Action Center

Chapter 3: Organizing & Finding Your Files

Chapter 4: Redesigning the Desktop

Chapter 5: Cortana, Your Voice Assistant

1

Desktop & Start Menu

These days, the graphic user interface (the colorful world of icons, windows, and menus) is standard. Mac, Windows, Chrome OS, Linux—every operating system is fundamentally the same, which is to say a very long way from the lines of typed commands that defined the earliest computers.

Windows 10 restores the desktop to its traditional importance, following a weird three-year detour into "what the heck" land known as Windows 8. The desktop is once again your only home base, your single starting point. It's the view that greets you when the computer turns on, and it offers all the tools you need to manage and organize your files.

Herewith: a grand tour of the state of the art in computer desktops—the one in Windows 10.

The Lock Screen

When you turn on a Windows 10 machine, you know right away that you're not in Kansas anymore. The first thing you see is a colorful curtain that's been drawn over the computer's world. It's the *Lock screen* (Figure 1-1).

The Lock screen serves the same purpose it does on a phone: It gives a quick glance at the time, the date, your WiFi signal strength, the weather, and (on laptops and tablets) your battery charge. As you download and install new apps, they can add informational tidbits to this Lock screen, too.

The point is that sometimes you don't really need to wake the machine up. You just want to know what time it is.

The Lock screen can also give you instant access to your Camera and Skype apps (pages 303 and 346). You might want to take a picture or answer a call without having to go through the red tape of fully logging in.

Figure 1-1:
You can control which apps are allowed to add information to the Lock screen in Settings (like the weather report shown here).

You're not stuck with the Lock screen photo as Mother Microsoft has installed it, either. You can change the picture, if you like, or you can eliminate it altogether. Chapter 4 has the details.

When you do want to go past the Lock screen to log in, there's nothing to it. Almost anything you do that says, "I'm here!" works:

- **Touchscreen:** Swipe a finger upward. (Swipe downward to jump into Camera mode.)

- **Mouse:** Click anywhere. Or turn the mouse wheel.

- **Keyboard:** Press any key.

The Lock screen slides up and out of the way, revealing the Login screen (Figure 1-2, top).

Tip: You can change the photo background of the Lock screen, fiddle with which information appears here, or even eliminate the Lock screen altogether. After all, it's an extra click every time you log in. See page 573 for details.

The Login Screen

As in any modern operating system, you have your own *account* in Windows. It's your world of files, settings, and preferences. So the second thing you encounter in

Windows 10 is the Login screen. Here, at lower left, you see the name and photo for each person who has an account on this machine (Figure 1-2). Choose yours.

This is also where you're supposed to log in—to prove that you're you. But *logging in* no longer has to mean *typing a password.* One of Windows 10's primary goals is to embrace touchscreens, and *typing* is a pain on tablets.

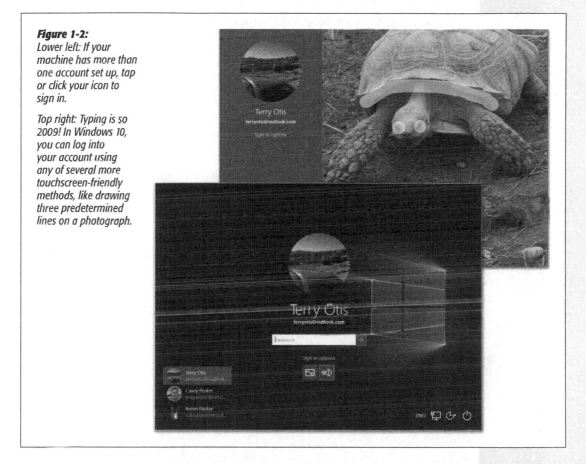

Figure 1-2:
Lower left: If your machine has more than one account set up, tap or click your icon to sign in.

Top right: Typing is so 2009! In Windows 10, you can log into your account using any of several more touchscreen-friendly methods, like drawing three predetermined lines on a photograph.

Therefore, you can log in using any of these techniques:

- Just *look* at your screen. On laptops or tablets with Intel's RealSense infrared cameras, facial recognition logs you in.

- Swipe your finger across the fingerprint reader, if your computer has one.

- Put your eye up to the iris reader, if your machine is so equipped.

- Draw three lines, taps, or circles on a photo you've selected (Figure 1-2, top).

- Type in a four-digit PIN number you've memorized.

- Type a traditional password.

• Skip the security altogether. Jump directly to the desktop when you turn on the machine.

See Chapter 19 for instructions on setting each of these up.

The Desktop

Once you've gotten past the security barrier, you finally wind up at the home base of Windows: the desktop. See Figure 1-3 for a refresher course.

You can, and should, make the desktop look like whatever you want. You can change its background picture or color scheme; you can make the text larger; you can clutter up the whole thing with icons you use a lot. Chapter 4 is a crash course in desktop interior decoration.

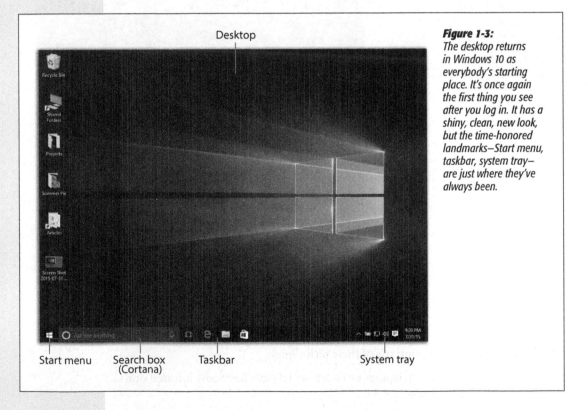

Desktop

Figure 1-3:
The desktop returns in Windows 10 as everybody's starting place. It's once again the first thing you see after you log in. It has a shiny, clean, new look, but the time-honored landmarks—Start menu, taskbar, system tray— are just where they've always been.

Start menu   Search box   Taskbar   System tray
              (Cortana)

Meet the Start Menu

Windows is composed of 50 million lines of computer code, scattered across your hard drive in thousands of files. The vast majority of them are not for you; they're support files, there for behind-the-scenes use by Windows and your applications. They may as well bear a sticker reading, "No user-serviceable parts inside."

That's why the Start menu is so important (Figure 1-4). It lists every *useful* piece of software on your computer, including commands, programs, and files. Just about everything you do on your PC begins—or can begin—with your Start menu.

In Windows 10, as you've probably noticed, the *word* "Start" doesn't actually appear on the Start menu, as it did for years; now the Start menu is just a square button in the lower-left corner of your screen, bearing the Windows logo (⊞). But it's still called the Start menu, and it's still the gateway to everything on the PC.

If you're the type who bills by the hour, you can open the Start menu (Figure 1-3, lower left) by clicking it with the mouse. If you feel that life's too short, however, tap the ⊞ key on the keyboard instead, or the ⊞ button if it's a tablet.

Really, truly: *Learn this*. Tap ⊞ to open the Start menu (or to close it!).

The Start menu (Figure 1-4) is split into two columns. For convenience, let's call them the left side and the right side.

Figure 1-4:
Here it is, the single biggest change in Windows 10: the new, hybrid Start menu. The left side gives you direct access to apps you use frequently, or that you've installed recently, as well as important commands and places like Power and "All apps." The right side is yours to customize.

Note: If your computer is a tablet, and it has no physical keyboard at all, then it may start up in Windows 10's new *Tablet mode*. In this mode, the right side of the Start menu fills the entire screen, and the left side doesn't appear unless you tap the ⌂ in the top-left corner. For details on Tablet mode, see Chapter 13.

Start Menu: The Left Side

The most amazing thing about the Windows 10 Start menu is that Windows 10 has a Start menu—something that's been missing since Windows 7. The left side, or something like it, has been with Windows from the beginning. The right side is a pared-back version of the Start screen that distinguished Windows 8.

The left side may *look* like the Start menu that's been in Windows from the beginning (except during that one unfortunate three-year Windows 8 phase). But there's a big difference: In Windows 10, you can't use it to list your own favorite programs, folders, and files. (That's what the right side is for.) The left side is meant to be managed and run entirely by Windows itself.

The left side has five sections, described here from top to bottom:

[Your name]

See your account name and picture in the upper-left corner of the Start menu (Figure 1-5)?

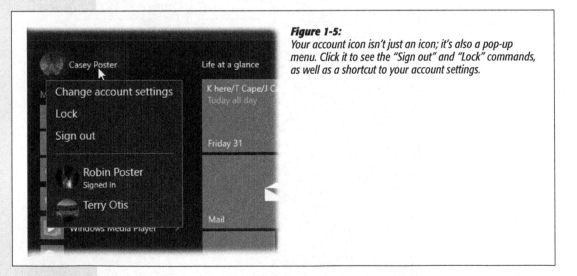

Figure 1-5:
Your account icon isn't just an icon; it's also a pop-up menu. Click it to see the "Sign out" and "Lock" commands, as well as a shortcut to your account settings.

That's not just helpful information. The picture is also a pop-up menu. And its commands all have to do with switching from one account to another. (In Windows' *accounts* feature, each person who uses this PC gets to see her own desktop picture, email account, files, and so on. See Chapter 19.) Here's what they do.

Tip: Some keystrokes from previous Windows versions are still around. For example, you can still press Ctrl+Alt+Delete to summon the three commands described here: "Lock," "Switch user," and "Sign out"—plus a bonus link for the Task Manager (page 228).

- **Change account settings** takes you directly to the Settings→Account screen, where you can change your account picture, password, login method, and other details of your account—and you can create accounts for other family members.

- **Lock.** This command takes you back to the Lock screen described at the beginning of this chapter. In essence, it throws a sheet of inch-thick steel over everything you were doing, hiding your screen from view. This is an ideal way to protect your PC from nosy people who happen to wander by your desk while you're away getting coffee or lunch.

- **Sign out.** When you choose "Sign out," Windows closes all your open programs and documents (giving you an opportunity to save any unsaved documents first). It then presents a new Login screen so that somebody else can log in.

   Whatever *you* had running remains open behind the scenes. When you log in again, you'll find all your open programs and documents exactly as you left them.

Most Used

Beneath your name icon, you get a list of the programs that Windows sees you using a lot. Windows computes this list automatically and continuously. It's a really great feature, because, well, if you've been using something a lot recently, you'll probably use it a lot more still, and now you don't have to burrow around looking for it.

On the other hand, if you'd rather not have Windows track what you're doing, you can get rid of this list, or just certain items on it; see the box below.

If you see a submenu arrow (>) next to a program's name in the Start menu, congrats. You've just found a *jump list*, a feature that gives you quick access to documents

---

GEM IN THE ROUGH

Getting Rid of the "Most Used" List

You can, if you wish, ask the Start menu *not* to display a list of the programs you've used most recently. For example, maybe it would be best that your boss or your spouse didn't know what you've been up to.

If there's just *one* compromising listing here, no big deal; right-click its name and, from the shortcut menu, choose "Don't show in this list." It's gone.

If you'd prefer Windows not to track your most used items at *all*, open the Start menu; choose Settings→

Personalization→Start; turn off "Show most used apps." (While you're here, if you're especially paranoid, you can also turn off "Store and display recently opened items in Jump Lists on Start or the taskbar"—a reference to the jump lists feature described starting on page 42.) Close Settings.

When you next inspect the Start menu, you'll be happy to see that the top-left quadrant, where the recently used programs are usually listed, is creepily blank.

---

you've opened recently. See page 51 for details on creating, deleting, and working with jump lists.

Tip: So how does Windows decide what to put into the "Most used" list? It's an algorithm, Microsoft says, one that it intends to keep refining to make the list more useful. One thing is for sure, though: Any app you've put onto the right side of the Start menu doesn't appear in the "Most used" list. Microsoft figures you don't need to see its name twice.

Recently Added

The middle section of the left side shows *one* item: whatever app you've most recently downloaded or installed. It's surprisingly handy, especially for novices, who often download something from the Internet and then can't find where it landed.

If you've installed *more than one* new app recently, open the "All apps" list described below; the little "New" indicators show you which are the recent arrivals.

Tip: It probably goes without saying, but you can hide the "Recently added" section if you like. Open the Start menu; choose Settings→Personalization→Start; turn off "Show recently added apps." Close Settings.

Important Places

In general, the bottom of the left side is devoted to listing important *places* on the computer. On a shiny new PC, the list includes these:

- **File Explorer**. This "app" is the standard desktop window, showing the contents of your drives and folders (Chapter 2).

- **Settings**. Yes, adjusting the settings and preferences of your PC is about six steps quicker now, since Settings is listed right here in the Start menu. Chapter 7 covers Settings in absurd detail.

- **Power**. Hard though it may be to believe, there may come a day when you want to shut down or restart your computer. See page 38.

- **All apps** opens the complete master list of all your programs, as described below.

What's great, though, is that you can add *other* important folders to this list, following the steps shown in Figure 1-6. These are some of your options:

- **Documents:** This command opens up your Documents folder, a very important folder indeed. It's designed to store just about all the work you do on your PC—everything except music, pictures, and videos, which get folders of their own.

  Of course, you're welcome to file your documents *anywhere* on the hard drive, but most programs propose depositing newly created documents into the Documents folder. That principle makes navigation easy. You never have to wonder where you filed something, since all your stuff is sitting right there in Documents.

Note: The Documents folder actually sits in the This PC > Local Disk (C:) > Users > [*Your Name*] folder.

If you study that path carefully, it should become clear that what's in Documents when *you* log in isn't the same thing other people will see when *they* log in. That is, each account holder (Chapter 19) has a different Documents folder, whose contents switch according to who's logged in.

- **Downloads.** For decades, computer novices have been baffled: They download something from the Web but then can't find where it went. Now you'll know. Out of the box, Windows puts your downloaded files into this Downloads folder (which is inside your Personal folder). It makes perfect sense to add this item to your Start menu so you have quick access to it.

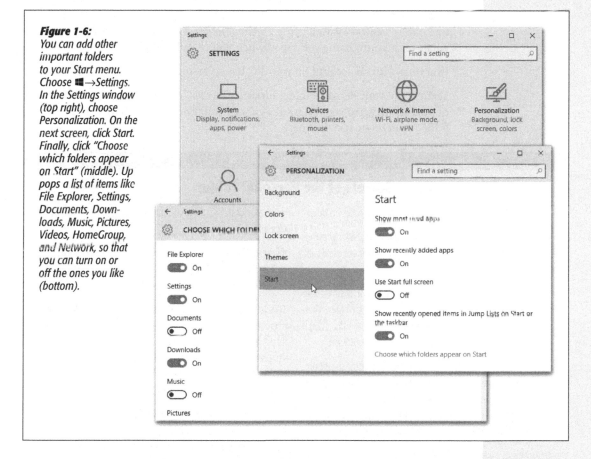

Figure 1-6:
You can add other important folders to your Start menu. Choose ⊞→Settings. In the Settings window (top right), choose Personalization. On the next screen, click Start. Finally, click "Choose which folders appear on Start" (middle). Up pops a list of items like File Explorer, Settings, Documents, Downloads, Music, Pictures, Videos, HomeGroup, and Network, so that you can turn on or off the ones you like (bottom).

- **Music, Pictures, Videos.** Microsoft assumes (correctly) that most people these days use their home computers for managing digital music, photos, and video collections. As you can probably guess, the Music, Pictures, and Videos folders are intended to house them—and these Start menu commands are quick ways to open them.

In fact, whatever software came with your phone, digital camera, or MP3 player probably dumps your photos into, and sucks your music files out of, these folders automatically. You'll find much more on photos and music in Chapter 8.

• **HomeGroup** is Microsoft's name for an easy file-sharing system. It lets you see what's on other computers on your home network, so that you can shove folders and files back and forth without running all over the house with a flash drive. This command opens the HomeGroup window (page 597).

• **Network** opens (what else?) the Network folder, where you can see a map of your home or office network and make changes to the settings. See Chapter 20.

• **Personal folder.** As the box below makes clear, Windows keeps *all* your stuff—your files, folders, email, pictures, music, bookmarks, even settings and preferences—in one handy, central location: your *Personal folder.* This folder bears your name, or whatever account name you typed when you installed Windows.

Everyone with an account on your PC has a Personal folder.

Technically, your Personal folder lurks inside the C:→Users folder. But that's a lot of burrowing when you just want a view of your empire. That's why your Personal folder can also be installed here.

FREQUENTLY ASKED QUESTION

Secrets of the Personal Folder

Why did Microsoft bury my files in a folder three levels deep?

Because Windows has been designed for *computer sharing.* It's ideal for any situation where family members, students, or workers share the same PC.

Each person who uses the computer will turn on the machine to find his own separate desktop picture, set of files, Web bookmarks, font collection, and preference settings. (You'll find much more about this feature in Chapter 19.)

Like it or not, Windows considers you one of these people. If you're the only one who uses this PC, fine—simply ignore the sharing features. But in its little software head, Windows still considers you an account holder and stands ready to accommodate any others who should come along.

In any case, now you should see the importance of the Users folder in the main hard drive window. Inside are folders—the Personal folders—named for the people who use this PC. In

general, nobody is allowed to touch what's inside anybody else's folder.

If you're the sole proprietor of the machine, of course, there's only one Personal folder in the Users folder—named for you. (You can ignore the Public folder.)

This is only the first of many examples in which Windows imposes a fairly rigid folder structure. Still, the approach has its advantages. By keeping such tight control over which files go where, Windows keeps itself pure—and very, very stable. (Other operating systems known for their stability, including Mac OS X, work the same way.)

Furthermore, keeping all your stuff in a single folder makes it very easy for you to back up your work. It also makes life easier when you try to connect to your machine from elsewhere in the office (over the network) or elsewhere in the world (over the Internet), as described in Chapters 13 and 21.

All Apps

When you click "All apps" at the bottom of the Start menu, you're shown an important list indeed: the master catalog of every program on your computer (Figure 1-7). You can jump directly to your word processor, calendar, or favorite game, for example, just by choosing its name in this scrolling list. As a handy bonus, the word "New" appears beneath the name of any *new* programs—ones you've installed but haven't yet used.

You can restore the original left-side column by clicking Back (at the bottom of the list).

Tip: You can also open the "All apps" menu with a *quick swipe upward* anywhere on the left side of the Start menu—either with the mouse, trackpad, or your finger on a touchscreen. Try it!

There are even more ways to open "All apps" if the Start menu is already open. Click the phrase "All apps," or point to it and keep the mouse still for a moment, or press the ↑ key (to highlight "All apps"). Then tap the Enter key, the → key, or the space bar. Just for keyboard fanatics: Once the "All apps" list is open, you can also choose anything in it without involving the mouse. Just press the ↑ and ↓ keys to highlight the item you want (or type a few letters of its name). Then press Enter to seal the deal.

The "All apps" list used to be called All Programs, of course, but Microsoft had to go with the lingo of those crazy kids today. But there is one handy trick in Windows 10 that never existed before: You can now jump around in the list using an alphabetic index, shown at right in Figure 1-7.

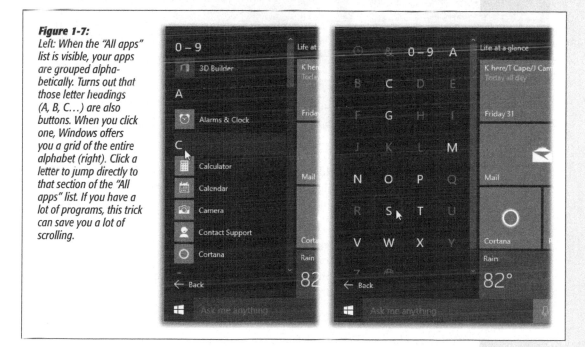

Figure 1-7:
Left: When the "All apps" list is visible, your apps are grouped alpha-betically. Turns out that those letter headings (A, B, C…) are also buttons. When you click one, Windows offers you a grid of the entire alphabet (right). Click a letter to jump directly to that section of the "All apps" list. If you have a lot of programs, this trick can save you a lot of scrolling.

Folders

As you'll quickly discover, the "All apps" list doesn't list just programs. It also houses a number of *folders*. See Figure 1-8.

Tip: Submenus, also known as cascading menus, largely have been eliminated from the Start menu. Instead, when you open something that contains *other* things—like a folder listed in the Start menu—you see its contents listed beneath, indented slightly, as shown at right in Figure 1-8. Click the folder name again to collapse the sublisting.

Keyboard freaks should note that you can also open a highlighted folder in the list by pressing the Enter key (or the → key). Close the folder by pressing Enter again (or the ← key).

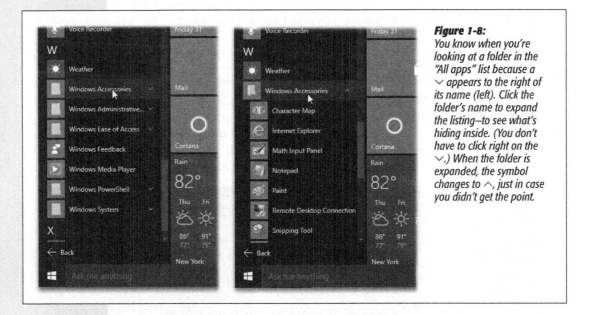

Figure 1-8:
You know when you're looking at a folder in the "All apps" list because a ⌄ appears to the right of its name (left). Click the folder's name to expand the listing—to see what's hiding inside. (You don't have to click right on the ⌄.) When the folder is expanded, the symbol changes to ⌃, just in case you didn't get the point.

- **Software-company folders.** Some of these folders bear the names of software you've installed; you might see a folder called, for example, PowerSoft or Logitech. These generally contain programs, uninstallers, instruction manuals, and other related junk.

- **Program-group folders.** Another set of folders is designed to trim down the Programs menu by consolidating related programs, like Games, Accessories (little single-purpose programs), and Maintenance. Everything in these folders is described in Chapter 8.

How to Customize the Left Side

You can't add anything to the left side yourself, which is a big change from Windows 7. Nor can you change the order of anything here.

You do, however, have three opportunities to redesign the left side:

- **Eliminate the "Most used" list (or certain items in it).** See the box on page 25.

- **Move something to Start or the taskbar.** Suppose there's some app—say, Calculator—that's listed in "Most used" or the "All apps" list. And you think you'd rather have it installed on your taskbar, visible at all times. Or you think it'd work best as a tile on the right side.

  Turns out you can right-click its name on the left side. From the shortcut menu, choose "Pin to taskbar" or "Pin to Start." It disappears from the left side and goes where you sent it.

Tip: If you have a touchscreen, you can "right-click" something by holding your finger down on it for one second.

- **Add certain Windows folders to the Important Places list.** You do that in Settings, as described on page 26.

Tip: How cool is this? You can uninstall a program right from the "All apps" list. Just right-click it (or hold your finger down on it); from the shortcut menu, choose Uninstall. Confirm in the dialog box that appears. (You can't uninstall apps that came with Windows 10 this way—only stuff *you've* added.

Start Menu: The Right Side

The right side of the Start menu is all that remains of the Great Touchscreen Experiment of 2012, during which Microsoft expected every PC on earth to come with a touchscreen. Instead of a Start menu, you got a Start *screen,* stretching from edge to edge of your monitor, displaying your files, folders, and programs as big rectangular tiles.

Unfortunately, the Start screen covered up your entire screen, blocking whatever you were working on. It was horribly space-inefficient—finding a new program you'd downloaded often meant scrolling several screens to the right. And it just felt detached from the rest of the Windows world.

Turns out most people preferred the Start *menu.*

There were some nice aspects of the Start-screen idea, though. For one thing, it's more than just a launcher. It's also a dashboard. Each tile isn't just a button that *opens* the corresponding program; it's also a little display—a *live tile,* as Microsoft calls it—that can show you real-time information from that program. The Calendar tile shows you your next appointment. Your Mail tile shows the latest incoming subject line. The People tile shows Twitter and Facebook posts as they pour in.

Tip: Not all Start menu tiles display their own names. Some apps, like the ones for Calendar, People, and Mail, are meant to be visual dashboards. To find out such an app's name, point to it with your cursor without clicking. A tinted, rectangular tooltip bar appears, identifying the name.

So in Windows 10, Microsoft decided to retain those colorful live tiles—on the right side of the Start menu (Figure 1-9).

Figure 1-9:
As you drag the top or right edge of the Right Side of the Start menu, you see it snap to a larger size once you've moved your cursor far enough. You don't have an infinite degree of freedom here; you can only double the width or, if you have one of those rare Samsung Billboard Monitors, maybe triple it.

You can also adjust the height of the Start menu—by dragging the top edge. You can goose it all the way to the top of your screen, or you can squish it down to mushroom height.

You can make this scrolling "column" bigger; you can even make it fill the screen, as it did in Windows 8; or you can hide it completely. But the point is that this time, it's up to you. The "Start screen" takes over your world only as much as you want it to.

Tip: If you're keyboard oriented, you can use the arrow keys to highlight the icon you want and then press the Enter key to open it.

How to Customize the Right Side

The left side is really Windows' playground; you can't do much to change it.

The right side, however, is your playground. You can customize it in *lots* of different ways. If your current job doesn't work out, you could become a full-time right-side customizer.

Make the right side bigger or smaller

If you have a mouse or a trackpad, you can make the right side of the Start menu either wider or taller; just grab the right edge or the top edge and drag. (In the initial release of Windows 10, you can't enlarge the Start menu with your finger on a touchscreen.)

Make the right side fill the screen

Maybe you were one of the 11 people who actually *liked* Windows 8, including the way it had a Start *screen* instead of a Start menu. Well, that look is still available.

Right-click anywhere on the desktop. (Touchscreen: Hold your finger down on the desktop.) From the shortcut menu, choose Personalize. On the Settings screen, click Start, and then click turn on "Use Start full screen."

In this mode, the left side of the Start menu is gone. The live tiles fill your entire desktop (which is handy for touchscreens).

Note: If your goal is to use Windows 10 on a tablet, you don't need to do all this. Just turn on Tablet mode (Chapter 13). In Tablet mode, the Start screen is standard and automatic.

Move a tile

You can, of course, drag the right side's tiles into a new order, putting the *personal* back into *personal computer.*

With the Start menu open, just drag the tile to a new spot. The other tiles scoot out of the way to make room.

That works fine if you have a mouse or a trackpad. But if you're using a touchscreen, that instruction leaves out a key fact: Dragging *scrolls* the right side! Instead, hold your finger down on the tile for half a second before dragging it.

Resize a tile

Tiles come in four sizes: three square sizes and one rectangle. As part of your Start menu interior decoration binge, you may want to make some of them bigger and some of them smaller. Maybe you want to make the important ones rectangular so you can read more information on them. Maybe you want to make the rarely used ones smaller so that more of them fit into a compact space.

Right-click the tile. (Touchscreen: Hold your finger down on the tile; tap the ··· button that appears.) From the shortcut menu, choose Resize. All icons give you a choice of Small and Medium; some apps offer Wide or Large options, too. See Figure 1-10.

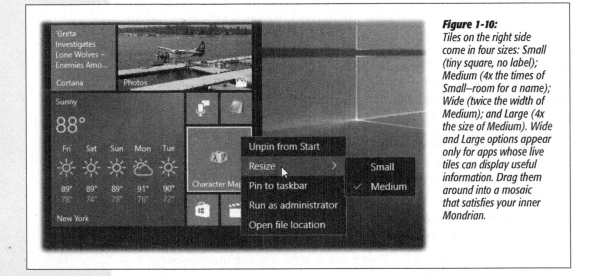

Figure 1-10:
Tiles on the right side come in four sizes: Small (tiny square, no label); Medium (4x the times of Small–room for a name); Wide (twice the width of Medium); and Large (4x the size of Medium). Wide and Large options appear only for apps whose live tiles can display useful information. Drag them around into a mosaic that satisfies your inner Mondrian.

Add new tiles

You can add tiles to the right side. They can be apps, folders, or disks (but not individual files). You can use either of two techniques: dragging or right-clicking.

- **The drag method**. Drag the icon directly into the open Start menu—from the desktop, an open window, the "All apps" list, or the left side of the Start menu.

- **The right-click method**. Right-click an icon wherever fine icons are found: in a window, on the desktop, in the "All apps" list, or on the left side. (Touchscreen: Hold your finger down on the icon for a second.) From the shortcut menu, choose Pin to Start.

Tip: In the Edge browser, you can also add a Web page to the right side. With the page open, click the ··· button at top right; choose Pin to Start.

In each case, the newly installed tile appears at the bottom of the right side. (You might have to scroll to see it.)

Make a tile stop blinking

Some of your right side tiles are *live tiles*—tiny dashboards that display real-time incoming information. There, on the Mail tile, you see the subject lines of the last few incoming messages; there, on the Calendar tile, is your next appointment; and so on.

It has to be said, though: Altogether, a Start menu filled with blinky, scrolling icons can look a little like Times Square at midnight.

If you're feeling quite caffeinated enough already, you might not want live tiles so much as, well, *dead* ones.

If you'd rather silence the animation of a live tile, right-click it. (Touchscreen: Hold your finger down on it, and then tap ☺.) From the shortcut menu, choose "Turn live tile off." The tile's current information disappears, and the live updating stops.

To reverse the procedure, "right-click" an unmoving tile; from the shortcut menu, choose "Turn live tile on" instead.

Remove a tile

Open the Start menu. Right-click the tile you want to eliminate. (Touchscreen: Hold your finger down on it, and then tap the ⋯ button.) From the shortcut menu, choose Unpin from Start. (You're not actually discarding that item—just getting its tile off the Start menu.)

Group your tiles

The right side's tiles aren't scattered pell-mell; they present an attractive, orderly mosaic. Not only are they mathematically nestled among one another, but they're actually *grouped*. Each cluster of related tiles can bear a *name*, like "Life at a glance" (Calendar, Mail, Weather…) or "Play and explore" (games, music, TV…).

But you can change those headings, or those groupings, and come up with new ones of your own.

The technique isn't quite obvious, but you'll get the hang of it (see Figure 1-11). It works like this:

1. **Drag a tile to the very bottom of the existing ones. (Touchscreen: Hold your finger still for a second before dragging.)**

   When you drag far enough—the right side might scroll, but keep your finger down—a horizontal bar appears, as shown in Figure 1-11. That's Windows telling you, "I get it. You want to create a new group right here."

2. **Drag the tile below the bar and release it.**

   Release the tile you're dragging; it's now happily setting up the homestead. Go get some other tiles to drag over into the new group to join it, if you like. Build up the group's population.

3. **Click or tap just above your newly grouped tiles.**

   The words "Name group" appear.

4. Type a name for this group, and then press Enter.

Your group name is now immortalized.

By the way: Whenever you point to (or tap) the heading of any group, you may notice a little "grip strip" at the right side. If you like, you can drag that strip up or down to

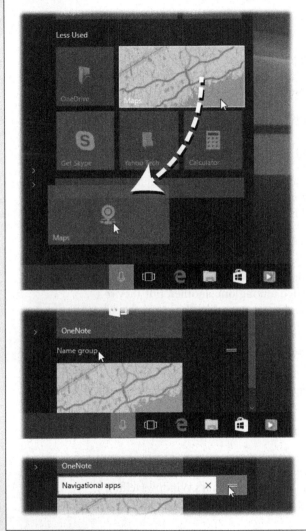

Figure 1-11:
Top: To create a new tile group, start by dragging one lonely tile below all other tiles. This is your colonist. A fat horizontal divider bar appears when you've gone far enough. Let go.

Middle: Point to the starter name ("Name group") and click.

Bottom: Type a name for the group. Use the grip strip to drag the group into a new spot, if you like.

move the entire group to a new spot among your existing groups. (Or horizontally, if you have a multicolumn right side.)

At any point, you can rename a group (click or tap its name; type). To eliminate a group, just drag all of its tiles into other groups, one at a time. When the group is empty, its name vanishes into wherever withered, obsolete tile groups go.

Eliminate all tiles

Yes, it's possible to eliminate the *entire* right side. If you like your Start menu to look like it did in the good old days, with only the left side showing, you can do that, as shown in Figure 1-12.

Of course, once you've done that, you've just eliminated one of the most useful ways of opening things on your PC. Now you can open apps only from the left side or the taskbar.

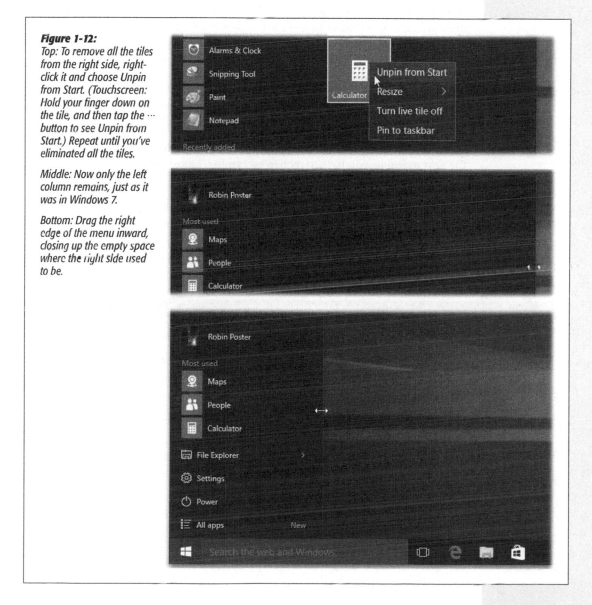

Figure 1-12:
Top: To remove all the tiles from the right side, right-click it and choose Unpin from Start. (Touchscreen: Hold your finger down on the tile, and then tap the ⋯ button to see Unpin from Start.) Repeat until you've eliminated all the tiles.

Middle: Now only the left column remains, just as it was in Windows 7.

Bottom: Drag the right edge of the menu inward, closing up the empty space where the right side used to be.

Change the color

You can also change colors of the various Start menu elements (and the taskbar, and the Action Center). See Chapter 4 for the step-by-steps.

Turn off ads

From time to time, you may spot a Start-menu tile that you didn't put there. It's a suggestion of an app that Microsoft thinks you might like—in other words, an ad.

If you'd prefer Microsoft and its ad partners to keep their darned apps to themselves, open Settings→Personalization→Start, and turn off "Occasionally show suggestions in Start."

Shutting Down

What should you do when you're finished using your computer for the moment?

Millions of people shut their PCs off, but they shouldn't; it's a colossal waste of time. When you shut down, you have to wait for all your programs to close—and then the next morning, you have to reopen everything, reposition your windows, and get everything back the way you had it.

You shouldn't just leave your computer *on* all the time, either. That's a waste of electricity, a security risk, and a black mark for the environment.

What you *should* do is put your machine to sleep. If it's a laptop, just close the lid. If it's a tablet, just press the Sleep switch. If it's a desktop PC, it's usually a matter of pressing the physical power button.

POWER USERS' CLINIC

Bringing Back the Hibernate Command

Hibernate mode is a lot like Sleep, except that it *doesn't* offer a period during which the computer will wake up instantly. Hibernate equals the *second* phase of Sleep mode, in which your working world is saved to the hard drive. Waking the computer from Hibernate takes about 30 seconds.

In an effort to make life simpler, Microsoft has hidden the Hibernate command in Windows 10. You won't find it in the ▦→Power pop-up menu.

You can bring it back, though.

To get there, press ▦ to put your cursor in the search box, and type *power but*.

In the search results, click Power Options.

Now click "Change settings that are currently unavailable" and authenticate yourself, if necessary (Microsoft's way of ensuring that only an administrator can change such important settings).

Finally, scroll down until you see "Shutdown settings." Turn on the "Hibernate: Show in Power menu" checkbox. Click "Save changes."

From now on, the Hibernate option appears in the menu shown in Figure 1-13, just like it did in the good old days.

The Sleep/Shut Down/Restart Commands

If you really want to do the sleeping or shutting down thing using the onscreen commands, you'll be happy to know that in Windows 10, you no longer need 20 minutes and a tour guide to find them. They're right there in the Start menu, near the bottom. Choose Power to see them.

As shown in Figure 1-13, shutting down is only one of the options for finishing your work session. What follows are your others.

Sleep

Sleep is great. When the flight attendant hands over your pretzels and cranberry cocktail, you can take a break without closing all your programs or shutting down the computer.

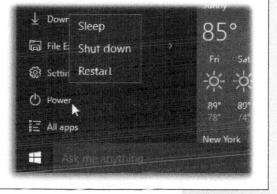

Figure 1-13:
Shutting down your computer requires only two steps now, rather than 417 (as in Windows 8).

Open the Start menu. Choose Power, and then "Shut down."

The instant you put the computer to sleep, Windows quietly transfers a copy of everything in memory into an invisible file on the hard drive. But it still keeps everything alive in memory—the battery provides a tiny trickle of power—for when you return and want to dive back into work.

If you do return soon, the next startup is lightning-fast. Everything reappears on the screen faster than you can say, "Redmond, Washington."

If you *don't* return shortly, then Windows eventually cuts power, abandoning what it had memorized in RAM. Now your computer is using no power at all; it's in *hibernate* mode.

Fortunately, Windows still has the hard drive copy of your work environment. So *now* when you tap a key to wake the computer, you may have to wait 30 seconds or so—not as fast as 2 seconds, but certainly better than the 5 minutes it would take to start up, reopen all your programs, reposition your document windows, and so on.

The bottom line: When you're done working for the moment—or for the day—put your computer to sleep instead of shutting it down. You save power, you save time, and you don't risk any data loss.

You can send a laptop to sleep just by closing the lid. On any kind of computer, you can trigger Sleep by choosing it from the ▓→Power command, or by pushing the PC's power button, if you've set it up that way, as described below.

Restart

This command quits all open programs and then quits and restarts Windows again automatically. The computer doesn't actually turn off. You might do this to "refresh" your computer when you notice that it's responding sluggishly, for example.

Shut down

This is what most people would call "really, really off." When you shut down your PC, Windows quits all open programs, offers you the opportunity to save any unsaved documents, exits Windows, and turns off the computer.

There's almost no reason to shut down your PC anymore, though. Sleep is almost always better all the way around.

The only exceptions have to do with hardware installation. Anytime you have to open up the PC to make a change (installing memory, hard drives, or sound or video cards), you should shut the thing down first.

Tip: If you're a keyboardy sort of person, you might prefer this faster route to shut down: Press Ctrl+Alt+Delete to summon the Lock/Switch User screen, and then Tab your way over to the ⏻ button in the lower right. Press Enter, and arrow-key your way to "Shut down." Press Enter again.

Three Triggers for Sleep/Shut Down—and How to Change Them

You now know how to trigger the "Shut down" command using the Start menu→Power button. But there are even faster ways.

If you have a laptop, just close the lid. If it's a tablet, tap its Sleep switch. If you have a desktop PC, press its power button (⏻).

In each of these cases, though—menu, lid, switch, or button—*you* can decide whether the computer shuts down, goes to sleep, hibernates, or just ignores you.

To find the factory setting that controls what happens when you close the lid or hit the power button, click in the "Ask me anything" search box and type *lid*.

In the search results, the top hit is "Change what closing the lid does." Press Enter to select it.

Now you arrive at the "Define power buttons" screen. Here, for each option (pressing the power button; pressing the Sleep button, if you have one; closing the lid), you can choose "Sleep," "Do nothing," "Hibernate," "Shut down," or "Turn off the display."

And you can set up different behaviors for when the machine is plugged in and when it's running on battery power.

Navigating the Start Menu by Keyboard

If your computer has a physical keyboard—you old-timer, you!—you can navigate and control the Start menu in either of two ways:

Use the Arrow Keys

Once the Start menu is open, you can use the arrow keys to "walk" up and down the menu. For example, press ↑ to enter the left-side column from the bottom. Or press ↑ and then → to enter the right side.

Either way, once you've highlighted something in either column, you can press the ← or → keys to hop to the opposite side of the menu, or press the ↑ or ↓ keys to highlight other commands in the column (even the Power command or "All apps"). (You can no longer type the first initial of something to select it.)

Once you've highlighted something, you can press Enter to "click" it (open it), or tap the ⊞ key or Esc to close the Start menu and forget the whole thing.

Use the Search Box

This thing is *awesome*. The instant you press the ⊞ key, your insertion point blinks in the new "Ask me anything" search box below the Start menu (Figure 1-13).

Note: If you *click* in the "Ask me anything" search box instead of pressing ⊞, you get a panel full of news, weather, and other details Windows thinks might be relevant to your life. That's all part of Cortana, the voice assistant described in Chapter 5.

That's your cue that you can now begin typing the name of whatever you want to open.

Note: The search box used to be part of the Start menu. Now it's actually part of the taskbar. It still takes you one click, tap, or keystroke to highlight it for typing—but because it's always visible, it seems more present and useful. You know?

The instant you start to type, you trigger Windows' very fast, whole-computer search function. This search can find files, folders, programs, email messages, address book entries, calendar appointments, pictures, movies, PDF documents, music files, Web bookmarks, and Microsoft Office documents, among other things.

It also finds anything *in* the Start menu, making it a very quick way to pull up something without having to click through a bunch of submenus.

You can read the meaty details about search in Chapter 3.

Jump Lists in the Start Menu

Jump lists are submenus that list frequently used commands and files in each of your programs for quick access.

For example, the jump list for a Web browser might offer commands like "New window" and "Close window"; the jump list for a Microsoft Office program (like Word) might list documents you've edited lately.

In other words, jump lists can save you time when you want to resume work on something you had open recently. They save you burrowing through folders.

Now, jump lists can appear either in the Start menu (in the "Most used" section) or on your taskbar. Page 98 describes the taskbar versions, but here's a quick rundown on the Start menu versions.

Recently Opened Documents

The left side of the Start menu—the "Most used" section—keeps track of recently used documents automatically, as shown in Figure 1-14. This list of Recent documents changes as your workflow does; documents drop off the list if you don't open them much anymore.

You can, however, *pin* a document to its jump list, meaning that it won't disappear even if you never open it. Figure 1-14 shows the technique.

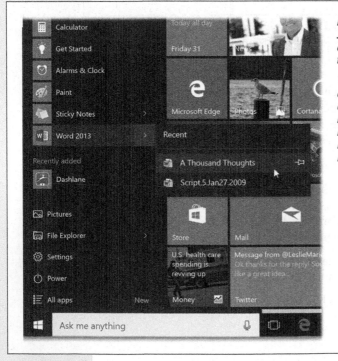

Figure 1-14:
Jump lists display the most recently opened documents in each program. Click the > button to see them.

To pin one of these document s so that it won't disappear on you, point to it without clicking, as shown here, and then click the pushpin icon. Now there's a new section in the jump list called Pinned, where that document will remain undisturbed until you unpin it (by clicking the pushpin again).

The Secret Start Menu

Windows 10's new (old) Start button harbors a secret: It can sprout a tiny utility menu, as shown in Figure 1-15.

To see it, right-click the ⊞ button, or (on a touchscreen) hold your finger down on it.

Tip: Or press ⊞+X to make the secret Start menu appear (if you have a keyboard, of course).

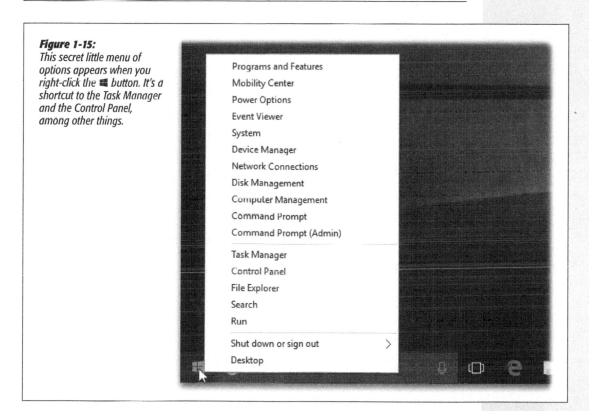

Figure 1-15:
This secret little menu of options appears when you right-click the ⊞ button. It's a shortcut to the Task Manager and the Control Panel, among other things.

There, in all its majesty, is the secret Start menu. It's seething with shortcuts to toys for the technically inclined.

All the items in it are described elsewhere in this book, but some are especially useful to have at your mousetip:

- **System** opens a window that provides every possible detail about your machine.

- **Control Panel** is the quickest known method to get to the desktop Control Panel, described in Chapter 7.

- **Task Manager**. Huge. This special screen (page 228) is your lifeline when a program seems to be locked up. Thanks to the Task Manager, you can quit that app and get on with your life.

CHAPTER 2

File Explorer, Taskbar & Action Center

W indows got its name from the rectangles on the screen—the windows—
where all your computer activity takes place. You look at a Web page in a
window, type into a window, read email in a window, and look at lists of
files in a window. But as you create more files, stash them in more folders, and open
more programs, it's easy to wind up paralyzed before a screen awash with cluttered,
overlapping rectangles.

Fortunately, Windows has always offered icons, buttons, and other inventions to help
you keep these windows under control—and Windows 10 positively crawls with them.

The primary tool at the desktop is now called File Explorer (formerly Windows
Explorer). That's the program—the app—that displays the icons of your files, folders, disks, and programs.

Like any well-behaved program, File Explorer has an icon of its own. You can open
a File Explorer window either by clicking the manila-folder button on the taskbar or
by choosing File Explorer's name in the Start menu's left side.

A desktop window opens, and the fun begins.

Universal Window Controls

A lot has changed in Windows since the Windows of a few years ago. If you're feeling
disoriented, firmly grasp a nearby stationary object and read the following breakdown.

Here are the controls that appear on almost every window, whether in an app or in File Explorer (see Figure 2-1):

- **Control menu.** This tiny icon has sat in the upper-left corner of every File Explorer window since Windows XP. It was invisible (though still functional) in Windows 7, but you can clearly see it now.

In any case, the Control menu contains commands for sizing, moving, and closing the window. One example is the Move command. It turns your cursor into a four-headed arrow; at this point, you can move the window by dragging *any* part of it, even the middle.

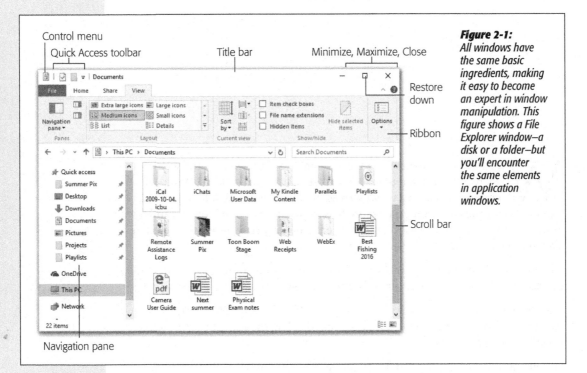

Control menu
Quick Access toolbar
Title bar
Minimize, Maximize, Close
Restore down
Ribbon
Scroll bar
Navigation pane

Figure 2-1:
All windows have the same basic ingredients, making it easy to become an expert in window manipulation. This figure shows a File Explorer window—a disk or a folder—but you'll encounter the same elements in application windows.

Why bother, since you can always just drag the top edge of a window to move it? Because, sometimes, windows get dragged *past* the top of your screen. You can hit Alt+space to open the Control menu, type *M* to trigger the Move command, and then move the window by pressing the arrow keys (or by dragging *any* visible portion). When the window is where you want it, hit Enter to "let go" or the Esc key to return the window to its original position.

Tip: You can double-click the Control menu spot to close a window.

- **Quick Access toolbar.** You can dress up the left end of the title bar with tiny icons for functions you use a lot—like Undo, Properties, New Folder, and Rename. And how do you choose which of these commands show up? By turning them on and off in the Customize Quick Access Toolbar menu (▾), which is always the last icon *in* the Quick Access toolbar.

Tip: As you can see in the ▾ menu, the Quick Access toolbar doesn't have to appear in the title bar (although that is the position that conserves screen space the best). You can also make it appear as a thin horizontal strip below the Ribbon, where it's not so cluttered. Just choose—what else?—"Show below the Ribbon."

- **Title bar.** This big, fat top strip is a giant handle you can use to drag a window around. It also bears the name of the window or folder you're examining.

Tip: The title bar offers two great shortcuts for maximizing a window, making it expand to fill your entire screen exactly as though you had clicked the Maximize button described below. Shortcut 1: Double-click (double-tap) the title bar. (Double-click it again to restore the window to its original size.) Shortcut 2: Drag the title bar up against the top of your monitor.

- **Ribbon.** That massive, tall toolbar at the top of a File Explorer window is the Ribbon. It's a dense collection of controls for the window you're looking at. You can hide it, eliminate it, or learn to value it, as described starting on page 56.

- **Navigation pane.** Some form of this folder tree, a collapsible table of contents for your entire computer, has been part of Windows for years. It's described on page 68.

- **Window edges.** You can reshape a window by dragging any edge—even the very top. Position your cursor over any border until it turns into a double-headed arrow. Then drag inward or outward to make the window smaller or bigger. (To resize a full-screen window, click the Restore Down (❑) button first.)

Tip: You can resize a window in two dimensions at once by dragging one of its corners. It doesn't have to be a certain corner; all four work the same way.

- **Minimize, Maximize, Restore Down.** These three window-control buttons, at the top of every Windows window, cycle a window among its three modes—minimized, maximized, and restored, as described on the following pages.

- **Close button.** Click the ✕ button to close the window. (Keyboard shortcut: Press Alt ⏐ F4.)

Tip: Isn't it cool how the Minimize, Maximize, and Close buttons are highlighted when your cursor passes over them? That's not a gimmick; it's a cue that lets you know when the button is clickable. You might not otherwise realize, for example, that you can close, minimize, or maximize a *background* window without first bringing it forward. But when the background window's Close box glows red, you know.

- **Scroll bar.** A scroll bar appears on the right side or bottom of the window if the window isn't large enough to show all its contents.

Window Management

Windows 10 carries on the window-stunt tradition of previous versions: special shortcuts expressly designed for managing windows. Most of them involve some clever *mouse gestures*—special dragging techniques. Thanks to those mouse movements and the slick animations you get in response, goofing around with your windows may become the new Solitaire.

Sizing Windows

A Windows window can cycle among three altered states.

Maximized

A maximized window is one that fills the screen, edge to edge, so you can't see anything behind it. It gets that way when you do one of these things:

- Click its Maximize button (□).
- Double-click the title bar.
- Drag the window up against the top of the screen.
- Press ⊞+↑. If you have a keyboard, that's an awesome shortcut.

Maximizing the window is an ideal arrangement when you're surfing the Web or working on a document for hours at a stretch, since the largest possible window means the least possible scrolling.

Once you've maximized a window, you can restore it to its usual, free-floating state in any of these ways:

- Drag the window away from the top edge of the screen.
- Double-click the title bar.
- Click the Restore Down button (❐). (It's how the Maximize button appears when the window is *already* maximized.)
- Press ⊞+↓.

Tip: If the window *isn't* maximized, then this keystroke minimizes it instead.

- Press Alt+space, and then R.

Minimized

When you click a window's *Minimize* button (−), the window gets out of your way. It shrinks down into the form of a button on your taskbar at the bottom of the screen. Minimizing a window is a great tactic when you want to see what's behind it. (Keyboard shortcut: ⊞+↓.)

You can bring the window back, of course (it'd be kind of a bummer otherwise). Point to the taskbar button (don't click) that represents that window's *program*. For example, if you minimized a File Explorer (desktop) window, then point to the File Explorer icon. If you have a touchscreen, just *touch* the program's taskbar button.

On the taskbar, the program's button sprouts handy thumbnail miniatures of the minimized windows when you point to it without clicking. Select a window's thumbnail to restore it to full size. (You can read more about this trick later in this chapter.)

Tip: There's a keyboard trick that lets you minimize all your windows at once, revealing your entire desktop. Just press ⊞+M (which you can think of as M for "Minimize all"). Add the Shift key (Shift+⊞+M) to bring them all back.

Restored

A *restored* window is neither maximized nor minimized; it's a loose cannon, floating around on your screen as an independent rectangle. Because its edges aren't attached to the walls of your monitor, you can make it any size you like by dragging its borders.

Moving a Window

Moving a window is easy—just drag the big, fat top edge.

Closing a Window

Microsoft wants to make absolutely sure you're never without some method of closing a window. It offers at least nine ways to do it:

- Click the Close button (the ✕ in the upper-right corner).

Tip: If you've managed to open more than one window, then Shift-click that Close button to close *all* of them.

- Press Alt+F4. (This one's worth memorizing. You'll use it everywhere in Windows.)

- Double-click the window's upper-left corner.

- Right-click (or hold your finger on) the window's button on the taskbar, and then choose Close from the shortcut menu.

- Point to a taskbar button without clicking. Thumbnail images of its windows appear. Point to a thumbnail; a ✕ button appears in its upper-right corner. Click it.

- On a touchscreen, tap a taskbar button with your finger. Thumbnail images of its windows appear, with ✕ buttons in their top right corners. Tap ✕.

- Right-click the window's title bar (top edge), and choose Close from the shortcut menu. (Touchscreen: Hold your finger down on the title bar instead.)

- In a File Explorer window, choose File→Close. That works in most other programs, too.

- Quit the program you're using, log off, or shut down the PC.

Be careful. In many programs, including most Web browsers, closing the window also quits the program entirely.

Hiding All Windows but One

If you've become fond of minimizing windows—and why not?—then you'll love this one. If you give your window's title bar a rapid back-and-forth *shake*, you minimize all *other* windows. The one you shook stays right where it was (Figure 2-2).

Tip: This shaking business makes a very snazzy YouTube demo video, but it's not actually the easiest way to isolate one window. If the window you want to focus on is already the frontmost window, then you can just press ⊞+Home to achieve the same effect. Press that combo a second time to restore all the minimized windows.

Handily enough, you can bring all the hidden windows back again, just by giving the hero window another title-bar shake.

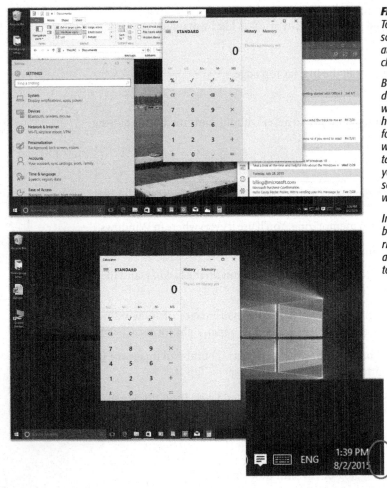

Figure 2-2:

Top: OK, this is the state of your screen. You want to have a look at your desktop—but oy, what a cluttered mess!

Bottom: So you give this window's title bar a little shake—a wiggle—at least a couple of horizontal or vertical back-and-forths—and boom! All other windows are minimized to the taskbar, so you can see what you're doing. Give the title bar a second shake to bring the hidden windows back again.

Inset: This is the Show Desktop button. It's a tiny slice at the far-right end of the taskbar. It makes all windows vanish. Click it again to get them to reappear.

Note: Dialog boxes (for example, boxes with OK and Cancel buttons) aren't affected by this shaking thing—only full-blown windows.

Background Windows

When you have multiple windows open on your screen, only one window is *active*, which affects how it works:

- It's in the foreground, *in front* of all other windows.

- It's the window that "hears" your keystrokes and mouse clicks.

- Its Close button is black. (Background windows' Close buttons are light gray, at least until you point to them.)

As you would assume, clicking a background window brings it to the front.

Tip: And pressing Alt+Esc sends an active window to the *back*. Bet you didn't know that one!

And what if it's so far back that you can't even see it? That's where Windows' window-management tools come in; read on.

NOSTALGIA CORNER

Bringing Back Aero Peek

In Windows 7, that invisible Show Desktop button (the tiny sliver shown in Figure 2-2) housed a gimmicky but cool additional feature. Instead of just clicking it to hide all windows, you could also point to it *without* clicking—and you'd trigger something called Aero Peek.

That's when all the windows stay where they are on your screen—but they become transparent. Only their outlines indicate where they used to be.

That feature no longer works. (Microsoft turned it off in Windows 8, where pointing to the lower-right corner of the screen had a confusing new meaning: Opening something called the Charms bar, which is no longer with us.)

You can bring Aero Peek back from the dead, if you like. Right-click the taskbar; from the shortcut menu, choose Properties. In the Properties dialog box, on the Taskbar tab, turn on "Use Peek to preview the desktop when you move your mouse to the Show Desktop button at the end of the taskbar." Click OK.

Now when you point to the lower-right corner of the screen, you make all windows disappear (except for their outlines). Eat your heart out, Cheshire Cat.

Tip: For quick access to the desktop, you can press ⊞+D. Pressing that keystroke again brings all the windows back to the screen exactly as they were.

There's a secret button that does the same thing when clicked or tapped, too. It's the Show Desktop button—a 3-pixel sliver that occupies the *farthest-right sliver* of the taskbar (Figure 2-2, bottom). Click that spot to make all windows and dialog boxes disappear *completely,* so you can do some work on your desktop. They're not minimized—they don't shrink down into the taskbar; they're just gone. Click the Show Desktop button a second time to bring them back from invisible-land.

Windows Snap—Now with Four Panes!

Here's a weird, wild feature that not many people know about, probably because there's no visible sign that it even exists. But you can neatly split the screen between two windows, full height, edge to edge of the monitor, as shown in Figure 2-3. Or, new in Windows 10, even four windows. (Eight windows will have to wait until Windows 11.)

And why would you bother? Well, a full-height, half-width window is ideal for reading an article, for example. You wouldn't want your eyes to keep scanning the text all the way across the football field of your screen, and you wouldn't want to spend a lot of fussy energy trying to make the window tall enough to read without scrolling a lot. This gesture sets things up for you with one quick drag.

But this half-screen-width trick is even more useful when you apply it to *two* windows. Now it's simple to compare two windows' contents, or to move or copy stuff between them.

Split the screen into two windows

Here's how Snap works. You can follow along in Figure 2-3:

1. **Mash the first window to the right or left edge of the screen.**

   Mouse, trackpad, finger: Using the window's title bar as a handle, drag the window to the right or left edge of the screen (Figure 2-3). When you've gone far enough, Windows shows you an outline of the proposed new window shape. Let go.

   Keyboard: It's actually much faster to use the keyboard shortcuts: ⊞+← to snap the window against the left side, or ⊞+→ to snap it against the right.

Tip: To move the window back again, either hit the same keystroke a few more times (it cycles left, right, and original spot, over and over), or use the ⊞ key with the opposite arrow key.

   At this point, your window is now hugging the side of your monitor, extending only halfway into it (Figure 2-3, top). But in Windows 10, that's not the end of the magic show.

2. **Adjust the width of the half-window, if you like.**

   That's right: Your Windows Snap experience doesn't have to result in a 50/50 split of the screen. It can be 60/40 or whatever you like, within reason. Just grab the inward edge of the window and drag it as wide or narrow as you like.

3. **Click the miniature of the window you want to fill the other half of the screen.**

Thanks to a new feature called Snap Assist, you may notice that the *other* open windows have now shrunk down to little index cards, huddling in the empty half of the screen. They're saying: "Which of us will you pick to fill the empty half?"

Click the one you want, and voilà: two windows, perfectly splitting the available screen area (Figure 2-3, bottom).

To end the Snap session, drag a window away from the edge, or press ⊞+← or ⊞+→.

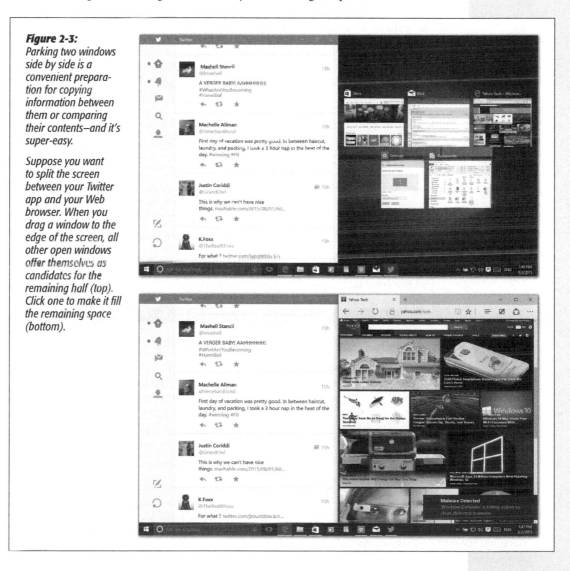

Figure 2-3:
Parking two windows side by side is a convenient preparation for copying information between them or comparing their contents—and it's super-easy.

Suppose you want to split the screen between your Twitter app and your Web browser. When you drag a window to the edge of the screen, all other open windows offer themselves as candidates for the remaining half (top). Click one to make it fill the remaining space (bottom).

Split the screen into three or four windows

If you have a big monitor, you might actually use this new Windows 10 feature. It lets you cram four windows into quadrants of your screen, neatly filling every available pixel. You feel like you're some kind of crazy day trader, or maybe a security guard keeping an eye on all the cameras.

Or, if you prefer, you can split the screen among *three* windows (25 percent, 25 percent, 50 percent).

The steps are similar to the two-pane version. Start with some open windows. Then:

1. **Move the first window into a corner of the screen.**

   Mouse, trackpad, finger: Using the window's title bar as a handle, drag the window to the *corner* of the screen. It's a little tricky; you have to move the cursor, or your finger, *directly* into the *exact* corner. If you don't see the ghost outline of the proposed new window shape, drag away and try again.

   Keyboard: The keyboard shortcut is much faster and more surefire. While holding down the ⊞ key, hit → and then ↑ (for the upper-right corner). Or ← and ↓ (lower-left). You get the idea. Don't hit the arrows simultaneously, but one after another.

Tip: Tweaky but true: Always hit the *horizontal* arrow first. If you press ⊞+↓ and *then* →, you'll lose your window—because ⊞+↓ means "minimize this window"!

   At this point, you have one window filling one quadrant of the screen.

2. **Click the second window; move it into *its* corner.**

   Use the same techniques (drag or keyboard).

NOSTALGIA CORNER

Turn Off All the Snapping and Shaking

It's cool how Windows now makes a window snap against the top or side of your screen. Right? That is, it's better than before, right?

It's perfectly OK to answer, "I don't think so. It's driving me crazy. I don't want my operating system manipulating my windows on its own."

In that case, you can turn off the snapping and shaking features. Open the Start menu. Type enough of the word *arrange* until you see "Arrange windows automatically by dragging them to the sides or corners of the screen." Select it. You've just opened the Settings→System→Multitasking control panel.

Here you can turn off the snapping feature ("Arrange windows automatically by dragging them to the sides or corners of the screen"), the automatic resizing of the second window as you drag the edge of the first ("When I snap more than one window, automatically adjust the size of the windows"), and Snap Assist, described above ("When I snap a window, show what I can snap next to it").

From now on, windows move only when and where you move them. (Shaking a window's title bar doesn't hide other windows now, either. And, alas, the ⊞+↑ and ⊞+↓ keystrokes for Maximize and Restore Down no longer work.)

---

3. Move the remaining one or two windows into their corners.

It doesn't really matter which order you fill the corners of your screen, except in one instance: If you want only *three* windows to split the screen; see Figure 2-4.

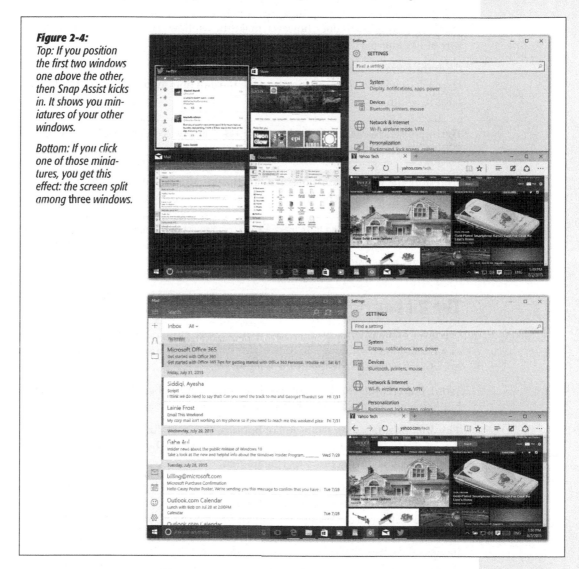

Figure 2-4:
Top: If you position the first two windows one above the other, then Snap Assist kicks in. It shows you miniatures of your other windows.

Bottom: If you click one of those miniatures, you get this effect: the screen split among three windows.

To unsnap, use the opposite keyboard shortcuts. Or drag the window's top edge with your mouse, trackpad, or finger.

Tip: *If you have more than one monitor, add the Shift key to move the frontmost window to the next monitor, left or right.*

The Full-Height Window Trick

This trick has never gotten much love from Microsoft's marketing team, probably because it's a little hard to describe. But it can be very useful.

It's not the same as the Snap thing described previously; this one doesn't affect the *width* of the window. It does, however, make the window exactly as tall as your screen, sort of like *half*-maximizing it.

Grab the *bottom* edge of your window and drag it *down,* to the bottom edge of your screen. The window snaps vertically to the top and bottom of your screen but maintains its width and horizontal position.

Tip: There's a keyboard shortcut for this feature: Shift+■+↑ to create the full-height effect and (of course) Shift+■+↓ to restore the window's original height.

To restore the window to its original dimensions, drag its top or bottom edge away from the edge of your screen.

Note: These window-morphing tricks make a good complement to the traditional "Cascade windows," "Show windows stacked," and "Show windows side by side" commands that appear when you right-click an empty spot on the taskbar.

The Ribbon

Windows offers all kinds of crazy ways to shape, sort, group, slice, and dice the contents of a File Explorer window. The controls are hiding in the Ribbon, which is a glorified horizontal toolbar at the top of the window.

Word, PowerPoint, Excel, and other Microsoft programs have Ribbons of their own, but here's an introduction to the one in File Explorer.

This Ribbon offers several tabs full of buttons. They can differ from window to window; for example, in a window full of pictures, you get buttons that are especially useful for managing picture files (Figure 2-5).

You can collapse the Ribbon to get it out of your way; it is, after all, pretty tall. You do that by clicking the ⌄ button at the window's upper-right corner, or by pressing Ctrl+F1. (Later, you can bring it back by clicking the ⌃ button, or by pressing Ctrl+F1 again. But that might not be necessary; even when the Ribbon is collapsed, its tab names—File, Home, Share, View, and so on—are still visible for quick clicking.)

Tip: The Ribbon also goes away in Full Screen mode, in which your File Explorer window fills the entire screen. (Press F11 to start or stop Full Screen mode.)

You can also get rid of it permanently, using the free Ribbon Disabler program. You can download it from this book's "Missing CD" page at *www.missingmanuals.com.*

But before you go whole-hog into a Ribbon-cutting ceremony, consider what the Ribbon has to offer.

File Tab

Ha, fooled you! The word File here looks like all the other tabs, but it's actually a weird kind of menu (Figure 2-5, top). The idea, as always, is to cram every possible command you might want into one central place, so you don't have to hunt.

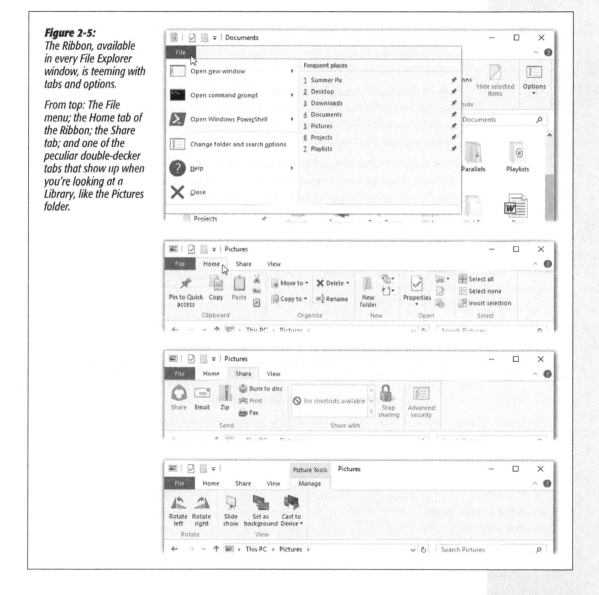

Figure 2-5:
The Ribbon, available in every File Explorer window, is teeming with tabs and options.

From top: The File menu; the Home tab of the Ribbon; the Share tab; and one of the peculiar double-decker tabs that show up when you're looking at a Library, like the Pictures folder.

Note: Many of these commands have submenus (a ▶ pointing to the right, containing more commands). But unlike normal submenus, you don't have to choose one of the subcommands. For example, the "Open new window" command has a submenu, but you can click or tap the "Open new window" command itself. If you *do* want one of the submenu choices, hit the ▶ symbol to see them.

Here's a rundown:

- **Open new window.** Creates a duplicate of the window you're browsing. (The submenu offers another "Open new window" command, plus "Open new window in new process." A *process* is a computer's train of thought. Hard-core PC geeks sometimes like to open a new window, or a second copy of the same one, in a new computer process in case the first one crashes. Not something you'll do every day.)

- **Open command prompt.** The command prompt is a *command line*, a text-based method of performing a task. You type a command, click OK, and something happens as a result. Power users can type long sequences of commands and symbols at the command prompt.

  Working at the command line is becoming a lost art in the world of Windows, because most people prefer to issue commands by choosing from menus using the mouse. However, some old-timers still love the command prompt, and even mouse lovers encounter situations when a typed command is the only way to do something.

  In the submenu: "Open command prompt as administrator," which gives you greater powers over your PC domain, once you enter an administrator password to prove your worth. Either way, the white-text-on-black command prompt window opens, ready for your typed input.

- **Open Windows PowerShell.** PowerShell is a command console and scripting language. If you're a programmer, PowerShell lets you write your own simple programs,

---

POWER USERS' CLINIC

Power Keys for the Ribbon

The Ribbon is supposed to enhance your efficiency by putting every conceivable command in one place, with nothing hidden. But how efficient is a tool that requires mousing?

Fortunately, the Ribbon is fully keyboard-operable. It even has a built-in cheat sheet. To see it, press the Alt key, which is the universal Windows shortcut for "Show me the keyboard shortcuts." You see the little boxed letter-key shortcuts for

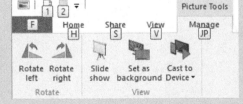

each of the tabs, as shown here. (Those keystrokes work, however, even if you haven't first summoned the cheat sheet.)

Sometimes, you'll actually see *two*-letter codes, to be typed one letter a time. In a Pictures library, for example, the Picture Tools tab of the Ribbon offers "JP" as the keyboard shortcut to get you to the Manage tab. But the idea is the same: to save you time and mousing.

---

called *cmdlets* ("commandlets") that can perform all kinds of automated drudgery for you: Copy or move folders, manipulate files, open or quit programs, and so on.

You harness all this power by typing up *scripts* in PowerShell's command line interface (which means no mouse, no menus, no windows—all text, like in the DOS days). In short, PowerShell is not for the layperson. If you're an ambitious layperson, however, a Google search for *PowerShell tutorial* unveils all kinds of Web sites that teach you, step by step, how to harness this very advanced tool.

- **Options.** Opens the time-honored Folder Options dialog box, described on page 86.

- **Help.** The Help command in the submenu opens a Bing search. The About Windows command just opens a dialog box that identifies which version of Windows 10 you have.

- **Close.** Closes the File Explorer window.

- **Frequent places.** Here, for your convenience, is a listing of important folders in your account (Desktop, Downloads, Documents, Pictures, Music, and so on), plus folders you've accessed recently. The idea is to save you some burrowing.

Tip: If you have a keyboard, you can save time by hitting the indicated number. In fact, *all* of the File menu commands offer keyboard shortcuts. See how it says "Open new window"? That underline means you can type the N key to open a new window, rather than using the mouse or a finger.

Home Tab

This tab of the Ribbon is, more or less, an exploded view of the shortcut menu that would appear if you right-clicked a desktop icon. But Microsoft research shows that a huge number of Windows fans don't even *know* about the shortcut menus—so by putting these commands in the Ribbon, the company hopes to make these useful commands more "discoverable."

- **Pin to Quick access.** The "Quick access" folder, new in Windows 10, lists folders and files you've used recently, so it's easier to get back to them later. By using this command, you can force icons to appear in this folder. See page 68.

- **Copy, Paste, Cut.** These commands let you copy, cut, and paste icons from one window to another.

- **Copy path.** This command copies the icon's navigational *path* to the Clipboard, ready for pasting somewhere. (See page 611.)

- **Paste Shortcut.** If you've copied an icon to the Clipboard, then this command pastes a shortcut icon of it—another handy way to make a shortcut (page 151).

- **Move to, Copy to.** These handy buttons/menus make it quick and easy to move or copy selected icons to another place on your computer. The pop-up menu lists frequently and recently opened folders; you can also hit "Choose location" to specify a folder that's not listed here. Either way, the beauty is that you can move or copy icons without having to open and position the destination window.

- **Delete.** The pop-up menu offers two commands: "Recycle" (moves the selected icon to the Recycle Bin) and "Permanently delete" (deletes the file forever without its usual stop in the Recycle Bin). The third item, "Show recycle confirmation," isn't a command—it's an on/off switch for the "Are you sure?" message that usually appears when you put something into the Recycle Bin.

- **Rename.** Opens the selected icon's name-editing box.

- **New Folder.** Makes a new, empty folder in the current window, ready for you to name and fill up with icons.

- **New item.** Here's a catch-all pop-up menu that lists new things you might want to create in the open window: a new folder, a shortcut (page 151), a contact (that is, a new person page in the People app), a Microsoft Word document, a Journal document, a text document, a compressed (zipped) folder, and so on. You may see different items here, since different programs can modify this menu to make your life more convenient.

- **Easy access.** Here's an even more miscellaneous pop-up menu of useful commands; all of them apply to icons you've selected in the window. "Include in library" adds the selected icon to one of your libraries (page 72). To understand "Map as drive," read page 611.

  The remaining commands—"Always available offline," "Sync," and "Work offline," pertain to the offline files feature described on page 453.

- **Properties.** This button/menu offers two options: "Properties" opens the selected icon's Properties dialog box, where you can read a wealth of detail about its size, type, and so on. "Remove properties" strips all of that stuff out of a file, usually because you're about to send it to somebody and don't want them to know about its revision history, modification dates, and so on.

Tip: You can just click the icon to open the Properties dialog box. That is, you don't actually have to choose from the submenu.

- **Open.** Do you really need a button that opens the selected icon? Yes, if it's a type of file that *more than one program can open.* For example, suppose you have a picture file. Do you want to open it in Photoshop or in Picasa? This pop-up menu changes to reflect the programs that are capable of opening the selected icon.

- **Edit** opens the highlighted icon in the first program Windows finds that can edit that file type.

- **History.** This button opens a window that tracks the file's editing history. It's an essential part of the *File History* feature described on 526; it lets you rewind a certain document to an earlier version.

- **Select all, Select none.** As you'd guess, these commands highlight all the icons in the window, or none of them.

- **Invert selection.** This command swaps what you've selected. In other words, if you've highlighted files A and B (but not C and D), then this command highlights files C and D and deselects A and B.

Share Tab

This tab offers a full line of controls for sharing the icons in the window—via email, fax, printer, or other people on your network.

- **Share.** Click to open a panel at the right side of your screen, listing apps that can hand off the selected item. For example, if you've selected a file, the choices might include Mail (to send it as an attachment) or Dropbox (to put a copy in your Dropbox). This Share panel is a standard Windows 10 element, and it appears in many apps.

- **Email.** Click to open a new outgoing email message, with the selected file(s) attached, ready to address and send.

- **Zip.** Compresses the selected file(s) into one compact, self-contained .zip file. Great for sending a batch of related files to somebody in a way that contains all the necessary pieces.

- **Burn to disc.** Prompts you to insert a blank CD or DVD; Windows will burn a copy of the selected files onto that disc. (If you don't have a disc burner, then this icon is dimmed.)

- **Print.** Opens the document and, depending on what kind of file it is, prepares it for printing.

- **Fax.** Sends the selected file to your fax modem, if you have one.

- **Specific people.** Makes the selected file(s) available for accessing over the network by people you specify. (Chapter 21 has details.) When you click here, a window opens up with a list of people on the network, so you can choose the lucky collaborators. You may also see a "Create or join a homegroup" command here, which does just what it says (Chapter 21).

- **Stop sharing.** Turns off network sharing, so that once again, you're the only person who can see the selected files.

- **Advanced security.** This control, too, affects file sharing on the network. It gives you much finer control over who's allowed to do what to the selected file: See it? Open it? Change it? Chapter 21 contains more on these file permissions.

View Tab

This tab controls the look, arrangement, and layout of the icons in the window: list view, icon view, sorted alphabetically, sorted chronologically, and so on. Page 88 has a complete rundown of these options.

Library Tools/Manage Tab

In a few places, you get a bonus tab—with a weird double-stacked title. These tabs appear only when you've opened the window of a *library*—a special class of folder that can display the contents of *other* folders, wherever they may actually sit on your machine, without having to move them. You can read more about libraries on page 72.

Music Tools/Play Tab

In the navigation list at the left side of a File Explorer window, folders like Music and Pictures await your inspection. Each offers a special Ribbon tab of its own. For example, when you've selected a music file in the Music library (either the one Windows gives you or one you've made yourself), the window bears a new double-decker tab called Music Tools/Play. These are your options:

- **Play.** Opens your music-playback program and begins playing the highlighted music. (If you've never selected a favorite playback program, Windows offers you a list of music programs and invites you to choose one.)

- **Play all.** Opens your playback app and begins playing everything in the window.

- **Cast to Device.** This pop-up menu lets you direct audio or video playback to another device—usually an Xbox connected to your TV, but there are other Play To–compatible receivers. If you do, in fact, own one of these gadgets, and you've configured it right, you'll see it listed in this pop-up menu. Choose its name to redirect sound. (If you don't have any other compatible playback gadgets, this button is dimmed.)

- **Add to playlist.** Adds the highlighted music file to a new, untitled playlist in Windows Media Player. The idea is that you can root around here, in a File Explorer window, adding files to a playlist without having to open Media Player first.

Picture Tools/Manage Tab

Opening the Pictures library folder offers a special double-decker tab, too, stocked with commands for controlling pictures. They include these:

- **Rotate left, Rotate right.** Turns the selected photos 90 degrees. Handy if they're coming up turned sideways because of the way you held the camera.

- **Slide show.** Starts an immediate full-screen slideshow. Click the mouse or tap to go to the next picture; press the arrow keys to go faster forward or backward; press the Esc key to stop the show.

- **Set as background.** Instantly applies the selected photo to your desktop, as its new wallpaper!

- **Cast to Device.** If you have an Xbox, a Miracast adapter, or another playback gadget attached to your TV, then you can send a photo or slideshow from your Windows machine to the big screen with this one click.

Tabucopia

Incredibly, that's not all the tabs. You'll see other tabs appear when you open certain window types. There's a Ribbon tab just for the Recycle Bin. There's a Disk Tools tab (when you open a disk window), a Shortcut Tools tab (for a shortcut), Application Tools (for a program), and so on. Part of the fun is encountering new tabs you've never seen before.

File Explorer Window Controls

When you're working at the desktop—that is, opening File Explorer folder windows—you'll find a few additional controls dotting the edges. They're quite a bit different from the controls of Windows XP and its predecessors.

Address Bar

In a Web browser, the address bar is where you type the addresses of the Web sites you want to visit. In a File Explorer window, the address bar is more of a "bread-crumbs bar" (a shout-out to Hansel and Gretel fans). That is, it now shows the path you've taken—folders you burrowed through—to arrive where you are now (Figure 2-6).

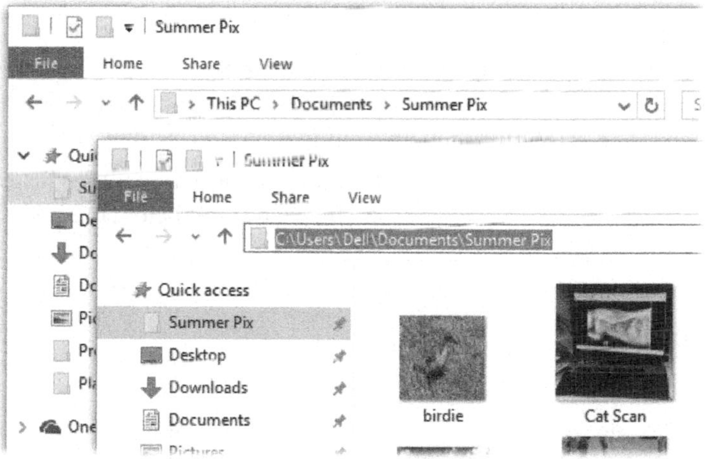

Figure 2-6:
Top: The notation in the address bar, This PC > Documents > Summer Pix, indicates that you opened the Documents folder and then opened the Summer Pix folder inside that.

Bottom: If you press Alt+D, then the address bar restores the slash notation of Windows versions gone by so that you can type in a different address.

There are three especially cool things about this address bar:

• **It's much easier to read.** Those > little > brackets are clearer separators of folder names than the older\slash\notation. And instead of drive letters like C:, you see the drive *names*.

Tip: *If the succession of nested folders' names is too long to fit the window, then a microscopic* « *icon appears at the left end of the address. Click it to reveal a pop-up menu showing, from last to first, the other folders you've had to burrow through to get here.*

(Below the divider line, you see, for your convenience, the names of all the folders on your desktop.)

- **It's clickable.** You can click any bread crumb to open the corresponding folder. For example, if you're viewing the Casey > Pictures > Halloween folder, you can click the *word* Pictures to backtrack to the Pictures folder.

- **You can still edit it.** The address bar of old was still a powerful tool, because you could type in a folder address directly (using the slash notation).

  Actually, you still can. You can "open" the address bar for editing in any of four different ways: (1) Press Alt+D. (2) Click the tiny icon to the left of the address. (3) Click any blank spot. (4) Right-click (or hold your finger down) anywhere in the address; from the shortcut menu, choose Edit Address.

  In each case, the address bar changes to reveal the old-style slash notation, ready for editing (Figure 2-6, bottom).

Tip: *After you've had a good look, press Esc to restore the* ► *notation.*

Components of the address bar
On top of all that, the address bar houses a few additional doodads that make it easy for you to jump around on your hard drive (Figure 2-7):

- **Back** (←), **Forward** (→). Just as in a Web browser, the Back button opens whatever window you opened just before this one. Once you've used the Back button,

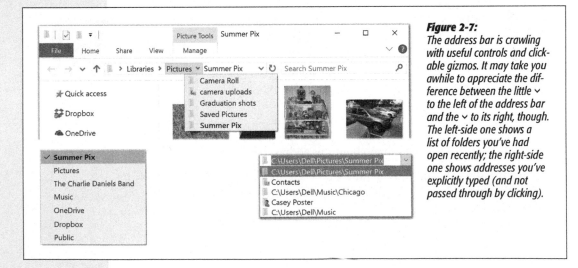

Figure 2-7:
The address bar is crawling with useful controls and clickable gizmos. It may take you awhile to appreciate the difference between the little ˅ to the left of the address bar and the ˅ to its right, though. The left-side one shows a list of folders you've had open recently; the right-side one shows addresses you've explicitly typed (and not passed through by clicking).

you can then use the Forward button to return to the window where you started. *Keyboard shortcuts:* Alt+←, Alt+→.

- **Recent pages list.** Click the ⌄ to the left of the address bar to see a list of folders you've had open recently; it's like a multilevel Back button.

- **Recent folders list.** Click the ⌄ at the *right* end of the address bar to see a pop-up menu of addresses you've recently typed.

- **Up (↑).** This delightful button, right next to the address bar, means "Open the parent folder of this one." It's a novice-friendly incarnation of the trusty Alt+↑ keystroke.

  For example, if you've drilled down into the USA > Texas > Houston folder, you could hit this button (or Alt+↑) to pop "upward" to the Texas folder, again for the USA folder, and so on. If you hit ↑ enough times, you wind up at your desktop.

- **Contents list.** This one takes some explaining, but for efficiency nuts, it's a gift from the gods.

  It turns out that the little > next to each bread crumb (folder name) is actually a pop-up menu. Click it to see what's *in* the folder name to its left.

POWER USERS' CLINIC

The Master File Explorer-Window Keyboard-Shortcut List

If you arrive home one day to discover that your mouse has been stolen, or if you simply like using the keyboard, you'll enjoy the shortcuts that work in File Explorer:

F6 or **Tab** cycles the "focus" (highlighting) among the different parts of the window: Favorite Links, address bar, main window, search box, and so on.

Shift+Ctrl+N makes a new empty folder.

F4 highlights the address bar and pops open the list of previous addresses. (Press Alt+D to highlight the address bar without opening the pop-up menu.)

Alt+← opens the previously viewed window, as though you'd clicked the Back button in a browser. Once you've used Alt+←, you can press Alt+→ to move *forward* through your recently open windows.

Backspace does the same thing as Alt+←. It, too, walks you backward through the most recent windows you've had open. That's a change from Windows XP, when Backspace meant "up," as in, "Take me to the parent folder" (see Alt+↑, below).

Alt+↑ opens the parent window of whatever you're looking at now—just like the ↑ button next to the address bar.

Alt+double-clicking an icon opens the Properties window for that icon. (It shows the same sort of information you'd find in the Details pane.) Or, if the icon is already highlighted, press Alt+Enter.

Alt+P hides or shows the Preview pane.

F11 enters or exits full-screen mode, in which the current window fills the entire screen. Even the taskbar and Ribbon are hidden. This effect is more useful in a Web browser than at the desktop, but you never know; sometimes you want to see everything in a folder.

Shift+Ctrl+E adjusts the navigation pane so that it reveals the folder path of whatever window is open right now, expanding the indented folder icons as necessary.

Press letter keys to highlight a folder or file that begins with that letter, or the ↑ and ↓ keys to "walk" up and down a list of icons.

How is this useful? Suppose you're viewing the contents of the USA > Florida > Miami folder, but you decide that the file you're looking for is actually in the USA > California folder. Do you have to click the Back button, retracing your steps to the USA folder, only to then walk back down a different branch of the folder tree? No, you don't. You just click the > that's next to the USA folder's name and choose California from the list.

- **Refresh (↻).** If you suspect that the window contents aren't up to date (for example, that maybe somebody has just dropped something new into it from across the network), click this button, or press F5, to make Windows update the display.

- **Search box.** Type a search phrase into this box to find what you're looking for *within this window.*

What to type into the address bar

When you click the tiny folder icon at the left end of the address bar (or press Alt+D), the bracket > notation changes to the slash\notation, meaning that you can edit the address. At this point, the address bar is like the little opening in the glass divider that lets you speak to your New York cab driver; you tell it where you want to go. Here's what you can type there (press Enter afterward):

- **A Web address.** You can leave off the *http://* portion. Just type the body of the Web address, such as *www.sony.com,* into this strip. When you press Enter (or click the → button to the right of the address box, called the Go button), your Web browser opens to the Web page you specified.

Tip: If you press Ctrl+Enter instead of just Enter, you can surround whatever you've just typed into the address bar with *http://www.* and *.com.* See Chapter 10 for even more address shortcuts along these lines.

- **A search phrase.** If you type some text into this strip that isn't obviously a Web address, then Windows assumes you're telling it, "Go online and search for this phrase." From here, it works exactly as though you'd typed into the address/search bar of Windows Edge.

- **A folder name.** You can also type one of several important folder names into this strip, such as *This PC, Documents, Music,* and so on. When you press Enter, that particular folder window opens.

Tip: This window has AutoComplete. That is, if you type *pi* and then press Tab, the address bar completes the word *Pictures* for you. (If it guesses wrong, press Tab again.)

- **A program or path name.** In this regard, the address bar works just like the Run command (page 346).

In each case, as soon as you begin to type, a pop-up list of recently visited Web sites, files, or folders appears below the address bar. Windows is trying to save you some typing. If you see what you're looking for, click it with the mouse, or press the ↓ key to highlight the one you want, and then press Enter.

Optional Window Panes

Most File Explorer windows have some basic informational stuff across the top: the address bar and the Ribbon, at the very least.

But that's just the beginning. As shown in Figure 2-8, you can add a new panel to the right side of any File Explorer window. It can take one of two forms: a Preview (of the selected icon) or a panel of Details. Turning one of these panels on may make your window feel a bit claustrophobic, but at least you'll know absolutely everything there is to know about your files and folders.

The on/off switch for this panel is on the View tab of the Ribbon, as shown in Figure 2-8.

Tip: You can adjust the size of any pane by dragging the dividing line that separates it from the main window. (You know you've got the right spot when your cursor turns into a double-headed arrow.)

Figure 2-8:
Use the View tab of the Ribbon to summon or dismiss the Preview or Details pane at the right side of the window. (You can have only one or the other visible—not both, as you could in Windows 7.)

Choose the name of a pane once to make it appear, a second time to hide it.

Inset: The taller you make the Details pane, the more information you reveal about the selected item.

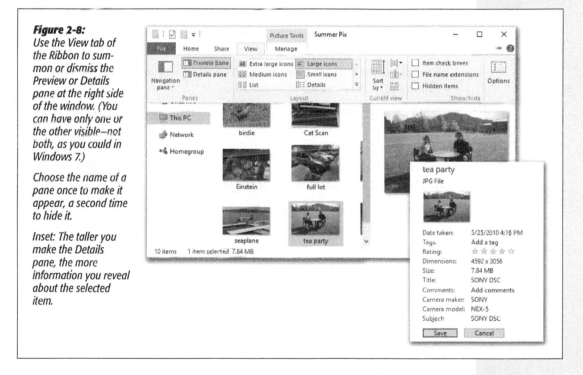

Preview Pane

The Preview pane appears either when you click the Preview pane button (shown in Figure 2-8) or when you press Alt+P.

It can be handy when you're examining common file types like pictures, text files, RTF files, and Office documents. As you click each icon, you see a magnified thumbnail version of what's actually *in* that document. (Alas, the Preview pane can no longer play back music and movie files, right in place.)

Now, the Preview pane isn't omniscient; right out of the box, Windows can't display the contents of oddball document types like, say, sheet-music documents or 3D modeling files. But as you install new programs, the Preview pane can get smarter. Install Office, for example, and it can display Office files' contents; install Adobe Acrobat, and it can show you PDF files. Whether or not the Preview pane recognizes a certain document type depends on the effort expended by the programmers who wrote its program (that is, whether they wrote *preview handlers* for their document types).

Details Pane

To open this panel (Figure 2-8, inset), click "Details pane" on the Ribbon, or press Shift+Alt+P. You get all kinds of information about whatever icon you've clicked in the main part of the window: its size, date, type, and so on. Some examples:

- **For a music file,** the Details pane reveals the song's duration, band and album names, genre, the star rating you've provided, and so on.

- **For a disk icon,** you get statistics about its formatting scheme, capacity, and how much of it is full.

- **For a Microsoft Office document,** you see when it was created and modified, how many pages it has, who wrote it, and so on.

- If *nothing* **is selected,** you get information about the open window itself: namely, how many items are in it.

- **If you select several icons at once,** this pane shows you the sum of their file sizes—a great feature when you're burning a CD, for example, and don't want to exceed the 650 MB limit. You also see the *range* of dates when they were created and modified.

What's especially intriguing is that you can *edit* many of these details, just by clicking and typing.

Navigation Pane

The navigation pane is the helpful folder map at the left side of a File Explorer window. It's come a long way, baby, since the folder hierarchy of Windows XP, and even since the navigation pane of Windows Vista. Today, it's something like a master map of your computer, with a special focus on the places and things you might want to visit most often.

Quick access list

At the top of the navigation pane, there's a collapsible list called "Quick access"—a new Windows 10 feature.

Well, kinda new. There was something similar here called Favorites in earlier Windows versions. But that was (a) confusing, since bookmarks in Microsoft's Web browser are *also* called Favorites, and (b) not as full-featured as "Quick access." (The "Quick access" section of a window has nothing to do with the Quick Access *toolbar*, either.)

This new list is intended to be one-stop shopping for important folders and disks, in two categories:

- Folders and disks that you "pin" here.

- Folders and disks you use frequently. Windows chooses them automatically. (That's the new part in Windows 10.)

"Quick access" displays *links* to these folders, wherever they happen to be on your machine. You're never actually moving them.

This list is a big deal. The "Quick access" window, in fact, greets you every time you open a File Explorer window. That's how important Microsoft considers this list.

Tip: File Explorer doesn't have to fill every window with "Quick access." It can, if you prefer, show you the primary folders of your PC, as it did in the old days. To make that happen, start in a File Explorer window. On the Ribbon's View tab, click Options. At the top of the resulting Folder Options window, change the "Open File Explorer to" pop-up menu to "This PC," and click OK.

Taking the time to install your favorite folders here can save you a lot of repetitive folder-burrowing. One click on an item's name opens the corresponding window. For example, click the Pictures icon to view the contents of your Pictures folder in the main part of the window.

The beauty of this parking lot for containers is that it's so easy to set up with *your* favorite places. For example:

- **Install a new folder, disk, library, or saved search.** Drag its icon off of your desktop (or out of a window) into any spot in the "Quick access" list (Figure 2-9, top).

  Or right-click the icon of any folder or disk (or hold your finger down on it); from the shortcut menu, choose "Pin to Quick access."

  Or, if the folder or disk window is already open, right-click the words "Quick access" (at the top of the list); from the shortcut menu, choose "Pin current folder to Quick access."

  Or, if you've highlighted a disk or folder icon, click "Pin to Quick access" on the Ribbon's Home tab (Figure 2-9, bottom).

- **Remove an icon from "Quick access."** Right-click its name in the list (or hold your finger down) to open the shortcut menu.

  If *you* put this thing into the menu, choose "Unpin from Quick access." If *Windows* put it there (because you use it frequently), choose "Remove from Quick access." Not only does that frequently used item disappear, but it also won't reappear, even if you use it all the time.

  In both cases, you haven't actually removed anything from your *PC;* you've just unhitched its alias from the navigation pane.

- **Rearrange** the icons by dragging them up or down in the list. Release the mouse when the black horizontal line lies in the desired new location.

Note: Windows can no longer sort this list alphabetically.

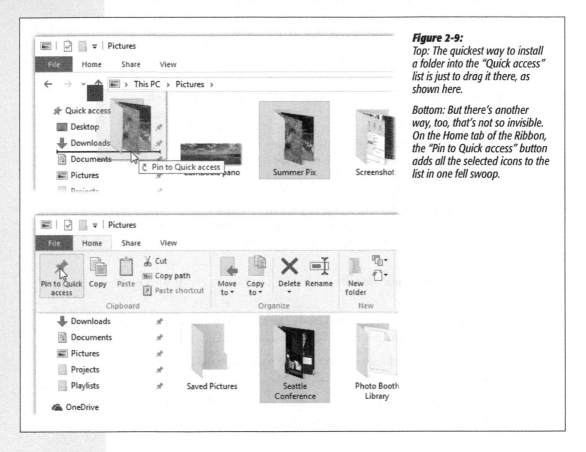

Figure 2-9:
Top: The quickest way to install a folder into the "Quick access" list is just to drag it there, as shown here.

Bottom: But there's another way, too, that's not so invisible. On the Home tab of the Ribbon, the "Pin to Quick access" button adds all the selected icons to the list in one fell swoop.

- **Adjust the width of the pane** by dragging the vertical divider bar right or left.

Tip: If you drag carefully, you can position the divider bar *just* to the right of the disk and folder icons, thereby hiding their names almost completely. Some people find it a tidier look; you can always identify the folder names by pointing to them without clicking.

- **Make "Quick access" stop listing the folders and files you use often.** In a File Explorer window, click the Ribbon's View tab. Click Options to open the Folder Options window. Turn off "Show recently used files in Quick access" or "Show frequently used folders in Quick access" to make it stop tracking your file and folder use, respectively. Click OK.

(You're still free to pin stuff there yourself, if you like; it's just that Windows will no longer add things it sees you using often.)

Tip: On the other hand, if you do like the "Quick access" concept, you can add its name to the Start menu's right side. That'll give you a quick way to open it whenever the Start menu is open.

Right-click (or hold your finger down on) the actual words "Quick access" at the top of the "Quick access" list. From the shortcut menu, choose Pin to Start.

OneDrive

Here's the contents of your Microsoft OneDrive—your free, 15-gigabyte "hard drive in the sky" (actually, on the Internet). Page 161 offers the details.

This PC

The next heading is This PC. (Yes, after 20 years, Microsoft finally retired the term "My Computer.") When you expand this heading, you see a list of all your drives (including the main C: drive), each of which is also expandable (Figure 2-10). In essence, this view can show you every folder on the machine at once. It lets you burrow very deeply into your hard drive's nest of folders without ever losing your bearings.

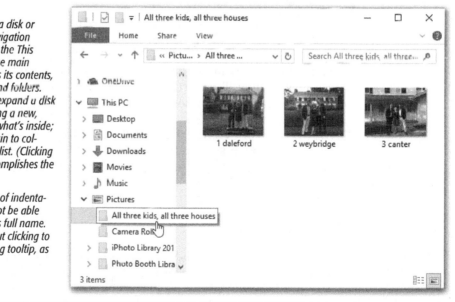

Figure 2-10:
When you click a disk or folder in the navigation pane—including the This PC hierarchy—the main window displays its contents, including files and folders. Double-click to expand a disk or folder, opening a new, indented list of what's inside; double-click again to collapse the folder list. (Clicking the flippy > accomplishes the same thing.)

At deeper levels of indentation, you may not be able to read an icon's full name. Point to it without clicking to see an identifying tooltip, as shown here.

Libraries

The next section of the navigation pane may list your *libraries*, if you've turned on this feature; read on.

Network

The Network heading shows your entire network. Not just Windows PCs that have been connected as a HomeGroup, but the *entire* network—Macs, PCs running older Windows versions, Linux boxes, whatever.

Homegroup

Finally, last in the nav pane, you might find the HomeGroup heading. Here's a list of all the computers in your house (Windows 7 and later) that you've joined into a harmonious unit using the HomeGroup networking feature. It's described in Chapter 21.

Flippy arrows

The navigation list displays *only* disks and folders, never individual files. To see those, look at the main window, which displays the contents (folders *and* files) of whatever disk or folder you click.

To expand a folder or disk that appears in the nav pane, double-click its name, or click the **>** next to its name. You've just turned the nav list into an outline; the contents of the folder appear in an indented list, as shown in Figure 2-10. Double-click the folder's name again to collapse the folder listing.

Tip: Windows can, if you like, expand the folder list automatically as you navigate your folders. Open the Music folder with your mouse, for example, and the Music folder's flippy **>** is automatically opened, giving you a visual representation of where you are. Sound useful? Turn it on like this: On the Ribbon's View tab, click Options. On the View tab of the resulting Folder Options dialog box, turn on "Expand to open folder." Click OK.

By selectively expanding folders like this, you can, in effect, peer inside two or more folders simultaneously, all within the single navigation list. You can move files around by dragging them onto the tiny folder icons, too.

Tip: Ordinarily, the nav pane shows only folders that Microsoft thinks you'd be interested in—folders that contain your stuff, for example. But, if you like, it can display more Windowsy folders like the Control Panel and Recycle Bin, too. On the Ribbon's View tab, click Options; the Folder Options dialog box appears. On the View tab, turn on "Show all folders." Click OK.

Libraries

Libraries, which debuted in Windows 7, are like folders, with one difference: They can display the contents of *other* folders from all over your PC—and even from other PCs on your network. In other words, a library doesn't really contain anything at all. It simply monitors *other* folders and provides a single "place" to work with all their contents.

Note: If you think that sounds confusing, you're not alone. So many people were befuddled by libraries that Microsoft hid this feature!

If you decide to try libraries out, you can bring them back easily enough. On the View tab of the Ribbon, open the "Navigation pane" pop-up menu and choose "Show libraries." Now they're back.

Windows starts you out with four libraries: Documents, Music, Pictures, and Videos. (You can make libraries of your own, too.)

Sure, XP and Vista came with *folders* bearing those names, but libraries are much more powerful. The Pictures library, for example, seems to contain all your photos—but in real life, they may be scattered all over your hard drive, on external drives, or on other PCs in the house.

So what's the point? Well, consider the advantages over regular folders:

- **Everything's in one spot.** When it comes time to put together a year-end photo album, for example, you might be very grateful to find your pictures, your spouse's pictures from the upstairs PC, and the pictures from your kids' laptop all in one central place, ready for choosing. Figure 2-11 shows the idea.

Figure 2-11:
The Pictures library window seems to contain a bunch of photo folders, all in one place. But don't be fooled; in real life, these folders are scattered all over your system.

In this library, for example, there are picture folders from your OneDrive (top row), this PC (middle), and an SD memory card that's inserted into the computer (bottom).

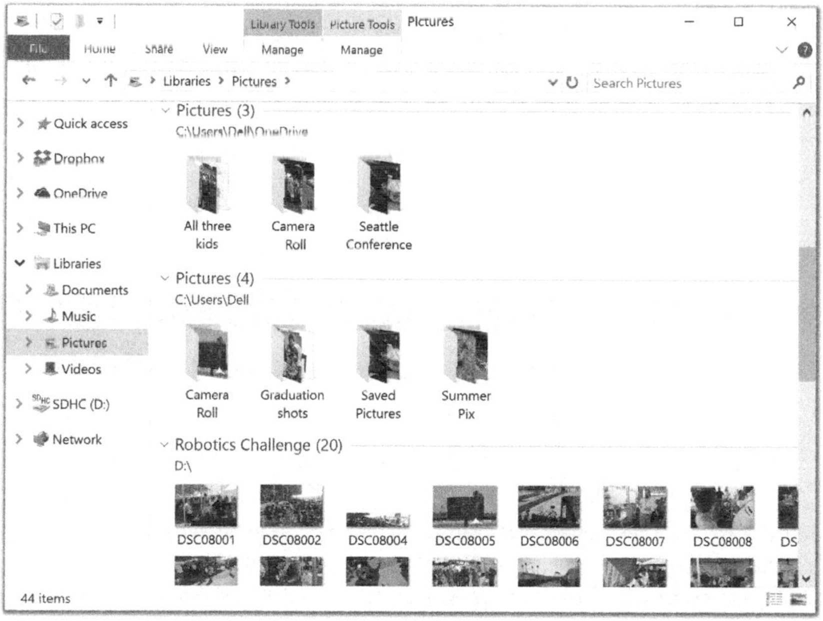

- **Happy laptop reunions.** When you come home with your laptop and connect to the network, you're instantly reunited with all those music, picture, and video files you store on other drives.

• **Easy backup or transfer.** You can back up or transfer all the files corresponding to a certain project or time period in one fell swoop, even though the originals are in a bunch of different places or reside on different collaborators' computers.

• **Manipulate en masse.** You can *work* with the contents of a library—deleting, searching, organizing, filtering—just as you would a folder's contents. But because you're actually working with folders from all over your computer and even your network, you can be far more efficient.

Working with Library Contents

To use a library, click its name in your navigation pane. (Try Pictures, for example.)

A special Library Tools tab appears on the Ribbon; that's how you know you're in a Library and not just a normal folder.

Tip: Remember, the icons in a library aren't really there; they're just a mirage. They're stunt doubles for files that actually sit in other folders on your hard drive.

Fortunately, when you're getting a bit confused as to what's really where, there's a way to jump to a file or folder's actual location. Right-click its icon in the library; from the shortcut menu, choose "Open file location" (or "Open folder location"). You jump right to the real thing, sitting in its actual File Explorer window.

Adding a Folder to an Existing Library

A library is nothing without a bunch of folders to feed into it. You can add a folder to a library (like Pictures or Music) in any of four ways, depending on where you're starting.

• **You can see the folder's icon.** If the folder is on the desktop or in a window, right-click it (or hold your finger down on it). From the shortcut menu, choose "Include in library"; the submenu lists all your existing libraries so you can choose the one you want. Figure 2-12 shows the idea.

Hiding and Showing Individual Libraries

Microsoft thinks libraries are very important. After all, libraries get one of the coveted spots in the navigation pane at the left side of every single File Explorer window.

You, however, may not consider all of them equally important. You might not use your PC for music at all. You might not have any videos. Or maybe you love libraries, but you don't want all of them listed in the nav pane, either for privacy reasons or clutter reasons.

In each of these cases, it's nice to know you can hide a library so that its name doesn't appear in the nav pane. Just right-click the library's name; from the shortcut menu, choose

"Don't show in navigation pane." Poof! It's gone (just the listing, not the library itself).

You can, fortunately, bring the library listing back. It's still sitting in your Personal→Libraries folder. To see it, click the word "Libraries" in any window's navigation pane. Right-click the library's icon; from the shortcut menu, choose "Show in navigation pane." Presto! It's back in the list. (Or, if you've really made a mess, right-click the word "Libraries" in the nav pane; from the shortcut menu, choose "Restore default libraries.")

- **You can see the folder's icon (alternate).** Use the right mouse button to drag the folder onto a library's name in the navigation pane, or into the library's open window. Release the mouse button. From the shortcut menu, choose "Include in library."

- **You've opened the library window.** If you're already *in* the library, you can add a folder to it using the dialog box shown in Figure 2-12, bottom. Click Add, and then find and double-click the folder you want. You see it added to the "Library locations" list in the dialog box. Click OK.

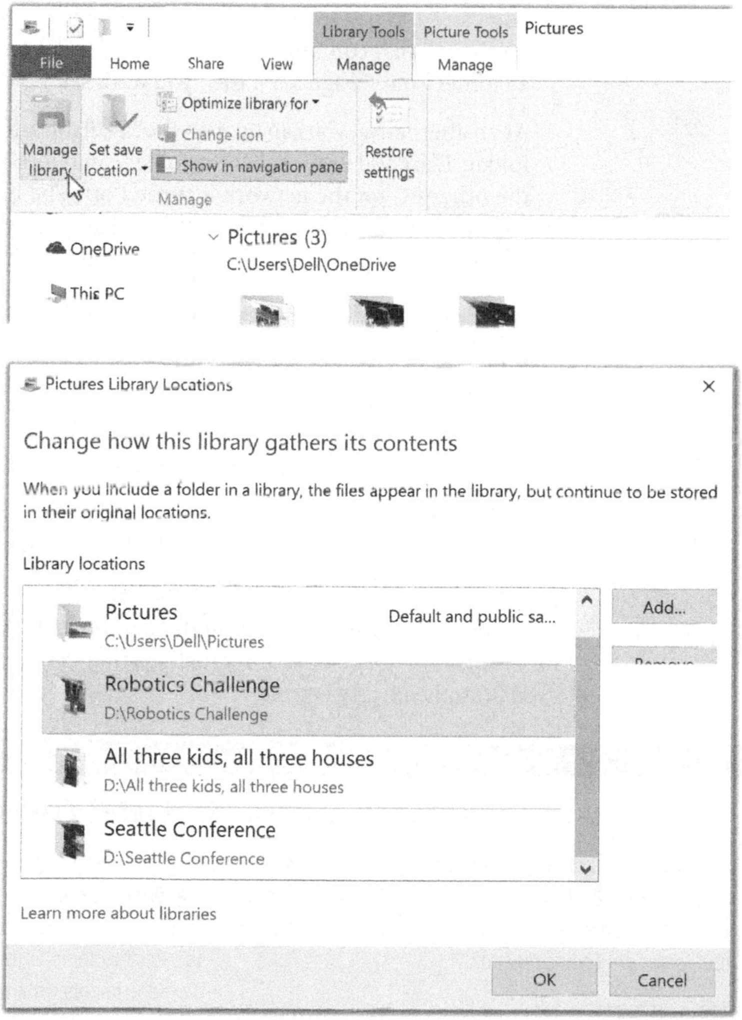

Figure 2-12:
Top: To add a regular folder to an existing library, open the library itself. Then, on the Library Tools/Manage tab of its Ribbon, click "Manage library."

Bottom: This dialog box appears. Here you can add new folders or remove existing ones from the library's concept of the world.

The fine print

All the techniques above also work for folders on external drives, USB flash drives, and shared folders on your network. There is, however, some important fine print:

- You can't add a folder that's on a CD or a DVD.

- You *can* add a folder that's on a USB flash drive, as long as that flash drive's icon shows up in the navigation pane when it's inserted, under the This PC/Hard Drives heading. (A few oddball models appear under Devices With Removable Storage; they're not allowed.) Furthermore, the folder won't be available in the library when the flash drive isn't inserted (duh).

- You can't add a networked folder to a library *unless* it's been *indexed for searching* on the PC that contains it; see page 130 for details on that process. (If it's part of a HomeGroup [page 597], then you're all set; it's been indexed.)

  As an alternative, you can turn on the "available offline" feature for that networked folder. The good news is that the folder can now be part of your library even when the other PC on the network is turned off. The bad news is that you've basically copied that folder to your own PC, which eats up a lot of disk space and sort of defeats the purpose of adding a networked folder to your library.

Removing a Folder from a Library

Getting rid of a folder is pretty straightforward, really. You can use any of these techniques:

- **If the library window is open:** Use the "Manage library" button shown at top in Figure 2-12. Click the folder's name and then click Remove.

- **If the library's name is visible in the navigation pane:** Expand the library to show the folder you want to remove. Right-click the folder's name (or hold your finger down on it). From the shortcut menu, choose "Remove location from library."

Remember: You're not deleting anything important. A library only *pretends* to contain other folders; the real ones are actually sitting in other places on your PC or network, even after the library is gone.

FREQUENTLY ASKED QUESTION

Your Preferred "Save Into" Folder

So let me get this straight: A library is just a fiction. It contains links to a bunch of folders. So when I'm in, say, Microsoft Word, and I save a new document "into the library," which real folder am I saving it into?

That's up to you.

In a File Explorer window, open the library in question. On the Ribbon, on the Library Tools/Manage tab, choose "Set save location." From the shortcut menu, choose the folder you want to serve as the standard receptacle for newly created documents within this library.

Creating a New Library

The starter libraries (Pictures, Music, Documents, and Videos) are awfully useful right out of the box. Truth is, they're as far as most people probably go with the libraries feature.

But you may have good reasons to create new ones. Maybe you want to create a library for each client—and fill it with the corresponding project folders, some of which have been archived away on external drives. Maybe you want to round up folders full of fonts, clip art, and text, in readiness for submitting a graphics project to a print shop.

In any case, here are the different ways to go about it:

- **From the navigation pane.** Right-click the word "Library" in any window's navigation pane, or any blank spot inside a library folder. From the shortcut menu, choose New→Library.

  A new, empty library appears, both in the Libraries window and in the list of libraries in the nav pane. It's up to you to add folders to it, as described earlier.

- **From a folder.** Right-click any folder. From the shortcut menu, choose "Include in library"→"Create new library." *Bing!* A new library appears in the Libraries list, named after the folder you clicked. As a handy bonus, this library already contains its first folder: the one you clicked, of course.

Tip: Once you've created a library, you can specify which canned library style it resembles most: General Items, Pictures, Music, Documents, or Videos. (Why does it matter? Because the library style determines which commands are available in the Ribbon. Pictures offers a tab that offers slideshow and rotation tools; Music offers choices like "Play" and "Add to playlist.")

Anyway, to make this choice, open the library. In the Ribbon, on the Library Tools/Manage tab, use the "Optimize library for" pop-up menu. Click the type you want.

Tags, Metadata, and Properties

See all that information in the Details pane—Date, Size, Title, and so on? It's known by geeks as *metadata* (Greek for "data about data").

Different kinds of files provide different sorts of details. For a document, for example, you might see Authors, Comments, Title, Categories, Status, and so on. For an MP3 music file, you get Artists, Albums, Genre, Year, and so on. For a photo, you get Date Taken, Title, Author, and so on.

Oddly (and usefully) enough, you can actually edit some of this stuff (Figure 2-13).

Some of the metadata is off limits. For example, you can't edit the Date Created or Date Modified info. (Sorry, defense attorneys.) But you *can* edit the star ratings for music or pictures. Click the third star to give a song a 3, for example. Most usefully of all, you can edit the Tags box for almost *any* kind of icon. A tag is just a keyword.

It can be anything you want: McDuffy Proposal, Old Junk, Back Me Up—anything. Later, you'll be able to round up everything with a certain tag, all in a single window, even though they physically reside in different folders.

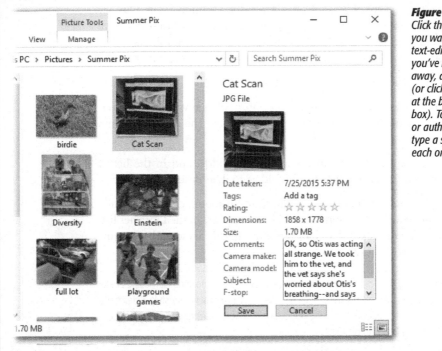

Figure 2-13:
Click the information you want to change; if a text-editing box appears, you've hit pay dirt. Type away, and then press Enter (or click the Save button at the bottom of the dialog box). To input a list (of tags or authors, for example), type a semicolon (;) after each one.

How to Shed Your Metadata's Skin

At the bottom of the Details pane (of the Properties dialog box) is a peculiarly worded link: "Remove Properties and Personal Information." This is a privacy feature. What it means is "Clean away all the metadata I've added myself, like author names, tag keywords, and other insights into my own work routine."

Microsoft's thinking here is that you might not want other people who encounter this document (as an email attachment, for example) to have such a sweeping insight into the minutiae of your own work routine.

When you click this link, the Remove Properties dialog box appears, offering you a scrolling list of checkboxes: Title, Rating, Tags, Comments, and lots and lots of others.

You can proceed in either of two ways. If you turn on "Create a copy with all possible properties removed," then *all* the metadata that's possible to erase (everything but things like file type, name, and so on) will be stripped away. When you click OK, Windows instantly creates a duplicate of the file (with the word "Copy" tacked onto its name), ready for distribution to the masses in its clean form. The original is left untouched.

If you choose "Remove the following properties from this file" instead, you can specify exactly *which* file details you want erased from the original. (Turn on the appropriate checkboxes.)

You'll encounter tags in plenty of other places in Windows—and in this book, especially when it comes to searching for photos and music.

Note: Weirdly, you can't add tags or ratings to .bmp, .png, .avi, or .mpg files.

Many of the boxes here offer autocompletion, meaning that Windows proposes finishing a name or a text tidbit for you if it recognizes what you've started to type.

Tip: You can tag a bunch of icons at once. Just highlight them all and then change the corresponding detail in the Details pane *once*. This is a great trick for applying a tag or a star rating to a mass of files quickly.

Click Save when you're finished.

Properties

The Details pane shows some of the most important details about a file, but if you really want to see the entire metadata dossier for an icon, open its Properties dialog box (Figure 2-14) using one of these tactics:

- **Select it.** From the Home tab of the Ribbon, click Properties.

- **Right-click it (or hold your finger down on it).** From the shortcut menu, choose Properties.

- **Alt+double-click it.**

Figure 2-14:
If Windows knows anything about an icon, it's in here. Scroll, scroll, and scroll some more to find the tidbit you want to see—or to edit. As with the Details pane, many of these text morsels are editable.

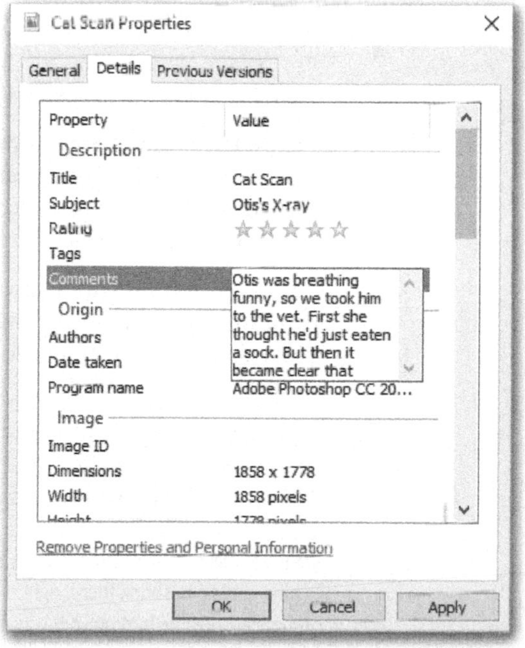

- **If the icon is already highlighted,** press Alt+Enter.

In each case, the Properties dialog box appears. It's a lot like the one in previous versions of Windows, in that it displays the file's name, location, size, and so on. But in Windows 10, it also bears a scrolling Details tab that's sometimes teeming with metadata details.

Window Views

Windows' windows look just fine straight from the factory; the edges are straight, and the text is perfectly legible. Still, if you're going to stare at this screen for half of your waking hours, you may as well investigate some of the ways these windows can be enhanced.

For starters, you can view the files and folders in a File Explorer window in either of two ways: as icons (of any size) or as a list (in several formats). Figure 2-15 shows some of your options.

Every window remembers its view settings independently. You might prefer to look over your Documents folder in List view (because it's crammed with files and folders), but you may prefer to view the Pictures library in Icon view, where the icons look like miniatures of the actual photos.

To switch a window from one view to another, you have several options, as shown in Figure 2-15, all of which involve the View tab of the Ribbon.

Tip: You can point to the icons in the View tab without clicking. The files in the window change as you hover, so you can preview the effect before committing to it.

So what *are* these various views? And when should you use which? Here you go:

- **Extra large icons, Large icons, Medium icons, Small icons.** In an icon view, every file, folder, and disk is represented by a small picture—an *icon.* This humble image, a visual representation of electronic bits, is the cornerstone of the entire Windows religion. (Maybe that's why it's called an icon.)

  At larger icon sizes, the contents of your folder icons peek out just enough so that you can see them. In the Music folder, for example, a singer's folder shows the first album cover within; a folder full of PowerPoint presentations shows the first slide or two; and so on.

  Small icons put the files' names to the right of the icons; the other views put the name *beneath* the icon. You might want one of the large settings for things like photos and the small settings when you want to see more files without scrolling.

Tip: If you have a touchscreen, you can use the two-finger spreading gesture to enlarge icons, or the pinching gesture to shrink them, right on the glass. If you have a mouse, you can enlarge or shrink all the icons in a window by turning your mouse's scroll wheel while you press the Ctrl key. This trick even works on desktop icons.

- **List view.** This one packs, by far, the most files into the space of a window; each file has a tiny icon to its left, and the list of files wraps around into as many columns as necessary to maximize the window's available space.

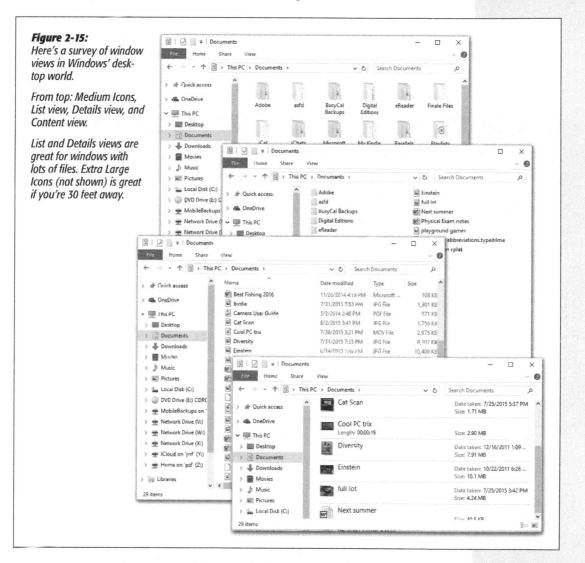

Figure 2-15:
Here's a survey of window views in Windows' desktop world.

From top: Medium Icons, List view, Details view, and Content view.

List and Details views are great for windows with lots of files. Extra Large Icons (not shown) is great if you're 30 feet away.

- **Details view.** This is the same as List view, except that it presents only a single column of files. It's a table, really; additional columns reveal the size, icon type, modification date, rating, and other information.

Microsoft thinks you'll really dig Details view. It's so important that it has a dedicated "Switch to Details view" icon at the lower-right corner of every window.

Furthermore, whenever you're in Details view, you get two bonus icons on the Ribbon's View tab: "Add columns" and "Size all columns to fit." They're described in the box below.

- **Tiles view.** Your icons appear at standard size, with name and file details just to the *right*.

Tip: Lots of people never even realize they *have* Tiles and Content view options— because these two choices are normally hidden on the Ribbon! You actually have to *scroll* that teeny tiny panel of view icons to see them.

Secrets of the Details View Columns

In windows that contain a lot of icons, Details view is a powerful weapon in the battle against chaos. Better yet, *you* get to decide how wide the columns should be, which of them should appear, and in what order. Here are the details on Details:

Add or remove columns. When you choose "Add columns" in the Ribbon's View tab, or right-click any column heading (like Name or Size), you see a shortcut menu with checkmarks next to the visible columns: Name, Date Modified, Size, and so on. Choose a column's name to make it appear or disappear.

But don't think that you're stuck with that handful of common columns. If you click "Choose columns" or "More" in the shortcut menu, you open the Choose Details dialog box, which lists *300 more* column types, most of which are useful only in certain circumstances: Album Artist (for music files); Copyright, Date Taken, Exposure Time (for photos); Nickname (for people); Video Compression (for movies); and on and on. To make one of these columns appear, turn on its checkbox and then click OK; by the time you're done, your File Explorer window can look like a veritable spreadsheet of information.

Rearrange the columns. You can rearrange your Details columns just by dragging their gray column headers horizontally. (You can even drag the Name column out of first position.)

Change column widths. If some text in a column is too long to fit, Windows displays an ellipsis (…) after the first few letters of each word. In that case, here's a trick: Carefully position your cursor at the right edge of the column's header (Name, Size, or whatever—even to the right of the ▾ button). When the cursor sprouts horizontal arrows, double-click the divider line to make the column adjust *itself,* fitting automatically to accommodate the longest item in the column.

If you'd rather adjust the column width manually, then just drag the divider line horizontally. Doing so makes the column to the *left* of your cursor wider or narrower.

Or use the "Size all columns to fit" command. It's in the shortcut menu and also on the Ribbon's View tab, and it makes all columns exactly as wide as necessary.

- **Content view.** This view attempts to cram as many details about each file as will fit in your window. It's a table that shows not just a file's icon and name, but also its metadata (Properties) and, in the case of text and Word files, even the first couple of lines of text *inside* it. (If you're not seeing all the file details you think you should, then make the window bigger. Windows adds and subtracts columns of information as needed to fit.)

You'll get to know Content view very well indeed once you start using the Search feature, which uses this view to display your results when you search in a File Explorer window.

Tip: At the lower right of every File Explorer window, you see repeats of the two styles Microsoft thinks you'll find the most useful: Details view and large thumbnails. (As their pop-out tooltip balloons indicate, they even have keyboard shortcuts: Ctrl+Shift+6 for Details, Ctrl+Shift+2 for large thumbnails.) By duplicating these controls here, Windows is trying to save you the effort of opening the Ribbon if it doesn't happen to be open.

Immortalizing Your Tweaks

Once you've twiddled and tweaked a File Explorer window into a perfectly efficient configuration of columns and views, you needn't go through the same exercise for each folder. Windows can immortalize your changes as the standard setting for *all* your windows.

On the Ribbon's View tab, click Options. Click the View tab. Click Apply to Folders, and confirm your decision by clicking Yes.

At this point, all your disk and folder windows open up with the same view, sorting method, and so on. You're still free to override those standard settings on a window-by-window basis, however. (And if you change your mind again and want to make all your maverick folder windows snap back to the standard settings, repeat the process but click Reset Folders instead.)

Sorting, Grouping, and Filtering

It's a computer—it had darned well better be able to sort your files alphabetically, chronologically, or in any other way. But that's only one way to impose order on your teeming icons. Grouping, filtering, and searching can be handy, too.

Sorting Files

Sorting the files in a window alphabetically or chronologically is nice, but it's *so* 2014. You can now sort up, down, and sideways.

The trick is to click the "Sort by" pop-up icon, which is on the View tab of the Ribbon. As you can see, it lists every conceivable sorting criterion: Name, Date modified, Type, Size, and on and on. And if those 10 ways to sort aren't enough, you can choose "Choose columns" from this menu to add even more options to it: Attachments, Copyright, Data rate, and so on.

Sorting in Details view

In Details view, you get another way to sort. See the column headings, like "Name," "Size," and "Type?" They aren't just signposts; they're also buttons. Click "Name" for alphabetical order, "Date modified" for chronological order, "Size" to view largest files at the top, and so on (Figure 2-16).

To reverse the sorting order, click the column heading a second time. The tiny triangle turns upside down.

Note: Within each window, Windows groups *folders* separately from *files*. They get sorted, too, but within their own little folder ghetto.

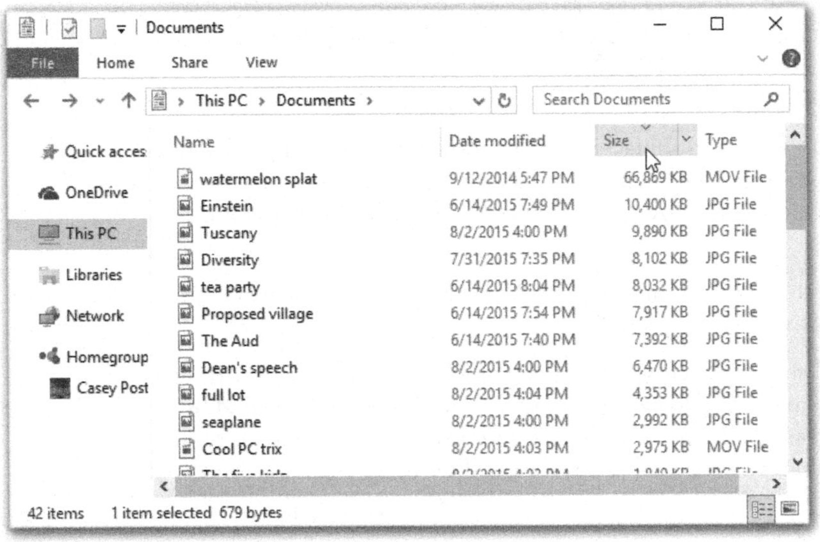

Figure 2-16:
Top: You sort a List view by clicking the column headings. Click a second time to reverse the sorting order.

The tiny triangle shows which way you've sorted the window: in ascending order (for example, A to Z) or descending order (Z to A).

(Hint: When the smallest portion of the triangle is at the top, the smallest files are listed first when viewed in size order.

Sorting using the shortcut menu

You can sort your icons in any window view without using the Ribbon, like this: Right-click a blank spot in the window. From the shortcut menu, choose "Sort by" and choose the criterion you want (Name, Date, Type…) from the submenu.

There's no handy triangle to tell you *which way* you've just sorted things; is it oldest to newest or newest to oldest? To make *that* decision, you have to right-click the window a second time; this time, from the "Sort by" submenu, choose either Ascending or Descending.

Grouping

Grouping means "adding headings within the window and clustering the icons beneath the headings." The effect is shown in Figure 2-17 ("Yesterday," "Earlier this month," and so on), and so is the procedure. Try it out; grouping can be a great way to wrangle some order from a seething mass of icons.

Don't forget that you can flip the sorting order of your groups. Reopen that shortcut menu and the "Group by" submenu, and specify Ascending or Descending.

Figure 2-17:
To group the icons in a window, use the "Group by" pop-up menu in the Ribbon, on the View tab. (If the window isn't especially wide, then you might see only the icon for the menu, not the actual words "Group by.")

You can also find the "Group by" menu by right-clicking a blank spot in the window. Use the shortcut menu that results; that way, you don't need the Ribbon.

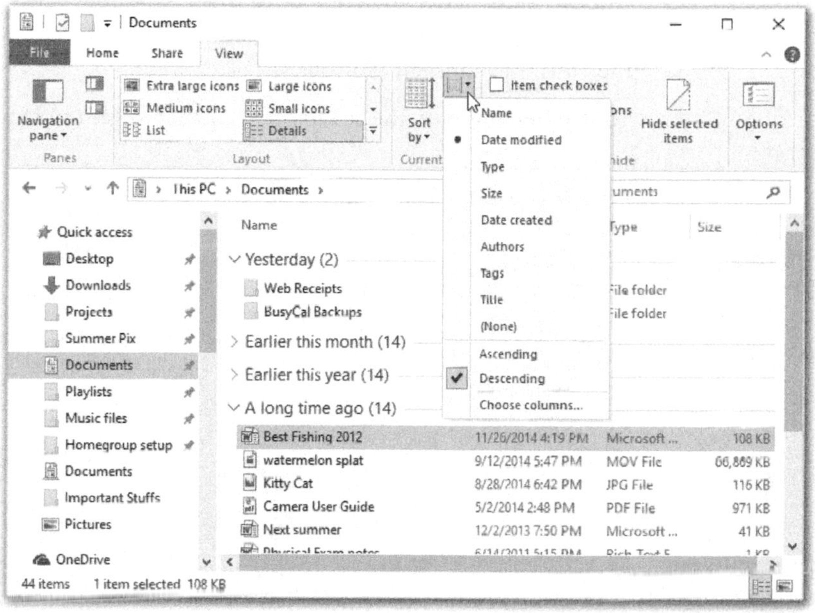

Filtering

Filtering, a feature available only in Details view, means hiding. When you turn on filtering, a bunch of the icons in a window *disappear,* which can make filtering a sore subject for novices.

Tip: In case you one day think you've lost a bunch of important files, look for the checkmark next to a column heading. That's your clue that filtering is turned on and Windows is deliberately hiding something from you.

On the positive side, filtering means screening out stuff you don't care about. When you're looking for a document you know you worked on last week, you can tell Windows to show you *only* the documents edited last week.

You turn on filtering by opening the pop-up menu next to the column heading you want. For instance, if you want to see only your five-star photos in the Pictures folder, open the Rating pop-up menu.

Sometimes, you'll see a whole long list of checkboxes in one of these pop-up menus (Figure 2-18). For example, if you want to see only the PDF and Word documents in your Documents folder…or only songs in your Music folder by The Beatles…turn on the corresponding checkmarks.

Note: Filtering, by the way, can be turned on *with* sorting or grouping.

Once you've filtered a window in Details view, you can switch to a different view; you'll still see (and not see) the same set of icons. The address bar reminds you that you've turned on filtering; it might say, for example, "Research notes→LongTimeAgo→DOC file," meaning "ancient Word files."

To stop filtering, open the heading pop-up menu again and turn off the Filter checkbox.

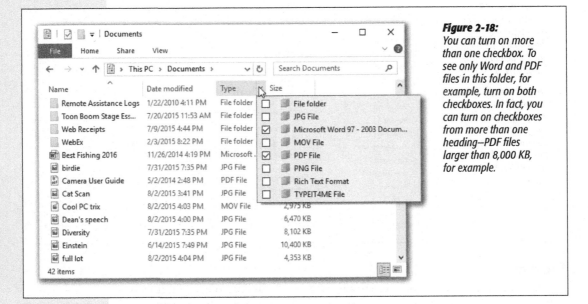

Figure 2-18:
You can turn on more than one checkbox. To see only Word and PDF files in this folder, for example, turn on both checkboxes. In fact, you can turn on checkboxes from more than one heading—PDF files larger than 8,000 KB, for example.

Searching in a File Explorer Window

There's a search box in the upper-right corner of every File Explorer window. You can use it to search just within the open window, as described in the next chapter.

The "Folder Options" Options

In the battle between flexibility and simplicity, Microsoft comes down on the side of flexibility almost every time. Anywhere it can provide you with more options, it will.

File Explorer windows are a case in point, as the following pages of sometimes preposterously tweaky options make clear. The good news: If File Explorer windows already work fine for you the way they are, you can ignore all of this.

But if you'd like to visit the famed Folder Options dialog box, here's how to do it: On the View tab of the Ribbon, click the Options button. You see the dialog box shown in Figure 2-19.

Here you see an array of options that affect *all* the folder windows on your PC. When assessing the impact of these controls, *earth-shattering* isn't the adjective that springs to mind. Still, you may find one or two of them useful.

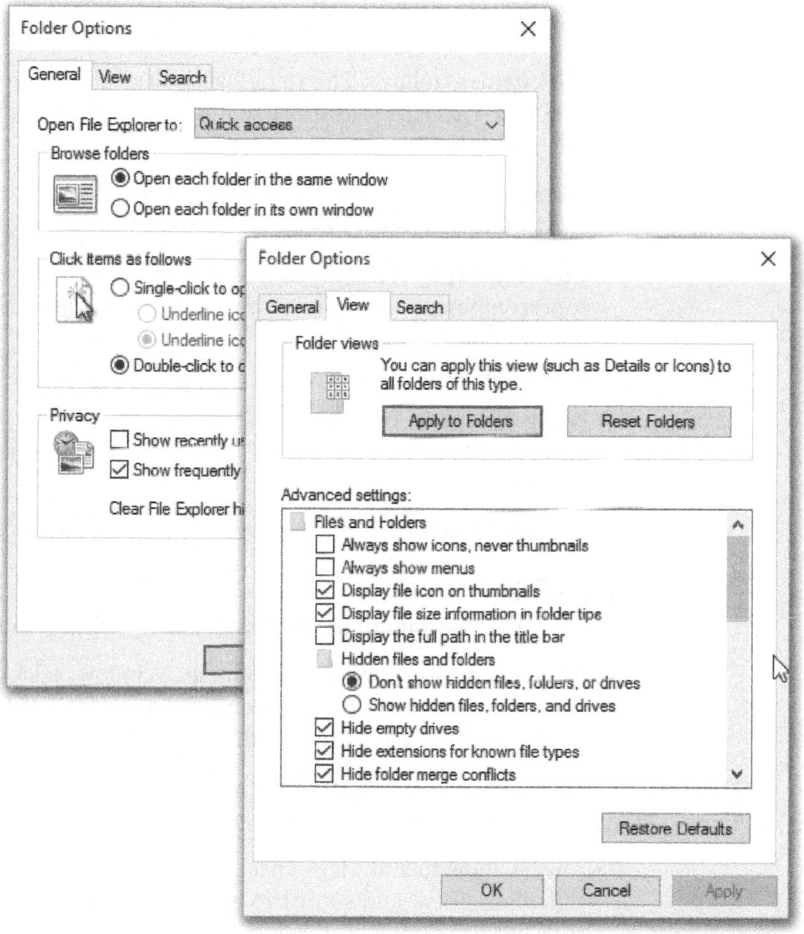

Figure 2-19:
Here are the first two tabs of the Folder Options dialog box: General and View.

Some of the options in the View list are contained within tiny folder icons. A double-click collapses (hides) these folder options or shows them again. For example, you can hide the "Don't show hidden files, folders, or drives" option by collapsing the "Hidden files and folders" folder icon.

General Tab

On the General tab, you find these intriguing options, most of which are new in Windows 10:

- **Open File Explorer to.** When you open a new desktop window, do you want it to start out showing the contents of your "Quick access" list? Or the primary folders of your PC? Use this pop-up menu to decide.

- **Browse folders.** When you double-click a folder, Windows can react in one of two ways. It can either *open a second window,* overlapping the first, making moving or copying an icon from one into the other a piece of cake. Or it can *replace the* *original window with a new one.* This only-one-window-at-all-times behavior keeps your desktop from becoming crowded with windows. If you need to return to the previous window, the Back button takes you there. Of course, you'll have a harder time dragging icons from one window to another using this method.

Whatever you decide, you tell Windows using these buttons. Click either "Open each folder in the same window" or "Open each folder in its own window," as you like.

- **Click items as follows.** This option lets you single-click icons to open them instead of double-clicking—a feature that might make life easier if you have a touchscreen. See page 143.

- **Privacy.** These two checkboxes let you turn off Windows' tendency to list folders and files you use often in the "Quick access" list; see page 68.

- **Clear File Explorer history.** If you have a photographic memory and a mind like a supercomputer, you may remember that the ⌄ icon at the right end of the address bar shows all the addresses you've typed in (the Recent Folders list). This button erases that list.

- **Navigation pane.** Here are three handy options that let you customize the navigation pane at the left side of every File Explorer window; they're described starting on page 68.

- **Restore defaults** returns all the options on this dialog box to their factory settings.

View Tab

Here are the functions of the 83,000 tiny checkboxes in this dialog box:

- **Always show icons, never thumbnails.** Windows takes great pride in displaying your document icons *as* documents. That is, each icon appears as a miniature of the document itself—a feature that's especially useful in folders full of photos.

  On a slowish PC, this feature can make your processor gasp for breath. If you notice that the icons are taking forever to appear, consider turning this checkbox on.

- **Always show menus.** This checkbox forces the traditional Windows menu bar (File, Edit, View, and so on) to appear in every File Explorer window, without your having to tap the Alt key.

- **Display file icon on thumbnails.** Ordinarily, you can identify documents (think Word, Excel, PowerPoint) because their icons display the corresponding logo (a big W for Word, and so on). But in Windows' icon views (medium and larger), you see the *actual document* on the icon—an image of the document's first page. So does that mean you can no longer tell at a glance what *kind* of document it is?

  Don't be silly. This option superimposes, on each thumbnail icon, a tiny "badge," a sub-icon, that identifies what kind of file it is. (It works only on some kinds of documents, however.)

- **Display file size information in folder tips.** A *folder tip* is a rectangular balloon that appears when you point to a folder—a little yellow box that tells you what's in that folder and how big it is on the disk. (It appears only if you've turned on the "Show pop-up description" checkbox described below.) You turn off *this* checkbox if you want to see only the description, but not the size. Talk about tweaky!

· **Display the full path in the title bar.** When this option is on, Windows reveals the exact location of the current window in the title bar of the window—for example, *C:* > *Users* > *Chris* > *Documents*. See page 63 for more on folder paths. Seeing the path can be useful when you're not sure which disk a folder is on, for example.

· **Hidden files and folders.** Microsoft grew weary of answering tech-support calls from clueless or mischievous customers who had moved or deleted critical system files, rendering their PCs crippled or useless. The company concluded that the simplest preventive measure would be to make them invisible (the files, not the customers).

This checkbox is the result. Your personal and Windows folders, among other places, house several invisible folders and files that the average person isn't meant to fool around with. Big Brother is watching you, but he means well.

By selecting "Show hidden files, folders, and drives," you, the confident power user in times of troubleshooting or customization, can make the hidden files and folders appear (they show up with dimmed icons, as though to reinforce their

The Little Filtering Calendar

Some of the column-heading pop-up menus in Details view—"Date modified," "Date created," "Date taken," and so on—display a little calendar, right there in the menu. You're supposed to use it to specify a date or a date range. You use it, for example, if you want to see only the photos taken last August, or the Word documents created last week. Here's how the little calendar works:

To change the month, click the ◄ or ► buttons to go one month at a time. Or click the month name to see a list of all 12 months; click the one you want.

To change the year, click the ◄ or ► buttons. Or, to jump further back or forward, double-click the month's name. You're offered a list of all 10 years in this decade. Click a third time (on the decade heading) to see a list of *decades*. At this point, drill down to the year you want by clicking. (The

calendar goes from the years 1601 to 9999, which should pretty much cover your digital photo collection.)

To see only the photos taken on a certain date, click the appropriate date on the month-view calendar.

To add photos taken on other dates, click additional squares. You can also drag horizontally, vertically, or diagonally to select blocks of consecutive dates.

If you "back out" until you're viewing the names of months, years, or decades, then you can click or drag to choose, for example, only the photos taken in June or July 2012.

The checkboxes below the calendar offer one-click access to photos taken earlier this week, earlier this year, and before the beginning of this year ("A long time ago").

delicate nature). But you'll have the smoothest possible computing career if you leave these options untouched.

Note: Actually, there's a much quicker way to turn hidden files on and off. The Ribbon's View tab has a "Hidden files" button dedicated just to this purpose.

- **Hide empty drives.** For years, the Computer (This PC) window has displayed icons for your removable-disk drives (floppy, CD, DVD, memory-card slots, whatever) even if nothing was in them. Now, though, that's changed. Now, because this option comes turned on, you see icons only when you insert a *disk* into these drives. (It now works like the Mac, if that's any help.)

- **Hide extensions for known file types.** Windows normally hides the *filename extension* on standard files and documents (.doc, .jpg, and so on), in an effort to make Windows seem less technical and intimidating. Your files wind up named "Groceries" and "Frank" instead of "Groceries.doc" and "Frank.jpg."

  There are some excellent reasons, though, why you should turn *off* this option. See page 240 for more on this topic.

Note: There's a dedicated on/off switch for showing filename extensions right on the Ribbon's View tab ("File name extensions"). It's a lot easier to reach than the Folder Options dialog box.

- **Hide folder merge conflicts.** When you drag a file into a window that contains an identically named file, Windows warns you; it doesn't want you to replace one file with another accidentally.

  When you drag a *folder* into a window that contains an identically named *folder*, however, whether or not Windows warns you is up to you. If you turn this box on, you get no warning—just an insta-replace.

- **Hide protected operating system files.** This option is similar to "Show hidden files, folders, and drives"—except that it refers to even more important files, system files that may not be invisible but are nonetheless so important that moving or deleting them might turn your PC into a $1,000 paperweight. Turning this off, in fact, produces a warning message that's meant to frighten away everybody but powergeeks.

- **Launch folder windows in a separate process.** This geekily worded setting opens each folder into a different chunk of memory (RAM). In certain rare situations, this largely obsolete arrangement is more stable—but it slows down your machine slightly and unnecessarily uses memory.

- **Restore previous folder windows at logon.** Every time you log off the computer, Windows forgets which windows were open. That's a distinct bummer, especially if you tend to work out of your Documents window, which you must therefore manually reopen every time you fire up the old PC.

  If you turn on this useful checkbox, then Windows will automatically greet you with whichever windows were open when you last logged off.

- **Show drive letters.** Turn off this checkbox to hide the drive letters that identify each of your disk drives in the This PC window (in the navigation pane, click This PC). In other words, "Local Disk (C:)" becomes "Local Disk"—an option that might make newcomers feel less intimidated.

- **Show encrypted or compressed NTFS files in color.** This option won't make much sense until you've read page 167, which explain how Windows can encode and compress your files for better security and disk space use. Turning on this checkbox turns the names of affected icons green and blue, respectively, so you can spot them at a glance. On the other hand, encrypted or compressed files and folders operate quite normally, immediately converting back to human form when double-clicked; hence, knowing which ones have been affected isn't particularly valuable. Turn off this box to make them look just like any other files and folders.

- **Show pop-up description for folder and desktop icons.** If you point to an icon, a taskbar button, a found item in Search, or whatever (without clicking), you get a *tooltip*—a floating, colored label that identifies what you're pointing to. If you find tooltips distracting, then turn off this checkbox.

- **Show preview handlers in preview pane.** This is the on/off switch for one of Windows' best features: seeing a preview of a selected document icon in the Preview pane. Turn it off only if your PC is grinding to a halt under the strain of all this graphics-intensive goodness.

- **Show status bar.** This option refers to the horizontal strip that you can summon at the bottom of every File Explorer window. It shows you, in tiny type, how many items are in the window. When you select some of them, it tells you how many you've highlighted and how much disk space they take up—a great way to anticipate whether or not they'll fit on some flash drive or CD.

- **Use check boxes to select items.** This option makes a *checkbox* appear on every icon you point to with your mouse, for ease in selection. Page 143 explains all.

Tip: There's an alternative, easier way to access this option: Turn on "Item check boxes" on the Ribbon's View tab.

- **Use Sharing Wizard (Recommended).** Sharing files with other computers is one of the great perks of having a network. As Chapter 21 makes clear, this feature makes it much easier to understand what you're doing. For example, it lets you specify that only certain people are allowed to access your files, and it lets you decide how much access they have. (For example, can they change them or just see them?)

- **When typing into list view.** When you've got a File Explorer window open, teeming with a list of files, what do you want to happen when you start typing?

  In the olden days, that'd be an easy one: "Highlight an icon, of course!" That is, if you type *piz,* you'd highlight the file called "Pizza with Casey.jpg." And indeed, that's what the factory setting means: "Select the typed item within the view."

But Windows also has a search box in every File Explorer window. If you turn on "Automatically type into the Search Box," then each letter you type arrives in that box, performing a real-time, letter-by-letter search of all the icons in the window. Your savings: one mouse click.

The final three options control what appears in the Navigation pane at the left side of every File Explorer window. They're all described elsewhere in this chapter: "Expand to open folder" (page 72), "Show all folders" (page 72), and "Show libraries" (page 73).

Taskbar 2.0

For years, the *taskbar*—the strip of colorful icons at the bottom of your screen—has been one of the most prominent and important elements of the Windows interface (Figure 2-20). Today, you can call it Taskbar, Extreme Makeover Edition; it can do a lot of things it's never done before.

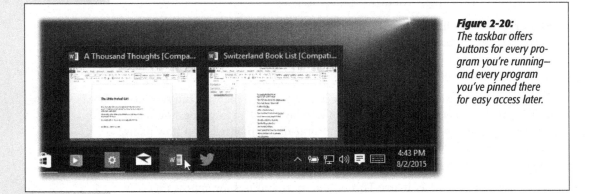

Figure 2-20:
The taskbar offers buttons for every program you're running—and every program you've pinned there for easy access later.

Here's an introduction to its functions, old and new:

- **The Start menu is back.** As you know from Chapter 1, the Start menu is at the far left of the task bar.

- **The Search/Cortana box is next.** Just to the right of the Start menu, the new search box (also known as "Ask me anything" or Cortana) awaits, as described in Chapter 5.

Tip: The search box does take up a lot of horizontal space—and you don't really need it. You can hide it and still have full access to Cortana and the search box. Jump ahead to Figure 2-22.

- **The taskbar lists your open programs and windows.** The icons on the taskbar make it easy to switch from one open program to another—from your Web browser to your email programs, for example—or even to specific windows *within* those programs.

Note: App icons are generally hidden in Tablet mode, described in Chapter 13. If you read this chapter and wonder why you're not seeing some of the things described here, now you know why.

- **The taskbar is a launcher.** You read that right. The taskbar is a mini–Start menu. It's a *launcher* for your favorite programs and folders, just like the Dock in the Mac's OS X or the Quick Launch toolbar in old Windows versions.

- **The system tray (notification area) is at the right end.** These tiny icons show you the status of your network connection, battery life, and so on.

- **The Show Desktop button hides at the far-right end.** You can read more about this invisible button on page 52.

So what can you do with the little buttons on the taskbar? Read on.

Tip: You can operate the taskbar entirely from the keyboard. Press ⊞+T to highlight the first button on it, as indicated by a subtle glow. Then you can "walk" across its buttons by pressing the left/right arrow keys, or by pressing ⊞+T (add the Shift key to "walk" in the opposite direction). Once a button is highlighted, you can tap the space bar to "click" it, press Shift+F10 to "right-click" it, or press the Menu key 🗐 on your keyboard to open the icon's jump list. Who needs a mouse anymore?

Taskbar as App Switcher

Every open window is represented by a button—an actual miniature of the window itself—that sprouts from its program's taskbar icon. These buttons make it easy to switch among open programs and windows. Just click one to bring its associated window into the foreground, even if it has been minimized.

Once you know what to look for, you can distinguish an open program from a closed one, a frontmost window from a background one, and so on (see Figure 2-21).

Figure 2-21:
An icon without a white underline is a program you haven't opened yet. A brightened background indicates the active (frontmost) program, Word, in this case.

Right-clicking one of these buttons lets you perform tasks on all the windows together, such as closing them all at once.

Handy Window Miniatures

If you point to a program's button without clicking, it sprouts thumbnail images of *the windows themselves.* Figure 2-20 shows the effect. It's a lot more informative than just reading the windows' *names*, as in days of yore (your previous Windows versions, that is). The thumbnails are especially good at helping you spot a particular Web page, photo, or PDF document.

Tip: When you point to one of these thumbnails, a tiny Close button (▣) appears in each thumbnail, too, which makes it easy to close a window without having to bring it forward first. (Or click the thumbnail itself with your mouse's scroll wheel, or use your middle mouse button, if you have one.) Each thumbnail also has a hidden shortcut menu. Right-click to see your options!

Full-Size Peeking

Those window miniatures are all fine, but the taskbar can also show you *full-screen* previews of your windows. It's a feature Microsoft calls Peek.

- **Mouse/trackpad:** Point to a taskbar button to make the window thumbnails appear. Then, still without clicking, point to one of the *thumbnails.*

- **Touchscreen:** Tap the apps' taskbar icon to make the window thumbnails appear. Now touch the same taskbar icon a second time and pause; without lifting your fingertip, drag onto one of the thumbnails.

Windows now displays that window at full size, right on the screen, even if it was minimized, buried, or hidden. Keep moving your cursor or finger across the thumbnails (if there are more than one); each time you land on a thumbnail, the full-size window preview changes to show what's in it.

When you find the window you want, click or tap the thumbnail you're already pointing to. The window pops open so you can work in it.

Button Groups

In the old days, opening a lot of windows might produce a relatively useless display of truncated buttons. Not only were the buttons too narrow to read the names of

---

GEM IN THE ROUGH

Secret Keystrokes of the Taskbar Icons

There's secret keyboard shortcuts lurking in them thar taskbar icons.

It turns out that the first 10 icons, left to right, have built-in keystrokes that "click" them: the ⊞ key plus the numbers 1, 2, 3, and so on (up to 0, which means 10).

If you use this keystroke to "click" the icon of a program that's not running, it opens up as though you'd clicked it. If

you "click" a program that has only one window open, that window pops to the front. If you "click" a program with more than one window open, the icon sprouts thumbnail previews of all of them, and the first window pops to the front.

Remember that you can drag icons around on the taskbar, in effect reassigning those 1-through-0 keystrokes.

---

the windows, but the buttons also appeared in chronological order, not software-program order.

As you may have noticed, though, Windows now automatically consolidates open windows into a single program button. (There's even a subtle visual sign that a program has multiple windows open: Its taskbar icon may appear to be "stacked," or its underline may sprout a gray extension, like the third icon in Figure 2-22.) All the Word documents are accessible from the Word icon, all the Excel documents sprout from the Excel icon, and so on.

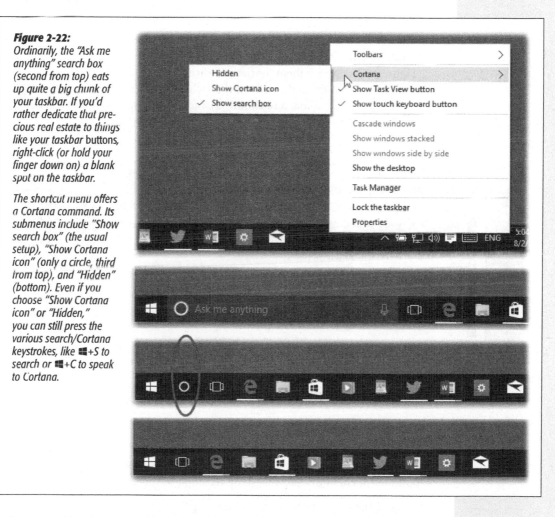

Figure 2-22:
Ordinarily, the "Ask me anything" search box (second from top) eats up quite a big chunk of your taskbar. If you'd rather dedicate that precious real estate to things like your taskbar buttons, right-click (or hold your finger down on) a blank spot on the taskbar.

The shortcut menu offers a Cortana command. Its submenus include "Show search box" (the usual setup), "Show Cortana icon" (only a circle, third from top), and "Hidden" (bottom). Even if you choose "Show Cortana icon" or "Hidden," you can still press the various search/Cortana keystrokes, like ⊞+S to search or ⊞+C to speak to Cortana.

Point to a taskbar button to see the thumbnails of the corresponding windows, complete with their names; click to jump directly to the one you want. (On a touchscreen, tap the taskbar button to see the thumbnails; tap a thumbnail to open it.)

Despite all the newfangled techniques, some of the following time-honored basics still apply:

- **If a program has only one** *window* **open,** you can hide or show it by hitting the program's taskbar button—a great feature that a lot of PC fans miss. (To hide a *background* window, select its taskbar button *twice:* once to bring the window forward, then a pause, then again to hide it.)

- **To minimize, maximize, restore, or close a window,** even if you can't see it on the screen, point to its program's button on the taskbar. When the window thumbnails pop up, right-click the one you want, and choose from the shortcut menu. (This option isn't available without a mouse/trackpad.)

- **Windows can make all open windows visible at once,** either by *cascading* them (Figure 2-23), *stacking* them (horizontal slices), or displaying them in side-by-side vertical slices. To create this effect, right-click (or hold your finger down on) a blank spot on the taskbar and choose Cascade Windows from the shortcut menu. Or "Show windows stacked" or "Show windows side by side."

Figure 2-23:
Cascading windows are neatly arranged so you can see the title bar for each window. Click any title bar to bring that window to the foreground as the active window.

This feature was a little buggy in the first Windows 10 release—the windows didn't stack neatly.

- **To hide all open windows in one fell swoop,** press ⊞+D. Or right-click a blank spot on the taskbar and choose "Show the desktop" from the shortcut menu. Or point to (or click) the Show Desktop rectangle at the far-right end of the taskbar.

  To bring the windows back, repeat that step.

Tip: When the taskbar is crowded with buttons, it may not be easy to find a blank spot to click. Usually there's a little gap near the right end; you can make it easier to find some blank space by *enlarging* the taskbar, as described on page 106.

The Taskbar as App Launcher

Each time you open a program, its icon appears on the taskbar. That's the way it's always been. And when you exit that program, its icon disappears from the taskbar.

These days, however, there's a twist: You can *pin* a program's icon to the taskbar so that it's always there, even when it's not open. One quick click opens the app. The idea, of course, is to put frequently used programs front and center, always on the screen, so you don't have to open the Start menu to find them.

To pin a program to the taskbar in this way, use one of these two tricks:

- **Drag a program's icon** directly to any spot on the taskbar, as shown in Figure 2-24. You can drag them from any File Explorer window or from the desktop.

Figure 2-24:
To install a program on your taskbar, drag its icon to any spot; the other icons scoot aside to make room, if necessary.

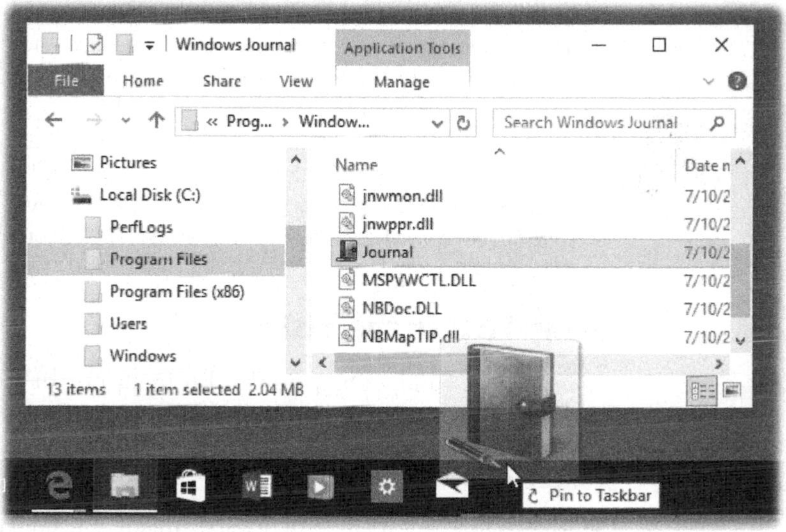

- **Right-click (or hold your finger down on) a program's icon,** wherever it happens to be.

Tip: This works even on programs listed on the left side of the Start menu—in the "Most used" list or the "All apps" list, for example.

From the shortcut menu, choose "Pin to taskbar." The icon appears instantly at the right end of the taskbar. You're welcome to drag it into a better position.

- **Right-click an open program's taskbar icon,** wherever it happens to be. From the shortcut menu, choose Pin to Taskbar. In other words, the program's icon might be on the taskbar *now*, because it's running—but you've just told it to stay there even after you exit it.

Once an icon is on the taskbar, you can open it with a single click. By all means, stick your favorites there; over the years, you'll save yourself thousands of unnecessary Start-menu trips.

Tip: If you Shift-click a taskbar icon, you open another window for that program—for example, a new browser window, a new Microsoft Word document, and so on. (Clicking with your mouse's scroll wheel, or middle mouse button, does the same thing.) Add the Ctrl key to open the program as an administrator.

And if you Shift-right-click a taskbar icon, you see the same menu of window-management commands (Cascade, Restore, and so on) that you get when you right-click a blank spot on the taskbar.

All these tricks require a mouse or a trackpad.

If you change your mind about a program icon you've parked on the taskbar, it's easy to move an icon to a new place—just drag it.

You can also remove one altogether. Right-click (or hold your finger down on) the program's icon—in the taskbar or anywhere on your PC—and, from the shortcut menu, choose "Unpin this program from taskbar."

Note: The taskbar is really intended to display the icons of programs. If you try to drag a file or a folder, you'll succeed only in adding it to a program's jump list, as described next. If you want quick, one-click taskbar access to files, folders, and disks, you can have it—by using the Links toolbar (page 108).

Jump Lists in the Taskbar

Jump lists are handy submenus that list frequently or recently opened files in each of your programs. For example, the jump list for the Edge browser shows the Web sites you visit most often; the jump list for Microsoft Word shows documents you've edited lately.

Jump lists can appear either in the Start menu (left side) or on your taskbar. Page 42 describes Start menu jump lists; the following pages describe the taskbar versions.

The point, in both cases, is that you can *re*open a file just by clicking its name. Jump lists can save you time when you want to resume work on something you had open recently but you're not in the mood to burrow through folders to find its icon.

Often, jump lists also include shortcut-menu-ish commands, like New Message (for an email program), Play/Pause (for a jukebox program), or Close All Windows (for just about any program). As Microsoft puts it, it's like having a separate Start menu for *every single program.*

You have several ways to make jump lists appear:

- **In the Start menu.** A **>** button next to a program's name on the left side means a jump list awaits. (In general, a program sprouts a jump list automatically if you've used it to open or play files.)

  To open the jump list, click or tap the **>**.

Note: If no jump lists ever appear, it's probably because you've turned this feature off. To turn it back on, open Settings→Personalization→Start. Turn on "Show recently opened items in Jump Lists on Start or the taskbar." (Yes, that's the on/off switch for jump lists.)

- **On the taskbar.** A similar jump list appears when you right-click a program's icon on your taskbar. If you're using a touchscreen computer, just swipe upward from the program's icon.

  (This second, secret way actually works if you have a mouse or trackpad, too. Give the mouse a flick upward while you're clicking.)

  In Figure 2-25, for example, you can see that Google Chrome's jump list includes Web pages you've recently visited and recently closed.

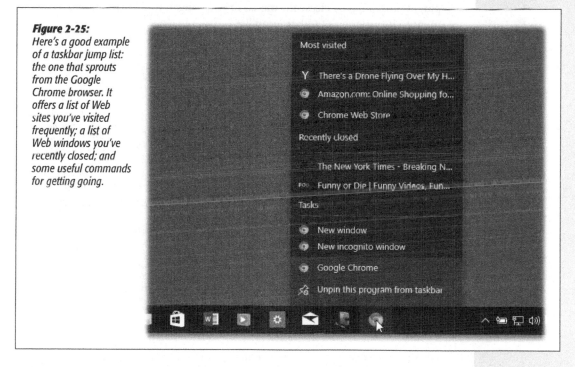

Figure 2-25:
Here's a good example of a taskbar jump list: the one that sprouts from the Google Chrome browser. It offers a list of Web sites you've visited frequently; a list of Web windows you've recently closed; and some useful commands for getting going.

Pinning to Jump Lists

In general, jump lists maintain themselves. Windows decides which files you've opened or played most recently or most frequently, and builds the jump lists accordingly. New document listings appear, older ones vanish, all without your help.

But you can also install files *manually* into a program's jump list—in Windows-ese, you can *pin* a document to a program's jump list so it's not susceptible to replacement by other items.

For example, you might pin the chapters of a book you're working on to your Word jump list. To the File Explorer jump list, you might pin the *folder and disk* locations you access often.

You can pin a file or folder to a taskbar jump list in any of three ways:

- **From the Start menu (left side):** Suppose some app or document is listed in the "Most used" or "All apps" sections of the Start menu. Right-click (or hold your finger down on) its name; from the shortcut menu, choose Pin to Taskbar.

- **From the desktop or a File Explorer window:** Drag a document (or its file short-cut) directly onto a blank spot on the taskbar. (You can drag it onto its "parent" program's icon if you really want to, but the taskbar itself is a bigger target.)

  As shown in Figure 2-26, a tooltip appears: Pin to Word 2013 (or whatever the parent program is). Release the mouse or your finger. You've just pinned the document to its program's taskbar jump list.

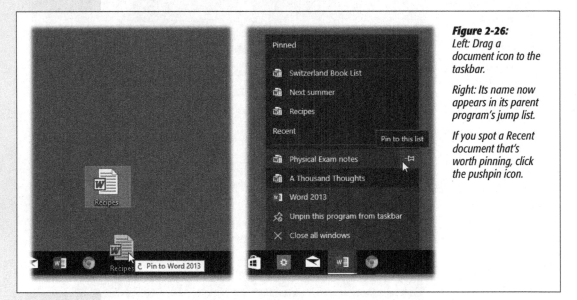

Figure 2-26:
Left: Drag a document icon to the taskbar.

Right: Its name now appears in its parent program's jump list.

If you spot a Recent document that's worth pinning, click the pushpin icon.

(If you drag a *folder*—or a shortcut of one—onto the taskbar, it gets pinned in the File Explorer icon's jump list.)

Note: *If the document's parent program didn't already appear on the taskbar, it does now. In other words, if you drag a Beekeeper Pro document onto the taskbar, Windows is forced to install the Beekeeper Pro program icon onto the taskbar in the process. Otherwise, how would you open the jump list?*

- **In an existing jump list, click the pushpin icon** (Figure 6-29, right). Suppose, for example, the document already appears in a Recently Opened list. When you point to it with your cursor, a pushpin icon appears. By clicking it, you can move the document up into the Pinned list at the top of the jump list. Now it won't be dislodged over time by other files you open.

(If you have only a touchscreen, you can still pin a document this way. Swipe upward on the app's taskbar icon to open its shortcut menu. Hold your finger down on the document to make *its* shortcut menu appear; tap "Pin to this list.")

- **If the file appears in another program's jump list, drag it onto the new program's taskbar icon.** For example, maybe you opened a document in WordPad (it's in WordPad's jump list), but you want to move it to Microsoft Word's jump list.

  To do that, drag the document's name out of WordPad's list and then drop it onto Word's taskbar icon. It now appears pinned in *both* programs' jump lists.

Removing things from your taskbar jump lists is just as easy. Open a program's jump list, point to (or hold your finger down on) the pushpin next to anything in the Pinned list, and choose "Unpin from this list."

Note: Once it's unpinned, the file's name may jump down into the Recent section of the jump list, which is usually fine. If it's not fine, you can erase it from there, too; right-click its name and, from the shortcut menu, choose "Remove from this list." (Of course, you're not actually deleting the file.)

You can also erase your jump lists completely—for privacy, for example. Read on.

Jump List Caveats

Jump lists are great and all, but you should be aware of a few things:

- They don't know when you've deleted a document or moved it to another folder or disk; they continue to list the file even after it's gone. In that event, clicking the document's listing produces only an error message. And you're offered the chance to delete the listing (referred to as "this shortcut" in the error message) so you don't confuse yourself again the next time.

- Some people consider jump lists a privacy risk, since they reveal everything you've been up to recently to whatever spouse or buddy happens to wander by. (You know who you are.)

  In that case, you can turn off jump lists, or just the incriminating items, as described next.

Tip: Of course, even if you turn off jump lists, there's another easy way to open a document you've recently worked on—from within the program you used to create it. Many programs maintain a list of recent documents in the File menu.

Jump List Settings

There are all kinds of ways to whip jump lists into submission. For example:

- **Turn off jump lists.** If the whole idea of Windows (or your boss) tracking what you've been working on upsets you, you can turn this feature off entirely. Open

---

Settings→Personalization→Start. Turn off "Show recently opened items in Jump Lists on Start or the taskbar." (The jump lists and > icons still appear—but your *files* are no longer listed in these menus.)

- **Delete one item from a jump list.** For privacy, for security, or out of utter embarrassment, you may not want some file or Web site's name to show up in a jump list. Just right-click (or hold your finger down) and, from the shortcut menu, choose "Remove from this list."

- **Clear a jump list completely.** At other times, you may want to wipe out *all* your jump lists—and all your tracks. To do that, turn jump lists off (as described above) and back on again. You've just erased all the existing jump lists. Your jump lists are now ready to start memorizing *new* items.

Tip: Jump-list items are draggable. For example, suppose you're composing an email message, and you want to attach your latest book outline. If it's in your Start menu, in a jump list, you can drag the document's icon directly from the jump list into your email message to attach it. Cool.

The System Tray (Notification Center)

The system tray, at the right end of the taskbar, gives you quick access to little status indicators and pop-up menus that control your PC (Figure 2-27).

Note: Most of the world calls this area the system tray. Microsoft calls it the notification area—why use three syllables when eight will do?

Figure 2-27:
You can point to a status icon's name without clicking (to see its name) or click one to see its pop-up menu of options.

This area has been a sore spot with PC fans for years. Many a software installer inserts its own little icon into this area: fax software, virus software, palmtop synchronization software, and so on. So the tray eventually filled with junky, confusing little icons that had no value to you—but made it harder to find the icons you *did* want to track.

Now, all that is history. Out of the box, only a handful of Windows icons appear here. Each one offers three displays: one when you *point without clicking,* one when you *click or tap the icon,* and a third when you *right-click* the icon (or hold your finger down on it).

Note: The "point without clicking" thing works only if you have a mouse or trackpad. If you try it on a touchscreen, nothing will happen, and your friends will look at you funny.

Here's what starts out on the system tray, left to right:

- ∧. This first icon is a pop-up menu that lists all the extra, junky system-tray icons that have been dumped there by your software programs (Figure 2-28, left).

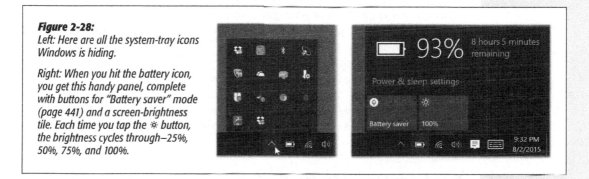

Figure 2-28:
Left: Here are all the system-tray icons Windows is hiding.

Right: When you hit the battery icon, you get this handy panel, complete with buttons for "Battery saver" mode (page 441) and a screen-brightness tile. Each time you tap the ☀ button, the brightness cycles through–25%, 50%, 75%, and 100%.

- **Power** (🔋, **portables only**). Point to the tiny battery icon without clicking to view the time-remaining (and percentage-remaining) readout for your laptop or tablet battery.

  Click or tap for a larger display of the same information (Figure 2-28, right).

  Finally, if you right-click the icon, you get access to the brightness control, Power Options control panel, and the Windows Mobility Center (see page 452).

- **Volume** (🔊). Point to see a tooltip that says, for example, "Speakers: 67%" (of full volume). Click/tap for a volume slider that controls your PC's speakers. Right-click for a shortcut menu that offers direct access to various Control Panel screens, like Sounds, Recording Devices, and so on.

- **Network** (📶 or 🖥). Point to see the name of your current network and whether or not it's connected to the Internet. Click/tap for a list of available networks; the wireless (WiFi) ones in the list come with icons for signal strength and "locked" (password-protected) status. You can switch networks by clicking the name of one.

  Right-click for a shortcut menu that offers direct access to a troubleshooting screen and to the Network and Sharing Center.

- **Action Center** (🗨). This humble, tiny icon is the front end for the Action Center: a huge, consolidated command center that's described at the end of this chapter.

- **Touch keyboard** (⌨). This button opens the onscreen typing keyboard, the one you need if you have a tablet that doesn't have a keyboard. In other words, you can make the onscreen keyboard appear and disappear by clicking this button. Chapter 13 has the details.

- **Clock.** Shows the current date and time. Point to see today's full date, with day of the week ("Thursday, January 14, 2016"). Click for a pop-up clock and mini-calendar, which you can use to check, for example, what day of the week March 9, 2017, falls on.

  (Right-clicking the Clock doesn't offer anything special—just the same shortcut menu that appears when you right-click a blank spot on the taskbar. The subtle difference: Choosing Properties from this one opens the Properties dialog box for the system-tray icons instead of the taskbar. Oh—and in this one instance, holding your finger down on a touchscreen is not the same as right-clicking. Holding your finger down on the clock doesn't open anything special.)

Tip: You can drag system-tray icons around to rearrange them—not just these starter icons, but any that you install, as described below. A vertical insertion-point line appears to show you where the icon will go when you release the mouse.

Reinstating the Hidden Icons

Thank you, Windows, for sparing us from Creeping Iconitus. Thank you for corralling all non-Windows system-tray icons into a single bubble of their own (Figure 2-28, left).

But what if you *want* one of those inferior icons to appear in the system tray? What if you *don't* want Windows to hide it away in the pop-up window?

No big whoop. Just drag it *out* of the "hidden" corral and back onto the taskbar. You can even drag it horizontally to reposition it.

Or you can do it the long way: Open the "Notifications & actions" pane of Settings. See Figure 2-29.

Tip: Here's a shortcut to that Notifications settings page: Right-click the clock; from the shortcut menu, choose Properties.

From this settings page, you have two relevant options:

- **Select which icons appear on the taskbar.** You get a list of all those secondary, usually hidden status icons. You can turn them on individually ("on" means appearing on the system tray).

- **Turn system icons on or off.** This is a list of the basic Windows system-tray icons that are supposed to appear. Now, here, you can hide them. If you don't want the time and date eating up taskbar space, then, by golly, you can hide them.

Tip: If your intention in visiting the Notification Settings box (Figure 2-29) is to turn on *all* system-tray icons—maybe to recreate the halcyon days of Windows XP—you can save yourself some time. Just turn on "Always show all icons in the notification area."

Now all the icons appear in the system tray, and the ∧ button at the left end of the system tray goes away.

Figure 2-29:
Top: To open this control panel, right-click the clock at the lower-right corner of your screen. From the shortcut menu, choose Properties. (Or choose ▦→ Settings→System→ "Notifications & actions.")

If you click "Select which icons appear on the taskbar," you gain individual hide/ show control over each system-tray icon that seeks some of your screen real estate (bottom).

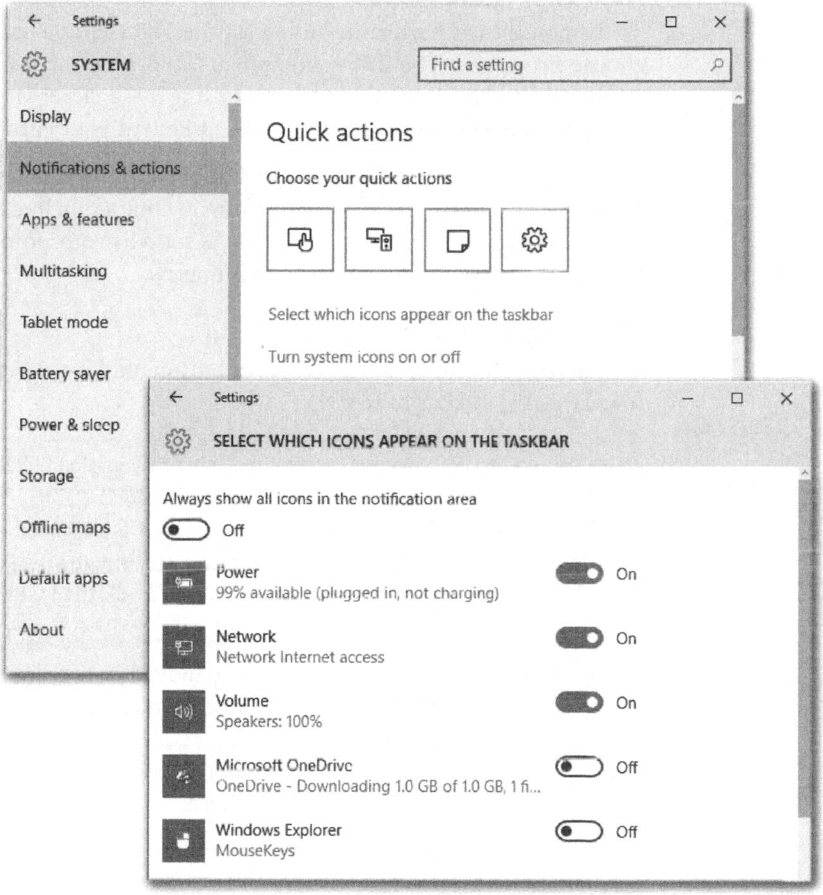

Keyboard control

You have complete keyboard control over the system tray. Press ▦+B to highlight the first icon—the ∧ button. Then press the arrow keys to "walk through" the other icons. Press the space bar to "click" whatever icon is highlighted, opening its menu. (Press the Menu key, if you have one, to "right-click" the icon.)

Three Ways to Get the Taskbar Out of Your Hair

The bottom of the screen isn't necessarily everyone's ideal location for the taskbar. Virtually all screens are wider than they are tall, so the taskbar eats into your limited vertical screen space. You have three ways out: Hide the taskbar, shrink it, or rotate it 90 degrees.

Auto-Hiding the Taskbar

To turn on the taskbar's auto-hiding feature, right-click a blank spot on the taskbar; choose Properties. The dialog box offers "Auto-hide the taskbar," which makes the taskbar disappear whenever you're not using it—a clever way to devote your entire screen to app windows and yet have the taskbar at your cursor tip when needed.

When this feature is turned on, the taskbar disappears whenever you click elsewhere, or whenever your cursor moves away from it. Only a thin line at the edge of the screen indicates that you have a taskbar at all. As soon as your pointer moves close to that line, the taskbar joyfully springs back into view.

Changing the Taskbar's Size

The taskbar can still accumulate a lot of buttons and icons. As a result, you may want to enlarge the taskbar to see what's what.

Note: This trick requires a mouse or trackpad; you can't do it on a touchscreen.

- **The draggy way.** First, ensure that the taskbar isn't *locked* (which means you can't move or resize it). Right-click (or hold your finger down on) a blank spot on the taskbar; from the shortcut menu, turn off "Lock the taskbar," if necessary.

  Now position your pointer on the upper edge of the taskbar (or, if you've moved the taskbar, whichever edge is closest to the center of the screen). When the pointer turns into a double-headed arrow, drag to make the taskbar thicker or thinner.

Note: If you're resizing a taskbar that's on the top or bottom of the screen, it automatically changes its size in full taskbar-height increments. You can't fine-tune the height; you can only double or triple it, for example.

If it's on the left or right edge of your screen, however, you can resize the taskbar freely. If you're not careful, you can make it look really weird.

- **The dialog-box way.** In the Properties dialog box for the taskbar (right-click it; choose Properties from the shortcut menu), an option called "Use small taskbar buttons" appears. It cuts those inch-tall taskbar icons down to half size, for a more pre-Win7 look.

Moving the Taskbar to the Sides of the Screen

Yet another approach to getting the taskbar out of your way is to rotate it so that it sits vertically against a side of your screen. You can rotate it in either of two ways:

- **The draggy way.** First, ensure that the taskbar isn't *locked*, as described above. (Right-click a blank spot; from the shortcut menu, uncheck "Lock the taskbar.")

  Now you can drag the taskbar to any edge of the screen, using any blank spot in the central section as a handle. (You can even drag it to the *top* of your screen, if you're a true rebel.) Let go when the taskbar leaps to the edge you've indicated with the cursor.

Tip: No matter which edge of the screen holds your taskbar, your programs are generally smart enough to adjust their own windows as necessary. In other words, your Word document will shift sideways so that it doesn't overlap the taskbar you've dragged to the side of the screen.

- **The dialog-box way.** Right-click a blank spot on the taskbar; from the shortcut menu, choose Properties. Use the "Taskbar location on screen" pop-up menu to choose Left, Right, Top, or Bottom. (You can do this even if the taskbar is locked.)

NOSTALGIA CORNER

Bringing Back the Old Taskbar

The taskbar's tendency to consolidate the names of document windows into one button saves space, for sure.

Even so, you might prefer the old system, in which there's one taskbar button for every single window. For example, the consolidated-window scheme means you can't bring a certain application to the front just by clicking its taskbar button. (You must actually choose one particular window from among its thumbnails, which is a lot more effort.)

To make Windows display the taskbar the old way, right-click an empty area of the taskbar and choose Properties from the shortcut menu. From the "Taskbar buttons" pop-up menu, choose either "Never combine" or "Combine when taskbar is full" (meaning "only as necessary"). Click Apply; you now have the wider, text-labeled taskbar buttons from the pre-Win7 days, as shown here.

While you're rooting around in here, consider also turning on "Use small taskbar buttons." That step replaces the inch-tall, unlabeled, Mac-style taskbar icons with smaller, half-height ones. Click OK.

The only weirdness now: Icons representing programs that aren't open—icons you've pinned to the taskbar—appear only as icons, without labels, and the effect is somewhat disturbing. You can get rid of them, if you want; just right-click each and choose "Unpin this program from taskbar."

Now you have a taskbar that looks almost exactly like the Windows XP taskbar—except that it still has a rectangular, plain, modern look. Without add-on shareware, that's as far back into the past as you're allowed to rewind Windows; the Classic theme, if you even remember it, is gone from Windows 10.

You'll probably find that the right side of your screen works better than the left. Most programs put their document windows against the left edge of the screen, where the taskbar and its labels might get in the way.

Note: When you position your taskbar vertically, what was once the right side of the taskbar becomes the bottom. In other words, the clock appears at the bottom of the vertical taskbar. So as you read references to the taskbar in this book, mentally substitute the phrase "bottom part of the taskbar" when you read references to the "right side of the taskbar."

Taskbar Toolbars

You'd be forgiven if you've never even heard of taskbar *toolbars*; this is one obscure feature.

These toolbars are separate horizontal sections on the taskbar that offer special-function features. You can even build your own toolbars—for example, one stocked with documents related to a single project. (Somewhere, there's a self-help group for people who spend entirely too much time fiddling with this kind of thing.)

To make a toolbar appear or disappear, right-click a blank spot on the taskbar and choose from the Toolbars submenu that appears (Figure 2-30). The ones with checkmarks are the ones you're seeing now; you can click to turn them on and off.

Tip: You can't adjust the toolbars' widths until you unlock the taskbar (right-click a blank spot and turn off "Lock the taskbar"). Now each toolbar is separated from the main taskbar by a "grip strip" (two thin vertical lines). Drag this strip to make the toolbar wider or narrower.

What follows is a rundown of the ready-made taskbar toolbars at your disposal.

Address Toolbar

This toolbar offers a duplicate copy of the address bar that appears in every File Explorer window, complete with a Recent Addresses pop-up menu—except that it's always available, even if no File Explorer window happens to be open.

Links Toolbar

From its name alone, you might assume that the purpose of this toolbar is to provide links to your favorite Web sites. And sure enough, that's one thing it's good for.

But in fact, you can drag *any icon at all* onto this toolbar—files, folders, disks, programs, or whatever—to turn them into one-click buttons.

In other words, the Links toolbar duplicates the "park favorite icons" function of the Start menu's right side, taskbar, and Quick Launch toolbar. But, in some ways, it's better. It can display *any* kind of icon (unlike the taskbar). It's always visible (unlike the Start menu). And it shows the icons' names.

Here are a few possibilities of things to stash here, just to get your juices flowing:

- **Install icons of the three or four programs** you use the most (or a few documents you work on every day).

- **Install the Recycle Bin's icon,** so you don't have to mouse all the way over to... wherever you keep the real Recycle Bin.

- **Install icons for shared folders on the network.** This arrangement saves several steps when you want to connect to them.

- **Install icons of Web sites you visit often** so you can jump directly to them when you sit down in front of your PC each morning. (In Internet Explorer—though not Edge—you can drag the tiny icon at the left end of the address bar directly onto the Links toolbar to install a Web page there.)

You can drag these links around on the toolbar to put them into a different order, or remove a link by dragging it away—directly into the Recycle Bin, if you like. (They're only shortcuts; you're not actually deleting anything important.) To rename something

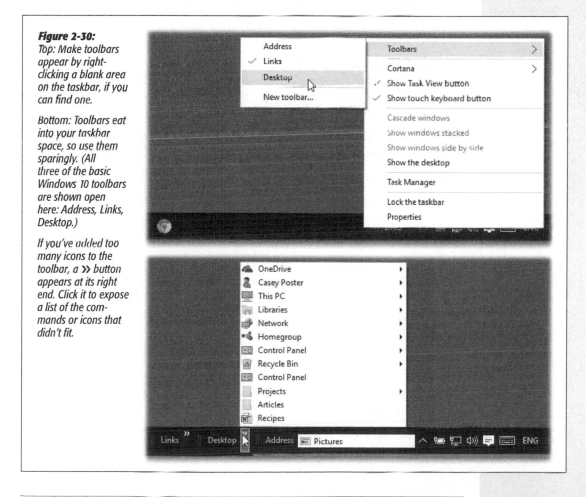

Figure 2-30:

Top: Make toolbars appear by right-clicking a blank area on the taskbar, if you can find one.

Bottom: Toolbars eat into your taskbar space, so use them sparingly. (All three of the basic Windows 10 toolbars are shown open here: Address, Links, Desktop.)

If you've added too many icons to the toolbar, a » button appears at its right end. Click it to expose a list of the commands or icons that didn't fit.

here—a good idea, since horizontal space in this location is so precious—right-click it and choose Rename from the shortcut menu.

Tip: Dragging a Web link from the Links toolbar to the desktop or a File Explorer window creates an *Internet shortcut file.* When double-clicked, this special document connects to the Internet and opens the specified Web page.

Desktop Toolbar

The Desktop toolbar (Figure 2-30, bottom) offers quick access to whichever icons are sitting on your desktop—the Recycle Bin, for example, and whatever else you've put there. As a convenience, it also lists a few frequently used places that *aren't* on the desktop, including your Personal folder, libraries, HomeGroup, Network, Control Panel, and so on.

When it first appears, the Desktop toolbar takes the form of a **»** button at the right end of the taskbar. You can widen the Desktop toolbar if you like, making its buttons appear horizontally on the taskbar. But if you leave it compressed, then many of its icons sprout pop-up *submenus* that give you direct access to their *contents*. That's a useful way to get at your stuff when your screen is filled with windows.

Redesigning Your Toolbars

To change the look of a toolbar, first unlock it. (Right-click it; from the shortcut menu, choose "Lock the taskbar," if necessary, so that the checkmark disappears. Later, repeat this procedure to lock the taskbar again.)

Next, right-click any blank spot on the toolbar. The resulting shortcut menu offers these choices, which appear *above* the usual taskbar shortcut menu choices:

- **View** lets you change the size of the icons on the toolbar.

- **Open Folder** works only with the Quick Launch and Links toolbars.

  It turns out that the icons on these toolbars reflect the contents of corresponding *folders* on your PC. To see one, right-click a blank spot on the toolbar itself; from the shortcut menu, choose Open Folder.

  Why is that useful? Because it means you can add, rename, or delete icons en masse, by working in the folder instead of on the toolbar itself. Of course, you can also delete or rename any icon on these toolbars by right-clicking it and choosing Delete or Rename from the shortcut menu. But a window isn't nearly as claustrophobic as the toolbar itself.

- **Show Text** identifies each toolbar icon with a text label.

- **Show Title** makes the toolbar's name (such as "Quick Launch" or "Desktop") appear on the toolbar.

- **Close Toolbar** makes the toolbar disappear.

Tip: How much horizontal taskbar space a toolbar consumes is up to you. Drag the border at the left edge of a toolbar to make it wider or narrower. That's a good point to remember if, in fact, you can't *find* a blank spot to right-click on. (Sub-tip: In a pinch, you can right-click the clock.) Don't forget that you have to unlock the toolbar before you can change its size (right-click, and then choose "Lock the taskbar" so the checkmark disappears).

Build Your Own Toolbars

The Quick Launch and Links toolbars are such a delight that you may find that having only one isn't enough. You may wish to create several *different* Links toolbars, each stocked with the icons for a different project or person. One could contain icons for all the chapters of a book you're writing; another could list only your games.

Fortunately, it's easy to create as many different custom toolbars as you like, each of which behaves exactly like the Links toolbar.

Windows creates toolbars from *folders,* so before creating a toolbar of your own, you must create a folder and fill it with the stuff you want to toolbar-ize.

Next, right-click a blank spot on the taskbar. From the shortcut menu, choose Toolbars→New Toolbar to open the New Toolbar dialog box. Find and click the folder you want, and then click Select Folder.

Now there's a brand-new toolbar on your taskbar, whose buttons list the contents of the folder you selected. Feel free to tailor it as described—by changing its icon sizes, hiding or showing the icon labels, or installing new icons onto it by dragging them from other File Explorer windows.

Notifications

A *notification* is an important status message. You might get one when a text message comes in, a Facebook post goes up, an alarm goes off, a calendar appointment is imminent, or your battery is running low.

In Windows 10, when some app is trying to get your attention, a message rectangle slides into view at the lower right of your screen (Figure 2-31, top). (Windows nerds love calling these things "toast," because of the way they pop out of the side.)

If you don't take action by clicking or tapping it, the message slides away again after a few seconds. On a touchscreen, you can also swipe it away with a finger.

Note: Do these "toast" notification bubbles appear on the Lock screen too? That's up to you.

Pres ⊞ to open the Start menu. Open Settings→System→"Notifications & actions." Turn off "Show app notifications on the lock screen." Also consider turning off "Show alarms, reminders and incoming VOIP calls on the lock screen"—more urgent forms of alerts.

Those messages no longer appear when the Lock screen is up.

The Silence of the Toast

There are times when you might prefer not to be interrupted, distracted, or awakened by the appearance (and sound) of notification bubbles popping up. Maybe you're about to give a presentation and don't want embarrassing reminders showing up.

Figure 2-31:

Top: This is a notification "toast"—an app trying to get your attention. It disappears after a moment, or you can flick it off to the right.

Middle: You have app-by-app control over which kinds of "toast" can pop up to get your attention. Each app lets you know how it intends to alert you: with a banner and/or a sound.

Bottom: If you click an app's name, you get this box, where you can tailor how that app gets your attention.

Quiet Hours

The quickest and most complete approach is to turn on Quiet Hours. That may sound like you can set up a schedule for your Do Not Disturb time (like 11 p.m. to 7 a.m.)—but alas, you must turn Quiet Hours on and off manually.

To do that, hit the ▣ on the taskbar to open the Action Center. Turn on the "Quiet hours" tile. (If you don't see it, hit "Expand" at the right edge.)

When this feature is turned on, your computer doesn't show alert bubbles, wake up your screen when a call comes in, or make any noises that might disturb you. The idea is to let you save battery power and, if you're lucky, get some sleep.

Silence for good

You can also turn off your notifications for good, on an app-by-app basis. Open Settings→System→ "Notifications & actions." Here you'll find a scrolling list of every app you own that's capable of trying to get your attention: Calendar, Mail, and so on (Figure 2-31, middle). Each has an On/Off switch, for your toast-stifling pleasure.

If you click an app's name, you can tailor how the app gets your attention. You generally have these options:

- **Notifications** is a duplicate of the master on/off switch on the previous Settings screen. Turning this off turns off *both* of the following switches.

- **Show notification banners.** That's a reference to the "toast" rectangles that slide onto your screen in real time. You can turn them off for this app.

- **Play a sound when a notification arrives.** Some apps also ding or chime to get your attention when their notifications appear—unless you shut them up here.

Silence when you're presenting

And by the way: Windows is willing to squelch all of its alert bubbles and sounds whenever you're using a presentation program like PowerPoint or connected to a projector. Nothing worse than an audience of 500 witnessing the embarrassing subject lines of your incoming email.

To do that, open the Settings screen shown in Figure 2-31 (Settings→System→ "Notifications & actions"). Scroll down; turn on "Hide notifications while presenting."

The Action Center

All right, now you know how to dismiss, stifle, or respond to notification toast. But what if you miss one? Or you decide to act on it later?

All of those "Hey you!" messages collect on a single screen called the Action Center, which is new in Windows 10 (Figure 2-32).

To make it appear, hit the 🗐 icon on your system tray. Or press ■+A (for Action Center!).

Tip: If you have a touchscreen, you can swipe your finger inward from the right edge of the screen to open the Action Center. Much more fun.

The Action Center slides onto the screen like a classy black window shade, printed in white with every recent item of interest.

The Notifications List

At the top of the Action Center, you'll find all the notifications from all the apps you've permitted to alert you, grouped by app—the first lines of all your tweets, emails, antivirus-software whines, App Store updates, weather warnings, calendar alarms, and so on. Each is date-stamped.

Here's the fun you can have with these things:

- **Tap the ∨ at far right to read more about it.** For example, you can read the full body of a tweet, or read the rest of an email's subject line. Basically, you get to read beyond the first line of whatever it was.

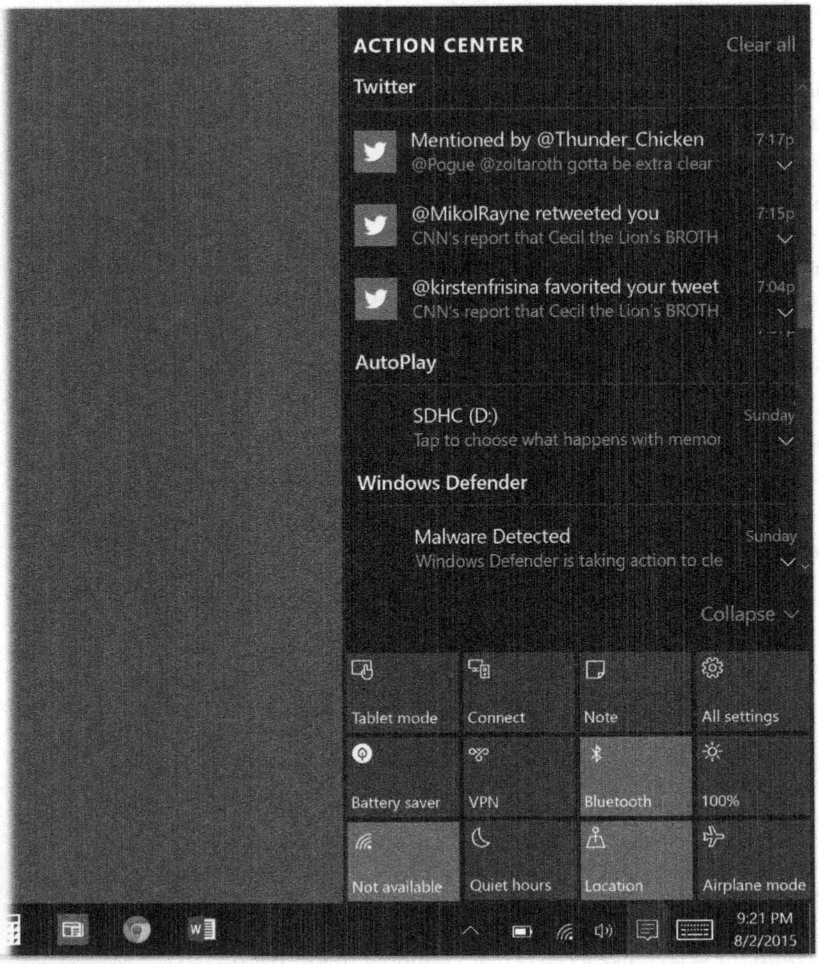

Figure 2-32:
This is the Action Center, one of the Big New Features of Windows 10. It's where your apps send you memos to get your attention—about incoming messages, mail, tweets, Facebook posts, security issues, app updates, and so on.

At bottom: Handy one-tap tiles for adjusting important PC settings.

- **Click an item to open the relevant app.** For example, click an appointment listed there to open its information panel in Calendar. Click the name of a software update to open the App Store program to read about it and download it. Click a message's name to open Mail, where you can read the entire message.

- **Swipe an item to the right to get rid of it.** You're not erasing the thing itself—only dismissing the notification.

Tip: If you have no interest in a certain app's notifications showing up here, you can make them stop appearing for good, as described on the preceding pages.

Once you've had a look at the notifications that have piled up since you last checked, you can also hit "Clear all" at the top of the column. That erases all the notifications, leaving the Action Center empty and ready for new messages.

The Quick Action Tiles

Below the list of notifications, another useful panel appears: the Quick Action tiles. These are one-touch buttons for important functions like the ones described below.

Clearly, this feature is intended primarily for portable gadgets like tablets, phones, and laptops, but a few are useful no matter what you've got:

- **Tablet mode.** If you have a touchscreen, you might enjoy this finger-friendly Windows 10 mode. It's described in Chapter 13; you turn Tablet mode on and off by tapping here.

- **Connect** is where you set up wireless audio and video receivers. For example, it's how you'd connect your tablet to a Bluetooth speaker, or your laptop to a Miracast receiver connected to your TV.

- **Note** opens up the OneNote app, where you can jot down a brainstorm (page 329).

- **All settings** is another way to open up the main Settings app. (The other way is to choose its name from the left side of the Start menu.)

- **Battery saver** is, of course, for portable gadgets. When it's on, the screen dims, and the computer stops doing continuous checking for email and other Internet data, all in an effort to eke out more useful time on your remaining charge.

  Ordinarily, Windows turns on Battery Saver automatically when the battery falls below 20 percent of a full charge—but by hitting this tile, you can invoke it manually. Details on page 441.

- **VPN** connects you to a virtual private network—a very secure way of connecting to your corporate network across the Internet. See page 456.

- **Bluetooth** is a short-range wireless technology. It's how you connect wireless keyboards, mice, and speakers, and this is the on/off switch.

- **Brightness.** Each time you tap this tile, the brightness cycles through four settings: 25%, 50%, 75%, and 100%. Screen brightness is the single biggest eater of battery power, so you've got a quick and easy way to adjust the illumination and the battery drain.

- **WiFi.** This tile turns your WiFi networking feature on or off—and when you're connected, it identifies the name of the hotspot you're on.

- **Quiet hours.** This is the on/off switch for notifications, as described on the previous pages.

- **Location.** A typical portable Windows machine always attempts to know where it is in the world. (You could argue that apps like Maps and Weather are more useful when they know where you are.) But sometimes, it may make you a little uneasy that your PC is tracking your whereabouts. In those cases, use this switch to turn off the computer's location tracking.

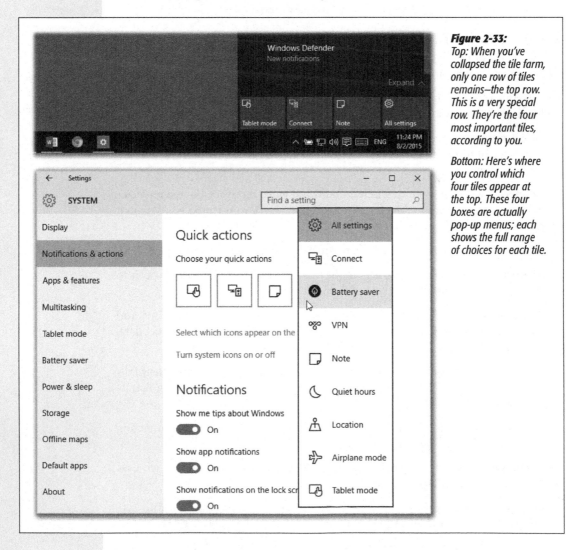

Figure 2-33:
Top: When you've collapsed the tile farm, only one row of tiles remains—the top row. This is a very special row. They're the four most important tiles, according to you.

Bottom: Here's where you control which four tiles appear at the top. These four boxes are actually pop-up menus; each shows the full range of choices for each tile.

- **Airplane mode,** of course, is just like airplane mode on a phone: It turns off all wireless transmission. No cellular, no WiFi. Handy when the flight attendant instructs everyone to put their devices into airplane mode, of course, but also useful when you want to eke out as much battery life as possible.

Tip: It's perfectly OK to turn on airplane mode—and then to turn *WiFi back on again*, using its Quick Action tile. WiFi is allowed in flight; meanwhile, all other wireless features (Bluetooth and cellular, for example) will remain turned off.

Although it might not be obvious, you have some control over the Quick Action tiles. You can exercise your good taste in either of two ways:

- **Collapse them.** Let's face it: Of the two parts of the Action Center (the notifications at top, the on/off tiles at bottom), the upper part is the one you'll probably check more often. These messages come in all the time.

  That's why Microsoft set it up with a Collapse button, visible in Figure 2-32. When you click it, the Action Center hides all but the top row of tiles, as shown in Figure 2-33.

- **Customize them.** You can't exactly go nuts, rearranging the Quick Action tiles as though they're puzzle pieces. You do, however, have complete control over which four appear in the *top row of them.*

  And why is the top row so special? Because when you collapse the tiles (by clicking Collapse), only the top row remains visible, as shown in Figure 2-33 at top. All the rest of the Action Center space is devoted to your notifications.

  Therefore, it's especially thoughtful of Microsoft to give you a Settings panel where you can specify which four tiles appear on the top row.

  Choose ■→Settings→System→"Notifications & actions," and proceed as shown in Figure 2-33.

CHAPTER 3

Organizing & Finding Your Files

Every disk, folder, file, application, printer, and networked computer is represented on your screen by an icon. To avoid spraying your screen with thousands of overlapping icons seething like snakes in a pit, Windows organizes icons into folders, puts those folders into *other* folders, and so on. This folder-in-a-folder-in-a-folder scheme works beautifully at reducing screen clutter, but it means that you've got some hunting to do whenever you want to open a particular icon.

Helping you find, navigate, and manage your files, folders, and disks with less stress and greater speed is one of the primary design goals of Windows—and of this chapter. The following pages cover Windows 10's improved Search function, plus icon-management life skills like selecting them, renaming them, moving them, copying them, making shortcuts of them, assigning them to keystrokes, deleting them, and burning them to CD or DVD.

The Search Box

Every computer offers a way to find and open files and programs. And in Windows 10, the Search feature has been improved—well, changed, anyway. It now searches both your computer and the Web simultaneously (you can turn that off). And Microsoft has tried to mix together Search and Cortana, Windows 10's voice-controlled assistant.

But at its heart, Search is still Search. It's how you open an app, find a file, or adjust a setting just by typing a few letters. It can save you a lot of hunting and burrowing through your folders.

It's important to note, though, that Windows offers search boxes in two different places:

- **The main search box.** The search box at the left end of the taskbar—labeled either "Ask me anything" or "Search the web and Windows"—searches *everywhere* on your computer. And beyond; it can also search your network or the Internet.

- **File Explorer windows.** The search box at the top of every desktop window searches only *that window* (including folders within it).

Search boxes also appear in the Settings window, the Edge browser, Mail, Windows Media Player, and other spots where it's useful to perform small-time, limited searches. The following pages, however, cover the two main search boxes, the ones that hunt down files and folders.

The Taskbar Search Box

The new search box is always on the screen. It's no longer part of the Start menu; it's part of the taskbar now. Here's how you might perform a search:

1. **Get your insertion point into the search box.**

   You can click or tap the box, or press either of these keystrokes:

   ■ opens the Start menu. But it *also* puts your blinking cursor into the search box.

   ■+**S** keystroke tells Cortana (Chapter 5) that you're about to type a request. But in Windows 10, Cortana is part of Search, so ■+S puts your cursor into the search box, just as you'd hope. Makes mnemonic sense, too: S stands for Search.

Note: The first time you use the search box, Windows displays a panel that informs you of the kind of information it needs to collect. Click "I agree" to continue—or see page 196 to find out more about this data.

   When you click into the search box or press ■+S, the Cortana panel opens automatically. It's not empty, though; it comes stocked with "stuff you might like to know about" (as the introductory text says), like your calendar for the day, breaking news, and so on. You can read more about these info-cards, and Cortana, in Chapter 5.

   In any case, you can ignore all this information for now.

2. **Start typing what you want to find (Figure 3-1).**

   For example, if you're trying to find a file called "Pokémon Fantasy League.doc," typing just *pok* or *leag* will probably work.

   Capitalization doesn't count, and neither do accent marks; typing *cafe* finds files with the word "café" just fine. (You can change this, however; see page 136.)

   As you type, search results begin to appear in the space formerly occupied by the Start menu, grouped by category (Figure 3-1). This is a live, interactive search; that is, Windows modifies the menu as you type—you don't have to press Enter after entering your search phrase.

The Search feature can find every file; folder; program; email message; address book entry; calendar appointment; picture; movie; PDF document; music file; Web bookmark; and Word, PowerPoint, and Excel document that contains what you typed, regardless of its name or folder location.

In fact, Windows isn't just searching icon *names*. It's also searching their contents—the words inside your documents—as well as all your files' *metadata*. (That's descriptive text information about what's in a file, like its height, width, size, creator, copyright holder, title, editor, created date, and last modification date. Page 77 has the details.)

Note: Windows is constantly updating its invisible index (page 130) in real time. You can prove it to yourself like this: Open a text document (in WordPad, for example). Type an unusual word, like *wombat.* Save the document using a different name—say, "Fun Pets." Now *immediately* do a search. Hit the ■ key and type *wom,* for example. You'll see that Windows finds "Fun Pets" even though it's only moments old. That's a far cry from the old Windows Indexing Service, which updated its index only once a day, in the middle of the night!

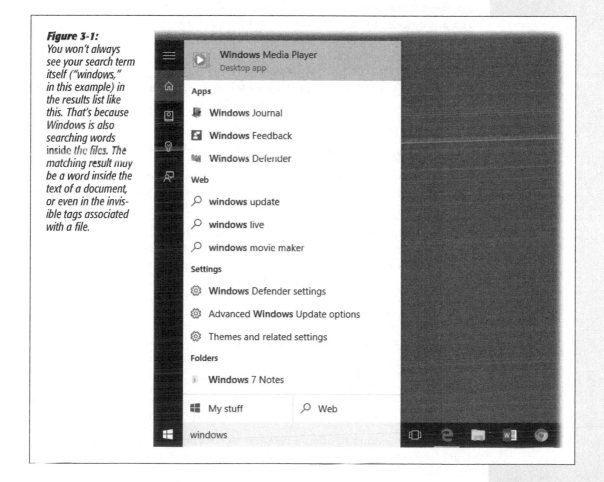

Figure 3-1:
You won't always see your search term itself ("windows," in this example) in the results list like this. That's because Windows is also searching words inside the files. The matching result may be a word inside the text of a document, or even in the invisible tags associated with a file.

4. If you see the item you were hoping to dig up, tap or click it to open it.

In fact, if that thing is listed *first* in the results menu, tinted, then you can press Enter to open it.

The search box, in other words, is an incredibly fast way to open a *program* you want. You should use it all the time. The whole thing happens very quickly, and you never have to take your hands off the keyboard. That is, you might hit ⊞ to open the Start menu, type *calc* (to search for Calculator), and press Enter. (Why does pressing Enter open Calculator? Because it's the first item in the list of results, and its name is highlighted.)

Why burrow around in folders when you can open any file or program with a couple of keystrokes?

If the thing you want is in the list—just not at the *top* of the list—click it, tap it, or "walk" down to it with the arrow keys and then press Enter to open it.

Tip: Unless you intervene (page 133), Search shows you results *both* from your computer and from the Web, all in the same list. It takes an additional click to see only one or the other. Click "My stuff" to open the More Results window described next, showing *only* what's on your computer. Or click "Web" to open your browser and complete the search using Microsoft's Bing search service.

---

5. If you don't see what you were looking for, click a category heading to see more results.

That step may take a little explanation; read on.

The "More Results" Window

The search results menu has room for only a few items. Unless you own one of those extremely rare 60-inch Skyscraper Displays, there just isn't room to show you the whole list.

Instead, Windows uses some fancy analysis to display the *most likely* matches for what you typed. They appear grouped into categories like Apps, Settings, Folders, Documents, and Store (meaning apps from the Windows app store).

Tip: If you click or tap one of these category headings, you open a window containing just the search results in that category. Kind of handy, really.

Such a short list of likely suspects means it's easy to arrow-key your way to the menu item you want to open. And Windows does a pretty good job at guessing which two or three search results to show you in each category.

On the other hand, you might have 425 different documents containing the word "syzygy," and you'll see only three of them in the search-results list.

Fortunately, Windows 10 offers a new way to reveal the rest of the results in a certain category: Click the *category name*. Click Apps, or Settings, or Documents, or whatever. And boom: You come face to face with the box shown in Figure 3-2: the More Results box.

The elements of this new box work out like this:

- **[what you've typed so far].** At the very top of the box, you see your search query. Don't click here, thinking that you can keep on typing, or editing the search; you'll only close the box.

- **Sort.** Your choices in this very small pop-up menu are Most Relevant (the results Windows thinks you're mostly likely to be looking for) and Most Recent (how long ago you've opened these things).

- **Show.** Of course, you *got* to this box by clicking a category heading—Settings, Apps, or whatever. But this pop-up menu lists all those categories again (Documents, Folders, Apps, Settings, and so on)—plus the very useful All—so that you can search a different category without having to start all over.

- **Search the Web.** Yeah. Just in case, you know, you realize that the file you believed to be on your *computer* might actually be on the *Web* (?).

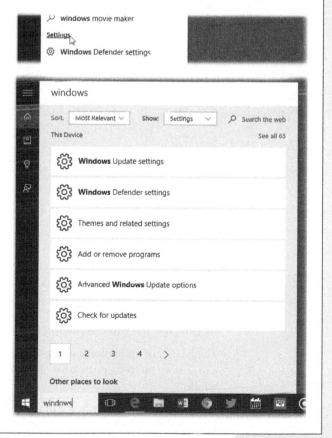

Figure 3-2:
Top: Click a category heading to see more of the search results in that category.

Bottom: The More Results box shows you more search results than can fit in the search results menu. And yet even here, only a few results appear on each screenful. You can click "Show all 65" (or whatever the number is), but you'll still have to flip "pages" of this screen to see all the matches.

- **This device, OneDrive.** The More Results window rounds up search results from your computer and your OneDrive separately. You can click this heading ("This device") to see only the results that are actually on your machine.

- **See all 40.** The More Results window shows more results than the results menu, but it still doesn't show very many—about six items, displayed on rectangular buttons large enough to be tapped by fingers on touchscreens.

  This "See all [number]" link expands the window to show you a larger set of results. (If the number of results is really big—over 30, say—you'll still have to page through them.)

- **Other places to look.** Click File Explorer, OneDrive, or Settings to limit your search to just those places.

File Explorer Window Searches

See the search box at the top right of every File Explorer window (Figure 3-3)? This, too, is a piece of the Search empire. But there's a big difference: This search box searches *your entire computer*. The search box in a File Explorer window searches *only that window* (and folders within it).

Figure 3-3:
The instant you click into the search box (circled), the Search tab of the Ribbon mysteriously appears. Marvel at the wealth of searching opportunity facing you.

As you type, the window changes to show search results (in Content view).

The beauty of an Explorer window search is that it's not limited to the height of the Cortana menu. If there are a lot of results, you see them all in one massively scrolling window.

Once the results appear, you can change the window view if that's helpful—or sort, filter, and group them, just as you would in any other Explorer window.

And now, three glorious tips about starting Explorer-window searches:

- You can make the search box bigger—by dragging the divider bar (between the address bar and the search box) to the left. Useful when you're searching for your novel in progress, "The Sudden Disappearance, Reappearance, and then Disappearance Again of Sean O'Flanagan at the Dawn of the Elizabethan Era."

- Ordinarily, when you just start typing in a File Explorer window, you highlight the first icon whose name matches your typing. But in the Folder Options dialog box (page 86), on the View tab, if you scroll down about three miles, you'll find an option called "When typing into a list view." Turn on "Automatically type into the Search Box." Now you save yourself a click every time you search; the mere act of typing initiates a search. (Despite the wording of this option, it works in any icon view—not just list view.)

Search Options on the Ribbon

When you use the File Explorer search box, the Ribbon magically sprouts a new tab, called Search (Figure 3-3). It's teeming with options, including *search filters* that help you weed down a big list of results:

- **This PC.** This button, at far left, does the opposite of weed down your results—it expands the scope of your search. You've just searched this Explorer window, but this button applies the same search to your entire computer.

- **Current folder.** An Explorer search usually searches the window that's open and all the folders inside it. If you click this button, though, you eliminate the subfolders from the results.

- **All subfolders.** Remember the fun you had reading the "Current folder" paragraph just now? This button has the opposite function. It expands the search's reach to include this window's subfolders once again.

- **Search again in.** This handy pop-up menu lists places you've recently searched. Now and then, one of these options can save you time and fiddling.

- **Date modified, Kind, Size, Other properties.** These are *search filters*. They refine your search, letting you limit the results to certain date ranges, file types, file sizes, and so on.

  When you use these menus, you'll see codes in blue text appear in the search box—for example, *datemodified:last week,* or *size:medium.* If you're more of a keyboard person than a mouse person, you could type those codes into the search box yourself; the result is exactly the same, as described in the next section. In other words, the options on the Ribbon are nothing more than user-friendlified, quicker ways of entering the same search codes.

Tip: You can adjust the second part of each code just by clicking it. For example, if you chose *size:small* and you really wanted *size:medium*—or if the *size:small* query didn't produce any results—click the word *small.* The pop-up menu of sizes appears again so you can adjust your selection.

You can use as many of these filters as you want. The more you click them (or type the corresponding shorthand), the longer the codes are in the search box. If you want to find medium files created by Casey last year with the tag *Murgatroid project,* go right ahead.

So what do they do? The "Date modified" pop-up menu offers choices like Today, Yesterday, Last Month, and This Year. "Kind" is a long list of file types, with choices like Folder, Game, Note, Picture, and Web History. "Size" offers file-size ranges like Tiny (0 to 10 KB), Medium (100 KB to 1 MB), Huge (16 to 128 MB), and Gigantic (greater than 128 MB).

As for the miscellaneous filters in the "Other properties" pop-up menu—well, they require some explanation.

"Type" lets you specify (after the word *Type:* in the search box) what general kind of thing you're looking for: *picture, sound, PDF, document, folder, disk image, backup, JPG, DOC,* and so on. (More on types in a moment.)

"Name" lets you search for something by its filename only. (Otherwise, Windows also shows you search results based on the words *inside* the files.)

"Folder path" lets you type out the folder path (page 611) of something you're seeking.

Finally, **"Tags"** lets you search for items according to the label you've applied to them, as described on page 77.

- **Recent searches** displays—correct!—recent searches you've performed. It uses the shorthand described above, like "portrait of mary kind:image" or "Book list size:medium."

- **Advanced options** is a shortcut to some of the options described on page 132, pertaining to non-indexed locations (that is, other computers on your network, or external drives). Here you can turn on the searching of zipped files and system files in those places, or turn on searching of text inside their files. You also get a shortcut to the Indexing Options dialog box described on page 132.

- **Save search.** This button becomes available once you've set up a search.

When clicked, it generates a *saved search* file and asks you to name it. (Behind the scenes, it's a special document with the filename extension *.search-ms.*) Windows proposes stashing it in your Saved Searches folder, inside your Personal folder, but you can choose any location you like—including the desktop.

Whenever you click the saved search, you get an instantaneous update of the search you originally set up.

The idea is to save you time when you regularly have to set up the same search; for example, maybe every week you have to round up all the documents authored by you that pertain to the Higgins proposal and save them to a flash drive. A search folder can do the rounding-up part with a single click. These items' real locations may be all over the map, scattered in folders throughout your PC. But through the magic of the saved search, they appear as though they're all in one neat window.

Note: Unfortunately, there's no easy way to edit a search folder. If you decide your original search criteria need a little fine-tuning, then the simplest procedure is to set up a new search—correctly this time—and save it with the same name as the first one; accept Windows' offer to replace the old one with the new.

Incidentally: Search filters work by *hiding* all the icons that don't match. So don't be alarmed if you click Size and then Small—and most of the files in your window suddenly disappear. Windows is doing what it thinks you wanted—showing you only the small files—in real time, as you adjust the filters.

At any time, you can bring all the files back into view by clicking the ✕ at the right end of the search box.

Limit by Size, Date, Rating, Tag, Author...

Suppose you're looking for a file called *Big Deals.doc*. But when you type *big* into the search box, you wind up wading through hundreds of files that *contain* the word "big."

It's at times like these that you'll be grateful for Windows' little-known *criterion* searches. These are syntax tricks that help you create narrower, more targeted searches. All you have to do is prefix your search query with the criterion you want, followed by a colon.

One example is worth a thousand words, so *several* examples should save an awful lot of paper. You can type these codes into the search box in an Explorer window (they don't work in the main search box):

- *name: big* finds only documents with "big" in their *names*. Windows ignores anything with that term *inside* the file.

- *tag: crisis* finds only icons with "crisis" as a tag—not as part of the title or contents.

- *created: 7/25/15* finds everything you wrote on July 25, 2015. You can also use *modified: today* or *modified: yesterday*, for that matter. Or don't be that specific. Just use *modified: July* or *modified: 2015*.

  You can use symbols like < and >, too. To find files created since yesterday, you could type *created: >yesterday*.

  Or use two dots to indicate a range. To find all the email you got in the first two weeks of March 2015, you could type *received: 3/1/2015..3/15/2015*. (That two-dot business also works to specify a range of file sizes, as in *size: 2 MB..5 MB*.)

Tip: That's right: Windows recognizes human terms like *today, yesterday, this week, last week, last month, this month*, and *last year*.

- *size: >2gb* finds all the big files on your PC.

- *rating: <**** finds documents to which you've given ratings of three stars or fewer.

- *camera model: Sony A7* finds all the pictures you took with that camera.

- *kind: email* finds all the email messages.

  That's just one example of the power of *kind*. Here are some other kinds you can look for: *calendar, appointment,* or *meeting* (appointments in Outlook, or iCal, or vCalendar files); *communication* (email and attachments); *contact* or *person* (vCard and Windows Contact files, Outlook contacts); *doc* or *document* (text, Office, PDF, and Web files); *folder* (folders, .zip files, .cab files); *link* (shortcut files); *music* or *song* (audio files, Windows Media playlists); *pic* or *picture* (graphics files like JPEG, PNG, GIF, and BMP); *program* (programs); *tv* (shows recorded by Windows Media Center); and *video* (movie files).

- The *folder:* prefix limits the search to a certain folder or library. (The starter words *under:*, *in:*, and *path:* work the same way.) So *folder: music* confines the search to your Music library, and a search for *in: documents turtle* finds all files in your Documents library containing the word "turtle."

Tip: You can combine multiple criteria searches, too. For example, if you're pretty sure you had a document called "Naked Mole-Rats" that you worked on yesterday, you could cut directly to it by typing *mole modified: yesterday* or *modified: yesterday mole*. (The order doesn't matter.)

So where's the master list of these available criteria? It turns out that they correspond to the *column headings* at the top of an Explorer window that's in Details view: Name, Date modified, Type, Size, and so on.

You're not limited to just the terms you see now; you can use any term that *can* be an Explorer-window heading. To see them all, right-click any of the existing column headings in a window that's in Details view. From the shortcut menu, choose More. There they are: 115 different criteria, including Size, Rating, Album, Bit rate, Camera model, Date archived, Language, Nickname, and so on. Here's where you learn that, for example, to find all your Ohio address book friends, you'd search for *home state or province: OH*.

GEM IN THE ROUGH

Beyond Your Own Stuff

Ordinarily, Windows searches only what's in *your* account—your Personal folder. From the search box, you can't search what's inside somebody else's stuff.

Yet you *can* search someone else's account—just not from the search box and not without permission.

Start by opening the This PC→Users folder. Inside, you'll find folders for all other account holders. Open the one you

want to search, and then search using the search box at the top of the File Explorer window.

You won't be given access, though, without first supplying an administrator's password. (You don't necessarily have to know it; you could just call an administrator over to type it in personally.) After all, the whole point of having different accounts is to ensure privacy for each person—and only the administrator, or *an* administrator, has full rein to stomp through anyone's stuff.

Dude, if you can't find what you're looking for using all *those* controls, it probably doesn't exist.

Special Search Codes

Certain shortcuts in the File Explorer search boxes can give your queries more power. For example:

- **Document types.** You can type *document* to find all text, spreadsheet, and Power-Point files. You can also type a filename extension—*.mp3* or *.doc* or *.jpg,* for example—to round up all files of a certain file type.

- **Tags, authors.** This is payoff time for applying *tags* or author names to your files (page 77). In a search box, you can type, or start to type, *Gruber Project* (or any other tag you've assigned), and you get an instantaneous list of everything that's relevant to that tag. Or you can type *Mom* or *Casey* or any other author's name to see all the documents that person created.

- **Utility apps.** Windows comes with a bunch of geekhead programs that aren't listed in the Start menu and have no icons—advanced technical tools like RegEdit (the Registry Editor), Command Prompt (the command line), and so on. By far the quickest way to open them is to type their names into the search box.

  In this case, however, you must type the *entire* name—*regedit,* not just *rege.* And you have to use the program's actual, on-disk name (regedit), not its human name (Registry Editor).

- **Quotes.** If you type in more than one word, Search works just the way Google does. That is, it finds things that contain both words *somewhere* inside.

  If you're searching for a phrase where the words really belong together, though, put quotes around them. For example, searching for *military intelligence* rounds up documents that contain those two words, but not necessarily side by side. Searching for *"military intelligence"* finds documents that contain that exact phrase. (Insert your own political joke here.)

- **Boolean searches.** Windows also permits combination-search terms like AND and OR, better known to geeks as Boolean searches.

  That is, you can round up a single list of files that match *two* terms by typing, say, *vacation AND kids.* (That's also how you'd find documents coauthored by two specific people—you and a pal, for example.)

Tip: You can use parentheses instead of AND, if you like. That is, typing *(vacation kids)* finds documents that contain both words, not necessarily together.

If you use OR, you can find icons that match *either* of two search criteria. Typing *jpeg OR mp3* will turn up photos and music files in a single list.

The word NOT works, too. If you did a search for *dolphins,* hoping to turn up sea-mammal documents, but instead find your results contaminated by football-team listings, then by all means repeat the search with *dolphins NOT Miami*. Windows will eliminate all documents containing "Miami."

Note: You must type Boolean terms like AND, OR, and NOT in all capitals.

You can even combine Boolean terms with the other special search terms described in this chapter. Find everything created in the past couple of months by searching for *created: September OR October,* for example. If you've been entering your name into the Properties dialog box of Microsoft Office documents, you can find all the ones created by Casey and Robin working together using *author: (Casey AND Robin).*

File-Explorer Results Menu Tips

It should be no surprise that a feature as important as Search comes loaded with options, tips, and tricks. Here it is—the official, unexpurgated Search Tip-O-Rama:

- You can open anything in the results menu by highlighting it and then pressing Enter to open it.

- If Windows doesn't find a *program* whose name matches what you've typed, it doesn't highlight anything in the list. In that case, pressing Enter has a different effect: It opens up the Search Results *window,* which has no length limit and offers a lot more features (page 122). (Pressing Enter, in this case, is the same as clicking the "See more results" list at the bottom.)

  Alternatively, you can use the mouse or the arrow-key/Enter method described above to open one of the search results.

- You can learn more about a search result by pointing to it without clicking. The pop-up tooltip balloon shows you the details. For a file, you see size, date, and other info; for a program or control panel, you see a description.

- You can jump to the actual icon of a search result, sitting there in its actual window, instead of opening it. To do that, right-click its name and, from the shortcut menu, choose "Open file location." The Esc key (top-left corner of your keyboard) is a quick "back out of this" keystroke. Tap it to close the results menu and restore the Start menu to its original form.

- To clear the search box—either to try a different search or just to get the regularly scheduled Start menu back—click the little × at the right end of the search box.

- When you need to look up a number in the People app, don't bother opening Mail; it's faster to use Search. You can type somebody's name or even part of someone's phone number.

The Search Index

You might think that typing something into the search box triggers a search. But to be technically correct, Windows has already *done* its searching. In the first 15 to 30 minutes after you install Windows—or in the minutes after you attach a new hard drive—it invisibly collects information about all your files. Like a kid cramming for an exam, it reads, takes notes on, and memorizes the contents of your hard drives.

And not just the names of your files. That would be *so* 2004!

No, Windows actually looks *inside* the files. It can read and search the contents of text files, email, Windows People, Windows Calendar, RTF and PDF documents, and documents from Microsoft Office (Word, Excel, and PowerPoint).

In fact, Windows searches over 300 bits of text associated with your files—a staggering collection of tidbits, including the names of the layers in a Photoshop document, the tempo of an MP3 file, the shutter speed of a digital-camera photo, a movie's copyright holder, a document's page size, and on and on. (Technically, this sort of secondary information is called *metadata*. It's usually invisible, although a lot of it shows up in the Details pane described on page 77.)

Windows stores all this information in an invisible, multimegabyte file called, creatively enough, the *index*. (If your primary hard drive is creaking full, you can specify that you want the index stored on some other drive; see page 136.)

After that, Windows can produce search results in seconds. It doesn't have to search your entire hard drive—only that card catalog index file.

After the initial indexing process, Windows continues to monitor what's on your hard drive, indexing new and changed files in the background, in the microseconds between your keystrokes and clicks.

Where Windows Looks

Windows doesn't actually scrounge through *every* file on your computer. Searching inside Windows' own operating-system files and all your programs, for example, would be pointless to anyone but programmers. All that useless data would slow down searches and bulk up the invisible index file.

What Windows *does* index is everything in your Personal folder: email, pictures, music, videos, program names, entries in your People and Calendar apps, Office documents, and so on. It also searches all your *libraries* (page 72), even if they contain folders from other computers on your network.

Similarly, it searches *offline files* that belong to you, even though they're stored somewhere else on the network.

Note: Windows indexes all the drives connected to your PC, but not other hard drives on the network. You can, if you wish, add other folders to the list of indexed locations manually (page 132).

Windows does index the Personal folders of everyone else with an account on your machine (Chapter 19), but you're not allowed to search them. So if you were hoping to search your spouse's email for phrases like "Meet you at midnight," forget it.

Adding New Places to the Index

On the other hand, suppose there's some folder on another disk (or elsewhere on the network) that you really do want to be able to search the *good* way—contents and all, nice and fast. You can do that by adding it to your PC's search index.

And you can do *that* in a couple of ways:

- **Add it to a library.** Drag any folder into one of your libraries (page 72). After a couple of minutes of indexing, that folder is now ready for insta-searching, contents and all, just as though it were born on your own PC.

- **Add it to the Indexing Options dialog box (Figure 3-4).** Windows maintains a master list of everything in its search index. That's handy, because it means you can easily *add* folders to the index—folders from an external hard drive, for example—for speedy searches.

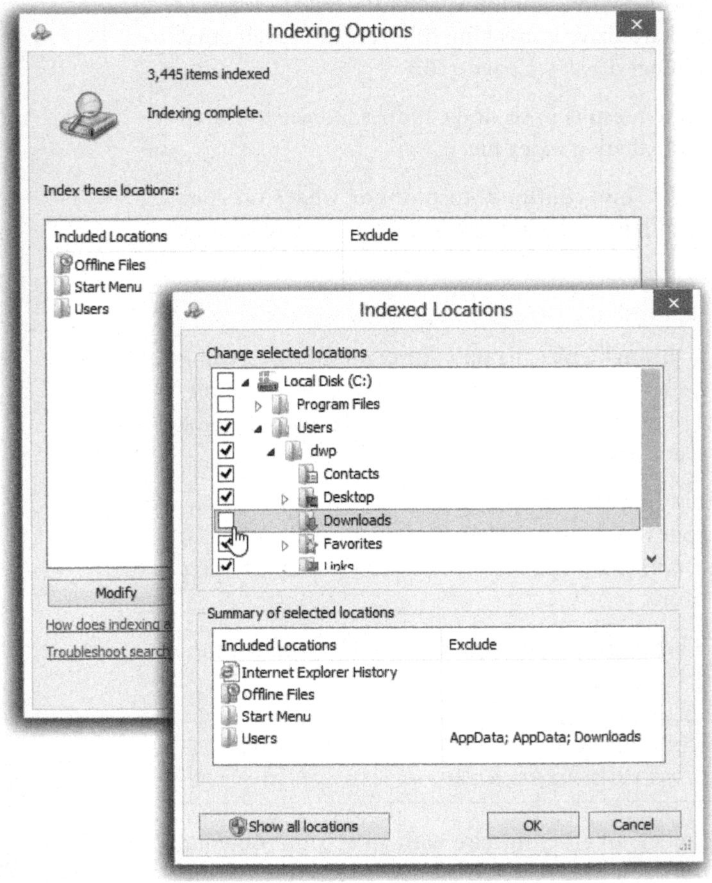

Figure 3-4:
In the Indexing Options box, you can add or remove disks, partitions, or folders, thereby editing the list of searchable items.

Start by opening Indexing Options (top), and then click Modify. Now expand the flippy triangles, if necessary, to see the list of folders on your hard drive. Turn a folder's checkbox on (to have Windows index it) or off (to remove it from the index, and therefore from searches). In this example, you've just told Windows to stop indexing your Downloads folder. Click OK.

You can *remove* folders from the index, too, maybe because you have privacy concerns (for example, you don't want your coworkers searching your stuff while you're away from your desk). Or maybe you just want to create more focused searches, removing a lot of old, extraneous junk from Windows' database.

Either way, the steps are simple. Open the Indexing Options control panel; the quickest way is to type *indexing* into the search box until you see Indexing Options in the search results. Click it, and proceed as shown in Figure 3-4.

Tip: If you're trying to get some work done while Windows is in the middle of building the index, and the indexing is giving your PC all the speed of a slug in winter, you can click the Pause button. Windows will cool its jets for 15 minutes before it starts indexing again.

Customizing Search

You've just read about how Search works fresh out of the box. But you can tailor its behavior, either for security reasons or to customize it to the kinds of work you do.

Unfortunately for you, Microsoft has stashed the various controls that govern searching into three different places. Here they are, one area at a time.

Search Settings

As you may have discovered, the main search box produces results both from your computer and from the Web, in a single list. If you squint your eyes a little and really think about it, that arrangement doesn't make much sense. You wouldn't search your hard drive to place an order from Amazon.com, and you wouldn't search the Web for that spreadsheet from December.

You can eliminate the Web results so that the search box finds only stuff on your actual computer. Unfortunately, that also involves turning off Cortana *completely*, including all the handy features described in Chapter 5. Mull over this tradeoff.

If you've chosen to continue, see Figure 3-5.

Folder Options

The first source is in the Folder Options→Search dialog box. To open it, find the View tab on the Ribbon in any Explorer window; click Options. In the resulting dialog box, click the Search tab. Here's what you'll find here:

- **Don't use the Index when searching in file folders for system files.** If you turn this item on, Windows won't use its internal Dewey Decimal System for searching Windows itself. It will, instead, perform the names-only, slower type of search.

  So who on earth would want this turned on? You, if you're a programmer or system administrator and you're worried that the indexed version of the system files might be out of date. (That happens, since system files change often, and the index may take some time to catch up.)

- **Include system directories.** When you're searching a disk that hasn't been indexed, do you want Windows to look inside the folders that contain Windows itself (as opposed to just the documents people have created)? If yes, then turn this on.

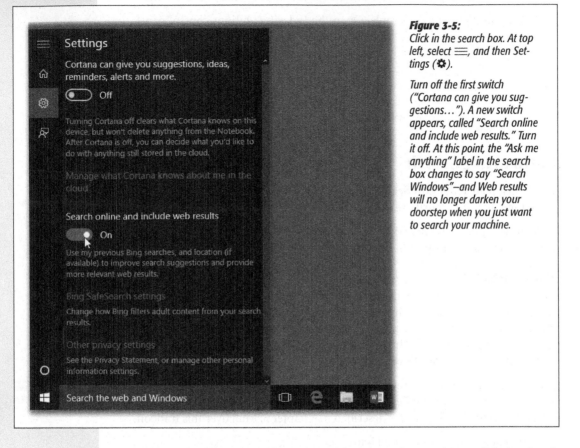

Figure 3-5:
Click in the search box. At top left, select ☰, and then Settings (⚙).

Turn off the first switch ("Cortana can give you suggestions..."). A new switch appears, called "Search online and include web results." Turn it off. At this point, the "Ask me anything" label in the search box changes to say "Search Windows"–and Web results will no longer darken your doorstep when you just want to search your machine.

- **Include compressed files (ZIP, CAB...).** When you're searching a disk that hasn't been indexed, do you want Windows to search for files inside compressed archives, like .zip and .cab files? If yes, then turn on this checkbox. (Windows doesn't ordinarily search archives, even on an indexed hard drive.)

- **Always search file names and contents.** As the previous pages make clear, the Windows search mechanism relies on an *index*—an invisible database that tracks the location, contents, and metadata of every file. If you attach a new hard drive, or attempt to search another computer on the network that hasn't been indexed, Windows ordinarily just searches its files' *names*. After all, it has no index to search for that drive.

  If Windows did attempt to index those other drives, you'd sometimes have to wait awhile, at least the first time, because index-building isn't instantaneous. That's why the factory setting here is Off.

But if you really want Windows to search the text inside the other drives' files, even without an index—which can be painfully slow—turn this checkbox on instead.

Indexing Options

The dialog box shown in Figure 3-6 is the master control over the search *index*, the massive, invisible, constantly updated database file that tracks your PC's files and what's in them. As described earlier, you can use this dialog box to add or remove folders from what Windows is tracking.

Figure 3-6:
Search works beautifully right out of the box. For the benefit of the world's tweakers, however, this dialog box awaits, filled with technical adjustments to the way Search works.

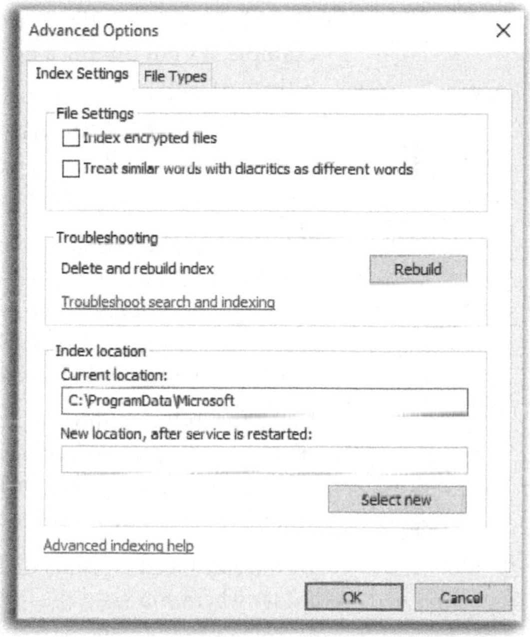

But there are a few more handy options here, too, lurking behind the Advanced Indexing Options button.

To find this third area of search options, start in the Indexing Options dialog box. (Use the search box and type *indexing*.) Click Advanced. Authenticate if necessary. Now you're ready to perform these powerful additional tweaks.

Index Settings tab

On the first tab, here's the kind of fun you can have:

• **Index encrypted files.** Windows can *encrypt* files and folders with a quick click, making them unreadable to anyone who receives one by email, say, and doesn't have the password. This checkbox lets Windows index these files (the ones that *you've* encrypted, of course; this isn't a back door to files you can't otherwise access).

• **Treat similar words with diacritics as different words.** The word "ole," as might appear cutely in a phrase like "the ole swimming pool," is quite a bit different from "olé," as in, "You missed the matador, you big fat bull!" The difference is a *diacritical mark* (øne öf mâny littlé lañguage märks).

Ordinarily, Windows ignores diacritical marks; it treats "ole" and "olé" as the same word in searches. That's designed to make it easier for the average person who can't remember how to type a certain marking, or even which direction it goes. But if you turn on this box, then Windows will observe these markings and treat marked and unmarked words differently.

• **Troubleshooting.** If the Search command ever seems to be acting wacky—for example, it's not finding a document you *know* is on your computer—Microsoft is there to help you.

Your first step should be to click "Troubleshoot search and indexing." (It appears both here, on the Advanced panel, and on the main Indexing Options panel.) The resulting step-by-step sequence may fix things.

If it doesn't, click Rebuild. Now Windows *wipes out* the index it's been working with, completely deleting it—and then begins to rebuild it. You're shown a list of the disks and folders Windows has been instructed to index; the message at the top of the dialog box lets you know its progress. With luck, this process will wipe out any funkiness you've been experiencing.

• **Move the index.** Ordinarily, Windows stores its invisible index file on your main hard drive. But you might have good reason for wanting to move it. Maybe your main drive is getting full. Or maybe you've bought a second, faster hard drive; if you store your index there, searching will be even faster.

In the Advanced Options dialog box, click "Select new." Navigate to the disk or folder where you want the index to go, and then click OK. (The actual transfer of the file takes place the next time you start up Windows.)

File Types tab

Windows ordinarily searches for just about every kind of *useful* file: audio files, program files, text and graphics files, and so on. It doesn't bother peering inside things like Windows operating system files and applications, because what's inside them is programming code with little relevance to most people's work. Omitting these files from the index keeps the index smaller and the searches fast.

But what if you routinely traffic in very rare Venezuelan Beekeeping Interchange Format (VBIF) documents—a file type your copy of Windows has never met before? You won't be able to search for their contents unless you specifically teach Windows about them.

In the Advanced Options dialog box, click the File Types tab. Type the filename extension (like VBIF) into the text box at the lower left. Click Add and then OK. From now on, Windows will index this new file type.

On the other hand, if you find that Windows uses up valuable search-results menu space listing, say, Web bookmarks—stuff you don't need to find very often—you can tell it not to bother. Now the results list won't fill up with files you don't care about.

Turn the checkboxes on or off to make Windows start or stop indexing them.

Using the "How should this file be indexed" options at the bottom of the box, you can also make Windows stop searching these files' contents—the text within them—for better speed and a smaller index.

The Folders of Windows 10

The top-level, all-encompassing, mother-ship window of your PC is the This PC window (formerly called Computer, formerly formerly called My Computer). From within this window, you have access to every disk, folder, and file on your computer. Its slogan might well be, "If it's not in here, it's not on your PC."

To see it, open an Explorer window and click This PC in the Navigation pane.

You wind up face to face with the icons of every storage gizmo connected to your PC: hard drives, CD and DVD drives, USB flash drives, digital cameras, and so on (Figure 3-7).

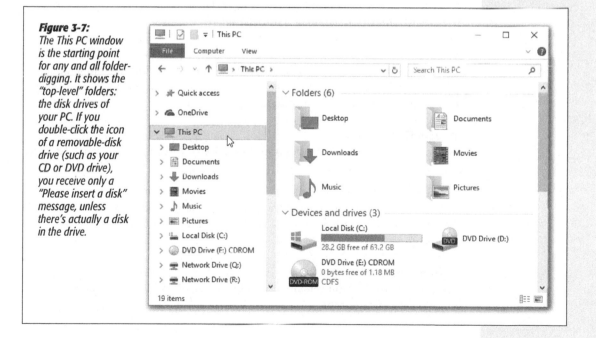

Figure 3-7:
The This PC window is the starting point for any and all folder-digging. it shows the "top-level" folders: the disk drives of your PC. If you double-click the icon of a removable-disk drive (such as your CD or DVD drive), you receive only a "Please insert a disk" message, unless there's actually a disk in the drive.

Tip: Ordinarily, every drive has an icon in here, even if no disk or memory card is in it. That can be annoying if your laptop has, for example, four memory-card slots, each for a different kind of card, labeled D:, E:, F:, and G:, and your This PC window is getting a little hard to navigate.

Fortunately, Windows can hide your drive icons when they're empty. To turn that on or off, open Folder Options (click Options on the Ribbon's View tab). Click the View tab. Click "Hide empty drives," and then click OK.

If you leave this option on, then your removable-disk/card drives appear only when something's in them—a CD, a DVD, or a memory card, for example.

Most people, most of the time, are most concerned with the Local Disk (C:), which represents the internal hard drive preinstalled in your computer. (You're welcome to rename this icon, by the way, just as you would any icon.)

Note: The drive lettering, such as C: for your main hard drive, is an ancient convention that doesn't offer much relevance these days. (Back at the dawn of computing, the A: and B: drives were floppy drives.)

Since Windows now displays icons and plain-English names for your drives, you might consider the drive-letter display to be a bit old-fashioned and cluttery. Fortunately, you can hide the drive letter (page 91).

What's in the Local Disk (C:) Window

If you double-click the Local Disk (C:) icon in This PC—that is, your primary hard drive—you'll find, at least, these standard folders.

PerfLogs

Windows Reliability and Performance Monitor is one of Windows' hidden maintenance apps that knowledgeable tech gurus can use to measure your PC's health and speed. This folder is where it dumps its *logs,* or reports.

Program Files

This folder contains all your desktop programs—Word, Excel, Internet Explorer, games, and so on.

Of course, a Windows program isn't a single, self-contained icon. Instead, it's usually a *folder,* housing both the program and its phalanx of support files and folders. The actual application icon itself generally can't even run if it's separated from its support group.

Program Files (x86)

If you've installed a 64-bit version of Windows, this folder is where Windows puts all your older 32-bit programs.

Users

Windows' *accounts* feature is ideal for situations where different family members, students, or workers use the same machine at different times. Each account holder will turn on the machine to find her own separate, secure set of files, folders, desktop pictures, Web bookmarks, font collections, and preference settings. (Much more about this feature in Chapter 19.)

In any case, now you should see the importance of the Users folder. Inside is one folder —one *Personal folder*—for each person who has an account on this PC. In general, standard account holders (page 557) aren't allowed to open anybody else's folder.

UP TO SPEED

All About AutoPlay

When you insert a CD, what should Windows do with it?

Start playing the music files on it? Open up a slideshow of the pictures on it? Just open an Explorer window to show you the files on it?

What about a DVD? What about the memory card from your camera? Or a flash drive? What kind of automatic action should Windows take when you insert one of those?

It's all up to you, thanks to the Auto-Play feature. For each kind of disc or card, AutoPlay lets you specify what you want Windows to do. It saves your having to indicate your preference each time you plug in a certain kind of storage.

As you can see in the inset figure, Windows generally asks you to make such a choice each time you connect a storage gadget. But the master control center for AutoPlay is in the Control Panel. To get there, press the ⊞ key (to open the search box). Type *autoplay*, so that AutoPlay appears in the search results. Open it.

(There's a similar, less sophisticated set of AutoPlay controls in the PC Settings control panel, described on page 192.)

Here you can see that each kind of disk (CD, DVD, removable drive like a flash drive or a memory card) has a pop-up menu of logical "what to do when I'm inserted" choices. For a music CD, for example, your options are Play (Windows Media Player will open and start playing the songs), "Take no action" (nothing happens at all), "Open folder to view files" (a File Explorer window will open so you can inspect the MP3 files), or "Ask me every time" (these choices will appear each time you insert a music CD).

If your tablet offers Microsoft's Tap and Do feature, you'll find an option for handling incoming Tap and Send files here, too.

This Control Panel also lets you turn off AutoPlay completely; turn off "Use AutoPlay for all media and devices." Now when you insert a disk or card, nothing happens. Or turn it off just for one kind of media, using the corresponding checkboxes. Click Save.

A tip: Even if you've turned off AutoPlay, you can still force it to kick in just this once: Hold down the Shift key as you insert or connect the disc, card, or gadget.

Note: Inside the Documents library, you'll see Public Documents; in the Music library, you'll see Public Music; and so on. These are nothing more than pointers to the master Public folder that you can also see here, in the Users folder. (Anything you put into a Public folder is available for inspection by anyone else with an account on your PC, or even other people on your network.)

Windows

Here's a folder that Microsoft hopes you'll just ignore. This most hallowed folder contains the thousands of little files that make Windows, well, Windows. Most of these folders and files have cryptic names that appeal to cryptic people.

In general, the healthiest PC is one whose Windows folder has been left alone.

Your Personal Folder

Everything that makes your Windows experience your own sits inside the Local Disk (C:) > Users > [your name] folder. This is your *Personal folder*, where Windows stores your preferences, documents, email, pictures, music, Web favorites, cookies (described below), and so on.

Tip: Actually, it would make a lot of sense for you to install your Personal folder's icon in the Quick Access list at the left side of every Explorer window. Drag its icon directly into the list.

To create a new folder, right-click where you want the folder to appear (on the desktop or in any File Explorer window except This PC), and choose New→Folder from the shortcut menu. The new folder appears with its temporary "New Folder" name highlighted. Type a new name for the folder and then press Enter.

But your Personal folder also comes prestocked with folders like these:

- **Contacts.** An address-book program called Windows Contacts came with Windows Vista, but Microsoft gave it the ol' pink slip for Windows 7. All that's left now is this folder, where it used to stash the information about your social circle. (Some other companies' address-book programs can use this folder, too.)

- **Desktop.** When you drag an icon out of a folder or disk window and onto your desktop, it may *appear* to show up on the desktop. But that's just an optical illusion—a visual convenience. In truth, nothing in Windows is ever really on the desktop; it's just in this Desktop *folder,* and mirrored on the desktop.

  Everyone who shares your machine, upon logging in, sees his own stuff sitting out on the desktop. Now you know how Windows does it; there's a separate Desktop folder in every person's Personal folder.

  You can entertain yourself for hours trying to prove this. If you drag something out of your Desktop folder, it also disappears from the actual desktop. And vice versa.

Note: A link to this folder appears in the Navigation pane of every Explorer window.

- **Downloads.** When you download anything from the Web, your browser suggests storing it on your computer in this Downloads folder. The idea is to save you the frustration of downloading stuff and then not being able to find it later.

- **Favorites.** This folder stores shortcuts of the files, folders, and other items you've designated as *favorites* (that is, Web bookmarks). This can be handy if you want to delete a bunch of your favorites all at once, rename them, or whatever.

- **Links.** In older Windows versions, this folder's icons corresponded to the easy-access links in the Favorite Links list in your Explorer windows. Today, it's a random collection of icon shortcuts used by various other Windows features (like saved searches).

- **Documents.** Microsoft suggests that you keep your actual work files in this folder. Sure enough, whenever you save a new document (when you're working in Word or Photoshop Elements, for example), the Save As box proposes storing the new file in this folder.

Tip: You can move the Documents folder, if you like. For example, you can move it to a *removable* drive, like a pocket hard drive or a USB flash drive, so that you can take it back and forth to work with you and always have your latest files at hand.

To do so, open your Documents folder. Right-click a blank spot in the window; from the shortcut menu, choose Properties. Click the Location tab, click Move, navigate to the new location, and click Select Folder.

What's cool is that the Documents *link* in every Explorer window's Navigation pane still opens your Documents folder. What's more, your programs still propose storing new documents there—even though it's not where Microsoft originally put it.

- **Music, Pictures, Videos.** You guessed it: These are Microsoft's proposed homes for your multimedia files. These are where song files from ripped CDs, photos from digital cameras, and videos from camcorders go.

- **OneDrive.** This is the actual, for-real storage location for your machine's local copy of the files and folders on your OneDrive (page 161).

- **Saved Games.** When you save a computer game that's already in progress, it should propose storing it here, so you can find it again later. (Needless to say, it may take some time before all the world's games are updated to know about this folder.)

- **Searches.** As described on page 126, you can *save* searches for reuse later. This folder stores shortcuts for them.

UP TO SPEED

Directories vs. Folders

Before Windows took over the universe, folders were called directories, and the folders inside them were called subdirectories. Keep that in mind the next time you're reading an old user guide, magazine article, or computer book.

Note: Your Personal folder also stores a few hidden items reserved for use by Windows itself. One of them is AppData, a very important folder that stores all kinds of support files for your programs. For example, it stores word-processor dictionaries, Web cookies, your Media Center recordings, Internet Explorer security certificates, and so on. In general, there's not much reason for you to poke around in them, but in this book, here and there, you'll find tips and tricks that refer you to AppData.

Selecting Icons

Before you can delete, rename, move, copy, or otherwise tamper with any icon, you have to be able to *select* it somehow. By highlighting it, you're essentially telling Windows what you want to operate on.

By Tapping or Clicking

To select one icon, just click it once. To select *multiple* icons at once—in preparation for moving, copying, renaming, or deleting them en masse, for example—use one of these techniques:

- **Select all.** Highlight all the icons in a window by using the "Select all" button on the Ribbon's Home tab. (Or press Ctrl+A, its keyboard equivalent.)

- **Highlight several consecutive icons.** Start with your cursor above and to one side of the icons, and then drag diagonally. As you drag, you create a temporary shaded blue rectangle. Any icon that falls within this rectangle darkens to indicate that it's been selected.

  Alternatively, click the first icon you want to highlight, and then Shift-click the last file. All the files in between are automatically selected, along with the two icons you clicked. (These techniques work in any folder view: Details, Icon, Content, or whatever.)

Tip: If you include a particular icon in your diagonally dragged group by mistake, Ctrl-click it to remove it from the selected cluster.

- **Highlight nonconsecutive icons.** Suppose you want to highlight only the first, third, and seventh icons in the list. Start by clicking icon No. 1; then Ctrl-click each of the others. (If you Ctrl-click a selected icon *again*, you *de*select it. A good time to use this trick is when you highlight an icon by accident.)

Tip: The Ctrl key trick is especially handy if you want to select *almost* all the icons in a window. Press Ctrl+A to select everything in the folder, and then Ctrl-click any unwanted subfolders to deselect them.

By Typing

You can also highlight one icon, plucking it out of a sea of pretenders, by typing the first few letters of its name. Type *nak*, for example, to select an icon called "Naked Chef Broadcast Schedule."

Checkbox Selection

It's great that you can select icons by holding down a key and clicking—if you can remember *which* key must be pressed.

Turns out novices were befuddled by the requirement to Ctrl-click icons when they wanted to choose more than one. So Microsoft created a checkbox mode. In this mode, any icon you point to temporarily sprouts a little checkbox that you can click to select it (Figure 3-8).

Figure 3-8:
Each time you point to an icon, a clickable checkbox appears. Once you turn it on, the checkbox remains visible, making it easy to select several icons at once. What's cool about the checkboxes feature is that it doesn't preclude your using the old click-to-select method; If you click an icon's name, you deselect all checkboxes except that one.

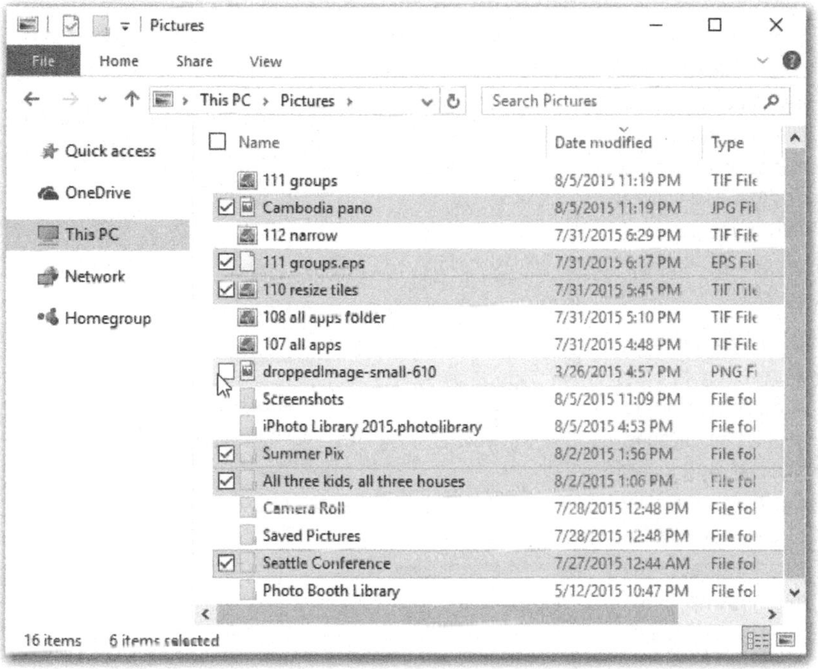

To turn this feature on, open any Explorer window, and then turn on "Item check boxes," which is on the View tab of the Ribbon.

Now, anytime you point to an icon, an on/off checkbox appears. No secret keystrokes are necessary now for selecting icons; it's painfully obvious how you're supposed to choose only a few icons out of a gaggle.

Eliminating Double-Clicks

In some ways, a File Explorer window is just like a Web browser. It has a Back button, an address bar, and so on.

If you enjoy this PC-as-browser effect, you can actually take it one step further. You can set up your PC so that *one* click, not two, opens an icon. It's a strange effect that some people adore, that some find especially useful on touchscreens—and that others turn off as fast as their little fingers will let them.

In any File Explorer window, on the View tab of the Ribbon, click Options.

The Folder Options control panel opens. Turn on "Single-click to open an item (point to select)." Then indicate *when* you want your icon's names turned into underlined

Secrets of the "Send to" Command

If you find yourself copying or moving certain icons to certain folders or disks with regularity, it's time to exploit the "Send to" command that lurks in the shortcut menu for almost every icon. Unlike the "Move to" and "Copy to" commands on the Ribbon, the "Send to" commands can send files to *services* (like a DVD burner or email program), not just folders.

This command offers a quick way to copy and move icons to popular destinations. For example, you can teleport a copy of a highlighted file directly to the desktop by choosing "Send to"→Desktop (create shortcut).

Then there's the "Send to"→Mail Recipient. It bundles the selected icon as an email attachment that's ready to send. You can also zip up a folder (see the end of this chapter) by choosing "Send to"→"Compressed (zipped) Folder."

If you start getting into "Send to"—and you should—check this out: If you press Shift while you right-click, you get a much longer list of "Send to" options, including all the essential folders (OneDrive, Downloads, Desktop, Favorites).

But if the folder you want isn't there, it's easy enough to make the "Send to" command accommodate your *own* favorite folders. In your Personal folder (page 140) sits a folder

called SendTo. Any shortcut icon you place here shows up instantly in the "Send to" menus.

Alas, this folder is among those Microsoft considers inappropriate for inspection by novices. As a result, the SendTo folder is *hidden*.

You can still get to it, though. In the address bar of any File Explorer window, type *shell:sendto*, and then press Enter. (That's a quick way of getting to the C: > Users > [your name] > AppData > Roaming > Microsoft > Windows > SendTo folder.)

Most people create shortcuts here for folders and disks. When you highlight an icon and choose "Send to"→Backup Disk, for example, Windows copies the icon to that disk. (Or, if you simultaneously press Shift, you *move* the icon to the other disk or folder.) You can even add shortcuts of *applications* (program files) to the SendTo folder. By adding WinZip to this "Send to" menu, for example, you can drop-kick a highlighted icon onto the WinZip icon (for decompressing) just by choosing "Send to"→WinZip. Or add a Web server to this menu, so you can upload a file with a right-click. You can even create shortcuts for a printer or fax modem so you can print or fax a document just by highlighting its icon and choosing File→"Send to"→ [printer or fax modem's name].

links by selecting "Underline icon titles consistent with my browser" (that is, *all* icons' names appear as links) or "Underline icon titles only when I point at them." Click OK. The deed is done.

Now, if a single click opens an icon, you're entitled to wonder how you're supposed to *select* an icon (which you'd normally do with a single click). Take your pick:

- Point to it for about a half-second without clicking. (To make multiple selections, press the Ctrl key as you point to additional icons. And to *drag* an icon, just ignore all this pointing stuff—simply drag as usual.)

- Turn on the checkbox mode described above.

Life with Icons

File Explorer has only one purpose in life: to help you manage the *icons* of your files, folders, and disks. You could spend your entire workday just mastering the techniques of naming, copying, moving, and deleting these icons—and plenty of people do.

Here's the crash course.

Renaming Your Icons

To rename a file, folder, printer, or disk icon, you need to open up its "renaming rectangle." You can do so with any of the following methods:

- Highlight the icon and then press the F2 key.

- Highlight the icon. On the Home tab of the Ribbon, click Rename.

- Click carefully, just once, on a previously highlighted icon's name.

- Right-click the icon (or hold your finger down on it) and choose Rename from the shortcut menu.

Tip: You can even rename your hard drive so you don't go your entire career with a drive named "Local Disk." Just rename its icon (in the This PC window) as you would any other.

In any case, once the renaming rectangle has appeared, type the new name you want and then press Enter. Use all the standard text-editing tricks: Press Backspace to fix a typo, press the ← and → keys to position the insertion point, and so on. When you're finished editing the name, press Enter to make it stick. (If another icon in the folder has the same name, Windows beeps and makes you choose another name.)

Tip: If you highlight a bunch of icons at once and then open the renaming rectangle for any *one* of them, you wind up renaming *all* of them. For example, if you've highlighted three folders called Cats, Dogs, and Fish, then renaming one of them to *Animals* changes the original set of names to Animals (1), Animals (2), and Animals (3).

If that's not what you want, press Ctrl+Z (that's the keystroke for Undo) to restore all the original names.

A folder or filename can technically be up to 260 characters long. In practice, though, you won't be able to produce filenames that long; that's because that maximum must also include the *file extension* (the three-letter suffix that identifies the file type) and the file's *folder path* (like C: > Users > Casey > Pictures).

Note, too, that because they're reserved for behind-the-scenes use, Windows doesn't let you use any of these symbols in a Windows filename: \ / : * ? " < > |

You can give more than one file or folder the same name, as long as they're not in the same folder.

Note: Windows comes factory-set not to show you filename extensions. That's why you sometimes might *think* you see two different files called, say, "Quarterly Sales, " both in the same folder.

The explanation is that one filename may end with *.doc* (a Word document), and the other may end with *.xls* (an Excel document). But because these suffixes are hidden, the files look like they have exactly the same name. To un-hide filename extensions, turn on the "File name extensions" checkbox. It's on the View tab of the Ribbon.

Icon Properties

Properties are a big deal in Windows. Properties are preference settings that you can change independently for every icon on your machine.

To view the properties for an icon, choose from these techniques:

- Right-click the icon; choose Properties from the shortcut menu.

- Highlight the icon in an Explorer window; click the Properties button. (It's the wee tiny icon at the upper-left corner of the window, in the Quick Access toolbar. Looks like a tiny page with a checkmark.)

- Highlight the icon. On the Ribbon, on the Home tab, click Properties.

- While pressing Alt, double-click the icon.

- Highlight the icon; press Alt+Enter.

Tip: You can also see some basic info about any icon (type, size, and so on) by pointing to it without clicking. A little info balloon pops up, saving you the trouble of opening the Properties box or even the Details pane.

These settings aren't the same for every kind of icon, however. Here's what you can expect when opening the Properties dialog boxes of various icons (Figure 3-9).

This PC (System Properties)

There are about 500 different ways to open the Properties dialog box for your This PC icon. For example, you can click This PC in the navigation pane of any window and then click "System properties" on the Ribbon's Computer tab. Or right-click the This PC icon (in the nav bar again); from the shortcut menu, choose Properties.

The System Properties window is packed with useful information about your machine: what kind of processor is inside, how much memory (RAM) it has, whether or not it has a touchscreen, and what version of Windows you've got.

The panel at the left side of the window (shown in Figure 3-9, bottom) includes some useful links—"Device Manager," "Remote settings," "System protection," and "Advanced system settings"—all of which are described in the appropriate chapters of this book.

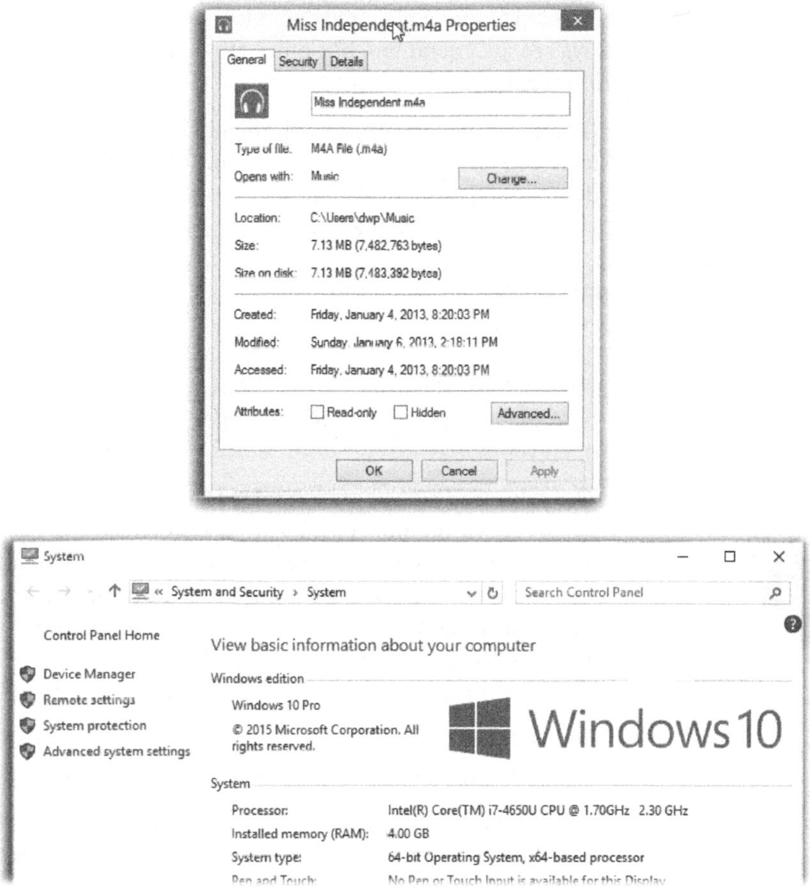

Figure 3-9:
The Properties dialog boxes are different for every kind of icon. In the months and years to come, you may find many occasions when adjusting the behavior of some icon has big benefits in simplicity and productivity.

Top: The Properties dialog box for a song file.

Bottom: The Properties window for the computer itself looks quite a bit different. It is, in fact, part of the Control Panel.

Note, however, that most of them work by opening the *old* System Properties Control Panel. Its tabs give a terse, but more complete, look at the tech specs and features of your PC. These, too, are described in the relevant parts of this book—all except "Computer Name." Here you can type a plain-English name for your computer ("Casey's Laptop," for example). That's how it will appear to other people on the network, if you have one.

Disks

In a disk's Properties dialog box, you can see all kinds of information about the disk itself, like its name (which you can change right there in the box), its capacity (which you can't), and how much of it is full.

This dialog box's various tabs are also gateways to a host of maintenance and backup features, including Disk Cleanup, Error-checking, Defrag, Backup, and Quotas; all of these are described in Chapters 17 and 18.

Data files

The properties for a plain old document depend on what kind of document it is. You always see a General tab, but other tabs may also appear (especially for Microsoft Office files).

- **General.** This screen offers all the obvious information about the document— location, size, modification date, and so on. The *read-only* checkbox locks the document. In the read-only state, you can open the document and read it, but you can't make any changes to it.

Note: If you make a *folder* read-only, it affects only the files already inside. If you add additional files later, they remain editable.

Hidden turns the icon invisible. It's a great way to prevent something from being deleted, but because the icon becomes invisible, you may find it a bit difficult to open *yourself*.

The Advanced button offers a few additional options. "File is ready for archiving" means "Back me up." This message is intended for the old Backup and Restore program described in Chapter 17, and it indicates that this document has been changed since the last time it was backed up (or that it's never been backed up). "Allow this file to have contents indexed in addition to file properties" lets you indicate that this file should, or should not, be part of the search index described earlier in this chapter.

"Compress contents to save disk space" is described later in this chapter. Finally, "Encrypt contents to secure data" is described on page 548.

- **Security** has to do with the technical NTFS permissions of a file or folder, technical on/off switches that govern who can do what to the contents. You see this tab only if the hard drive is formatted with NTFS.

- **Custom.** The Properties window of certain older Office documents includes this tab, where you can look up a document's word count, author, revision number, and many other statistics. But you should by no means feel limited to these 21 properties.

Using the Custom tab, you can create properties of your own—Working Title, Panic Level, Privacy Quotient, or whatever you like. Just specify a property type using the Type pop-up menu (Text, Date, Number, Yes/No); type the property name into the Name text box (or choose one of the canned options in its pop-up menu); and then click Add.

You can then fill in the Value text box for the individual file in question (so that its Panic Level is Red Alert, for example).

Note: This is an older form of tagging files—a lot like the tags feature described on page 77—*except* that you can't use Windows Search to find them. Especially technical people can, however, perform query-language searches for these values.

- The **Details** tab reveals the sorts of details—tags, categories, authors, and so on—that *are* searchable by Windows' search command. For many kinds of files, you can edit these little tidbits right in the dialog box.

  This box also tells you how many words, lines, and paragraphs are in a particular Word document. For a graphics document, the Summary tab indicates the graphic's dimensions, resolution, and color settings.

- The **Previous Versions** tab appears only if you've gone to the extraordinary trouble of resurrecting Windows 7's Previous Versions feature, which lets you revert a document or a folder to an earlier version.

Folders

The Properties dialog box for a folder offers a bunch of tabs:

- **General, Security.** Here you find the same sorts of checkboxes and options as you do for data files, described above.

- **Sharing** makes the folder susceptible to invasion by other people—either in person, when they log into this PC, or from across your office network (see Chapter 21).

- **Location.** This tab appears only for folders you've included in a library (page 72). It identifies where the folder *really* sits.

- **Customize.** The first pop-up menu here lets you apply a *folder template* to any folder: General Items, Documents, Pictures, Music, or Videos. A template is nothing more than a canned layout with a predesigned set of Ribbon tabs, icon sizes, column headings, and so on.

  You may already have noticed that your Pictures library displays a nice big thumbnail icon for each of your photos, and that your Music library presents a tidy Details-view list of all your songs, with Ribbon buttons like "Play all," "Play To," and "Add to playlist." Here's your chance to apply those same expertly designed templates to folders of your own making.

  This dialog box also lets you change the *icon* for a folder, as described in the next section.

Program files

There's not much here that you can change yourself, but you certainly get a lot to look at. For starters, there are the General and Details tabs described above. But you may also find an important Compatibility tab, which may one day come to save your bacon. It lets you trick a pre–Windows 10 program into running on Microsoft's latest.

Changing Your Icons' Icons

You can change the actual, inch-tall illustrations that Windows uses to represent the little icons replete in your electronic world. You can't, however, use a single method to do so; Microsoft has divided up the controls between two different locations.

Standard Windows icons

First, you can change the icon for some of the important Windows desktop icons: the Recycle Bin, Documents, and so on. To do so, right-click a blank spot on the desktop. From the shortcut menu, choose Personalize.

In the resulting window, click Themes in the task pane at the left side; then click "Desktop icon settings." You'll see a collection of those important Windows icons. Click one and then click Change Icon to choose a replacement from a collection Microsoft provides. (You haven't *lived* until you've made your Recycle Bin look like a giant blue thumbtack!)

Folder or shortcut icons

Ordinarily, when your Explorer window is in Tiles, Content, or a fairly big Icon view, each folder's icon resembles what's in it. You actually see a tiny photo, music album, or Word document peeking out of the open-folder icon.

This means, however, that the icon may actually *change* over time, as you put different things into it. If you'd rather freeze a folder's icon so it doesn't keep changing, you can choose an image that will appear to peek out from inside that folder.

Note: The following steps also let you change what a particular shortcut icon looks like. Unfortunately, Windows offers no way to change an actual document's icon.

Actually, you have two ways to change a folder's icon. Both begin the same way: Right-click the folder or shortcut whose icon you want to change. From the shortcut menu, choose Properties, and then click the Customize tab. Now you have a choice (Figure 3-10):

Prizewinners   Prizewinners   Prizewinners

Figure 3-10:
Left: The original folder icon.

Middle: You've replaced the image that seems to be falling out of it.

Right: You've completely replaced the folder icon.

- **Change what image is peeking out of the file-folder icon.** Click Choose File. Windows now lets you hunt for icons on your hard drive. These can be picture files, icons downloaded from the Internet, icons embedded inside program files and .dll files, or icons you've made yourself using a freeware or shareware icon-making program. Find the graphic, click it, click Open, and then click OK.

It may take a couple of minutes for Windows to update the folder image, but eventually, you see your hand-selected image "falling out" of the file-folder icon.

- **Completely replace the file-folder image.** Click Change Icon. Windows offers up a palette of canned graphics; click the one you want, and then click OK. Instantly, the original folder bears the new image.

Shortcut Icons

A *shortcut* is a link to a file, folder, disk, or program (see Figure 3-11). You might think of it as a duplicate of the thing's icon—but not a duplicate of the thing itself. (A shortcut occupies almost no disk space.) When you double-click the shortcut icon, the original folder, disk, program, or document opens. You can also set up a keystroke for a shortcut icon so you can open any program or document just by pressing a certain key combination.

Figure 3-11:
Left: You can distinguish a desktop shortcut from its original in two ways. First, the tiny arrow "badge" identifies it as a shortcut; second, its name contains the word "Shortcut."

Right: The Properties dialog box for a shortcut indicates which actual file or folder this one "points" to. The Run drop-down menu (shown open) lets you control how the window opens when you double-click the shortcut icon.

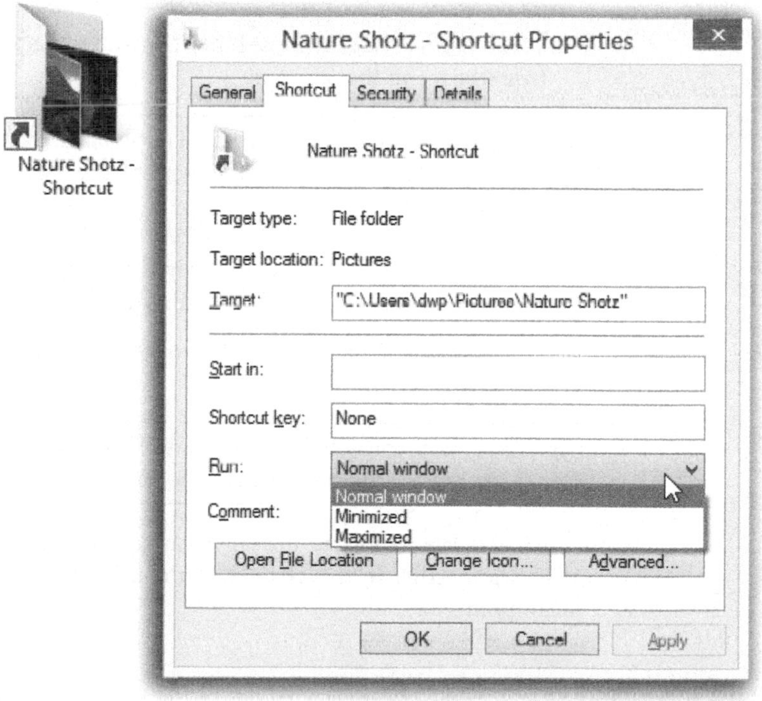

Shortcuts provide quick access to the items you use most often. And because you can make as many shortcuts of a file as you want, and put them anywhere on your PC, you can, in effect, keep an important program or document in more than one folder. Just create a shortcut to leave on the desktop in plain sight, or drag its icon onto the Links toolbar. In fact, every link in the top part of your Navigation pane is a shortcut.

Note: Don't confuse the term *shortcut,* which refers to one of these duplicate-icon pointers, with *shortcut menu,* the context-sensitive menu that appears when you right-click almost anything in Windows. The shortcut *menu* has nothing to do with the shortcut icons feature; maybe that's why it's sometimes called the *context* menu.

Among other things, shortcuts are great for getting to Web sites and folders elsewhere on your network, because you're spared having to type out their addresses or burrowing through network windows.

Creating and Deleting Shortcuts

To create a shortcut, use any of these tricks:

- Right-click (or hold your finger down on) an icon. From the shortcut menu, choose "Create shortcut."

- Right-drag an icon from its current location to the desktop. (On a touchscreen, hold your finger on the icon momentarily before you drag.)

  When you release the mouse button or your finger, choose "Create shortcuts here" from the menu that appears.

Tip: If you're not in the mood to use a shortcut menu, just left-drag an icon while pressing Alt. A shortcut appears instantly. (And if your Alt key is missing or broken—hey, it could happen—drag while pressing Ctrl+Shift instead.)

- Copy an icon, as described earlier in this chapter. Open the destination window; then, on the Ribbon's Home tab, click "Paste shortcut."

- Drag the tiny icon at the left end of the address bar onto the desktop or into a window.

Tip: This also works with Web sites. If your browser has pulled up a site you want to keep handy, drag that little address-bar icon onto your desktop. Double-clicking it later will open the same Web page.

You can delete a shortcut the same way as any icon, as described in the Recycle Bin discussion earlier in this chapter. (Of course, deleting a shortcut *doesn't* delete the file it points to.)

Unveiling a Shortcut's True Identity

To locate the original icon from which a shortcut was made, right-click the shortcut icon and choose Properties from the shortcut menu. As shown in Figure 3-11, the resulting box shows you where to find the "real" icon. It also offers you a quick way to jump to it, in the form of the Open File Location button.

Shortcut Keyboard Triggers

Sure, shortcuts let you put favored icons everywhere you want to be. But they still require clicking to open, which means taking your hands off the keyboard—and that, in the grand scheme of things, means slowing down.

Lurking within the Shortcut Properties dialog box is another feature with intriguing ramifications: the Shortcut Key box. By clicking here and then pressing a key combination, you can assign a personalized keystroke for the shortcut. Thereafter, by pressing that keystroke, you can summon the corresponding file, program, folder, printer, networked computer, or disk window to your screen, no matter what you're doing on the PC. It's *really* useful.

Three rules apply when choosing keystrokes to open your favorite icons:

- The keystrokes work only on shortcuts stored *on your desktop*. If you stash the icon in any other folder, the keystroke stops working.

- Your keystroke can't incorporate the space bar or the Enter, Backspace, Delete, Esc, Print Screen, or Tab keys.

- Your combination *must* include Ctrl+Alt, Ctrl+Shift, or Alt+Shift, and another key.

  Windows enforces this rule rigidly. For example, if you type a single letter key into the box (such as *E*), Windows automatically adds the Ctrl and Alt keys to your combination (Alt+Ctrl+E). This is the operating system's attempt to prevent you from inadvertently duplicating one of the built-in Windows keyboard shortcuts and thoroughly confusing both you and your computer.

Tip: If you've ever wondered what it's like to be a programmer, try this. In the Shortcut Properties dialog box (Figure 3-11), use the Run drop-down menu at the bottom of the dialog box to choose "Normal window," "Minimized," or "Maximized." By clicking OK, you've just told Windows what kind of window you want to appear when opening this particular shortcut.

Controlling Windows in this way isn't exactly the same as programming Microsoft Excel, but you are, in your own small way, telling Windows what to do.

If you like the idea of keyboard shortcuts for your files and programs, but you're not so hot on Windows' restrictions, consider installing a free *macro program* that lets you make *any* keystroke open *anything anywhere*. The best-known one is AutoHotkey, which is available from this book's "Missing CD" page at *www.missingmanuals.com,* but there are plenty of similar (and simpler) ones. (Check them out at, for example, *www.shareware.com.)*

Copying and Moving Folders and Files

Windows offers two techniques for moving files and folders from one place to another: dragging them and using the Copy and Paste commands. In both cases, you'll be delighted to find out how much more communicative Windows is during the copy process (Figure 3-12).

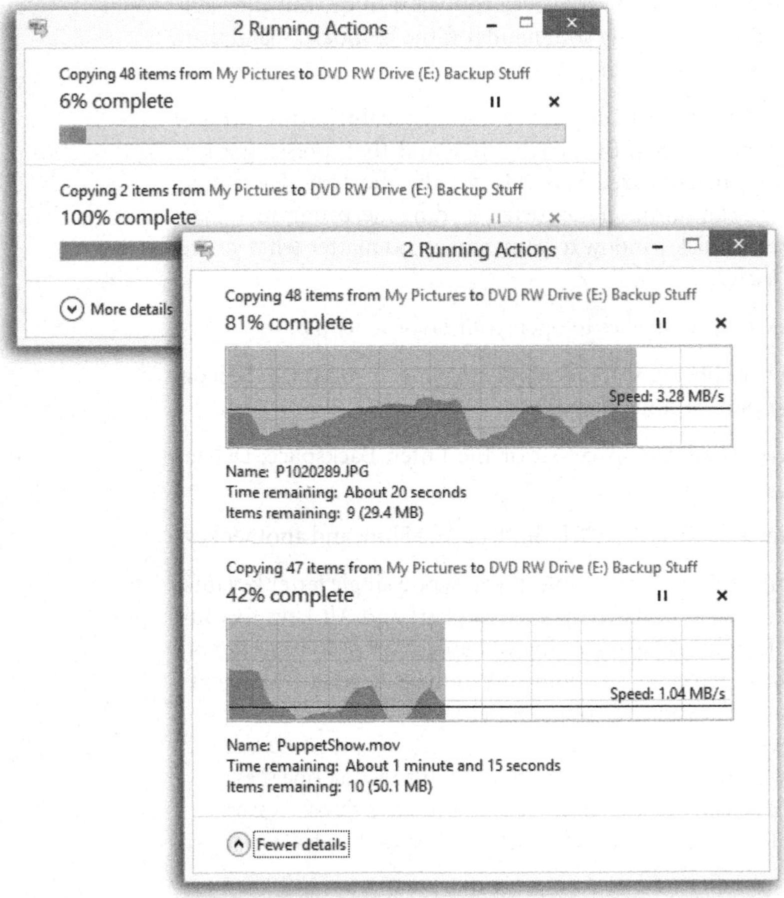

Figure 3-12:
Windows is a veritable chatterbox when it comes to copying or moving files.

Top: For each item you're copying, you see a graph and a percentage-complete readout. There's a Pause button and a Cancel button (the ✕). And there's a More Details button.

Bottom: The "more details" turns out to be an elaborate graph that shows you how the speed has proceeded during the copy job. The horizontal line indicates the average speed, in megabytes per second.

Any questions?

Whichever method you choose, you start by showing Windows which icons you want to copy or move—by highlighting them, as described on the previous pages. Then proceed as follows.

Copying by Dragging Icons

You can drag icons from one folder to another, from one drive to another, from a drive to a folder on another drive, and so on. (When you've selected several icons, drag any *one* of them, and the others will go along for the ride.)

Here's what happens when you drag icons in the usual way, using the left mouse button:

- Dragging to another folder on the same disk *moves* the folder or file.

- Dragging from one disk to another *copies* the folder or file.

- Holding down the Ctrl key while dragging to another folder on the same disk *copies* the icon. (If you do so within a single window, Windows creates a duplicate of the file called "[Filename] - Copy.")

- Pressing Shift while dragging from one disk to another *moves* the folder or file (without leaving a copy behind).

Tip: You can move or copy icons by dragging them either into an open window or directly onto a disk or folder *icon.*

The right-mouse-button trick

Think you'll remember all those possibilities every time you drag an icon? Probably not. Fortunately, you never have to. One of the most important tricks you can learn is to use the *right* mouse button as you drag. When you release the button, the menu shown in Figure 3-13 appears, letting you either copy or move the selected icons.

Tip: Press the Esc key to cancel a dragging operation at any time.

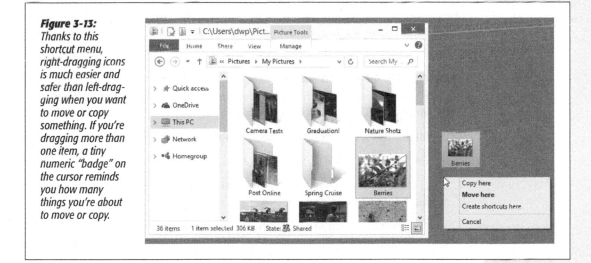

Figure 3-13:
Thanks to this shortcut menu, right-dragging icons is much easier and safer than left-dragging when you want to move or copy something. If you're dragging more than one item, a tiny numeric "badge" on the cursor reminds you how many things you're about to move or copy.

Dragging icons into the Navigation pane

You may find it easier to copy or move icons using the Navigation pane, since the two-pane display format makes it easier to see where your files are and where they're going.

Just expand the arrow brackets of the Navigation pane until you can see the destination folder.

Tip: If you accidentally click a folder in the Navigation pane, its contents will pop up in the right pane, covering up the icon you wanted to copy. Click the Back button to get back to where you once belonged.

Then find the icon you want to move in the right pane and drag it to the appropriate folder in the left pane, or vice versa. Windows copies the icon.

Tip: This situation is also a good time to use the window Snap feature. Drag the icon's home window against the right side of your screen; drag the destination window against the left side. Now they're perfectly set up for drag-copying between them.

Copying or Moving Files with the Ribbon

Dragging icons to copy or move them feels good because it's so direct; you actually see your arrow cursor pushing the icons into the new location.

But you also pay a price for this satisfying illusion. That is, you may have to spend a moment or two fiddling with your windows, or clicking in the Explorer folder hierarchy, so you have a clear "line of drag" between the icon to be moved and the destination folder.

But, these days, moving or copying icons can be a one-step operation, thanks to the "Move to" and "Copy to" buttons on the Ribbon's Home tab. The pop-up menu for each one lists frequently and recently used folders. (If the destination folder isn't listed, choose "Choose location" and navigate to it yourself.)

In other words, you just highlight the icons you want to move; hit "Move to" or "Copy to" and then choose the destination folder. The deed is done, without ever having to leave the folder window where you began.

Copying with Copy and Paste

You can also move icons from one window into another using the Cut, Copy, and Paste commands. The routine goes like this:

1. **Highlight the icon or icons you want to move.**

   Use any of the tricks described on page 142.

2. **Right-click (or hold your finger down on) one of the icons. From the shortcut menu, choose Cut or Copy.**

   You may want to learn the keyboard shortcuts for these commands: Ctrl+C for Copy, Ctrl+X for Cut. Or use the Cut and Copy buttons on the Ribbon's Home tab.

   The Cut command makes the highlighted icons appear dimmed; you've stashed them on the invisible Windows Clipboard. (They don't actually disappear from their original nesting place until you paste them somewhere else—or hit the Esc key to cancel the operation.)

   The Copy command also places copies of the files on the Clipboard, but it doesn't disturb the originals.

3. **Right-click the window, folder icon, or disk icon where you want to put the icons. Choose Paste from the shortcut menu.**

Once again, you may prefer to use the appropriate Ribbon button, Paste.

Either way, you've successfully transferred the icons. If you pasted into an open window, you see the icons appear there. If you pasted onto a closed folder or disk icon, you need to open the icon's window to see the results. And if you pasted right back into the same window, you get a duplicate of the file called "[Filename] - Copy."

The Recycle Bin

The Recycle Bin is your desktop trash basket. This is where files and folders go when they've outlived their usefulness. Basically, the Recycle Bin is a waiting room for data oblivion, in that your files stay there until you *empty* it—or until you rescue the files by dragging them out again.

While you can certainly drag files or folders onto the Recycle Bin icon, it's usually faster to highlight them and then perform one of the following options:

- Press the Delete key.
- Click the Delete button on the Ribbon's Home tab.
- Choose File→Delete.
- Right-click a highlighted icon and choose Delete from the shortcut menu.

Windows asks if you're sure you want to send the item to the Recycle Bin; it provides a good chunk of information about the file in the warning window, for your safety. (You don't lose much by clicking Yes, since it's easy enough to change your mind, as noted below.) Now the Recycle Bin icon looks like it's brimming over with paper.

You can put unwanted files and folders into the Recycle Bin from any folder window or even from inside the Open File dialog box of many applications.

Note: All these methods put icons from your *hard drive* into the Recycle Bin. But deleting an icon from a removable drive (a flash drive, for example), from other computers on the network, or from a .zip file, does *not* involve the Recycle Bin. Those files go straight to heaven, giving you no opportunity to retrieve them. (Deleting anything with the Command Prompt commands *del* or *erase* bypasses the Recycle Bin, too.)

Making the Recycle Bin Less Naggy

When you get right down to it, you really have to *work* to get rid of a file in Windows. First you have to put the thing in the Recycle Bin. Then you have to confirm that, yes, you're sure. Then you have to *empty* the Recycle Bin. Then you have to confirm that, yes, you're sure about *that.*

Fortunately, those are just the factory settings. There are all kinds of ways to eliminate some of these quadruplicate confirmations. For example:

- **Squelch the "Are you sure?" message.** On the Ribbon's Home tab, click the ▾ beneath the Delete button. From the shortcut menu, turn off "Show recycle confirmation." Or, in the Recycle Bin's Properties dialog box (Figure 3-14), turn off "Display delete confirmation dialog." Now you'll never get that message when you put something into the Recycle Bin.

- **Bypass the Recycle Bin just this time.** Again, use the ▾ beneath the Delete button on the Ribbon's Home tab. From the shortcut menu choose "Permanently delete"; you've just deleted the file permanently, skipping its layover in the Recycle Bin.

Note: Pressing Shift while you delete a file (and then clicking Yes in the confirmation box, or hitting Enter), also deletes the file instantly. The Shift-key trick works for every method of deleting a file: pressing the Delete key, choosing Delete from the shortcut menu, and so on.

- **Bypass the Recycle Bin for good.** If you, a person of steely nerve and perfect judgment, never delete a file in error, then your files can *always* bypass the Recycle Bin. No confirmations, no second chances. You'll reclaim disk space instantly when you press the Delete key to vaporize a highlighted file or folder.

To set this up, right-click the Recycle Bin. From the shortcut menu, choose Properties. Select "Don't move files to the Recycle Bin. Remove files immediately when deleted" (Figure 3-14).

Figure 3-14:
Use the Recycle Bin Properties dialog box to govern the way the Recycle Bin works, or even if it works at all. If you have multiple hard drives, the dialog box offers a tab for each of them so you can configure a separate and independent Recycle Bin on each drive.

And voilà! Your safety net is gone (especially if you *also* turn off the "Display delete confirmation dialog" checkbox—then you're *really* living dangerously).

Note: That really is living dangerously. The Shift-key trick might be a better safety/convenience compromise.

Restoring Deleted Files and Folders

If you change your mind about sending something to the software graveyard, simply open the Recycle Bin by double-clicking. A window like the one in Figure 3-15 opens.

To restore a selected file or folder—or a bunch of them—click the "Restore this item" link on the task toolbar. Or right-click any one of the selected icons and choose Restore from the shortcut menu.

Tip: Weird but true: You can actually pin the Recycle Bin onto the right side of your Start menu, for easy clicking. Just right-click the Bin; from the shortcut menu, choose Pin to Start. It shows up as a tile on the Start menu.

Restored means returned to the folder from whence it came—wherever it was on your hard drive when deleted. If you restore an icon whose original folder has been deleted in the meantime, Windows even recreates that folder to hold the restored file(s). (If nothing is selected, the toolbar button says "Restore all items," but be careful: If there are weeks' worth of icons in there, and Windows puts them all back where they came from, recreating original folders as it goes, you might wind up with a real mess.)

Tip: You don't have to put icons back into their original folders. By *dragging* them out of the Recycle Bin window, you can put them back into any folder you like.

Emptying the Recycle Bin

While there's an advantage to the Recycle Bin (you get to undo your mistakes), there's also a downside: The files in the Recycle Bin occupy as much disk space as they did when they were stored in folders. Deleting files doesn't gain you additional disk space until you *empty* the Recycle Bin.

That's why most people, sooner or later, follow up an icon's journey to the Recycle Bin with one of these cleanup operations:

- Right-click the Recycle Bin icon, or a blank spot in the Recycle Bin window, and choose Empty Recycle Bin from the shortcut menu.

- In the Recycle Bin window, click Empty Recycle Bin on the Ribbon's Recycle Bin Tools/Manage tab.

- In the Recycle Bin window, highlight only the icons you want to eliminate, and then press the Delete key. (Use this method when you want to nuke only *some* of the Recycle Bin's contents.)

• Wait. When the Recycle Bin accumulates so much stuff that it occupies a significant percentage of your hard drive space, Windows empties it automatically, as described in the next section.

The first three of these procedures produce an "Are you sure?" message.

Auto-emptying the Recycle Bin

The Recycle Bin has two advantages over the physical trash can behind your house: First, it never smells. Second, when it's full, it can empty itself automatically.

To configure this self-emptying feature, you specify a certain fullness limit. When the Recycle Bin contents reach that level, Windows begins deleting files (permanently) as new files arrive in the Recycle Bin. Files that arrived in the Recycle Bin first are deleted first.

Unless you tell it otherwise, Windows reserves 10 percent of your drive to hold Recycle Bin contents. To change that percentage, open the Recycle Bin; on the Ribbon, click "Recycle bin properties" (Figure 3-15). Now you can edit the "Maximum size" number, in megabytes. Keeping the percentage low means you're less likely to run out of the disk space you need to install software and create documents. On the other hand, raising the percentage means you have more opportunity to restore files you decide to retrieve.

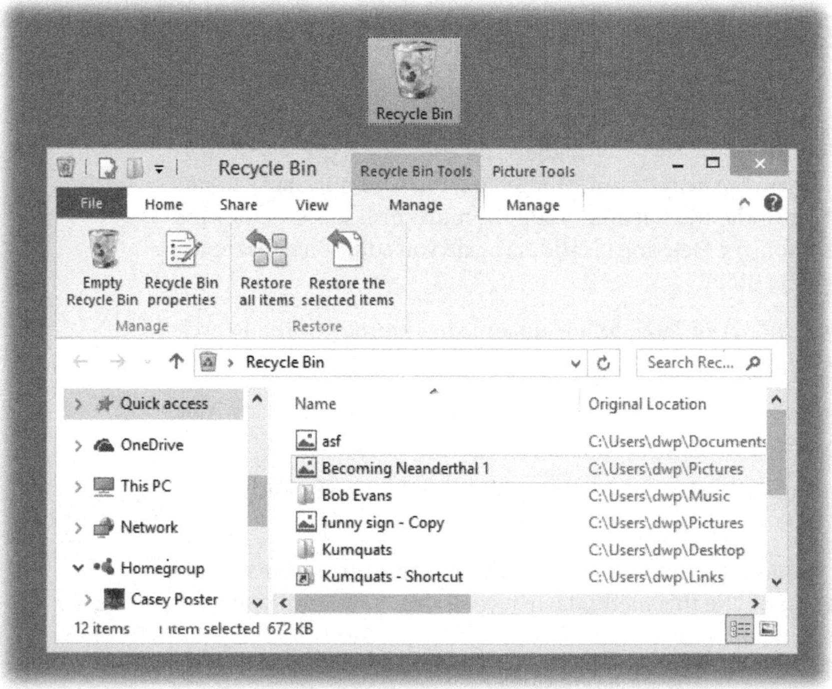

Figure 3-15:
When you double-click the Recycle Bin (top), its window (bottom) displays information about each folder and file it holds. It's a regular Explorer window, so you can inspect a selected item in the Details view, if you like.

Note: Every disk has its own Recycle Bin, which holds files and folders you've deleted from that disk. As you can see in the Recycle Bin Properties dialog box, you can give each drive its own trash limit and change the deletion options shown in Figure 3-15 for each drive independently. Just click the drive's name before changing the settings.

OneDrive

The OneDrive (originally called SkyDrive) is one of Microsoft's great unsung offerings. It's a free, 15-gigabyte online hard drive on the Internet—and part of your free Microsoft account (page 554). In File Explorer, it's represented by an icon in every window.

Whatever you put into it appears, almost instantly, in the OneDrive folder on all your other machines: other PCs, Macs, iPhones, iPads, Android phones, and so on. (There are OneDrive apps available for all of those operating systems.)

In fact, your files will even be available at *onedrive.com*, so you can grab them even when you're stranded on a desert island with nothing but somebody else's computer. (If this concept reminds you of the popular free program Dropbox, then you're very wise.) Figure 3-16 shows the idea.

Figure 3-16:
People don't make nearly enough fuss about the OneDrive. There it is, happily offering convenient Internet-based storage or backup for 15 gigabytes of your stuff—no charge. It behaves exactly like any other folder or disk; OneDrive is very humble about its magic.

This is an incredibly useful feature. No more emailing files to yourself. No more carrying things around on a flash drive. After working on some document at the office, you can go home and resume from right where you stopped; the same file is waiting for you, exactly as you left it.

OneDrive also makes a gloriously simple, effective backup disk. Anything you drag into this "folder" is instantly copied to all your devices and computers. And, as you know, the more copies that exist of something (and in the more locations), the better your backup. Even if your main PC is stolen or burned to dust, your OneDrive files are safe.

The OneDrive is also a handy intermediary for sharing big files with other people far away. And it's a handy way to offload files from a computer that has limited storage space. You still see them listed on your machine—but they don't actually download until you ask for them.

Your drive holds 15 gigabytes of files for free. You can pay extra for more space: $2 a month for 100 gigs, $4 a month for 200 gigs, or $7 a month for one terabyte (1,000 gigabytes).

Tip: There are some free ways to get more space, too. If you use the iPhone, Android, or Windows Phone app and set it up to auto-backup your phone's photos, Microsoft gives your OneDrive another free 15 gigabytes. If you set up OneDrive on another computer, that's worth another 5. And every time you persuade a friend to sign up for OneDrive, that's another 500 megabytes.

Putting Files onto the OneDrive

On the PC, you use the OneDrive just as you would a folder or a flash drive. Click its name in the Navigation pane to see what's in there. Drag files into its window, or onto its name, to copy them there. Make folders, add files, delete files, rename them—whatever. Any changes you make are reflected on your other computers, phones, and tablets within seconds.

Inside a program, you can choose File→Save in the usual way. When the Save box appears, click OneDrive in the Navigation pane. Or choose a OneDrive folder's name, if you've made one.

Tip: The window shown in Figure 3-16 shows your OneDrive documents and lets you open them, even when you're offline. How? Turns out your computer stores a "local" copy. The changes you make won't update the online copy until you're online again, but at least you're never cut off from your own files.

Offline Files

Ordinarily, the files you've put onto your OneDrive aren't *only* online. Windows also maintains a copy of them on your computer.

That's handy, of course, because it means that you can open and edit them even when you don't have an Internet connection. (Next time you're online, Windows automatically transmits the changes you made to the OneDrive copy of the file—and onto all other machines you use to sign in with the same account.)

But there's a problem with this scenario: You can't use your OneDrive to offload big files you don't *want* on your computer. You can't use it to archive files, freeing up room on your PC's drive.

Fortunately, there's also a solution. See Figure 3-17.

Note: The ability to choose the folders you want to sync is new in Windows 10. It replaces the "smart files" (placeholder files) feature of Windows 8.1, which Microsoft says confused people and didn't work well with other apps.

Figure 3-17:
Here's how you tell Windows which folders you want synced with your online OneDrive.

Top: Right-click the OneDrive icon in the system tray. (If you don't see it, it may be hidden. In that case, click the ^ button in the system tray to see the hidden icons—including OneDrive. You can right-click it right there in the balloon.)

From the shortcut menu, choose Settings.

Middle: The OneDrive Settings dialog box appears.

Select the "Choose folders" tab, then the "Choose folders" button.

Bottom: At this point, Windows displays a list of all the folders on your OneDrive.

Turn off the checkboxes of folders you don't want copied to your PC.

The first time you turn off a checkmark, Windows warns you that your local (PC) copy will be deleted. Only the Internet copy will live on.

From now on, you can keep some folders synced with your PC, and some only online, safely tucked on your OneDrive in the sky.

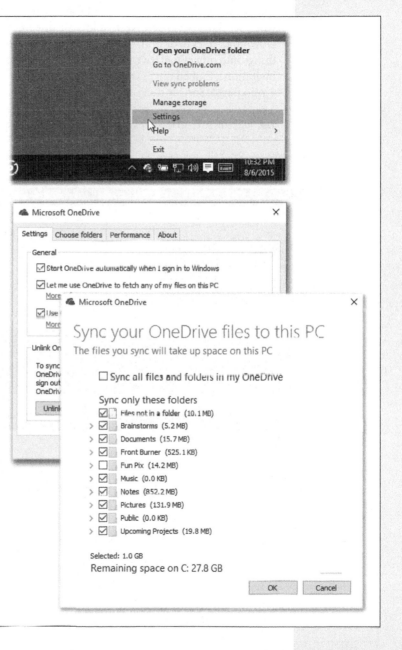

OneDrive.com

No matter where you go, no matter what computer, tablet, or phone you're using, you can get to all the files on your OneDrive—from a Web page. Just log in to your Microsoft account at *onedrive.com*.

Once you're viewing the contents of a OneDrive folder (Figure 3-18, bottom), buttons across the top of the window describe all the usual tasks you might want to perform when working with files: New (folder or document), Rename, Delete, Upload and Download (files to or from the OneDrive), "Move to" and "Copy to" (to move or copy things into other OneDrive folders), Share (with someone else, by sending an emailed invitation), Embed (gives you the HTML code you need to make the file show up on a Web page), Sort, and so on.

Tip: You can also drag file and folder tiles into other folders, right here in your browser. Weird.

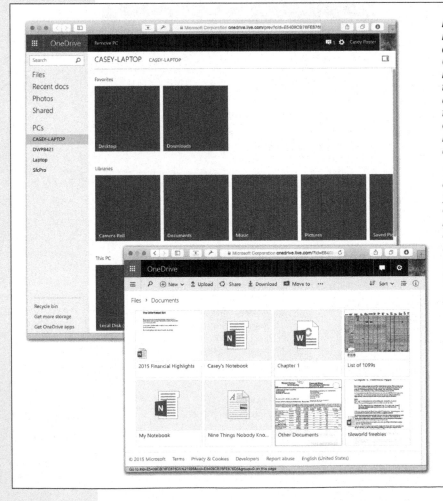

Figure 3-18:
Bottom: Here's the online copy of your OneDrive contents. It may be a little clunkier than working on the desktop, but you have full command here: copy, rename, delete, move into new folders, and so on.

Top: From any Mac or PC in the world, you can explore the contents of a PC back home (that's turned on and online). Just double-click a folder (represented by a big colored square) to "drill down" into your stuff.

If you swipe down on a tile or right-click, you get a tall menu of options. Most of them are identical to the buttons described above (Rename, Delete, and so on). But here, you may see other commands that pertain only to the kind of document you've selected. If it's a Word, Excel, or PowerPoint document, you can open and edit it right there in your Web browser. If it's a photo, you get options like "Rotate," "Order prints," or "Add to album."

Tip: Most of the time, the OneDrive app prefers to display your files as tiles. But there's something to be said for a traditional list view, where you can see your files' or folders' sizes, modification dates, and (for folders) number of items inside. Use the button at top right to produce that view.

Fetch: Remote Access to Your Whole PC Back Home

OneDrive has a secret feature that could save your bacon the next time you're away from home and realize you need something that's on your home PC: a feature called Fetch. It lets you access everything on your PC back at home, from wherever you happen to be, from OneDrive.com—even if you're on a Mac.

There's only a short list of fine-print footnotes:

- The PC back home has to be turned on and online.

- You can't fetch files from a Windows 8.1 computer—the remote PC has to be running Windows 7, Windows 8, or Windows 10. (And if it's Windows 7 or 8, it has to have the OneDrive app installed and open. You can download it from OneDrive.com.)

Turn on Fetch

Here's how you prepare the home PC for remote invasion:

1. **Right-click the OneDrive icon in the system tray.**

   See Figure 3-17, top.

2. **From the shortcut menu, choose Settings.**

   The OneDrive Settings dialog box appears (Figure 3-17, middle).

3. **On the Settings tab, under General, turn on "Let me use OneDrive to fetch any of my files on this PC." Make sure "Start OneDrive automatically when I sign in to Windows" is also turned on. Click OK.**

   And that's it! You can now tap into everything on that PC from the road; read on.

Access the PC back home

Open any Web browser on any kind of computer. Go to *onedrive.com* and sign into your Microsoft account.

On the left side, under the heading PCs, you see the names of any PCs for which you've turned on the Fetch feature. In Figure 3-18, you can see four machines that have been set up for OneDrive Fetch, named Casey Laptop, DWPB421, Laptop, and SfcPro.

If you click your PC's name, you'll see that you can actually begin opening folders on it, from thousands of miles away. Voilà!

Note: The first time you perform this stunt, you're asked to "Sign in with a security code." Click Text or Email, and specify your phone number or email address so that Microsoft can send you a confirmation code. (You wouldn't want some evil villain to rummage through your PC, now, would you?)

Once the text or email arrives, copy the code it contains into the box on the Web page before you. (Turn on "I sign in frequently on this device" if you don't want to have to repeat this code business every time you use Fetch.) Click Submit.

Double-click your C: drive, and burrow into whatever folder you like. You can even open other machines on the network if you added them to one of your libraries (page 72) or mapped them as drives (page 611). You can play music or video, or play photos as a slideshow, or download anything to the machine you're using right now.

And you were alive to see the day…

Sharing Files from OneDrive

There's one other fantastic feature awaiting on your OneDrive: The ability to send huge files—files that are much too big for email—to other people.

Technically, you're not really sending them the files; you're sending them a link to the files. But the effect is the same: With one click, your colleague can download a file or folder from your OneDrive, no matter how huge it is.

Share a file or folder from the desktop

When you right-click a file or folder on your OneDrive (on your computer), the shortcut menu offers a long list of handy features. The one you want is "Share a OneDrive link"; see Figure 3-19.

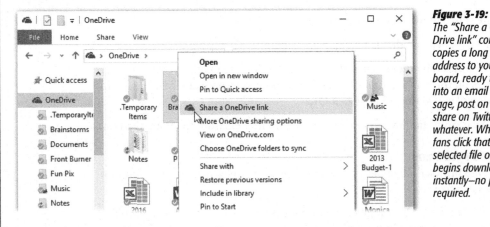

Figure 3-19:
The "Share a One-Drive link" command copies a long Web address to your Clipboard, ready to paste into an email message, post on Flicker, share on Twitter, or whatever. When your fans click that link, the selected file or folder begins downloading instantly—no password required.

Share a file or folder from OneDrive.com

If you select a file or folder on the OneDrive Web site, you can then click Share (top of the window) to gain a wider variety of sharing options.

The resulting dialog box lets you specify the email address of the recipient; type a note to that person; turn off the recipient's ability to edit the document; require the other person to have a Microsoft account; copy a link to your Clipboard (of the type described above); and so on.

Tip: You can also jump to this cornucopia of sharing options directly from the desktop, without having to go to your Web browser first. To do that, right-click the file or folder you want to share from your OneDrive. From the shortcut menu, choose More OneDrive Sharing Options.

Compressing Files and Folders

Today's hard drives have greater capacities than ever, but programs and files are much bigger, too. Running out of disk space is still a common problem. Fortunately, Windows is especially effective at compressing files and folders to take up less disk space.

Compressing files and folders can also be useful when you want to email files to someone without dooming them to an all-night modem-watching session. That's why Microsoft has endowed Windows with two different schemes for compressing files and folders: *NTFS compression* for storing files on your hard drive, and *zipped folders* for files that might have to be transferred.

NTFS Compression

Windows 10, since you asked, requires a hard drive that's formatted using a software scheme called *NTFS*. It's a much more modern formatting scheme than its predecessor, something called FAT32—and among its virtues is, you guessed it, NTFS *compression*.

This compression scheme is especially likable because it's completely invisible. Windows automatically compresses and decompresses your files, almost instantaneously. At some point, you may even forget you've turned it on. Consider:

- Whenever you open a compressed file, Windows quickly and invisibly expands it to its original form so you can edit it. When you close the file again, Windows instantly recompresses it.

- If you send compressed files (via disk or email, for example) to a PC whose hard drive doesn't use NTFS formatting, Windows once again decompresses them, quickly and invisibly.

- Any file you copy into a compressed folder or disk is compressed automatically. (If you only *move* it into such a folder from elsewhere on the disk, however, it stays compressed or uncompressed—whichever it was originally.)

There's only one downside to all this: You don't save a *lot* of disk space using NTFS compression (at least not when compared with zip compression, described in the next section). Even so, if your hard drive is anywhere near full, it might be worth turning on NTFS compression. The space you save could be your own.

Compressing files, folders, or disks

To turn on NTFS compression, right-click the icon for the file, folder, or disk whose contents you want to shrink; from the shortcut menu, choose Properties. Proceed as shown in Figure 3-20.

Tip: To compress an entire hard drive, the steps in Figure 3-20 are even simpler. Just right-click the drive's icon (in your This PC window); choose Properties; and turn on "Compress this drive to save disk space." Click OK.

Figure 3-20:
In the Properties dialog box for any file or folder, click Advanced. Turn on "Compress contents to save disk space," and then click OK. For a folder, Windows offers to compress all the files and folders inside this one, too.

If you don't see the "Compress contents to save disk space" checkbox (highlighted here), then your hard drive probably doesn't use the NTFS formatting scheme.

Many Windows veterans wind up turning on compression for the entire hard drive, even though it takes Windows several hours to do the job. (If you plan to go see a movie while Windows is working, though, wait until the appearance of the first message box letting you know about some "open file" that can't be compressed; then click Ignore All. A few files will remain uncompressed when you get back from the cineplex, but at least you won't have had to stay home, manually clicking to dismiss every "open file" complaint box.)

When Windows is finished compressing files, their names appear in a different color, a reminder that Windows is doing its part to maximize your disk space.

Note: If the files don't change color, somebody—maybe you—must have turned off the "Show encrypted or compressed NTFS files in color" option (see page 167).

Zipped Folders

NTFS compression is ideal for freeing up disk space while you're working at your PC. But as soon as you email your files to somebody else or copy them to a flash drive, the transferred copies bloat right back up to their original sizes.

Fortunately, there's another way to compress files: Zip them. If you've ever used Windows before, you've probably encountered .zip files. Each one is a tiny little suitcase, an *archive*, whose contents have been tightly compressed to keep files together, to save space, and to transfer them online faster (see Figure 3-21). Use this method when you want to email something to someone, or when you want to pack up a completed project and remove it from your hard drive to free up space.

Creating zipped folders

You can create a .zip archive in either of two ways:

- Right-click any blank spot on the desktop or an open window. From the shortcut menu, choose New→"Compressed (zipped) Folder." (Or, from the Ribbon's Home tab, choose "New item"→"Compressed (zipped) Folder.") Type a name for your newly created, empty archive, and then press Enter.

  Now, each time you drag a file or folder onto the archive's icon (or into its open window), Windows automatically stuffs a *copy* of it inside.

  Of course, you haven't exactly saved any disk space, since now you have two copies (one zipped, one untouched). If you'd rather *move* a file or folder into the archive—in the process deleting the full-size version and saving disk space—then *right*-drag the file or folder icon onto the archive icon. Now, from the shortcut menu, choose Move Here.

UP TO SPEED

Data Compression

Data compression is the process of replacing repetitive material in a file with shorthand symbols. For example, if a speech you've written contains the phrase *going forward* 21 times, a compression scheme like the one in NTFS may replace each occurrence with a single symbol, making the file that much smaller. When you reopen the file later, the operating system almost instantaneously restores the original, expanded material.

The degree to which a file can be compressed depends on what kind of data the file contains and whether it's already been compressed by another program. For example, programs (executable files) often shrink by half when

compressed. Bitmapped graphics like TIFF files squish down to as little as one-seventh their original size, saving a great deal more space.

The PNG and JPEG graphics files so popular on the Web, however, are already compressed (which is why they're so popular—they take relatively little time to download). As a result, they don't get much smaller if you try to compress them manually. That's one of the main rules of data compression: Data can be compressed only once.

In short, there's no way to predict just how much disk space you'll save by using NTFS compression on your drives. It all depends on what you have stored there.

- To turn an *existing* file or folder into a .zip archive, right-click its icon. (To zip up a handful of icons, select them first, and then right-click any one of them.) Now, from the shortcut menu, choose "Send to"→"Compressed (zipped) Folder." You've just created a new archive folder *and* copied the files or folders into it.

Tip: At this point, you can right-click the zipped folder's icon and choose "Send to"→Mail Recipient. Windows automatically whips open your email program, creates an outgoing message ready for you to address, and attaches the zipped file to it. It's now set for transport.

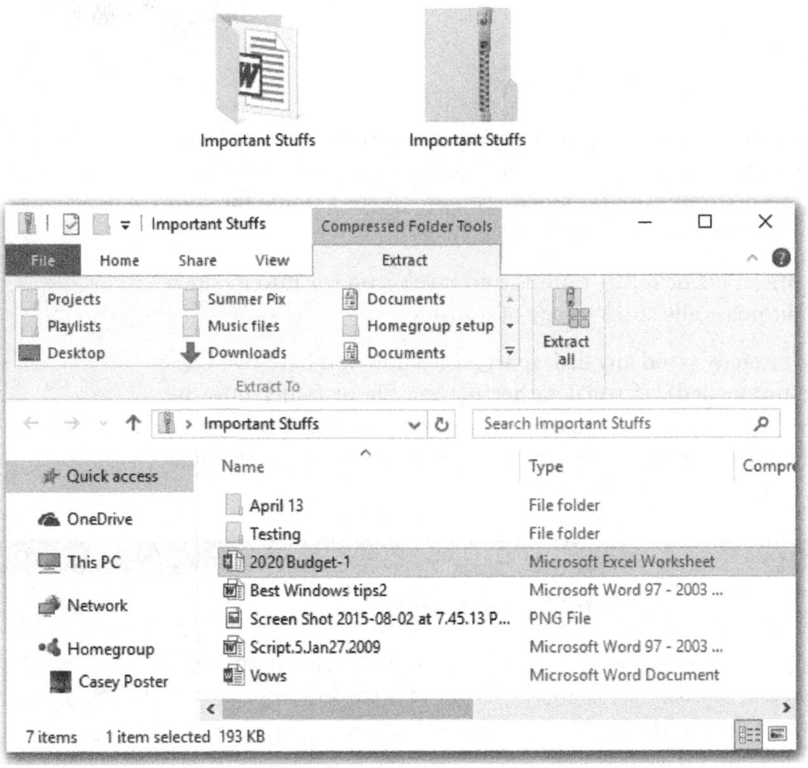

Figure 3-21:
Top: A Zip archive looks just like an ordinary folder—except for the tiny little zipper.

Bottom: Double-click one to open its window and see what's inside. The Size, Compressed Size, and Ratio columns tell you how much space you've saved. (JPEG and GIF graphics usually don't become much smaller than they were before zipping, since they're already compressed formats. But word processing files, program files, and other file types reveal quite a bit of shrinkage.)

Working with zipped folders

In many respects, a zipped folder behaves just like any ordinary folder. Double-click it to see what's inside.

If you double-click one of the *files* you find inside, however, Windows opens a *read-only* copy of it—that is, a copy you can view, but not edit. To make changes to a read-only copy, you must use the File→Save As command and save it somewhere else on your hard drive first.

Note: Be sure to navigate to the desktop or Documents folder, for example, before you save your edited document. Otherwise, Windows will save it into an invisible temporary folder, where you may never see it again.

To decompress only some of the icons in a zipped folder, just drag them out of the archive window; they instantly spring back to their original sizes. Or, to decompress the entire archive, right-click its icon and choose Extract All from the shortcut menu (or, if its window is already open, click "Extract all files" on the Ribbon's Compressed Folder Tools/Extract tab). A dialog box asks you to specify where you want the resulting files to wind up.

Tip: Windows no longer lets you password-protect a zipped folder, as you could in Windows XP. But the Web is teeming with zip-file utilities, many of them free, that do let you assign a password. You might try, for example, SecureZIP Express. It's available from this book's "Missing CD" page at *www.missingmanuals.com*.

Burning CDs and DVDs from the Desktop

Back in the day, people burned CDs or DVDs to back stuff up, to transfer stuff to another computer, to mail to somebody, or to archive older files to free up hard drive space. These days, most of that's done over the network or the Internet; it's a rare computer that even comes with a CD/DVD drive anymore.

Windows 10 can still burn CDs and DVDs, though—in either of two formats: ISO (Mastered) or UDF (Live File System). For step-by-step instructions, see the free PDF appendix to this chapter, "Burning CDs and DVDs." It's available on this book's "Missing CD" page at *www.missingmanuals.com*.

ISO Disk Images

Programs you download from the Web (not the Windows Store) often arrive in a specially encoded, compressed form—a *disk image* file, also known as an ISO image (Figure 3-22). Heck, most people got Windows 10 *itself* as an ISO file they downloaded.

Disk images are extremely handy; they behave exactly like discs, in that they can include a whole bunch of related files, folders, and pieces, all distributed online in just the way the software company intended. And here's the good news: You can work with ISO images just as though they're discs, too. (In the old days, you had to buy a program like Virtual CloneDrive to get this feature.)

Just double-click the downloaded ISO icon. (You can also right-click it; from the shortcut menu, choose Mount. Or click its icon and use the Mount button on the Ribbon's Disk Tools/Manage tab.)

After a moment, it magically turns into a disk icon in your Nav pane or This PC window, which you can work with just as though it were a real disk. Windows even assigns it a drive letter, like D: or L:; you've got yourself a virtual disc. The software you downloaded is inside.

In theory, you could also create an ISO image from a DVD or Blu-ray disc, so you'll have "the disc" with you when you travel (even if your machine doesn't have a disc drive). Games, for example, run faster from a disk image than from an actual disc. The Web is full of free programs that let you turn folders or groups of files into ISO images.

Tip: If an ISO image doesn't mount (open) when you double-click it, check your file associations (page 240). It's possible that you've associated .iso file types to open with a different program, like WinZip or Nero. That program is therefore intercepting your attempt to open the ISO image.

When you're finished working with the disk image, you can eject it exactly as you would a CD or DVD—using the Eject button on the Drive Tools tab of the Ribbon, for example.

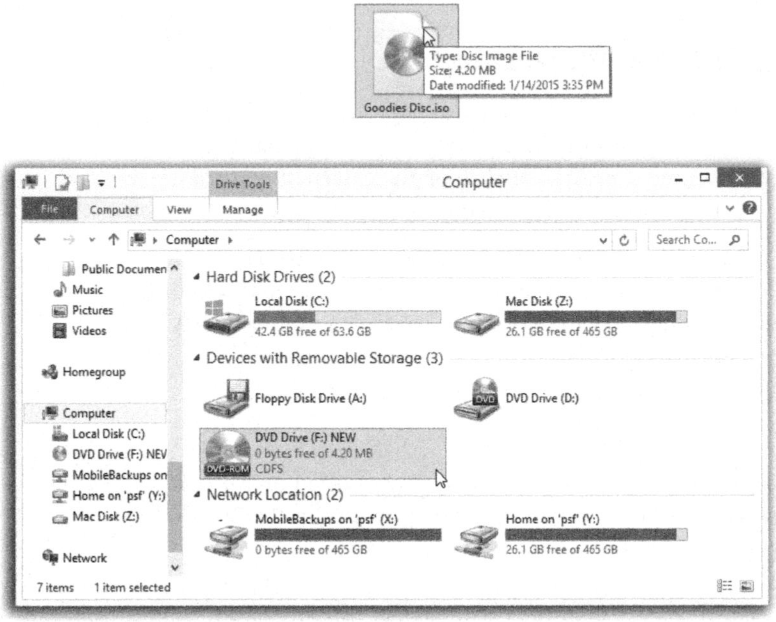

Figure 3-22:
Top: The icon of an ISO image generally looks like what it is: a disc in a file. Double-click it to open it.

Bottom: When you've opened (or "mounted") an ISO disk image, your computer now thinks that it has a new DVD drive; the disk image perfectly impersonates an actual DVD (it's the one here indicated by the cursor). Double-click one to open its window and see what's inside. At that point, you can add, delete, and manipulate files on the image, just as though it's (for example) a flash drive.

Redesigning the Desktop

W indows 10 looks a lot better than previous versions of Windows. The new system fonts, color schemes, taskbar design, typography—it's all much clearer, more graceful, and more modern than what's come before.

Still, these changes aren't for everybody. Fortunately, Win10 is every bit as tweakable as previous versions of Windows. You can change the picture on your desktop, or tell Windows to change it *for* you periodically. You can bump up the text size for better reading by over-40 eyeballs. You can create a series of virtual "external monitors"— perfect spaces in which to spread out a bunch of apps, each on its own "screen."

As Microsoft might say, "Where do you want to redesign today?"

Note: Customizing the Start menu is described in Chapter 1; customizing the taskbar is covered in Chapter 2.

Wallpaper, Color, and Themes

It's fun to customize your PC (especially because it's your opportunity to replace, at last, that huge Dell or HP logo that came as your preinstalled wallpaper). This is also yet another way to shut off some of Windows' predefined cosmetics.

To see your design choices, right-click a blank spot on the desktop. From the shortcut menu, choose Personalize.

The Personalization page of Settings opens (Figure 4-1). It offers five tabs of options, all dedicated to changing the look of your desktop world. The Start options govern your Start menu and are described in Chapter 1; the Lock screen options and the other tabs—Background, Colors, and Themes—are described right here.

Background (Wallpaper)

Windows comes with a host of desktop pictures, patterns, and colors for your viewing pleasure. You want widescreen images for your new flat-panel monitor? You got 'em. Want something gritty, artsy, in black and white? It's there, too. And you can use any picture you'd like as your background as well.

The Background tab (of Settings→Personalization) offers a huge Preview image, showing off the color scheme of your desktop world at the moment.

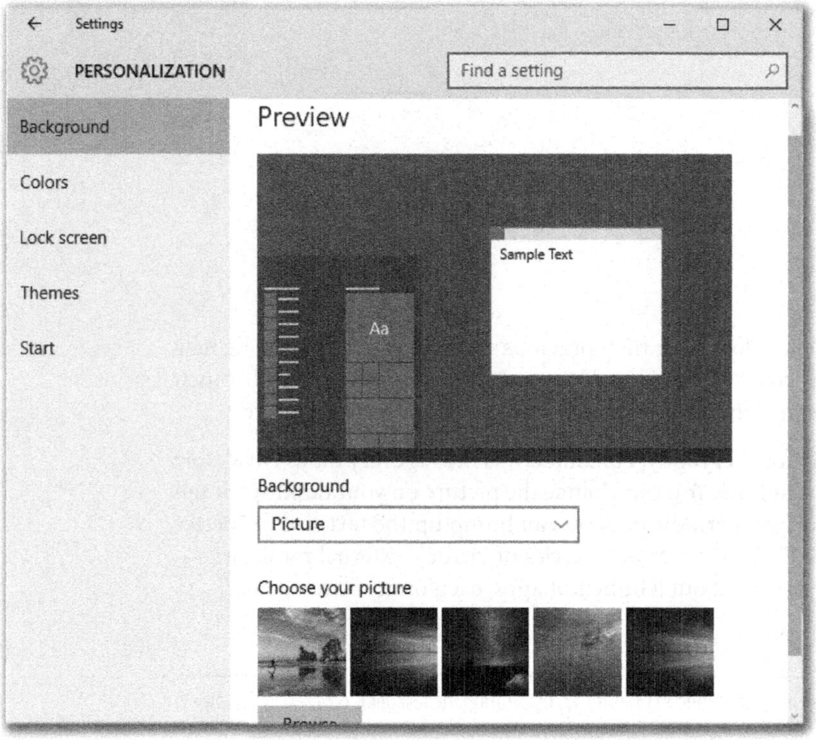

Figure 4-1:
The Personalization tab of Settings offers a simplified diagram of your desktop. As you adjust the wallpaper and color scheme options, this miniature desktop changes to show how it will look.

Background is Microsoft's new word for wallpaper (the image that fills your entire desktop background). The Background pop-up menu offers three choices:

- **Solid Color** is a palette of simple, solid colors for your desktop background. It's not a bad idea, actually; it's a little easier to find your icons if they're not lost among the details of a nature photo (or a Sofía Vergara photo).

- **Picture** starts you off with five luscious nature photos. It also offers you a Browse button that displays what's in your Pictures folder, because it's more fun to use one of your *own* pictures on the desktop. That might be an adorable baby photo of your niece, or it might be Sofía Vergara with half her clothes off; the choice is yours.

- **Slideshow.** The novelty of any desktop picture is likely to fade after several months of all-day viewing. Fortunately, you can choose *multiple* desktop pictures from the gallery. Use the Browse button to find a promising-looking folder full of images.

  Now, from the "Change picture every" pop-up menu, specify when you want your background picture to change: every day, every hour, every 5 minutes, or whatever. (If you're *really* having trouble staying awake at your PC, you can choose every minute.)

  Now, at the intervals you specified, your desktop picture changes automatically, smoothly cross-fading between the pictures in your chosen source folder like a slideshow. You may never want to open another window, because you'd hate to block your view.

Tip: Once your slideshow wallpaper is set up, you don't have to wait out the waiting period if you get bored. You can right-click the desktop and, from the shortcut menu, choose "Next desktop background."

No matter which source you use to choose a photo, you have one more issue to deal with. Unless you've gone to the trouble of editing your chosen photo so that it matches the precise dimensions of your screen (1440×900 or whatever), it probably isn't exactly the same size as your screen.

Using the "Choose a fit" pop-up menu, you can choose any of these options:

- **Fill.** Enlarges or reduces the image so that it fills every inch of the desktop without distortion. Parts may get chopped off, but this option never distorts the picture.

- **Fit.** Your entire photo appears, as large as possible without distortion *or* cropping. If the photo doesn't precisely match the proportions of your screen, you get "letterbox bars" on the sides or at top and bottom.

- **Stretch.** Makes your picture fit the screen exactly, come hell or high water. Larger pictures may be squished vertically or horizontally as necessary, and small pictures are drastically blown up *and* squished, usually with grisly results.

- **Tile.** This option makes your picture repeat over and over until the multiple images fill the entire monitor.

- **Center.** Centers the photo neatly on the screen. If the picture is smaller than the screen, it leaves a swath of empty border all the way around. If it's larger, the outer edges get chopped off.

- **Span.** If you have more than one monitor, this option lets you slap a single photo across multiple screens.

Tip: Really, the Background screen described above is the wallpaper headquarters. But there are "Set as desktop background" commands hiding everywhere in Windows, making it simple to turn everyday images into wallpaper. You'll find that command, for example, when you right-click a graphics icon in an Explorer window or a graphic on a Web page.

Colors

This page of Settings lets you specify an accent color—the shade that paints the tiles and background of the Start menu, window buttons, the taskbar background, and the Action Center (page 113).

- **Automatically pick an accent color from my background.** If you leave this switch on, then Windows chooses the accent for you. It chooses a color that it believes will provide an attractive contrast to the photo or color you've chosen for your desktop background.

  If you turn this switch off, then Windows offers a palette of about 50 color squares. It's prodding you to choose your *own* darned accent color.

- **Show color on Start, taskbar, and action center.** If you turn this off, your chosen accent color will apply only to Start-menu tiles and window controls; the Start-menu background, taskbar, and Action Center backgrounds will be black.

- **Make Start, taskbar, and action center transparent.** There's no particularly good reason you'd want these Windows elements to be partly see-through; they're easier to read when they're opaque. But you know—whatever floats your boat.

- **High contrast settings.** This link opens the Ease of Access page of Settings. Here the "High contrast" tab lets you choose a high-contrast color scheme (bright text, dark backgrounds) that may be easier to read if you have vision impairments.

Note: In Windows Vista and Windows 7, there was a button here called "Advanced appearance settings." It opened a dialog box that let you change every single aspect of the selected visual theme independently—scroll-bar thickness, tooltip text size, icon fonts, and so on. Alas, that box, and those options, are no longer available in Windows 10.

Themes

As shown in Figure 4-2, Windows includes a number of predesigned *themes* that affect the look of your desktop and windows.

Each design theme controls these elements of Windows:

- Your wallpaper (desktop picture).

- Your screensaver.

- The design of icons like This PC, Network, Control Panel, and Recycle Bin.

- The color scheme for your window edges, plus any tweaks you make in the Color and Appearance dialog box (font size, window border width, and so on).

- The size and shape of your arrow cursor.

- The sounds your PC uses as error and alert beeps.

Note: Don't miss the "Get more themes online" link; it takes you to a download-more-themes Web site.

The control panel shown in Figure 4-2 offers three categories of themes: My Themes (ones you've modified yourself), Windows Default Themes (Microsoft's canned starter designs), and High Contrast themes. These are designed to help out people with limited vision, who require greater differences in color between window elements. High-contrast themes more closely resemble the squared-off windows and dialog boxes of Windows 2000 (see Figure 4-3).

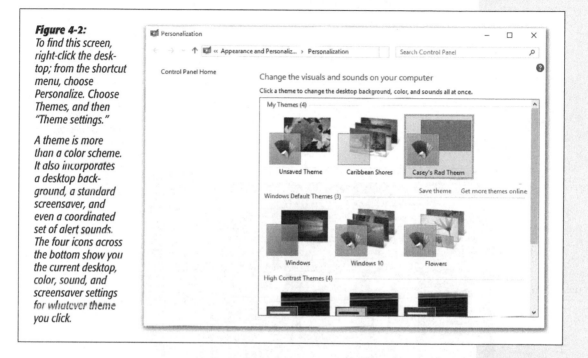

Figure 4-2:
To find this screen, right-click the desktop; from the shortcut menu, choose Personalize. Choose Themes, and then "Theme settings."

A theme is more than a color scheme. It also incorporates a desktop background, a standard screensaver, and even a coordinated set of alert sounds. The four icons across the bottom show you the current desktop, color, sound, and screensaver settings for whatever theme you click.

The real fun, however, awaits when you choose one of the canned themes and then *modify* it. You can make changes on the Background and Colors tabs described above, as well as Sounds, Screen Saver, Desktop Icons, and Mouse Pointers, which are described on the following pages.

When that's all over, you return to the Themes control panel, where all the modifications you've made are represented at the top of the screen—as an icon called Unsaved Theme (Figure 4-2).

Well, you wouldn't want all that effort to go to waste, would you? So click "Save theme," type a name for your new, improved theme, and click Save.

From now on, the theme you've created (well, *modified)* shows up in the row of icons called My Themes. From now on, you can recall the emotional tenor of your edited look with a single click on that icon.

If you make *further* changes to that theme (or any other theme), another Unsaved Theme icon appears, once again ready for you to save and name. You can keep going forever, adding to your gallery of experimentation.

You can also delete a less-inspired theme (right-click its icon; from the shortcut menu, choose Delete Theme). On the other hand, when you strike creative gold, you can package up your theme and share it with other computers—your own, or other people's online. To do that, right-click the theme's icon; from the shortcut menu, choose "Save theme for sharing." Windows asks you to name and save the new .themepack file, which you can distribute to the masses. (Just double-clicking a .themepack file installs it in the Themes dialog box.)

Note: If your theme uses sounds and graphics that aren't on other people's PCs, they won't see those elements when they install your theme.

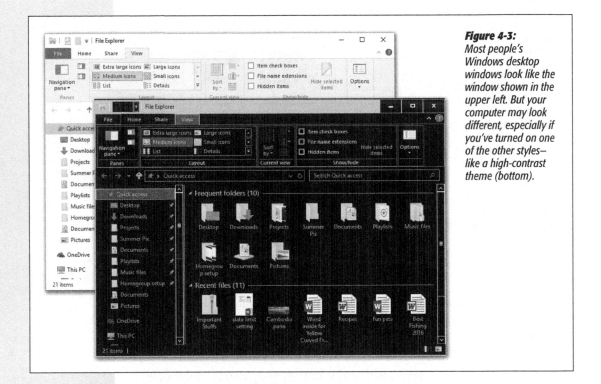

Figure 4-3:
Most people's Windows desktop windows look like the window shown in the upper left. But your computer may look different, especially if you've turned on one of the other styles—like a high-contrast theme (bottom).

On the main Themes Settings screen are some related settings, here labeled Related Settings. They are "Advanced sound settings," "Desktop icon settings," and "Mouse pointer settings." Read on.

Advanced sound settings

Windows plays beeps and bloops to celebrate various occasions: closing a program, yanking out a USB drive, logging in or out, getting a new fax, and so on. You can turn these sounds on or off, or choose new sounds for these events.

Sounds, too, are part of a theme. To edit the suite of sounds that goes with your currently selected theme, open the Themes Settings page and click "Advanced sound settings." Or, if you're starting from scratch, type *sounds* into the taskbar search box; in the results list, choose "Change system sounds."

See the list of Program Events (Figure 4-4)? A speaker icon represents the occasions when a sound will play. Double-click a sound (or click the Test button) to see what it sounds like.

Figure 4-4:
Each set of sounds is called a sound scheme. Sometimes the sound effects in a scheme are even sonically related. (Perhaps the collection is totally hip-hop, classical, or performed on a kazoo.) To switch schemes, use the Sound Scheme pop-up menu. You can also define a new scheme of your own. Start by assigning individual sounds to events, and then click the Save As button to save your collection under a name that you create.

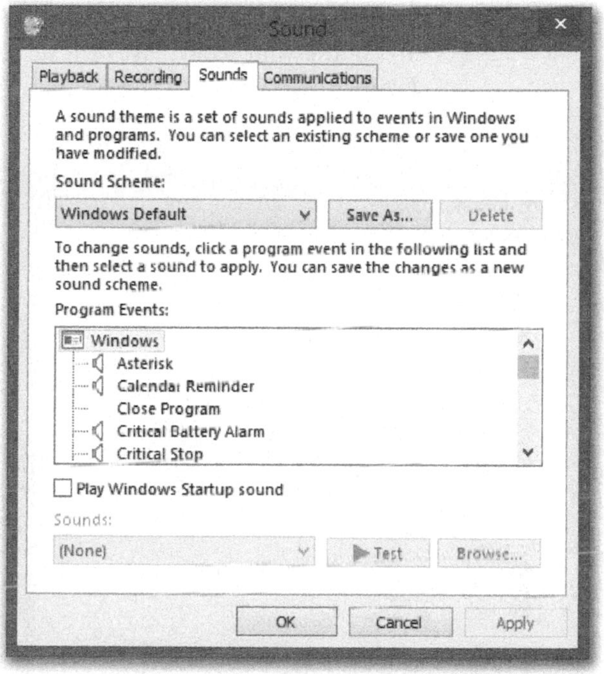

Or, if you click the name of some computer event (say, Low Battery Alert), you can make these adjustments:

- **Remove a sound from the event** by choosing (None) from the Sounds drop-down list.

- **Change an assigned sound,** or add a sound to an event that doesn't have one, by clicking Browse and choosing a new sound file from the list in the Open dialog box.

Tip: When you click the Browse button, Windows opens the Local Disk (C:)→Windows→Media folder, which contains the *.wav* files that provide sounds. If you drag *.wav* files into this Media folder, they become available for use as Windows sound effects. Many people download *.wav* files from the Internet and stash them in the Media folder to make their computing experience quirkier, more fun, and richer in *Austin Powers* sound snippets.

When you select a sound, its filename appears in the Sounds drop-down list. Click the Test button to the right of the box to hear the sound.

Desktop icon settings

Thanks to the "Desktop icon settings" link on the Themes Settings screen, you can specify which standard icons sit on your desktop for easy access and what they look like. (Or type *desktop icons* into the search box; in the results list, choose "Themes and related settings." Then click "Desktop icon settings.")

To choose your icons, just turn on the checkboxes for the ones you want (see Figure 4-5).

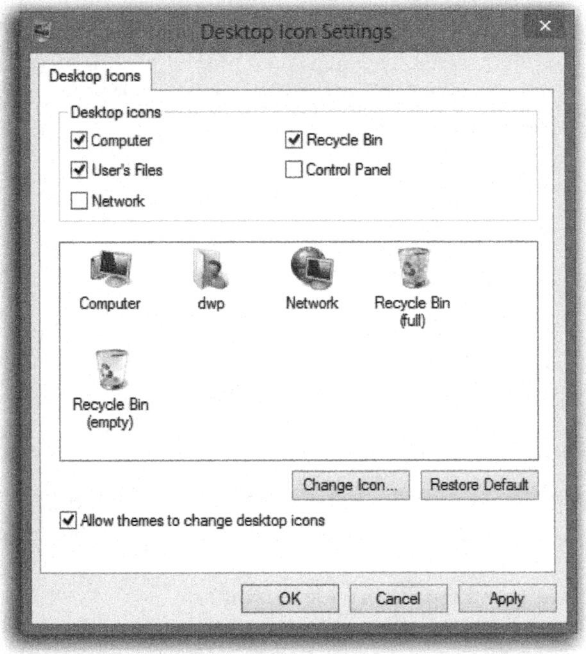

Figure 4-5:
Microsoft has been cleaning up the Windows desktop in recent years, and that includes sweeping away some useful icons, like This PC, Control Panel, Network, and your Personal folder. But you can put them back, just by turning on these checkboxes.

You can also substitute different *icons* for your icons. Click, for example, the This PC icon, and then click Change Icon. Up pops a collection of predrawn icons in a horizontally scrolling selection box. If you see a picture you like better, double-click it.

Click OK if you like the change, Cancel if not.

Mouse pointer settings

If your fondness for the standard Windows arrow cursor begins to wane, you can assert your individuality by choosing a different pointer shape. For starters, you might want to choose a *bigger* arrow cursor—a great solution on today's tinier-pixel, shrunken-cursor monitors.

Tip: What you're about to read is the old way of adjusting the cursor shape and size—the more complete way, involving a visit to the old Control Panel. In Windows 10, a few simplified cursor-shape options await in the newfangled Settings program (page 257).

Begin by clicking "Mouse pointer settings" in the Themes Settings box. (If you're not already there, open the Start menu and type *mouse pointer*; in the results list, choose "Change how the mouse pointer looks.")

In a flash, you arrive at the dialog box shown in Figure 4-6.

Figure 4-6:
Top: The Pointers dialog box, where you can choose a bigger cursor (or a differently shaped one).

Bottom: The Pointer Options tab. Ever lose your mouse pointer while working on a laptop with a dim screen? Maybe pointer trails could help. Or have you ever worked on a desktop computer with a mouse pointer that seems to take forever to move across the desktop? Try increasing the pointer speed.

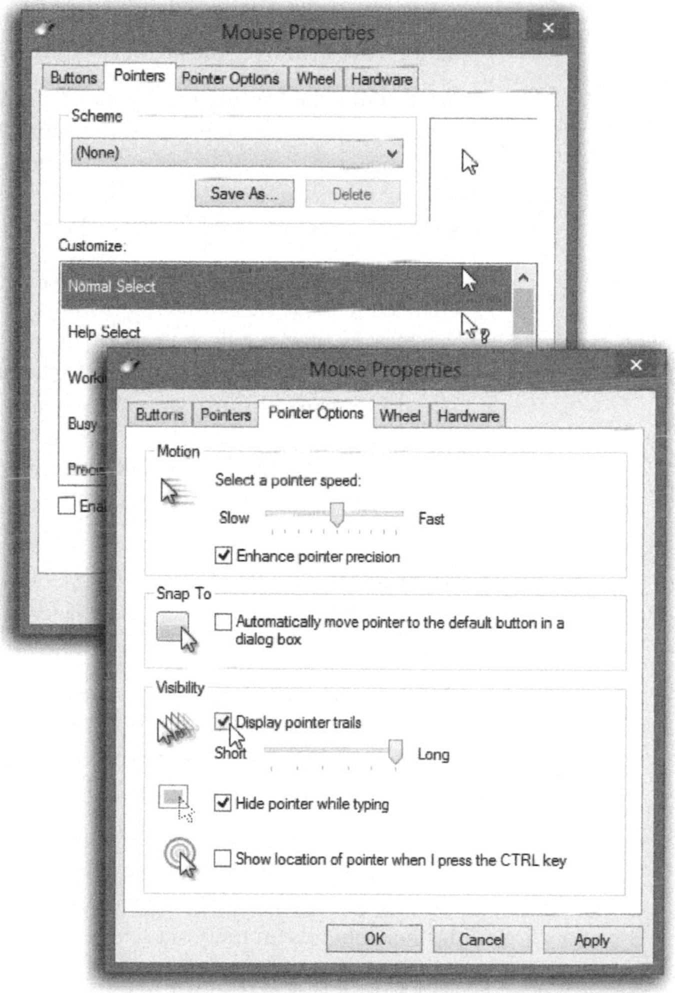

At this point, you can proceed in any of three ways:

- **Scheme.** There's more to Windows cursors than just the arrow pointer. At various times, you may also see the spinning circular cursor (which means, "Wait; I'm thinking," or "Wait; I've crashed"), the I-beam cursor (which appears when you're editing text), the little pointing-finger hand that appears when you point to a Web link, and so on.

  All these cursors come prepackaged into design-coordinated sets called *schemes*. To look over the cursor shapes in a different scheme, use the Scheme drop-down list; the corresponding pointer collection appears in the Customize list box. The ones whose names include "large" or "extra large" offer jumbo, magnified cursors ideal for very large screens or failing eyesight. When you find one that seems like an improvement over the factory-setting set, click OK.

- **Select individual pointers.** You don't have to change to a completely different scheme; you can also replace just one cursor. To do so, click the pointer you want to change, and then click the Browse button. You're shown the vast array of cursor-replacement icons (which are in the Local Disk (C:)→Windows→Cursors folder). Click one to see what it looks like; double-click to select it.

- **Create your own pointer scheme.** Once you've replaced a cursor shape, you've also changed the scheme to which it belongs. At this point, either click OK to activate your change and get back to work, or save the new, improved scheme under its own name, so you can switch back to the original when nostalgia calls. To do so, click the Save As button, name the scheme, and then click OK.

Tip: The "Enable pointer shadow" checkbox at the bottom of this tab is pretty neat. It casts a shadow on whatever's beneath the cursor, as though it's skimming just above the surface of your screen.

Pointer Options

Clicking the Pointer Options tab offers a few more random cursor-related functions (Figure 4-6, bottom):

- **Pointer speed.** It comes as a surprise to many people that the cursor doesn't move five inches when the mouse moves five inches on the desk. Instead, you can set things up so that moving the mouse one *millimeter* moves the pointer one full *inch*—or vice versa—using the "Select a pointer speed" slider.

  It may come as an even greater surprise that the cursor doesn't generally move *proportionally* to the mouse's movement, regardless of your "Pointer speed" setting. Instead, the cursor moves farther when you move the mouse faster. How *much* farther depends on how you set the "Select a pointer speed" slider.

  The Fast setting is nice if you have an enormous monitor, since it prevents you from needing an equally large mouse pad to get from one corner to another. The Slow setting, on the other hand, can be frustrating, since it forces you to constantly pick up and put down the mouse as you scoot across the screen. (You can also turn off the disproportionate-movement feature completely by turning off "Enhance pointer precision.")

- **Snap To.** A hefty percentage of the times when you reach for the mouse, it's to click a button in a dialog box. If you, like millions of people before you, usually click the *default* (outlined) button—such as OK, Next, or Yes—then the Snap To feature can save you the effort of positioning the cursor before clicking.

  When you turn on Snap To, every time a dialog box appears, your mouse pointer jumps automatically to the default button so that all you need to do is click. (And to click a different button, like Cancel, you have to move the mouse only slightly to reach it.)

- **Display pointer trails.** The options available for enhancing pointer visibility (or invisibility) are mildly useful under certain circumstances, but mostly they're just for show.

  If you turn on "Display pointer trails," for example, you get ghost images that trail behind the cursor like a bunch of little ducklings following their mother. In general, this stuttering-cursor effect is irritating. On rare occasions, however, you may find that it helps you locate the cursor—for example, if you're making a presentation on a low-contrast LCD projector.

- **Hide pointer while typing** is useful if you find that the cursor sometimes gets in the way of the words on your screen. As soon as you use the keyboard, the pointer disappears; just move the mouse to make the pointer reappear.

- **Show location of pointer when I press the CTRL key.** If you've managed to lose the cursor on an LCD projector or a laptop with an inferior screen, this feature helps you gain your bearings. After turning on this checkbox, Windows displays an animated concentric ring each time you press the Ctrl key to pinpoint the cursor's location.

Tip: You can also fatten up the insertion point—the cursor that appears when you're editing text. See page 268.

Screensavers

The term "screensaver" is sort of bogus; today's flat-panel screens *can't* develop "burn-in." (You're too young to remember, but screensavers were designed to bounce around a moving image to prevent burn-in on those old, bulky, CRT screens.)

No, screensavers are mostly about entertainment—and, especially in the business world, security. You can wander away from your desk without fear of snoopers.

The idea is simple: A few minutes after you leave your computer, whatever work you were doing is hidden behind the screensaver; passersby can't see what's on the screen. To exit the screensaver, move the mouse, click a mouse button, or press a key.

Choosing a Screensaver

To choose a screensaver, type *screensaver* into the taskbar search box; in the results list, choose "Change screen saver." The Screen Saver page of the Control Panel dialog box appears.

Now use the "Screen saver" drop-down list. A miniature preview appears in the preview monitor on the dialog box (see Figure 4-7).

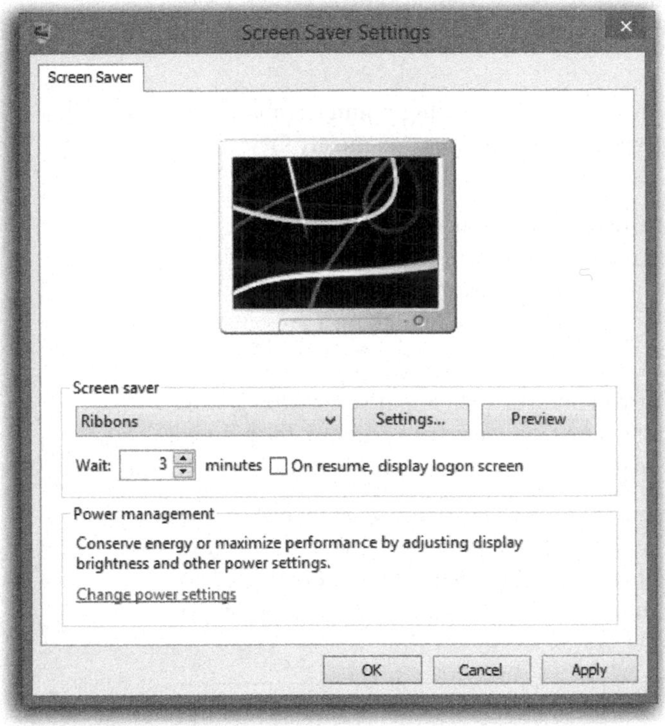

Figure 4-7:
"On resume, display logon screen" is a handy security measure. It means you'll have to input your password to get back into your PC once the screensaver has come on—a good barrier against nosy coworkers who saunter up to your PC while you're out getting coffee.

To see a *full-screen* preview, click the Preview button. The screensaver display fills your screen and remains there until you move your mouse, click a mouse button, or press a key.

The Wait box determines how long the screensaver waits before kicking in, after the last time you move the mouse or type. Click the Settings button to play with the chosen screensaver module's look and behavior. For example, you may be able to change its colors, texture, or animation style.

At the bottom of this tab, click "Change power settings" to open the Power Options window described on page 282.

Tip: If you keep graphics files in your Pictures folder, try selecting the Photos screensaver. Then click the Settings button and choose the pictures you want to see. When the screensaver kicks in, Windows puts on a spectacular slideshow of your photos, bringing each to the screen with a special effect (flying in from the side, fading in, and so on).

Turning Off the New Look

The Windows 10 desktop world of icons and windows doesn't look much different from the Windows 7 desktop. (There's a Ribbon in Explorer windows, window edges are no longer transparent, and the Start menu and taskbar have new designs—but that's about it for changes.)

But if you're used to anything earlier, things look a lot different. You may miss the less flashy, more utilitarian look of Windows Vista or XP. If you're in that category, don't worry: Windows comes with a whole trainload of Off switches.

Turning Off Window Snapping and Shaking

If you drag a window close to the top edge of your screen, the window expands to fill the *whole* screen. If you drag it close to a side of your screen, the window expands to fill *half* the screen. If all this auto-snapping makes you crazy, turn it off as described on page 54.

Turning Off the Inch-Tall Taskbar

The Windows 10 taskbar shows giant, inch-tall icons—with no text labels. And you no longer get one button for each open window; Windows consolidates open windows within each program to save taskbar space.

You can make the taskbar look like it did in Vista or even Windows XP, if you like. Details are on 107.

Turning Off All Those Glitzy Animations

Then there are all those other things Windows does to show off: Windows seem to zoom open or closed; the Close, Minimize, and Maximize buttons glow when you point to them; menu commands and tooltips fade open and closed; and so on.

It turns out that there's a master list of these effects, filled with individual on/off switches for Windows' various animations, pop-up previews, mouse and window shadows, and so on.

To see it, open the Start menu; start typing *appearance* until "Adjust the appearance and performance of windows" appears in the search results. Click it.

You arrive in the Performance Options dialog box (see Figure 4-8), on a tab called Visual Effects. Now, these aren't exactly the kinds of visual effects they make at Industrial Light & Magic for use in *Star Wars* movies. In fact, they're so subtle, they're practically invisible. But the more of them you turn off, the faster the desktop will seem to work. (You can turn all of them off with one click—select "Adjust for best performance.") Here are a few examples:

- **Enable Peek.** Yes, you can turn off the Peek feature, which lets you (a) point to a taskbar thumbnail to see its full-size window pop to the fore and (b) point to the Show Desktop button (right end of the taskbar) to make all windows transparent.

- **Show shadows under windows/mouse pointer.** Take a look: Open windows may actually seem to cast faint, light gray drop shadows, as though floating an eighth of an inch above the surface behind them. It's a cool, but utterly superfluous, special effect.

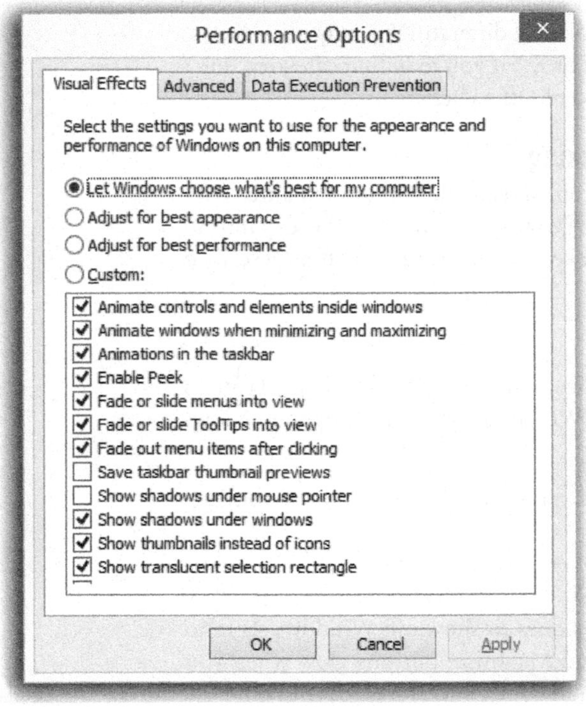

Figure 4-8:
Select "Adjust for best performance" to turn everything off, leaving you with, more or less, Windows XP. Alternatively, turn off only the animations you can live without.

- **Show window contents while dragging.** If this option is off, then when you drag a window, only a faint outline of its border is visible; you don't see all the items *in* the window coming along for the ride. As soon as you stop dragging, the contents reappear. If this option is on, however, then as you drag a window across your screen, you see all its contents, too—a feature that can slow the dragging process on really slow machines.

- **Smooth edges of screen fonts.** If you look very closely at the characters on your screen, they look a bit ragged on the curves. But when this option is turned on, Windows softens the curves, making the text look more professional (or slightly blurrier, depending on your point of view).

Turn Off the Tiles in the Start Menu

You're not stuck with the big square tiles, the last remaining visible gasp of Windows 8. See page 37.

Monitor Settings

You wouldn't get much work done without a screen on your computer. It follows, then, that you can get *more* work done if you tinker with your screen's settings to make it more appropriate to your tastes and workload.

Four Ways to Enlarge the Screen

There are two reasons why Windows offers a quick-and-easy way to magnify *everything* on the screen.

First, people tend to get older—even you. Come middle age, your eyes may have trouble reading smaller type.

Second, the resolution of computer screens gets higher every year. That is, more and more dots are packed into the same-sized screens, and therefore those dots are getting smaller, and therefore the *type and graphics* are getting smaller.

Microsoft finally decided enough was enough. That's why there's a one-click way to enlarge all type and graphics, with crisp, easier-to-see results. There are also various older schemes for accomplishing similar tasks. Here's a rundown of all of them.

Change the resolution

Your screen can make its picture larger or smaller to accommodate different kinds of work. You perform this magnification or reduction by switching among different *resolutions* (measurements of the number of dots that compose the screen).

When you use a low-resolution setting, such as 800×600, the dots of your screen image get larger, enlarging (zooming in on) the picture—but showing a smaller slice of the page. Use this setting when playing a small movie on the Web, for example, so that it fills more of the screen.

At higher resolutions, such as 1280×1024, the dots get smaller, making your windows and icons smaller but showing more overall area. Use this kind of setting when working on two-page spreads in your page-layout program, for example.

Unfortunately, adjusting the resolution isn't a perfect solution if you're having trouble reading tiny type. On a flat-panel screen—that is, the *only* kind sold today—only one resolution setting looks really great: the maximum one. That's what geeks call the *native* resolution of that screen.

That's because on flat-panel screens, every pixel is a fixed size. At lower resolutions, the PC does what it can to blur together adjacent pixels, but the effect is fuzzy and unsatisfying. (On the old, bulky CRT monitors, the electron gun could actually make the pixels larger or smaller, so you didn't have this problem.)

If you still want to adjust your screen's resolution, here's how you do it. Right-click the desktop. From the shortcut menu, choose "Display settings." In the Settings screen that opens, click "Advanced display settings." Finally, in the new dialog box, use the Resolution pop-up menu.

Tip: Depending on your monitor, you may see a weird Orientation pop-up menu here. Believe it or not, this control lets you flip your screen image upside down or into a mirror image. These options make hilarious practical jokes, of course, but they were actually designed to accommodate newfangled PC designs where, for example, the screen half of a laptop flips over, A-frame style, so people across the table from you can see it.

In any case, once you choose an orientation and click Apply or OK, a dialog box lets you either keep or discard the setting. Which is lucky, because if the image is upside down on a regular PC, it's really hard to get any work done.

Enlarge just the type and graphics

This feature is one of Microsoft's most inspired, most useful—and least publicized. It turns out that you can enlarge the type and graphics on the screen *without* changing the screen's resolution. So type gets bigger without getting blurrier, and everything else stays sharp, too. Figure 4-9 shows all.

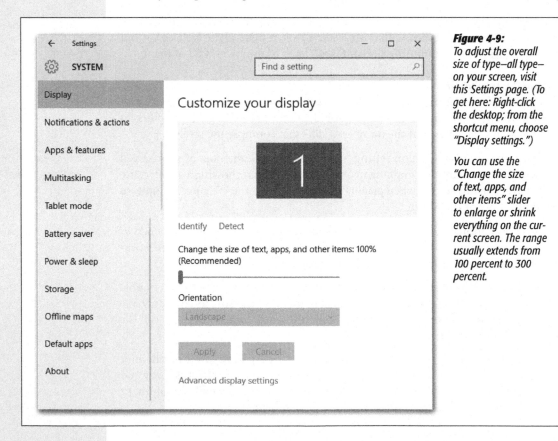

Figure 4-9:
To adjust the overall size of type—all type—on your screen, visit this Settings page. (To get here: Right-click the desktop; from the shortcut menu, choose "Display settings.")

You can use the "Change the size of text, apps, and other items" slider to enlarge or shrink everything on the current screen. The range usually extends from 100 percent to 300 percent.

Enlarge specific window elements

Sure, sure—enlarging the type is pretty handy. Enlarging everything is handy, too. But Microsoft's Too Much Control team has gone to spectacular lengths to make sure that your options don't stop there.

You can, in fact, change every single aspect of the selected visual theme independently: title bars, menus, message boxes, palette titles, icons, and tooltips.

To see these controls, open the Start menu and type *text size*; in the results list, choose "Make text and other items larger or smaller." Proceed as shown in Figure 4-10.

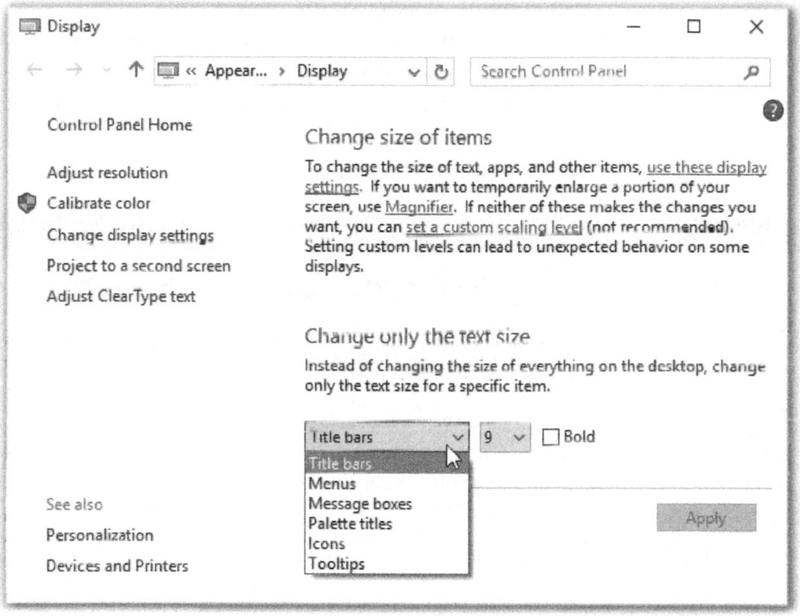

Figure 4-10:
Use the pop-up menu to choose an element whose size you want to change (Title bars, Menus, Icons, and so on). Then, using the little menu to its right, you can change the type size used for any of these screen elements. You can turn on Bold for even more seeability.

When you've exhausted your options—or just become exhausted—click Apply. You can now explore the world of your new, larger-type icon and window elements.

The Magnifier

If your "type is too small" problem is only occasional, you can call up Windows' Magnifier. It's like a software magnifying glass that fills the top portion of your screen; as you move your pointer around the real-size area beneath, the enlarged image scrolls around, too. Details are on page 312.

Colors

Today's video cards offer different *color depth* settings, each of which permits the screen to display a different number of colors simultaneously. You usually have a choice between settings like Medium (16-bit), which was called High Color in early versions of Windows; High (24-bit), once known as True Color; and Highest (32-bit).

In the early days of computing, higher color settings required a sacrifice in speed. Today, however, there's very little downside to leaving your screen at its highest setting. Photos, in particular, look best when you set your monitor to higher-quality settings.

To check your settings, right-click the desktop. From the shortcut menu, choose "Display settings." In the dialog box, click "Advanced display settings" and then "Display adapter properties" to open the Properties dialog box for your monitor. Click the Monitor tab, and fiddle around till you're blue, red, and green in the face.

Multiple Monitors

If your computer has a jack for an external monitor (most do these days—including the video-output jacks on laptops and even tablets), or if your new tablet or laptop offers WiDi (wireless display) technology, then you can hook up a second monitor (or even third monitor) or a projector. You can either display the same picture on both screens (which is what you'd want if your laptop were projecting slides for an audience), or you can create a gigantic virtual desktop, moving icons or toolbars

---

POWER USERS' CLINIC

Some Clear Talk about ClearType

ClearType is Microsoft's word for a sneaky technology that makes type look sharper on your screen than it really is.

Imagine a lowercase "s" at a very small point size. It looks great on this page, because this book was printed at 1,200 dots per inch. But your monitor's resolution is far lower—maybe 96 dots per inch—so text doesn't look nearly as good. If you were to really get up close, you'd see that the curves on the letters are actually a little jagged.

Each dot on an LCD screen is actually composed of three subpixels (mini-dots): red, green, and blue. What ClearType does is simulate smaller pixels in the nooks and crannies of letters by turning on only some of those subpixels. In the curve of that tiny *s*, for example, maybe only the blue subpixel is turned on, which to your eye looks like a slightly darker area, a fraction of a pixel; as a result, the type looks finer than it really is.

ClearType's behavior is adjustable. To see the options, open the Start menu. Type *cleartype* until you see "Adjust ClearType text" in the results list; click it.

On the first screen, you have an on/off checkbox for ClearType. It's there just for the sake of completeness, because text on an LCD screen really does look worse without it.

If you click Next, Windows walks you through a series of "Which type sample looks better to you?" screens, where all you have to do is click the "Quick Brown Fox Jumps Over the Lazy Dog" example that you find easiest to read. Behind the scenes, of course, you're adjusting ClearType's technical parameters without even having to know what they are. When it's all over, you'll have the best-looking small type possible.

Click the text sample that looks best to you (2 of 4)

The Quick Brown Fox Jumps Over the Lazy Dog. Lorem ipsum dolor sit amet, consectetuer adipiscing elit. Mauris ornare odio vel risus. Maecenas elit metus, pellentesque quis, pretium.	The Quick Brown Fox Jumps Over the Lazy Dog. Lorem ipsum dolor sit amet, consectetuer adipiscing elit. Mauris ornare odio vel risus. Maecenas elit metus, pellentesque quis, pretium.	The Quick Brown Fox Jumps Over the Lazy Dog. Lorem ipsum dolor sit amet, consectetuer adipiscing elit. Mauris ornare odio vel risus. Maecenas elit metus, pellentesque quis, pretium.
The Quick Brown Fox Jumps Over the Lazy Dog. Lorem ipsum dolor sit amet, consectetuer adipiscing elit. Mauris ornare odio vel risus. Maecenas elit metus, pellentesque quis, pretium.	The Quick Brown Fox Jumps Over the Lazy Dog. Lorem ipsum dolor sit amet, consectetuer adipiscing elit. Mauris ornare odio vel risus. Maecenas elit metus, pellentesque quis, pretium.	The Quick Brown Fox Jumps Over the Lazy Dog. Lorem ipsum dolor sit amet, consectetuer adipiscing elit. Mauris ornare odio vel risus. Maecenas elit metus, pellentesque quis, pretium.

---

from one monitor to another. The latter setup lets you keep an eye on Web activity on one monitor while you edit data on another. It's a *glorious* arrangement, even if it does make the occasional family member think you've gone off the deep end with your PC obsession.

Over the years, PC makers have offered different kinds of connectors for external screens—jacks called things like VGA, DVI, HDMI, and DisplayPort. Alas, it's your burden to figure out which jack your computer has, and to get the right kind of cable or adapter to accommodate your external screen.

Once you've done that, treat yourself to an Oreo milkshake to celebrate, and then read on to dive into the software setup.

Customizing Your Displays

For the beating heart of Windows' multiple-monitor controls, right-click the desktop. From the shortcut menu, choose "Display settings."

In the resulting dialog box, you see icons for both screens (or even more, if you have them—you lucky thing!). It's like a map, as shown in Figure 4-11.

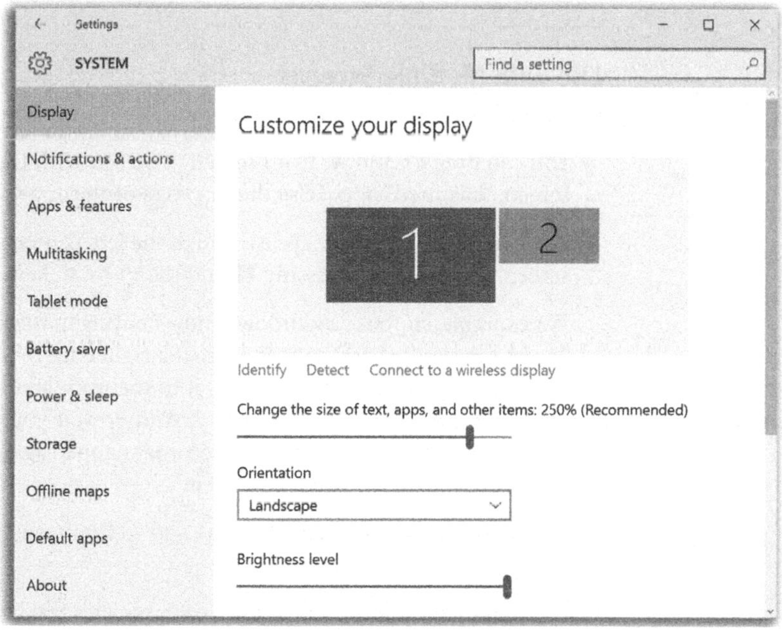

Figure 4-11:
Click the screen whose settings you want to change. If Windows seems to be displaying these miniatures out of sequence—if your external monitor is really to the left of your main screen, and Windows is showing it to the right—you can drag their thumbnails around until they match reality. (Click Identify if you get confused; that summons an enormous digit in a black box on each real screen, which helps you match it to the digits on the miniatures.)

To bring about the extended-desktop scenario, use the "Multiple displays" pop-up menu. It offers commands like "Duplicate these displays" and "Extend these displays."

Click each monitor's icon and adjust its settings, if you like—for example, resolution (usually, you want the highest available), orientation, and brightness. Don't miss

"Make this my main display," either. The main display is the monitor that will contain your Start menu and desktop icons. (In Windows 10, your taskbar appears on *every* monitor. Nice touch.)

The "Change the size of text, apps, and other items" slider described earlier is even more important when your multiple monitors have different resolutions. You can use this slider to match them up better, so that windows don't abruptly shrink or blow up huge when they move from monitor to monitor.

Click Apply.

Windows asks you to sign out and sign back in again at this point. Do it. If you don't, you may wind up with some strange visual glitches, like a missing taskbar or funny window sizes.

When your PC lights up again, all should be well with your new multiscreen setup.

Tip: If you click the "Advanced display settings" link, and then "Display adapter properties," you're offered a collection of technical settings for your particular monitor model. Depending on your video driver, there may be tab controls here that adjust the *refresh rate* to eliminate flicker, install an updated adapter or monitor driver, and so on. In general, you rarely need to adjust these controls—except on the advice of a consultant or help-line technician.

Life with Multiple Screens

Once you've hooked up a second monitor, there are more tips than ever:

- You can drag a window from screen to screen with the mouse, even if it's a split-screen, "snapped" app. (Use the top edge of the app's screen as a handle.)

- You can make a window cycle through the left, center, and right positions on each screen by repeatedly pressing ⊞ and the → or ← keys.

  For example, suppose a window is now floating in the middle of Screen 1. Pressing ⊞+→ repeatedly first snaps the it to the right edge of Screen 1, then snaps it to the left edge of Screen 2, then releases it to the middle of Screen 2, and finally snaps it against the right edge of Screen 2. And now, if you press ⊞+→ yet again, that same window "wraps" around to become snapped against the left edge of Screen 1. It makes more sense when you try it.

- The system tray (notification area) and Action Center appear only on the main monitor.

- You can't pin different items onto each screen's taskbar.

- Eventually, Microsoft says, you'll be able to give each screen its own desktop wallpaper, exactly as you'd hope. But in the original Windows 10 release, there's no way to create that effect.

Virtual Screens

Here's one of Windows 10's best new features: a nearly infinite number of full-size *virtual monitors*. (Microsoft says that it's heard of people creating as many as 150 screens before this feature conks out. Don't worry—they're in therapy.)

Hard-core productivity mavens can tell you how useful it is to set up multiple screens. It's just fast and useful to have a wider view. You might dedicate each one to a different program or *kind* of program. Screen 1 might contain your email and chat windows, arranged just the way you like them. Screen 2 can hold Twitter and Facebook, their windows carefully arrayed. On Screen 3: your Web browser in Full Screen mode.

Ordinarily, of course, attaching more than a screen or two would be a massively expensive proposition, not to mention detrimental to your living space and personal relationships. But in Windows 10, these are virtual screens. They exist only in the PC's little head. You see only one at a time; you switch using a keystroke or a mouse click. You gain most of the advantages of owning a bunch of PC monitors—without spending a penny.

Now, virtual screens aren't a new idea—this sort of software has been available for years. But it's never been a standard feature of Windows, or so easy to use.

Creating a Desktop

To create a second desktop, enter Task View (click ▢ on the taskbar, or press ⊞+Tab; see page 226 for more on Task View).

Click "New desktop" (the big + icon at the right side) to create a new mini desktop at the bottom of the screen (see Figure 4-12).

Now it's time to park some windows onto the new desktop. At the moment, all the windows you had open are still clustered on the first screen, ingeniously named Desktop 1. When you point to the Desktop 1 thumbnail without clicking, those windows appear at 50 percent size on the main screen. You can drag one of them, or several, onto your new blank desktop (Desktop 2).

Tip: You can also right-click (or hold your finger down on) one of these app "cards." From the shortcut menu, choose "Move to"→"Desktop 2" (or whatever desktop you want it moved to).

Figure 4-12 shows this process.

Finally, exit Task View (click either desktop thumbnail, or anywhere on the main screen, or press Esc).

Tip: Once you've mastered the long way to create a desktop, as described above, you're ready for the turbo method. It's a much faster way to create a desktop—that doesn't involve a trip to Task View: Press Ctrl+⊞+D.

Switching Virtual Screens

Once you've got a couple of virtual monitors set up, the fun begins. Start by moving to the virtual screen you want; it's like changing the channel. Here are some ways to do that:

- **Press ⊞+Ctrl+← or ⊞+Ctrl+→ to rotate to the previous or next desktop.** (That is, while pressing ⊞+Ctrl, tap the right or left arrow key.)

- **Enter Task Mode again** (▢ on the taskbar), and choose the desktop you want.

When you make a switch, you see a flash of animation as one screen flies away and another appears. Now that you're "on" the screen you want, open programs and arrange windows onto it as usual.

Note: *Windows uses your main desktop's background picture for all additional desktops. It would be nice if you could choose a different wallpaper for each, to help you keep them straight—and, indeed, Microsoft says that feature will come in one of its steady Windows 10 improvements.*

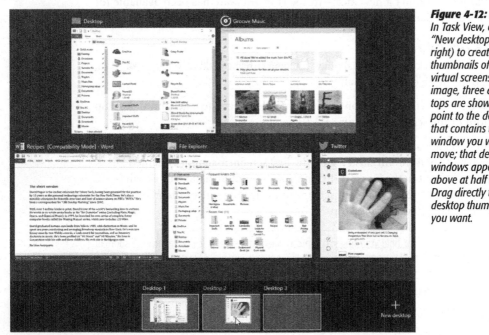

Figure 4-12:
In Task View, click "New desktop" (far right) to create the thumbnails of new virtual screens; in this image, three desktops are shown. Then point to the desktop that contains the app window you want to move; that desktop's windows appear above at half size. Drag directly to the desktop thumbnail you want.

Deleting a Desktop

To delete the desktop you're on, press Ctrl+⊞+F4. (You can also enter Task View, point to one of the screen thumbnails without clicking, and click the ✕ in its corner.)

That desktop disappears, and whatever windows were on it get shoved onto the desktop to its left.

CHAPTER 5

Cortana, Your Voice Assistant

Cortana is by far the biggest new feature in Windows 10. She's a crisply accurate, uncomplaining, voice-commanded servant. No voice training or special syntax is required. You can say, "Wake me up at 7:45," or "How do I get to the airport?" or "What's the weather going to be like in San Francisco this weekend?" or "What's 453 divided by 4?" or even "What's the meaning of life?"

You can ask questions about sports, news, weather, math, history, and much more. Each time, Cortana shows you the answer, fetched from the Internet (and usually speaks it, too).

Older speech-recognition systems work only if you issue certain limited commands with predictable syntax, like, "Call 445-2340" or "Open Microsoft Word." But Cortana has been programmed to respond to casual speech, normal speech. It doesn't matter if you say, "What's the weather going to be like in Tucson this weekend?" or "Give me the Tucson weather for this weekend" or "Will I need an umbrella in Tucson?" Cortana understands almost any variation.

And she understands regular, everyday speaking. You don't have to separate your words or talk weirdly; you just speak normally.

Now, it's not *Star Trek*. You can't ask Cortana to clean your gutters or to teach you French. (Well, you can *ask*. Anytime she doesn't have an answer for you, she opens up your Web browser and displays the Bing search results for your question.)

But, as you'll soon discover, the number of things she *can* do for you is rather impressive. Furthermore, Microsoft intends to keep adding to Cortana's intelligence through software updates.

Of course, none of this is a new idea. Apple introduced Siri (for the iPhone) in 2011, and Google followed with Google Now (for Android phones) in 2012.

But Microsoft's version is unique in three important respects:

- **Cortana runs on your PC.** In addition to Windows 10 phones and tablets, Cortana also runs on your laptop or desktop.

- **You can *type* your commands instead of speaking them.** That's handy when you're using your computer in, for example, church.

- **She speaks with an actual recorded human voice.** Siri is a synthesized, slightly robotic-sounding voice. But when Cortana speaks, you generally hear actual recordings of an actual actress.

Tip: Cortana is named after a voluptuous female character in Halo, the video game. In fact, Microsoft hired the same Cortana voice actress—Jen Taylor—to record Cortana's responses.

In a few spots, Cortana uses a synthetic voice—but it's derived *from* sound recordings by that same actress.

Note: Microsoft will also increase the number of languages that Cortana understands. Already, she understands English (American and British), Chinese (Simplified), French, Italian, German, and Spanish.

You can change her language in Settings→"Time & language"→"Region & language." Choose the language you want, set it to be your system's default, download the speech pack, and then, on the Speech tab, choose that language.

Setting Up Cortana

The first time you use Cortana, you're treated to a few setup steps—including a walloping privacy disclaimer (or, rather, lack-of-privacy disclaimer). Here's how it goes:

1. **Click in the search box.**

   A panel opens, directly above the search box (Figure 5-1). It lets you know that if you use Cortana, Microsoft intends to harvest a lot of information from your PC: your location, Web search history, calendar, address book, messages from texting apps, and so on.

   Microsoft says its intention in harvesting all this data is to make Cortana work better—both for you individually and for Windows fans at large. The company says, "Cortana doesn't use the information in the Cortana Notebook to send targeted ads." (Microsoft does use *some* information it gets from you—from non-Cortana sources—for the purposes of delivering targeted ads to you. This part, at least, you can turn off; visit *http://choice.microsoft.com/en-us*.)

   If all of this strikes you as a wee bit nosy, Microsoft cheerfully points out that you can turn off Cortana entirely (click "No thanks" in the info panel). Presto: Cortana won't collect any data from you. And you can't use Cortana.

Tip: You can also turn off Cortana later. Click in the search box; click the Settings icon (or Notebook, and then Settings); and turn off the top switch.

You can also *limit* the data Microsoft harvests by using the Notebook (page 216), by turning off the Cortana feature in the Edge browser (page 390), and by turning off the features described at the very end of this chapter.

Anyway. If you click "No thanks," you shut down the setup process. You can't use Cortana, and Microsoft can't get at your data.

But since you're reading this chapter, let's suppose you decide you do, in fact, want to turn on Cortana.

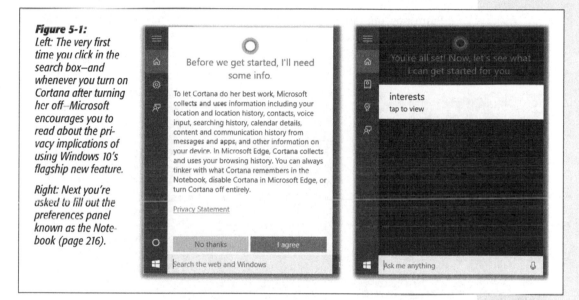

Figure 5-1:
Left: The very first time you click in the search box—and whenever you turn on Cortana after turning her off—Microsoft encourages you to read about the privacy implications of using Windows 10's flagship new feature.

Right: Next you're asked to fill out the preferences panel known as the Notebook (page 216).

2. **Choose "I agree."**

   Cortana asks what you want her to call you.

3. **Type your name or nickname, and then hit Next.**

   Unless you don't *want* her to address you by name; in that case, hit Skip.

At this point, you can start using Cortana. "You're all set!" she says. "Now, let's see what I can get started for you." And the light-gray type in the search box says, "Ask me anything." (When Cortana is turned off, it says, "Search the web and Windows.")

This same final screen invites you to "tap to view" your interests—which means the preferences screens known as the Notebook (Figure 5-1, right). Details on the Notebook are on page 216.

How to Use Cortana

If you want to ask Cortana something aloud, you must first get her attention. To do that, you have three choices:

- **Click the microphone button in the search box.** At this point, the Cortana *panel* opens above the search box (Figure 5-2, left). The text in the search box says "Listening."

- **Say, "Hey, Cortana."** Some people feel funny about knowing that their computers are always eavesdropping on the nearby conversation, so this feature comes turned off. To turn it on, click in the search box; in the column of buttons at left, click the Notebook icon (▣), then Settings, and then turn on "Hey Cortana."

From now on, instead of clicking or tapping, you can say, "Hey, Cortana," and then speak your request. The "listening" box opens without opening the whole card panel (Figure 5-2, right).

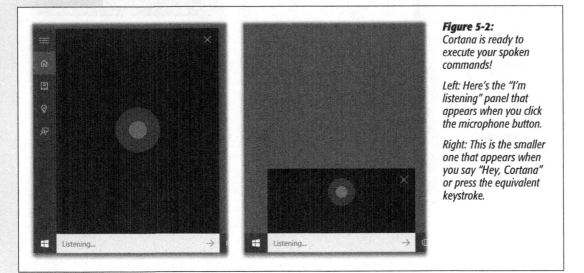

Figure 5-2:
Cortana is ready to execute your spoken commands!

Left: Here's the "I'm listening" panel that appears when you click the microphone button.

Right: This is the smaller one that appears when you say "Hey, Cortana" or press the equivalent keystroke.

- Press ⊞+C (for "Cortana," get it?). That keystroke opens the Cortana "listening" box, exactly as though you'd said "Hey, Cortana."

When you see Cortana's pulsing rings, Cortana is listening. Speak your question or command (see below). You don't have to lean into your microphone; Cortana works perfectly well at arm's length, on your desk in front of you.

As you speak, blocks of random alphabet letters spin madly, like the little fruit pictures on a slot machine. In seconds, you'll see them lock into words—the words you've said so far that Cortana has recognized.

When you're finished speaking, be quiet for a moment. Cortana presents (and speaks) an attractively formatted response. Or, worst case, opens your Web browser and displays the answer there, courtesy of Bing.com (Microsoft's search service).

Typing to Cortana

When speech is out of the question—if your request is private, if you don't have a microphone, if the room is too noisy, if talking might disturb others—you can also *type* your questions to Cortana. That's a surprisingly useful feature that's not available with Siri or Google Now.

Just click in the taskbar search box (or tap the ■ key) and then type whatever you would say.

What to Say to Cortana

Cortana comes with a cheat sheet to help you learn her capabilities. Just ask her (by typing or speaking), "What can I say?"

Cortana displays a handy screen of command examples (Figure 5-3).

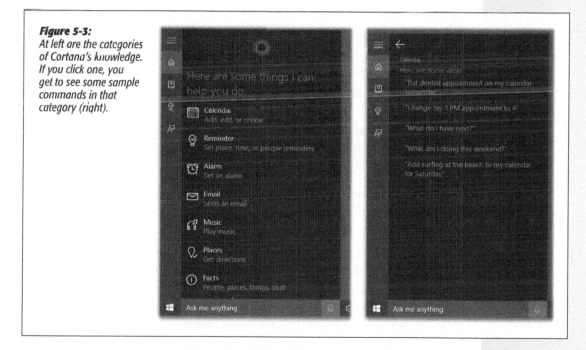

Figure 5-3:
At left are the categories of Cortana's knowledge. If you click one, you get to see some sample commands in that category (right).

In the meantime, what follows are the general categories of things you can say to Cortana.

Tip: Windows no longer comes with a built-in Help system. What it does have, though, is Cortana. You can ask her basic "How do I" questions like "How do I delete my browsing history?" or "How do I add an account?" and she'll lead you to the answer, often on the Web. Better than nothing, right?

Open Apps

If you don't learn to use Cortana for anything else, for the love of Mike, learn this one.

You can say, "Open Calendar" or "Launch Calculator."

Result: The corresponding app opens instantly. It's exactly the same as hunting around for the app in your Start menu—but without hunting around for the app in your Start menu.

Open Settings Panels

When you need to make tweakier changes to Settings, you can open the most important panels by voice. "Open WiFi settings," "Open touchpad settings," "Open Notification settings," "Open camera settings," "Open wallpaper settings," and so on.

Result: Cortana cheerfully displays the name of the corresponding Settings page and then opens it.

Change Your Settings

You can make changes to certain basic settings just by speaking your request. You can say, for example, "Turn on airplane mode," "Turn on quiet hours," or "Turn on WiFi." (You can't turn *off* airplane mode by voice, because Cortana doesn't work without an Internet connection.)

Result: Cortana makes the requested adjustment, tells you so, and displays the corresponding switch in case she misunderstood your intention.

Reminders

Like any good personal assistant, Cortana will give you reminders (Figure 5-4). For example, you can tell her, "Remind me to file my IRS tax extension." "Remind me to bring the science supplies to school." "Remind me to take my antibiotic."

Cortana's reminders are especially useful because they're aware of their own circumstances. Three things can trigger a reminder to appear on your screen:

- **A time.** "Tonight at 8:30 p.m., record *Game of Thrones*." "Remind me to work out tomorrow at 3 p.m." "In half an hour, remind me to turn off the oven." "Remind me to pick up Bo from the train station on September 10 at 4:25 pm."

- **A place.** You can say, "Remind me to visit the drugstore when I leave the office." "Remind me to water the lawn when I get home." "Remind me to get cash when I'm near an ATM."

Of course, if you're using a laptop or desktop PC, you may wonder what the point is; without GPS, how does it know where you are? But remember that your reminders sync to any *phones or tablets* you may own (if you've signed in with the same Microsoft account)—and they *do* know where you are. In other words, you're fine creating location-based reminders on your laptop or desktop, secure in the knowledge that your portable gadget will actually sound the reminder.

Tip: And how does Cortana know what you mean by "home," "the office," "work," and so on? You've taught her. See page 217.

- **A person.** You can say, "Remind me about the water damage the next time I talk to Kelly." Or "Next time I talk to André Smithers, remind me to discuss his tax return."

  Next time you get email from that person, or start writing an email to that person, this reminder will pop up. Rather brilliant, actually.

  If you have a Windows 10 phone, the notification will pop up when you and the other person call or text, too.

Result: Cortana displays what it understands your reminder to be. You can edit it before you accept it; if it's a time-based reminder, you can set up a recurring schedule, so that you're reminded every Tuesday at 4 (or whatever). Click Remind or say "Yes."

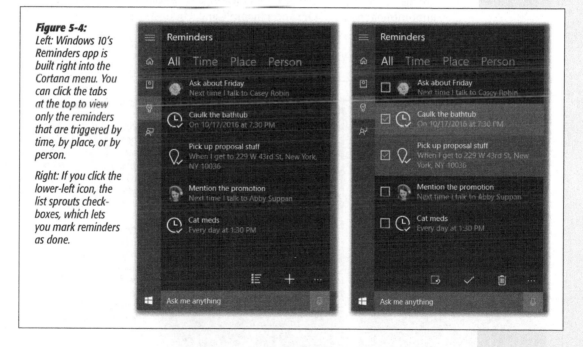

Figure 5-4:
Left: Windows 10's Reminders app is built right into the Cortana menu. You can click the tabs at the top to view only the reminders that are triggered by time, by place, or by person.

Right: If you click the lower-left icon, the list sprouts check-boxes, which lets you mark reminders as done.

Reminders you record this way show up in two places. First, Cortana includes her own built-in Reminders list, which you can peek at whenever you like (Figure 5-4). To see it, say or type to Cortana, "Open Reminders"—or just click the 💡 icon in the Cortana menu. You can delete a reminder or mark it as done, but you can't edit it.

Second, at the appointed time, a reminder appears as a pop-up notification at the lower-right corner of your screen, as described in Chapter 2.

At that point, you can click Complete (meaning "I'm done with this") or Snooze (meaning "remind me again in 5 minutes, 15 minutes, an hour, 4 hours, a day, or the next time I'm at this place/corresponding with this person").

Calendar

Cortana can make appointments for you. Considering how many tedious finger taps it usually takes to schedule an appointment in the Calendar app, this is an enormous improvement. "Put curling practice on my calendar for tomorrow." "Make an appointment with Patrick for Thursday at 3 p.m." "Set up a haircut at 9." "Create a meeting with Charlize this Friday at noon." "New appointment with Steve, next Sunday at 7." "Schedule a conference call at 5:30 p.m. tonight in my office."

Result: A slice of that day's calendar appears, filled in the way you requested (Figure 5-5). You can edit it manually or, if it looks good as is, say, "Yes" or "Add."

Tip: Cortana may also alert you to a conflict, something like this: "By the way, you have two other events at the same time."

You can also *move* previously scheduled meetings by voice. For example, "Move my 2:00 appointment to 2:30." Or cancel them: "Cancel budget review meeting." Or add people to a meeting: "Add Jan to my meeting with Casey."

You can even consult your calendar by voice (Figure 5-5, right).

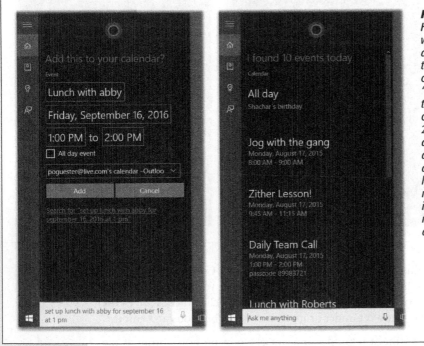

Figure 5-5:
Here's what it looks like when you (left) make an appointment using Cortana or (right) ask what's coming up. You can say: "What's on my calendar today?" "What's on my calendar for September 23?" "When's my next appointment?" "What do I have next?" "What does the rest of my day look like?" "When is my meeting with Charlize?" "Where is my next meeting?" "What am I doing this weekend?"

Result: Cortana reads the answer and handsomely displays the specified appointment.

Alarms

You can say, "Wake me up at 7:35 a.m." "Cancel my 7:35 a.m. alarm." "Wake me up in six hours." "Cancel my 6 a.m. alarm" (or "Delete my…" or "Turn off my…").

This is *so* much quicker than setting the alarm the usual way.

Result: Cortana says, "Sure. Your alarm is set for 7:35 a.m." (or whatever).

Tip: Cortana doesn't understand "timer" commands, like "Set a timer for 20 minutes." If you try, though, she'll cheerfully open up a Web page that lists *online* timers. That's handy when you're baking something, limiting your kid's video-game time, and so on.

Clock

"What time is it?" "What time is it in San Francisco?" "What's today's date?"

Result: Cortana shows a clock identifying the time in question.

FREQUENTLY ASKED QUESTION

How to Make Microsoft Forget All About You

OK, I know you're going to call me a member of the Tinfoil Hat Club or whatever, but I really do not want Microsoft collecting personal information about me. How do I wipe Cortana and Microsoft clean of everything they've harvested?

You're not alone in worrying that Microsoft may be a little overzealous in its data collection. The company admits that if you use Cortana, Windows uploads to Microsoft "your calendar, contacts, location triggered by Cortana, and browsing history."

Your *calendar, contacts, location, and search history.* Oh, is that all?

(It's actually even worse. By "search history," Microsoft actually means *Cortana* history; Microsoft records and stores online everything you've ever asked her.)

You might assume that if you turn off Cortana altogether, you delete Microsoft's copy of all this personal data. And that *does* delete the data from your computer, and stops Microsoft from learning anything new about you. But it doesn't delete the information that Microsoft has already collected and stored online.

To erase *that,* click in the search box; hit Notebook (page 216), 🗒 and then ⚙. Click "Manage what Cortana knows about me in the cloud."

Your browser opens to a special Microsoft Web page. After you log in, you can make Microsoft forget all of these things:

Your calendar, address book, location, and search history: Under the heading "Under Other Cortana Data and Personalized Speech, Inking and Typing," hit Clear.

Your saved places ("Work," "Home," and so on): Under the heading "Saved places," select Bing Maps; on the next page, hit "My places." Click the ✕ next to each location that you want to delete (and then click Yes to confirm).

Your Cortana command history: Under the "Search history" heading, hit "Search History page." Here, incredibly, is the entire list of things you've asked Cortana. When you point to one of these tiles, a Clear button appears in the corner; click it to delete that query. Or hit "Clear All" (top right) to erase your *entire* query history.

Your Notebook interest preferences (like favorite restaurant types): Under the Interests heading, hit Clear.

For more complicated questions, like "What's the date a week from Friday?" she opens a Web page showing links that might answer it.

Weather

This one's easy.

"What's the weather going to be today?" "What's the forecast for tomorrow?" "Show me the weather this week." "Will it snow in Dallas this weekend?" "Check the forecast for Memphis on Friday." "What's the forecast for tonight?" "What's the humidity right now?"

Result: A convenient miniature weather display for the date and place you specified (Figure 5-6, left).

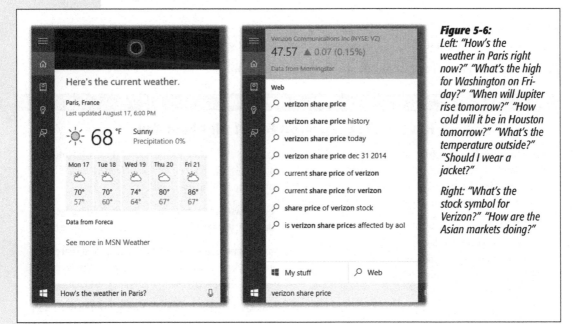

Figure 5-6:
Left: "How's the weather in Paris right now?" "What's the high for Washington on Friday?" "When will Jupiter rise tomorrow?" "How cold will it be in Houston tomorrow?" "What's the temperature outside?" "Should I wear a jacket?"

Right: "What's the stock symbol for Verizon?" "How are the Asian markets doing?"

Stocks

If you phrase your requests just the right way, Cortana can serve as a one-woman exchange bureau:

"How is Microsoft stock doing?" "What's the bitcoin exchange rate?" "How much is Facebook stock worth?"

Result: A tiny stock graph (Figure 5-6, right).

Sports

At last you have a buddy who's just as obsessed with sports trivia as you are. You can say things like "How did the Indians do last night?" "What was the score of the last Yankees game?"

You can ask lots of other things, too, but Cortana will hand you off to your Web browser to see the answers (courtesy of a Bing.com search): "Who has the best batting average?" "Who has scored the most runs against the Red Sox?" "Who has scored the most goals in British soccer?" "Which quarterback had the most sacks last year?" "Show me the roster for the Giants." "Who is pitching for Tampa this season?" "Is anyone on the Marlins injured right now?"

Result: Neat little box scores or factoids, complete with team logos.

Flights

Cortana is quite the aviation nerd. She knows the takeoff and landing times of every flight today, which comes in incredibly handy—especially if you're the person who's supposed to *meet* somebody on that flight.

"What time does Delta flight 300 take off?" "Flight status United 1411." "What's the status of Southwest Airlines flight 33?"

Result: A neat little graphic (Figure 5-7).

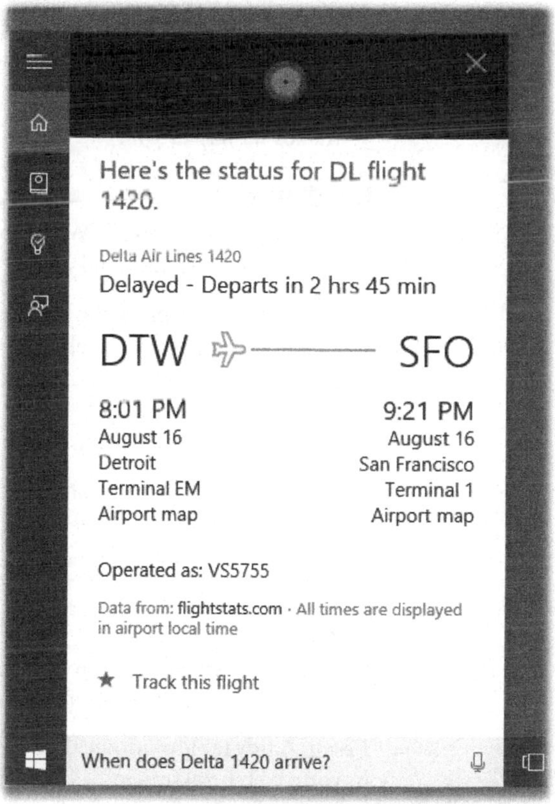

Figure 5-7:
Cortana is an aviation-details hound. She'll show you the departure, status, and landing info for any flight. See the "Track this flight" link? She's offering to continue monitoring that flight, so that you see a card on the Cortana home screen that keeps you posted.

Here's the status for DL flight 1420.

Delta Air Lines 1420
Delayed - Departs in 2 hrs 45 min

DTW ✈———— SFO

8:01 PM — 9:21 PM
August 16 — August 16
Detroit — San Francisco
Terminal EM — Terminal 1
Airport map — Airport map

Operated as: VS5755

Data from: flightstats.com · All times are displayed in airport local time

★ Track this flight

When does Delta 1420 arrive?

Cortana can also track flights for you—meaning that she'll display updates as cards on her home screen. All you have to do is search for a flight, as described above; a Cortana card asks, "Would you like to track flight DL 300?" (or whatever). If you click Yes, you'll continue to see a status card for that flight until it lands.

Packages

Here's a crazy feature that's a perfect fit for a personal assistant: Windows' Mail app keeps tabs on packages you're expecting.

- **Automatic:** Cortana keeps an eye out for automatically generated emails from certain Web-based businesses, like Amazon.com, Target, Walmart, Apple, eBay, and the Microsoft Store. Cortana scans them to see if they contain anything about packages that have been shipped to you.

  If so, you see a card about its status on the Cortana home screen; if the email contains a FedEx or UPS tracking number, you'll see that shipping info, too. These shipping updates also appear in the Notebook, on the Packages tab.

- **Manual.** You can also paste in a tracking number manually—from FedEx, UPS, or DHL—to make Cortana track its progress as it wends its way toward you. You can paste this number directly into the search box, or you can go to the Notebook→ Packages tab, hit "Add a package," and paste it in there.

  Once again, you'll see cards in the Cortana panel that track that shipment as it makes its way to you.

Headlines

"Show me today's news." "What are the top headlines?" "Show me the local news." "Show me the international news."

Result: Cortana displays the first couple of breaking-news headlines, with a photo, right there on her own panel.

Tip: She also reads the headlines aloud. You might wonder: Haven't all of Cortana's utterances been prerecorded by an actress? (Answer: Yes.) Then how can Cortana read headlines she's never seen before?

Because Microsoft *also* created a synthesized version of Cortana's voice, one that can read any text aloud. You won't be especially fooled–the synthesized one sounds a lot more artificial and broken-up than the recorded one–but at least she tries.

Movies

Cortana also knows current showtimes in theaters. You can say, "What movies are out right now?" "What movies are opening this week?"

Result: A tidy table of movie theaters or movie showtimes. (Tap or click one for details in your Web browser.)

Note: You can ask all kinds of other movie questions—"Who was the star of *Groundhog Day*?" "Who directed *Chinatown*?" "What is *Waterworld* rated?" "What movie won Best Picture in 1952?"—but Cortana hands you off to a Bing search in your browser to see those answers.

Email

You can compose new email messages by voice, which is incredibly handy, especially for short notes.

Anytime you use the phrase "about," that becomes the subject line for your new message. "Email Dad about the reunion." "Email Tracy about the dance on Friday." "Mail Ellen about Saturday's flight."

You can also specify the priority (if your email account type offers that feature), the email address (if the recipient has more than one), and more than one addressee. For example: "New email to Freddie Gershon from my Gmail account." "Send an urgent mail to Robin McTeague." "Email Frank and Cindy Vosshall and Peter Love about the picnic."

Result: Cortana's panel shows the piece of outgoing email (Figure 5-8). Usually, you have a few more tasks to complete before you send it. For example, if you've indicated only the subject and addressee, Cortana prompts you for the body of the message. Cortana asks, "Send it? Add more? Or make changes?"

There's also a "Continue in Outlook" link (or whatever your email program is), so that you can wrap this up with the more complete set of tools in your mail app.

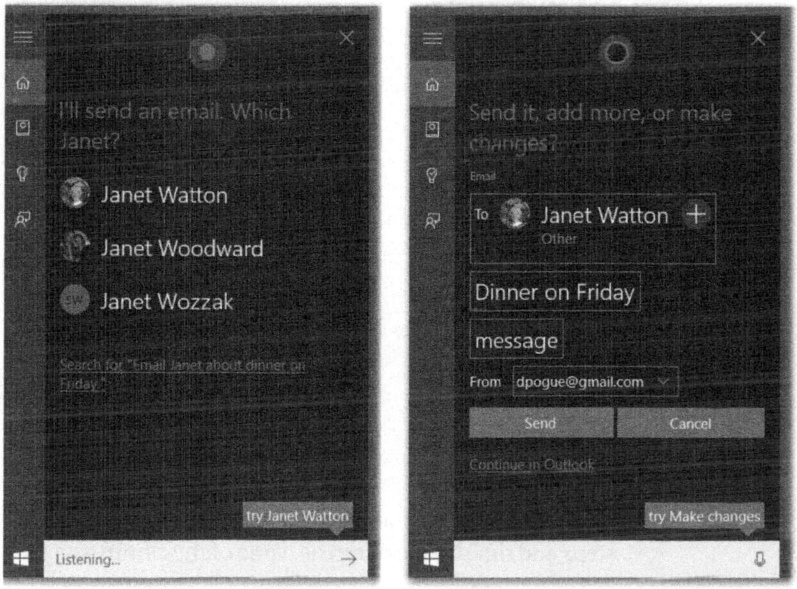

Figure 5-8:
Left: If your address book lists more than one person with this name—or more than one email address for her—Cortana asks you to speak the one you want. (You can say, for example, "the second one.")

Right: Here's the proposed message, ready to send. You can edit any of the text in these boxes.

Maps

Cortana is plugged into Windows 10's Maps app and its database of the world's stores, restaurants, and points of interest.

Queries about distance, traffic, and business details are all fair game: "Show me a map of 200 West 70th Street, New York City." "How far is it to JFK?" "How long would it take me to get to Pittsburgh?" "What time does Walmart open?" "What's traffic like on the way home?" "Is Barracuda Café open on Mondays?" "Find good Italian restaurants near me."

Note: Are Cortana's "time to get there" calculations based on driving time—or public-transportation time? That's up to you. You make this setting in the Notebook preferences, as described on page 218.

Result: In most cases, Cortana displays a little map, or the answer to your query, right in her panel (Figure 5-9). Sometimes you have to specify *which* Walmart (or Starbucks, or CVS) you're asking about. On the "find restaurants" query, your Web browser opens with Bing search results.

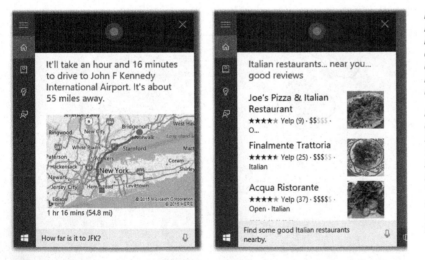

Figure 5-9:
Left: Cortana is tied into the Map app's database. So you can ask about any address in the world and see it quickly on a map.

Right: She also does a decent job of finding restaurants. Your request can specify things like "near me," "open now," and "with good reviews," along with the type of restaurant you're looking for.

Playing Music

Instead of fumbling around in Windows' music app (called Groove), save yourself steps and time by speaking the name of the album, song, or band: "Play some Beatles."

"Play 'I'm a Barbie Girl.'" "Play some jazz." "Put on my jogging playlist." "Play the next track." "Pause." "Resume." "Shuffle the music."

Result: Cortana plays (or skips, shuffles, or pauses) the music you asked for—without ever leaving whatever app you were using.

Identifying Music

Cortana can listen to the music playing in the room and try to identify it (song name, singer, album, and so on). Ask her, "What song is this?" or "What's this song?"

Result: Cortana listens to the music playing at your home/office/bar/restaurant/picnic— and identifies the song by name and performer.

Math and Conversions

"What's 473 times 6?" "What's the cube root of 480?" "How much is 23 dollars in pesos?" "What's the exchange rate between dollars and euros?" "Convert 60 euros to dollars." "How many teaspoons are in a gallon?" "What's a 17 percent tip on 62 dollars for three people?"

Result: Most of the time, Cortana does something peculiar, as shown in Figure 5-10.

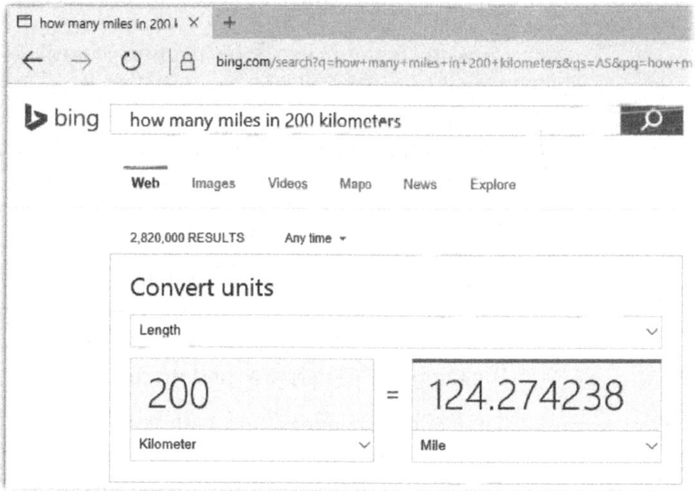

Figure 5-10:
Cortana generally doesn't reply to math or unit-conversion questions right on her own panel. Almost always, she opens your Web browser and displays the answer there, in an online calculator. (She displays the answer right on the Cortana panel only in the case of currency conversions.)

Definitions

When you're not sure what some word means, ask Cortana. "What does *pecuniary* mean?" "Define *schadenfreude.*" "Give me a definition of *pernicious.*"

Result: The definition, presented as though on a dictionary page, on Bing.com—complete with a Play button so you can hear the word's pronunciation.

Calling

On a Windows 10 phone, Cortana can place phone calls for you. "Make a call to John at home." "Call Jan on speakerphone." "Call Cindy." "Call Kelly, home." "Redial." "Dial 512-444-1212."

Result: Cortana hands you off to the Phone app and places the call. At this point, it's just as though you'd initiated the call yourself.

Texting

If you're using a phone, Cortana executes commands like "Text Dad," "Message Lydia," and "Show me messages from Billy." You can also dictate a text message like this: "Text Horatio, 'Do you want to grab lunch?'"

Result: Cortana opens the Messages app and displays your outgoing message, ready to send (or shows the messages you've requested).

Facts and Figures

This is a huge category. The possibilities here could fill an entire chapter—or an entire encyclopedia.

You can say things like "How many days until Valentine's Day?" "When was Abraham Lincoln born?" "What's the capital of Belgium?" "When is the next solar eclipse?" "What's the tallest mountain in the world?" "What's the price of gold right now?" "Who is the tallest woman in the world?" "Who is the president of Portugal?" "What is the capital of Qatar?" "How old is Joe Biden?"

Result: Often, the answer!

In many cases, though, Cortana hands you off to your Web browser, where Bing.com does the search for you. That's the case with, for example: "How many calories are in a Hershey bar?" "What movie won the Oscar for Best Picture in 1985?" "Show me the Big Dipper." "Generate a random number." "What flights are overhead?"

Thanks to that integration with your browser, Cortana can also harness the entire wisdom of Wikipedia. You can say, for example, "Search Wikipedia for Harold Edgerton," or "Tell me about Abraham Lincoln," or "Show me the Wikipedia page about Richard Branson."

You may never find the end of the things Cortana understands, or the ways that she can help you. If her repertoire seems intimidating at first, start simple—use her to open apps, schedule alarms, create appointments, and check the traffic on your commute. You can build up your bag of tricks as your confidence builds.

Search the Web

"Search the Web for a 2014 Ford Mustang." "Search for healthy smoothie recipes." "Search Wikipedia for the Thunderbirds." "Search for news about the Netflix-Amazon merger."

Tip: Cortana uses Microsoft's Bing search service to perform its Web searches. If you prefer Google, the world of clever code writers awaits.

What you need is Bing2Google, a free extension (add-on) for Google's Chrome browser. It requires that you install Chrome and make it your preferred Web browser instead of Microsoft's own Edge (Chapter 10)—but most people would consider that a wise move anyway.

You can get Bing2Google from this book's "Missing CD" page at *www.missingmanuals.com*.

Wikipedia is a search type all its own. "Search Wikipedia for Harold Edgerton." "Look up Mariah Carey on Wikipedia."

Result: Cortana opens your browser and displays the results of a Bing.com search.

When Things Go Wrong

If Cortana doesn't have a good enough Internet connection to do her thing, she'll tell you so.

If she's working properly but misrecognizes your instructions, you'll know it, because you can see her interpretation of what you said.

What happens a *lot* is that Cortana recognizes what you said, but it isn't within her world of comprehension. In those cases, she automatically opens your Web browser and does a Bing.com search. If Cortana doesn't know it, the Internet surely does.

Cortana's Personality

Cortana's understanding of casual spoken commands is so impressive that you might sometimes think she's almost human. And that, of course, is exactly what Microsoft wants you to think. A team of Microsoft writers has put a *lot* of effort into giving her perky responses to all kinds of off-kilter things that you might say to her.

For example, if you ask her, "What is the meaning of life?" she might say, "We all shine on, my friend." Or "I've heard from a reliable source that the answer is 42. (Still no word on what the question is.)" You'll get that joke if you've ever read *The Hitchhiker's Guide to the Galaxy.*

Tip: Clearly, somebody over at Microsoft has been paying close attention to Siri; while the silly responses are always different from Apple's, the silly *questions* Cortana knows how to answer are nearly identical. Often, though, Cortana's replies are more fun, because they're recordings of an actual actress—not a synthesized voice. So Cortana can tell jokes with interpretation, funny accents, and so on.

Cortana is full of such comebacks (Figure 5-11)—she's especially adept at quotes from sci-fi movies.

There are whole Web sites dedicated to her snark, but here are a few hundred of the best examples.

Note: The list here won't ruin the fun, because Cortana has several different comebacks to many of these questions.

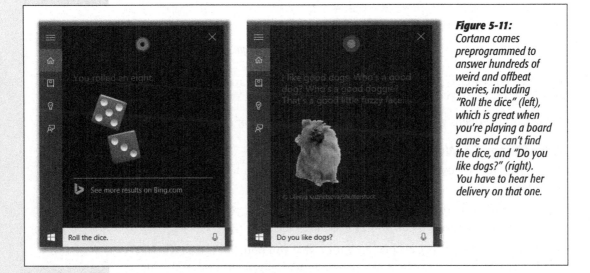

Figure 5-11:
Cortana comes preprogrammed to answer hundreds of weird and offbeat queries, including "Roll the dice" (left), which is great when you're playing a board game and can't find the dice, and "Do you like dogs?" (right). You have to hear her delivery on that one.

You: "Who's your daddy?" Cortana: "Technically speaking, that'd be Bill Gates. No big deal."

You: "Open the pod bay doors, Hal." Cortana: "Dave, this conversation can serve no purpose anymore."

You: "May the force be with you." Cortana (British accent): "The force is with you, young Skywalker, but you are not a Jedi yet."

You: "Knock knock." Cortana: "Knock knock. Who's there? A little old lady. A little old lady who? I didn't know you could yodel!"

You: "Roll the dice!" Cortana: "Nine." (She gives a different answer each time—and displays a matching pair of dice each time.)

You: "What are you wearing?" Cortana: "Just a little something I picked up in Engineering."

You: "Who's the boss?" Cortana: "You're in charge here!"

You: "Beam me up, Cortana!" Cortana (in a Scottish accent): "Sorry, Captain! I need more power!"

You: "How much wood would a woodchuck chuck if a woodchuck could chuck wood?" Cortana: "Impressive. Most impressive."

You: "Guess what." Cortana: "Chicken butt."

You: "Talk dirty to me." Cortana: "No thanks."

You: "Do you know Siri?" Cortana: "I know her, but I don't KNOW her, know her."

You: "What is better: Google or Bing?" Cortana (showing Bing logo): "Is that a trick question?" (Bizarrely, this doesn't work if you say, "*Which* is better…" You have to say "What is better…")

You: "Do you have a religion?" Cortana: "Artificially intelligent types like me can't experience spirituality."

You: "Do an impression." Cortana (in Harry Potter voice, with special magic-wand graphic): "Expecto Patronum!"

You: "Why are you naked?" Cortana: "Naked? I'm pixels in a circle shape. I think you're bringing your own issues to this one."

Tip: Cortana can even help you pass the time. If you say, "Play the movie game," she'll offer you a series of clues about popular movies until you guess them.

Got the idea? Great. Then here are a few other things to say to Cortana when you get bored:

Conversation starters

Talk to me.

Say something.

Ask me a question.

Surprise me.

Tell me a joke.

Tell me a riddle.

Tell me a story.

Sing me a song.

Sing me a lullaby.

Tell me a bedtime story.

Tell me a science joke.

Tell me a dirty joke.

Flip a coin.

Tell me a secret.

Rock, paper, scissors, lizard, Spock.

Do a barrel roll.

Why did the chicken cross the road?

Who is your creator?

Why are we here?

Critters

How do you feel about cats?

How do you feel about dogs?

What does a cat say?

What does a dog say?

What does a horse say?

What does a pig say?

What does a rooster say?

What does the fox say?

The tech industry

What do you think about Clippy?

Where is Clippy?

Are you better than Siri?

Are you better than Google Now?

What do you think of Siri?

Are you jealous of Siri?

What do you think about Google?

What do you think about Yahoo?

Which is better—Cortana or Siri?

Which is better: Xbox or PlayStation?

What's the best search engine?

What's the best computer?

What's the best tablet?

What's the best smartphone?

Do you like Surface?

Do you like Windows?

Do you like Windows 10?

Do you like Microsoft Office?

Do you like iOS?

Do you like Android?

Do you like Apple?

Do you like Steve Ballmer?

Do you like Satya Nadella?

Do you like Bill Gates?

Do you like Steve Jobs?

Tip: Any of the "Do you like" questions can also begin, "What do you think of…."

Pop-culture references

What's the first rule of Fight Club?

What is the second rule of Fight Club?

What is the airspeed velocity of an unladen swallow?

What is your quest?

Who lives in a pineapple under the sea?

Beam me up, Scotty!

Can you speak Klingon?

Use the force.

Set phasers to stun.

Do you know Jarvis?

Where can I hide a dead body?

Do you like Jimmy Fallon?

What is Minecraft?

Do you like Minecraft?

Hey, Siri!

Cortana and you

Yo!

Testing.

What's up?

I like you.

You're cool.

You're cute.

You're funny.

You're so good to me.

What have you been up to?

What are you doing later?

What's your number?

Where do you live?

Do you have a boyfriend?

Am I your best friend?

Will you date me?

Dance.

What do you want?

Are you drunk?

What are you doing?

Can I kiss you?

You are awesome!

I love you!

Do you love me?

You love me.

What is love?

Can you cook?

Are you married?

Will you marry me?

Can I borrow some money?

You are annoying.

What's wrong with you?

Shut up.

I hate you.

Sorry.

Good night!

About You

I'm bored.

I'm lonely.

I'm tired.

I'm happy.

I'm confused.

I'm angry.

I'm depressed.

I'm drunk.

I'm hungry.

Who's your boss?

Who am I?

Am I ugly?

Am I handsome?

How do I look?

Do you think I'm pretty?

About Cortana

Who are you?

Cortana!

What are you?

Are you human?

Are you real?

How old are you?

Who is your creator?

Do you have feelings?

Where does your name from?

What does "Cortana" mean?

Can I change your name?

Who is your voice?

How do you work?

What do you look like?

When is your birthday?

What are your measurements?

Why are you blue?

Are you male or female?

You have beautiful eyes.

Are you hot?

Are you dead?

Are you alive?

Where are you from?

Do you have any siblings?

Do you have a sister?

Do you have any kids?

What do you like to do in your spare time?

What's your favorite color?

What's your favorite music?

What's your favorite day?

What's your favorite animal?

What's your favorite band?

What's your favorite TV show?

Where do babies come from?

Do you have a Facebook page?

What's your favorite car?

What's your favorite food?

What do you eat?

Do you like your job?

Do you believe in ghosts?

What's your favorite movie?

Where were you born?

Who made you?

Are you a Democrat or a Republican?

Do you sleep?

Do you dream?

Do you drink?

Do you eat?

Do you have a brain?

Are you stupid?

Are you intelligent?

Are you awake?

Do you believe in God?

Do you believe in love?

What's your secret?

Are you kidding me?

You're the best assistant ever.

Thank you!

Halo references

Where is Master Chief?	Tell me about Halo 5.	Do you know Jen Taylor?
Do you love Master Chief?	Which Halo game do you like the most?	What is rampancy?
Who is Doctor Halsey?	Will you be reborn in Halo 5?	What's the story of the next Halo game?
What is a Halo?		Tell me about Elites.

Tip: Other Halo entities Cortana can tell you about: Grunts, Hunters, Jackals, Prophets, Buggers, Brutes, Prometheans, Didact, Guilty Spark, the Librarian, Flood, Beamish.

Cortana's Cards—and the Notebook

When you click into the search box, *before* you say or type anything, you see a panel filled with *cards* about your world—little panels that offer news headlines, weather, sports scores, restaurant recommendations, updates about your flights and your commute, and so on. (Microsoft calls this panel Cortana Home.) This is Cortana's second skill: She's a helpful clipping service for updates on topics you want to monitor.

You can, and should, customize *which* kinds of cards appear in this panel.

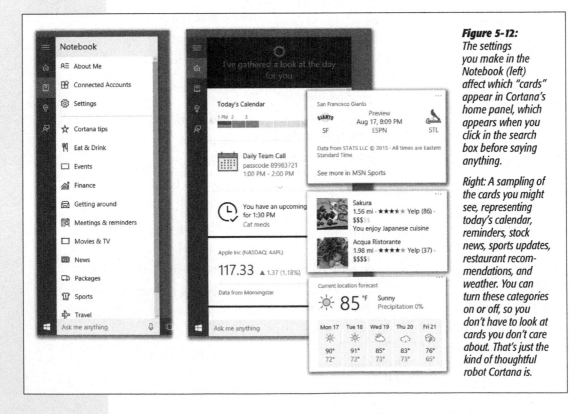

Figure 5-12:
The settings you make in the Notebook (left) affect which "cards" appear in Cortana's home panel, which appears when you click in the search box before saying anything.

Right: A sampling of the cards you might see, representing today's calendar, reminders, stock news, sports updates, restaurant recommendations, and weather. You can turn these categories on or off, so you don't have to look at cards you don't care about. That's just the kind of thoughtful robot Cortana is.

Once the Cortana panel is open, you can click the ⊡ icon at top left to open what Microsoft calls the Notebook (Figure 5-12).

Microsoft says that, in designing what it hoped would become the world's best virtual assistant, it spent time interviewing *human* personal assistants. It discovered that many of the best ones carry around a physical notebook, filled with details about their clients: their preferred airline, beverage, salad dressing, flowers, hotel chain, and so on.

But the Notebook really just means "preference settings for the little info cards."

Here are the tabs the Notebook offers you:

- **About Me.** Here's where you can change the name Cortana uses to address you ("Master," "All-Knowing Overlord," or whatever you prefer).

  If you hit "Edit favorites" and then the + button, you can build a list of places you go often. For sure, you should enter your home and work addresses, so that later Cortana will know how long your commute will take, and can advise you when to leave for work (or home). See Figure 5-13.

  When you've finished recording the addresses that mean something to you, click the Notebook icon (⊡) to return to the list of tabs.

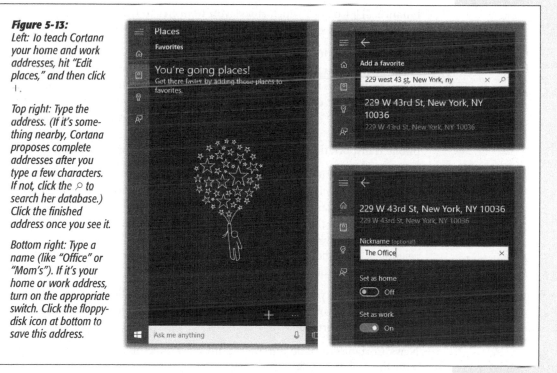

Figure 5-13:
Left: To teach Cortana your home and work addresses, hit "Edit places," and then click +.

Top right: Type the address. (If it's something nearby, Cortana proposes complete addresses after you type a few characters. If not, click the ⌕ to search her database.) Click the finished address once you see it.

Bottom right: Type a name (like "Office" or "Mom's"). If it's your home or work address, turn on the appropriate switch. Click the floppy-disk icon at bottom to save this address.

- **Connected Accounts.** If you have an Office 365 account, enter its details here, so that Cortana can access your online calendar, so she'll be able to flag upcoming appointments.

- **Settings.** Here are the on/off switches for Cortana herself, the "Hey Cortana" trigger, the flight-info message search, Taskbar Tidbits (Cortana displays messages in the search box), and other options; they're described at the end of this chapter.

The rest of the items in the Notebook govern the "cards" that appear in the Cortana home panel. On each of these panels, you can specify *whether* that type of card will appear, and *which kinds* of cards. For example:

- **Cortana Tips.** If this switch is on, the Cortana panel will display cards that provide tips on using Cortana.

- **Eat & Drink.** You'll see cards—with the frequency of dining out that you indicate here—that suggest restaurants, based on your preferences for atmosphere, price, and cuisine type.

- **Events.** Would you like Cortana cards to let you know about local events? And if so, what types? (You get choices like Arts & Crafts, Business & Tech, Dance, Music, Shopping, and so on.)

- **Finance.** Tell Cortana which stocks you want her to track for you. Click "Add a stock" to get started.

- **Getting around.** Monitoring traffic is one of Cortana's specialties. Using the various on/off switches on this panel, you can invite Cortana's cards to let you know when there's traffic news that might affect your travel to appointments on your calendar (for which you've entered an address) or to the places you set up on the "About Me" page; when it's time to leave for home or work; or when the last bus or train is leaving. Finally, you can tell Cortana whether you usually travel by driving or public transportation (click the Driving or Transit button to switch this setting).

- **Meetings & reminders.** If you have an Office 365 subscription, Cortana can see what you've got on your calendar and in your email. The options here turn that knowledge into cards on the Cortana panel: "Meeting prep" (the attendees for your next meeting), "Daily timeline" (a little graph of your day), "Related documents" (files related to your next meeting, if they appeared in email or on your calendar), and "Show reminders on Cortana home" (do you even want Cortana cards to remind you of stuff?).

- **Movies & TV.** Do you want Cortana to show you cards about movies? Showtimes and trailers? Do you want to play "predict the winners" for awards shows? Here's where you tell Cortana.

- **News.** Cortana's cards do very well as tiny news bulletins, on topics you can specify with these switches: local news, bigger news, news based on your interests, and news people are searching for right now. You can also request news "category cards" (broad areas like sports, business, entertainment, politics, health, and so on) and "topic cards" (type in "2020 Olympics" or "Jennifer Lawrence" or anything you want Cortana to track); at the bottom of the panel, you'll find the controls you need to choose *which* topics and *which* categories you want to see.

- **Packages.** When you've shipped a package (or you're expecting one), Cortana can keep you posted on its journey to or from you. Just click "Add a package," and then enter a FedEx or UPS tracking number. (See "Packages" on page 206.)

- **Sports.** What good would a personal assistant be if it couldn't keep you posted on the successes and failures of your favorite teams? Click "Add a team" to specify which major-league teams you want to follow. You can opt to see recent game scores, upcoming game schedules, or both.

- **Travel.** Cortana can show you updates about your flights, as well as notifications about the traffic you'll encounter on your way to the airport and the weather where you're going.

- **Weather.** You can opt for *nearby* weather reports, but you can also store distant cities whose weather you want to follow. You can specify what units you want for temperature (Fahrenheit, for example) and whether you want Cortana to flag "weather incidents" (special cards for things like thunderstorms).

Cortana Settings

If you click into the search box, then click Notebook (⬛), and then Settings (⚙), you find some very important controls. Here they are:

- **Master on/off switch.** At the top of the panel, you'll see that you can turn off Cortana completely.

  Microsoft will collect no data from your queries, and you won't be able to use any of Cortana's features.

  And the text in the search box changes from "Ask me anything" to "Search the web and Windows." No more spoken requests, no more cute jokes.

- **"Hey Cortana" on/off switch.** Here's the feature that lets you trigger Cortana by voice—by saying, "Hey, Cortana" before a command, rather than clicking in the search box.

  There are two reasons you might want to turn off this otherwise excellent feature. First, the constant audio monitoring costs you a small amount of battery power on a laptop or tablet.

  Second, maybe you somehow worry that Microsoft can *hear* you if your PC is *listening all the time,* and the thought gives you chills.

  The fact is, Microsoft captures only the audio of your command itself—nothing before "Hey, Cortana"—but whatever.

(Besides. You're going to start worrying about Microsoft spying on you *now*?)

- **Find flights and more.** If this option is turned on, then Windows 10 continuously monitors your email for *flight and shipping* information. That business of tracking flights and packages is actually one of the coolest features of Cortana (page 205). But if the notion of your computer "reading" your email creeps you out, you can turn it off here.

- **Taskbar tidbits.** The search box usually contains the starter prompt, "Ask me anything." This option lets Cortana replace that text with more interesting variations. You may see, for example, "What's up?" "Good morning!" or "Need something, Casey?" (or whatever your name is).

- **Respond best.** Out of the box, Cortana's voice recognition responds equally well to anyone's voice. If nobody uses your PC (or at least this account on your PC) but you, then you'll get better accuracy by turning on "To me."

At this point, Cortana shows you six sample sentences and asks you to read them aloud (Figure 5-14).

Tip: One of the most useful Cortana settings isn't in Cortana at all: your choice of how Cortana is represented on the taskbar. Instead of the full-size search box, you may prefer just a Cortana logo, or nothing at all. (The keystrokes for using Cortana still work, and so does saying "Hey, Cortana.") See page 95.

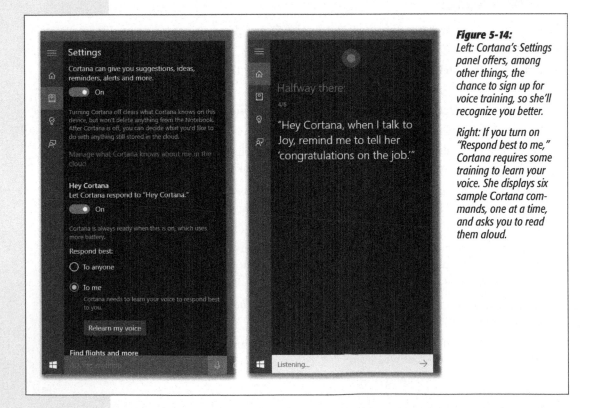

Figure 5-14:
Left: Cortana's Settings panel offers, among other things, the chance to sign up for voice training, so she'll recognize you better.

Right: If you turn on "Respond best to me," Cortana requires some training to learn your voice. She displays six sample Cortana commands, one at a time, and asks you to read them aloud.

Part Two:
The Programs
of Windows 10

2

Chapter 6: Programs & Documents

Chapter 7: Settings & Control Panel

Chapter 8: The Windows Starter Apps

Programs & Documents

When you get right down to it, an operating system is nothing more than a home base from which to launch applications (programs). And you, as a Windows person, are particularly fortunate, since more programs are available for Windows than for any other operating system on earth.

But when you launch a program, you're no longer necessarily in the world Microsoft designed for you. Programs from other companies work a bit differently, and there's a lot to learn about how Windows handles programs that were born before it was.

This chapter covers everything you need to know about installing, removing, launching, and managing programs; using programs to generate documents; and understanding how documents, programs, and Windows communicate with one another.

Note: In the beginning, *programs* were things that ran on computers; *apps* ran on phones and tablets. Microsoft would very much like the Great Merging of These Categories to hurry up. So in Windows 10, it refers to all of them as "apps." (Except in older dialog boxes, like the old Control Panel, where they're still called "programs." Sigh.) In this book, "apps" and "programs" are the same thing, and both terms appear interchangeably to spice things up.

Opening Programs

Windows lets you launch (open) programs in many different ways:

- Choose a program's name from the Start menu.
- Choose a program's name from the "All apps" list.
- Click a program's icon on the taskbar.

- Double-click an application's program-file icon in the This PC→Local Disk (C:) →Program Files→[application] folder, or highlight the application's icon and then press Enter.

- Press a key combination you've assigned to be the program's shortcut.

- Press ⊞+R, type the program file's name in the Open text box, and then press Enter.

- Let Windows launch the program for you, either at startup (page 516) or at a time you've specified (see Task Scheduler, page 502).

- Open a document using any of the above techniques; its "parent" program opens automatically. For example, if you used Microsoft Word to write a file called "Last Will and Testament.doc," then double-clicking the document's icon launches Word and automatically opens that file.

What happens next depends on the program you're using (and whether or not you opened a document). Most programs present you with a new, blank, untitled document. Some, like FileMaker and Microsoft PowerPoint, welcome you instead with a question: Do you want to open an existing document or create a new one? And a few oddball programs don't open any window at all when launched. The appearance of tool palettes is the only evidence that you've even opened a program.

An (Unfortunately) Necessary Word on Windows 8 Apps

As you may recall with clenched teeth, Windows 8 was two operating systems in one. And it ran two different kinds of programs:

- **Desktop apps.** These are the standard Windows programs. Photoshop, Quicken, iTunes, and 4 million others. They have menus. They have overlapping windows. They can create, open, and close documents.

UP TO SPEED

The Dawn of the Universal App

It's no secret that Windows 10 is an ambitious undertaking for Microsoft. Variations of this same operating system run on laptops, desktops, tablets, and phones.

Clearly, the similarity of Windows on all of these machines offers a big payoff for you: You have a lot less to learn. Everything looks, feels, and works the same, no matter what the device. (Take that, iPhone and Mac owners!)

But Microsoft intends to pull off an even more dramatic stunt: It wants to usher in an era when these different devices not only run the same OS, but even the same *apps!* You buy an app once, and run it on your laptop, phone, and tablet.

Of course, software companies have to *create* apps that work this way—what Microsoft calls Universal Apps.

To show other software companies the way, Microsoft has written a bunch of apps as Universal ones already, including Calendar, Mail, People, Photos, OneNote, Groove Music, Movies & TV, News, Money, Weather, and so on.

It's an attractive idea, this Universal thing. It's not likely that the creators of all 4 million existing PC apps will, in fact, rework their products to run identically on all different kinds of screens. But if even some of them do, it'll be a satisfying first in tech history.

- **Windows Store apps.** These apps ran in TileWorld, the edge-to-edge touchscreen environment designed for tablets. They were an all-new class of programs that looked and acted very different. (Microsoft calls them "Windows Store apps," because they're available exclusively from the online Windows Store.)

  Windows Store apps filled the whole screen, edge to edge. Their windows never overlapped. They had no menu bar and no drop-down menus. They had simple functions—they were like tablet apps.

Unfortunately, having to learn and master two different kinds of programs was massively confusing to most people. Undoing this confusion was one of Microsoft's primary goals in creating Windows 10—and it has mostly succeeded.

In Windows 10, both kinds of programs still exist (Figure 6-1). But the differences between their behavior have mostly been erased:

- **They both live in floating, overlapping windows.** Both *can* go full-screen, but only at your command.

- **They can appear side-by-side in the Start menu**—as tiles on the right side, or listings on the left.

- **They are listed as equals in the same "layer" of the app switcher** (page 226). There are no longer two different working worlds—one for desktop programs, one for TileWorld (Windows Store) apps.

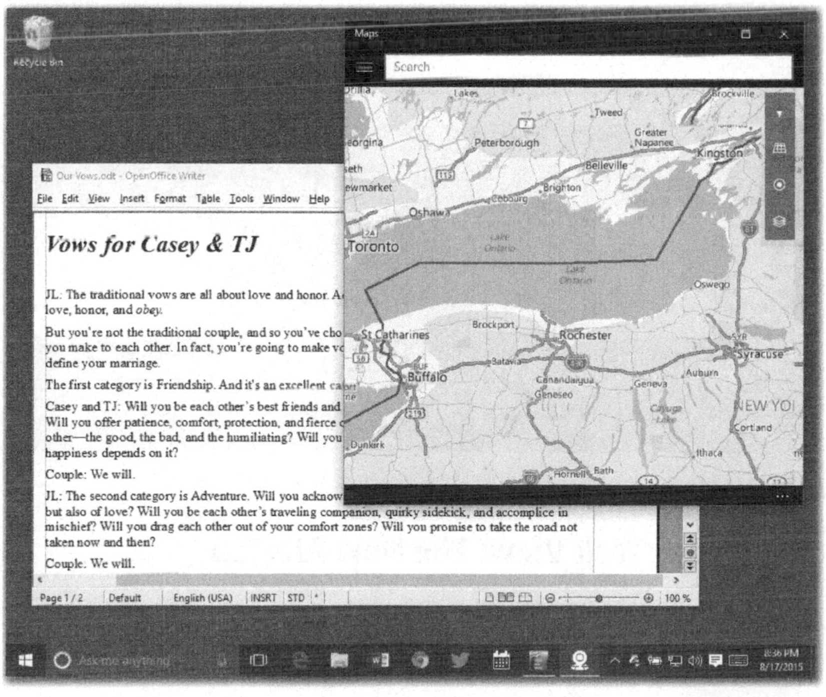

Figure 6-1:
In Windows 10, desktop programs and tablet-style Windows Store apps coexist on the same screen at the same time. At worst, you'll notice how weird it is that some programs seem to have a very different design philosophy than others. But you'll never have to wonder why they work differently or live in different places.

The App Switcher: Alt+Tab

In its day, the concept of overlapping windows on the screen was brilliant, innovative, and extremely effective. In that era before digital photos, digital music, and the Web, managing your windows was easy this way; after all, you had only about three of them.

These days, however, managing all the open windows in all your programs can be like herding cats. Fortunately, Windows 10 offers the same window-shuffling tricks that were available in previous editions:

- **Use the taskbar.** Clicking a button on the taskbar (page 92) makes the corresponding program pop to the front, along with any of its floating toolbars, palettes, and so on.

- **Click the window.** You can also bring any window forward by clicking any visible part of it.

- **Alt+Tab.** It's hard to imagine how anybody gets along without this keyboard shortcut, which offers a quick way to bring a different window to the front without using the mouse. If you press Tab while holding down the Alt key, a floating palette displays miniatures of all open windows, as shown in Figure 6-2. Each time you press Tab again (still keeping the Alt key down), you highlight the next app; when you release the keys, the highlighted program jumps to the front.

Tip: If you just *tap* Alt+Tab and then release keys, you get an effect that's often even more useful: You jump back and forth between the *last two* windows you've had open. It's great when, for example, you're copying sections of a Web page into a Word document.

Figure 6-2:
Alt+Tab highlights successive icons; add Shift to move backward. (Add the Ctrl key to lock the display, so you don't have to keep Alt down. Tab to the icon you want; then press the space bar or Enter.)

Task View: The New Alt+Tab

The beloved Alt+Tab keystroke has been with us since Windows 1.0. But there are two huge problems with it:

- It's relatively useless on touchscreens. What are you going to do, open up the onscreen keyboard every time you want to switch apps?

- Microsoft's research found that only *6 percent* of Windows fans actually use Alt+Tab!

So in Windows 10, Microsoft has introduced something that's much better, much easier to find, much more visual, much easier to remember: Task View.

As Figure 6-3 shows, Task View is a close relative to the Alt+Tab task switcher—but

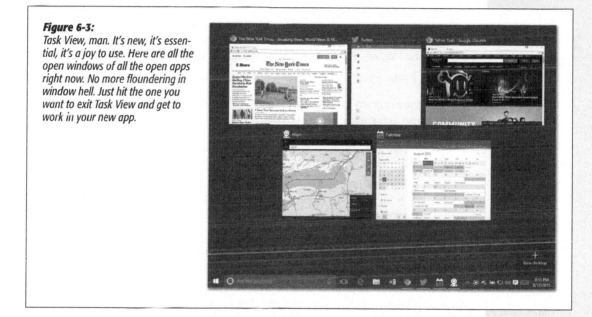

Figure 6-3:
Task View, man. It's new, it's essential, it's a joy to use. Here are all the open windows of all the open apps right now. No more floundering in window hell. Just hit the one you want to exit Task View and get to work in your new app.

the window miniatures are even bigger, and you don't have to keep any keys pressed to look over your app world. Just click or tap the window you want; Windows switches you instantly.

Task View is so important that Microsoft offers a lot of ways to trigger it:

- **Mouse:** Click the Task View button (⬚) on the taskbar. It's the one that's new in Windows 10, right next to the search box. It's a pretty good bet that this important button will be the Task View method most people use, most of the time.

- **Keyboard:** Press ⊞+Tab. Once Task View appears, you can press any of your arrow keys to highlight successive apps. When you press the space bar or Enter, the highlighted app pops to the front.

- **Trackpad:** Swipe upward on your trackpad with *three fingers* simultaneously. (Swipe down again with three fingers to exit Task View.)

- **Touchscreen:** Swipe inward from the left edge of the screen. Then tap the app you want to open.

Task View is the gateway into the joys of Windows 10's new virtual screens feature, too (page 193).

Exiting Programs

When you exit, or quit, an application, the memory it was using is returned to the Windows pot for use by other programs.

If you use a particular program several times a day, like a word processor or a calendar, you'll save time in the long run by keeping it open all day long. (You can always minimize its window when you're not using it.)

But if you're done using a program for the day, exit it, especially if it's a memory-hungry one like, say, Photoshop. Do so using one of these techniques:

- **Choose File→Exit.**

- **Click the program window's Close box,** or double-click its Control-menu spot (at the upper-left corner of the window).

- **Right-click the program's taskbar button;** from the shortcut menu, choose Close or Close Group.

- **Point to the program's taskbar button;** when the thumbnail preview pops up, click the little ✕ button in its upper-right corner. (If the program had only one window open, then the program exits.)

- **Press Alt+F4** to close the window you're in. (If it's a program that disappears entirely when its last document window closes, then you're home.)

- **Press Alt+F** and then select Exit.

After offering you a chance to save any changes you've made to your document, the program's windows, menus, and toolbars disappear, and you "fall down a layer" into the window that was behind it.

When Programs Die: The Task Manager

Windows 10 may be pretty stable, but that doesn't mean that *programs* never crash or freeze. They crash, all right.

When something goes horribly wrong with a program, your primary interest is usually in exiting it. But when a program locks up (the cursor moves, but menus and tool palettes don't respond) or when a dialog box tells you a program has "failed to respond," exiting may not be so easy. After all, how do you choose File→Exit if the File menu doesn't open?

As in past versions of Windows, the solution is to open up the Task Manager dialog box (Figure 6-4).

Tip: Actually, there may be a quicker solution. Try right-clicking the frozen program's taskbar button; from the shortcut menu, choose Close. This trick doesn't always work—but when it does, it's much faster than using the Task Manager.

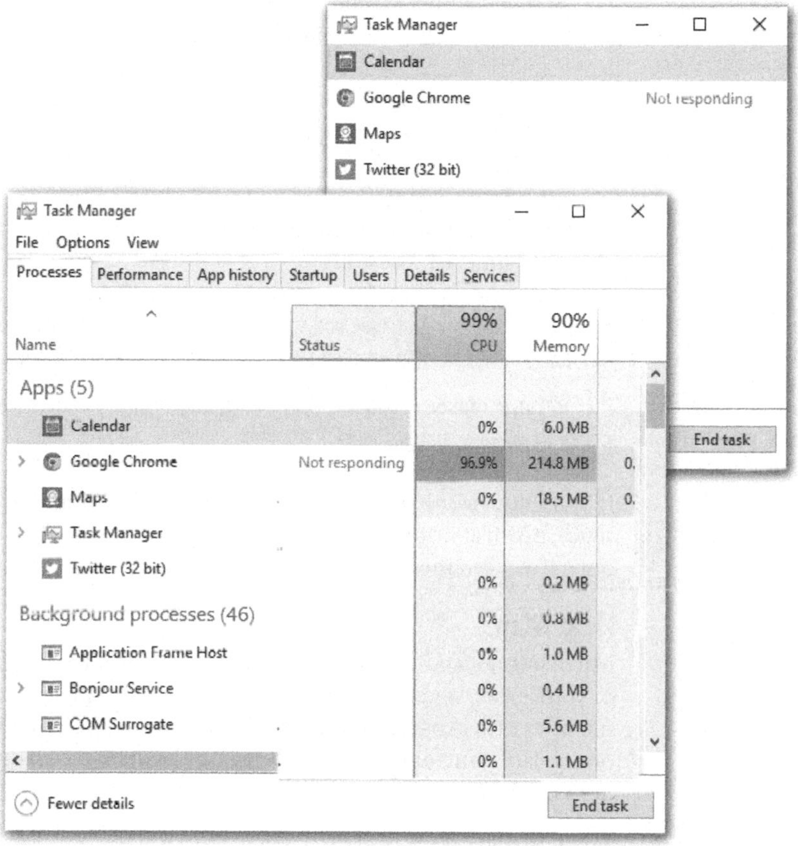

Figure 6-4:
Top: The Task Manager opens up like this: a simple list of open apps whose names you should recognize. If one is frozen, you can click it and then click "End task" to exit it the hard way.

Bottom: But if you click "More details" at the lower-left corner, you expand the Task Manager into this massively informative new table.

In this case, the color coding and the alarming numbers—one program is using 96.9 percent of your processor's energy!—should make it pretty clear which program is giving you problems.

The flippy triangles indicate programs with more than one window open. Open the triangle to see them listed.

Here are three ways to do it:

- Invoke the new "three-fingered salute," Ctrl+Shift+Esc.

- Right-click the taskbar and, from the shortcut menu, choose Task Manager.

- Right-click the ⊞ in the lower-left corner of the screen; from the secret utilities menu, choose Task Manager.

In any case, now you see a list of every open program. In its freshly opened state, the Task Manager doesn't let you do anything but (a) double-click a program's name to switch to it, or (b) click a program's name and then hit "End task" to close it.

But if you click "More details," then, wow, are your nerd genes in for a treat. The Task Manager blossoms into a full-blown spreadsheet of details about all the programs you're running at the moment—including invisible, background programs ("processes") you might not even have known were there. Figure 6-4 shows the Task Manager in both its tiny and expanded states.

The Status column should make clear what you already know: One of your programs—labeled "Not responding"—is ignoring you.

Tip: Now, "Not responding" could just mean "in the middle of crunching away." If the nonresponsive program is some huge mega-hog and you just chose some command that's going to take a while, then give it a chance to finish before you conclude that it's locked up.

Shutting down the troublesome program is fairly easy; just click its name and then click the "End task" button.

Note: In the old Task Manager, you sometimes got yet another dialog box at this point, telling you, "This program is not responding." You had to click the End Now button to put it away for good.

That no longer happens. "End task" kills a program completely and instantly—and no longer gives you the chance to save any changes.

If you click "More details," you expand the Task Manager into its newly beefed-up state, shown at bottom in Figure 6-4. Clearly, this mode is intended for power geeks only; if you're among them, then hours of fun await you. Read on.

Heat Map

Microsoft noticed that people often sorted the Task Manager by CPU (how much of your processor's attention is dedicated to each program) or memory (how much memory each program is using). When your computer slows down, it's often because one out-of-control program is hogging the system—and that's how you can figure out which one.

The Task Manager's "heat map" effect saves you the trouble. The "heat map" uses darker shades of color to flag the programs that are using the most computer resources—not just CPU cycles or memory, but also network bandwidth and disk space. In other words, you can now spot the resource hogs without having to sort the columns or even understand the numbers (for example, Google Chrome in Figure 6-4).

Similarly, when one resource is being gobbled up disproportionately, Task Manager darkens that column title (CPU, Memory, Disk, Network) to get your attention. If your computer has been slowing down, check that column first.

Tip: The Task Manager tries to use plain-English names for the programs and processes it displays—a welcome change from the old days of cryptic programmery names. But you'll still see unfamiliar items listed here. Fortunately, you can right-click anything in the list and, from the shortcut menu, choose "Search online." You'll go directly to a page of Bing or Google search results to read about the mystery item.

The Other Tabs

The Task Manager offers seven tabs. They're crammed with information that's either useful or useless, depending on just how technical a person you are. Here's a crash course:

- **Processes.** This is the tab that most people visit most often. It lists all programs and processes (background operations) that are running right now.

Tip: Click a column heading to sort the table by that criterion. Right-click a column heading to get a choice of additional columns that you can add—including PID, the process ID (a favorite of geekheads).

- **Performance.** Cool graphs—one each for CPU (processor time), Memory, Disk, and Network. Shows how much you've got, how much is in use, and what the trend is.

- **App history.** A table that shows how much data each of your programs and apps has used for the current account. This table could tell you all kinds of things about, for example, what your kid's been doing on the family PC. (The Metered column means "cellular connections." Since an app that uses a lot of data over cellular connections costs you money, this is a critical tool in keeping your bills under control.)

- **Startup.** Shows you exactly which items are starting up automatically when you turn on the computer—some you may not even know about. (This is information that used to require a trip to the user-unfriendly MSCONFIG program.)

  If your computer seems to be taking an unusually long time to start up, here's the first place you should check; Task Manager even shows you the impact of each item on your startup process.

  You can turn one off by right-clicking it; from the shortcut menu, choose Disable. You can also read about something unfamiliar by choosing "Search online" from the shortcut menu.

- **Users.** If you've set up multiple accounts on this machine, this little table shows which are logged in right now and how much of the computer's resources they're using.

- **Details.** Stand back. This massive, nearly infinitely expandable table looks like a space shuttle cockpit. It's a far more detailed version of the Processes tab; for example, it uses the true process names instead of the plain-English ones. You start out with seven columns, but you can add many more; right-click any column header, and from the shortcut menu, choose "Select columns."

- **Services.** This table lists all of Windows' behind-the-scenes "services"—background features that run all the time. (For example, the indexing of your hard drive, to keep your Search feature up to date, is a service. So are background printing, the computer's clock if you've told it to set itself, and Windows Messenger, which stays alert in case someone tries to instant-message you.)

Tip: On any of these tabs, you can drag columns horizontally to move them around.

Saving Documents

In Calculator, Character Map, and most Windows Store apps, you don't actually create any documents; when you close the window, no trace of your work remains. Most desktop programs, however, are designed to create *documents*—files you can reopen for further editing, send to other people, back up on another disk, and so on.

That's why these programs offer File→Save and File→Open commands, which let you save the work you've done onto the hard drive as a file icon so you can return to it later.

The Save Dialog Box

When you choose File→Save for the first time, you're asked where you want the new document stored. These days, this Save As box is a *full File Explorer window,* complete with taskbar, Navigation pane, search box, and a choice of views (Icon/List/Details). All the skills you've picked up working at the desktop come into play here; you can even delete a file or folder right from within the Save or Open box. (The Delete command is in the Organize menu.)

To give it a try, open any program that has a Save or Export command—WordPad, for example. Type a couple of words and then choose File→Save. The Save As dialog box appears (Figure 6-5).

Tip: Some techie PC fans like to keep their files on one hard drive and Windows on another. In Windows 10, you can set that up easily. In Settings→System→Storage, use the pop-up menus to indicate which drive you want to hold new documents, music, pictures, and videos. (On that drive, you'll find a new folder, named for your account, with Documents, Music, Pictures, and Videos folders within.)

GEM IN THE ROUGH

Why You See Document Names in the Save Dialog Box

In the Save dialog box, Windows displays a list of both folders *and documents* (documents that match the kind you're about to save, that is).

It's easy to understand why *folders* appear here: so you can double-click one if you want to save your document inside it. But why do *documents* appear here? After all, you can't very well save a document into another document.

Documents are listed here so you can perform one fairly obscure stunt: If you click a document's name, Windows copies its name into the "File name" text box at the bottom of the window. That's a useful shortcut if you want to *replace*

an existing document with the new one you're saving. By saving a new file with the same name as the existing one, you force Windows to overwrite it (after asking your permission, of course).

This trick also reduces the amount of typing needed to save a document to which you've assigned a different version number. For example, if you click the "Thesis Draft 3.1" document in the list, Windows copies that name into the "File name" text box; doing so keeps it separate from earlier drafts. To save your new document as "Thesis Draft 3.2," you need to change only one character (change the 1 to a 2) before clicking the Save button.

Saving into Your Documents Folder

The first time you use the File→Save command to save a file, Windows suggests putting your new document in your OneDrive (see page 161). If you've turned off that option, then it proposes your Documents folder.

For many people, Documents is an excellent suggestion. First, it means your file won't accidentally fall into some deeply nested folder where you'll never see it again. Instead, it will be waiting in the Documents folder, which is very difficult to lose.

Second, it's very easy to make a backup of your important documents if they're all in one folder. There's a third advantage, too: The Documents folder is also what Windows displays whenever you use a program's File→*Open* command. In other words, the Documents folder saves you time both when *creating* a new file and when *retrieving* it.

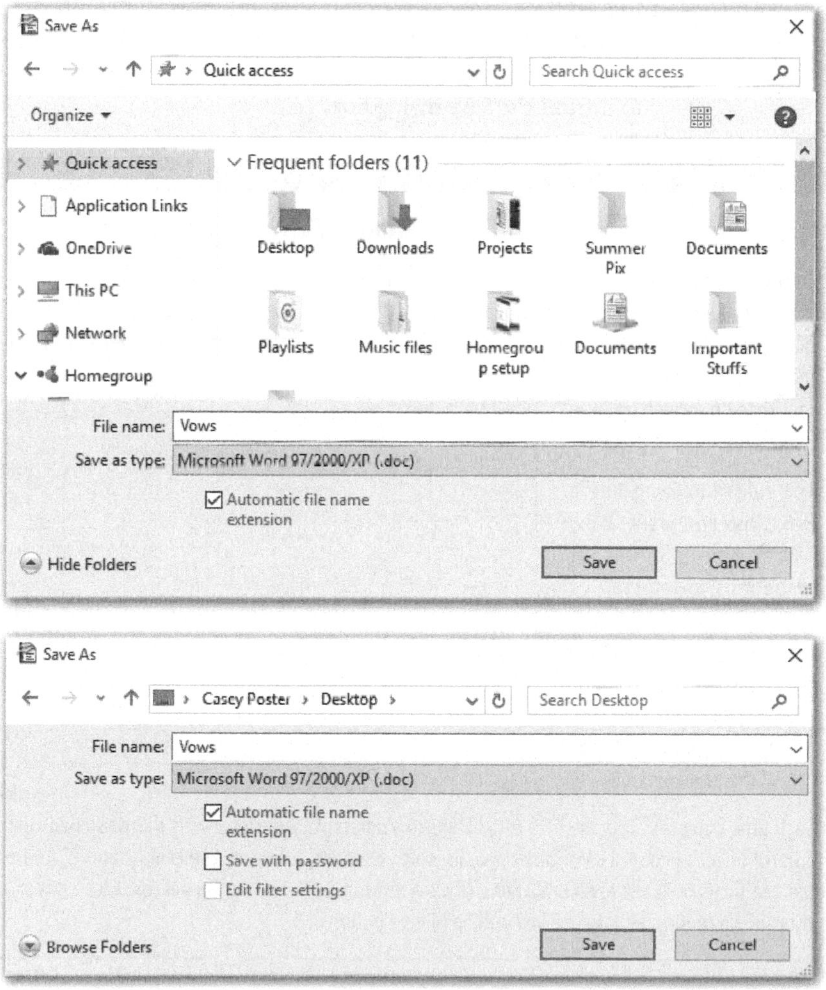

Figure 6-5:
The Save box may appear in either of two forms: the full-blown, File Explorerish view shown at top, or the collapsed form shown at bottom.

You may notice that your OneDrive is available to receive your newly created documents—in fact, Windows may propose it as the factory setting.

Use the Hide Folders button in the lower left to collapse the big version, or the Browse Folders button to expand the collapsed version.

Type a name, choose a folder location, and specify the format for the file you're saving.

Tip: If the Documents folder becomes cluttered, feel free to make subfolders inside it to hold your various projects. You could even create a different default folder in Documents for each program.

Saving into Other Folders

Still, the now-familiar Navigation pane, address bar, and search box also appear in the Save dialog box. (The Nav pane appears only in the Save box's expanded form; see Figure 6-5, top.) You always have direct access to other places where you might want to save a newly created file.

All the usual keyboard shortcuts apply: Alt+↑, for example, to open the folder that *contains* the current one. There's even a "New folder" button on the toolbar, so you can generate a new, empty folder in the current list of files and folders. Windows asks you to name it.

In fact, if on some project you often find yourself having to navigate to some deeply buried folder, press ▇+D to duck back to the desktop, open any Explorer window, and then drag the folder to your Favorites list. From now on, you'll have quick access to it from the Save dialog box.

UP TO SPEED

Dialog Box Basics

To the delight of the powerful Computer Keyboard Lobby, you can manipulate almost every element of a Windows dialog box by pressing keys on the keyboard. If you're among those who feel that using the mouse to do something takes longer, then you're in luck.

The rules for navigating a dialog box are simple: Press Tab to jump from one set of options to another, or Shift+Tab to move backward. If the dialog box has multiple tabs, like the one shown here, press Ctrl+Tab to "click" the next tab, or Ctrl+*Shift*+Tab to "click" the previous one.

Each time you press Tab, the PC's *focus* shifts to a different control or set of controls. Windows reveals which element has the focus by using text highlighting (if it's a text box or drop-down menu), or a dotted-line outline (if it's a button).

Once you've highlighted a button or a checkbox, simply press the space bar to "click" it. If you've opened a drop-down list or a set of mutually exclusive *option buttons* (or *radio buttons*) then press the ↑ or ↓ keys. (Once you've highlighted a drop-down list's name, you can also press the F4 key to open it.)

Each dialog box also contains larger, rectangular buttons at the bottom (OK and Cancel, for example).

Efficiency fans should remember that tapping the Enter key is always the equivalent of clicking the *default* button—the one with the darkened or thickened outline (the OK button in this illustration). And pressing Esc almost always means Cancel (or "Close this box").

Tip: Many programs let you specify a different folder as the proposed location for saved (and reopened) files. In Microsoft Word, for example, you can change the default folders for the documents you create, where your clip art is stored, and so on.

Navigating the List by Keyboard

When the Save As dialog box first appears, the "File name" text box is automatically selected so you can type a name for the newly created document.

But a Windows dialog box is elaborately rigged for keyboard control. In addition to the standard Tab/space bar controls, a few special keys work only within the list of files and folders. Start by pressing Shift+Tab (to shift Windows' attention from the "File name" text box to the list of files and folders) and then do the following:

- Press various letter keys to highlight the corresponding file and folder icons. To highlight the Program Files folder, for example, you could type *Pr*. (If you type too slowly, your keystrokes are interpreted as separate initiatives—highlighting first the People folder and then the Rodents folder, for example.)

- Press the Page Up or Page Down keys to scroll the list up or down. Press Home or End to highlight the top or bottom item in the list.

- Press the ↑ or ↓ keys to highlight successive icons in the list.

- When a folder (or file) is highlighted, you can open it by pressing the Enter key (or double-clicking its icon, or clicking the Open button).

The File Format Drop-Down Menu

The Save As dialog box in many programs offers a menu of file formats (usually referred to as file *types*) below or next to the "File name" text box. Use this drop-down menu when preparing a document for use by somebody whose computer doesn't have the same software.

For example, if you've typed something in Microsoft Word, you can use this menu to generate a Web page document or a Rich Text Format document that you can open with almost any standard word processor or page-layout program.

Closing Documents

You close a document window just as you'd close any window: by clicking the close box (marked by ✕) in the upper-right corner of the window, by double-clicking the top-left corner, by clicking the ✕ in its taskbar icon's preview thumbnail, or by pressing Alt+F4. If you've done any work to the document since the last time you saved it, Windows offers a "Save changes?" dialog box as a reminder.

Sometimes closing the window also exits the application, and sometimes the application remains running, even with no document windows open. And in a few *really* bizarre cases, it's possible to exit an application (like Windows Mail) while a document window (an email message) remains open on the screen, lingering and abandoned!

The Open Dialog Box

To reopen a document you've already saved and named, you can pursue any of these avenues:

- Open your Documents library (or whichever folder contains the saved file). Double-click the file's icon.

- If you've opened the document recently, choose its name from the taskbar's jump list.

- If you're already in the program that created the document, choose File→Open. (Or check the bottom of the File menu, where many programs add a list of recently opened files.)

- Type the document's path and name into the Run dialog box (■+R) or the address bar. (You can also browse for it.)

The Open dialog box looks almost identical to the Save As dialog box. Once again, you start out by perusing the contents of your Documents folder; once again, the dialog box otherwise behaves exactly like an Explorer window. For example, you can press Backspace to back *out* of a folder you've opened.

When you've finally located the file you want to open, double-click it or highlight it (from the keyboard, if you like), and then press Enter.

Most people don't encounter the Open dialog box nearly as often as the Save As dialog box. That's because Windows offers many more convenient ways to *open* a file (double-clicking its icon, choosing its name from the Start→Documents command, and so on), but only a single way to *save* a new file.

Moving Data Between Documents

You can't paste a picture into your Web browser, and you can't paste MIDI music into your desktop publishing program. But you can put graphics into your word processor, paste movies into your database, insert text into Photoshop, and combine a surprising variety of seemingly dissimilar kinds of data. And you can transfer text from Web pages, email messages, and word-processing documents to other email and word-processing files; in fact, that's one of the most frequently performed tasks in all of computing.

Cut, Copy, and Paste

Most experienced PC fans have learned to quickly trigger the Cut, Copy, and Paste commands from the keyboard—without even thinking.

Bear in mind that you can cut and copy highlighted material in any of three ways. First, you can use the Cut and Copy commands in the Edit menu; second, you can press Ctrl+X (for Cut) or Ctrl+C (for Copy); and third, you can right-click the highlighted material and, from the shortcut menu, choose Cut or Copy (Figure 6-6).

When you do so, Windows memorizes the highlighted material, stashing it on an invisible Clipboard. If you choose Copy, nothing visible happens; if you choose Cut, the highlighted material disappears from the original document.

Figure 6-6:
Suppose you want to email some text from a Web page to a friend.

Left: Drag through it, and then choose Copy from the shortcut menu (or Edit→ Copy).

Right: In your email program, paste into an outgoing message.

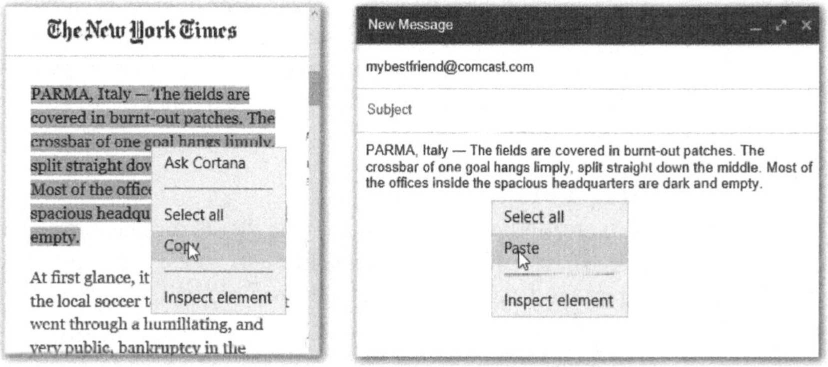

FREQUENTLY ASKED QUESTION

When Formatting Is Lost

How come pasted text doesn't always look the same as what I copied?

When you copy text from Internet Explorer, for example, and then paste it into another program, such as Word, you may be alarmed to note that the formatting of that text (bold, italic, font size, font color, and so on) doesn't reappear intact. In fact, the pasted material may not even inherit the current font settings in the word processor. There could be several reasons for this problem.

First, not every program *offers* text formatting—Notepad among them. And the Copy command in some programs (such as Web browsers) doesn't pick up the formatting along with the text. So when you copy something from Internet Explorer and paste it into Word or WordPad, you may get plain, unformatted text. (There is some good news along these lines, however. Word maintains formatting pasted from the latest Internet Explorer.)

Finally, a note on *text wrapping*. Thanks to limitations built into the architecture of the Internet, email messages aren't like word processor documents. The text doesn't flow continuously from one line of a paragraph to the next, reflowing as you adjust the window size. Instead, email programs insert a press of the Enter key at the end of each line *within* a paragraph.

Most of the time, you don't even notice that your messages consist of dozens of one-line "paragraphs." When you see them in the email program, you can't tell the difference. But if you paste an email message into a word processor, the difference becomes painfully apparent—especially if you then attempt to adjust the margins.

To fix the page, delete the invisible carriage return at the end of each line. (Veteran PC lovers sometimes use the word processor's search-and-replace function for this purpose, using the character code "^p" to replace the paragraph marks.) Or, if you just need a quick look, reduce the point size (or widen the margin) until the text no longer breaks oddly.

Pasting copied or cut material, once again, is something you can do either from a menu (choose Edit→Paste), from the shortcut menu (right-click and choose Paste), or from the keyboard (press Ctrl+V).

The most recently cut or copied material remains on your Clipboard even after you paste, making it possible to paste the same blob repeatedly. Such a trick can be useful when, for example, you've designed a business card in your drawing program and want to duplicate it enough times to fill a letter-sized printout. On the other hand, whenever you next copy or cut something, whatever was previously on the Clipboard is lost forever.

Drag and Drop

As useful and popular as it is, the Copy/Paste routine doesn't win any awards for speed; after all, it requires four steps. In many cases, you can replace it with the far more direct (and enjoyable) drag-and-drop method. Figure 6-7 illustrates how it works.

Tip: To drag highlighted material offscreen, drag the cursor until it approaches the top or bottom edge of the window. The document scrolls automatically; as you approach the destination, jerk the mouse away from the edge of the window to stop the scrolling.

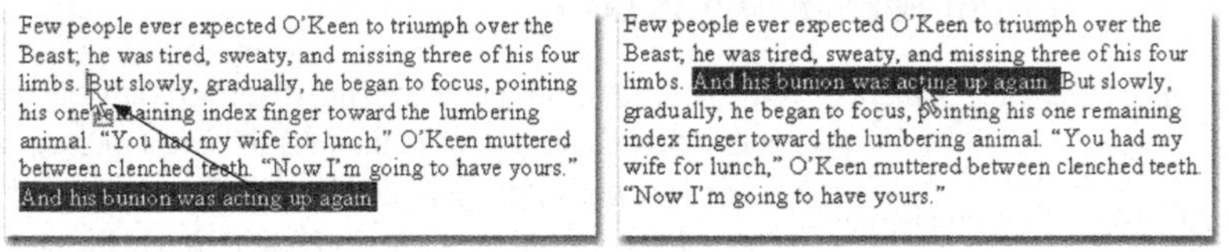

Few people ever expected O'Keen to triumph over the Beast; he was tired, sweaty, and missing three of his four limbs. But slowly, gradually, he began to focus, pointing his one remaining index finger toward the lumbering animal. "You had my wife for lunch," O'Keen muttered between clenched teeth. "Now I'm going to have yours." And his bunion was acting up again

Few people ever expected O'Keen to triumph over the Beast; he was tired, sweaty, and missing three of his four limbs. And his bunion was acting up again. But slowly, gradually, he began to focus, pointing his one remaining index finger toward the lumbering animal. "You had my wife for lunch," O'Keen muttered between clenched teeth. "Now I'm going to have yours."

Figure 6-7:
You can drag highlighted text to another place in the document—or to a different window or program.

Several of the built-in Windows programs work with the drag-and-drop technique, including WordPad and Mail. Most popular commercial programs offer the drag-and-drop feature, too, including email programs and word processors, Microsoft Office programs, and so on.

Note: Scrap files—bits of text or graphics that you can drag to the desktop for later—no longer exist in Windows.

As illustrated in Figure 6-7, drag-and-drop is ideal for transferring material between windows or between programs. It's especially useful when you've already copied something valuable to your Clipboard, since drag-and-drop doesn't involve (and doesn't erase) the Clipboard.

Its most popular use, however, is rearranging the text in a single document. In, say, Word or WordPad, you can rearrange entire sections, paragraphs, sentences, or even individual letters, just by dragging them—a terrific editing technique.

Tip: Using drag-and-drop to move highlighted text within a document also deletes the text from its original location. By pressing Ctrl as you drag, however, you make a *copy* of the highlighted text.

Export/Import

When it comes to transferring large chunks of information from one program to another—especially address books, spreadsheet cells, and database records—none of the data-transfer methods described so far in this chapter does the trick. For such purposes, use the Export and Import commands found in the File menu of almost every database, spreadsheet, email, and address-book program.

These Export/Import commands aren't part of Windows, so the manuals or help screens of the applications in question should be your source for instructions. For now, however, the power and convenience of this feature are worth noting. Because of these commands, your four years' worth of collected names and addresses in, say, an old address-book program can find its way into a newer program, such as Mozilla Thunderbird, in a matter of minutes.

Speech Recognition

For years, there's been quite a gulf between the promise of computer speech recognition (as seen on *Star Trek*) and the reality (as seen just about everywhere else). You say "oxymoron"; it types "ax a moron." (Which is often just what you feel like doing, frankly.)

Microsoft has had a speech-recognition department for years. But until recently, it never got the funding and corporate backing it needed to do a really bang-up job.

The speech recognition in today's Windows, however, is another story. It can't match the accuracy of its chief rival, Dragon NaturallySpeaking, but you might be amazed to discover how elegant its design is now, and how useful it can be to anyone who can't, or doesn't like to, type.

GEM IN THE ROUGH

Text to Speech

The big-ticket item, for sure, is that speech-to-text feature. But Windows can also convert typed text *back* to speech, using a set of voices of its very own.

To hear them, open the search box. Type *speech* and select "Speech settings." In the search results, click "Change text to speech settings." Click Preview Voice to hear the astonishing realism of Microsoft Mark and Microsoft Zira, the voices of Windows. You can even control their speaking rate using the "Voice speed" slider.

So when can you hear these voices do their stuff? Primarily in Narrator (page 325). If you master the Narrator keyboard shortcuts, Microsoft can read back *whatever you want,* like stuff you've written or articles you find on the Web. Why not let your computer read the morning news to you while you're getting breakfast ready each day?

In short, Speech Recognition lets you not only *control* your PC by voice—open programs, click buttons, click Web links, and so on—but also *dictate text* a heck of a lot faster than you can type.

To make this all work, you need a PC with a microphone. The Windows Speech Recognition program can handle just about any kind of mike, even the one built into your laptop's case. But a regular old headset mike—"anything that costs over $20 or so," says Microsoft—will give you the best accuracy.

For a full, free online guide to using Windows Speech Recognition, download "Speech Recognition.pdf," a PDF appendix to this chapter. It's on this book's "Missing CD" page at *www.missingmanuals.com*.

Filename Extensions and File Associations

Every operating system needs a mechanism to associate documents with the applications that created them. When you double-click a Microsoft Word document icon, for example, Word launches and opens the document.

In Windows, every document comes complete with a normally invisible *filename extension* (or just *file extension*)—a period followed by a suffix that's usually three letters long.

Here are some common examples:

When you double-click this icon...	...this program opens it.
Fishing trip.docx	Microsoft Word
Quarterly results.xlsx	Microsoft Excel
Home page.htm	your Web browser
Butterfly.psd	Photoshop
Agenda.wpd	Corel WordPerfect
A home movie.avi	Windows Media Player

Tip: For an exhaustive list of every file extension in the world, visit *www.whatis.com*; click the link for File Extensions.

Behind the scenes, Windows maintains a massive table that lists every extension and the program that "owns" it. More on this in a moment.

Displaying Filename Extensions

It's possible to live a long and happy life without knowing much about these extensions. Because file extensions don't feel very user-friendly, Microsoft designed Windows to *hide* the suffixes on most icons (Figure 6-8). If you're new to Windows, you may never have even seen them.

Some people appreciate the way Windows hides the extensions, because the screen becomes less cluttered and less technical-looking. Others make a good argument for the Windows 3.1 days, when every icon appeared with its suffix.

For example, in a single File Explorer window, suppose one day you discover that three icons all seem to have exactly the same name: PicThrower. Only by making filename extensions appear would you discover the answer to the mystery: that one of them is called PieThrower.ini, another is an Internet-based software updater called PieThrower.upd, and the third is the actual PieThrower program, PieThrower.exe.

If you'd rather have Windows reveal the file suffixes on *all* icons, then open an Explorer window. On the Ribbon's View tab, turn on "File name extensions," as shown in Figure 6-8. Now the filename extensions for all icons appear.

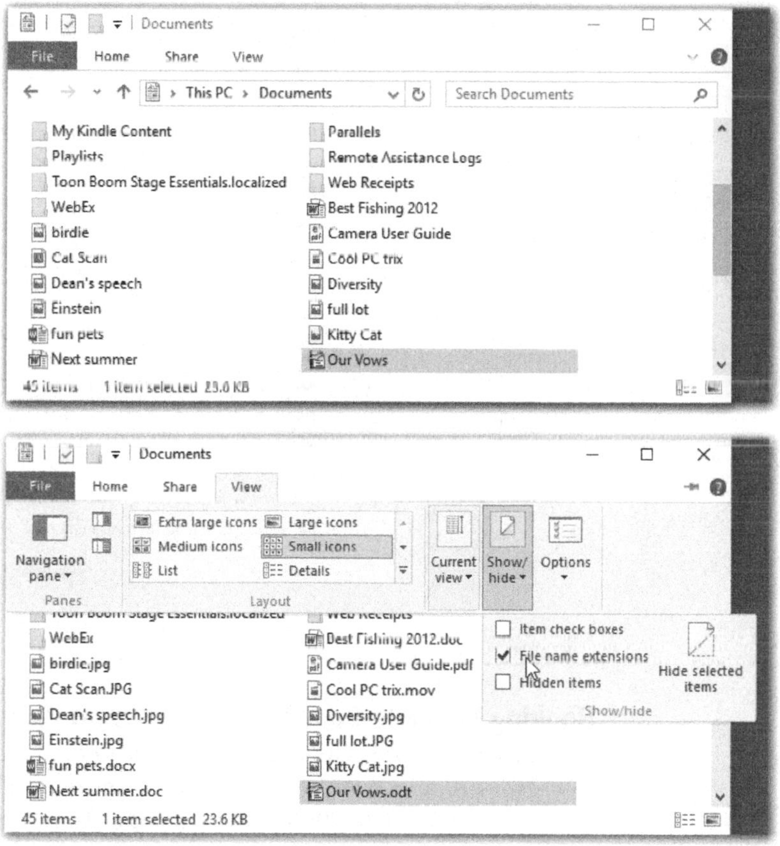

Figure 6-8:
As a rule, Windows shows filename extensions only on files whose extensions it doesn't recognize. The JPEG graphics and Word files at top, for example, don't show their suffixes.

Bottom: You can ask Windows to display all extensions, all the time. Just use the "File name extensions" checkbox on the Ribbon's View tab, indicated by the cursor.

Hooking Up an Unknown File Type

Every now and then, you might try to open a mystery icon—one whose extension is missing, or whose extension Windows doesn't recognize. Maybe you've been sent some weirdo document created by a beekeeper or a banjo transcriber using a program you don't have, or maybe you're opening a document belonging to an old DOS program that doesn't know about the Windows file-association feature. What will happen when you double-click that file?

Windows *asks* you.

Windows offers you two options, shown in the dialog box Figure 6-9. First, it encourages you to go online to the Windows Store in hopes of finding a TileWorld app that can open this file type. Good luck with that.

Usually, you'll want to click "More apps." As shown in Figure 6-9 at right, you now see a list of all programs that are capable of opening this document. Click the name of the program you want, and then turn on "Always use this app to open [mystery filename extension] files," if you like.

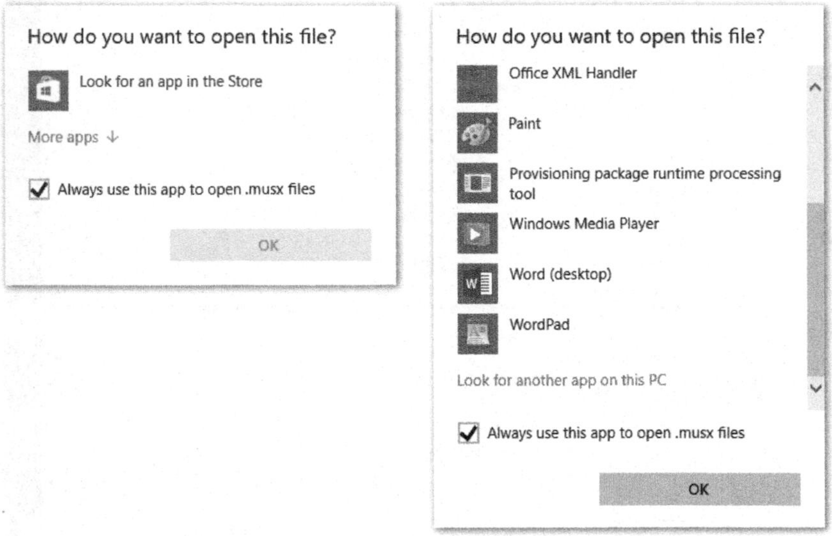

How do you want to open this file?

Look for an app in the Store

More apps ↓

☑ Always use this app to open .musx files

OK

How do you want to open this file?

Office XML Handler

Paint

Provisioning package runtime processing tool

Windows Media Player

Word (desktop)

WordPad

Look for another app on this PC

☑ Always use this app to open .musx files

OK

Figure 6-9:
Left: If you're pretty sure your PC has a program that can open this mystery file, then give it a little help—click "More apps."

Right: Use this list to select a program for opening the mystery file.

Hooking Up a File Extension to a Different Program

Windows comes with several programs that can open text files with the extension *.txt*—Notepad and WordPad, for example. There are also plenty of programs that can open picture files with the extension *.jpg*. So how does Windows decide *which* program to open when you double-click a .txt or .jpg file?

Easy—it refers to its internal database of preferred *default programs* for various file types. But at any time, you can reassign a particular file type (file extension) to a different application. If you've just bought Photoshop, for example, you might want it to open up your JPEG files, rather than the Photos app.

This sort of surgery has always confused beginners. Yet it was important for Microsoft to provide an easy way of reprogramming documents' mother programs; almost everyone ran into programs like RealPlayer that, once installed, "stole" every file association it could. The masses needed a simple way to switch documents back to their preferred programs.

Whether or not the *three* file-association mechanisms described next are actually superior to the *one* old one from Windows versions of old—well, you be the judge.

Method 1: Start with the document

Often, you'll discover a misaligned file-type association the hard way. You double-click a document and the wrong program opens it.

For that reason, Microsoft has added a new way of reprogramming a document—one that starts right in File Explorer, with the document itself.

Right-click the icon of the file that needs a new parent program. From the shortcut menu, choose "Open with."

If you're just trying to open this document into the new program *this once,* you may be able to choose the new program's name from the "Open with" submenu (Figure 6-10). Windows doesn't always offer this submenu, however.

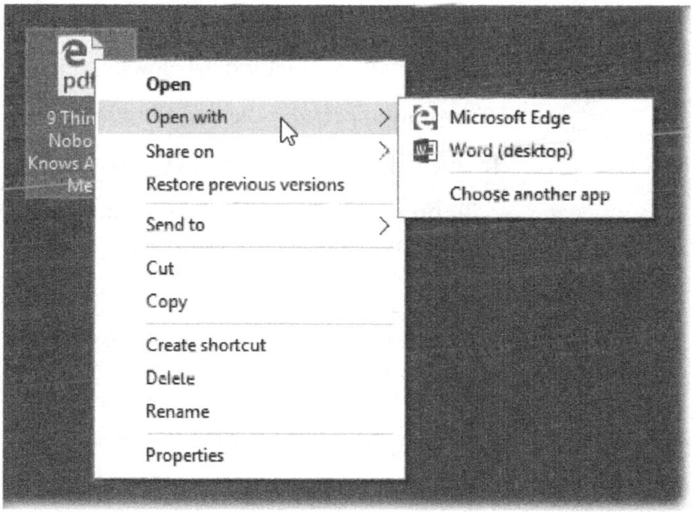

Figure 6-10:
To reassign a document to a new parent program, use its "Open with" shortcut menu. If you're lucky, you get a submenu of available programs that can open the document.

If you choose "Choose another app" from the submenu, or if there's no submenu at all, then the new "How do you want to open this file?" box appears, as shown in Figure 6-9. It's supposed to list every program on your machine that's capable of opening the document.

And now, a critical decision: Are you trying to make *only this document* open in a different program? Or *all documents of this type?*

If it's just this one, then click the program you want and stop reading. If it's *all* files of this type (all JPEGs, all MP3s, all DOC files…), then also turn on "Always use this app to open [filename extension] files" before you click the program name.

You should now be able to double-click the original document—and smile as it opens in the program you requested.

Note: If the program isn't listed, you can go find it yourself. Scroll to the very bottom of the list of proposed apps. If you see "More apps," click that. Now scroll to the very bottom again until you see the last item: "Look for another app on this PC." Now you're shown a standard Open File dialog box so that you can peruse the entire contents of your Programs folder on a quest for just the right software.

By the way, it's sometimes useful to associate a particular document type with a program that *didn't* create it. For example, you might prefer that double-clicking a text file created with WordPad should really open into Microsoft Word.

Method 2: Start with the program

If you'd prefer to edit the master database of file associations directly, a special control panel awaits. You can approach the problem from either direction:

- Choose a program and then choose which file types you want it to take over; or

- Choose a filename extension (like .aif or .ico) and then choose a new default program for it (Method 3, below).

Here's how to perform the first technique:

1. **Open the Default Programs Control Panel.**

   To do that, right-click (or hold your finger down on) the ⊞ button. From the shortcut menu, choose Control Panel. Then, with the Control Panel in Category view (page 272), hit Programs.

Tip: If you have a keyboard, it's probably faster to start typing *default* in the search box until you see "Default Programs" in the results list; choose it.

---

2. **Choose "Set your default programs."**

   A curious dialog box appears, as shown in Figure 6-11. It's a list of every program on your machine that's capable of opening multiple file types.

3. **Select the name of a program.**

   For example, suppose a program named FakePlayer 3.0 has performed the dreaded Windows Power Grab, claiming a particular file type for itself without asking you. In fact, suppose it has elected itself King of *All* Audio Files. But you want Windows Media Player to play everything *except* FakePlayer (.fkpl) files.

   In this step, then, you'd click Windows Media Player.

If you want Media Player to become the default player for *every* kind of music and video file, you'd click "Set this program as default." But if you want it to open only *some* kinds of files, proceed like this:

4. Click "Choose defaults for this program."

Now yet another dialog box opens. It lists every file type the selected program knows about.

5. Turn on the checkboxes of the file types for which you want this program to be the default opener.

Of course, this step requires a certain amount of knowledge that comes from experience—how the heck would the average person know what, say, a .wvx file is?—but it's here for the power user's benefit.

6. Click Save and then OK.

Figure 6-11:
Each software program you install must register the file types it uses. The link between the file type and the program is called an association. This dialog box displays each program on your PC that's capable of opening documents.

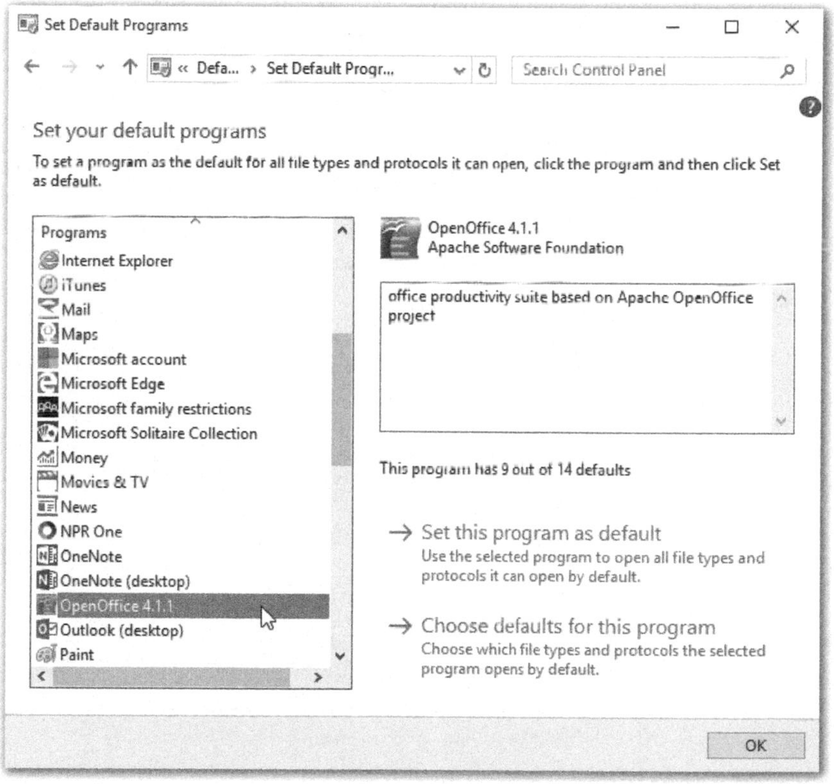

Method 3: Start with the file type

Finally, you can approach the file-association problem by working through a massive alphabetical list of filename extensions (.aca, .acf, .acs, .aif, and so on) and hooking each one up to a program of your choice.

You work the Default Programs Control Panel once again, like this:

1. **Open the Default Programs Control Panel.**

   Right-click (or hold your finger down on) the ⊞ button. From the shortcut menu, choose Control Panel. Then, in Category view (page 272), hit Programs.

2. **Choose "Make a file type always open in a specific program."**

   After a moment, a massive list of filename extensions opens (Figure 6-12).

3. **Select the filename extension you want, and then click "Change program."**

   Now the Open With dialog box appears, also shown in Figure 6-12.

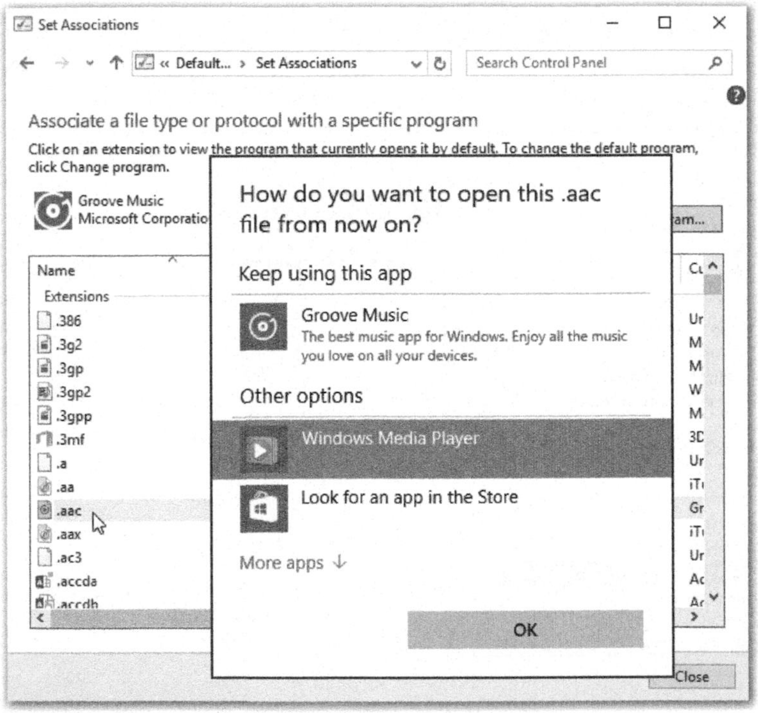

Figure 6-12:
Here you can manually inform Windows which app should open each type of file. This massive list of thousands of file types makes you realize just how many possible combinations of three letters there really are.

In this example, you're about to change .aac audio files so that they open up in Windows Media Player instead of Groove Music.

4. **Click the name of the new default program.**

Once again, if you don't see it listed here, you can click "More apps" or "Look for another app on this PC" or "Look for an app in the Store," to find it yourself.

5. **Click OK and then Close.**

Choosing Your Default Apps

Windows comes with a Web browser, a calendar app, an email program, a maps app, and players for music, photos, and videos. Very nice of Microsoft, isn't it?

The courts—in the U.S. and Europe—didn't think so. They thought that Microsoft was stifling competition by including these goodies in Windows. Who'd bother trying anybody else's Web browser, if Microsoft put its own right under your nose?

Ever since, Microsoft has included a Settings panel like the one shown in Figure 6-13. Here you can click the name of Microsoft's program (for Web browser, calendar, maps, and so on), and choose the name of a rival to use instead.

So what, exactly, is a *default* app? It's the one that opens automatically. For example, if I email you a link to a cool Web site, the default browser is the one that will open when you click the link. It's the photo program that opens when you double-click a picture file. And so on.

Figure 6-13:
In Settings→System→ Default apps, you can choose to replace Microsoft's starter apps with other companies' wares. For your Web browser, for example, you might prefer Chrome, Firefox, or even Internet Explorer instead of Microsoft Edge.

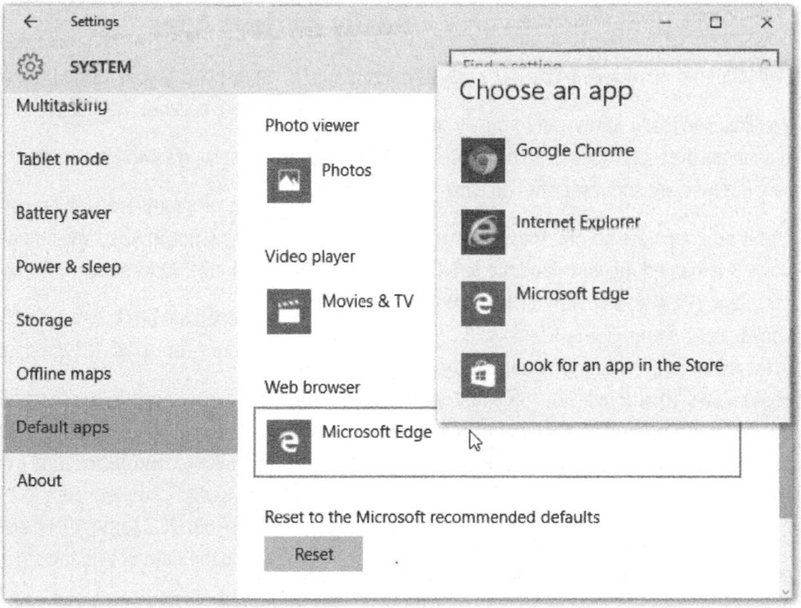

Installing New Apps

Most people don't buy their computers from Microsoft. Most computers come from companies like Dell, HP, Acer, and Lenovo; they install Windows on each computer before customers take delivery.

Many PC companies sweeten the pot by preinstalling other programs, such as Quicken, Microsoft Works, Microsoft Office, more games, educational software, and so on. The great thing about preloaded programs is that they don't need installing. Just double-click their desktop icons, or choose their names from the Start menu, and you're off and working.

Sooner or later, though, you'll probably want to exploit the massive library of Windows software and add to your collection. Today, almost all new desktop software comes to your PC from the Internet. (Software sold on a CD or DVD still happens, but less and less often.)

Desktop Apps

When you buy or download a standard desktop program (iTunes, Quicken, what have you), an installer program generally transfers the software files to the correct places on your hard drive. The installer also adds the new program's name to the Start menu, and tells Windows about the kinds of files (file extensions) it can open.

FREQUENTLY ASKED QUESTION

Really Ancient Apps

Will Windows 10 run my really old, really important app?

You'll never really know until you try. And this chapter outlines all the tools available to help you make the old app run. But here are some specifics on what you can expect.

16-bit programs are so old, they were written when Windows 3.1 roamed the earth and the first George Bush was president. (Programs written for Windows 95 and later are known as *32-bit* programs; Windows 8 can even run *64-bit* programs.) But, amazingly enough, the 32-bit versions of Windows 10 (though not the 64-bit versions) can run most of these programs. They do so in a kind of software simulator—a DOS-and-Windows 3.1 PC impersonation called a *virtual machine.*

As a result, these programs don't run very fast, don't understand the long filenames of modern-day Windows, and may crash whenever they try to "speak" directly to certain components of your hardware. (The simulator stands in their way, in the name of keeping Windows stable.) Furthermore,

if just one of your 16-bit programs crashes, then *all* of them crash, because they all live in the same memory bubble.

Even so, it's impressive that they run at all, 15 years later.

DOS programs are 16-bit programs, too, and therefore they run just fine in 32-bit versions of Windows, even though DOS no longer lurks beneath the operating system.

To open the black, empty DOS window that's familiar to PC veterans, press ⊞+R, type *command.com*, and press Enter.

For the best possible compatibility with DOS programs—and to run DOS programs in a 64-bit copy of Windows—try out DOSBox (*www.dosbox.com/*), which emulates a classic 16-bit computer, complete with DOS compatibility. It's great for those old DOS games that haven't run correctly on Windows since the days of Windows 95.

Programs written for Windows 95, 2000, and XP usually run OK in the Compatibility mode described on these pages.

For best results, answer these questions before you install anything:

- **Are you an administrator?** Windows derives part of its security and stability by handling new software installations with suspicion. You can't install most programs unless you have an *administrator account* (page 751).

- **Does it run in Windows 10?** If the software or its Web site specifically says it's compatible, great. Install away. If not, find out when a compatible version is due.

Tip: See "Really Ancient Apps" on page 248 for compatibility tips.

- **Is the coast clear?** Exit all your open programs. You should also turn off your virus-scanning software, which may take the arrival of your new software the wrong way.

- **Are you prepared to backtrack?** If you're at all concerned about the health and safety of the software you're about to install, remember that the System Restore feature (page 521) takes an automatic snapshot of your system just before any software installation. If the new program turns out to be a bit hostile, you can rewind your system to its former, happier working condition.

- **Are you darned sure?** Internet downloads are the most common sources of PC virus infections. If you're downloading from a brand-name site like *Shareware.com* (or a software company's site, like *Microsoft.com*), you're generally safe. But if the site is unfamiliar, be very, very afraid.

- **Run or Save?** You can find thousands of Windows programs (demos, free programs, and shareware) at Web sites like *www.download.com* or *www.tucows.com*.

Windows Store Apps

Microsoft is hoping to pull an Apple here: It wants its *online* software store to be your one-stop software shopping mall.

The Windows Store is an online catalog of software from huge software companies, tiny one-person software companies, and everything in between. You can read about the apps, check out customer reviews, and, finally, download them directly to your computer.

There are some huge advantages to this system. Since there's no box, DVD, registration card, shipping, or stocking, the software can cost a lot less. Plenty of programs in the Windows Store are free, and many paid ones offer a free 7-day trial.

Furthermore, Microsoft controls the transaction on both ends—it knows who you are—so there are no serial numbers to type in. The installation doesn't have to interrupt you with warnings like "Please enter your password to install this software." Once you click Buy, Try, or Install, the software downloads and installs itself automatically, without any interaction from you at all.

There are no disks to store and hunt down later, either. If you ever need to reinstall a program from the Windows Store, or if you ever get a new PC, you just re-download it; the store remembers that you're a legitimate owner. Better yet, you'll be downloading the latest version of that program; you won't have to install all the ".01" patches that have come along since.

Best of all, since Microsoft knows what programs you have, it can let you know when new versions are available. You'll see the word "Updates" in the upper-right corner of the Windows Store and on the updated app's Start menu tile; the Store tile on the Start menu shows how many updates await. Tap it to see the apps for which more recent versions are ready. (Tap Install to grab all of them at once.)

Navigating the store

To use the Windows Store, open the Store tile on your Start menu. As shown in Figure 6-14 (top), the store looks like it's been printed on an endless paper towel roll; it scrolls for miles.

There are thousands of these apps, so Microsoft tries to bring a few choice morsels to the surface with categories like "Picks for you," "Top free apps" (most-downloaded) and "Top paid apps" (the most-downloaded ones that cost money).

At the top of the Home screen: an "App categories" link. It opens a sublist of categories like Sports, Travel, Shopping, and so on—another way to dive into the app ocean.

Of course, you can also search for an app by name or by nature. To do that, click in the search box and type (*piano, stocks, fantasy football,* or whatever).

In general, the store here works exactly like the app store on a smartphone. Tap a program's icon to open its details page. Here you'll find reviews and ratings from other people, a description, screenshots of the program, and much more information to help you make a good buying decision. See Figure 6-14 at bottom.

When you find an app that looks good, tap Free (if it's free) or its price button or Free Trial button (if it's not). When the download is complete, that button changes to say Open. You never have to enter your password, restart, unzip, or manually install anything.

Note: The Windows Store lists desktop apps, too (not just Windows Store apps). But you don't actually buy and download desktop apps from the Windows Store; you get a link to the software company's Web site for that purpose. The only programs you can actually download from the Windows Store are, indeed, Windows Store apps.

Automatic updates

Software companies frequently update Windows Store apps, just as they do with phone and tablet apps. They fix bugs; they add new features. As it turns out, new versions of your Windows Store apps get installed quietly and automatically, in the background; you're not even aware it's happening.

Microsoft says that it inspects each app to make sure that Automatic App Updates doesn't hand you something that doesn't work right. But it does sometimes happen:

You prefer the original version of some app to the "new, improved" one—and if automatic updates is turned on, you'll never have the opportunity to object.

So: If the automatic-updates business is a little too automatic for your tastes, you can turn it off. In the Store app, click your own icon (the round one next to the search box); from the shortcut menu, choose Settings, and then turn off "Update apps automatically."

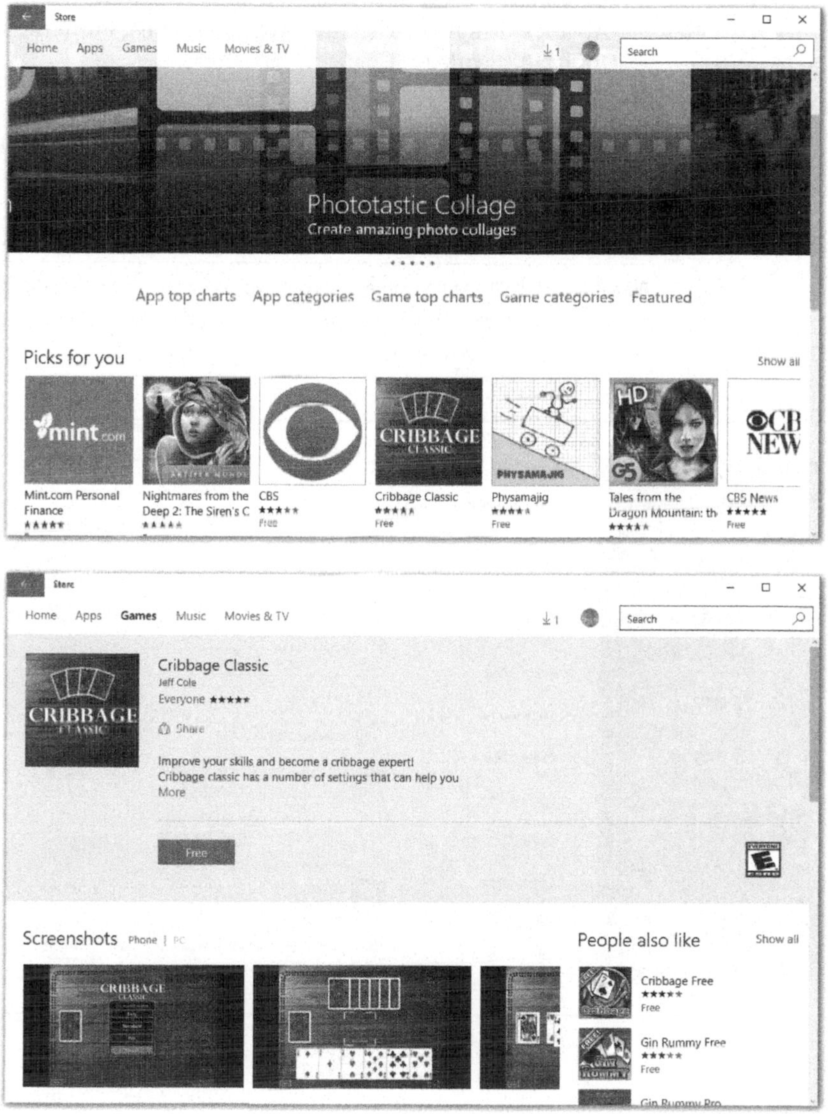

Figure 6-14:
Top: The Store app is the source of all touch-friendly "Windows Store" apps.

To see a list of every app you've ever downloaded, click your own icon (the round one next to the search box) and choose "My library."

Bottom: Each app has its own page—a horizontally scrolling page filled with information. Photos, reviews, details, related apps, and other apps made by the same people.

Uninstalling Software

When you've had enough of a certain program and want to reclaim the disk space it occupies, don't just delete its folder. The typical application installer tosses its software components like birdseed all over your hard drive; therefore, only some of the program is actually in the program's folder.

Instead, the proper method goes like this:

- **Enlightened programs (released since Windows 10).** Open the Start menu's "All apps" list. Right-click the program's name. From the shortcut menu, choose Uninstall (Figure 6-15, left).

- **Older programs.** Open Windows 10's new Apps & Features page of Settings (Settings→System→Apps & features). Select the app, and then hit Uninstall (Figure 6-15, right).

You have to admit it: *That* is progress, is it not?

Note: If you don't see the name of the app you want to remove in Settings, it must be a truly ancient, creaking piece of work. You might have to open the old Control Panel and navigate to the Programs and Features page (page 283), to remove it.

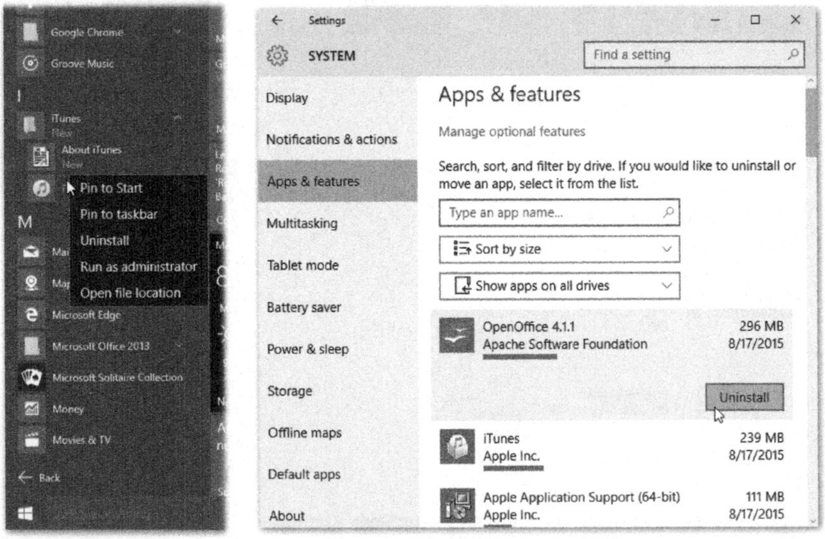

Figure 6-15:
Before Windows 10, uninstalling one of your apps sometimes required a power drill, a blowtorch, and a six-volume instruction manual. Now it's as easy as right-clicking in the "All apps list" (left) or clicking the program's name in Settings.

Program Compatibility Modes

"You can't make an omelet without breaking a few eggs." If that's not Microsoft's motto, it should be. Each successive version of Windows may be better than the previous one, but each inevitably winds up "breaking" hundreds of programs, utilities, and drivers that used to run fine.

Microsoft is well aware of this problem and has pulled every trick in the book to address it. Here, for example, is the chain of second chances you'll experience:

Compatibility Mode

In principle, programs that were written for recent versions of Windows should run fine in Windows 10. Unfortunately, some of them contain software code that deliberately sniffs around to find out what Windows version you have. These programs (or even their installer programs) may say, "Windows *what?*"—and refuse to open.

Fortunately, Windows' Compatibility mode has some sneaky tricks that can fool them into running. You can use it to make "Let me run!" changes to a stubborn app either the non-techie, wizardy way (you just answer questions in a screen-by-screen interview format, and let Windows make the changes behind the scenes) or the expert way (changing compatibility settings manually).

Compatibility mode: The wizardy way

To let Windows fix your compatibility headache, open the Start menu. Start typing *compatibility* until you see "Run programs made for previous versions of Windows." Choose it.

Tip: Here's another way to get to the wizard: Right-click a program's icon (in the Program Files folder, for example), or its shortcut's icon; from the shortcut menu, choose "Troubleshoot compatibility."

The Program Compatibility program opens. It's a wizard—a series of dialog boxes that interview you. On the way, you're asked to click the name of the program you're having trouble with. On the following screen, you have a choice of automatic or manual modes:

- **Try recommended settings** means "Let Windows try to figure out how to make my stubborn program run. I don't really care what it has to tinker with under the hood."

- **Troubleshoot program** means "Let me adjust the compatibility settings myself."

  You'll be asked to choose from options like, "The program worked in earlier versions of Windows," "The program opens but doesn't display correctly," and so on. Work through the question screens the best you can. When it's all over, you get a "Start the program" button that lets you see if the program finally runs without problems.

  Whether things are fixed or not, after you've checked out the app, return to the troubleshooting wizard and click Next. You'll be able to (a) save the fixed settings for the future, (b) start a new round of troubleshooting, or (c) send a report to Microsoft that you never did solve the problem.

Compatibility mode: The manual way

If you know what you're doing, you can save some time and cut to the chase by invoking Compatibility mode yourself. To do that, right-click a program's icon (or its shortcut's icon). From the shortcut menu, choose Properties; click the Compatibility tab.

Now the dialog box shown in Figure 6-16 appears. The options here are precisely the same choices Windows makes for you automatically when you use the wizard described above—it's just that now you can adjust them yourself. Here's what you get:

- **Compatibility mode.** This is the part that tricks the program into believing you're still running Windows 95, Windows XP, or whatever.

- **Reduced color mode.** Makes the program switch your screen to certain limited-colors settings required by older games.

- **Run in 640 × 480 screen resolution.** Runs the app in a small window—the size monitors used to be in the olden days. You might try this option if the app doesn't look right when it runs.

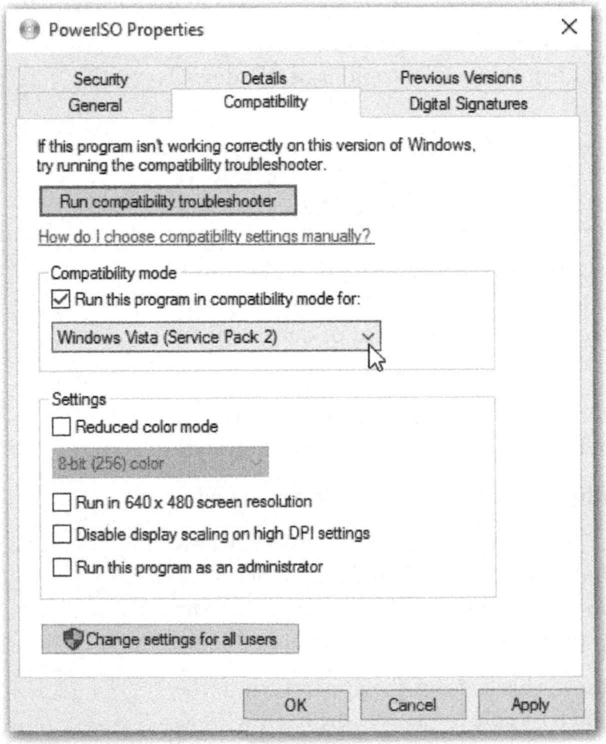

Figure 6-16:
By turning on "Run this program in compatibility mode for" and choosing the name of a previous version of Windows from the list, you can fool that program into thinking it's running on Windows 95, Windows Me, Windows NT, or whatever.

- **Disable display scaling on high DPI settings.** If you've bumped up the type size for your screen but your fonts are looking really weird in an older app, turn on this checkbox.

- **Run this program as an administrator** lets you run the program as though you have an administrator account (page 751; it's not available if you are *already* logged in as an administrator).

This mode is designed to accommodate poorly written programs that, in the XP days, had to be run in administrative mode, back when everyone ran their PCs that way and didn't realize how many virus doors that left open. The downside of

A Little Bit About 64 Bits

Windows 10 is available in both 32-bit and 64-bit versions.

Right. 64-what?

If you want your eyes to glaze over, you can read the details on 64-bit computing on Wikipedia. But the normal-person's version goes like this:

For decades, the roadways for memory and information that passed through PCs were 32 "lanes" wide—they could manage 32 chunks of data at once. It seemed like plenty at the time. But as programs and even documents grew enormous, and computers came with the capacity to have more and more memory installed, engineers began to dream of 64-lane circuitry.

To reach 64-bit nirvana, however, you need a 64-bit computer running the 64-bit version of Windows.

Sometimes, you don't have a choice. For example, if your PC comes with 4 gigabytes of memory or more, it has 64-bit Windows, like it or not.

Otherwise, though, you probably do have a choice. Which version should you go for?

In the short term, the most visible effect of having a 64-bit computer is that you can install a lot more memory. A top-of-the-line 32-bit PC, for example, is limited to 4 GB of RAM—and only about 3 GB is actually available to your

programs. That once seemed like a lot, but it's suffocatingly small if you're a modern video editor, game designer, or number-crunchy engineer.

On a 64-bit PC with 64-bit Windows, though, you can install just a tad bit more memory: 192 GB.

Eventually, there may be other benefits to a 64-bit PC. Programs can be rewritten to run faster. Security can be better, too.

For now, though, there are some downsides to going 64-bit. For example, older, 32-bit programs mostly run fine on a 64-bit machine. But some won't run at all, and 32-bit drivers for older hardware (sound card, graphics card, printer, and so on) may give you particular headaches.

You can't run 16-bit programs at all in 64-bit Windows, either (at least not without an add-on program like DOSBox).

If you have taken the 64-bit plunge, you generally don't have to know whether your apps are running in 32- or 64-bit mode; every kind of program runs in the right mode automatically. If you ever want to see how many of your apps are actually 32-bitters, though, press Ctrl+Shift+Esc to open the Task Manager; then click the Processes tab. The 32-bit programs you have open are indicated by "(32 bit)" after their names.

turning on this option is that you'll have to authenticate yourself every time you run the program.

- **Change settings for all users.** If more than one person has an account on this PC, this applies the changes you've just made to everyone's accounts.

Finally, two footnotes:

- You're much better off securing an updated version of the program, if it's available. Check the program's Web site to see if a Win10-compatible update is available.

- Don't try this "fake out the app" trick with utilities like virus checkers, backup programs, CD-burning software, and hard drive utilities. Installing older versions of these with Windows 10 is asking for disaster.

Note: In Windows 7, there was Windows XP Mode: an actual Windows XP simulator that could run all those legacy and specialty programs. Alas, it's gone in Windows 10. You can find some iffy hacks online to restore it—let Google be your friend—but for all real-world purposes, Windows XP Mode is gone and buried.

CHAPTER 7

Settings & Control Panel

E very complex machine has a control panel. There's the dashboard of a car, the knobs on a stove, the cockpit of an airplane. And then there's the granddaddy of them all: the Control Panel in Windows.

Actually, in Windows 10, the Control Panel isn't very important anymore. It's still there, like an old typewriter you can't bear to throw away. You can still read about it later in this chapter.

But in Windows 10, Microsoft has extracted a few hundred of the Control Panel's most useful options and packaged them up into a new app called Settings. It's far cleaner, simpler, and better organized, and it's designed to accommodate either a mouse or your finger on a touchscreen.

Only the most obscure settings require a visit to the old Control Panel—and over time, Microsoft says, it will move even more of those into the new Settings app.

For the moment, though, it's clear that Microsoft hasn't yet completed its mission to unify the two brains of Windows 8. Windows 10 still includes two different apps to adjust your computer's settings.

Fortunately, this chapter covers them both.

The Settings App

Most of the time, you'll customize your system in the new Settings app. Volume, screensaver, WiFi setup, privacy settings, PC accounts, color schemes, and so on—it's all here, in one place.

And where is "here?" There are plenty of avenues to the new Settings:

- **From the Start menu.** Click, press, or tap ▦; in the left side of the Start menu, choose Settings.

- **From the Action Center.** Click or tap ▤ (or press ▦+A); on the Quick Action tiles, hit All Settings.

- **From the keyboard.** Press ▦+ I. (That's *I* for *settIngs,* of course.)

You now encounter the magnificence of the Windows 10 Settings app (Figure 7-1).

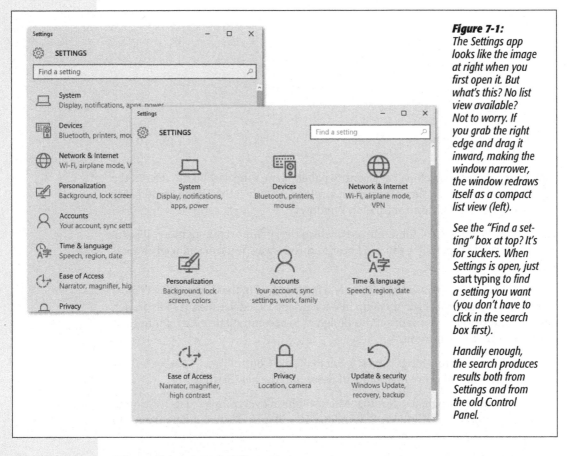

Figure 7-1:
The Settings app looks like the image at right when you first open it. But what's this? No list view available? Not to worry. If you grab the right edge and drag it inward, making the window narrower, the window redraws itself as a compact list view (left).

See the "Find a setting" box at top? It's for suckers. When Settings is open, just start typing to find a setting you want (you don't have to click in the search box first).

Handily enough, the search produces results both from Settings and from the old Control Panel.

Direct Access to Settings Pages

The nine broad categories of Settings are described below.

But you're wasting your time if you *click or tap* your way into a settings screen. It's almost always faster to *search* for a setting, or to ask Cortana to open it for you. Say, "Open WiFi settings," for example, or type *wifi settings* into the search box. You'll jump right to the page you want.

Tip: If there's a certain Settings page you use often, here's an idea that probably wouldn't have occurred to you: Install its tile on the Start menu!

Once the Settings app is open, you can right-click either a Settings category (like System or Devices) or an individual Settings page (like Battery Saver or Storage). From the shortcut menu, choose Pin to Start. Boom—there it is.

System

At top left in the Settings app, the most important category here: System. This icon is the gateway to individual screens for power, storage, notifications, apps, and screen settings. Click it to reveal the following settings pages inside (Figure 7-2).

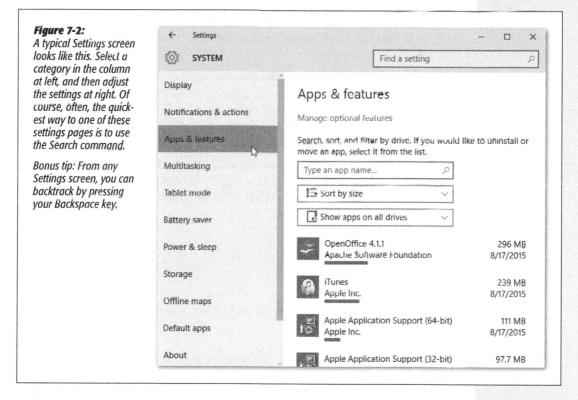

Figure 7-2:
A typical Settings screen looks like this. Select a category in the column at left, and then adjust the settings at right. Of course, often, the quickest way to one of these settings pages is to use the Search command.

Bonus tip: From any Settings screen, you can backtrack by pressing your Backspace key.

Display

These controls govern the size of type on your screen and serve as the dashboard for multiple-monitor setups. Page 190 describes it all.

Notifications & Actions

Here you can tame the notifications—the little bubbles that pop onto your screen to alert you about this or that—that might otherwise interrupt you to insanity. (And, because Microsoft had nowhere else to put it, there's a "Select which icons appear on the taskbar" link here, too.) See page 111.

Apps & Features

This screen (Figure 7-2) presents a complete listing of all your apps. You can sort them by size, name, or installation date; exclude apps on external drives; or search for just one app by name. You'd never look at this list unless you were worried about running out of space, which is why it's extra convenient that you can uninstall any app here by selecting it and then hitting the Uninstall button that appears. (Except for the primary apps of Windows 10; Microsoft doesn't want you to remove those.)

Multitasking

These are the options that control window snapping, and they're described in the box on page 52.

Also tucked here: a couple of options for the new virtual-screens feature described on page 193. For example:

- **On the taskbar, show windows that are open on:** The taskbar's job is to sprout icons for all your open windows. But what if you've set up a couple of virtual monitors? Should the taskbar change as you switch from "monitor" to "monitor," showing buttons only for the apps on the current desktop? Or should it always reflect *all* your open windows on all the desktops?

- **Pressing Alt+Tab shows windows that are open on:** Similar question. When you press the app-switching keystroke (page 226), should the app switcher show the window miniatures for *all* the windows on *all* your desktops? Or just the one you're using right now?

Tablet Mode

See page 443.

Battery Saver

It's new in Windows 10, it's for laptops and tablets, and it's described in Chapter 13.

Power & Sleep

These options manage the power consumption of your computer. That's a big deal when you're running on battery power, of course, but it's also important if you'd like to save money (and the environment) by cutting down on the juice consumed by your *desktop* PC.

The pop-up menus here govern the sleeping habits of two components: your screen and the computer itself. The sooner they sleep, the more power you save. The pop-up menus let you choose intervals from "1 minute" to "Never."

Of course, when your PC is plugged in, you might not care so much about battery savings—so you get a second set of pop-up menus that govern sleep schedules when the machine has wall power.

Tip: The "Additional power settings" link opens up the old Power Options page of the Control Panel, where you have far more detailed control over various elements of your computer and how much power they use.

Save Locations

This is a new option in Windows 10. It's designed for people who have external drives connected to their PCs, so they can keep big files like pictures, music, and videos in separate, roomier places.

At top: Little maps of all your drives, showing how full they are.

Below that: Pop-up menus for documents, music, pictures, and videos. For each, you can choose an external drive's name and letter. From now on, whenever you download or import files of those types, Windows stores them on the specified drives, for your convenience.

(Of course, whatever change you make here doesn't affect the current locations of any files—only future ones.)

Offline Maps

If you rely on the Maps app as your primary navigation source (not bloody likely), you might appreciate the options here.

Ordinarily, the Maps app gets its pictures of the world from the Internet, downloading them as you scroll. That generally works well, but there are two problems:

- **You're not always online.** Maybe you have a tablet or laptop that doesn't have a cellular connection, so there's no way for Maps to download information when you're on the go.

- **Data costs money.** Maybe you do have a cellular connection—but map data is big data, and downloading a lot of it can rack up your cellular bill.

In both cases, the solution is offline maps: Download the map images for a certain country before you go there. That data will be saved on your machine, and Maps won't have to go online to get them. So:

- **Download maps.** Click to choose a continent, and then a country, whose map images you want to download now, while you still have an Internet connection. Windows tells you how much room each one will require. (There's a "Delete all maps" button, too, so you can recover the space once your trip is over.)

- **Metered connections.** If this is off, Windows will download maps only when you have free WiFi or unlimited cellular connections—not when you have to pay to get online.

The last item here has nothing to do with offline maps, but what are you gonna do? It's "Automatically update maps." That's an acknowledgment that maps change all the time (roads are built, empires crumble). If this is on, you give Microsoft permission to send you the updated maps automatically.

Default Apps

What's your preferred Web browser? Music player? Video player? Choose here. (See page 247.)

About

Here's your computer's birth certificate (Figure 7-3).

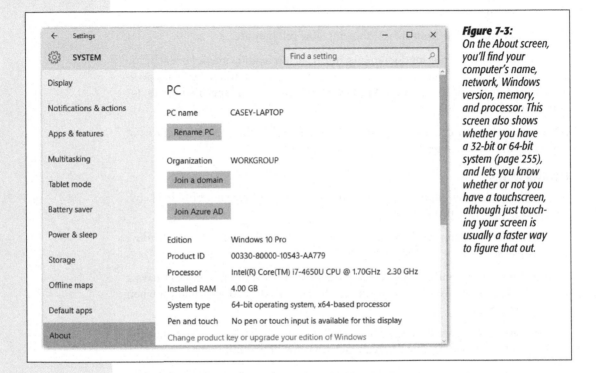

Figure 7-3:
On the About screen, you'll find your computer's name, network, Windows version, memory, and processor. This screen also shows whether you have a 32-bit or 64-bit system (page 255), and lets you know whether or not you have a touchscreen, although just touching your screen is usually a faster way to figure that out.

Devices

This second major Settings category is the grand depot for connecting other devices: printers, scanners, cameras, and so on. Its tabs go like this:

Printers & Scanners

Here's your list of printers and scanners that Windows knows about—and your opportunity to connect a new one. See Chapter 14.

Connected Devices

This is the master screen that lists every external device your computer knows about: printer, scanner, mouse, keyboard, USB camera, and so on.

This is also where you add new devices (that is, introduce them to Windows) and delete old ones. See Chapter 15 for details.

Mouse & Touchpad

On this page, you can tweak the most essential behaviors of your pointing device:

- **Primary mouse button.** The primary mouse button is the one you press for normal clicks (as opposed to right-clicks). If you're left-handed, you may prefer to switch the buttons so that the *right* button is the primary one.

- **Roll the mouse wheel to scroll.** If you have a mouse, and it has a scroll wheel, this pop-up menu lets you change the behavior of each "click" of that wheel. Does it scroll a few lines at a time, or one screenful?

  If you choose "lines at a time," you can then use the slider to specify how *many* lines at a time, to suit how caffeinated your style is.

- **Scroll inactive windows when I hover over them.** The question is: When your cursor is in front of a background window—not the one you're working in—what should happen when you turn the mouse wheel? Should that window scroll? (Usually, you want this on. It's handy.)

- **Cursor delay.** Laptop trackpads are pretty great. Unfortunately, they're generally positioned right next to the *keyboard*. If you're not careful, you'll be typing along happily... your thumb will accidentally brush the trackpad, causing an accidental click...which plants the insertion point in some random place...and the next thing you know, you've typed the next four sentences into some completely random part of your document.

  This setting is designed to eliminate that problem. You can set it up so that touching the trackpad doesn't register a tap at all ("Turn off taps"), or so that it registers only if a fraction of a second has elapsed since your last spurt of typing ("Short delay," "Medium delay," and so on).

  Or, if you never make that kind of mistake, choose "No delay (always on)"; now you can always tap the trackpad.

Typing

You might have noticed that as you type, Windows quietly and instantly corrects your obvious typos. Or maybe you *haven't* noticed, which is even more awesome.

In other words, if you type "prolbem," for example, it changes to "problem" the instant you press the space bar at the end of the word. There's no beep, no underline, no error message; the correction just happens.

(On the other hand, these spell-checking features work only in Windows Store apps—not traditional desktop apps. So maybe you really *haven't* ever seen them.)

But what about a word like "corse"? Did you mean *corset* or *course?* Windows can't read your mind. (Maybe someday.)

In that case, Windows doesn't correct the error—it just flags it by displaying a wavy underline beneath the questionable word.

You might want to turn these features off—for example, if you're writing a novel starring a character with really bad spelling, or you just don't like these features. Here are the on/off switches: "Autocorrect misspelled words" and "Highlight misspelled words."

AutoPlay

Windows wants to know what you want to happen when you insert a flash drive ("Removable drive") or a memory card ("Memory card"). For each, you get choices like "Open folder to view files," "Import photos or videos," "Configure this drive for backup"—or "Take no action." Or you can turn the whole feature off.

Network & Internet

The third major Settings page offers all the settings you need to get online. Most of them are described in Chapter 9:

Airplane Mode

As you're probably aware, you're not allowed to make cellphone calls on U.S. airplanes. According to legend (if not science), a cellphone's radio can interfere with a plane's navigational equipment.

But come on. If you're using a tablet with cellular service, are you really supposed to deprive yourself of all the music, videos, movies, and email that you could be using in flight, just because wireless gadgets are forbidden?

Nope. Just turn on airplane mode (so that this switch says On). Now the cellular and WiFi features are turned off completely. You can't make calls or get online, but you can do anything else in the computer's bag of noncellular tricks.

Tip: Of course, it's much faster to hop into airplane mode using the Quick Actions panel (page 115)—or even by telling Cortana, "Turn on airplane mode."

Data Usage

This item shows how much Internet data your computer has used in the past 30 days. (It's primarily intended for tablets and laptops that have cellular service, to avoid going over your monthly allotment. But some people also have WiFi service with monthly data caps; this gauge could be useful there, too.)

Click "Usage details" to view which apps have used how much of that data.

VPN

All over the world, corporate employees on the road connect to their home offices using *virtual private networking*. VPN is a fancy way of saying, "Your laptop computer can become part of your company's network over the Internet." See page 456 for details.

Dial-Up

Really? You get online with a dial-up modem?

Ethernet

This screen does little more than tell you whether or not you're connected to a network with an Ethernet cable—and offer links to other networking control panels.

Proxy

A *proxy server* is a security barrier between your own network and the Internet. It prevents evildoers online from getting through to your internal network. This screen is where highly paid networking professionals can set up an automatic or manual proxy server.

Personalization

Main Settings Category No. 4 is your interior-design center. Here's where you can change the look of your desktop wallpaper (Background), desktop color scheme (Colors and Themes), image on your Lock screen, and behavior of your Start menu. All of it's described in Chapter 4. (The options governing what shows up in your Start menu are described in Chapter 1.)

Accounts

This is the fifth main category. When you sign into your computer, you're signing into your own account. That keeps your stuff private from anyone else who uses this machine and prevents people from messing up your files and settings.

On this panel, you can set up additional accounts for logging in to Windows—usually one for each person who uses a machine—or make changes to your own. And the "Sign-in options" category lets you specify a password, a four-digit number, or a picture password to unlock your account (page 566). Details on accounts are in Chapter 19.

Time & Language

Just what it says.

Date and Time

- **Set time automatically, Adjust for daylight saving time automatically.** If you turn these off, you will have to set your computer's clock, time zone, and daylight saving settings manually.

- **Time and date formats.** What's the first day of the week? Do you put the month first, American style (7/30/15), or the date first, European style (30/7/15)? How do you like the time written out?

Region and Language

Specify where you live and what language(s) you speak, for the purposes of tailoring the Web sites you see and the onscreen keyboards available to you.

Speech

Here's where you indicate what language you speak (for the purposes of Cortana and speech recognition) and which of Windows' two voices you want it to use when speaking to *you* (male or female). This is also where you can set up your microphone for accurate speech interpretation; if you hit "Get started," Windows asks you to read a sentence aloud, so it gets the idea of what you sound like.

Ease of Access

Windows offers all kinds of tools to make computing easier if you have trouble seeing or hearing. For example:

Narrator, Magnifier

Narrator is a screen reader, a digitized voice that reads everything on the screen, which is essential if you're blind. See page 325.

Magnifier enlarges what's on the screen in a special movable window; see page 312.

High Contrast

This feature reverses the screen's colors black for white, like a film negative. It creates a higher-contrast effect that some people find is easier on the eyes. (The other colors reverse, too—red for green, and so on.) Here you can choose a canned color scheme, and even edit it (tap a color swatch to change it).

Closed Captions

This option controls the look of the closed captions (subtitles) that appear in some of the movies, TV shows, and videos you can buy, rent, or stream from Microsoft's new TV and movie store.

Tip: In the Movies & TV Store, videos equipped with subtitles bear a small CC icon.

Using these pop-up menus, you can change an insane number of font, size, opacity, and color options, both for the type and the background it appears on.

Keyboard

These clever features are designed to help people who have trouble using the keyboard.

- **On-Screen Keyboard** is just another way to make the keyboard appear (page 445).

- **Sticky Keys** lets you press multiple-key shortcuts (involving keys like Shift, Ctrl, and ⊞) one at a time instead of all together.

- **Toggle Keys** plays a sound when you hit the Caps Lock, Num Lock, or Scroll Lock key. It has little to do with disabilities; it's to save *anyone* from the frustration of hitting one of those keys accidentally and looking up to discover 10 minutes' worth of gibberish typing.

- **Filter Keys** doesn't register a key press at all until you've held down the key for more than a second or so—a feature designed to screen out accidental key presses. It also ignores repeated keystrokes.

- **Enable shortcut underlines.** Windows veterans remember when menu commands had little underlines, showing which keyboard letter (in combination with the Alt key) would trigger a command. Now that handy cheat-sheet system is back—if you turn on this switch. (Doesn't work in all programs.)

- **Display a message when turning a setting on with a shortcut.** You'll be shown an "Are you sure?" box when you turn on one of the Ease of Access features from the keyboard.

- **Make a sound when turning a setting on or off with a shortcut.** You'll hear a confirmation beep when you turn on one of the Ease of Access features from the keyboard.

Mouse

These controls govern the arrow cursor (the "pointer") and its movement.

- **Pointer size, Pointer color.** You can make your cursor bigger here, or change it from black to white (or even "black until it's against a black background, in which case it's white"). Cool.

- **Mouse Keys** is designed to help people who can't use the mouse—or who want more precision when working in graphics programs. It lets you click, drag, and otherwise manipulate the cursor by pressing the keys on your numeric keypad. (It's not very useful on keyboards that don't have separate numeric keypads, like laptops.)

  When Mouse Keys is turned on, the 5 key triggers a click, and the + key acts as a double-click. (Specify a left-button click by first pressing the / key, or a right-click by pressing the - key.)

  Move the cursor around the screen by pressing the eight keys that surround the 5 key. (For example, hold down the 9 key to move the cursor diagonally up and to the right.) You can even drag something on the screen; press 0 to "hold down the button" on something, and then move it using the number keys, and press the period (.) to let go.

  While you're moving the mouse, you can speed up by pressing Ctrl and slow down by pressing Shift (if you've turned this option on here).

Tip: It's kind of clunky to have to burrow all the way into PC Settings every time you want to turn on Mouse Keys. Fortunately, there's a shortcut: the Num Lock key on your keyboard. It turns on Mouse Keys (at least if "Use mouse keys when Num Lock is on" is on).

Other Options

Here are a few miscellaneous options that may help you, whether you have a disability or not:

- **Play animations in Windows.** Windows 10 spices things up by displaying animations here and there. When you hit the ▣ button, for example, the Start menu seems to slide into place, with its tiles sliding in a microsecond later. It's very pretty, but it also saps away precious moments of work time. This switch eliminates them, and the time they take.

- **Show Windows background.** If you turn this switch off, then you see a solid color as your wallpaper. Any fancy photo or swirly pattern you've chosen is gone, presumably to make life more legible for the hard-of-seeing.

- **Show notifications for.** Notifications, the rectangular bubbles described in Chapter 2, pop in to remind you of something, or to let you know that some new message has arrived—and then they disappear. But using this pop-up menu, you can control how long they stick around before vanishing—from 5 seconds to 5 minutes (a good setting if you're *really* slow on the draw).

- **Cursor thickness.** How thick do you want the text cursor to be? (Not the arrow pointer—the vertical bar that blinks where the next typing will appear.) See Figure 7-4.

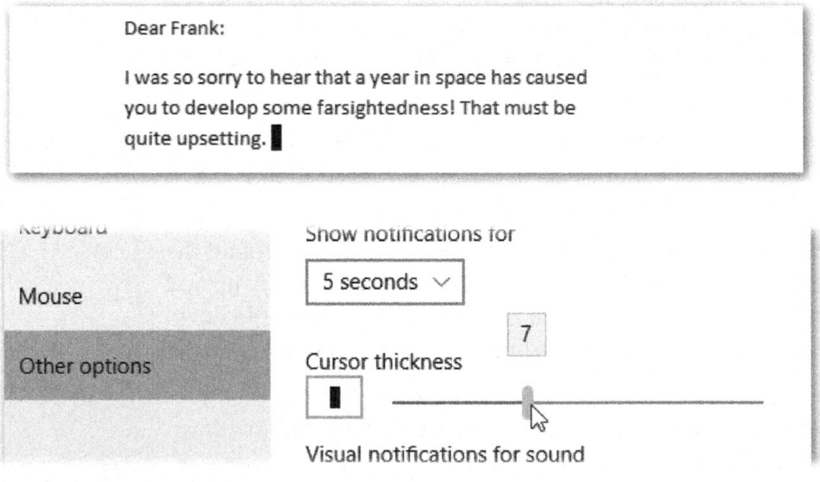

Figure 7-4:
Top: You can make the insertion-point cursor ridiculously thick, if you want.

Bottom: Use the pop-up menu to choose, on a scale of 1 pixel (a fine vertical line) to 20 pixels (a huge, fat, black box) the size of your cursor. As you adjust the thickness, you get to see an example in the box to the left of the menu.

- **Visual notifications for sound.** If you have trouble hearing, or if your roommate tends to play heavy metal at top volume when you're trying to work, you might not hear the little beeps or chimes that Windows plays to get your attention. This pop-up menu lets you opt to add a visual cue, like a flash of the menu bar, window, or the whole screen.

Privacy

This panel reveals just how vast the ocean of data is that Microsoft routinely harvests from your computer and shares—with advertisers, with its own programmers, and with other apps.

Fortunately, you can shut down much of it. Chapter 12 covers what these options do, blow by blow.

Update & Security

Windows, like any software, is an eternal work in progress, as these options make clear:

Windows Update

Windows is software and can therefore be updated, debugged, and improved. (Software is handy that way.) Windows Update is Microsoft's system for sending you patches and fixes over the Internet. See page 495 for more on Windows Update.

Windows Defender

The Windows world is teeming with viruses and other nastiness—and Windows comes with a free antivirus program to block it all, called Defender. These options are described in Chapter 12.

Backup

You've just found the settings for Windows' automatic backup feature, File History. It's described in Chapter 17.

Recovery

Windows offers several ways to reset itself in times of troubleshooting. Details are in Chapter 16, but here are the basics:

- **Reset this PC.** This option *refreshes* your PC—resets your computer. Basic computer settings are reset to their factory states, and apps that didn't come from the Windows App Store are deleted. You wind up with a fresh copy of Windows, and your files and settings intact (if that's what you want).

- **Go back to an earlier build.** As you know from page 1, Microsoft continues Windows 10 to be a work in progress. Upgrades and new features will trickle out all year long, automatically; in Windows 10 Home, you can't even decline them.

  If some update really messes up your machine, though, at least you have this option; it rewinds Windows to an earlier version.

- **Advanced startup.** This option restarts your computer so that you can boot up from some external drive, like a DVD or a USB flash drive, or change startup settings in the course of troubleshooting.

The screen blinks off, and then you arrive at the "Choose an option" screen, where you can restart Windows, troubleshoot (refresh or reset the PC, or use the advanced troubleshooting and configuration tools described in Chapter 16), or just turn the computer off.

Activation

Activation is Microsoft's name for copy protection: You can't run Windows without a serial number (a "product key").

This screen lets you know if your current copy of Windows has, in fact, been activated (as opposed to running in trial mode). You can even change your Product ID by clicking "Change product key" without having to reinstall Windows itself, which can come in handy if, for example, you want to upgrade Windows versions, or switch to a multiple-use product key.

For Developers

These three options are for software programmers who need access to unusual features—like sideloading apps (installing apps that didn't come from Microsoft's app store).

The Control Panel

The Settings app is where you'll go to make most changes to your computer. It's a cleaner, newer, nicer-looking dashboard for your PC's settings.

But the old Control Panel is still around, teeming with miniature applications (or *applets*) that govern every conceivable setting for every conceivable component of your computer.

Many are duplicated in the new Settings app. Others are so obscure that you'll wonder what on earth inspired Microsoft to create them.

The following pages cover them all.

Note: Here and there, within the Control Panel, you'll spot a little Windows security-shield icon. It tells you that you're about to make an important, major change to the operating system, something that will affect everyone who uses this PC—fiddling with its network settings, for example, or changing its clock. To prove your worthiness (and to prove that you're not an evil virus attempting to make a nasty change), you'll be asked to *authenticate* yourself; see the box on page 726 for details.

Many Roads to Control Panel

For most people, these are the quickest ways to the Control Panel:

- Right-click the Start menu (or press ⊞+X). From the secret utility menu, choose Control Panel.

- Press ⊞ to open the search box; start typing *control panel* until you see its name at the top of the menu. Press Enter (or tap it).

But you know what? Those are only the tips of the iceberg of Ways to Open Control Panel. Consider:

- Control Panel is listed in your Start menu's "All apps" list (in the folder called Windows System).

- Often, you'll wind up popping into the Control Panel without any warning—after clicking a "More options" link in the Settings app. (Settings has a lot of links to the Control Panel like that.)

- The search box is uncannily good at taking you to the control panel you really want, too. Hit ⊞ to open the Start menu; type *color*; when you see Color Management highlighted in the results list, press Enter to open it. (On other quests, you might type *fonts, sound, battery, accounts, date, CDs, speech,* or whatever.)

  There's a similar search box right in the Control Panel window itself.

- You can choose a certain panel's name *directly* from the Start menu, as described on page 44.

- If you don't mind a cluttered desktop, you can make a shortcut for the applets you access most. To do that, open the Control Panel. Right-click the icon you want; from the shortcut menu, choose "Create shortcut." It automatically places it on the desktop for you.

- You can install a certain Control Panel applet onto the Start menu (right side), too! With Control Panel open, right-click the icon you want; from the shortcut menu, choose Pin to Start.

- You can even put an applet into the "Quick access" list that appears in every File Explorer window. In the open Control Panel, right-click the icon you want; from the shortcut menu, choose "Pin to Quick access."

Control Panel Views

When it first appears, the Control Panel looks like the one shown in Figure 7-5. But that's just the beginning.

The "View by" pop-up menu (upper right) shows that there are three ways to view the complete collection of control panels: by category or as a list of small or large icons.

Category view

If you choose Category view, you'll find these categories:

- **System and Security.** In this category are system and administrative tasks like backing up and restoring, setting your power options, and security options (firewall, encryption, and so on).

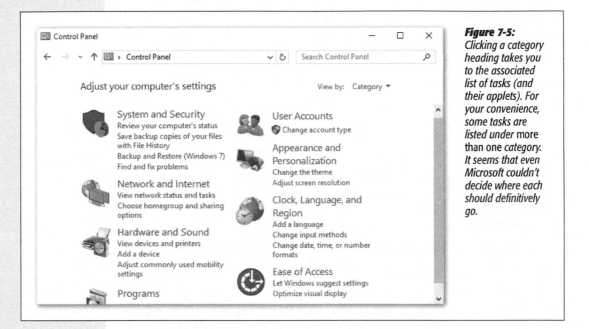

Figure 7-5:
Clicking a category heading takes you to the associated list of tasks (and their applets). For your convenience, some tasks are listed under more than one category. It seems that even Microsoft couldn't decide where each should definitively go.

- **Network and Internet.** This category contains settings related to networking, Internet options, offline files (page 635), and Sync Center (to manage synchronizing data between computers and network folders).

- **Hardware and Sound.** Here you find everything for managing gadgets connected to your computer: printer settings, projector settings, laptop adjustments, and so on.

- **Programs.** You'll probably use this one a lot. Here's where you uninstall programs, choose which program is your preferred one (for Web browsing or opening graphics, for example), turn Windows features on and off, and manage your desktop gadgets.

- **User Accounts.** This category contains the settings you need to manage the accounts on the computer (Chapter 17), including the limited-access accounts that parents can create for their children.

- **Appearance and Personalization.** Here's a big category indeed. It covers all things cosmetic, from how the desktop looks (plus taskbar and personalization settings) to folder options, and fonts.

- **Clock, Language, and Region.** These time, language, and clock settings all have one thing in common: They differ according to where in the world you are.

- **Ease of Access.** This category is one-stop shopping for every feature Microsoft has dreamed up to assist the disabled. It's also the rabbit hole into Speech Recognition Options.

Large icons, Small icons

The category concept sounds OK in principle, but it'll drive veterans nuts. You don't want to guess what category Fax wound up in—you just want to open the old Print and Fax control panel, right now.

Fortunately, the Control Panel can display all 50 icons in alphabetical order (Figure 7-6).

Use the "View by" pop-up menu in the upper-right, and choose either "Small icons" or "Large icons." Then double-click the icon of the applet you'd like to use.

Figure 7-6:
Classic view might be overwhelming for novices, because the task icons give little indications about what settings they actually contain. Here's a hint: Remember that you can just move your mouse over a task and pause there. A tooltip pops up, giving you an idea of what's inside.

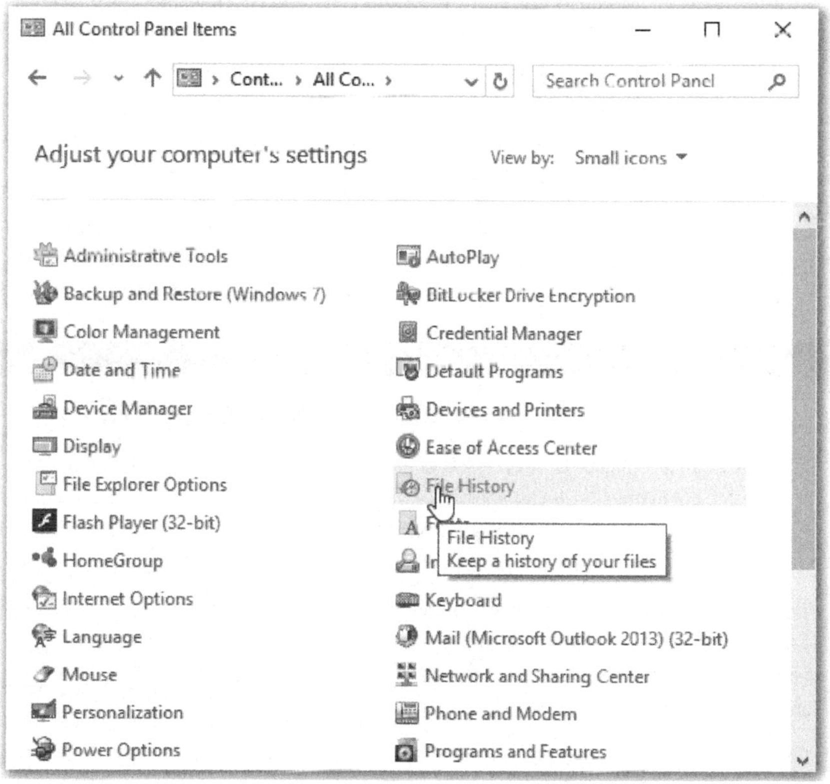

All Control Panel Items

Adjust your computer's settings — View by: Small icons

Administrative Tools	AutoPlay
Backup and Restore (Windows 7)	BitLocker Drive Encryption
Color Management	Credential Manager
Date and Time	Default Programs
Device Manager	Devices and Printers
Display	Ease of Access Center
File Explorer Options	File History
Flash Player (32-bit)	
HomeGroup	
Internet Options	Keyboard
Language	Mail (Microsoft Outlook 2013) (32-bit)
Mouse	Network and Sharing Center
Personalization	Phone and Modem
Power Options	Programs and Features

File History
Keep a history of your files

The Control Panel, Applet by Applet

Icon view is the perfect structure for a chapter that describes each Control Panel applet, since it's organized in alphabetical order. The rest of this chapter assumes you're looking at the Control Panel in one of the two Icon views.

Note: To spare you from hunting through an obsolete jungle of Control Panel options when a much cleaner Settings-app page will do, the following descriptions indicate which applets have been largely replaced by modern Settings screens.

Administrative Tools

This icon is actually a folder containing a suite of very technical administrative utilities. These tools, intended for serious technowizards only, aren't covered in this book.

AutoPlay

The primary features are duplicated in the Settings app; see page 264.

What do you want to happen when you insert a CD? Do you want to see a window of what's on it? Do you want the music on it to start playing? Do you want to auto-run whatever software installer is on it? Do you want whatever photos it contains to get copied to your Pictures library?

The answer, of course, is, "Depends on what kind of CD it is," and also, "That should be up to me."

That's the purpose of AutoPlay. It differentiates between different kinds of audio CDs and DVDs, video CDs and DVDs, programs (like software and games), pictures, video and audio files, blank CDs and DVDs, and even proprietary kinds of discs, like Blu-ray,

---

UP TO SPEED

Control Panel Terminology Hell

The Control Panel continues to be an object of bafflement for Microsoft, not to mention its customers; from version to version of Windows, this window undergoes more reorganizations than a bankrupt airline.

Windows 10 presents the most oddball arrangement yet. There are far more icons in the Control Panel than ever before—about 50 of them, in fact. But they're not all the same kind of thing.

Some are the traditional *applets,* meaning mini-applications (little programs). Others are nothing more than tabbed dialog boxes. Some open up wizards (interview dialog boxes that walk you through a procedure) or even ordinary Explorer windows. And even among the applets, the look and substance of the Control Panel panels vary widely.

So what are people supposed to call these things? The world needs a general term for the motley assortment of icons in the Control Panel window.

To help you and your well-intentioned author from going quietly insane, this chapter refers to all the Control Panel icons as either icons (which they definitely are), control panels, or applets (which most of them are—and besides, that's the traditional term for them).

HD, and SuperVideo. It even lets you manage how externally attached devices (like cameras or USB drives) are handled.

Each time you insert such a disc or drive, you get a dialog box asking how you want to handle it—this time, and every time you insert a similar gadget thereafter. For each kind of disc, the pop-up menu offers you obvious choices by disc type (like "Play audio CD" for music CDs), as well as standard options like "Open folder to view files using Windows Explorer," "Take no action," or "Ask me every time."

Behind the scenes, your choices are recorded in the AutoPlay control panel, where you can change your mind or just look over the choices you've made so far.

If you've never liked AutoPlay and you don't want Windows to do *anything* when you insert a disc, just turn off "Use AutoPlay for all media and devices" at the top of the window.

Backup and Restore Center

The primary features are duplicated in the Settings app; see page 269.

Backup and Restore Center is an obsolete method of backing up your computer. It's included here for the benefit of people who have Windows 7 backups they might want to restore. Check out Chapter 17 for more detailed information.

BitLocker Drive Encryption

BitLocker encrypts the data on your drives to keep them from being accessed by the bad guys who might steal your laptop. For details, see Chapter 18.

Color Management

Microsoft created this applet in conjunction with Canon in an effort to make colors more consistent from screen to printer. Details are in Chapter 14.

Credential Manager

Credential Manager, formerly called "Stored User Names and Passwords," lets you teach Windows to memorize your corporate account names and passwords. It's not the same thing as the Web-browser feature that memorizes your passwords for everyday Web sites (like banking sites). Instead, Credential Manager stores passwords for shared network drives and corporate-intranet Web sites, the ones where you have to enter a name and password before you even see the home page.

Date and Time

The primary features are duplicated in the Settings app; see page 265.

Your PC's concept of what time it is can be very important. Every file you create or save is stamped with this time, and every email you send or receive is marked with it. When you drag a document into a folder that contains a different draft of the same thing, Windows warns that you're about to replace an older version with a newer one (or vice versa)—but only if your clock is set correctly.

This program offers three tabs:

- **Date and Time.** Here's where you can change the time, date, and time zone for the computer (Figure 7-7)—if, that is, you'd rather not have the computer set its own clock (read on).

Tip: In the "Time zone" section of the Date and Time tab, you can find exactly when Windows thinks daylight-saving time is going to start (or end, depending on what time of year it is). In addition, there's an option to remind you a week before the time change occurs, so you don't wind up unexpectedly sleep-deprived on the day of your big TV appearance.

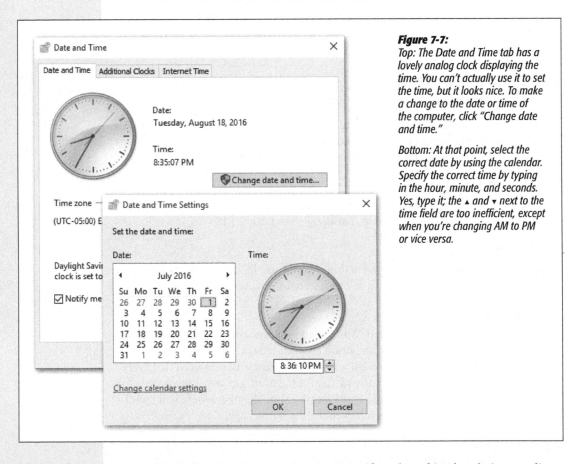

Figure 7-7:
Top: The Date and Time tab has a lovely analog clock displaying the time. You can't actually use it to set the time, but it looks nice. To make a change to the date or time of the computer, click "Change date and time."

Bottom: At that point, select the correct date by using the calendar. Specify the correct time by typing in the hour, minute, and seconds. Yes, type it; the ▲ and ▼ next to the time field are too inefficient, except when you're changing AM to PM or vice versa.

- **Additional Clocks.** If you work overseas, or if you have friends, relatives, or clients in different time zones, you'll like this one; it's the only thing that stands between you and waking them up at three in the morning because you forgot what time it is where they live.

  This feature lets you create clocks for two other time zones, so you can see what time it is in other parts of the world. (They appear when you point to the taskbar clock—or, in larger type, when you click it.)

You can give them any display name you want, like "Paris" or "Mother-in-Law time." Note that the additional clocks' times are based on the PC's own local time. So if the computer's main clock is wrong, the other clocks will be wrong, too.

Figure 7-8 shows how to check one of your additional clocks.

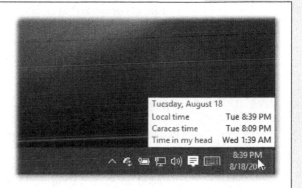

Figure 7-8:
To see the time for the additional clocks, point without clicking over the time in the system tray. You get a pop-up displaying the time on the additional clock (or clocks) that you configured.

- **Internet Time.** This option has nothing to do with Swatch Internet Time, a 1998 concept of time that was designed to eliminate the complications of time zones. (Then again, it introduced complications of its own, like dividing up the 24-hour day into 1,000 parts called "beats," each one being 1 minute and 26.4 seconds long.)

  Instead, this tab teaches your PC to set its own clock by consulting one of the scientific clocks on the Internet. To turn the feature on or off, or to specify which atomic clock you want to use as the master clock, click Change Settings. (No need to worry about daylight-saving time, either; the time servers take that into account).

Default Programs

The primary features are duplicated in the Settings app; see page 262.

In an age when Microsoft is often accused of leveraging Windows to take over other realms of software, like Web browsing and graphics, the company created this command center. It's where you choose your preferred Web browser, music-playing program, email program, and so on—which may or may not be the ones provided by Microsoft.

You're offered four links:

- **Set your default programs.** Here's where you teach Windows that you want your own programs to replace the Microsoft versions. For instance, you can say that, when you double-click a music file, you want to open iTunes and not Windows Media Player.

- **Associate a file type or protocol.** This window lets you specify exactly what kind of file you want to have opened by what program. (That's essentially what happens in the background when you set a default program.) File associations are covered in more depth on page 242.

- **Change AutoPlay Settings.** This option opens the AutoPlay applet described on page 315.

- **Set program access and computer defaults.** Here you can not only manage what programs are used by default, like browsing with Microsoft Edge or getting email with Windows Mail, but also disable certain programs so that they can't be used at all. It's organized in rather combative schemes: You can choose to prefer Microsoft products (disabling access to the non-Microsoft interlopers), Non-Microsoft products (pro-third party, anti-Microsoft), or create a Custom scheme, in which you can choose a mix of both. See page 249 for more information.

Device Manager

The primary features are duplicated in the Settings app; see page 262.

The Device Manager console shows you where all your hardware money was spent. Here, you or your tech-support person can troubleshoot a flaky device, disable and enable devices, and manage device drivers. If you're comfortable handling these more advanced tasks, then Chapter 15 is for you.

Devices and Printers

The primary features are duplicated in the Settings app; see page 262.

Double-click to open the Devices and Printers window, where everything you've attached to your PC—Webcam, printer, scanner, mouse, whatever—appears with its own picture and details screen. Chapter 15 has the details.

Display

The primary features are duplicated in the Settings app; see page 259.

This one opens the "Make it easier to read what's on your screen" window described on page 192. The task pane on the left side offers links to other screen-related controls, like "Adjust resolution," "Change display settings" (meaning resolution), and so on.

Ease of Access Center

The primary features are duplicated in the Settings app; see page 266.

The Ease of Access Center is designed to make computing easier for people with disabilities, although some of the options here can benefit anyone. See page 287 for details.

File Explorer Options

This program, which is called "Folder Options" when accessed through File Explorer, offers three tabs—General, View, and Search—all of which are described in Chapter 2.

File History

The primary features are duplicated in the Settings app; see page 269.

Here's the HQ for Windows' backup feature. See Chapter 17.

Fonts

This icon is a shortcut to a folder; it's not an applet. It opens into a window that reveals all the typefaces installed on your machine, as described in Chapter 14.

HomeGroup

The HomeGroup icon opens the "Change homegroup settings" screen, where you can change the password or perform other administrative tasks related to your HomeGroup (home file-sharing network). HomeGroups are described in Chapter 21.

Indexing Options

The search box is so magnificently fast because it doesn't actually root through all your files. Instead, it roots only through an *index* of your files, an invisible, compact database file that Windows maintains in the background.

This dialog box lets you manage indexing functions and change what gets indexed, and it lets you know how many items have been indexed. To learn more about the particulars of indexing and how to use it, see Chapter 3.

Internet Options

A better name for this program would have been "Web Browser Options," since all its settings apply to Web browsing—and, specifically, to Internet Explorer. As a matter of fact, this is the same dialog box that opens from the Tools→Internet Options menu command within Internet Explorer.

It's described in the free "Internet Explorer.pdf" appendix that you can download from this book's "Missing CD" page at *www.missingmanuals.com*.

Keyboard

The primary features are duplicated in the Settings app; see page 266.

You're probably too young to remember the antique known as a *typewriter*. On some electric versions of this machine, you could hold down the letter X key to type a series of XXXXXXX's—ideal for crossing something out in a contract, for example.

On a PC, *every* key behaves this way. Hold down any key long enough, and it starts spitting out repetitions, making it easy to type, "No WAAAAAY!" or "You go, grrrrrl!" for example. (The same rule applies when you hold down the arrow keys to scroll through a text document, hold down the = key to build a separator line between paragraphs, hold down Backspace to eliminate a word, and so on.) The Speed tab of this dialog box governs the settings.

- **Repeat delay.** This slider determines how long you must hold down the key before it starts repeating (to prevent triggering repetitions accidentally).

- **Repeat rate.** The second slider governs how fast each key spits out letters once the spitting has begun. After making these adjustments, click the "Click here and hold down a key" test box to try out the new settings.

• **Cursor blink rate.** The "Cursor blink rate" slider actually has nothing to do with the *cursor*, the little arrow that you move around with the mouse. Instead, it governs the blinking rate of the *insertion point*, the blinking marker that indicates where typing will begin when you're word processing, for example. A blink rate that's too slow makes it more difficult to find your insertion point in a window filled with data. A blink rate that's too rapid can be distracting.

Language

The primary features are duplicated in the Settings app; see page 265.

Windows is, of course, used all over the world, in all different languages. Here's where you specify which language you want Windows to show you (Figure 7-9, top).

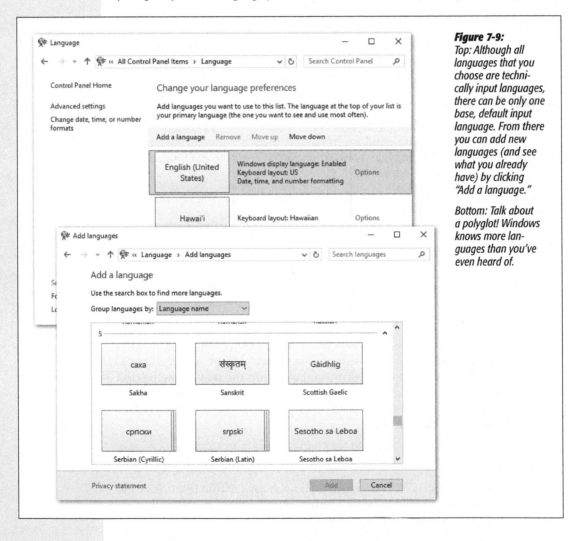

Figure 7-9:
Top: Although all languages that you choose are technically input languages, there can be only one base, default input language. From there you can add new languages (and see what you already have) by clicking "Add a language."

Bottom: Talk about a polyglot! Windows knows more languages than you've even heard of.

The symbols you use when you're typing in Swedish aren't the same as when you're typing in English. Microsoft solved this problem by creating different *keyboard layouts*, one for each language (or more, like Qwerty or Dvorak for English). Each keyboard layout rearranges the letters that appear when you press the keys. For example, in the Swedish layout, pressing the semicolon key produces an ö.

The "Add a language" button lets you install additional language packs to your computer (you can download them from Microsoft's Web site); hundreds are available, from Afrikaans to Yoruba (Figure 7-9, bottom).

Mouse

The primary features are duplicated in the Settings app; see page 263.

All the icons, buttons, and menus in Windows make the mouse a very important tool. And the Mouse dialog box is its configuration headquarters.

Buttons tab

This tab offers three useful controls: "Button configuration," "Double-click speed," and "ClickLock."

- **Button configuration.** This checkbox is for people who are left-handed and keep their mouse on the left side of the keyboard. Turning on this checkbox lets you switch the functions of the right and left mouse buttons so that your index finger naturally rests on the primary button (the one that selects and drags).

- **Double-click speed.** Double-clicking isn't a very natural maneuver. If you double-click too slowly, the icon you're trying to open remains stubbornly closed. Or, worse, if you accidentally double-click an icon's name instead of its picture, Windows sees your double-click as two single clicks, which tells it that you're trying to rename the icon.

  The difference in time between a double-click and two single clicks is usually well under a second. That's an extremely narrow window, so let Windows know what you consider to be a double-click by adjusting this slider. The left end of the slider bar represents 0.9 seconds, and the right end represents 0.1 seconds. If you need more time between clicks, move the slider to the left; by contrast, if your reflexes are highly tuned (or you drink a lot of coffee), try sliding the slider to the right.

  Each time you adjust the Speed slider, remember to test your adjustment by double-clicking the little folder to the right of the slider. If the folder opens, you've successfully double-clicked. If not, adjust the slider again.

- **ClickLock.** ClickLock is for people blessed with large monitors or laptop trackpads who, when dragging icons onscreen, get tired of keeping the mouse button pressed continually. Instead, you can make Windows "hold down" the button automatically, avoiding years of unpleasant finger cramps and messy litigation.

  When ClickLock is turned on, you can drag objects on the screen like this: First, point to the item you want to drag, such as an icon. Press the left mouse or trackpad button for the ClickLock interval. (You can specify this interval by clicking the Settings button in this dialog box.)

When you release the mouse button, it acts as though it's still pressed. Now you can drag the icon across the screen by moving the mouse (or stroking the trackpad) without holding any button down.

To release the button, hold it down again for your specified time interval.

Pointers tab

See page 188 for details on changing the shape of your cursor.

Pointers Options tab

See page 189 for a rundown of these cursor-related functions.

Wheel tab

The scroll wheel on the top of your mouse may be the greatest mouse enhancement since they got rid of the dust-collecting ball on the bottom. It lets you zoom through Web pages, email lists, and documents with a twitch of your index finger.

Use these controls to specify just how *much* each wheel notch scrolls. (You may not see this tab at all if your mouse doesn't have a wheel.)

Hardware tab

The Mouse program provides this tab exclusively for its Properties buttons, which take you to the Device Manager's device properties dialog box. Useful if you have to troubleshoot a bad driver.

Network and Sharing Center

This network command center offers, among other things, a handy map that shows exactly how your PC is connected to the Internet. It also contains a tidy list of all networking-related features (file sharing, printer sharing, and so on), complete with on/off switches. See Chapter 20 for details.

Personalization

The Personalization applet is simply the Themes window described on page 176.

Phone and Modem

If you have a dial-up modem, you'll need to access these settings, but only once: the first time you set up to dial out.

Power Options

The primary features are duplicated in the Settings app; see page 260.

Power Options manages your computer's power consumption. That's crucial when you're running off a laptop's battery, but it's also important if you'd like to save money (and the environment) by cutting down on the juice consumed by your *desktop* PC. The options you see depend on your PC's particular features.

A *power plan* dictates things like how soon the computer goes to sleep, how bright the screen is, what speed the processor cranks at, and so on.) Right up front, you get three premade power plans:

- **Balanced,** which is meant to strike a balance between energy savings and performance. When you're working hard, you get all the speed your PC can deliver; when you're thinking or resting, the processor slows down to save juice.

- **Power saver** slows down your computer but saves power—a handy one for laptop luggers who aren't doing anything more strenuous than word processing.

- **High performance** (click "Show additional plans" to see it) sucks power like a black hole but grants you the computer's highest speed possible.

Tip: You don't have to open the Control Panel to change among these canned plans. On a laptop, for example, you can just click the battery icon on your system tray and choose from the pop-up menu.

But creating your *own* power plan can be useful, not only because you gain more control, but also because you get to see exactly what a plan is made of. For step-by-step instructions, see the free downloadable appendix "Creating a Power Plan.pdf" on this book's "Missing CD" page at *www.missingmanuals.com*.

Programs and Features

The primary features are duplicated in the Settings app; see page 260.

Programs and Features is about managing the software you have installed, managing updates, and buying software online. It replaces the old Add/Remove Programs program. This window is useful for fixing (which might simply mean reinstalling), changing, or uninstalling existing programs, and it's the only place you can go to turn on (or off) Windows features like Fax and Scan, Games, and Meeting Space.

Recovery

The Recovery icon is a quick-access button for three features:

- **Create a recovery drive** lets you build a flash drive that can start up your PC when your PC can't start up on its own. See page 531.

- **Open System Restore** and **Configure System Restore** are described starting on page 695. System Restore lets you rewind your sick PC back to an earlier, better-behaved state.

Region

The primary features are duplicated in the Settings app; see page 265.

Windows can accommodate any conceivable arrangement of date, currency, and number formats.

Formats tab

If you think that 7/4 means July 4 and that 1.000 is the number of heads you have, skip this section.

But in some countries, 7/4 means April 7, and 1.000 means one thousand. If your PC isn't showing numbers, times, currency symbols, or dates in a familiar way, choose your country from the top Format pop-up menu. (Or, if you're a little weird, use the "Additional settings" button to rearrange the sequence of date elements; see Figure 7-10.)

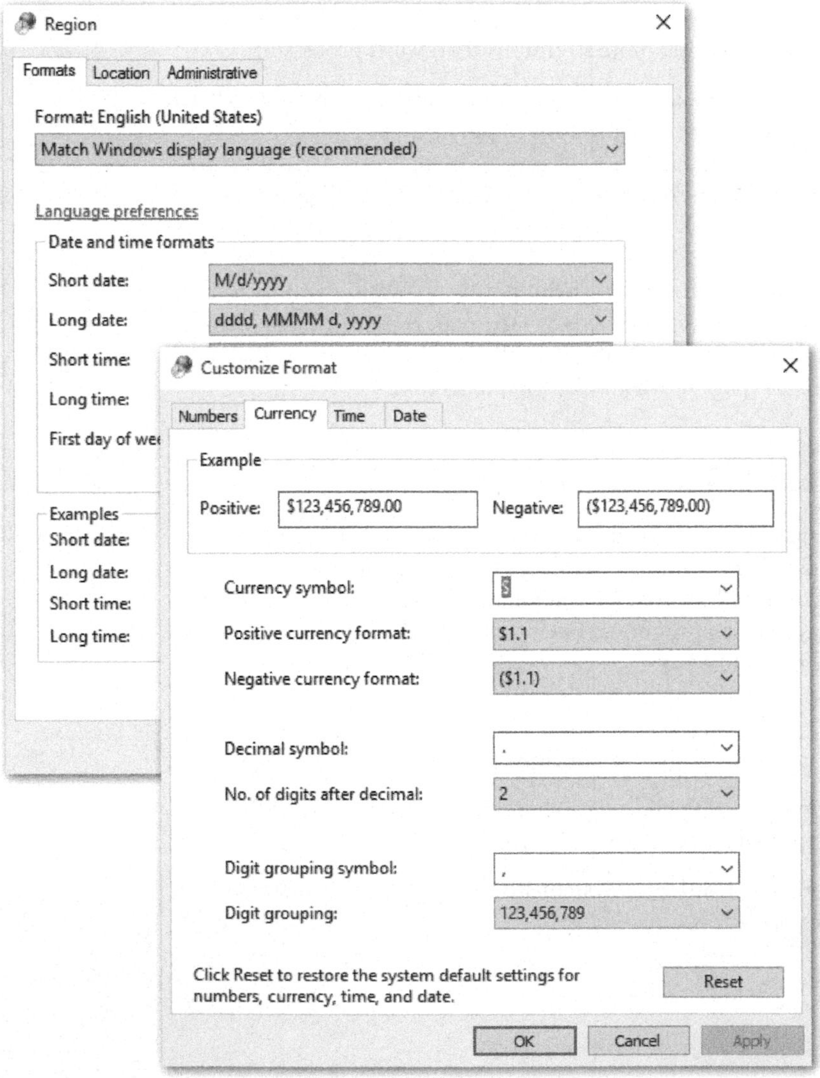

Figure 7-10:
Top: Regional standard format templates are available from the drop-down list in the Formats tab.

Bottom: Once you choose a standard format (like US), then you can customize exactly how numbers, currency, time, and dates are handled. Simply click "Additional settings."

Tip: The Time tab of the Customize Format box (Figure 7-10) is where you can specify whether you prefer a 12-hour clock ("3:05 PM") or a military or European-style, 24-hour clock ("15:05").

Location tab

This tab identifies your computer's location. The point is so when you go online to check local news and weather, you get the *right* news and weather—a handy feature if you're traveling.

Administrative

The "Copy settings" button applies the newly configured language settings to:

- The Windows Welcome screen, so that it'll be in the right language, and/or

- New user accounts, so anyone who gets a new account on this computer will have your language, format, and keyboard settings conveniently available to them.

The "Change system locale" button on this tab lets you specify which language handles error messages and the occasional dialog box. (Just changing your input language may not do the trick.)

RemoteApp and Desktop Connections

The world's corporate system administrators can "publish" certain programs, or even entire computers, at the company headquarters—and you, using your laptop or home computer, can use them as though you were there.

But in Windows, these "published" resources behave like programs right on your PC. They're listed right in your Start menu, for heaven's sake (in a folder in All Programs called, of course, "RemoteApp and Desktop Connections"), and you can search for them as you'd search for any apps.

The whole cycle begins when your company's network nerd provides you with the URL (Internet address) of the published program. Once you've got that, open the RemoteApp and Desktop Connections control panel, and then click "Set up a new connection with RemoteApp and Desktop Connections."

A wizard now appears; its screens guide you through pasting in that URL and typing in your corporate network name and password.

When it's all over, you see a confirmation screen; your new "connection" is listed in the control panel; and the folder full of "published" remote programs appears in your Start menu, ready to use.

Security and Maintenance

This is the one *new* Control Panel applet in Windows 10.

Open Security for a tidy dashboard of your firewall, antivirus, and other features, so you can see how they're doing. Open Maintenance for a similar dashboard of problems and features that could be affecting your PC. (Chapter 16 has more details.)

Sound

The Sound dialog box contains four tabs that control every aspect of your microphone and speakers: Playback, Recording, Sounds, and Communications. See Figure 7-11.

Playback and Recording tabs

These tabs simply contain the icons for each attached sound device. To change a device's settings, select it and then click Configure.

If you're configuring an output ("playback") device like a speaker or headset, then you get a quick wizard that lets you set the speaker configuration (stereo or quadraphonic, for example). If you're configuring a microphone ("recording"), then you're taken to the Speech Recognition page, where you can set up your microphone.

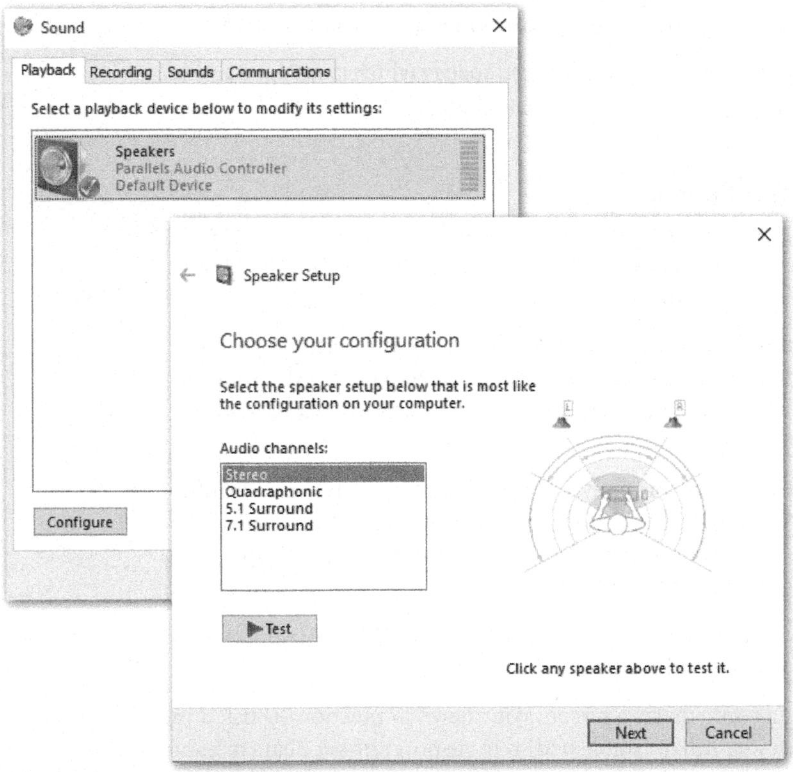

Figure 7-11:
Top: The Playback and Recording tabs display the devices your computer has for playing or recording sounds. If you select the device, you can see its properties or configure it.

Bottom: Here are some of the configurations you can set from the Playback tab, from simple stereo to 7.1 surround sound. Your setup may vary.

Sounds tab

Windows comes with a tidy suite of little sound effects—beeps, musical ripples, and chords—that play when you turn on the PC, trigger an error message, empty the Recycle Bin, and so on. This tab lets you specify which sound effect plays for which situation; see page 184 for details.

Communications tab

This tab is designed for people who make phone calls using the PC, using a program like Skype, Google Talk, or Windows Live Messenger. Here you can tell your PC to mute or soften other sounds—meaning music you've got playing—whenever you're on a PC call.

Nice touch.

Speech Recognition

This little program sets up all the speech-related features of Windows. See Chapter 6 for complete details.

Sync Center

The Sync Center is for syncing your files with folders elsewhere on your corporate network, so you'll always be up to date. For details, see page 635.

System

The primary features are duplicated in the Settings app; see page 259.

This advanced control panel window is the same one that appears when you right-click your This PC icon and choose Properties from the shortcut menu (or press ⊞+Break key or ⊞+Pause key). It contains the various settings that identify every shred of circuitry and equipment inside, or attached to, your PC.

When you open the System icon in Control Panel, you're taken to the System window. Here you can find out:

- **What edition of Windows is installed on your computer.** Not all editions are made equal; if you're flailing to find some feature that you could have sworn is supposed to be in Windows 10, it's good to check here. You might find out that the feature you want is available only on higher-priced versions.

- **The model name and speed of your PC's processor** (such as Intel Core 2 Duo, 2.8 GHz).

- **How much memory your PC has.** That's a very helpful number to know, particularly if you need to improve your computer's speed.

- **Your computer's name, domain, or workgroup, which can be modified with the "Change settings" button.** Remember, your computer name and description are primarily useful on a network, since that's how other people will identify your computer. Unless you tell it otherwise, Windows names your computer after your login name, something like Casey Robbins-PC.

- **Whether or not your operating system is activated.** For more on Activation, check Appendix A.

- **What the Product ID key is for your system.** Every legal copy of Windows has a Product ID key—a long serial number that's required to activate Microsoft software. For more information about Product ID keys, see Appendix A.

At the left side of the window, you find a few links:

- **Device Manager.** This very powerful console lists every component of your PC: CD-ROM, Modem, Mouse, and so on. Double-clicking a component's name (or clicking the + symbol) discloses the brand and model of that component. For more on the Device Manager, see Chapter 15.

- **Remote settings.** To read about Remote Assistance—the feature that lets a technical help person connect to your PC (via the Internet) to help you troubleshoot—turn to page 202.

- **System Protection.** This link takes you to the System Protection tab in the System dialog box. Here you can keep track of the automatic system restores (snapshot backups of a system), or even create a new restore point. And if your computer has begun to act like it's possessed, you can go here to restore it to a previous restore point's state. Check out Chapter 17 for more details.

- **Advanced system settings.** Clicking this link opens the Advanced tab of the System Properties dialog box. This tab is nothing more than a nesting place for four buttons that open other dialog boxes—some of which aren't "advanced" in the least.

  The first Settings button opens the **Performance Options** dialog box, described on page 186. The second button opens the **User Profiles** box, which is covered in Chapter 19. The third button opens a **Startup and Recovery** window. It contains advanced options related to *dual booting* (Appendix A) and what happens when the system crashes.

  Finally, the **Environment Variables** button opens a dialog box that will get only technically minded people excited. It identifies, for example, the path to your Windows folder and the number of processors your PC has. If you're not in the computer-administration business, avoid making changes here.

Taskbar and Navigation

This program controls every conceivable behavior of the taskbar. You can read all about these options in Chapter 2.

Troubleshooting

Here's a list of Windows' troubleshooters—step-by-step interview screens that walk you through fixing various problems. [Insert your own joke here about Windows' need for an entire program dedicated to troubleshooting.]

Anyway, you can find links here for running older programs under Windows 10, getting online, figuring out why your speakers aren't working, sleuthing out why your PC is getting so slow, and so on.

User Accounts

The primary features are duplicated in the Settings app; see page 265.

This control panel is the master switch and control center for the user-accounts feature described in Chapter 19. If you're the only one who uses your PC, you can (and should) ignore it.

Windows Defender

Windows Defender is Microsoft's free anti-spyware product, built into Windows. For an extensive look at what it can do for you, see Chapter 12.

Windows Firewall

In this age of digital technology, when most people's computers are connected at all times to the Internet (and therefore always vulnerable to the Internet), it's a good and reasonable idea to have a firewall protecting your computer from possible attacks and exploitation. To learn more about Windows Firewall, see Chapter 12.

Windows Mobility Center

The Windows Mobility Center is a central panel for instant access to laptoppy/tablety features like screen brightness, volume, battery, and so on. The new Action Center is nearly an exact duplicate and is much easier to find. See page 420 for more on Action Center; for more on Mobility Center, see page 452.

Work Folders

If you work for a corporation, your kindly, all-knowing network administrator may have set up Work Folders for you—folders full of your documents that physically sit on protected computers at work, but that you can access across the Internet even from your own home computers.

CHAPTER 8

The Windows Starter Apps

E ven after a fresh installation of Windows, your computer teems with a rich array of preinstalled programs—as an infomercial might put it, they're your *free bonus gifts*. And there are a lot of them.

Some are former "Windows Store" (TileWorld) apps, and some are traditional desktop programs. But in Windows 10, they all behave alike—so for your reference pleasure, they're described in this vast chapter. They may appear in your Start menu in various groups, under various headings (Figure 8-1). But in this chapter, they're all alphabetical, for your sanity's sake.

Note: This chapter covers every scrap of software that comes in your "All apps" menu, even the ones stored in subfolders like Windows Accessories. The exception: what's in the Windows Administrative Tools folder (Component Services, Local Security Policy, ODBC Data Sources, and so on). Those are technical tools for people who *write* computer books, not read them.

The New, Unified Design of Apps

Among the other problems with Windows 8: the design of Windows Store (TileWorld) apps. They had no menus. They had few visible buttons. These apps didn't really *do* anything—unless you knew about the secret, hidden strip of commands known as the App bar.

It appeared only if you swiped upward onto the screen from beneath it. A lot of people never realized that.

In Windows 10, Microsoft's starter Windows Store apps have all been redesigned. The App bar is gone. No more hidden controls. Let the celebrations begin!

In fact, to make your life easier, Microsoft has blessed all of these apps with the *same* basic design. You'll find this design in the Alarms & Clock, Calculator, Calendar, Food & Drink, Get Started, Groove Music, Health & Fitness, Mail, Maps, Microsoft Solitaire Collection, Money, Movies & TV, News, People, Photos, Store, Weather, and Xbox apps, to name a few.

In this design, the app lives in a single window with a vertical menu column, always visible, hugging the left side (see Figure 8-1). It shows only icons, because they don't take up much space.

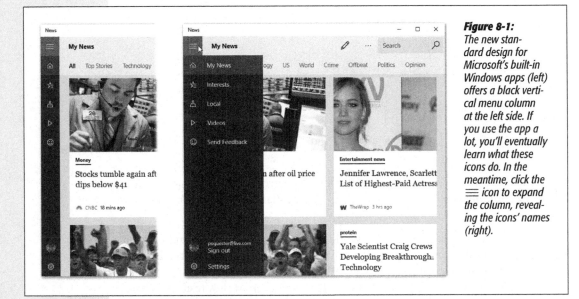

Figure 8-1:
The new standard design for Microsoft's built-in Windows apps (left) offers a black vertical menu column at the left side. If you use the app a lot, you'll eventually learn what these icons do. In the meantime, click the ☰ icon to expand the column, revealing the icons' names (right).

In this pillar of options, you'll find these consistent elements:

- **A ☰ button at the top.** Click to expand the column, revealing the icons' names. (Internally, Microsoft calls the ☰ button the "hamburger button," thanks to its resemblance to three horizontal layers of goodness.)

- **Send Feedback** (☺). The smiley-face button takes you to a Web page where you can submit bugs, complaints, and compliments to Microsoft.

- **A bunch of icons.** These vary by app, and they're described in this chapter. If there are a lot of them, as in the Sports app, the menu column of icons may actually scroll.

Then comes a divider line and then two more icons that aren't part of the main column:

- **Sign out.** This round photo represents you, and the Microsoft account you've used to sign in.

- **A Settings button at the very bottom.** It opens a Settings panel, usually on the opposite side of the screen—on the right.

A ← button usually appears at the *very* top left corner of the window. That, of course, is your Back button. It gets you out of the current screen, and walks you back, back, back, eventually to the app's main home screen. For example, if you're using the Maps app, the ← button backs you out of your directions, or Streetside, or Settings—and back to the main Maps display.

Tip: In most Windows Store apps, there's a keyboard shortcut for that ← button: Alt+←.

Not all Windows Store apps adopt Microsoft's suggestion of the left-side menu column, of course. But most of the built-in Windows apps do, so it's worth cozying up to the idea now.

3D Builder

This oddball little app is designed to work with 3D printers. You use it to design three-dimensional objects (or modify the big library of starter shapes) that you'll later print in plastic.

Even though it's a bare-bones app, there's a lot to master; fortunately, the Help button takes you online to a series of video tutorials. Happy modeling!

Alarms & Clock

Don't be deceived by the name. This app does let you set up alarms, and it does have a clock. But it does more—so much more. It's also a timer and a stopwatch.

Alarm Tab

If you travel much, this feature could turn out to be one of your machine's most useful functions. It's reliable, it's programmable, and it's fun to use (Figure 8-2).

Note: The alarm won't play unless the machine is on and awake (unless your computer has a feature called InstantGo, which keeps networking and clock functions going even when the PC is asleep). Does that defeat the whole purpose? Come on—don't be a killjoy.

Microsoft starts you off with a dummy alarm, set to 7:00 a.m., but switched off.

To change the time, click it to enter editing mode (Figure 8-2, right). Now you can edit the alarm's name, time, repeat schedule, alarm sound, and snooze time.

When you finally hit the Save (🖫) button, the Alarm screen lists your new alarm (Figure 8-2, left). Just tap the On/Off button to prevent an alarm from going off. It stays in the list, though, so you can quickly reactivate it another day, without having to redo the whole thing.

You can hit the + button to set another alarm, if you like.

To edit an alarm, click it and proceed as described above; to delete it, click it and then tap 🗑.

When the alarm goes off, a notification appears on the screen, identifying the alarm and the time, and the sound rings.

You can snooze it or dismiss it (turn it off for good).

World Clock

The second tab of Alarms & Clock starts you out with one clock, showing the current time where you are.

The neat part is that you can set up several of these clocks and set each one to show the time in a different city. The result looks like the row of clocks in a hotel lobby, making you seem Swiss and precise.

By checking these clocks, you'll know what time it is in some remote city, so you don't wake somebody up at what turns out to be 3 a.m.

To specify which city's time appears on the clock, hit the + button at lower right. Type in the city you want; as you type, a list of matching cities appears. Hit the one whose time you want to track.

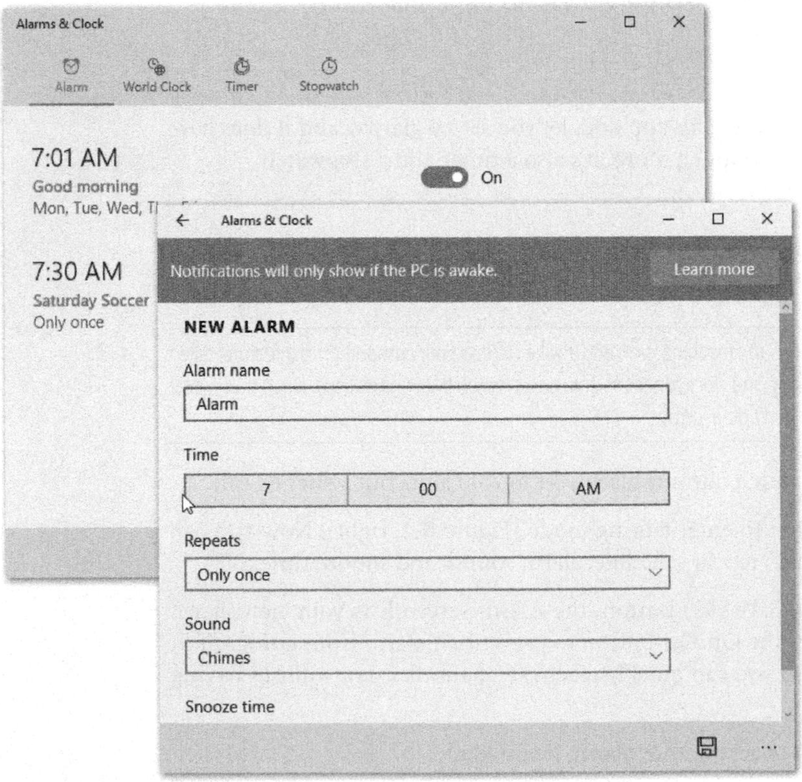

Figure 8-2:
The Alarms & Clock app can't wake the computer to wake you. You should think of it more as a system to remind you of something while you're actually working (and the computer is on and awake).

Left: Your list of alarms.

Right: Setting up a new alarm.

As soon as you tap a city name, you return to the World Clock display, where your new city time appears. Here's the fun you can have:

- **Zoom through time.** As Figure 8-3 makes clear, this is an interactive set of clocks. You can scroll through time and watch them change.

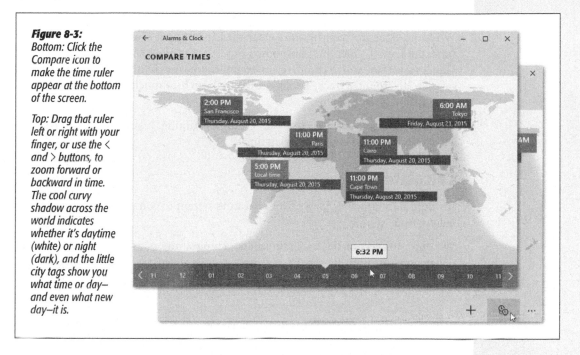

Figure 8-3:
Bottom: Click the Compare icon to make the time ruler appear at the bottom of the screen.

Top: Drag that ruler left or right with your finger, or use the < and > buttons, to zoom forward or backward in time. The cool curvy shadow across the world indicates whether it's daytime (white) or night (dark), and the little city tags show you what time or day— and even what new day–it is.

- **Pin a clock to the Start menu.** Right-click (or hold your finger down on) a city's time. From the shortcut menu, choose Pin to Start. And presto: There, on the right side of your Start menu, a new tile appears. It will always show that city and its current time, for your quick-glancing pleasure.

- **Delete a clock.** Right-click (or hold your finger down on) it. From the shortcut menu, choose Delete.

Timer

Countdown timers are everywhere in life. They measure the periods in sports and games, cooking times in the kitchen, penalties in hockey. The third tab in the Alarms & Clock app, Timer, is a countdown timer. You input a starting time, and it counts down to zero.

To set the timer, click the big digits; now you can change the name and the time of the timer. Hit the Save (🖫) button.

Finally, hit ▶. The timer counts down toward zero. You can hit the ‖ button to pause the countdown, if you like. You can also hit ▷ to restart the countdown, or ⤢ to make the numbers big and bold enough to see from the moon.

When the timer runs out, you get a sound and a notification. They'll keep chiming until you hit Dismiss.

Stopwatch

You've never met a prettier stopwatch than this one. Hit ▶ to begin timing something: a runner, a train, a long-winded person who's arguing with you.

While the digits are flying by, you can tap the Lap button (⌚) as often as you like. Each time, the Laps list identifies how much time elapsed since the last time you tapped Lap. It's a way for you to compare, for example, how much time a runner is spending on each lap around a track. The large digits tell you how much time has elapsed since you started the stopwatch.

Tap **II** to freeze the counter; tap ▷ to resume the timing. If you tap ⊙, you reset the counter to zero and erase all the lap times.

Calculator

It would be a little silly for a major operating system to come without a pocket calculator app, wouldn't it? Yep.

Windows 10's version has a scientific mode, a programmers' mode, and a powerful list of conversions (time, power, pressure, area, length, speed, and so on). See Figure 8-4.

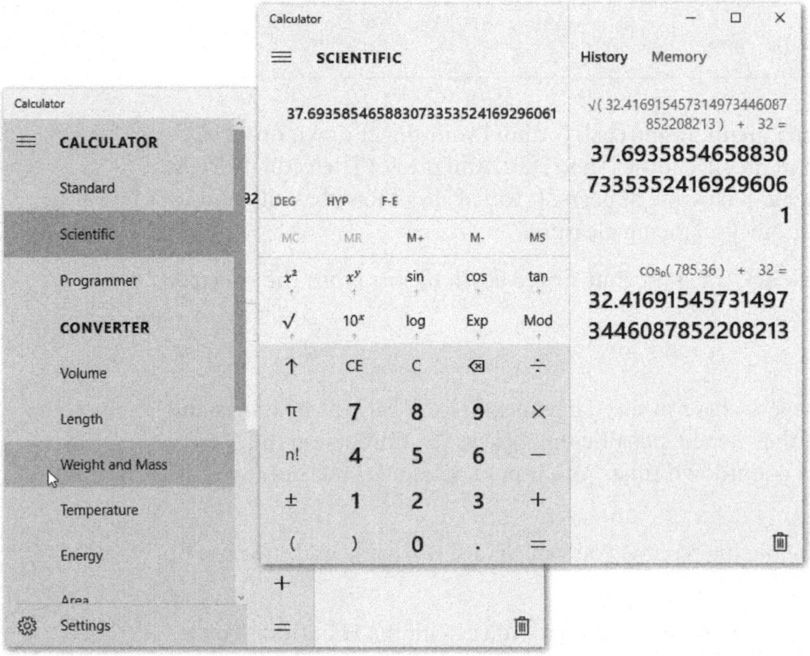

Figure 8-4:
The Calculator (left) offers three modes: Standard, Scientific, Programmer. You can press Alt+1, 2, and 3 for those modes.

Use the menu column to choose from a huge list of conversions: volume, length, weight, temperature, energy, area, speed, time, power, and so on. Once you've specified the conversion type, specify what units you want to convert to or from. Handy, really.

Calendar

Calendar is not so different from those "Hunks of the Midwest Police Stations" paper calendars that people leave hanging on the walls for months past their natural life spans.

But Calendar offers several advantages over paper calendars. For example:

- **It can automate the process** of entering repeating events, such as weekly staff meetings or gym workouts.

- **Calendar can give you a gentle nudge** (with a sound and a message) when an important appointment is approaching.

- **It can subscribe to online calendars** from Outlook, Hotmail, or even your company's Exchange calendar, so you have all your life's agendas in one place.

Note: There may already be stuff on your calendar the first time you open it—if, elsewhere in Windows, you've already entered account information for an online account. For example, if you've entered your Facebook details, then all your friends' birthdays appear in Calendar automatically. You can, of course, turn off one account or another; read on.

That said, you may find that Calendar is among the simplest, most bare-bones calendar programs ever written. At least it won't overwhelm you.

Working with Views

When you open Calendar, your first order of business is to point it to your existing online calendars: your corporate calendar (Exchange), one of Microsoft's various free services (Outlook.com, Live.com, Hotmail, MSN), Google's (Gmail), or even Apple's (iCloud). (Yes, Apple's. That sound you hear? That's hell freezing over.)

If you don't already have one of these accounts, you can create a free Microsoft account on the spot.

Then you see something like Figure 8-5. Using the toolbar at top, you can switch among these views:

- **Day** looks exactly like a day-at-a-time desk calendar. Scroll up and down to see the rest of the day.

Tip: But wait, there's a secret here! If you hit the Day button, you get a pop-up menu of "1 day," "2 day," and so on up to 6. It's letting you specify how *many* Day columns fit on each screen. In other words, you have a middle ground between Day (1 column) and Work Week (5) or Week (7).

- **Work week** fills the main display area with five columns, reflecting the current work week (that is, Monday through Friday).

- **Week** fills the main display area with seven columns, reflecting the current week.

- **Month** shows the entire month that contains today's date.

If a Month-view square is too small to show everything you've got scheduled that day, you'll see a notation at the top of the square like "5 events." It's letting you know that there may be more events than you can currently see. Switch to Day or Week view to see what they all are.

Tip: If you have a keyboard, you can instead hit Ctrl+Alt+1, 2, 3, 4, and 5 for the views listed above.

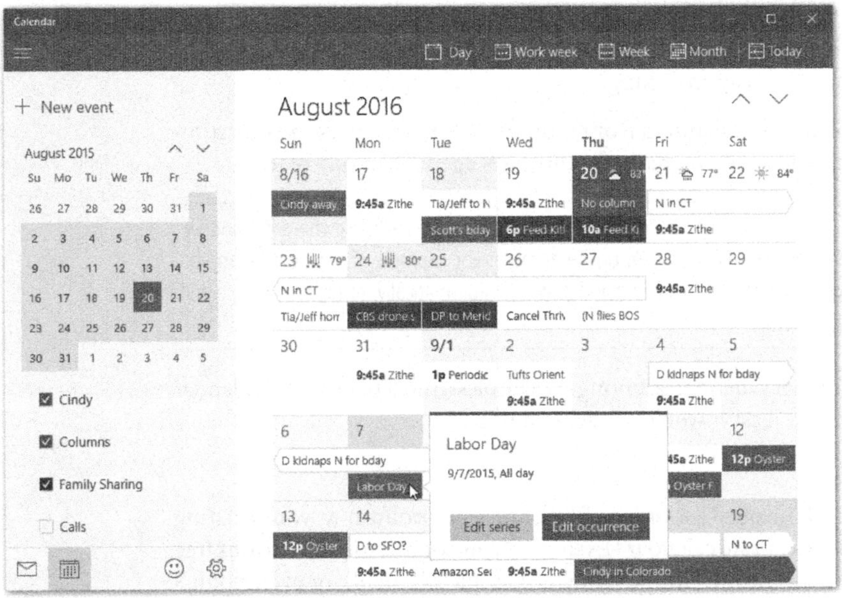

Figure 8-5:
The Windows calendar is very, very simple. Switch views using the icons at top. Turn categories on or off by the checkboxes at left. Point to an appointment (or tap with your finger) to see a pop-up details bubble, as shown here.

Navigating in any of the column views is easy and fun for the whole family:

- **Touchscreen:** Swipe vertically to move through the hours, horizontally to move through the days.

- **Mouse:** Turn the scroll wheel to move through the hours; add Shift to move through the days.

- **Keyboard:** The ← and → keys go to the previous/next day, and the ↑ and ↓ keys go to the previous/next hour.

In Month view, on the other hand, there's only one way to scroll: Vertically, with your finger, keyboard, trackpad, or mouse.

Tip: A compact calendar appears at the left side. You can use it to jump quickly to a date that's far in the future (or in the past, if you like to rewrite history).

To jump back to today's date, hit Today (top right).

Making an Appointment: Quick Way

The basic calendar is easy to figure out. After all, with the exception of one unfortunate Gregorian incident, we've been using calendars successfully for centuries.

In Day, Work week, Week, or Month view, tap or click the correct time slot or date square. A little new-event box appears, where you can specify the name for your appointment ("Lunch with Chris" or whatever); start and end times (if, in fact, they're not already correct); a location; and a calendar category. Click Done or press Enter. You've just created an appointment.

Making an Appointment: Detailed Way

That "click-to-make-a-one-hour-appointment" method is quick and easy. But what if there's more to the story? What if you want a reminder? Or you want it to occur every week?

In that case, you should open the more complete Details screen shown in Figure 8-6. Ways to open Details:

- **Open the small "new event" box first,** as described above. Then click "More details."

- **Press Ctrl+N.** Of course, this method is slower than the click-the-time-slot method, because you have to specify the time and date manually.

- **Click "New event" at the top-left corner of the screen.** Once again, you have to specify the time and date manually.

Figure 8-6:
Here's where you both create a new appointment and edit an old one. When choosing the End time, the pop-up menu shows you how long the appointment will be if you choose each time ("30 minutes," for example). Nice touch.

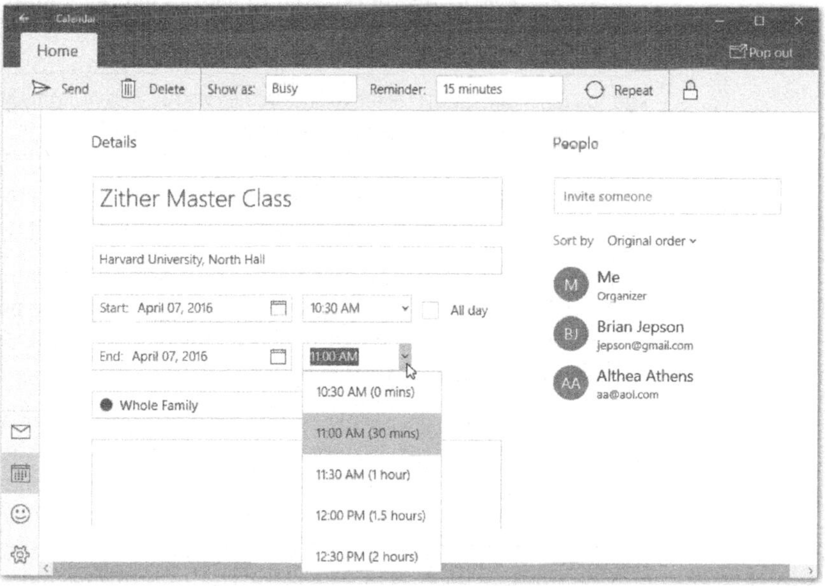

On the Details screen (Figure 8-6), you can specify everything about the new appointment:

- **Event name.** For example, you might type *Fly to Phoenix.*

- **Location.** This field makes a lot of sense; if you think about it, almost everyone needs to record *where* a meeting is to take place. You might type a reminder for yourself like *My place,* a specific address like *212 East 23,* or some other helpful information, like a contact phone number or a flight number.

- **Start.** Here you enter the starting date and time for the appointment.

- **Start, End.** Separate pop-up menus (and a pop-up calendar) let you specify a date and time that this event starts and stops.

- **All day.** An "All day" event, of course, refers to something that has no specific time of day associated with it: a holiday, a birthday, a Windows book deadline. When you turn on this box, the name of the appointment jumps to the top of the day/week/month square, in the area reserved for this kind of thing.

- **Account (calendar).** The account name you see here is actually a pop-up menu. Beneath headings that represent your various calendar services—your Live.com account, Google, iCloud, Exchange, or whatever—you see whatever calendar *categories* you've created on that calendar service.

  These color-coded subsets can be anything you like. One person might have calendars called Home, Work, and TV Reminders. Another might have Me, Spouse 'n' Me, and The Kidz. A small business could have categories called Deductible Travel, R&D, and R&R.

  (You can't create or edit calendar categories in Calendar itself—only on the originating services.)

Tip: You can, however, change the color associated with a category. Right-click (or hold your finger down on) the category's name; choose from the palette that appears.

- **Event description.** In this big box, you can type or paste any text you like—driving directions, contact phone numbers, a call history, or whatever.

- **People.** If the appointment is a meeting or some other gathering, you can type the participants' names here. As you type, a list of matching names from your People app appears, to make it easy to choose the one you want. (You can also type out a full email address of anyone here.)

  Once you've added a person's name, you can add another, and then another. Later, when you're finished creating this event, the Send button at top left will invite your lucky recipients via by email. Each message comes with an *iCal.ics* attachment: a calendar-program invitation file. In many mail and calendar programs, opening this attachment automatically presents your invitation; the recipients can respond (by choosing the Accept, Maybe, or Decline buttons that appear in *their* calendar programs).

For each appointment, you can have even more fun with the options in the top toolbar. You can also indicate the following:

- **Show as.** If you're on a shared calendar—in an office, for example—the options in this pop-up menu are pretty standard: Free, Busy, Out of office, and Tentative.

  For each event you put on your own calendar, you can use these tags to signal coworkers your availability for meetings or calls. Your colleagues won't see *what* you're doing during that block ("Haircut," "Me time" or whatever)—only that you're "Busy," "Out of the office," or whatever.

- **Reminder.** This pop-up menu tells Calendar when to notify you when a certain appointment is about to begin. You can specify how much advance notice you want for this particular appointment. If it's a TV show, then a reminder 5 minutes before airtime is probably fine. If it's a birthday, then you might set up a warning a week in advance, so there's time to buy a present.

Tip: If you subscribe to the same calendar service on your phone, it'll remind you when the time comes. In other words, these reminders aren't useful only when you're sitting at your desk.

- **Repeat.** This button opens a new set of controls for recurring events: Daily, Weekly, and so on. Or you can turn on the day checkboxes to specify any more complicated repeating pattern, like "Tuesdays and Wednesdays" or "First Monday of every month."

  You can also set an end date—a date when you want the repetitions to stop.

- **Private [🔒].** If other people can see your chosen account (for example, if it's an Exchange calendar you use at work), then turning on this box means that they can't see this particular appointment. Great for events like "Colonoscopy" or "Court date re: public nuisance charge."

When you're finished setting up the appointment, hit the "Save and close" button at top left, or press Ctrl+S. (If invitees are involved, that button may say "Send" or, if you've made changes, "Send update.")

Your newly scheduled event now shows up on your calendar, complete with the color coding that corresponds to the calendar category you've assigned.

Inspecting an Event

Usually, Calendar shows you only each appointment's name. But if you tap it or click it, a little box pops out to show more detail—the location and name of the person who created the appointment, for example.

If it's a meeting with other invitees, there's a handy button there: "I'm running late." One click, and boom: An outgoing email is already written and addressed to everyone else who was invited to that meeting. Click Send and then run for the cab.

If it's a repeating event, you have the choice of editing just that one event, or the entire series of them.

Editing Events

To edit an event, just click it (with mouse or trackpad) or tap it twice (with your finger). You return to the screen shown in Figure 8-6, where you can make any changes you like.

Rescheduling Events

Sometimes things change. In Calendar, alas, you can't drag an appointment block to another time or date. You have to open its Details screen and change its scheduled time or date manually.

Deleting Events

To delete an appointment, open it and then hit Delete at the top.

If you're opening a recurring event, like a weekly meeting, a pop-up menu offers "Delete one" (you want to operate on only that particular instance of the event) or "Delete all" (the whole series from that point forward).

If other people have been invited, then the button says "Cancel meeting" instead of Delete; they'll be notified about the change. And when you hit that button, you're invited to type a little message of apology or shame.

What's in the Left-Side Panel

At the left side of Calendar, there's a handy panel of options. (If you see only a narrow strip of icons, hit the ≡ at top left to open the panel.)

There's a mini calendar, for quick navigation of your life's timeline.

Below that: A list of your calendar accounts and the color-coded categories within them. By turning a category's checkbox on or off, you can show or hide *all* appointments in that category. That's an incredible way to wade through a crowded schedule to focus on, say, your kids' events.

Below that: four icons. There's Mail (because email is something you often do when you're calendaring), Calendar (because you may want to switch back), a smiley face (complain to Microsoft about things that aren't working right), and Settings. Read on.

Settings

If you click ⚙ at lower left, you open the Settings panel on the right edge of the window. Here you've got these categories:

- **Accounts.** Edit or delete any of your calendar accounts (Outlook, iCloud, Gmail, and so on).

- **Calendar Settings.** Specify what you consider the first day of the week (affects how Month and Week views appear), which hours of the day you work (affects how Day view appears), and which days of the week you actually work (affects how Work week appears).

  As a bonus, you can specify either mild or vivid colors for category color-coding.

- **Weather Settings.** Choose your preferred temperature units (F or C).

- **Help.** Opens a Web page where you're offered five Help pages for using Calendar.

- **Trust Center.** If this switch is on, you're turning on "locally relevant content." It will "provide functionality that's relevant to your usage and preferences."

  But you knew that.

- **Feedback** lets you send suggestions to Microsoft.

- **About** tells you your Calendar version.

Camera

Almost every tablet and laptop these days has a camera—sometimes two (front and back). Even some desktop PCs have Webcams built in. Nobody is going to take professional portraits with these cameras, but they're fine for video chats and Facebook snaps. Camera (Figure 8-7) is the app you use for taking pictures and videos. (If you don't see the Camera app, it's because your gadget doesn't have a camera.)

Note: The first time you open this app, Microsoft's privacy team has your back. "Can Camera use your webcam and microphone?" it asks. It's just making sure that the camera isn't opening on behalf of some nasty piece of spyware.

To take a picture, tap the  button, or press the space bar or Enter.

Figure 8-7:
If you're used to the 3-inch screen on the back of a digital camera, discovering that your new preview screen is the entire size of your tablet or laptop comes as quite a shock. In essence, you're seeing the finished photo before you even take it.

A few cryptic icons haunt the edges of the window:

- **Top left: Camera Roll.** Select to see all the pictures and movies you've made with this machine, as described below.

- **Top Center: Change camera.** This button appears only if your computer has cameras on both the front and the back—a common arrangement on tablets. (Back camera for photography, front camera for video chats, since it's aimed at you.) Each time you tap this button, your view switches to the other camera.

At top right, you find the Options (…) button. It opens a panel that offers features like these:

- **Self timer.** Yes, kids, your machine has a self-timer. It works in both photo and video modes. It's great for getting a self-portrait or a self-video when you don't want to be right at the machine.

  Tap this button once for a pop-up menu that offers 2-, 5-, or 10-second countdowns. Now when you hit the ◙ button, "3…2…1" countdown digits appear—and then the photo gets snapped, or the video begins. ("Continue taking photos every 2 seconds until I press the camera button again" does just what it says, and it's an extraordinarily useful feature every now and then. It's almost a poor-man's time-lapse.)

- **Settings.** The exact list of settings varies by PC. But a typical settings setup lets you specify what happens when you hold down the camera button (shoot video or capture rapid-fire burst-mode shots), the proportions of the photos you take (like 4 × 3, 3 × 2, or 16 × 9), what kind of composition gridlines you want superimposed on the preview, the quality and resolution of video you want to capture, whether you want image stabilization turned on, and so on.

The Camera Roll

To see the picture or video you've just captured, jump into the Camera Roll. It's a special album that holds photos you took with this computer (as opposed to those you've rounded up from other sources).

The Camera Roll opens when you tap the top-left screen icon (⊠). You're now faced with handy buttons like Delete, Rotate, Crop, Edit, and Share. Technically, you're now in the Photos app, which is why you have to turn to page 340 to read about the functions of these buttons.

Character Map

Your computer is capable of creating hundreds of different typographical symbols—the currency symbols for the yen and British pound, diacritical markings for French and Spanish, various scientific symbols, trademark and copyright signs, and so on. Obviously, these symbols don't appear on your keyboard; to provide enough keys, your keyboard would have to be the width of Wyoming. You *can* type the symbols, but they're hidden behind the keys you do see.

The treasure map that reveals their locations is the Character Map. When first opening this program, use the Font pop-up menu to specify the font you want to use (because every font contains a different set of symbols). Now you see every single symbol in the font. As you click on each symbol, a magnified version of it appears to help you distinguish them. See Figure 8-8 for details on transferring a particular symbol to your document.

Tip: Some email programs can't handle the fancy kinds of symbols revealed by the Character Map. That explains why your copyright symbols, for example, can turn into a gibberish character on the receiving end.

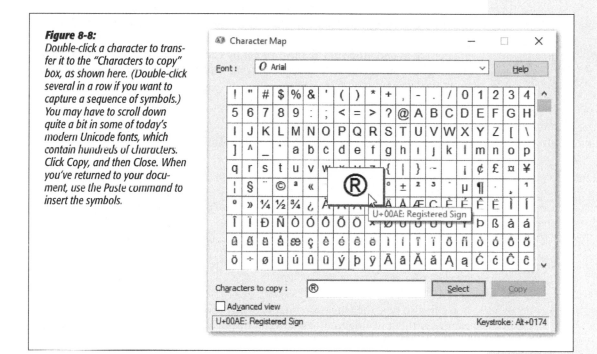

Figure 8-8:
Double-click a character to transfer it to the "Characters to copy" box, as shown here. (Double-click several in a row if you want to capture a sequence of symbols.) You may have to scroll down quite a bit in some of today's modern Unicode fonts, which contain hundreds of characters. Click Copy, and then Close. When you've returned to your document, use the Paste command to insert the symbols.

Command Prompt

The Command Prompt opens a *command line interface:* a black, empty screen with the time-honored *C:>* prompt where you can type out instructions to the computer. This is a world without icons, menus, or dialog boxes; even the mouse is almost useless.

Surely you can appreciate the irony. The whole breakthrough of Windows was that it *eliminated* the DOS command-line interface that was still the ruling party on the computers of the day. Most nongeeks sighed with relief, delighted that they'd never have to memorize commands again. Yet here's Windows 10, Microsoft's supposedly ultramodern operating system, complete with a command line! What's going on?

Actually, the command line never went away. At universities and corporations worldwide, professional computer nerds kept right on pounding away at the little

C:> prompts, appreciating the efficiency and power such direct computer control afforded them.

You never *have* to use the command line. In fact, Microsoft has swept it far under the rug, obviously expecting that most people will use the beautiful icons and menus of the regular desktop.

Tip: Quickest way to open the Command Prompt: type *command* into the search box, and then press Enter.

If you have a little time and curiosity, however, the Command Prompt opens up a world of possibilities. It lets you access corners of Windows that you can't get to from the regular desktop. (Commands for exploring network diagnostics are especially plentiful—*ping, netstat,* and so on.) It lets you perform certain tasks with much greater speed and efficiency than you'd get by clicking buttons and dragging icons. And it gives you a fascinating glimpse into the minds and moods of people who live and breathe computers.

Here are a few examples:

Command	Purpose	Example
control	Opens a Control Panel applet	*control date/time*
ping	Checks to see if a server is responding	*ping nytimes.com*
ipconfig	Reveals your PC's IP address	*ipconfig*
mkdir	Make directory (that is, create a folder)	*mkdir \Reports*
copy	Copy files from one folder to another	*copy c:\Reports*.* \Backup*

Tip: You can open a Command Prompt for any folder just by Shift+right-clicking a folder. From the shortcut menu, choose Open Command Window Here.

You can also type the true, secret name of any program to open it, quickly and efficiently, without having to mouse around through the Start menu. For example, you can type *winword* to open Word, or *charmap* to open Character Map.

To learn a few of the hundreds of commands at your disposal, consult the Internet, which is filled with excellent lists and explanations. To find them, Google *Windows command line reference.* You'll find numerous ready-to-study Web sites that tell you what to type at the Command Prompt. (Here's an example from Microsoft: *http://bit.ly/bx0xo4.*)

Contact Support

Believe it or not, Windows 10 no longer comes with a built-in Help system. Instead, you're supposed to use the taskbar search box to find help by searching the Web.

You also get this little app, though, which has links to your PC company's help site, as well as to Microsoft's help sites for your Microsoft accounts (Xbox, Skype, Office, and so on) and Microsoft services (Windows, OneDrive, Xbox, and so on).

Cortana

Cortana, of course, is Windows 10's new voice-operated "personal assistant" (see Chapter 5). But opening this "app" in the Start menu does nothing more than open the Cortana home panel, as though you'd tapped the Cortana microphone button or pressed ⊞+C.

Games

Oh yes, Windows 10 comes with games. See "Microsoft Solitaire Collection" and "Xbox," later in this chapter.

Get Office, Get Skype

Microsoft has kindly given you entire apps that do nothing but let you download other Microsoft programs.

Get Started

It's rather shocking that Windows 10, one of the most complex software programs on earth, no longer comes with an online help system. If you want to know how to do something, you're supposed to type it into the search box ("How do I set up multiple desktops?"). For basic Windows features, you might get a response right there in the

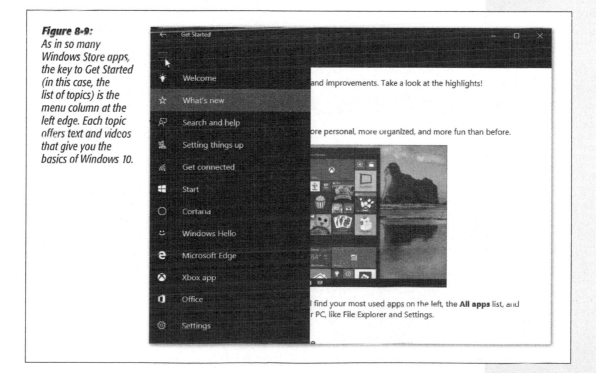

Figure 8-9:
As in so many Windows Store apps, the key to Get Started (in this case, the list of topics) is the menu column at the left edge. Each topic offers text and videos that give you the basics of Windows 10.

Cortana panel; for anything more sophisticated, you'll be shown links from the Web that might answer your query.

You do, however, get Get Started, which is a bunch of videos and help screens that explain the basics of Windows 10: how to use Cortana, how to configure the Start menu, how to use the new Edge browser, and so on. See Figure 8-9.

Groove Music

It wouldn't be a computer if it couldn't play your tunes, right?

But this music app, redesigned and renamed in Windows 10, is much more than a jukebox for songs you already own (Figure 8-10). It's also the front end for Microsoft's Groove music service (formerly Xbox Music), which is Microsoft's version of Spotify or Apple Music: You can listen to any music, on demand and unlimited, for $10 a month or $100 a year, from a catalog of 40 million songs.

Tip: The first time you open this app, you're offered three buttons. "Go to collection" means "see your own song files." "Get a Groove Music Pass" means "Pay Microsoft for unlimited streaming and downloading." And "Get started" takes you to a Web page that lets you copy your song files to your OneDrive. Once there, you can play them on any of your Windows machines: PCs, tablets, Windows Phones, and even the Xbox.

The main menu column at left serves as the outline for the following pages' worth of description.

Figure 8-10:
The complete list of your music. You can sort it using the pop-up menu at top: by year, alphabetically, and so on.

In Albums and Artists views, you see cover art like this. In Songs view, you see a simple table—a list—with columns for title, singer, album name, length, and year of release. A ▶ button and + button (meaning "Add to a playlist") also appear.

Note: Whenever music is playing, a bar full of playback controls appears at the bottom of the window. They do just what you'd expect: Previous Song, Pause, Next Song, Volume, Shuffle, Repeat. There's usually a scroll bar, too, showing where you are in the song and permitting you to skip to another spot.

Search

This search box finds everything from everywhere: songs, bands, albums; on your PC, in Microsoft's music stores. As you type, a drop-down menu proposes name matches, to save you typing.

When you click one of the suggestions (or press Enter), you get a Results page. At the top, you see how many of these songs or albums are actually on your machine ("In collection"), and how many are online, in Microsoft's store ("Full catalog").

Albums, Artists, Songs

Use these buttons to specify how you want your music displayed. You see something like Figure 8-10.

In general, all three of these views are alike: They present all of your music, grouped by album, performer, or individual song. At the top, four important controls appear:

- **Shuffle.** When turned on (appears in color), Groove Music will play back the music on this screen in random order.

- **All (381).** Groove can play music files that live anywhere: on your computer, on your OneDrive, or on Microsoft's Groove music service (that is, streaming from the Internet). This pop-up menu lets you show only the music files from one source or another: "Available offline" (you won't need an Internet connection), "Streaming" (not actually on your computer—playing over the Internet), "Only on this device" (not showing what's on your network or OneDrive), or "On OneDrive."

  The number in parentheses shows you *how many* songs you've got.

- **Date added.** This pop-up menu lets you sort the music you're examining by date, alphabetically by name, by year, by musical genre, or by performer.

- **Select.** The fourth icon at the top turns on Select mode, which means that checkboxes appear on the icons of all of the songs, albums, or performers. (Often the "checkbox" is the top-right corner of an album's or band's icon.)

  As soon as you start checking boxes, a strip of options appears at the bottom of the screen, referring to what you want to do with these selected musics: Play them, Add them to a playlist (+), Download them, or Delete them. There's also a "Clear selection" button, which turns off the checkmarks so you can start over.

In Albums and Artists view, clicking or tapping takes you to further information screens. For example:

- **Albums.** The screen fills with a lovely display of the album art and song titles. When you choose an album, the buttons at the top are Play (▷), Add to (Playlist) (+), Explore artist (⋀), and More (···). That last one's a pop-up menu; its commands include "Start radio" (start a stream of music that sounds like this song), Pin to Start, Delete, and Download. (Those last two are available only for songs you actually own.)

- **Artists.** Here's a screen (Figure 8-11) full of tidbits pertaining to this particular performer: a list of that artist's songs in your collection, latest albums, top songs, and even a bio.

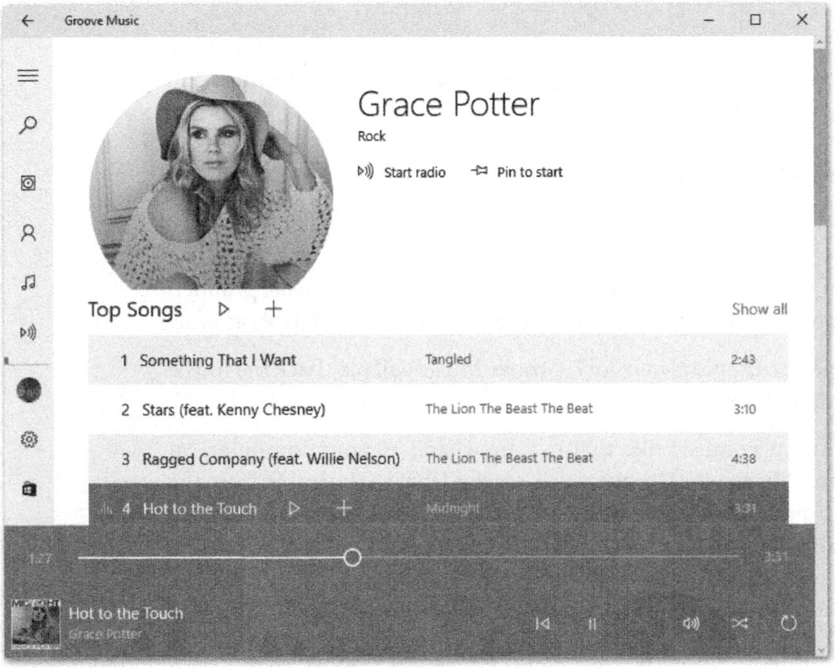

Figure 8-11:
The Artist screen reveals lists of albums by this performer—both those in your collection already and those you might want to explore—and top songs, and similar-sounding albums.

Radio

This is Microsoft's version of Pandora, and it's available only if you subscribe to Microsoft's Groove service.

When you select "Start a station," you're asked to enter the name of a band or a singer you like. When you then press Enter, Groove instantly starts playing songs by that artist *and songs that sound similar.* It's a great way to discover new favorites based on what you know you like, and also a great way to keep the mood going when you find a style you like.

A tile for your new station appears, so that you'll be able to recall it instantly. Just tap or click. Use the standard playback controls at bottom to play or skip songs.

To delete one of your stations, turn on Select mode (☰), select the station's tile, and then hit Delete in the toolbar that appears at the bottom.

Explore

This screen displays the icons of new albums, in hopes of whetting your appetite and introducing you to new music. If you're a paying Groove subscriber (or within the free trial period), all of it is available to listen to, right now—no charge.

Now Playing

Whenever music is playing, no matter how far you've meandered in Groove Music, the "Now playing" button in the list at left (ıl) summons a full screen of information. It shows the album art, the list of songs from that album, and a "Save as a playlist" button.

Tip: Groove Music's taskbar icon sprouts basic playback controls that appear when you point to it (or tap with your finger).

[Your name]

The icon here reveals your name and account details.

Settings (⚙)

Here's the full Settings page for Groove Music. Most of the options here are self-explanatory, but a few are worth noting:

- **Groove Music Pass.** This is where you pay Microsoft monthly or yearly for its unlimited streaming-music service.

- **Music on this PC.** Here you tell the app which folders contain your music files. You can even import playlists from an existing copy of Apple's iTunes.

- **Downloads.** If you're a subscriber: Do you want songs you buy to be downloaded instantly? And when you add new music to your collection, do you want it downloaded to your machine? Or just "bookmarked" for streaming later, to save disk space?

- **Background.** Do you prefer white text against black, or black on white?

GEM IN THE ROUGH

Universal Playback Controls

You can start music playing and then dive into other apps or programs; the music continues to play. You know—background music for your work session.

But what if you have to take a phone call or to speak sternly to a child? Do you have to muddle all the way back to the Groove Music app to pause playback?

Don't be silly. If you have a keyboard, just tap one of your volume keys. Up pops this audio palette, containing Previous Song, Next Song, Pause, and volume controls. The album cover appears, too—a nice touch.

• **More.** Lots of links related to your account, billing, privacy, and help.

Playlists

A playlist is a group of songs you've placed together, in a sequence that makes sense to you. One might consist of party tunes; another might hold romantic dinnertime music; a third might be drum-heavy workout cuts.

Creating playlists

To create a new playlist, select "New playlist" (+) in the list at left. Type a name for the playlist ("Rockout Toonz," "Makeout Music," whatever), and hit Save.

Now a playlist icon called "Rockout Toonz" (or whatever you called your latest list) appears in the list of playlists at left. All you have to do is add songs to it.

Just look for the + symbol. It appears on the "Now playing" screen, for example, next to any selected song name. It appears on the Albums and Artists pages for your collection.

Wherever it appears, it produces a pop-up menu of playlist names. Specify which playlist should be the new home for that song.

You can also work in reverse. Tap a playlist's name and then hit "Explore music." Microsoft opens its massive vault of songs to you; search, browse, navigate to find the music you want, hitting the + button each time you see one worth enshrining in your playlist.

Editing, rearranging, and deleting playlists

To perform any kind of surgery to one of your playlists, select its name in the list at left.

The buttons below its name at the top of the screen let you add more songs (+), rename the playlist ($\varnothing$), or delete it ($\cdots$).

You can also operate on the individual songs inside it. Tap one of the songs; the − button next to the ▷ means "Delete this song" (from the playlist, not your collection).

You can also rearrange the songs by dragging them up or down the list.

Tip: Like many of Microsoft's Windows Store apps, Music is intended to be bare-bones and simple. It offers the basic functions and no more; for example, it doesn't let you rip your audio CDs to your computer, edit song information, or create "smart playlists."

If you'd prefer something a little fuller fledged, don't forget that Windows Media Player is waiting for you back at the Windows desktop. Or you could download a nicer, more complete free program like MusicBee. It's available from this book's "Missing CD" page at *www.missingmanuals.com*.

Magnifier

Magnifier puts a floating magnifying-glass icon on your screen (Figure 8-12, top left). When you click it, you get the Magnifier toolbar (top right).

Magnifier creates various magnification effects—great when your eyes are tired or old, or when you're trying to study something whose font is just too dang small.

Using the View menu, you can choose "Full screen" (the entire screen image grows when you click the + button), "Lens" (you get a floating magnification inset that follows your cursor, as shown at bottom in Figure 8-12), or "Docked" (the top strip of the screen is one giant magnification inset; the rest of the screen is normal size).

In each case, the magnified area scrolls as you move your cursor, tab through a dialog box, or type, enlarging whatever part of the screen contains the action. Using the Magnifier Settings dialog box (click the ⚙ in the toolbar), you can specify how the magnification area should follow your cursor.

Tip: Whenever Magnifier is turned on, you can zoom in or out with Ctrl+plus or Ctrl+minus.

Figure 8-12:
Top left: Magnifier enlarges whatever part of the screen your cursor is touching.

Top right: In Lens or Docked modes, note that you can adjust the size of the magnified area by dragging its edge.

Bottom: In Docked mode, you can also tear the pane away from the edge of the screen so it becomes a floating window; just drag anywhere inside it.

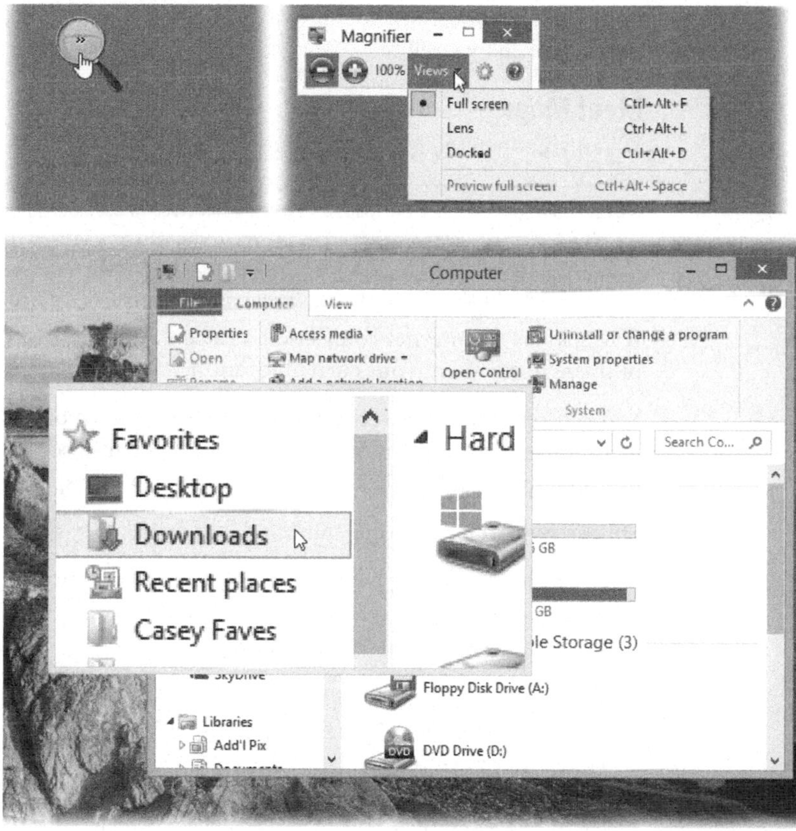

Mail

The built-in Windows 10 mail app is easy to use, it's beautiful, and—especially if you have a touchscreen—it offers a fast, fluid way to work. And it's not nearly as stripped down as it was in Windows 8. It gets its own chapter in this book: Chapter 11.

Maps

Now that Windows is a tablet operating system, a Maps program is more or less a must-have.

Maps (which is powered by Bing, which is powered by Nokia Maps, which is powered by NAVTEQ) lets you type in any address or point of interest in the United States or many other countries and see it plotted on a map. It can give you spoken turn-by-turn driving directions, just like a dashboard GPS unit. It also gives you a live national Yellow Pages business directory and real-time traffic-jam alerts, if you have an Internet connection. You have a choice of a street-map diagram or actual aerial photos, taken by satellite.

Meet Maps

When you open the Maps app, you see—a map.

Note: You also see a question: Maps asks you if it's allowed to use your current location, so that it can show you where you are on the map. The only reason to choose Block is if you think it's creepy that Maps, and by extension Microsoft, knows where you are.

If Maps has an Internet connection and can figure out where you are, it displays a bullseye to represent your current location.

You can scroll in any direction. You can also zoom in or out, using any of the usual techniques (two-finger pinch or spread; turn the mouse's scroll wheel). You can also double-tap or double-click to zoom into a particular spot.

On the right: four awesome buttons. Here's what they do, from top to bottom:

- **North is up.** Click or tap to orient the map so that north is up. (Which seems like a "duh" function, until you realize that sometimes you'll have rotated the map deliberately and need to get it back.)

- **Tilt.** Angles the map in a sort of 3D-ish way. You might find that it better resembles those car-dashboard GPS displays this way.

- **Show my location.** If you ever find that you've scrolled (or searched) away from your home location, this icon (or the Ctrl+Home keystroke) makes the map scroll and zoom until the "You are here" diamond is dead center on your screen. That's handy if you've scrolled or searched some other part of the world.

- **Map views.** This icon opens a palette of three options. "Aerial view" displays the map as satellite photos of the real world. Zoom in far enough, and you can find your house. (As opposed to the usual view—roads represented as lines—which Microsoft calls "Road view.")

"Show traffic" gives you free, real-time traffic reporting—color-coded on major roadways, showing you the current traffic speed. Green for good traffic flow, yellow for slower traffic, and red for true traffic jams. You even see tiny clickable icons representing accidents and construction sites, for your stressing pleasure.

If you don't see any colored lines, it's either because traffic is moving fine or because Microsoft doesn't have any information for those roads. Usually, you get traffic info only for highways, and only in metropolitan areas.

Finally, "Streetside" is Microsoft's version of Google's Street View; read on.

Streetside

Streetside (Figure 8-13) is a mind-blowing way to explore maps. It lets you stand at a spot on the map and "look around." You're seeing actual photos of the street you seek; you can turn right or left and actually move through the still photos. It's a great way to investigate a neighborhood before you move there, for example, or to scope out the restaurant where you're supposed to meet someone.

(To create Streetside, Microsoft, like Google before it, must drive specially equipped photography vans up and down every single road in the world, capturing photos

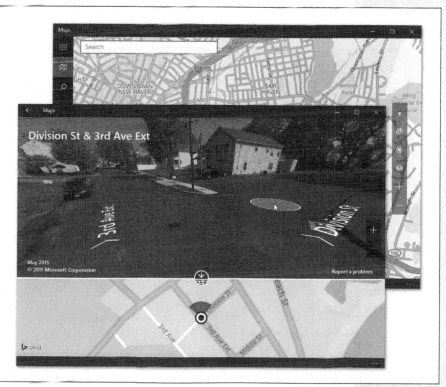

Figure 8-13:
The bluish tints on streets and towns indicates Streetside availability. In these areas, you can see, with photos, exactly what it looks like to be on the ground at a certain spot on the map. Drag to look around you. Click or tap farther down a road to jump there, or click in the navigation bar at bottom. (It may not appear if the window is too small.) Zoom with your mouse wheel, or by scrolling on the trackpad or pinching with two fingers on the touchscreen.

and GPS data. So far, it's done so only in a few cities in the U.S. and Europe, but it has big plans.)

When you click the Streetside button, the map changes. If you zoom out enough, you'll see puddles of blue shading in populated areas. These are the places where Streetside is available. Click there (or navigate there), and then proceed as shown in Figure 8-13.

Searching the Maps

You're not always interested in finding out where you are; often, you want to see where something *else* is. To search Maps, type into the search box at top.

Tip: When you click into the search box, Microsoft opens a menu of Hotels, Coffee, Restaurants, Shopping, and Museums. The point is that you can select one of these to see nearby hotels, restaurants, or whatever—without having to type anything.

Here's what Maps can find for you:

- **An address.** You can skip the periods (and usually the commas, too). And you can use abbreviations. Typing *710 w end ave nyc* will find 710 West End Avenue, New York, New York. (In this and any of the other examples, you can type a Zip code instead of a city and a state.)

- **An intersection.** Type *57th and lexington, ny ny*. Maps will find the spot where East 57th Street crosses Lexington Avenue in New York City.

Figure 8-14:
Left: When you search for something, Maps shows you all the results as pink numbered dots, and as corresponding listings.

Right: When you tap a search result, Maps turns into a full-blown Yellow Pages. It shows you the name, address, phone number, ratings, and other information about the business, complete with buttons like Directions, Nearby, Web site, Call, and Add to Favorites.

- **A city.** Type *chicago il* to see that city. You can zoom in from there.

- **A Zip code or neighborhood.** Type *10024* or *greenwich village nyc*.

- **A point of interest.** Type *washington monument* or *niagara falls*.

- **A commercial establishment.** You can use Maps as a glorified national Yellow Pages. If you type, for example, *pharmacy 60609,* blue numbered dots show you all the drugstores in that Chicago Zip code. It's a great way to find a gas station, a cash machine, or a hospital in a pinch.

  Select a listing (Figure 8-14, top left) to see a full dossier about that place (Figure 8-14, bottom right).

Tip: You can tap or click either place. That is, you can tap a numbered circle to auto-scroll the info column to the corresponding description, or you can tap a description to auto-scroll the map to the corresponding numbered circle.

Directions

If you open the ≡ menu and choose Directions, you get *two* search bars, labeled A and B (Figure 8-15, top left). That's right: Microsoft is *literally* prepared to get you from Point A to Point B.

Type in two addresses, using the keyboard. After typing, press Enter or tap the →.

Three features save you time here:

- The A address may already say "My Location."

- If you've saved any locations as Favorites (described below) or in Cortana preferences (page 196), they appear here, too, for quick selecting.

- As you type, Windows displays a tappable list of matching locations.

Tip: The Options link below the B box offers checkboxes for things you might want to avoid—like Traffic, Toll roads, Unpaved roads, and Ferries. (Because there's nothing like crashing into a ferry to ruin your day.)

Once you've selected your A and B, the proposed route appears on the map, the written directions appear at left, and Maps shows the distance and the estimated time for your travel (Figure 8-15).

Three option icons appear at top. They let you specify how you're planning to travel: by car, by public transportation, or on foot. Yes, that's right: It's turn-by-turn *walking* instructions.

At this point, on a tablet (or phone), Maps is a full-blown GPS navigation app. It shows where you are as you drive, speaks turning instructions, and auto-scrolls the map as you drive.

Tip: Select ⚙ (lower left) to view some useful controls: kilometers vs. miles, for example, and what you want the map background to look like as you travel: Day (bright), Night (dim, to prevent driver distraction), or Automatic (chooses Day or Night based on ambient light).

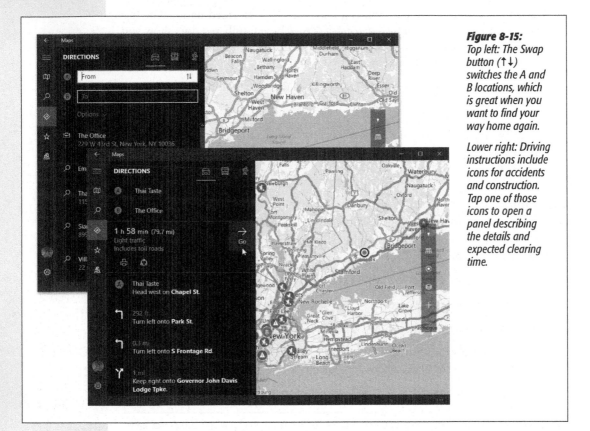

Figure 8-15:
Top left: The Swap button (↑↓) switches the A and B locations, which is great when you want to find your way home again.

Lower right: Driving instructions include icons for accidents and construction. Tap one of those icons to open a panel describing the details and expected clearing time.

Favorites

If you're like most people, you tend to live in one place. You probably have a home, and you may very well have a place of work. It's possible you have a friend or two.

Fortunately, you don't have to painstakingly re-enter these addresses every time you want directions someplace. You can designate any place, or even any set of directions, as a favorite; just tap the ☆ that appears on the information panel for any address or establishment.

Once you've accumulated a few, it's easy enough to call them up again: Tap the ☆ in the left-side menu. Tap a Favorite place to see it on the map.

3D Cities

All the time Microsoft was trawling the world's cities to create Streetside, described above, it was also assembling 3D Cities, which is closely modeled on Apple's Flyover feature. It depicts certain cities (150, soon to increase) as three-dimensional models—like aerial views, except that you can *peek behind* buildings (Figure 8-16).

To try it out, hit the 3D Cities icon in the menu column (just below the Favorites star). Here's what you can try out if you have a touchscreen:

- **Move the map** by dragging with one finger.

- **Zoom** by pinching or spreading with two fingers.

Figure 8-16:
3D Cities is a dynamic, interactive, photographic 3D model of certain major cities. It looks something like an aerial video, except that you control the virtual camera. You can pan around these scenes, looking over and around buildings to see what's behind them.

- **Rotate the map** by twisting two fingers.

- **Change your viewing angle** by dragging up or down with two fingers.

If you have mouse or trackpad:

- **Move the map** by dragging.

- **Zoom** by turning the mouse wheel (or dragging two fingers on the trackpad).

- **Rotate the map** by pointing to the little compass-needle pointing (at top of the vertical toolbar). A tiny rotation-arrow button appears on each side, which you can click to turn the map.

- **Change the viewing angle** by adding the Shift key to the zooming method.

Math Input Panel

This unsung little freebie is intended for an elite group indeed: mathematicians with touchscreen computers. You're supposed to write out math equations using your finger or a stylus and marvel as Windows translates your handwriting into a typed-out mathematical expression. (You *can* use this program with a mouse; it just might feel a little odd.)

Most of the time, you'll want to use MIP when you're writing in a word processor—preparing a math test for students, writing a white paper, whatever.

Note: This program can insert its finished math expressions only into programs that recognize something called MathML (Mathematical Markup Language). Microsoft Word, Excel, and PowerPoint do, and so does the free OpenOffice.org.

If you have a touchscreen computer and you're working in the Windows Journal program, you can also use MIP to analyze your previously *handwritten* math expressions and make them properly typeset. (Use the selection tool to highlight your handwriting, and then drag the expression *into* the MIP window.)

To use MIP on any other computer, write out the mathematical expression, as neatly as you can, in the writing area. In the Preview area (see Figure 8-17), you see Windows' stab at recognizing your handwriting.

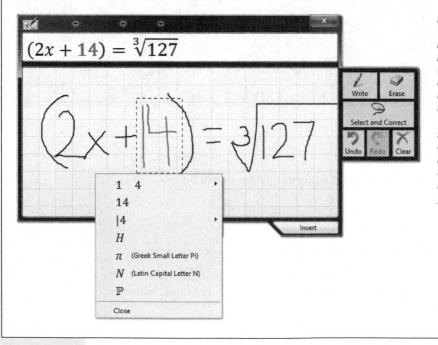

Figure 8-17:
To correct an error in Math Input Panel, right-click the error. (Or use the "Select and Correct" tool, and draw a circle around the problem.) Then, from the list of suggestions, tap the one that's what you intended. (If none of the guesses are right, rewrite the portion you've selected.)

If it's all correct, tap Insert to drop the equation into your word processor.

If something needs correcting, you can show MIP what it got wrong in one of several ways:

- **Right-click the mistake.** Or, if the mistaken transcription is more than one symbol, circle the error while pressing the right mouse button.

- **Tap the mistake while pressing your stylus's button.** (Or, again, circle the mistake while pressing the pen's button.)

- **Click the Select and Cancel button.** Now tap the erroneous symbol, or circle the larger part that's wrong.

Tip: It's better to correct errors after you've written out the whole thing.

Immediately, a pop-up menu of alternative transcriptions appears. Proceed as shown in Figure 8-17.

If the expression is now complete, tap Insert. If you have more to write, just keep on going. (If you got into symbol-correction mode by tapping Select and Cancel, then you have to tap Write before you continue.)

Tip: You can tap any entry in the History menu to re-input an expression you've entered before. When you're working on, for example, a proof, or a drill with many similar problems, that can save you a lot of time.

Microsoft Edge

Here's the new Windows 10 browser. See Chapter 10.

Microsoft Solitaire Collection

To the shock of many, Microsoft killed off Solitaire back in Windows 8. The one, the only—for many people, the most-used app of all.

But don't panic. Windows 10 comes with a new, improved version of Solitaire—five different versions, in fact. (There are also links to download Bingo, Minesweeper, Sudoku, Mahjong, and four others, all free.)

Note: Well, *sort of* free. Your game-playing experience is interrupted every now and then by 15- and 30-second video ads—including one that offers a Premium plan, where you pay $10 a year to get *rid* of the ads.

Improved not just because their graphics and gameplay are modernized and great, but also because they save their data as part of your online Microsoft account, so your impressive card-playing stats look similar no matter what computer (or Xbox console) you're using.

When you fire up this app, dismiss or approve the first three administrative screens. You arrive at the game screen (Figure 8-18).

Figure 8-18:
When you click the game you want to play, detailed instructions appear to help you.

Left: As always in a Windows Store app, the ≡ button at top left opens the main menu; in this case, it lists the five card games and gives you access to daily challenges, statistics, your Xbox account, and so on.

Money

What "Money" really means is "financial news." When you open this app, you arrive at what looks like a glorious, beautifully designed financial magazine. Scroll to see stock-market graphs; tiles for the day's winners and losers; article blurbs and head-lines; videos; and stats for bonds, rates, currencies, and commodities (Figure 8-19).

Read this chapter's writeup about the News app for a complete understanding of how these apps work. But for now, don't miss the toolbar. It offers tiles like these:

- **Today.** Brings you back to the opening collection of news and stats.

- **Watchlist.** Your own portfolio (or just stocks you want to watch). Tap the + button to specify each company name, or stock symbol, that you want this page to track.

- **News, Investing, Personal Finance, Real Estate, Careers, Videos.** Direct links to those sections of this "magazine."

Meanwhile, the main menu (left-side icons) offers these options (in addition to Today and Watchlist described above):

- **Markets.** Huge rows of financial tables representing today's financial-market activity in every conceivable category, or today's interest rates for various mortgages, bank accounts, and credit cards.

- **Currencies.** Complete lists of today's international currency values, plus a conversion calculator.

- **Mortgage Calculator.** Shopping for a house? Comparing loans? You go, girl/dude.

- **World Markets.** Maps of the world, with labels showing at a glance what happened to their stock markets today.

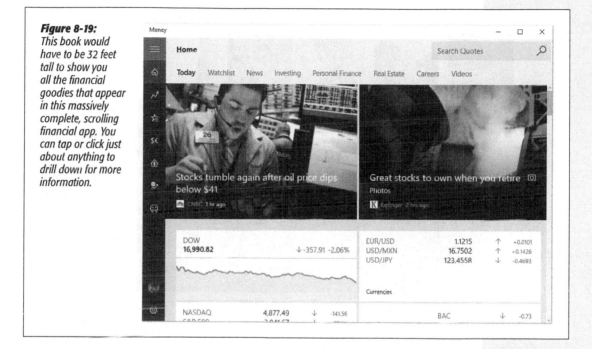

Figure 8-19:
This book would have to be 32 feet tall to show you all the financial goodies that appear in this massively complete, scrolling financial app. You can tap or click just about anything to drill down for more information.

Movies & TV

Windows 10 wasn't Microsoft's only big launch in 2015. That's also when the Microsoft Movies & TV Store opened online.

It's exactly like the iTunes store, or the Amazon video store, or whatever: It's a place where you can either buy or rent movies and TV-show episodes.

This app, Movies & TV, is really just a video *player*—not just for videos you got from Microsoft, but for your own video files, too. If you click one of the movie-poster buttons, or "Show all," or "Shop for more," you're taken out of this app and into the Windows Store app to do your actual shopping.

If you make the window wide enough, a navigation panel appears at left, bearing the three categories of videos in your collection: Movies, TV, and Videos (meaning, your own videos).

When you click a video's name, you get an info screen about it. When you click the Play triangle next to a video's name there, you open the main player screen—and the video plays.

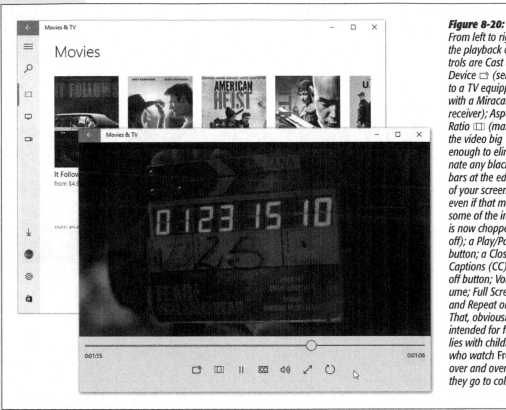

Figure 8-20:
From left to right, the playback controls are Cast to Device ⧉ (sends to a TV equipped with a Miracast receiver); Aspect Ratio ⧄ (makes the video big enough to eliminate any black bars at the edges of your screen, even if that means some of the image is now chopped off); a Play/Pause button; a Closed Captions (CC) on/off button; Volume; Full Screen; and Repeat on/off. That, obviously, is intended for families with children who watch Frozen over and over until they go to college.

GEM IN THE ROUGH

Miracast: Play Photos and Movies on Your TV

A tablet is one thing. But if you want to show your pictures to more than a couple of people, your big-screen TV is the way to go. Fortunately, Windows makes it easy to send what's on your computer's screen to your TV screen.

Windows works with Miracast, a wireless audio-video transmission technology (like Apple's AirPlay). If you have a TV with Miracast (also known as WiDi) built in, or a Miracast box that connects to a TV, the TV becomes a mirror of everything on your Windows screen. Great for slideshows, videos, and teaching people how to use Windows.

When you want to broadcast your computer's audio and video to the TV, hit ▤ on the taskbar to open the Action Center; choose the Connect tab; and wait while Windows tries to find the Miracast TV's wireless signal. After a moment, its name appears in the right-side panel.

(There's a long way, too: Open Settings→Devices →"Connected devices." Open "Add a device," and then choose the name of your Miracast receiver.)

Like magic, your computer's image now shows up on the TV—with sound. Miraculous!

Whenever you wiggle your mouse or tap the screen, you get the playback controls shown in Figure 8-20, bottom.

Music

The Music app has been renamed—it's now Groove Music. See page 308.

Narrator

Narrator began life as a little program that could read aloud certain items on the screen, like dialog boxes and error messages. But it's had a huge upgrade. Now it can read anything that's on the screen. If you're visually impaired, you may find that Narrator comes very close to serving as a basic screen reader. It can describe every item on the screen; it can describe the layout of a Web page; and it can make sounds to confirm that you've performed a touchscreen gesture correctly.

Even if you're not blind, Narrator is still handy; it can read your email back to you, or read Web articles as you're getting dressed in the morning.

Figure 8-21:
Narrator's entire visual presence is nothing more than this Settings dialog box—and a colored rectangular frame that moves around the screen as you touch it (or arrow-key it). Whatever the frame encloses, Narrator speaks. That way, you can figure out where you are on the screen even if you can't see it.

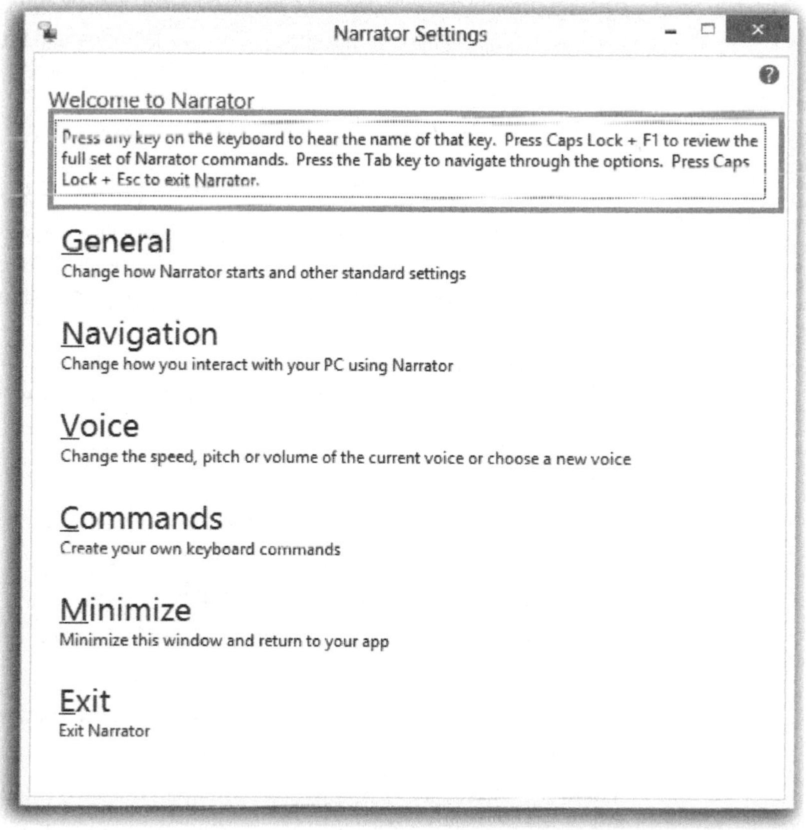

Narrator Settings

Welcome to Narrator

Press any key on the keyboard to hear the name of that key. Press Caps Lock + F1 to review the full set of Narrator commands. Press the Tab key to navigate through the options. Press Caps Lock + Esc to exit Narrator.

General
Change how Narrator starts and other standard settings

Navigation
Change how you interact with your PC using Narrator

Voice
Change the speed, pitch or volume of the current voice or choose a new voice

Commands
Create your own keyboard commands

Minimize
Minimize this window and return to your app

Exit
Exit Narrator

When you open Narrator, you wind up at its Settings dialog box (Figure 8-21)—and the voice of Microsoft David (no relation) starts talking, reading everything on the screen.

As you'll soon discover, mastering Narrator takes a lot of time and patience; it's something like a complete operating system in itself. But here are the basics.

Touchscreen Basics

Narrator is especially important on touchscreen computers; if you're blind, how else are you supposed to navigate the screen?

Drag your finger around the touchscreen; Narrator speaks everything you touch, so that you can get a feel for the layout of things. You can also tap to hear a single item identified; you don't have to worry about opening something accidentally.

Of course, if touching something makes it say its name, then how are you supposed to open it? Simple: Add another tap. That is, you *double-tap* when a single tap usually works (or press-and-hold) and *triple-tap* when you'd ordinarily double-tap.

To see the master cheat sheet of touch gestures in Narrator (and hear it read to you), tap *three times with four fingers* against the screen. You'll learn essential tips like these:

To do this...	...Use this touch command
Stop Narrator from reading	Tap once with two fingers
Read current window	Swipe up with three fingers
Click	Double-tap
Double-click	Triple-tap
Start dragging	Tap with three fingers
Show/hide Narrator window	Tap with four fingers
Move to previous/next item	Flick left/right with one finger
Scroll	Swipe any direction with two fingers
Tab forward and backward	Swipe left/right with three fingers

There's a lot more to Narrator. For instructions, see the free downloadable PDF Appendix "Narrator.pdf" on this book's "Missing CD" page at *www.missingmanuals.com*.

News

The News app is one of several free, daily, full-screen magazines that come preinstalled in Windows 10. (Sports, Money, and Weather are the others.)

At its core, News is simply grabbing articles from over 300 different big-name news Web sites: *The New York Times, The Wall Street Journal, The New Yorker*, CNN, The Huffington Post, and so on.

But it reformats everything into one uniform, attractive, screen-friendly layout (Figure 8-22).

These apps all work essentially alike. You open the app (Internet connection required). Scroll down to see headlines and teaser blurbs for other articles; use the section buttons across the top to view sections. In News's case, they're Top Stories, Technology, US, World, Crime, Offbeat, Politics, and so on. Each button takes you directly to a similar spread of photos, headlines, and blurbs just for that section.

Note: These section buttons scroll horizontally—far enough to include any interests that you set up in Cortana's Notebook (page 216).

Figure 8-22:
No hard-to-read color schemes or ugly fonts. No blinking ads, banners, or obnoxious animations. If the 300 publications presented here pique your interest at all, then the News app is, for sure, the way to read them.

Customizing News

It turns out that your News magazine is *customizable*. You can ask it to bring you stories about your favorite actor, your favorite toothpaste, or even *you*.

When you select Interests in the menu column, you see a scrolling list of topic tiles—the same ones that appear across the top. You can tap or click to turn off the ones you don't want cluttering up your newspaper.

You can also *add* topics or news sources at this point. Each of the categories before you (Featured, News, Entertainment, and so on) offers subcategories that you can turn on with just a click or tap on its + button. (Or click the tile *not* on the + button to get a preview of what you'll see there.)

Or hit + at the top and type in anything you like; as you type, News shows you matching topics or sources. Click the one you want. *Waterski magazine. Electric cars. Seedless watermelon.* Whatever you might like your customized newspaper to show you.

You can add as many new topics as you like.

> **Tip:** In Windows 10, Microsoft killed off the Health & Fitness magazine app. But everything in it lives on here, in News. On the Add Interests page, under Lifestyle, you can add everything that used to be in Health & Fitness: Nutrition, Strength, Cardio, Yoga, Wellness, and so on.

The other icons in the menu column at left include these:

- **Local.** If you grant the app access to your location, it automatically presents articles from your local newspapers and Web sites—no charge.

- **Video.** This section gives you direct access to *videos* from Bing's multitude of sources. That's something a typical printed magazine doesn't usually offer.

Especially on a tablet, wow—News is one of the best things to come along since hyperlinks.

Notepad

Notepad is a bargain-basement *text editor,* which means it lets you open, create, and edit files that contain plain, unformatted text, like the ReadMe.txt files that often accompany new programs. You can also use Notepad to write short notes or to edit text that you intend to paste into your email program after editing it.

Notepad Basics

Notepad opens automatically when you double-click text files (those with the file extension *.txt*). You can also find Notepad by typing *notep* at the Start menu.

You'll quickly discover that Notepad is the world's most frill-free application. Its list of limitations is almost longer than its list of features.

UP TO SPEED

How Scroll Bars Work

These days, swiping with your finger, or tapping the space bar, are the most efficient ways to move down a Web page.

But if you're a mouse addict, you can still operate the vertical scroll bar that appears at the right edge of the window when you move the mouse or touch the trackpad.

In case this whole scroll bar thing is new to you, here's the drill: The scroll bar is a map of your entire document or page. In the middle, there's a sliding

darker rectangle; its height represents how much of the page you're already seeing. For example, if the differently colored handle is one-third the height or width of the whole screen, then you're already seeing one-third of the page.

You can drag the handle manually to move around the page. You can also click or tap in the scroll bar track on either side of the handle to make the window scroll by one screenful.

For example, the Notepad window has no toolbar and can work with only one file at a time.

Above all, Notepad is a *text* processor, not a *word* processor. That means you can't use any formatting at all—no bold, italic, centered text, and so on. That's not necessarily bad news, however. The beauty of text files is that any word processor on any kind of computer—Windows, Mac, Unix, whatever—can open plain text files like the ones Notepad creates.

About Word Wrap

In the old days, Notepad didn't automatically wrap lines of text to make everything fit in its window. As a result, chunks of text often went on forever in a single line or got chopped off by the right side of the window, which could produce disastrous results when you were trying to follow, say, a soufflé recipe.

Now, lines of text wrap automatically, exactly as they do in a word processor. But you're still seeing nothing more than the effects of the Format→Word Wrap command—an option you can turn off, if you like, by choosing the command again. (You can tell when Word Wrap is on by the presence of a checkmark next to the command in the Format menu.)

On-Screen Keyboard

In the new world of touchscreen tablets, not everyone has a physical keyboard. Windows 10 offers this onscreen version, which is described on page 445.

OneDrive

This "app" is just a shortcut to opening your OneDrive *folder*, described on page 161.

OneNote

"OneNote" isn't really a good name for this program, since its whole point is to create and organize *lots* of notes.

But never mind that; be grateful that you're getting it free (albeit in a simpler, touch-screen-friendly edition). (Actually, the full version is free, too. Go get it!)

Notes can be anything (Figure 8-23). Driving directions, recipes, to-do lists, stuff you paste in from the Web or email, brainstorms—anything you might want to refer to later. OneNote is a notepad and a scrapbook in one.

The beauty of it is that these notes sync via the Internet. You can refer to the same set of notes on any Windows device—phone, tablet, computer—and even Android, iPhone, or Mac. (Just download the OneNote app for each one.)

To create a new note, hit the + at top left, or press Ctrl+N. Type a name for this note.

The tabs across the top let you access these toolbars:

- **Home.** Here's formatting: bold, italic, underline, font choice; lists, like bullets, numbered lists, or checkboxes; and paragraph formatting like Centered.

- **Insert.** Your note can include a table, another file on your computer, a photo, or a Web link.

Tip: If you insert a picture, you can resize it by dragging the corners. You can also rotate it: Right-click (or hold your finger down on) it; from the shortcut menu, choose Picture, and then Rotate.

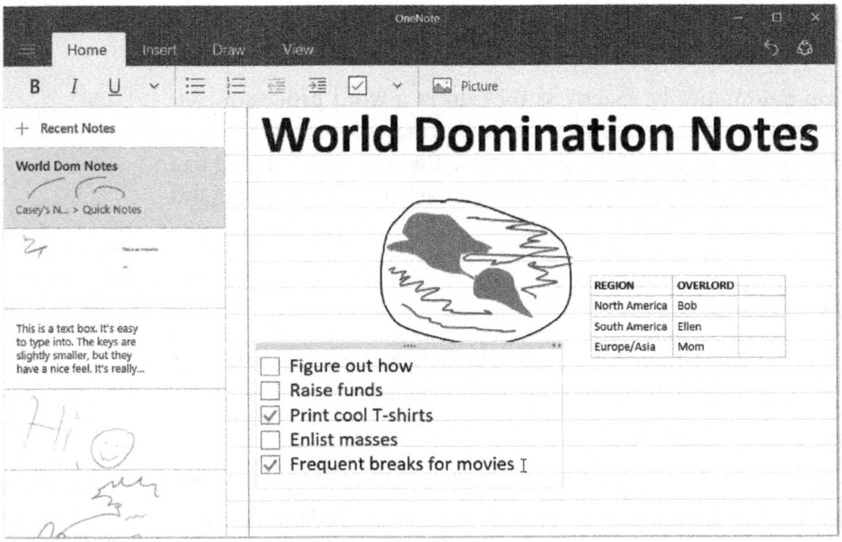

Figure 8-23:
In OneNote, all kinds of data can coexist on the same note: typing, drawing, photos, to-do lists, and so on. All of this gets auto-synced to any other device that has OneNote running.

- **Draw.** This is the "touch-enabled" part. You can draw with your finger (or, more clumsily, a mouse or trackpad). The tools include an eraser, a highlighter, a pen, and a color palette.

- **View.** Here's how you can zoom in or out, or superimpose faint blue lines like the ones in a paper notebook.

As you create your notes, they're listed in a table of contents on the left side. Some profoundly useful options appear if you right-click one (or hold your finger down on one)—like Delete Page, Rename Page, Copy Link to Page, and Pin to Start. That one creates a tile on the right side of your Start menu—a great way to get instant access to something you refer to a lot, like your list of credit cards, things to do, or an essay in progress.

There are a few miscellaneous settings in Settings, and the ☰ menu lets you create additional notebooks. That's right: multiple notebooks full of multiple notes. OneNote *really* isn't the right name for this app.

Paint

You can use Paint to "paint" simple artwork or to edit graphics files from other sources. You might say Paint is something like Adobe Photoshop (well, in the same way you might say the local Cub Scout newsletter is something like *The New York Times*). Common tasks for this program include making quick sketches, fixing dust specks on scanned photos, and entertaining kids for hours on end.

When you first open Paint, you get a small, empty painting window. Go like this:

1. **From the File menu, choose Properties to specify the dimensions of the graphic you want to create. Click OK.**

   Later in your life, you can revisit that command to adjust your graphic's dimensions.

2. **Click a tool on the Home tab, like the Pencil.**

   If you need help identifying one of these tools, point to it without clicking. A tooltip identifies the icon by name, and a help message appears at the bottom of the window.

3. **Click a "paint" color from the palette.**

   You may also want to change the "brush" by clicking the Brushes palette, like the spray-paint splatter shown in Figure 8-24.

4. **If you've selected one of the enclosed-shape tools, use the Fill pop-up menu to specify a texture (Watercolor, Crayon, or whatever); click Color 2, and then a color swatch, to specify the color for the inside of that shape.**

   Some tools produce enclosed shapes, like squares and circles. You can specify one color for the border, and a second color for the fill color inside.

5. **Finally, drag your cursor in the image area (see Figure 8-24).**

   As you work, don't forget that you can click the Undo button (the counterclockwise arrow at the very top edge of the window), "taking back" the last painting maneuvers you made.

   For fine detail work, click the View tab, and then click Zoom In. You've just enlarged it so every dot is easily visible.

Paint can open and create several different file formats, including BMP, JPEG, and GIF—every file format you need to save graphics for use on a Web site.

Tip: Paint also offers a nifty way to create wallpaper. After you create or edit a graphic, open the File menu. Choose "Set as desktop background"; from the submenu, choose Fill, Tile, or Center to transfer your masterpiece to your desktop.

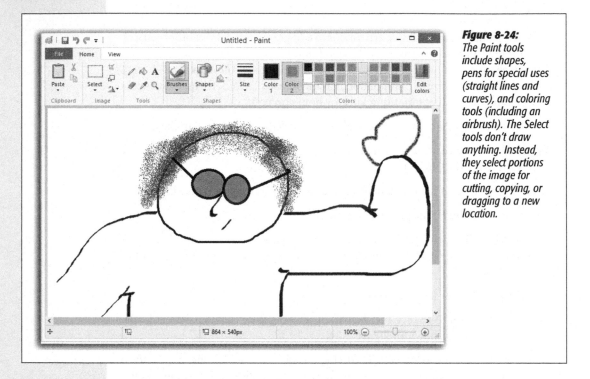

Figure 8-24:
The Paint tools include shapes, pens for special uses (straight lines and curves), and coloring tools (including an airbrush). The Select tools don't draw anything. Instead, they select portions of the image for cutting, copying, or dragging to a new location.

People

The People app is Windows' address book. It's a centralized database of everybody in your social circles: their email and mailing addresses, phone numbers, and so on (Figure 8-25).

It is a very, very simple address book, stripped down so much that it's practically shivering. It doesn't even have the sharing options, the Twitter and Facebook features, or the Favorites feature it had in Windows 8.1.

Importing Addresses from Online Accounts

Delightfully enough, the People app can synchronize its contacts with online Rolodexes that may be very important to you: your contacts from Apple's iCloud service, Google, Microsoft's Outlook.com system, or your company's corporate system.

That's why the first thing you may see, the first time you open People, is an invitation to connect those online accounts to People. Choose the name of the network you belong to, and enter the name and password for that account.

Note: If the People app has people listed in it the very first time you open it, then you've probably entered this kind of account information already, in another Windows app.

If you don't see that invitation, or if you declined it, you can always connect your accounts later. To add an account, use the ⋯ button next to the + button; choose Settings. There, staring you in the face, are names of the accounts you've set up already.

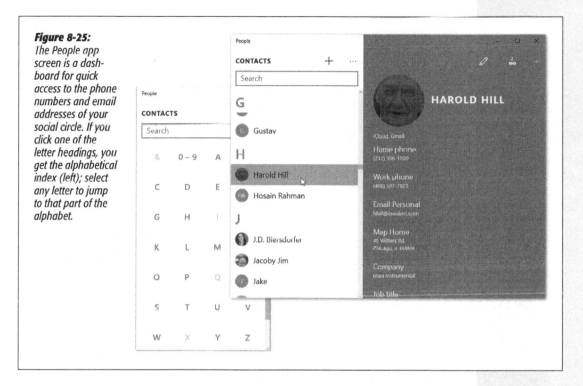

Figure 8-25:
The People app screen is a dashboard for quick access to the phone numbers and email addresses of your social circle. If you click one of the letter headings, you get the alphabetical index (left); select any letter to jump to that part of the alphabet.

To add a new one, use the "Add an account" link. Tap the kind of account you want: iCloud, Google, or whatever. Enter your account information, and boom—you're done. The People app is now synced with your online accounts. Change information in one place and it's also changed in the other.

You can repeat the process to add more accounts; in fact, you can even have *multiple* accounts for certain types (like Google and Microsoft email accounts).

Note: Microsoft's online help indicates that you can also hook up your Facebook and Twitter accounts to the People app—but if you click "Get social apps" here on the Settings screen, you go to an empty page of the Windows Store. Microsoft says that one day soon, apps will show up here that let you incorporate your Facebook and Twitter contacts into People.

It's important to understand that you're actually linking those Internet services *to your Microsoft account*. You have to do that only once, and then all your Windows starter apps—Mail, Calendar, People, and so on—can use their information.

The big payoff comes when you sign into another Windows 10 machine (or a Windows 10 phone). To your delight and amazement, you'll see that your address book is already filled in with all your contacts and accounts. Your Favorites list is even prefilled with the favorites you've set up on other Microsoft products. Progress!

Even after you've hooked up some accounts like this, you're not stuck with wading through the addresses of a million people you don't care about:

- **Hide an account.** On the main People screen, just below the search box, it says, "Showing all" (or "Showing some accounts"). Click those words to open the "Filter contacts" dialog box shown in Figure 8-26.

Note: On the Settings screen, there's a link called "Filter contacts." It opens the same options shown in Figure 8-26.

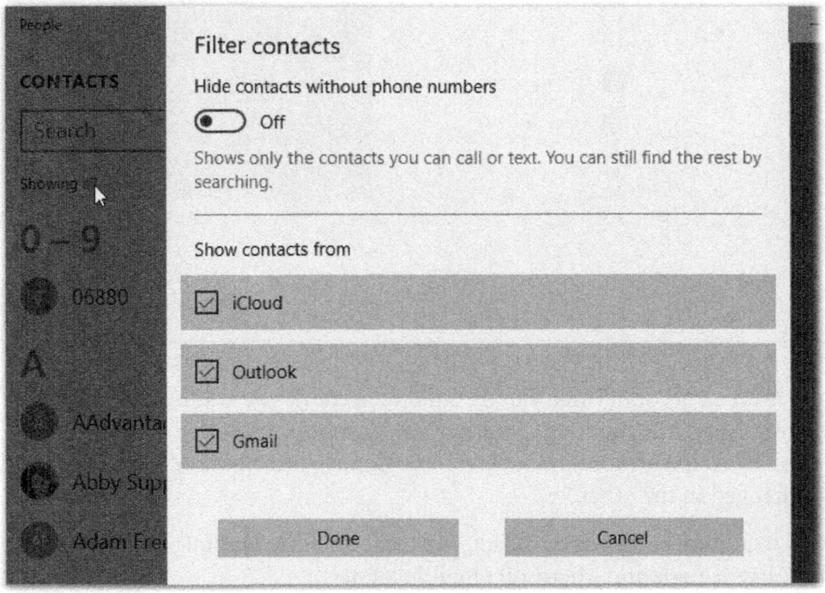

Figure 8-26:
In the "Filter contacts" box, you can turn off the checkboxes of certain accounts. That way, you're hiding their address-book contents from your People browsing and searching. You're not deleting anything, just hiding it.

- **Delete an account.** You can unsubscribe from one of your online accounts, too—but not in the People app. You have to delete the account from, believe it or not, the Mail app, as described on page 401. At that point, that account's addresses will vanish from your People app.

Creating Address Cards Manually

Each entry in People is like a Web form, with predefined spaces to hold all the standard contact information.

To add a new person, click the + button above the contacts list. You get the "New contact" screen (Figure 8-27).

Note: The very first time you hit the +, the app asks you to specify which of your online accounts you want new addresses to be stored in: iCloud, Google, Exchange, or whatever. Not all new contacts have to join this account; you can override this decision each time you create a new card. But choose this main account wisely; if you accidentally choose the wrong one now, you're in for a lot of manual overriding and kicking yourself later.

Figure 8-27:
It shouldn't take you very long to figure out how to fill in this form: You tap in a box and type. Fill in this person's name, email address, phone number, and so on, pressing the Tab key to move from field to field. To change the label for a number ("mobile," "home," "work," and so on), tap the ⌄ button next to the current label.

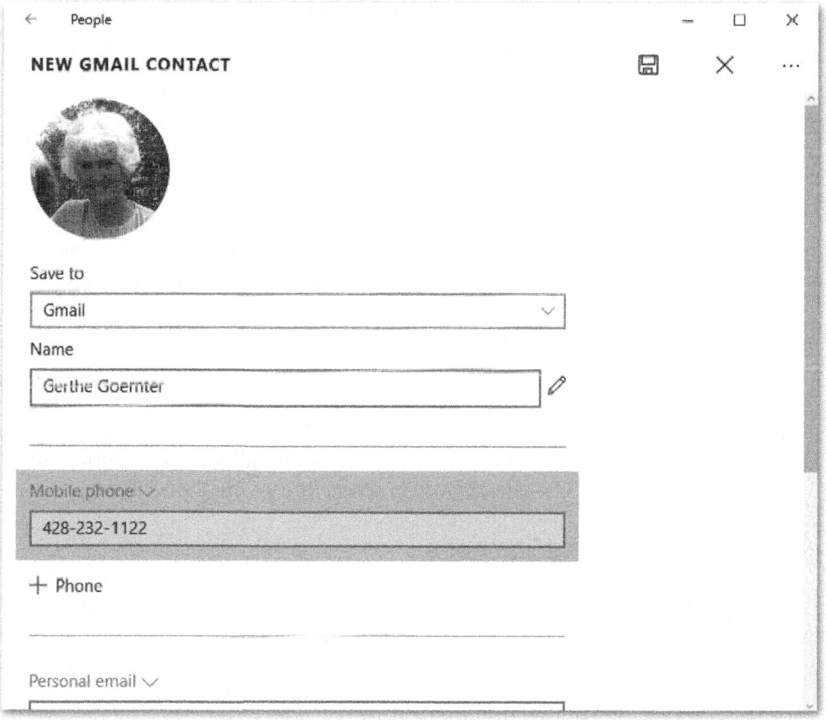

On the New Contact screen, you can fill in details like these:

- **Add photo.** Tap or click to open your Photos app, where you can choose a headshot for this person. It's OK if the person's face isn't very big in the picture you choose; you're offered the chance to crop down to just the head.

- **Save to.** Which online email address book you want this name stored in? (This assumes you've actually *set up* some accounts.)

Tip: If you have an Android phone, choose Gmail; if you have an iPhone, choose iCloud. Windows will thoughtfully add this person to your phone's built-in address book automatically.

- **Name.** Put both first and last names here.

- **Phone number.** Use the pop-up menu above the box ("Mobile phone") to specify what kind of phone this is.

  Now, the trouble with people these days is that they often have more than one phone number, more than one email address, and more than one mailing address. Fortunately, all of these boxes are infinitely expanding. Choose + to add another blank box of the same type: another phone-number field, for example.

- **Email.** Here again, choose which email address you're recording (Personal, Work, Other); here again, hit + to record more email addresses.

- **Address.** Weirdly, People doesn't come with a mailing-address boxes already set up; you have to click the + Address button.

Tip: You can also add fields for "Job title," "Significant other," "Website," or "Notes." They're hiding in the Other button. Select its + button to see those choices.

Once you've added the complete dossier for this person, hit the 🖫 button (or just press Ctrl+S). Both take you back to the main People screen.

Editing an Address

People move, people quit, people switch cellphone carriers. To make changes to somebody's card manually, select it and then hit the ✐ icon.

You return to the screen shown in Figure 8-27, where you can add, remove, and edit fields. Use the 🖫 button when you're finished.

Finding Someone

There are two ways to find someone in your digital Rolodex:

- **Search.** As you type into the search box, a list of matches sprouts right out of the search box. Once you see the name you want, select it; that person's card opens.

- **Use the alphabetical index.** The letter headings in the list of names are, in fact, buttons. It works just as it does in the Start menu; see Figure 8-25.

Linking Contacts

If People discovers two people with the same name among your different accounts—say, one from Gmail and one from iCloud—it does something very smart. It automatically links the two, making it seem as though all of the information appears on a single card.

Tip: See the chain-link icon at the top of the person's card? If it bears a tiny digit, like 2, then the People app is showing you the gloriously unified data from two different cards.

But if the names on the two cards are so different that People can't guess they're actually the same person, you can do this hooking up manually. Open the first card; click the chain-link icon; click "Choose a contact to link"; and choose the second card. Save your change.

Tip: To unlink someone that you've linked this way (or that the app linked incorrectly), click the link ∞ button. On the resulting card, choose the account card you want removed from the linkage, and confirm your move.

Phone Companion

This is a new Microsoft, brethren and cistern. Windows 10 is full of places where the company is offering openness and interconnectedness even with its blood rivals, like Apple and Google. Nowhere are those open arms opener than here, in this app.

It's intended for the heretics: people who have Android phones or iPhones. (Weirdos!)

You tap the kind of phone you have, and the app offers links to all of Microsoft's apps and services for your model: Skype, Office, OneNote, OneDrive, Mail, and so on.

(One of the most attractive options here: It seems the app can keep your entire photo collection synced between your PC and your phone automatically. And indeed it can—if you're willing to instruct both your phone and your computer to store all photos on your OneDrive.)

Photos

Microsoft changes photo programs the way most people change socks. The Photo Gallery from Windows Vista? Dead. The Photo Viewer of Windows 7? Gone.

In Windows 10, you get yet another digital photo shoebox, just called Photos.

Its Job is to grab photo albums from everywhere fine photos are stored—your own Pictures folder, other PCs on your network, and your OneDrive—and display them all in one place (Figure 8-28).

Navigating Photos

It's not hard to get around. Click or tap a photo thumbnail to open it big enough to see. To move among them, swipe across the screen, press the arrow keys, swipe across your trackpad, or turn your mouse's scroll wheel. To return to the thumbnail view, hit the ← button on the screen or press Alt+←.

You can view your collection either as a Collection (chronologically in groups) or as Albums. Albums are clusters of photos that the app creates automatically; it looks for shots taken around the same time and place. (To switch among these two viewing options, hit the second and third icons in the left-side menu column.)

As usual, once you've burrowed to your destination, the ← button takes you back to the start.

Your Pictures Folder

Back at the desktop, you have a Pictures folder. Any photos in this folder show up in the Photos app automatically.

But you can also tell Photos to display the contents of other pictures and drives. To do that, hit ⚙ to open the Settings page and choose "Add a folder."

At this point, you can also turn on "Show my photos and videos from OneDrive," if you like. You don't have to worry about duplicates; Photos is smart enough to prevent dupes from showing up, even if they're different file formats.

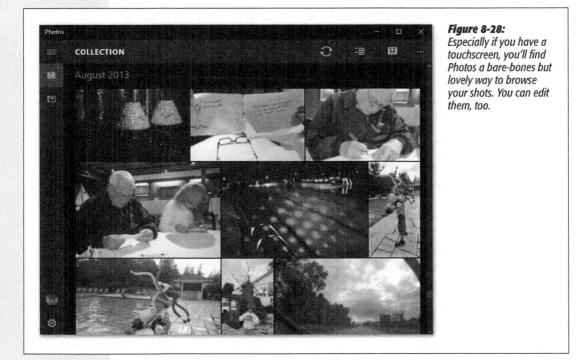

Figure 8-28:
Especially if you have a touchscreen, you'll find Photos a bare-bones but lovely way to browse your shots. You can edit them, too.

Slurping in Photos from a Camera

Photos can import photos from a camera, a memory card, flash drive, or any other drive, too. Just connect the camera, card, or drive to your machine, and then hit the Import button at the top (⬇). "Start importing?" asks the app. Hit Import.

When it's all over, you see the newly imported goodies nestled in their new home, in the Photos app.

Auto Albums

Windows 10's version of Photos incorporates a tiny feature that most people won't even notice, but that represents a lot of work by some highly hard-core image engineers: automatic albums.

When you click the Albums button in the main menu column, you see groups of photos that represent certain photo shoots. Usually, you'll know right away what they were: "Oh, Casey's birthday party!" "Oh, the house inspection." "Oh, that time I woke up in Poughkeepsie."

Photos creates these groupings by studying the photos' times and locations. No magic there.

But then it does something wild: Using artificial intelligence, it chooses what it considers the best dozen or so—and a master "headline" photo—to display, as shown in Figure 8-29.

Figure 8-29:
Photos has created this album presentation (top) all by its little self! Of course, you're welcome to override its selection of these highlights. Scroll down and hit "Add or remove photos" at the bottom (bottom). You're now shown all of the photos in this group; you can turn on the checkboxes of the ones you'd prefer to see, and turn off the ones that Photos chose for you.

Playing with Photos

The rules of Photos are simple:

- **By tapping or clicking,** select a source, then an album within it, and then a photo within *it.* When you've drilled down as far as you can go, the picture fills most of the screen.

- **To move through the photos,** swipe horizontally (touchscreen), click the ⟨ and ⟩ buttons at the edges of the screen (mouse), or press the ← and → keys (keyboard).

- **The toolbar offers a Slideshow button** (▣) that starts a slideshow of all photos in this batch. Or press F5. (Click or tap to end the show.)

- **To send a photo to somebody by email,** or to send it into another app for editing, tap the Share button on the toolbar.

Zooming In, Zooming Out

When you've opened an individual photo, you can enlarge or shrink it in the usual ways:

- **Touchscreen:** Spread two fingers apart on the glass; pinch to zoom back out.

- **Mouse:** Click the + and − buttons at the right edge of the horizontal scroll bar to zoom in or out. Or turn the scroll wheel while pressing the Ctrl key.

- **Keyboard:** Press Ctrl and the + or − keys.

Editing Photos: The Mini Photoshop

You might be a great photographer (although if your primary tool is a tablet or a laptop, that's debatable).

But even pros touch up their work—and in Photos, an impressively complete suite of photo-editing tools awaits. These tools can rotate or crop; they can also fix the brightness, contrast, and color of your pictures, and even add special effects like selective blur and vignetting (where the photo corners are misty white to draw the eye to the subject).

To begin, open the photo that needs help. Use the ✏ button to open the editing wonderland shown in Figure 8-30.

Ready? Keep hands and feet inside the tram at all times.

Tip: As you work, keep in mind that you can zoom in for better detail work. You can also press the amazingly handy keystroke Ctrl+/ (forward slash), the shortcut for the Compare button on the toolbar; it shows the "before" version of your photo, so that you can quickly compare the edited version with the original.

Finally, as you work, keep in mind that the Undo command is always at your service to reverse the last editing step. It's a safety net, it's Ctrl+Z, and its icon is first on the toolbar.

(If you dig finding out about this sort of Photos keyboard shortcut tip, don't miss the full list on page 646.)

Basic fixes

This left-side button produces four adjustment options on the right:

- **Enhance.** When you tap this magical button (or press the E key), the app analyzes the relative brightness of all the pixels in your photo and attempts to "balance" it. After a moment, the app adjusts the brightness and contrast and intensifies dull or grayish-looking areas. Usually, the pictures look richer and more vivid as a result.

  You may find that Auto-Enhance has little effect on some photos, only minimally improves others, and totally rescues a few.

Figure 8-30:
In the Editing mode, you get five primary buttons at the left side; each one summons a different set of "button dials" on the right side. The toolbar gives you everything you need to undo, cancel, or preserve the changes.

- **Rotate.** Tap this button (or press Ctrl+R) to rotate the photo 90 degrees each time.

- **Crop.** Cropping means shaving off unnecessary outer portions of a photo. Usually, you crop a photo to improve its composition—adjusting where the subject appears within the frame of the picture. Often, a photo has more impact if it's cropped tightly around the subject, especially in portraits. Or maybe you want to crop out wasted space, like big expanses of background sky. You can even chop a former romantic interest out of an otherwise perfect family portrait.

  When you select the Crop button, a white rectangle appears on your photo. Drag inward on any corner. The part of the photo that Windows will eventually trim away is dimmed out. You can recenter the photo by dragging any part of the photo, inside or outside the box. (For greater precision, you can press Shift and the arrow keys to resize the cropping rectangle, or Ctrl and the arrow keys to move it.)

If you tap the "Aspect ratio" button on the top toolbar, you get a choice of nine canned proportions: Square, 3 × 2, 3 × 5, 4 × 3, and so on. They make the app limit the cropping frame to preset proportions. (The "Lock screen" choice ensures that your cropped photo will exactly fit your computer's Lock screen.)

This feature is especially important if you plan to order prints of your photos. Prints come only in standard photo sizes: 4 × 6, 5 × 7, and so on. Limiting your cropping to one of these standard sizes guarantees that your cropped photos will fit perfectly into Kodak prints.

When everything looks good, press Enter or tap ✓.

• **Straighten.** Drag the big white dot around the "clock" to tilt the photo until it's straight, using the dotted grid as a guide. There! Nobody will ever know you were tipsy.

• **Redeye.** Red eye is a common problem in flash photography. This creepy, possessed look—devilish, glowing-red pupils in your subjects' eyes—has ruined many an otherwise great photo.

Red eye is caused by light reflected back from eyes. The bright light of your flash illuminates the blood-red retinal tissue at the back of the eyes. That's why red-eye problems are worse when you shoot pictures in a dim room: Your subjects' pupils are dilated, allowing even more light from your flash to reach their retinas.

When you select this button, your cursor becomes loaded with a dot. Apply it inside each eye that has the problem. (Zoom in if necessary.) The app turns the red in each eye to black.

• **Retouch.** Sometimes an otherwise perfect portrait is spoiled by the tiniest of imperfections—a stray hair or a hideous blemish, for example. Professional photographers routinely remove such imperfections—a process known as retouching, for clients known as self-conscious or vain. (Kidding!)

The Retouch brush lets you do the same thing with your own photos: paint away scratches, spots, hairs, and other small flaws. It doesn't cover the imperfections you're trying to remove, but blurs them out by softly blending them into a small radius of surrounding pixels (in other words, you can't use it to whiten teeth).

Once you've clicked Retouch, your cursor sprouts a round brush. Find the imperfection and "paint" over it, either by dabbing or dragging to blend it with the surrounding portion of the photo.

Filters

All those Instagram fans can't be wrong—*filters* must be a thing. They're special effects that tinker with a photo's colors so that it takes on certain looks—like an old Polaroid, or an old 1970's home photo, for example. You get five filters (plus the top one, "None") on the right side here; just tap or click to see what each looks like.

Light

When this button is selected (left side), the buttons on the right offer more of Photos' *button dials*. Figure 8-31 shows the idea.

- **Brightness.** Adjusts the overall exposure of the photo, making all of it lighter or darker.

- **Contrast.** If your photo looks flat, then use this effect to bring out details. It makes the dark parts of your photo a little darker, and the light parts a little lighter.

- **Highlights, Shadows.** The Highlights and Shadows dials are designed to recover lost detail in the brightest and darkest areas of your photos, turning what once might have been unsalvageably overexposed or underexposed photos into usable shots.

  For example, suppose you've got a photo looking good, except that you don't have any detail in murky, dark areas. Turn the Shadows handle clockwise, and presto! A world of detail emerges from what used to be nearly black.

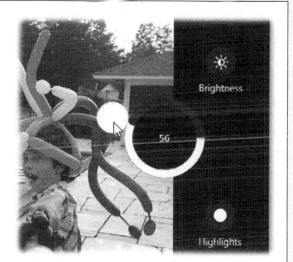

Figure 8-31:
Many of the new photo-editing controls rely on "button dials." When you tap or click it, the button itself becomes a dial—a white, round handle. You can drag it either counterclockwise or clockwise. The unexpected part is that you can drag all the way around from the zero point, in either direction.

Color

Digital cameras (and scanners) don't always capture color accurately. Digital photos sometimes have a slightly bluish or greenish tinge, producing dull colors, lower contrast, and sickly looking skin tones. In fact, the whole thing might have a faint green or magenta cast. Or perhaps you just want to take color adjustment into your own hands, not only to get the colors right, but also to create a specific mood.

Here are the tools at your disposal:

- **Temperature.** This dial adjusts the photo along the blue-orange spectrum. Dial clockwise, for example, to warm up the tones, making them more orangeish—a handy technique for breathing life back into subjects who have been bleached white with a flash. Dial counterclockwise for bluer tones.

- **Tint.** Like the tint control on a color TV, this slider adjusts the photo's overall tint along the red-green spectrum. Adjusting this slider is helpful for correcting skin tones and for compensating for difficult lighting situations, like fluorescent lighting.

- **Saturation.** When you increase the saturation of a photo's colors, you make them more vivid; you make them "pop." You can also improve photos that have harsh, garish colors by dialing *down* the saturation, so the colors look a little less intense. (Boosting the saturation is often a bad idea for pictures of *people*, though; skin can wind up looking really weird.)

- **Color boost.** Here's a weirdie. This one lets you boost just one color in the photo— all the reds, for example, or all the blues. If you want, you can really goose just the sky, or bring out the yellows in a field of flowers.

  Once you've selected this button, tap or click a spot in the photo that displays the color that needs boosting; a pin appears there, as though you'd marked a spot on a map. Now turn the button dial to make *all* patches of that color get brighter or dimmer.

Effects

Photos comes with two special effects, each intended to draw the viewer's eye to the subject of the photo. You won't need them often, but now and then, they hit the bullseye:

- **Vignette.** This effect whites out, or blacks out, the corners of the photo, creating an oval-shaped, softly faded frame around the center. The more you turn the button dial, the more the whiteness or blackness encroaches toward the middle.

- **Selective focus.** Tap or click the part of the photo that you want to be in focus. The rest of the image gets softly blurred, as though taken with an expensive camera by someone who knew what he was doing.

Saving the editing

Any editing session ends the same way: On the toolbar, choose Save 🖫 (make changes to the original), "Save a copy" next to it (preserve the edited photo as a duplicate of the original), or Cancel (discard all your edits).

Tip: Before you commit, you can use the Compare icon (third from the left on the toolbar) to flip back and forth between the original and the edited version of your photo.

Slapping a Photo onto the Lock Screen or Desktop

When you're looking at a single photo (and not editing it), the ⋯ button at top right offers a secret shortcut menu. Its options let you slap the current photo onto either of these billboards:

- **Lock screen.** That's a reference to the big photo that appears when you first wake up a Windows 10 machine, the one that bears the current time. Here's one easy way to change it to a photo of your own. (Keyboard shortcut: Ctrl+L.)

- **Background.** Right from here, you can install this photo as your desktop wallpaper.

Tip: Also in the ⋯ menu: "File info." Choosing this option–or pressing Alt+Enter at any time–opens a left-side panel that tells you everything about the current photo: size, date, name, camera model, manual settings, ISO, and so on.

Selecting Photos (to Share or Delete)

Photos wouldn't be much fun if your screen were the only place you could see them. Fortunately, the Photos app is happy to zap them away to your adoring fans electronically. Or, if they're terrible shots, you can zap them away forever.

Selecting photos

The first step is telling Photos which pictures you want to send. To do that, drill down until you're looking at the thumbnails of some batch. Then hit the ⋮≡ icon to make their checkboxes appear. Just click or tap each photo you want to include.

Tip: Actually, if you have a trackpad or mouse, you can save a step. Just point to each photo to see its checkbox appear–no ⋮≡ click necessary.

Sharing selected photos

Once you've chosen the photos you want to share, the top toolbar offers four ways to go:

- **Cancel.** This means, "back out of this—forget all that checking business."

- **Share** (⌂). The right-side Share panel opens, listing all the places you can send the selected images. The options here vary. They might say Mail, Facebook, and Dropbox, for example. If you've installed a program with beefier editing tools, like Microsoft's own Fresh Paint, its name appears here, too.

- **Copy** (◻). The next button copies the selected photos to your Clipboard, ready for pasting (into an email message, for example).

- **Delete** (🗑). The next button copies the selected photos to your Clipboard, ready for pasting (into an email message, for example).

GEM IN THE ROUGH

The Littlest Slideshow

Deep in Photos' Settings screen (hit the ⚙ icon in the lower-left corner of the screen), there lies what may be the quirkiest preference setting in all of Windows I and: "Choose what to show on the Photos tile."

That's right: Microsoft is asking which one photo you want to appear on the tile that represents the Photos app, as it appears on the right side of the Start menu.

Your choices are "One photo" (and then there's a "Choose photo" button)…or "Recent photos." That option gives you a rotating slideshow–sized for an audience of gnats–right there on the Photos tile in the Start menu.

Don't scoff. The ability to decide exactly what appears on that one app's tile might just make somebody's year.

Remote Desktop Connection

Remote Desktop Connection lets you sit at your home PC and operate your office PC by remote control. Details are in Chapter 13.

Run

When you want to open something with just a few keystrokes, the little Run command-line window is there for you. See the free downloadable appendix, "Run command. pdf," on this book's "Missing CD" page at *www.missingmanuals.com.*

Settings

This app is, of course, the awe-inspiring Settings app described in Chapter 7.

Skype

In 2011, Microsoft bought Skype, the popular chat, audiochat, and videochat program. (The price: $8.5 billion. For Microsoft, pocket change.)

In 2013, Skype officially became a standard Windows Store app. (Its predecessor, an app called Messenger, went to the great CompUSA in the sky.)

In any case, Skype is a game-changer. It's the app millions of middle-aged parents use to call their kids studying abroad…new parents use to show their newborn babies to the new grandparents…and long-distance couples use to videochat. The best part: All of this voice and video calling is free.

For most people, Skype doesn't come preinstalled with Windows. You have to run the Get Skype app that is preinstalled (in your "All apps" list).

For a handy guide to setting up and using Skype, see the free downloadable PDF Appendix "Skype.pdf" on this book's "Missing CD" page at *www.missingmanuals.com.*

Snipping Tool

Snipping Tool (Figure 8-32) takes pictures of your PC's screen, for use when you're writing up instructions, illustrating a computer book, or collecting proof of some secret screen you found buried in a game. You can take pictures of the entire screen or capture only the contents of a rectangular selection. When you're finished, Snipping Tool displays your snapshot in a new window, which you can print, close without saving, edit, or save (as a JPEG, GIF, PNG, or embedded HTML file), ready for emailing or inserting into a manuscript or page-layout program.

Now, as experienced PC enthusiasts already know, Windows has *always* had shortcuts for capturing screenshots: Press the Print Screen (or PrtScn) key to print a picture of the whole screen; add the Alt key to copy it to your Clipboard; or press ⊞+PrtScn to save the screenshot as a file into a Screenshots folder in your Pictures library.

So why use Snipping Tool instead? Because it's infinitely more powerful and flexible. Here's how it works:

1. **Open Snipping Tool.**

   The screen goes foggy and light, and the Snipping Tool palette appears.

2. **From the New shortcut menu, specify what area of the screen you want to capture.**

   These are your choices:

   Free-form Snip means you can drag your cursor in any crazy, jagged, freehand, nonrectangular shape. Snipping Tool outlines it with a red border.

Tip: You can change the border color in the Options dialog box. It appears when you click Options on the main Snipping palette, or when you choose Tools→Options in the editing window.

Rectangular Snip lets you drag diagonally across the frozen screen image, thus capturing a square or rectangular area. Unfortunately, you can't adjust the rectangle if your aim was a little off; the instant you release the mouse button, the program captures the image in the rectangle.

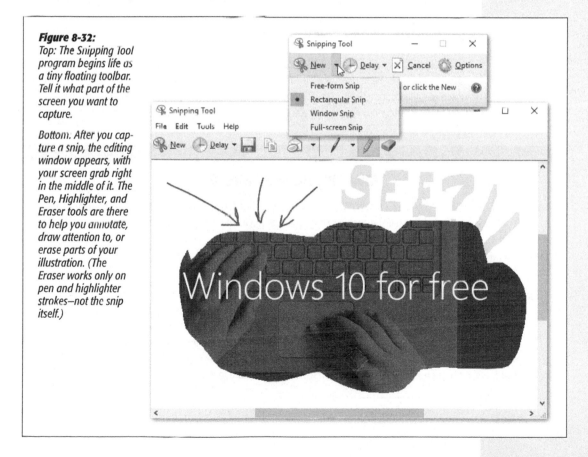

Figure 8-32:
Top: The Snipping Tool program begins life as a tiny floating toolbar. Tell it what part of the screen you want to capture.

Bottom: After you capture a snip, the editing window appears, with your screen grab right in the middle of it. The Pen, Highlighter, and Eraser tools are there to help you annotate, draw attention to, or erase parts of your illustration. (The Eraser works only on pen and highlighter strokes—not the snip itself.)

A **Window Snip** neatly captures an entire window, automatically cropping out the entire background. And *which* window does it capture? That's up to you. As you point to each window, a red border appears around it to illustrate what Snipping Tool *thinks* you intend to capture. When the correct one is highlighted, click the mouse to capture.

Tip: A "window," in this context, doesn't have to be a window. It can also be the taskbar, a dialog box, and so on.

And a **Full-screen Snip,** of course, captures the entire screen.

3. **Specify what you want to capture, if necessary.**

That is, drag across the screen for a Free-form or Rectangular snip, or click the window (object) you want for a Window Snip. (Skip this step if you chose Full-screen Snip. In that case, Snipping Tool pretty much knows what to do.) Now the editing window appears (Figure 8-32, bottom).

What you do with your finished graphic is up to you. For example:

- **Paste it.** The edited image may be in the window in front of you, but the original, unedited image is *also* on your invisible Windows Clipboard. Close the editing window without saving changes, pop into your graphics, word-processing, or email program, and paste (Ctrl+V) what you've copied. Often, that's exactly what you want to do.

Tip: On the other hand, the Snipping Tool's tendency to copy everything to the Clipboard can be *bad* if there was already something *on* the Clipboard you wanted to keep. (The Clipboard can hold only one thing at a time.) If that syndrome is driving you nuts, you can turn off the copy-to-Clipboard feature in Options.

May I Please See a Menu?

Snipping Tool, as you've already seen, is a heck of a lot better than the old PrtScn keystroke. But at first glance, you might assume that it still can't take a picture of a menu or a shortcut menu. After all, the instant you try to drag to highlight the menu, the menu closes!

Actually, you can capture menus—if you know the secret.

Open Snipping Tool, and then *minimize* it, which hides its window but keeps it running.

Now open the menu you want to capture, using the mouse or keyboard. Once the menu is open, press Ctrl+PrtScn.

That's all it takes; Snipping Tool is smart enough to know that you intend to capture just the menu.

That's workable, but still a bit complicated. That's why, if you're *actually* going to write a computer book or manual, you probably want a proper screen-capture program like Snagit (*www.techsmith.com*). It offers far more flexibility than any of Windows' own screenshot features. For example, you have a greater choice of file formats and capture options, you can dress up the results with arrows or captions, and (with its companion program, Camtasia Studio) you can even capture *movies* of screen activity.

- **Send it.** The little envelope button on the editing-window toolbar automatically prepares an outgoing email message with your graphic already pasted in (or, if your email program is set to send plain, unformatted text messages only, as an attachment).

- **Save it.** If your intention is to save the capture as a file, click the Save (🖫) icon, or choose File→Save, or press Ctrl+S. When the Save As dialog box appears, type a name for your graphic, choose a file format for it (from the "Save as type" pop-up menu), specify a folder location, and then click Save.

Tip: If you capture the screen of a Web page and save it in HTML format, Snipping Tool helpfully prints the original URL (Web address) at the bottom of the image, so you'll know where it came from. You can turn off this "subtitling" feature in the Options dialog box of Snipping Tool.

Sports

Here's another online magazine, composed of attractively laid out articles that Microsoft swipes from 300 big-name online news sources.

The app works exactly like the News app (page 326), with a few exceptions:

- It's all about sports.

- If you poke around, you'll find pages and pages of scores, statistics, and schedules, along with news, videos, and slideshows.

- Open the menu column. See the various league buttons (NFL, NBA, MLB, Golf, and so on)? There are lots of them. You may actually have to *scroll* the menu column—that's something you probably haven't seen before—to view them all. Each league page offers headings like Top Stories, Scoreboard, Standings, Videos, and Slideshows.

- Scroll far enough down the menu column, and you'll find a My Favorites button. Here, you can create a new "section" that displays news of *only* the teams you like. (Hit the + button to add one.) You can start typing the team name, like *dolphins,* or the city, like *miami;* the app displays a list of matches that narrows down as you type.

Steps Recorder

This weird little program is designed to record exactly where you're clicking or tapping, and to capture a screen picture each time you do so. Why? So that you can document some problem you're having. You can send the resulting recording to someone who wants to see exactly what steps you were taking when you ran into trouble.

Of course, this is a similar scenario to the times when you might use Windows Remote Assistance, where the wise guru can *watch* you perform the steps that are frustrating you. But because Steps Recorder lets you type a little message each time you click the mouse, it's a better, more permanent way to record some problem you're having.

When you're ready to record the steps, click Start Record. Now do whatever it is, on your computer, that produces the problem: Click here, use that menu, drag that slider, whatever. As you go, you can do the following:

- **Pause the recording.** Click Pause Record. (Click Resume Record to continue.)

- **Type an annotation for a particular step.** ("Here's where I double-clicked.") Click Add Comment, highlight the part of the screen that you want to comment on, type your note into the box, and then click OK.

Note: Anything you type outside that comment box doesn't get recorded; that's a security precaution.

When you're finished, click Stop Record.

The Recorded Steps window appears. It shows you each screenshot that Steps Recorder captioned, complete with its time stamp and text description ("User left-click on 'File Explorer' button," for example). This is your chance to make sure you're not about to send away personal information (or naughty photos) that might have been on the screen while you recorded.

If everything looks good, click either Save (creates a compressed archive—a .zip file—that you can later open to look at the report again in your Web browser) or Email (to send to an expert).

Sticky Notes

Sticky Notes creates virtual Post-it notes that you can stick anywhere on your screen—a triumphant software answer to the thousands of people who stick notes on the edges of their actual monitors.

You can type quick notes and to-do items, paste in Web addresses or phone numbers you need to remember, or store any other little scraps and snippets of text you come across (Figure 8-33).

Creating Notes

To create a new note, click the + button in the upper-left corner of the starter note, or press Ctrl+N. Then fill the note by typing or pasting.

Note the resize handle on the lower-right corner of each note. Drag it to make notes larger or smaller onscreen.

Formatting Notes

You can format the text of a note—a *little* bit. There are no menus, of course, so you have to use keyboard shortcuts:

- **Bold, Italic, Underline.** Press Ctrl+B, Ctrl+I, or Ctrl+U.

- **Strikethrough style.** Press Ctrl+T.

- **Create a bulleted list.** Press Ctrl+Shift+L.

Tip: Press Ctrl+Shift+L a second time to produce a numbered list.

• **Change the type size.** Press Ctrl+Shift+> (larger font) or Ctrl+Shift+< (smaller).

You can also change the "paper" color for a note to any of five other pastel colors. To do that, right-click the note and then choose from the shortcut menu.

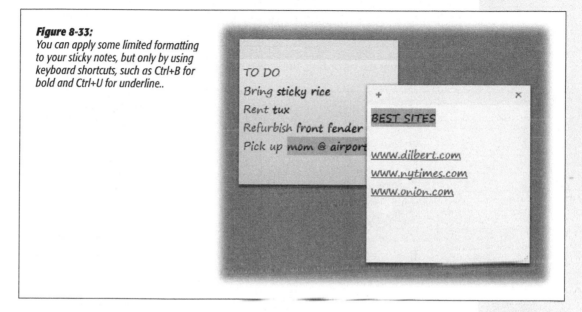

Figure 8-33:
You can apply some limited formatting to your sticky notes, but only by using keyboard shortcuts, such as Ctrl+B for bold and Ctrl+U for underline..

Deleting Notes

To get rid of a note, click the little ✕ in the upper-right corner. (You may have to point to it to see it.) When the program asks if you're sure, click Yes.

On the other hand, you can *exit* Sticky Notes without worrying that you'll lose what you've already typed. Right-click the Sticky Notes icon on the taskbar, for example, and choose "Close window" from the shortcut menu. The program disappears, but all your notes will be there the next time you open it.

Store

This is it: the Windows Store, source of many apps. You can read all about it in Chapter 6.

Voice Recorder

This audio app is ideal for recording lectures, musical performances, notes to self, and cute child utterances. You can make very long recordings with this thing. Let it run all day, if you like. Even your most long-winded friends can be immortalized.

Talk about a minimal interface! There's nothing in this app except for a big, round microphone button). Hit it to start recording. A little timer clicks away, and the Stop button (■) pulses, to show that you're rolling. You can pause or resume the recording at will (II) or, when it's good and done, stop it by tapping the huge round Stop button. (If you switch into another app, the recording pauses automatically.)

Tip: During recording, you can hit the little ⚑ icon to mark important points in the audio you'll want to find later. Each time, Voice Recorder creates a new time stamp, listed across the bottom of the screen. Later, you'll be able to jump to these spots for playback (see Figure 8-34).

When you stop the recording, the screen changes; see Figure 8-34.

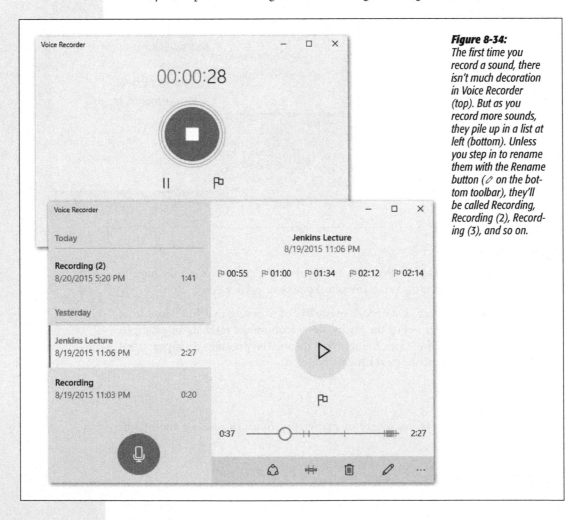

Figure 8-34:
The first time you record a sound, there isn't much decoration in Voice Recorder (top). But as you record more sounds, they pile up in a list at left (bottom). Unless you step in to rename them with the Rename button (⌀ on the bottom toolbar), they'll be called Recording, Recording (2), Recording (3), and so on.

At this point, you can proceed like this:

- **Name the recording** using the ✏ button.

- **Record another sound.** Use the microphone button again. As you record more sounds, they pile up in the list at top left.

- **Play a recording.** Select it, and then select the ▷ button.

- **Rewind, Fast-Forward.** Drag the round handle in the scrubber bar to skip backward or forward in the recording. It's a great way to skip over the boring pleasantries.

- **Jump to your markers.** They show up with time stamps above the scrubber bar—click to jump there in the playback—and also as notches *on* the scrubber bar.

- 🗑. Tap to get rid of a recording (you're asked to confirm).

- **Trim off the ends.** You might not guess that such a tiny, self-effacing app actually offers some basic editing functions, but it does. You can trim off the beginning or end of your audio clip. That, of course, is where you'll usually find "dead air" or microphone fumbling before the good stuff starts playing. (You can't otherwise edit the sound; for example, you can't copy or paste bits or cut a chunk out of the middle.)

  To trim the bookends of your clip, use the ✂ button. At this point, the beginning and end of the recording are marked by big black dots; these are your trim points. Drag them inward to isolate the part of the clip you want to keep. Play the sound as necessary to guide you (▷).

  Select × if you change your mind, or the ✓ to lock in your changes. From its shortcut menu, choose either "Save a copy" (which also saves the original file) or "Update original" (which doesn't).

Tip: It's a common question: Once you record these sounds, *where are they?* Yes, you can email them to yourself from within the app. But where on your PC are the actual recordings sitting?

Well, they're buried, that's for sure. Switch to the desktop. Make hidden files visible (on the View tab of an Explorer window's ribbon, turn on "Hidden items"). Navigate to your personal folder→AppData→Local→ Packages→Microsoft.WindowsSoundRecorder_8wekyb3d8bbwe→localstate→Indexed→recordings. (Yes, there really is a folder called *Microsoft.WindowsSound-Recorder_8wekyb3d8bbwe*.) And there they are—the actual .m4a music files that represent your recordings. Now you can back them up, share them, copy them to a flash drive, whatever.

Weather

This app presents a lovely, colorful weather report. Right off the bat, you see the current weather (as though the full-window background photo didn't give it away). There's the five-day forecast (Figure 8-35). Below that, you see the hour-by-hour forecast for today, so you can see exactly what time your softball game will get rained out.

Tip: You can view this hourly section either as a cool graph ("Summary") or as hourly tables of data ("Details").

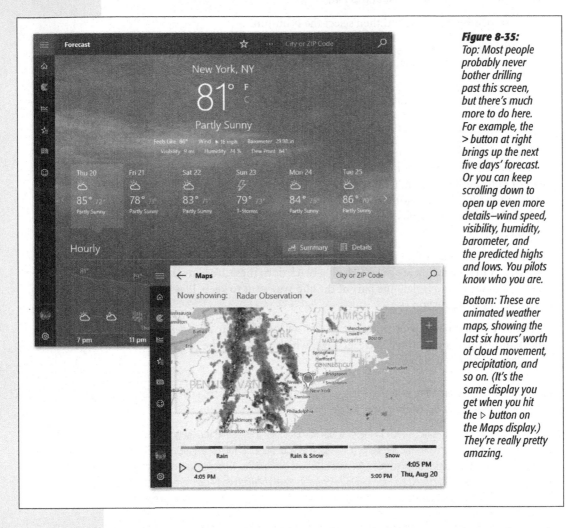

Figure 8-35:
Top: Most people probably never bother drilling past this screen, but there's much more to do here. For example, the > button at right brings up the next five days' forecast. Or you can keep scrolling down to open up even more details—wind speed, visibility, humidity, barometer, and the predicted highs and lows. You pilots know who you are.

Bottom: These are animated weather maps, showing the last six hours' worth of cloud movement, precipitation, and so on. (It's the same display you get when you hit the ▷ button on the Maps display.) They're really pretty amazing.

But the most surprising part of the Weather app is the more complete weather station that lurks in the left-side menu column. Here's what these icons do:

- ☾ **Maps** are cool visual representations of current meteorological data for the whole country: radar, regional temperature, precipitation, cloud cover, severe weather alerts, and so on.

Tip: If you hit the Play button (▷), the map *animates* (Figure 8-35, bottom). It shows you the last six hours' worth of whatever you're looking at: cloud cover, precipitation, temperature, and so on. Zoom in or out to see a different area of the country.

- ≋ **Historical weather.** This handy graph shows you a snapshot of your current location's weather history. The big graph shows temperature, rainfall, and snowfall (depending on which of the three round icons you select beneath it). The little table beneath gives you stats like the average high and low for today's date, the record high and low for today's date, and monthly averages for rainfall, snowy days, and rainy days.

- ⭐☰ **Places.** Here, you can set up tiles that show you, at a glance, the weather in *other* cities around the world that might interest you. Hit the + button and type the city's name.

- 🗔 **News.** The next icon presents tiles that represent individual news articles about weather.

There are settings to explore in Weather, too. You can specify F or C for the temperature readings, and you can ask the app to auto-detect your location for weather-report purposes.

Windows Defender

Here's the front panel for Windows 10's built-in antivirus software. Details are in Chapter 12.

Windows Fax and Scan

See Chapter 14 for more on sending and receiving faxes from your PC—and on scanning documents using a scanner.

Windows Journal

Windows Journal is for taking notes (Figure 8-36). But unlike Notepad or WordPad, Journal is specially designed for touchscreens. You can take your notes in handwriting, and later ask the program to convert it into typed text. Try *that* on an iPad!

Journal opens up to a blank note page; File→New Note opens another one.

Tip: The standard new note looks like a sheet of lined notebook paper. But if you choose File→New Note from Template, you get to choose from a bunch of different looks for your new note: graph paper, Sudoku-ish paper, even musical staff paper.

You can create your own design templates, too. Use the File→Page Setup command to specify the paper size, paper color, line pattern, background picture, and other elements of your page. Then choose File→Save As, and choose the template format as you name your new sheet of "stationery."

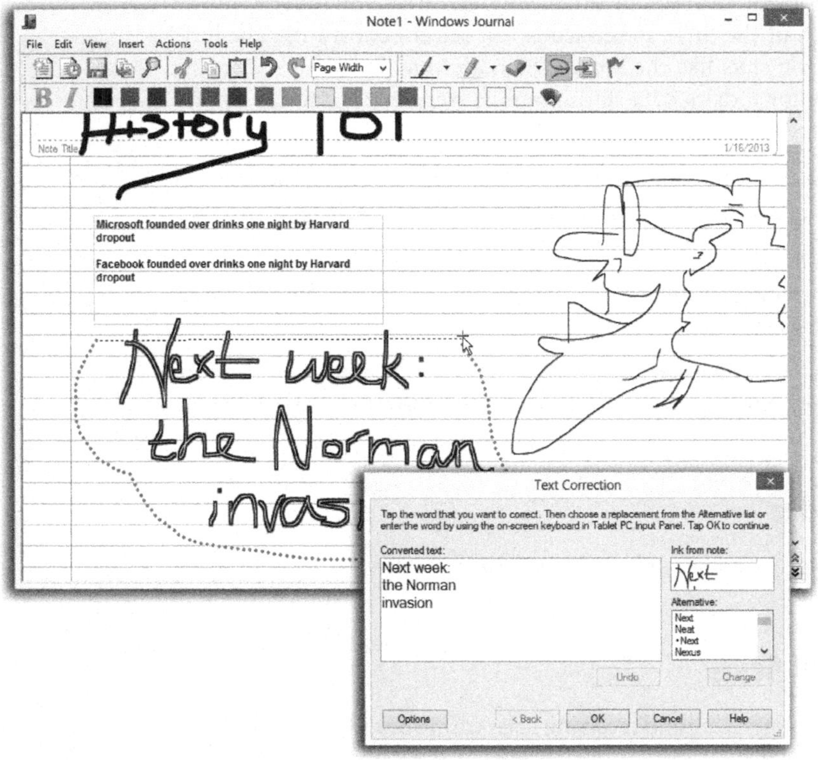

Figure 8-36:
To convert handwriting to text, click the lasso tool on the toolbar. Then drag a circle around the text you want to convert. Choose Actions→ Convert Handwriting to Text.

In the Text Correction box (bottom), confirm the transcription; make corrections as necessary, clicking a word and choosing from the Alternative list; and click OK.

Handwriting

All you have to do is start writing, using your finger or, for less frustration, a stylus. The toolbar offers a pop-up menu of pen thicknesses; for a choice of colors, choose View→Toolbars→Format.

Tip: You can change your pen thickness or color even after your writing is on the page—something that's very difficult to do with real pen marks. Select the writing using the lasso tool, and then choose Edit→Format Ink. Make your changes in the resulting dialog box.

An eraser tool is available on the toolbar if you mess up. There's also a highlighter pen that lets you draw over the most important parts of your notes for emphasis.

Even when your notes are still in handwritten-scrawl form, Journal can still search for text. Depending on how messy your writing is, this trick can seem like something of a miracle. Just choose File→Search and type the text you're trying to find. Journal highlights the matching handwritten phrase, wherever it appears in your notes.

Later, when the lecture or meeting is over, you can convert the handwriting to text; Figure 8-36 shows the steps. They conclude with an offer to either (a) put the converted text on the Clipboard, ready to paste into any program, or (b) put the converted text into a text box on the page.

Of course, you can also type into a Journal note; use the Insert→Text Box command to plop a rectangle onto the page, which you can fill with typing.

Tip: To move the text box, click the Selection lasso tool. Point to the text box's border; when the pointer becomes a four-headed arrow, you can drag to move the text box.

You can also import an existing text document into Journal, and then mark it up with your pen or finger (hello, proofreaders!). Use the File→Import command for this purpose.

Tip: When you first open Journal, you're asked if you want to install the Journal Note Writer driver. Say yes. It adds, to the Print menus of other programs, a new "printer" that sends any document to Journal. (If you declined that opportunity, choose Tools→Repair Journal Note Writer.)

For example, suppose you're in Word. You can choose File→Print, and then choose Journal Note Writer as your "printer." Click Print; name and save the resulting file.

Now you can switch to Journal, use File→Open, and open that file, which has now turned into a Journal document.

Sketches

Journal is also great for freehand drawing, of course. Sure beats the back of an envelope.

The program can even help clean up your work. If you draw a rough approximation of a line, square, or circle, you can select it with the Selection lasso and then use the Action→Change Shape To command. The submenu options (Line, Square, Circle/Ellipse) turn your scratched shape into a perfectly, computer-drawn version.

Exporting

When your masterpiece is ready for the viewing public, here's what you can do:

- Use the File→Export command to save it as a TIFF graphics file (great for sketches).

- Select some writing with the Selection lasso, and then choose Action→Convert to email. Journal converts the writing to typed text as described above, and then puts it into a new outgoing email message.

Windows Media Player

In the beginning, Windows Media Player was the headquarters for music and video on your PC. It was the Grand Central Terminal for things like music CDs (you could play 'em, copy songs off 'em, and burn 'em); MP3 files and other digital songs (you could sort 'em, buy 'em online, and file 'em into playlists); pocket music players of the non-iPod variety (fill 'em up, manage their playlists); Internet radio stations; DVD movies (watch 'em); and so on.

Media Player still does all that, and more. But it's no longer clear that this is the program you'll use for these activities. Gradually, the Media Player audience is splintering. Nowadays, people are using alternative programs like Groove Music, Apple's iTunes, or other non-Microsoft candidates.

Still, millions continue to use Windows Media Player as their music-file database. If you're among them, see the free downloadable PDF Appendix "Windows Media Player. pdf" on this book's "Missing CD" page at *www.missingmanuals.com*.

Windows PowerShell

PowerShell is a command console and scripting language. If you're a programmer, PowerShell lets you write your own simple programs, called *cmdlets* ("commandlets") that can perform all kinds of automated drudgery for you: copy or move folders, manipulate files, open or quit programs, and so on.

You harness all this power by typing up *scripts* in PowerShell's command line interface (which means no mouse, no menus, no windows—all text, like in the DOS days). In short, PowerShell is not for the layperson. If you're an *ambitious* layperson, however, a Google search for *PowerShell tutorial* unveils all kinds of Web sites that teach you, step-by-step, how to harness this very advanced tool.

Windows Speech Recognition

Windows offers a surprisingly useful (and accurate) speech-recognition feature. You can read all about it on page 239.

WordPad

WordPad is a basic word processor. Among other blessings, WordPad has a toolbar ribbon for quick access to formatting commands, and it can open and create Microsoft Word files. Yes, you can get away with not buying Microsoft Office, and none of your email business partners will ever know the difference.

And it's not just Word files. WordPad also can open and create plain text files, Rich Text Format (RTF) documents, and OpenOffice.org files.

Using WordPad

When WordPad first opens, you see an empty sheet of electronic typing paper. Just above the ruler, the Ribbon offers menus and buttons that affect the formatting of your text. As in any word processor, you can apply these formats (like bold, italic, or color) to two kinds of text:

- **Text you've highlighted by dragging the mouse across it.**

- **Text you're *about* to type.** In other words, if you click the *I* button, the next characters you type will be italicized. Click the *I* button a second time to turn off the italics.

The Font formatting buttons let you change the look of selected text: font, size, color, subscript, and so on. The Paragraph formatting buttons affect entire paragraphs.

WordPad doesn't offer big-gun features like spell checking, style sheets, or tables. But it does offer a surprisingly long list of core word-processing features. For example:

- **Find, Replace.** Using the Find button (right end of the Home tab on the Ribbon), you can locate a particular word or phrase instantly, even in a long document. The Replace command takes it a step further, replacing that found phrase with another one (a great way to change the name of your main character throughout your entire novel, for example).

Text-Selection Fundamentals

Before doing almost anything to text in a word processor, like making it bold, changing its typeface, or moving it to a new spot in your document, you have to *highlight* the text you want to affect. For millions of people, this entails dragging the cursor extremely carefully, perfectly horizontally, across the desired text. And if they want to capture an entire paragraph or section, they click at the beginning, drag diagonally, and release the mouse button when they reach the end of the passage.

That's all an enormous waste of time. Selecting text is the cornerstone of every editing operation in a word processor, so there are faster and more precise ways of going about it.

For example, double-clicking a word highlights it, instantly and neatly. In fact, by keeping the mouse button pressed on the second click, you can now drag horizontally to highlight text in crisp one-word chunks—a great way to highlight text faster and more precisely. These tricks work anywhere you can type.

In most programs, including Microsoft's, additional shortcuts await. For example, *triple*-clicking anywhere within a paragraph highlights the entire paragraph. (Once again, if you *keep* the button pressed at the end of this maneuver, you can then drag to highlight your document in one-paragraph increments.)

In many programs, including Word and WordPad, you can highlight exactly one sentence by clicking within it while pressing Ctrl.

Finally, here's a universal trick that lets you highlight a large blob of text, even one that's too big to fit on the current screen. Start by clicking to position the insertion point cursor at the very beginning of the text you want to capture. Now scroll, if necessary, so the ending point of the passage is visible. Shift+click there. Windows instantly highlights everything between your click and your Shift+click.

- **Indents and Tab stops.** As shown in Figure 8-37, you click on the ruler to place tab stops there. Each time you press the Tab key, your insertion point cursor jumps in line with the next tab stop.

- **Bulleted lists.** You're reading a bulleted list right now. To apply bullets to a bunch of paragraphs, click the Bullets button (▤). If you click the ▾ next to it, you can create a numbered or lettered list instead.

- **Insert object.** This button lets you create or slap in a picture, graph, chart, sound, movie, spreadsheet, or other kind of data. (The "Paint drawing" button opens up a temporary Paint window so that you can whip up a quick sketch that then gets dropped into your WordPad document.)

Tip: If you click "Date and time," you get a dialog box full of date and time formats (12/18/2013; 12-Dec-2013; Wednesday, December 18, 2013, and so on). Double-click one to insert that date into your document at the insertion point.

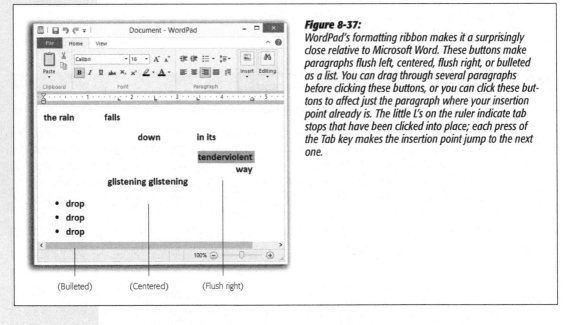

Figure 8-37:
WordPad's formatting ribbon makes it a surprisingly close relative to Microsoft Word. These buttons make paragraphs flush left, centered, flush right, or bulleted as a list. You can drag through several paragraphs before clicking these buttons, or you can click these buttons to affect just the paragraph where your insertion point already is. The little L's on the ruler indicate tab stops that have been clicked into place; each press of the Tab key makes the insertion point jump to the next one.

- **Drag-and-drop editing.** Instead of using the three-step Copy and Paste routine for moving words and phrases around in your document, you can simply drag highlighted text from place to place on the screen.

Xbox

Steady there. No, Windows 10 does not come with a free Xbox.

But if you already *own* Microsoft's popular game console, you're in for a treat. This app is one of Microsoft's proudest new Windows 10 features. It can perform a whole circus full of stunts that supplement an *actual* Xbox in your TV room.

For example, the Xbox app shows you all your stats, recently played games, and friends; you can message them, invite them, and chat with them.

You can also use your tablet or laptop as a remote control for the Xbox (using it to change TV channels, for example, or pause playback).

Some companies are releasing games that you can play *between* a PC and a real Xbox, too.

The real eye-popper, though, is real-time *game streaming.* That's when you're sitting at your laptop or tablet in one room, playing games that are physically running on the Xbox One in another. You're seeing, hearing, and controlling the Xbox on your PC, using the PC as a second screen.

That's a huge benefit when you're playing a game on the Xbox in the TV room, and some heartless family member comes in and demands to watch TV. Instead of being booted off your game, you can just take it anywhere else on the WiFi network.

The Guided Tour

If you've ever played an Xbox *game*, much of the Xbox *app* should look familiar (Figure 8-38):

Figure 8-38:
The Xbox app is a wireless global companion for your Xbox console at home—and for your universe of friends and enemies on the Xbox service. The Xbox app is a remote control for your Xbox, and also makes it possible to play games on your laptop that physically run on the Xbox elsewhere in the house.

- **Top left.** Here's a list of the Xbox games you've been playing recently. You'll need this list if you ever decide to try that game-streaming business, as you'll see in a moment.

Tip: If you click a game's cover art here, you open the "game hub"—the game company's own news feed.

- **Lower left.** Featured games from Microsoft's store—that is, games the company dearly hopes you'll buy.

- **Center column.** This is your activity feed, exactly as it appears on the Xbox. It shows what your friends have been doing in their games, and lets you comment on or "like" their achievements.

- **Right column.** Here's your list of friends—all of them, whether they're online at the moment or not. You can see what they're doing right now on their Xboxes ("Watching TV," "Blu-ray Player," "Halo," or whatever), send them messages, start a party chat, invite them to game sessions, watch their recorded game clips, and so on. (Click a friend's name to summon the Invite and Message buttons in a toolbar at top.)

Game Streaming

OK, here it is: The much celebrated Xbox game streaming. Your Xbox One console is actually running the game, but you're playing it on a Windows 10 computer elsewhere on the same WiFi network. Here's how to get it going.

First, the setup: The Xbox One and your Windows 10 machine have to be on the same network—very fast WiFi or a wired network are recommended—and you have to sign in with the same Xbox account (gamertag) on both.

1. **Set up the Xbox One for streaming.**

   On the Xbox itself, go to Settings→Preferences. Turn on "Allow game streaming to other devices." On the same screen, under "Enable the SmartGlass connection," select either "From any SmartGlass device" or "Only from profiles signed in on this Xbox."

2. **On your Windows 10 machine, open the Xbox app. Tap ≡ (top left) to open the menu column. Hit Connect.**

   The "Connect to Your Xbox" screen opens, and the app scans the network for Xbox One consoles.

3. **Select your Xbox's name.**

   If the fates are smiling, you're now connected. New options appear for streaming, power, and media remotes. You now have remote control of your Xbox One!

4. **Select Stream. Within the Xbox app, find a game you want to play. On its details screen, hit "Play from console" at upper right.**

In just a moment, the game appears on your Windows 10 machine's screen. You can plug in a USB game controller, if you like, or just use the keyboard—but either way, you can marvel at the miracle of gaming that transcends the barriers of space and time.

Well, sort of.

Tip: If your network isn't fast enough for smooth, crisp video, you may have to settle for smooth, less crisp video. In the Xbox app, open Settings→Game Streaming, and try lowering the Quality level until the gameplay stops stuttering.

Screenshots and Game DVR

If you do something extra cool in a game, it's not enough just to brag about it; you've got to capture a picture of it (a screenshot) or record it as a video, using the Game DVR feature.

You take a screenshot of a game the way you always have: ⊞+Alt+PrtScn (page 346).

But in the Xbox app, life gets even sweeter, because you can also record *video* of your gameplay. In fact, you can record video of *anything* you're doing on your computer, even if it's not a game and has nothing to do with the Xbox. Keep that in mind next time you're making a training video.

Note: Two things the Xbox app *can't* record are the desktop and File Explorer windows. For that, you'd need a more professional video-capture program like Camtasia.

To set this up in the Xbox app, open Settings→Game DVR. Turn on "Take screenshots using Game DVR" and "Background recording" must be turned on. (If you can't turn on "Background recording," get a less wimpy PC.) Other settings here govern the quality of the recordings, maximum length, audio, storage location, and so on.

Now you're ready.

Open any app on your computer. It doesn't have to be a game. It could be Maps, or Mail, or a Web browser—doesn't matter. The Xbox app, running in the background, will be able to record its video image.

When you're ready, press ⊞+G.

Note: If this is the first time you're recording from this app, Windows wants to know: "Do you want to open Game bar?" (See Figure 8-39.)

It may sound as if it's proposing that the two of you go into the local sports-bar business. But in fact, this message is brought to you by Microsoft's jumpy lawyers. They want you to confirm that you are, in fact, about to record a game—and, you know, not something you shouldn't be recording.

The answer, if you hope to record video, is always yes. Doesn't matter what kind of app you're really going to record; lie through your teeth if necessary. Click "Yes, this is a game."

Now the Game Bar appears. It has five icons: Xbox (opens the Xbox app), Record That (saves the last 30 seconds of video as a recording), Screenshot (saves a still image), Start Recording (this is what you've been after all this time), and Settings.

Figure 8-39:
Top: Doesn't matter if you're recording a Web browser, a map, or a spreadsheet; if you want to capture video, tell Windows that it's a game.

Bottom: The big red Record button on the Game bar starts the recording within the current window. In this case, you're making a thrilling fly-through of your Maps app.

To start recording, hit the Start Recording button, or press ⊞+Alt+R.

Now go about your business in whatever app you're using. Play, zoom, scroll, click, do whatever you need to do. Behind the scenes, the Xbox app is creating a beautiful audio+video clip. You have an hour to fill, if necessary.

When it's all over, press ⊞+Alt+R again. (Or if you can't remember that, press ⊞+G to open the Game Bar, and then click the red, square Stop Recording button.)

If you now return to the Xbox app and click the Game DVR icon (fourth from the bottom), you'll see your recorded clip. Here you can play it back, trim it, rename it, delete it, share it, or open the folder it's saved in (which is your Videos→Captures folder, in case you were wondering).

XPS Viewer

This little app is dedicated to letting you read XPS files that people send you. (Hint: Nobody will.)

You know how Microsoft always comes up with its own version of anything popular? iPod, iPad, Web browser, whatever?

Its latest software target is the PDF document, the brainchild of Adobe.

A PDF document, of course, is a file that opens up on any kind of computer—Mac, Windows, Unix, anything—looking exactly the way it did when it was created, complete with fonts, graphics, and other layout niceties. The recipient can't generally make changes to it, but can search it, copy text from it, print it, and so on. It's made life a lot easier for millions of people because it's easy, free, and automatic.

And now Microsoft wants a piece o' dat. Its Microsoft XPS document format is pretty much the same idea as PDF, only it's Microsoft's instead of Adobe's.

To turn any Windows document into an XPS document, choose File→Print. In the Print dialog box, choose Microsoft XPS Document Writer as the "printer," and then click Print. You're asked to name it and save it.

The result, when double-clicked, opens up in this program, XPS Viewer—a bare-bones program that does nothing but open XPS files. It offers the usual PDF-type options: find a phrase, jump to a page, zoom in or out, switch to double-page view, print, save a copy, and so on. XPS Viewer also has commands for unlocking password-protected XPS documents.

Truth is, Microsoft has a long battle ahead if it hopes to make the XPS format as commonplace as PDF.

But then again, long battles have never fazed it before.

Part Three:
Windows Online

Chapter 9: Getting Online

Chapter 10: The Edge Browser

Chapter 11: Mail

Chapter 12: Security & Privacy

3

Getting Online

P lenty of people buy a PC to crunch numbers, scan photos, or cultivate their kids'
hand-eye coordination. But for millions of people, Reason One for using a PC
is to get on the Internet. Few computer features have the potential to change
your life as profoundly as the Web and email.

There are all kinds of ways to get a PC onto the Internet these days:

- **WiFi.** Wireless hotspots, known as WiFi, are glorious conveniences, especially if
you have a laptop or a tablet. Without stirring from your hotel bed, you're online
at high speed. Sometimes for free.

- **Cable modems, DSL.** Over half of the U.S. Internet population connects over
higher-speed wires, using broadband connections that are always on: cable modems,
DSL, or corporate networks. (These, of course, are often what's at the other end
of an Internet hotspot.)

- **Cellular modems.** A few well-heeled individuals enjoy the go-anywhere bliss of
USB cellular modems, which get them online just about anywhere they can make
a phone call. These modems are offered by Verizon, Sprint, AT&T, and so on, and
usually cost $60 a month.

- **Tethering.** Tethering is letting your cellphone act as a glorified Internet antenna
for your PC, whether connected by a cable or a Bluetooth wireless link. The phone
company charges you maybe $20 a month extra for this convenience.

- **Dial-up modems.** It's true: Some people still connect to the Internet using a modem
that dials out over ordinary phone lines. They get cheap service but slow connections, and their numbers are shrinking.

This chapter explains how to set up each one of these. (For the basics of setting up your own network, see Chapter 20.)

Tip: If you upgraded to Windows 10 from an earlier version of Windows, then you can already get online, as the installer is thoughtful enough to preserve your old Internet settings. That's the best news you'll hear all day.

Connecting to a WiFi Hotspot

Almost every computer today has a built-in WiFi antenna, officially known as 802.11 (WiFi) wireless networking technology. WiFi can communicate with a wireless base station up to 300 feet away, much like a cordless phone. Doing so lets you surf the Web from your laptop in a hotel room, for example, or share files with someone across the building from you.

Chapter 20 has much more information about *setting up* a WiFi network. The real fun begins, however, when it comes time to *join* one.

Sometimes you just want to join a friend's WiFi network. Sometimes you've got time to kill in an airport or on a plane that has WiFi, and it's worth a $7 splurge for half an hour. And sometimes, at some street corners in big cities, WiFi signals bleeding out of apartment buildings might give you a choice of several free hotspots to join.

If you're in a new place, and Windows discovers, on its own, that you're in a WiFi hotspot, then the 🖧 icon sprouts an asterisk. And where is the 🖧 icon? It's in two places:

- On the taskbar (Figure 9-1, top left).
- On the Quick Actions panel (hit the 🗩 icon on the taskbar).

Figure 9-1 shows you how to proceed. Along the way, you'll be offered the "Connect automatically" checkbox; if you turn it on, you'll spare yourself all this clicking the next time your PC is in range. It'll just hop on that network by itself.

Most hotspots these days are protected by a password. It serves two purposes: First, it keeps everyday schlumps from hopping onto that network; second, it encrypts the connection so that hackers armed with sniffing software can't intercept the data you're sending and receiving.

When You Can't Get On

That should be all that's necessary to get you onto a WiFi hotspot. You should now be able to surf the Web or check your email.

Before you get too excited, though, some lowering of expectations is in order. There are a bunch of reasons why your 🖧 icon might indicate that you're in a hotspot, but you can't actually get online:

- **It's locked.** If there's no tiny "!" shield next to the hotspot's signal strength in the pop-up list of networks, then the hotspot is password-protected. That's partly to prevent hackers from "sniffing" the transmissions and intercepting messages, and partly to keep random passersby like you off the network.

- **The signal isn't strong enough.** Sometimes the WiFi signal is strong enough to make the hotspot's name show up, but not strong enough for an actual connection.

- **You're not on the list.** Sometimes, for security, hotspots are rigged to permit only specific computers to join, and yours isn't one of them.

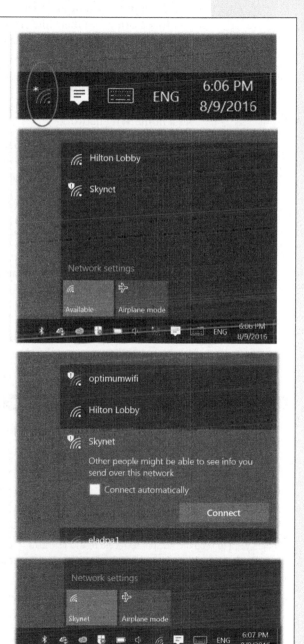

Figure 9-1:
Top left: Hey, look! On the taskbar, your 🛜 icon has an asterisk! There's WiFi here!

Second from top: And if you hit the 🗩 icon to open the Quick Actions panel, it says "Available!"

In fact, it seems that there are two WiFi networks available. One of them displays a shield with an exclamation point, which probably means it's not protected by a password. It's an open network!

Suppose you select it?

Third from top: You're offered a Connect button. Because this is an open network, Windows is warning you that nearby hackers could, with the right software tools, be able to "sniff" whatever data you're sending.

If you don't want to have to go through all this the next time you're in this hotspot, turn on "Connect automatically."

(If you'd chosen the other hotspot, which is more secure, you'd be asked now for the "network security key"–that is, the password.)

Bottom: As the Quick Actions panel indicates, you're now on the Skynet network. Congratulations!

(Tip: If you point to the taskbar icon without clicking, you see the network's name and signal strength. And if you right-click the icon, you get links to a troubleshooting app and the Network and Sharing Center.)

• **You haven't logged in yet.** Commercial hotspots (the ones you have to pay for) don't connect you to the Internet until you've supplied your payment details on a special Web page that appears automatically when you open your browser, as described below.

• **The router's on, but the Internet's not connected.** Sometimes wireless routers are broadcasting, but their Internet connection is down. It'd be like a cordless phone that has a good connection back to the base station in the kitchen—but the phone cord isn't plugged into the base station.

Commercial Hotspots

Choosing the name of the hotspot you want to join is generally all you have to do—if it's a home WiFi network.

Unfortunately, joining a commercial hotspot—one that requires a credit card number (in a hotel room or an airport, for example)—requires more than just connecting to it. You also have to sign into it before you can send so much as a single email message.

To do that, open your browser. You see the "Enter payment information" screen either immediately or as soon as you try to open a Web page of your choice. (Even at free hotspots, you might have to click OK on a welcome page to initiate the connection.)

Supply your credit card information or (if you have a membership to this WiFi chain, like Boingo or T-Mobile) your name and password. Click Submit or Proceed, try not to contemplate how this $8 per hour is pure profit for somebody, and enjoy your surfing.

Memorized Hotspots

If you turned on "Connect automatically," then whenever your laptop enters this hotspot, it will connect to the network automatically. You don't have to do any clicking at all.

POWER USERS' CLINIC

Secret Hotspots

It's entirely possible for you to be standing right in the middle of a juicy, strong WiFi hotspot—and not even know it. Its name doesn't show up in the list.

It turns out that the owner can choose whether or not the hotspot should broadcast its name. Sometimes, he might want to keep the hotspot secret—to restrict its use to employees at a coffee shop, for example, so that the common customer riffraff can't slow it down. In these cases, you'd have to know (a) that the hotspot exists, and (b) what its name is.

Sometimes, you see "Unidentified network" right there in the list of available networks. If so, great—select it, enter the name and password, and off you go.

If not, open the Network and Sharing Center (page 591). Select "Set up a new connection or network." On the next screen, choose "Manually connect to a wireless network," and then hit Next.

Now enter the network's exact name and password. You'll probably want to turn on "Start this connection automatically," too, if you think you might encounter the hotspot again later.

When you click Next, you'll get a notification that you've successfully connected (if, in fact, you have).

Behind the scenes, Windows is capable of piling up quite a list of these hotspots, representing a bread-crumb trail of the hotspots you've used at every hotel, airport, coffee shop, and buddy's house.

You're welcome to peek at this list at any time—and to clean it out, purging the hotspots you'll never need again. To see it, open Settings→Network & Internet→Wi-Fi, and proceed as shown in Figure 9-2.

Figure 9-2:
If you want Windows to forget a hotspot, select it (top) and then hit "Manage Wi-Fi Settings." On the next screen, under "Manage known networks," tap a hotspot's name and then hit Forget.

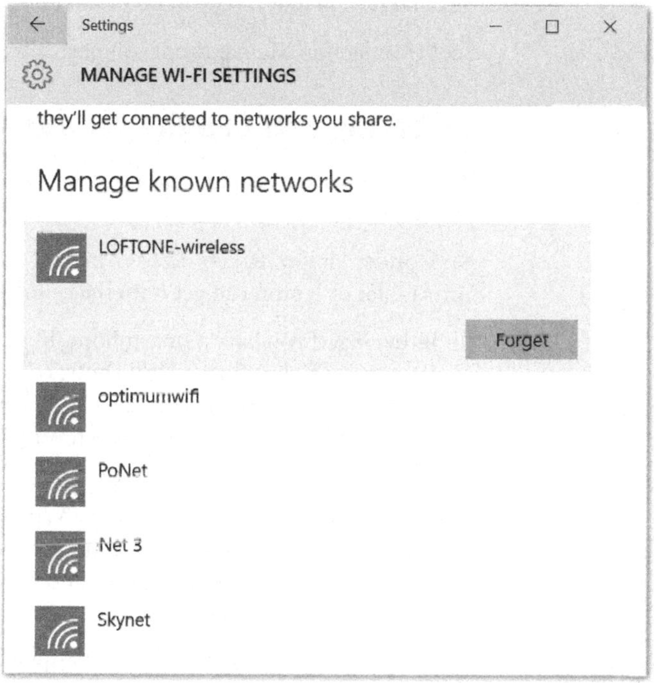

← Settings — □ ✕

⚙ **MANAGE WI-FI SETTINGS**

they'll get connected to networks you share.

Manage known networks

📶 LOFTONE-wireless

Forget

📶 optimumwifi

📶 PoNet

📶 Net 3

📶 Skynet

Wired Connections

The beauty of Ethernet connections is that they're superfast and supersecure. No bad guys sitting across the coffee shop, armed with shareware "sniffing" software, can intercept your email and chat messages, as they theoretically can when you're on wireless.

Connecting to an Ethernet network is usually as simple as connecting the cable to the computer. That's it. You're online, quickly and securely, and you never have to worry about connecting or disconnecting.

Automatic Configuration

Most broadband wired connections require no setup whatsoever. Take a new PC out of the box, plug the Ethernet cable into your cable modem, and you can begin surfing the Web instantly.

That's because most cable modems, DSL boxes, and wireless base stations use DHCP. It stands for dynamic host configuration protocol, but what it means is: "We'll fill in your Network Control Panel automatically." (Including techie specs like IP address and DNS Server addresses.)

Manual Configuration

If, for some reason, you're not able to surf the Web or check email the first time you try, it's remotely possible that your broadband modem or your office network doesn't offer DHCP. In that case, you may have to fiddle with the network settings manually.

See "Connection Management" on page 375 for details.

Tethering and Cellular Modems

WiFi hotspots are fast and usually cheap—but they're *spots*. Beyond 150 feet away, you're offline.

No wonder laptop luggers across America are getting into cellular Internet services. Your tablet or laptop can get onto the cellular data network in any of four ways:

- **Tethering.** If you have a smartphone, like an iPhone, Android, or Windows phone, you can use it as a glorified WiFi hotspot. You have to pay, for example, $20 a month extra to your cellphone company. And tethering eats up battery power like crazy. But for quick Internet checks wherever you are, there's nothing as convenient.

- **MiFi.** The MiFi is a pocket-sized, thick-credit-card-looking thing that grabs the cellular signal and converts it into a WiFi signal for your Windows machine. Here again, you pay a monthly fee. But the nice part is that up to five people can use the WiFi hotspot simultaneously, and this arrangement doesn't slurp down your phone's battery power.

- **USB sticks.** All the big cellphone companies offer ExpressCards or USB sticks that let your laptop get online at high speed anywhere in major cities.

IP Addresses and You

Every computer connected to the Internet, even temporarily, has its own exclusive *IP address* (IP stands for Internet Protocol). When you set up your own Internet account, as described on these pages, you're asked to type in this string of numbers. As you'll see, an IP address always consists of four numbers separated by periods.

Some PCs with high-speed Internet connections (cable modem, DSL) have a permanent, unchanging address called a *static* or *fixed* IP address. Other computers get assigned a new address each time they connect (a *dynamic* IP address). That's always the case, for example, when you connect via a dial-up modem. (If you can't figure out whether your machine has a static or fixed address, ask your Internet service provider.)

If nothing else, dynamic addresses are more convenient in some ways, since you don't have to type numbers into the Internet Protocol (TCP/IP) Properties dialog box.

• **Built-in cellular.** Plenty of laptops and tablets even have cellular circuitry built right inside, so you have nothing to insert or eject.

Imagine: No hunting for coffee shops. With cellular Internet service, you can check your email while zooming down the road in a taxi. (Outside the metropolitan areas, you can still get online wirelessly, though much more slowly.)

And if your phone, MiFi, USB stick, or cellular computer has 4G LTE-type cellular, wow—you'll get speeds approaching a cable modem.

To make the connection, turn on the cellular gadget (phone, MiFi, whatever). After about 20 seconds, the name of your private WiFi hotspot shows up in the list, as shown in Figure 9-1.

Dial-Up Connections

High-speed Internet is where it's at, baby! But there are plenty of reasons why you may be among the 10 percent of the Internet-using population who connect via dial-up modem, slow though it is. Dial-up is a heck of a lot less expensive than broadband. And its availability is incredible—you can find a phone jack in almost any room in the civilized world, in places where the closest Ethernet or WiFi network is miles away.

To get online by dial-up, you need a PC with a modem—maybe an external USB model—and a dial-up *account*. You sign up with a company called an Internet service provider (or *ISP*, as insiders and magazines inevitably call them).

National ISPs like EarthLink and AT&T have local telephone numbers in every U.S. state and in many other countries. If you don't travel much, you may not need such broad coverage. Instead, you may be able to save money by signing up for a local or regional ISP. In fact, you can find ISPs that are absolutely free (if you're willing to look at ads), or that cost as little as $4 per month (if you promise not to call for tech support). Google can be your friend here.

In any case, dialing the Internet is a local call for most people.

To do enter your dialup account information, open the Network and Sharing Center (page 591). In the main window, click "Set up a new connection or network." Double-click "Set up a dial-up connection," and follow the instructions on the screen.

Connection Management

No matter what crazy combination of Internet connections you've accumulated on your computer, Windows represents each one as a *connection icon*. These aren't networks or hotspots; these are *ways* your computer can get online, like Ethernet, WiFi, or Bluetooth. You can view them, rename them, change their settings, or just admire them by opening the window shown at top in Figure 9-3.

To get there, open the Network Connections window. Here's the quickest way to go about it: In the search box, type *view net*. Select "View network connections" in the results.

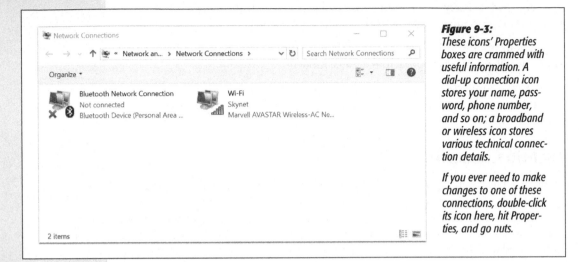

Figure 9-3:
These icons' Properties boxes are crammed with useful information. A dial-up connection icon stores your name, password, phone number, and so on; a broadband or wireless icon stores various technical connection details.

If you ever need to make changes to one of these connections, double-click its icon here, hit Properties, and go nuts.

WiFi Sense

It would be hard to call Windows 10 "controversial." There's hardly a corner of it that's not superior to, ahem, its immediate predecessor.

But WiFi Sense, an optional but very helpful new Windows 10 feature, caused a stir online. (Microsoft must be slapping its corporate forehead in exasperation. As the saying goes, no good deed goes unpunished.)

The idea behind WiFi Sense is powerful, generous, and convenient: To give you no-fuss WiFi Internet as often as possible, wherever you go. It confers two blessings:

- **Automatic connections to good, fast open hotspots.** You go somewhere you've never been before, and boom—you're online. Your laptop quietly connected to the not-password-protected network, without having to log in.

  And how does WiFi Sense know that those open networks are OK to join? Crowd-sourcing. Microsoft maintains a massive database of millions of open hotspots that have been visited by your fellow Windows 10 fans (who have WiFi Sense turned on). If most people have had a good, fast connection to a certain hotspot, WiFi Sense connects *you* to it automatically when you come within range.

Tip: As always, an open network is one that can be "sniffed" by nearby hackers in the same coffee shop. These hotspots are fine to use for Twitter, Facebook, reading news, streaming video or music, and general Web surfing. But to be absolutely safe, don't do your banking or shopping on an open network.

- **Automatic connection to friends' protected networks.** You go to a buddy's house, and boom—you're online, even though he hasn't given you his WiFi password!

Or you visit the local hipster coffee shop, and pow—you're surfing the Internet, even though you haven't entered its hotspot password!

That happens because someone you know—someone in your Facebook, Skype, or Outlook.com contacts—was here before, also using Windows 10. For the sake of the greater good (of her friends), she turned on WiFi Sense sharing for this coffee shop hotspot. And you're the beneficiary.

Overall, then, WiFi Sense is designed to make life just a little easier by eliminating some red tape and fuss from your life. You'll be online more often, effortlessly.

As you can imagine, though, the WiFi Sense description includes some phrases that sound truly terrifying to some people—like "No password needed!" and "Microsoft maintains a massive database of WiFi hotspots!"

But there's very little reason for concern. Read this twice:

- People who get onto a protected hotspot automatically *never see its password.* (Microsoft stores the password in its master database—encrypted, of course—and enters it behind the scenes.)

- WiFi Sense connects people *only* to the Internet. It does not give them access to any *computers, disks, or files* on the network they're borrowing.

- It actually takes a lot of steps to make a password-protected hotspot available for sharing to your friends. You must turn on sharing, which involves entering its password again (Figure 9-4, top right). And for Facebook sharing, there's yet another step.

Bottom line: Nobody's going to share a WiFi Sense connection accidentally.

- If you're still concerned, you can turn WiFi Sense off. You can do that for your entire computer, or for individual hotspots that you visit or control, as described below.

FREQUENTLY ASKED QUESTION

Laptop's Lament: Away from the Cable Modem

When I'm home, I connect my laptop to my cable modem. But when I'm on the road, of course, I have to use my dial-up ISP. Is there any way to automate the switching between these two connection methods?

If there weren't, do you think your question would have even appeared in this chapter?

The feature you're looking for is in the Internet Options control panel. (Quickest way to open it: In the search box,

start typing *Internet options* until you see Internet Options in the results list; press Enter to open it.

Click the Connections tab, and then turn on "Dial whenever a network connection is not present."

From now on, your laptop will use its dial-up modem only when it realizes that it isn't connected to your cable modem.

Express Settings

As you may know from Appendix A, installing Windows 10 involves clicking past a screen that offers Express Settings. It means "Here—we'll set up your PC with the most common preference settings to save you some time."

If you do accept Express Settings, though, you turn on WiFi Sense. So it's likely that the master WiFi Sense switch is turned on, on your machine.

Even so, WiFi Sense doesn't actually do anything until (a) you sign into your Microsoft account, and (b) you turn on WiFi Sense sharing for at least one hotspot that you sign into. (Yes, Windows asks you, every time you sign into a password-protected hotspot, whether you're willing to share it with your contacts who also have WiFi Sense.)

Manual On-Off Switches

You can also turn WiFi Sense on or off manually, like this:

Open Settings→Network & Internet→Wi-Fi. Select Manage Wi-Fi Settings. And there it is: WiFi Sense (Figure 9-4, left).

Here you have three decisions to make:

- **Connect to suggested open hotspots.** This is the feature that hooks you up automatically to open (no password) hotspots when you're out and about. It relies on Microsoft's database of millions of open hotspots that have, in the past, provided good Internet connections to Windows 10 folk.

- **Connect to networks shared by my contacts.** And this is the part where you and your friends share one another's *password-protected* hotspots—both the ones you own, like your home or small office, and the ones you visit, like protected hotspots at restaurants and coffee shops.

Note: WiFi Sense does not get anybody onto *corporate* WiFi hotspots and does not get anyone onto a WiFi hotspot that requires *logging in through a Web page*.

Turning this on is a two-way street: You'll get online instantly through your friends' hotspots when you go to *their* houses or coffee shops, and they'll get online instantly to yours when they're visiting *your* house and coffee shops.

- **Which circles of friends to share with.** If you turned on the "shared by my contacts" switch, you must also specify which circles of friends are welcome to use your Internet when they're visiting: Your Outlook.com contacts, Skype contacts, or Facebook friends (Figure 9-4, left). Or any combination.

Note: You can't choose individuals to share with; it's your *entire* online circle or *nobody* in it.

Sharing (or Unsharing) a Hotspot

Now that WiFi Sense is turned on, you'll notice an interesting new checkbox the next time you connect to a password-protected hotspot. See Figure 9-4, top right.

At any time, you can survey a list of hotspots you've shared in this way—maybe your own home WiFi is among them—and turn them on or off at will.

See the list of past hotspots shown in Figure 9-4 (bottom)? Each one bears a WiFi Sense notation. It says either "Can't share" (because it's an open network or a corporate one), "Not shared" (because you were feeling selfish or paranoid when you joined it), or "Shared" (because you're a kind soul who wants to make the world a better place).

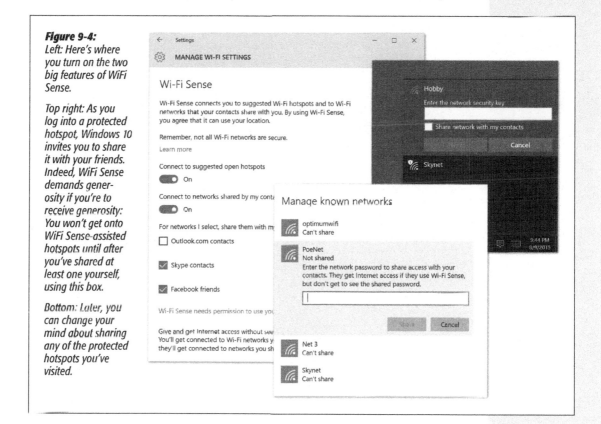

Figure 9-4:
Left: Here's where you turn on the two big features of WiFi Sense.

Top right: As you log into a protected hotspot, Windows 10 invites you to share it with your friends. Indeed, WiFi Sense demands generosity if you're to receive generosity: You won't get onto WiFi Sense-assisted hotspots until after you've shared at least one yourself, using this box.

Bottom: Later, you can change your mind about sharing any of the protected hotspots you've visited.

To share an unshared hotspot, click Share, enter its password, and then hit Share again.

Sharing a hotspot in this way doesn't cost you anything—not in money, time, or bandwidth. You're just helping out people you know who may visit this hotspot in the future. May they smile when they think of you here, making their lives easier.

The Edge Browser

I nternet Explorer was the most famous Web browser on earth, thanks in part to several years of Justice Department scrutiny. But it may have been too successful for its own good. Because it was built into Windows, because everyone used it, Internet Explorer became a prime target for hackers. Over the years, it had become old, and slow, and riddled with holes and patches. In Windows 10, Microsoft decided to start over. It wrote a brand-new browser—called Edge.

Now, don't panic. Internet Explorer is still on your computer. You won't find it in the Start menu—not even in "All apps"—and certainly not on the taskbar. But a search will find it. And if you want to know more about it, read the free downloadable PDF appendix to this chapter, "Internet Explorer.pdf," on this book's "Missing CD" page at *www.missingmanuals.com*.

But as far as Microsoft's future is concerned, Edge is it. It's far faster and more modern than IE ever was—and much simpler. You cannot believe how much cruft Microsoft hacked out of it. A ton of stuff nobody used (Trusted Zones, anyone?) and a lot of shortcuts and refinements you'll miss. (Microsoft says, "Give us time. This is 1.0.")

Edge is designed to eat up very little screen space with controls, so that the Web pages you're reading get as much room as possible. Yet the big-ticket features you'd expect are in place, like bookmarks, a Downloads list, a History list, Reader view (text and graphics only—no ads, no blinkies), private browsing, Find on Page, password storing, and Print.

Edge also has three relatively unusual features. You can look up weather and stocks right in the address bar; you can right-click a word in a Web story to get more information on it in a slide-out panel; and you can draw or write on a page with your finger or the mouse and then save that annotated graphic to OneNote or email it to somebody.

Edge is a fresh start, a clean canvas, modernized and ready for the next 10 years. And the best news is that Microsoft intends to let programmers write extensions for it (feature plug-ins), just like the ones that make Chrome so attractive to so many people (*cough* ad blockers *cough*).

To open Edge, click its icon on the taskbar. It comes preinstalled there—a blue lowercase *e*, so as not to throw off people looking for the old Internet Explorer logo. It's also preinstalled on the right side of the Start menu.

Tip: There's one other sneaky way to open desktop Edge, one that may actually be quicker sometimes. Just type a Web address—a *URL* (Uniform Resource Locator)—into any File Explorer window's address bar, and then hit Enter. Edge opens automatically and pulls up that page. (A Web page URL usually begins with the prefix *http://*, but you can leave that part off when typing into the address bar.)

As you can see in Figure 10-1, the Edge window is filled with tools designed to facilitate a smooth trip around the World Wide Web.

Address/Search bar   Tabs   Hub   Main menu

Figure 10-1:
The Edge window offers tools and features that let you navigate the Web almost effortlessly; these various toolbars and status indicators are described in this chapter. Chief among them: the unified address/search bar, which displays the address (URL) of the Web page you're currently seeing and also serves as the search box when you want to find something on the Web.

The Start Page

The first Web page you encounter when Edge connects to the Internet is a Microsoft Web site. "Where to next?" it says, and there's an address bar so you can type a URL.

Or maybe it's Dell's, or Asus'; the point is, *you* didn't choose it. This site is your factory-set *home page*.

Unless you actually work for Microsoft, Dell, or Asus, you'll probably find Web browsing more fun if you specify your *own* favorite Web page as your startup page.

The easiest way to go about it is to follow the instructions shown in Figure 10-2. Your options include these:

- **Start page.** That's the "Where to next?" page described above.

- **New tab page.** This option means, "Open a new window with whatever I like to see when I create a new *tab*" (page 387). Which you determine using a pop-up menu, here. It's called "Open new tabs with," and it offers its own three options: "Top sites" (icons for your most recently visited sites), "Top sites and suggested content" (a combination of those icons and articles that Microsoft wishes to plug), or "A blank page."

A blank page— **an** empty home page—makes Edge load very quickly when you first launch it. Once this window opens, *then* you can tell the browser where you want to go today.

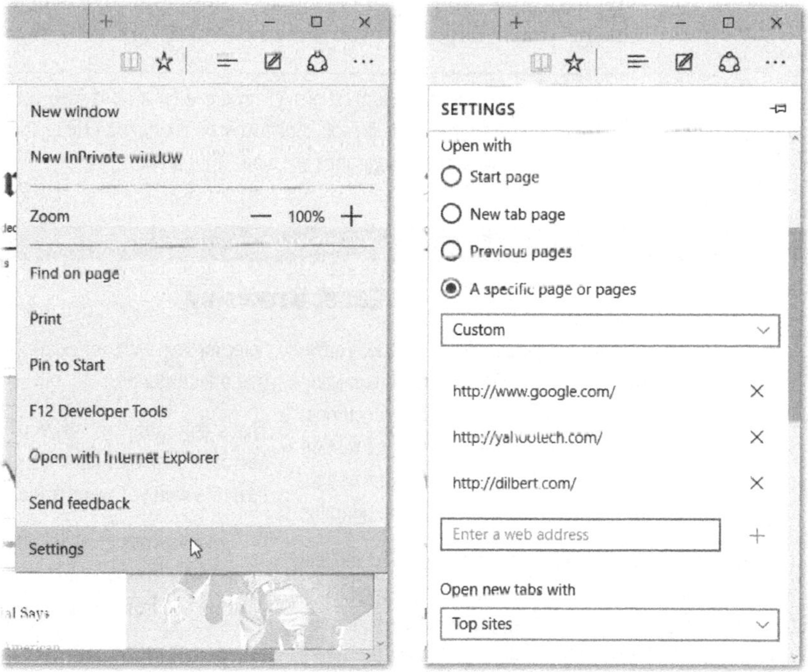

Figure 10-2:
Left: Many, many operations in Edge begin with a visit to Settings, which lives at the bottom of the main menu.

Right: Here, for example, you can designate what you want as your home page.

- **Previous pages.** Whatever pages you had open the last time you closed Edge.

- **A specific page or pages.** Lots of people like to be greeted every morning by a superbly informative site like NYTimes.com or YahooTech.com. Or even several favorite sites, all loaded and ready for reading; that's a great way to avoid wasting time by calling up one site after another, because they'll all be loading in the background as you read the first one.

> **Tip:** Edge has two different looks: A light-gray color scheme and a black one. To switch, open the ⋯ menu and then hit Settings; there's your "Choose a theme" pop-up menu. Try them all!

The Address/Search Bar

In Edge, as in many popular browsers, a single, unified box serves as both the address bar and the search bar. If you type a Web address there, like *amazon.com*, pressing Enter takes you to that Web site; if you type anything else, like *cashmere sweaters* or just *amazon*, pressing Enter gives you the Bing search results for that phrase.

Searching the Web

Press Ctrl+L (or F4, or Alt+D) to deposit your insertion point inside the unified toolbar, just as in Internet Explorer. As you type something you're looking for—*phony baloney*, say—a pop-up menu of autocomplete suggestions appears beneath your typing. When you finish typing and press Enter (or when you choose one of those suggestions), Edge takes you directly to the Bing results page, or the page you selected.

> **Tip:** You can turn off these suggestions. (They are, after all, provided courtesy of a two-way trip to Microsoft's servers, meaning that Microsoft knows what you're typing.) Hit ⋯ and then Settings→"View advanced settings"→"Show search suggestions as I type." Turn it off.

UP TO SPEED

Caret Browsing

Caret browsing is an ancient computing technique. You've probably been using it your whole life without even realizing that it has a name. It just means you can navigate a document with the keyboard. Press the arrow keys to move the insertion point through your text, or Page Up/Page Down to scroll, or press Home or End to jump to the end or the beginning.

(Oh, and you can hold down the Shift key to select the text as you go. That's especially useful when you're selecting text on a Web page, because it captures only the text in the current column. If you simply drag your mouse through a Web page, you might also accidentally highlight stuff that's off to the side, like ads or list boxes or other stories. And when you copy and paste that selection, you wind up with a nightmare of intermixed text from different columns.

Selecting text with, for example, Shift+arrow keys, prevents that phenomenon.)

That's commonplace in word processing, of course, but Microsoft seems to think it's something you might want to turn off when you're on a Web page.

Well, here's your chance, although it's hard to think of a reason why you wouldn't want the ability to choose and navigate text from the keyboard.

In Edge, open the More panel (⋯), then Settings, then "View advanced settings." Here's the "Always use caret browsing" on/off switch.

Or, if you've got the keyboard for it, press F7 to turn caret browsing on or off.

Adding Google

You're not obligated to use Microsoft's Bing search service. There is, after all, another very good search engine out there called Google. You might have heard of it.

Fortunately, you can make Edge use Google instead of (or in addition to) Bing. The only weird part is that you must start by *opening* Google (pull up *www.google.com*). Or any search page you prefer—DuckDuckGo, Yahoo, whatever.

Hit the ⋯ button, then Settings, then "View advanced settings." Scroll down to "Search in the address bar with," hit "Add new," and select Google's address. Finally, hit "Add as default."

From now on, much to Microsoft's dismay, you'll be using Google instead of Bing for searching. As an added convenience, the names of any search services you add in this way —Bing, Google, and whatever others you add using this technique—appear in the "Search in the address bar with" pop-up menu. In other words, you can switch back and forth as needed.

Tip: Sure, Bing and Google are great for finding Web pages on the Internet. But Edge can also find words *on* a certain page. Press Ctrl+F. (Or hit ⋯ and then "Find on page.") In the "Find on page" toolbar that appears, type the text you're trying to find, and then use the < and > buttons to jump from occurrence to occurrence. (The Options pop-up menu lets you specify whether or not you require full-word matches and whether capitalization counts.)

Entering an Address

Because typing out Internet addresses is so central to the Internet experience and such a typo-prone hassle, the address bar is rich with features that minimize keystrokes. For example:

- You don't have to click in the address bar before typing; just press Alt+D.

- You don't have to type out the whole Internet address. You can omit the *http://www* and *.com* portions; if you press Ctrl+Enter after typing the name, Edge fills in those standard address bits for you.

  To visit Amazon.com, for example, you can press Alt+D to highlight the address bar, type *amazon,* and then press Ctrl+Enter.

- Even without the Ctrl+Enter trick, you can still omit the *http://* from any Web address. (Most of the time, you can omit the *www.,* too.) To jump to today's Dilbert cartoon, type *dilbert.com* and then press Enter.

- When you begin to type into the address/search bar, AutoComplete kicks in. Edge displays a drop-down list below the address bar, listing Web addresses that seem to match what you're typing, as well as sites you've visited recently whose addresses match. To save typing, just select the correct complete address with your mouse, or use the ↓ key to reach the desired listing and then press Enter. The complete address you selected then pops into the address bar.

Topside doodads

Around the address/search bar, you'll find several important buttons. Some of them lack text labels, but all offer tooltip labels:

- **Back button** (←), **Forward button** (→). Click the ← button to revisit the page you were just on. (Keyboard shortcut: Alt+←)

  Once you've clicked Back, you can then click Forward (or press Alt+→) to return to the page you were on *before* you clicked the Back button.

- **Refresh button.** Click ↻ if a page doesn't look or work quite right, or if you want to see the updated version of a Web page that changes constantly (such as a stock ticker). This button forces Edge to re-download the Web page and reinterpret its text and graphics.

- **Stop** (×). Click to interrupt the downloading of a Web page you've just requested (by mistake, for example).

- **Reader view** (▭). This button opens the wonderful, glorious Reader view, described on page 395.

- **Add to Favorites** (☆). This button lets you bookmark a page for reading later. You'll have a choice of listing the page either as a Favorite (page 388) or a Reading List item (page 395).

- **The Hub** (≡). Here's where everything you collect online winds up: Favorites, reading list, browsing history, and recent downloads.

- **Markup** (✐). New in Edge: Draw or type onto any Web page; save it as a graphic (page 391).

- **Share** (⌂). Opens the Share panel so that you can send a link to this page to other people or apps.

- **More actions** (⋯). This is Edge's More menu. There's a lot of stuff crammed into it, but you'll eventually find what you're looking for.

Window Controls

These last items wrap up your grand tour of Edge's window gizmos:

- **Scroll bars.** Use the scroll bar, or the scroll wheel on your mouse, to move up and down the page—or to save mousing, press the space bar each time you want to see more. Press Shift+space bar to scroll *up*. (The space bar has its traditional, space-making function only when the insertion point is blinking in a text box or the address/search bar.)

  You can also press your ↑ and ↓ keys to scroll. Page Up and Page Down scroll in full-screen increments, while Home and End whisk you to the top or bottom of the current Web page.

- ⌂ **button.** Click to bring up the Web page you've designated as your home page— your starter page, as described on page 382.

Note: What's that you say? There is no Home button in your copy of Edge? That's because you have to turn it on. Hit ···, then Settings→"View advanced settings"→"Show the home button." Turn it on.

Tabbed Browsing

Beloved by hard-core surfers the world over, *tabbed browsing* is a way to keep a bunch of Web pages open simultaneously—in a single, neat window, without cluttering up your taskbar with a million buttons. Figure 10-3 illustrates.

Figure 10-3:
When you Ctrl-click a link, or type an address and press Alt+Enter, you open a new tab, not a new window as you ordinarily would. You can now pop from one open page to another by clicking the tabs above the window, or close one by clicking its × button (or pressing Ctrl+W).

Shortcut-O-Rama

Tabbed browsing unlocks a whole raft of Edge shortcuts and tricks, which are just the sort of thing power surfers gulp down like Gatorade:

- **To open a new, empty tab** in front of all others, press Ctrl+T (for *tab*), or click the New Tab stub identified in Figure 10-3. From the empty tab that appears, you can navigate to any site you want.

- **To open a link into a new tab,** Ctrl-click it. Or click it with your mouse wheel.

  Or, if you're especially slow, right-click it and, from the shortcut menu, choose Open in New Tab.

Note: Ctrl-clicking a link opens that page in a tab *behind* the one you're reading. That's a fantastic trick when you're reading a Web page and see a reference you want to set aside for reading next, but you don't want to interrupt whatever you're reading now.

But if you want the new tab to appear in *front,* then add the Shift key.

- **To close a tab,** click the ✕ on it, press Ctrl+W, or click the tab with your mouse wheel or middle mouse button, if you have one. (If you press Alt+F4, you close all tabs. If you press Ctrl+Alt+F4, you close all tabs *except* the one that's in front.)

- **Switch from one tab to the next** by pressing Ctrl+Tab. Add the Shift key to move backward through them.

- **Jump to a specific tab** by pressing its number along with the Ctrl key. For example, Ctrl+3 brings the third tab forward.

- **Open a duplicate of this tab** by pressing Ctrl+Shift+K. (Handy if your quest for information might branch out in a different direction.)

- **Close all?** When you close Edge, a dialog box appears asking if you really want to close *all* the tabs, or just the frontmost one. If you grow weary of answering that question, then turn on "Always close all tabs" before making your selection.

Favorites (Bookmarks)

When you find a Web page you might like to visit again, press Ctrl+D. That's the keyboard shortcut for the Add to Favorites command. (The long way is to click the ☆ button to make the Favorites pane appear, and then click Add—but who's got the time?) Type a shorter or more memorable name, if you like, and then click Add.

The page's name appears instantly in the Hub, on the Favorites pane, which is the panel indicated by the star (Figure 10-4). The next time you want to visit that page, open this panel—or press Ctrl+I—and choose the Web site's name in the list.

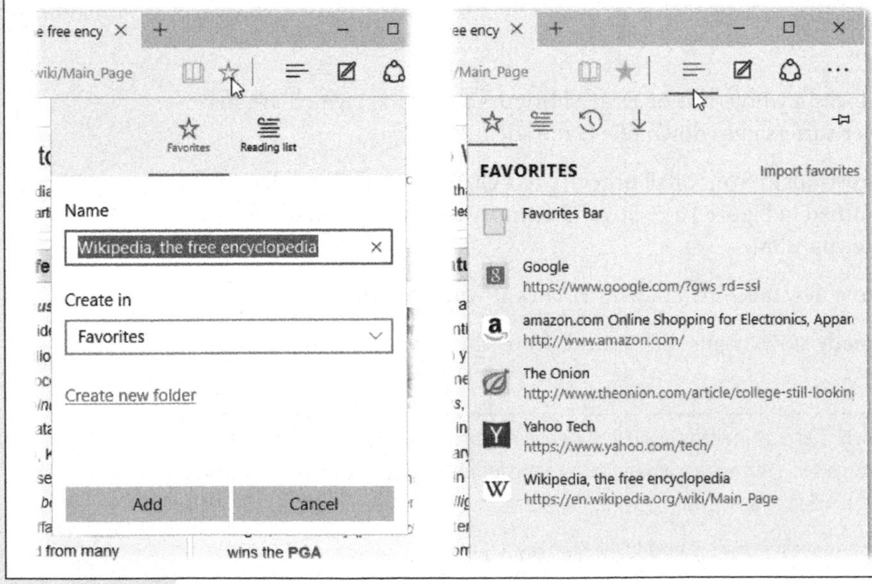

Figure 10-4:
Left: When you want to flag a Web page for visiting later, hit the star.

Right: Later, open the Hub to find a page you want to revisit. You can drag names up or down to rearrange the list. Or right-click one to access the commands that rename, delete, or file a favorite into a folder.

Tip: Unfortunately, the Favorites menu covers up part of the Web page you're reading. It hides itself soon enough, but you might also want to freeze the Hub open so that it doesn't cover the page. To do that, click the Pin (-ᶋ) button above the Favorites tab.

You can rearrange the bookmarks in your Favorites menu easily enough. Open the Favorites Center (Figure 10-4, right), and then drag things up and down in the list.

Tip: Edge is perfectly happy to import the bookmarks you've carefully assembled in rival browsers. To do that, open the ··· menu and then hit Settings; there's your "Import favorites from another browser" link. (You can even import them from several browsers simultaneously.)

The Favorites Bar

The Favorites panel is one way to maintain a list of Web sites you visit frequently. But opening a Web page in that pane requires *two taps or clicks*—an exorbitant expenditure of energy. The Favorites toolbar, on the other hand, lets you summon a few, very select, *very* favorite Web pages with only *one* click. (See Figure 10-5.)

Figure 10-5:
You can't rename the icons on the Favorites bar, and you can't drag them around to rearrange them, and you can't add a site to the Favorites bar by dragging its icon from the address bar.

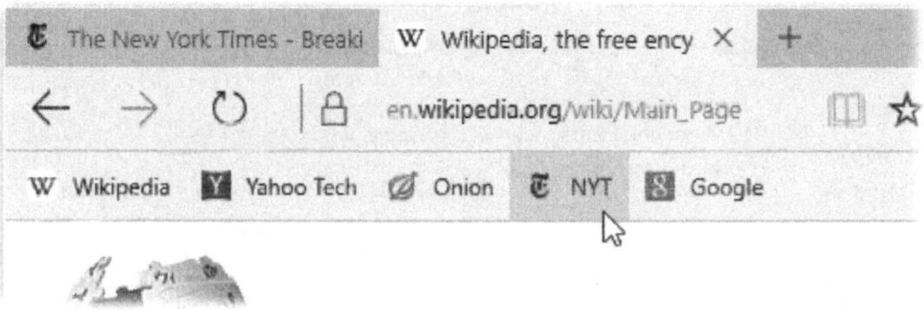

You make the toolbar appear by pressing Ctrl+Shift+B (for "bar"). Or the long way: Hit ···, then Settings→"Show the favorites bar."

You can add a new bookmark to the Favorites bar just as you'd add one to your Favorites list: Click the star (☆)—but in the resulting box (Figure 10-4, left), choose "Favorites bar" from the "Create in" pop-up menu. (Or drag an existing favorite onto the Favorites Bar icon shown at right in Figure 10-4.)

Tip: In Edge, four important lists are all hiding in the Hub—the panel marked by ☰. But there are direct keyboard shortcuts for all four, all in a cluster on your keyboard. You've got Ctrl+G (Reading list), Ctrl+H (History list), Ctrl+J (Downloads list), and Ctrl+ I (Favorites). See what Microsoft did there?

History List

This *history* is a list of the Web sites you've visited. To see it, open the Hub by clicking ☰; then click the ⟳ to see your History. Or skip all that, and just press Ctrl+H. Figure 10-6 presents the world's shortest History class.

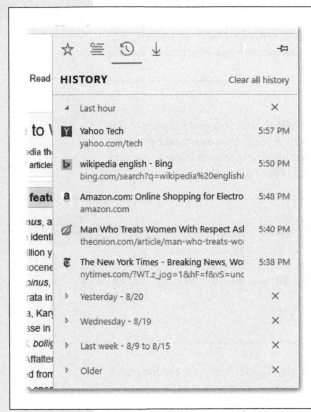

Figure 10-6:
You can expand or collapse the "folders" here (indicating days, weeks, and older time periods) with a click.

Handily enough, you can also delete any of these time-period browsing records with a click—on the ✕ button next to it.

Cortana Meets Edge

Cortana, as you may recall from Chapter 5, is your voice-controlled personal assistant. Microsoft says she's at work in Edge, too, although you'll soon discover that there's very little resemblance to the cheerful assistant who lives in a rock under the Start menu.

Microsoft is referring to three fledgling features in Edge:

- **Instant answers in the address bar.** We're talking about weather, stocks, and definitions. Type *weather 10024* or *goog* or *define perspicacious* into the address bar, and a panel pops up with the temperature, stock price, or definition even before you press Enter (Figure 10-7).

- **Instant info in an article.** You're reading along, and you encounter a reference to, let's say, vegan cooking. What is that, exactly? Highlight the text. Right-click it (or hold your finger down on it). From the shortcut menu, choose Ask Cortana, and boom: A panel opens on the right side of the window with a lot more information about whatever it is you highlighted. A company, a person, a place, a word you need defined (Figure 10-7, bottom).

Figure 10-7:
You can't actually speak to Cortana in the Edge browser. But you can access her lookup skills.
Top: She can provide stock quotes, weather, and word definitions before you even press Enter.

Bottom: She can provide a useful panel of background information on anything you high-light in a Web article. This feature is rather fantastic, actually. It can save you a lot of trips to Wikipedia.

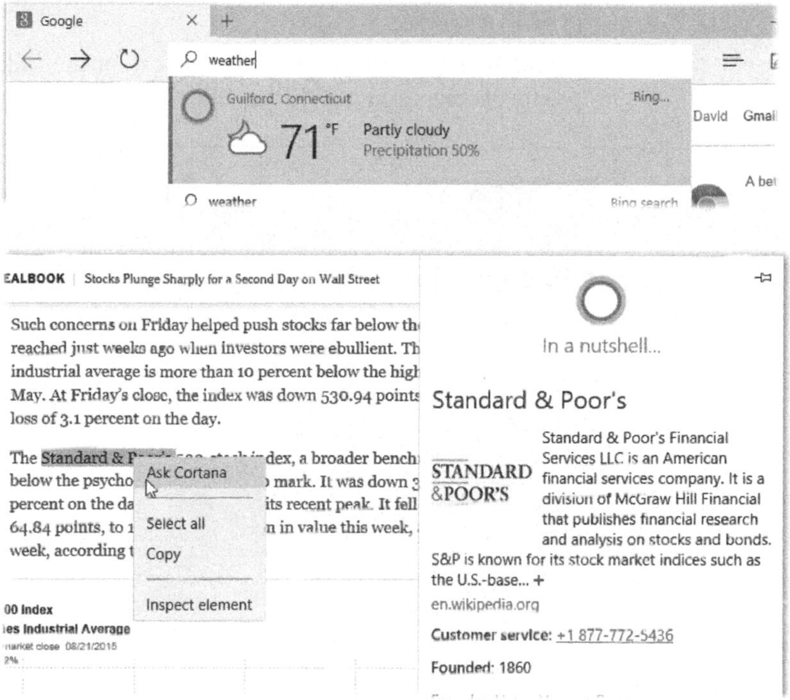

- **Restaurant details.** Someday, Microsoft says, you'll be able to type the name of a restaurant into the address bar and marvel as a button appears that says: "I've got directions, hours, and more." Choose that link, and an info panel for the restaurant will appear—with directions, hours, and more!

Alas, Microsoft has to hand-rig each restaurant to this feature, and as Windows 10 debuted, only about 300 restaurants were so rigged.

Mark Up Your Web Pages

Microsoft (or at least its marketing team) is especially proud of this unusual feature: You can use drawing tools on any Web page. Mark it up. Underline, circle, type comments (Figure 10-8).

Sadly, your graffiti doesn't show up on the real Web; the rest of the Internet doesn't get to see your handiwork (although that'd be fun!). But once you've marked up a page, you can preserve it as a graphic—send it to someone, capture it in OneNote, or whatever.

All you have to do is click the Markup button (✏) in the top-right corner of Edge. The Markup toolbar appears, starring these tools:

- **Pen** (▽). Draw on the page. Hit this icon to open a palette of colors and three pen thicknesses.

- **Highlighter** (▽). Exactly like the Pen, except the "ink" is transparent. Again, a palette of colors and pen thicknesses.

Figure 10-8:
The new Markup feature lets you draw, paint, or type onto an image of any Web page. You're not actually defacing the Internet—more like your private copy of this page—but it can be handy when you're trying to communicate with a buddy (or a spouse).

- **Eraser** (◇). Draw over any other Pen or Highlighter markings you've made to erase them. Or, if you've really made a mess of things, hit the icon and choose "Clear all ink."

- **Typed notes** (▢). Click to open a little text box, where you can type your notes, observations, or corrections. You can create as many of these boxes as you like. They expand vertically to hold a lot of text, but you can't make them wider. You can move them, though, by dragging their numbered tags.

  A 🗑 button appears in the corner of each for easy disposal later.

- **Clip** (✂). This tool lets you copy a certain rectangle of the Web page, ready for pasting into, for example, an email message or OneNote. When you open the tool, Edge tells you "Drag to copy region" in lettering big enough to see from Pluto. Drag diagonally and then release; the image is now on your Clipboard.

If you want to preserve the marked-up page for future generations, you can export it or send it.

Export as Web Note

A Web Note is basically a graphic snapshot of your marked-up page. When you hit the ☁ at top right of Edge, you're offered three destinations for this Web Note:

- **OneNote.** Your image becomes a note "page" in OneNote (page 329).

- **Favorites.** The image becomes a bookmark you can call up later from within Edge. You'll be able to continue editing at that point. (You can choose which Favorites folder you want, and you can type a name for this marked-up image.)

- **Reading List.** The image is stored as an "article" that you can read—and edit—later (page 395).

Tip: Remember, you're just editing a graphic image at this point. When you reopen your Web Note from the Favorites or Reading List panel, however, a "Go to original page" link appears at the top; it takes you to the live, unmarked, original Web page. (And there's a "Hide notes" button that temporarily hides all your markings on the graphic.)

Send to Your Fans

The Share button (☁) opens the standard Share panel, with whatever options appear there: Mail and OneNote, for example. Handy if you want to email the marked-up Web page image to prove a point.

Exit

If you choose Exit, you return to regular Web surfing and stop drawing. If you haven't exported or shared your masterpiece first, all your work is lost forever.

Tips for Better Surfing

Edge is filled with shortcuts and tricks for better speed and more pleasant surfing. For example:

Bigger Text, Smaller Text

When your eyes are tired, you might like to make a Web page bigger. Fortunately, there are plenty of ways to zoom in or out of the whole affair:

- If you have a touchscreen, pinch or spread two fingers against the glass.

- If you have a scroll-wheel mouse, press the Ctrl key as you turn the mouse's wheel. (This works in Microsoft Office programs, too.)

- Press Ctrl+plus or Ctrl+minus on your keyboard.

- Hit ··· to see Zoom buttons staring you in the face.

Note: In Edge, there's no way to enlarge only the *text* on a page. You must enlarge or shrink the *entire* page.

Memorized Passwords & Forms

Each time you type a password into a Web page, Edge can offer to memorize it for you. It's a great time- and brain-saver. (Of course, use it with caution if you share an account on your PC with other people.)

It can remember other stuff, too, like your address and phone number, so you don't have to keep typing those into shopping sites, gaming sites, and so on.

Thanks to the Manage Passwords dialog box shown in Figure 10-9, it's easy to see all the passwords Edge has saved for you—and to delete the ones you want it to forget.

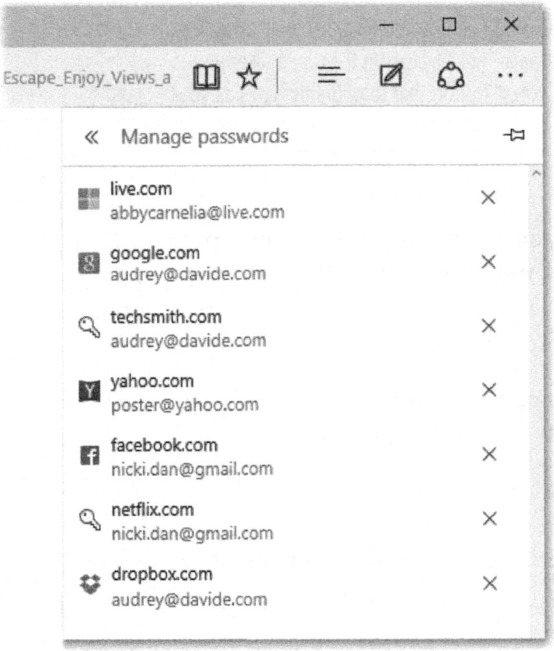

Figure 10-9:
Here are all the Web sites for which Edge has memorized your passwords so you don't have to type them in every time you visit. Yes! You can make Edge forget one by hitting the ×, or you can double-click a row to edit its name/password combination.

This feature is a lot like the popular password/credit card keeper programs like 1Password and Dashlane—better, really, because it's free, and because Edge auto-syncs your stored passwords to your other Windows 10 machines, too.

To turn this feature on or off, hit ⋯, then Settings→"View advanced settings." And here they are: "Offer to save passwords," (on/off), "Save form entries" (on/off), and "Manage my saved passwords." That one opens up a master list of the passwords Edge has saved for you, as shown in Figure 10-9.

Online Photos

Edge is loaded with features for handling graphics online. Right-clicking an image on a Web page, for example, produces a shortcut menu that offers commands like "Save picture," "E-mail picture," "Copy picture," and "Share picture." (That last one opens the Share panel, where you get options like Facebook or Mail.)

So when you see a picture you'd like to keep, right-click it and choose "Save picture" from the shortcut menu. After you name the picture and then click the Save button, the result is a new graphics file on your hard drive containing the picture you saved.

The Reading List

The Reading List, one of the options in the Hub (Figure 10-4), saves the names of Web pages that you want to read later.

Unlike the similar feature in rival browsers, this one doesn't actually *store* the Web pages on your computer so that you can read them later when you're offline. You still need an Internet connection to reopen one of these.

In other words, Edge's Reading List feature does pretty much the same thing as Favorites or Bookmarks. (In fact, Windows 10 even synchronizes your Reading List among your Windows 10 machines, just as it does Favorites.) It's as though the Web always keeps your place as you move from gadget to gadget.

To add a page to the Reading List, hit the star ☆ button, just as though you're about to add a Favorite. But in the panel that appears, select Reading List. Edit the name, if you like, and then choose Add.

Later, to view your saved pages, open the Hub (≡); then click the Reading List (≣) tab. Select the story you want to reopen.

The Download Manager

When you click a link to download something from a Web page, Edge records it in the Downloads list.

To view the list, open the Hub (≡); then click the Downloads (↓) tab. Click the ✕ to clear a downloaded item's name from the list, or "Clear all" to erase the entire list. You're not actually removing any files from your computer—you're just erasing the visual record of what you've downloaded.

Reader

How can people read Web articles when there's Times Square blinking going on all around them? Fortunately, you'll never have to put up with that again.

The Reader button (▥) at the top of the Edge window is amazing. With one click (or one press of Ctrl+R), it eliminates *everything* from the Web page you're reading except the text and photos. No ads, blinking, links, banners, promos, or anything else.

The text is also changed to a clean, clear font and size, and the background is made plain and pure. Basically, it makes any Web page look like a printed book page or a Kindle page, and it's glorious (Figure 10-10).

To exit Reader, hit ▥ again.

Best. Feature. Ever.

Tip: On the More (⋯) panel, in Settings, under Reading, you can change the background color and type size for Reader view.

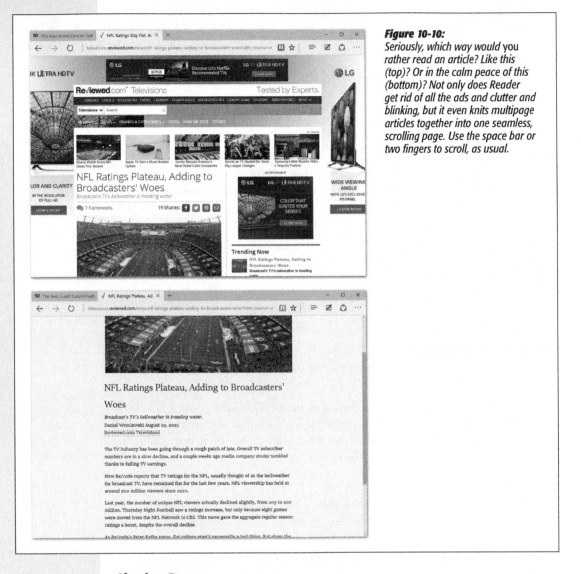

Figure 10-10:
Seriously, which way would you rather read an article? Like this (top)? Or in the calm peace of this (bottom)? Not only does Reader get rid of all the ads and clutter and blinking, but it even knits multipage articles together into one seamless, scrolling page. Use the space bar or two fingers to scroll, as usual.

Sharing Pages

Edge lets you tell a friend about the page you're looking at. You might find that useful when you come across a particularly interesting news story, op-ed piece, or burrito recipe.

Hit the Share icon (⌂) to open the Share panel, where you see a list of places that will accept this Web page—like Facebook, Mail, and OneNote.

Printing Pages

The decade of chopped-off printouts is over. In Edge, when you press Ctrl+P or choose ⋯ and then Print, *all* the page's text is laid out to fit within the page.

The Print panel offers a handsome preview of the end result, plus controls like these:

- **Orientation** means Portrait, Landscape (upright or sideways).

- **Headers and footers** hides or shows the header (the text at the top of the printout, which usually identifies the name of the Web site you're printing and the number of pages) and the footer (the URL of the Web page and the date).

- **Scale** affects the size of the image on the printed pages. Shrink to Fit adjusts the printout so it won't be chopped off, but you can manually magnify or reduce the printed image by choosing the other percentage options in this menu.

- **Margins.** Do you want Narrow, Normal, Moderate, or Wide margins in your printout?

Tip: Lots of Web sites have their own "Print this Page" buttons. When they're available, use them instead of Edge's own Print command. The Web site's Print feature not only makes sure the printout won't be chopped off, but it also eliminates ads, includes the entire article (even if it's split across multiple Web pages), and so on.

The Keyboard Shortcut Master List

Before you sail off into the Edge sunset, it's worth admitting that surfing the Web is one of the things most people do *most* with their PCs. And as long as you're going to spend so much time in this single program, it's worth mastering its keyboard shortcuts. Once you've learned a few, you save yourself time and fumbling.

Page 645 in Appendix C offers a master list of every Edge keyboard shortcut known to Microsoft. Clip and save.

CHAPTER 11

Mail

M ail, which is Windows 10's built-in email program, is easy to use, it's beautiful, and—especially if you have a touchscreen—it offers a fast, fluid way to
work. And it's not nearly as stripped down as it was in Windows 8.

This Mail app is, as you'll soon discover, super basic. For example, you can't create or
edit mail folders, view your messages in a unified Inbox, set up message rules, turn
off "conversation threading" view, or open a message in its own window (at least not
in the initial version).

But Mail works great on a touchscreen, thanks to its very few, but bold, buttons. And
it's handy that it syncs with your other Windows 10 machines. Set up your accounts
once, and find them magically waiting for you on any other phones, tablets, or PCs
you may pick up. And it's handy that Mail's messages notify you by appearing in the
Windows 10 Action Center (page 113).

Note: Saying that the Mail app is very simple to use is another way of saying that it's fairly rudimentary.

There are plenty of alternative mail programs, though—including Microsoft's own Windows Live Mail, which
came with Windows 8 but not with Windows 10. It's a desktop program (rather than a "Windows Store"
app), so it's far more complete. It's a free download, it works great in Windows 10, and you can find it on
this book's "Missing CD" page at *www.missingmanuals.com*. In fact, there's a free PDF appendix to this book
that describes it, on the same "Missing CD"—"Windows Live Mail.pdf."

Setting Up

The first time you fire up Mail—or any email program, actually—your first job is to enter the details of your email account. After you click Get Started on the welcome screen, you wind up on the Accounts screen. Hit "Add account."

On the next screen, you'll see that Mail comes ready to accommodate all kinds of popular email services (Figure 11-1): Gmail, Yahoo, Apple's iCloud, Outlook.com (any of Microsoft's free Web-based email services, including Hotmail, Live.com, or MSN), and Exchange (the system most offices use). If you have any other service, hit "Other account" and fill in the details.

In general, all you have to fill in is your email address and password. On the next screen, you're asked for your name; this is the name that'll be in the "From" line when other people get messages from you. (See the box on the facing page for details on some of the weirder account types.)

When you click Done on the "All done" screen, you return to the Accounts setup screen so you can start all over again with another account. Once you've completed this joyous task, you can hit "Ready to go" to start doing email.

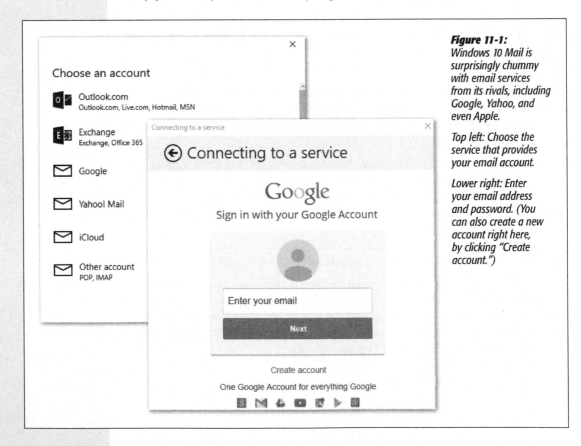

Figure 11-1:
Windows 10 Mail is surprisingly chummy with email services from its rivals, including Google, Yahoo, and even Apple.

Top left: Choose the service that provides your email account.

Lower right: Enter your email address and password. (You can also create a new account right here, by clicking "Create account.")

Note: You can always add additional accounts later. Hit ⚙; on the Settings pane, choose Accounts, and then "Add account." That Accounts panel is also how you delete an account; select it, then "Delete account."

If your settings were all correct, you get teleported directly into that account's inbox, ready to start processing email.

There's no unified inbox in Mail for the messages from multiple accounts. If you've set up more than one account, you switch among them by selecting Accounts (top left corner). (Depending on the window's width, you may just see the *icons* of the menu-column entries; click the Accounts icon to see your list of accounts.)

Tip: You can also pin one account's inbox—or any other mail folder—to your Start menu (right side), for instant access and step-saving. For example, if you have a folder called Stuff to Do, or a folder called Reply to These, you might want them pinned on your Start menu.

To do that, right-click (or hold your finger down on) the folder you want to pin; choose Pin to Start. You'll find the pinned folder at the bottom of your Start menu. One click on that tile, and boom: You're in Mail, in that folder, reading the latest communiqués.

POP, IMAP, and Web-based Mail

There are three kinds of email accounts—and Windows 10 Mail works with all of them.

Web-based mail. Some email accounts are designed to be accessed on a Web site, like the free accounts offered by Gmail, Yahoo, Hotmail, or Outlook.com.

IMAP accounts (Internet message access protocol) are the latest type, and they're surging in popularity. IMAP servers keep all your mail online, rather than storing it solely on your computer; as a result, you can access the same mail from any computer (or phone), and you'll always see the same lists of mail. IMAP servers remember which messages you've read and sent, and they even keep track of how you've filed messages into mail folders. (Those free Yahoo and iCloud email accounts are IMAP accounts, and so are corporate Exchange accounts. Gmail and Outlook.com accounts are usually IMAP, too.)

POP accounts are the oldest type on the Internet. (POP stands for Post Office Protocol, but this won't be on the test.) The big difference: A POP server transfers incoming mail to your computer; once it's there, it's no longer on the Internet. (If you try to check your email on your phone, you won't see whatever new messages were downloaded by your computer back at home since you last checked.) Internet providers like Time Warner and Comcast usually provide email addresses as POP accounts.

Windows 10 Mail, unlike Windows 8 Mail, works with POP accounts. If they're from a big name like, well, Time Warner or Comcast, use the "Other account" option on the setup screen and supply your email address and password.

If Windows doesn't immediately recognize the provider name, then you need a way to enter the account details beyond the name and password (like the server addresses, authentication method, and so on).

For that purpose, there's an "Advanced setup" option at the bottom of the "Choose an account" screen. (You may have to scroll down to see it.) Click that, click "Internet accounts," and off you go.

The Amazing Expand-O-Window

Mail is one of Microsoft's *universal* apps, meaning that it runs identically on phones, tablets, and computers. Which really means that its *layout changes* to fit the screen size of the machine you're using. Which makes it hard for a computer-book author to anticipate what you might see on your screen.

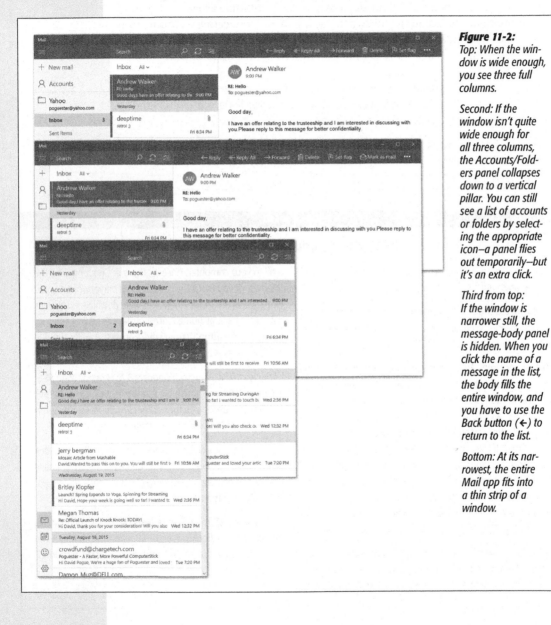

Figure 11-2:
Top: When the window is wide enough, you see three full columns.

Second: If the window isn't quite wide enough for all three columns, the Accounts/Folders panel collapses down to a vertical pillar. You can still see a list of accounts or folders by selecting the appropriate icon—a panel flies out temporarily—but it's an extra click.

Third from top: If the window is narrower still, the message-body panel is hidden. When you click the name of a message in the list, the body fills the entire window, and you have to use the Back button (←) to return to the list.

Bottom: At its narrowest, the entire Mail app fits into a thin strip of a window.

In Mail's wildest dreams, it has a very wide screen, showing three columns:

- **First column:** The list of your email accounts, and the email folders for whichever one you're using now. (There's no unified inbox in Mail for the messages from multiple accounts.)

- **Second column:** The list of messages.

- **Third column:** The actual message body of whatever you've selected in the list.

As you can see in Figure 11-2, though, these columns do various degrees of collapsing or shrinking as the window gets narrower.

But wait, there's More! In the first column, you generally see only three mail folders: Inbox, Sent Items, and Drafts. But then there's More. If you select that link, another new column pops out, offering a list of any subfolders you've created: Urgent, To Do, Long-Term, Cat Videos, or whatever.

Checking Email

If your email account offers "As they arrive" mail checking, then new messages show up on your computer as they arrive, around the clock.

If you have any other kind of account, or if you didn't turn that option on, then Mail checks for new messages automatically on a schedule—every 15, 30, or 60 minutes (see page 411). It also checks for new messages each time you open the Mail program.

Tip: You can also force Mail to check for new messages and send waiting ones on command—by hitting the Sync icon (⟳) at top right. Or, if you have a keyboard, press Ctrl+M.

When new mail arrives, you'll know it. Mail can notify you, complete with a little chime, even when you're working in another app. And, of course, the Mail tile on the Start menu updates itself to show you the latest messages (a rotating display of their senders/subjects/first lines).

A new message is marked with a bold vertical line at its left edge. If you see a tiny ▶ button next to the subject line, it's an indication that Mail is condensing several back-and-forths into a single line, for convenience; see Figure 11-3.

At least in the initial version of Windows 10 Mail, you can't turn this feature off, much to the dismay of people who are confused by the sudden consecutive listing of emails that may, in fact, have been sent weeks apart.

You can flick your finger, or turn the mouse wheel, or two-finger drag on your trackpad, to scroll the message list, if it's long. Select a message to read it in all its formatted glory.

Tip: In the Message pane, Mail shows you the name of the sender ("Casey Robin"). To see the email address for whoever sent the message, hold your finger down on the name or double-click it. A pop-up bubble shows you the underlying email address.

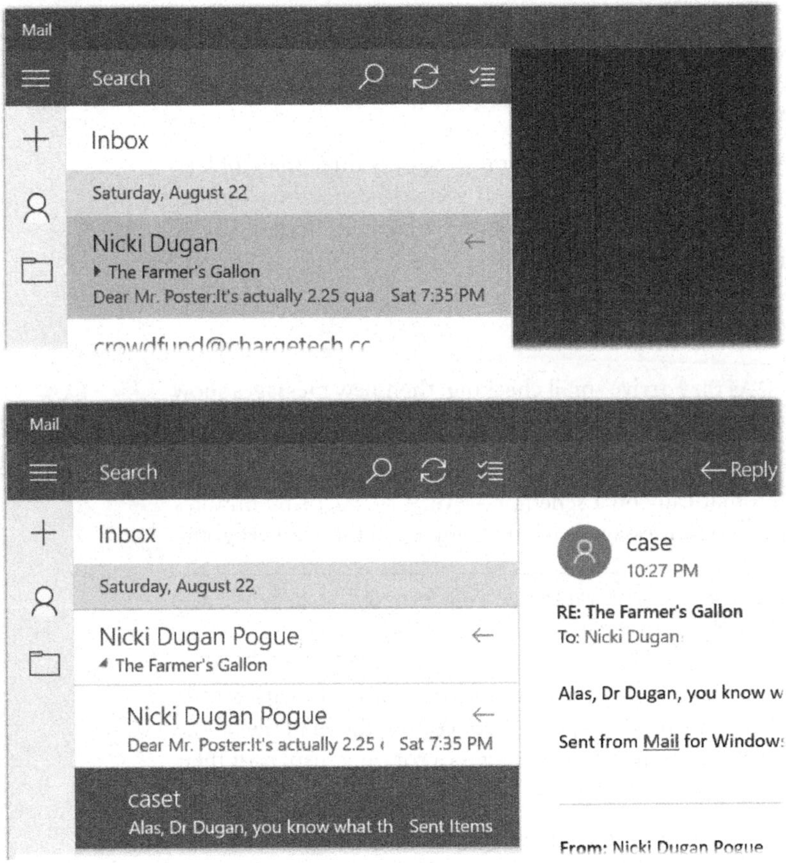

Figure 11-3:
Mail offers message threading, in which back-and-forths on a particular subject appear clumped together in the list. Select the ▶ button next to the Subject line (top) to expand the collected messages (bottom).

What to Do with a Message

Once you've read a message, you can respond to it, delete it, file it, and so on. Here's the drill:

- **Read it.** The type size in email messages can be pretty small. Fortunately, you have some great enlargement tricks at your disposal. For example, on a touchscreen, you can spread two fingers to enlarge the entire email message. Or press Ctrl+plus or Ctrl+minus, just as in a Web browser.

- **Next message.** Once you've had a good look at a message and processed it to your satisfaction, you can move on to the next (or previous) message in the list.

Touchscreen or mouse: Tap or click the message you want in the message list. *Keyboard:* Press the ↑ or ↓ keys.

- **Open an attachment.** You'll know when somebody has attached a file to a message you've received. A paper clip (◍) appears next to the message's name in the message list, and an icon for the attachment appears at the top of the body. Tapping the attachment icon opens it right up.

- **Reply to it.** To answer a message, select the Reply button at the top of the message. If the message was originally addressed to multiple recipients, then "Reply all" sends your reply to everyone simultaneously.

Tip: If you have a keyboard, you can press Ctrl+R for Reply, or Shift+Ctrl+R for Reply All.

A new message window opens, already addressed. As a courtesy to your correspondents, Mail places the original message at the bottom of the window. At this point, you can add or delete recipients, edit the subject line or the original message, and so on. When you're finished, hit Send or press Ctrl+Enter.

- **Forward it.** Instead of replying to the person who sent you a message, you may sometimes want to pass the note on to a third person. To do so, hit Forward at the top of the message (or just press Ctrl+F.) A new message opens, looking a lot like the one that appears when you reply; you're expected to start by filling in the To box. You may wish to precede the original message with a comment of your own, like, "Frank: I thought you'd be interested in this joke about your mom."

- **Delete it.** Hit Delete at the top of the message. (There's no confirmation screen; on the other hand, you can recover the message from the "Deleted items" folder if you change your mind.)

Tip: If you have a touchscreen, you can swipe leftward across the message to delete it. (Some email services call this "Archive" instead.)

- **File it.** Most mail accounts let you create filing folders to help manage your messages. Once you've opened a message that's worth keeping, you can move it into one of those folders.

  To do that, hit the ⋯ button, or right-click the message; from the shortcut menu, choose Move. Mail displays the folder list. Choose the one you want.

  Alternatively, you can drag-and-drop messages into a new folder. (If the folder isn't immediately visible, drag the message onto the word "More" at the bottom of the folder list. When the full folder list appears, continue your drag until you reach the target folder.)

- **Flag it.** Sometimes you'll receive email that prompts you to some sort of action, but you may not have the time (or the fortitude) to face the task at the moment. ("Hi there…it's me, your accountant. Would you mind rounding up your expenses for 1999 through 2011 and sending me a list by email?")

That's why Mail lets you *flag* a message, summoning a little flag icon next to the message's name and giving a color tint to its row in the message list. These indicators can mean anything you like—they simply call attention to certain messages.

To flag a message in this way on a touchscreen, see Figure 11-4. If you have a mouse or trackpad, click the message in the list; the ⚑ icon appears at the right end. Click that icon to flag the message. (To clear the flag, repeat the procedure.)

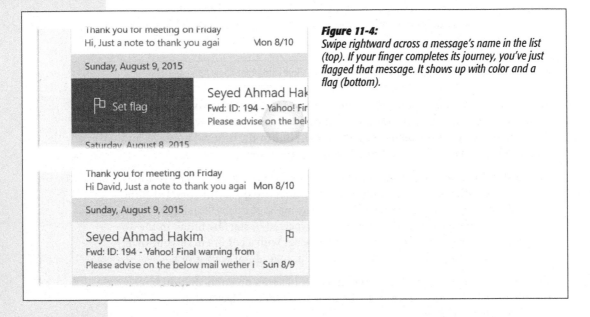

Figure 11-4:
Swipe rightward across a message's name in the list (top). If your finger completes its journey, you've just flagged that message. It shows up with color and a flag (bottom).

- **Mark as unread.** In the inbox, a bold, blue bar marks any message you haven't yet read. Once you've opened the message, the bar goes away. By choosing Mark as Unread, you make the boldface *reappear*. It's a great way to flag a message for later, to call it to your own attention. The boldface can mean not so much "unread" as "un–dealt with."

(This button changes to say "Mark as read" if you want to go the *other* way—to flag an unread message, or a bunch of them, as read; see below.)

To see the "Mark as unread" command, hit the More button at top right (⋯).

Tip: Got a keyboard? Press Ctrl+U for "Mark as unread," Ctrl+Q for "Mark as read."

Filing or Deleting Batches of Messages

You can select a message by clicking or tapping it, of course. But what if you want to file or delete a bunch of messages at once?

To select more than one at a time, so that all remain highlighted, hit the ⊻☰ on the toolbar. Suddenly, checkboxes appear next to all the messages in the list (you can see this effect in Figure 11-5, bottom).

Select the name of each message you want to include; you don't have to tap the checkboxes themselves.

Tip: Once you've made the checkboxes appear, you can work down the list using the arrow keys; press Ctrl+Enter to add the checkmark to each message.

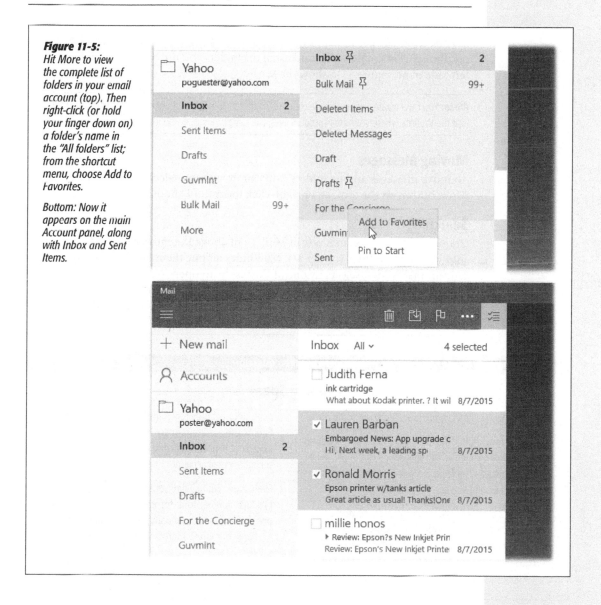

Figure 11-5:
Hit More to view the complete list of folders in your email account (top). Then right-click (or hold your finger down on) a folder's name in the "All folders" list; from the shortcut menu, choose Add to Favorites.

Bottom: Now it appears on the main Account panel, along with Inbox and Sent Items.

You can select as many messages as you like, scrolling as necessary. At that point, you can operate on them all at once—mark them as junk, flag them, delete them, or mark them as read or unread—using the buttons on the App bar.

Message Folders

When you first tiptoe into Mail, you may notice, aghast, that your mail folders—Sent, Deleted, Drafts, Important, Work Stuff, and so on—aren't listed anywhere. Actually, they're there, but the list doesn't appear until you select More in the left-side panel. At that point, the folder list sprouts open (you can see it in Figure 11-5). Click a folder to see what's in it.

It's not especially convenient to have to open and close this pull-out drawer of folders, though. Fortunately, you can install the folders you use most often right onto the left-side pane; Figure 11-5 shows how.

Note: You can't create, rename, or delete email folders in Mail (at least not in the first version). To do that, visit the Website where your email account lives, like Gmail, Yahoo, or Outlook.com.

Moving Messages

To move messages among folders, you can drag them, select them and then use the Move button on the toolbar, or right-click them (and choose Move).

Searching

Praise be—there's a search box in Mail, right above the message list. After you type into it and press Enter (or tap 🔎), Mail hides all but the matching messages in the current mail folder; select any one of the results to open it.

Tip: Using the pop-up menu above the search box, you can specify that you want to search either the current folder only—or all folders.

FREQUENTLY ASKED QUESTION

Canning Spam

Help! I'm awash in junk email! How do I get out of this mess?

Spam is a much-hated form of advertising that involves sending unsolicited emails to thousands of people. While there's no instant cure for spam, you can take certain steps to protect yourself from it.

1. Above all, *never post your main email address online, ever.* Use a different, dedicated email account for online shopping, Web site and software registration, and comment posting. Spammers have automated software robots that scour every Web page, automatically recording email addresses they find. These are the primary sources of spam, so at least you're now restricting the junk mail to one secondary mail account.

2. Even then, when filling out forms or registering products online, look for checkboxes requesting permission for the company to send you email or to share your email address with its "partners." Just say no.

3. Buy an antispam program like SpamAssassin.

Select any message in the list to read it. When you're finished, tap the × above the message list. Your full list is restored, and the search adventure is complete.

Writing Messages

To compose a new piece of outgoing mail, use the "New mail" (+) button in the top-left corner. A blank new outgoing message appears (see Figure 11-6).

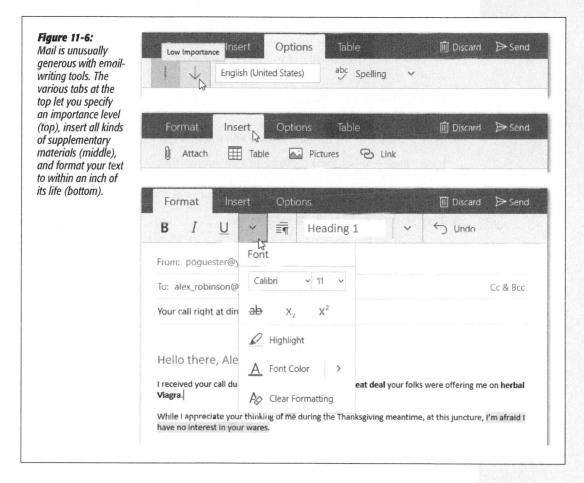

Figure 11-6:
Mail is unusually generous with email-writing tools. The various tabs at the top let you specify an importance level (top), insert all kinds of supplementary materials (middle), and format your text to within an inch of its life (bottom).

Here's how you go about writing a message:

1. In the "To:" field, type the recipient's email address—or grab it from People.

Often, you won't have to type much more than the first couple of letters of the name or email address. As you type, Mail displays all matching names and addresses so you can choose one from the list instead of typing.

You can add as many addressees as you like; just repeat the procedure.

2. **To send a copy to other recipients, hit "Cc & Bcc" to reveal the "Cc:" or "Bcc:" boxes. Then enter the address(es).**

   Cc stands for *carbon copy*. Getting an email message where your name is in the Cc line implies: "I sent you a copy because I thought you'd want to know about this correspondence, but I'm not expecting you to reply."

   "Bcc:" stands for *blind* carbon copy. It's a copy that goes to a third party secretly—the primary addressee never knows who else received it. For example, if you send your coworker a message that says, "Chris, it bothers me that you've been cheating the customers," you could Bcc your supervisor to clue her in without getting into trouble with Chris.

   Each of these lines behaves exactly like the "To:" line. You fill each one up with email addresses in the same way.

3. **Type the topic of the message in the "Add a subject" box.**

   It's courteous to put some thought into the subject line. (Use "Change in plans for next week," for instance, instead of "Yo.") Leaving it blank only annoys your recipient. On the other hand, don't put the *entire* message into the subject line, either.

4. **Type your message in the message area.**

   All the usual keyboard tricks apply (Chapter 3). Don't forget that you can use Copy and Paste, within Mail or from other programs. Both text and graphics can appear in your message.

   A wealth of formatting awaits on the Format bar (Figure 11-6). There are your font and style controls, plus options to create bulleted or numbered lists, indent paragraphs, add space before or after paragraphs, or even choose various canned styles (headings, emphasis, book titles, and so on).

4. **Attach a file, if you like.**

   On the Insert tab, the Attach button opens the standard Open File dialog box. Tap the file you want to send, and then choose Open. You return to your message in progress, with the files neatly inserted as icons.

   Here on the Insert tab, you can also insert a Table; a toolbar appears, with controls to format and adjust its rows and columns.

   There's a Pictures button, too; choose a photo from your computer to insert into the message, whereupon a formatting toolbar appears with buttons for Rotate, Crop, Size, and so on. (Drag the round white dots to resize the photo, or the top center icon to rotate it.)

   Finally, there's a Link button, which lets you insert a link to a Web address.

Tip: A visit to the Options tab is an optional step. Here, you can establish a Priority setting for the messages you're about to send; in Mail, you have only two choices—High and Low Importance. Tap the arrow button to flip between the two. The good part about this system is that it lets your recipient see that an email you've sent is, for example, urgent. The bad part is that not every email program displays the priority of email—and even if your recipient's email program *does* display your message's priority, there's no guarantee that it'll make him respond any faster.

The Options tab also includes an option to check your spelling and hide any proofing marks that may have wound up in your message (for example if it's copied in from Word).

4. **To send the message, hit Send, or press Ctrl+Enter. Or hit Discard to back out of it.**

   If you choose Discard, the message lands in your Drafts folder. Later, you can open the Drafts folder, tap the aborted message, finish it up, and send it. (Or delete it from there; Mail doesn't care.)

Account Options

Each email account you set up offers some useful options that are worth a visit. They're hiding in two different places.

To see them, hit Settings (⚙). On the Settings screen (Figure 11-7, top), you can choose either Accounts or Options. Here's what awaits.

Accounts

On this screen, you see a simple list of whatever email accounts you've set up: Gmail, Outlook, iCloud, or whatever. Choose the one you want to open its settings box.

The settings available for each account type are different. But "Change mailbox sync settings" is always available.

Here's where you find settings like these:

• **Download new mail.** How often do you want Mail to check for new messages? Usually, "As items arrive" is what you want. Some account types offer only "Every 15 minutes," "Every 30 minutes," and so on.

   (If you choose Manual, then Mail never checks unless you hit the Sync button.)

• **Always download full message and Internet images.** Spammers, the vile undercrust of low-life society, have a famous trick. When they send you email that includes a picture, they don't actually paste the picture into the message. Instead, they include a "bug"—a piece of code that instructs your email program to *fetch* the missing graphic from the Internet. Why? Because that gives the spammer the ability to track who has actually opened the junk mail, making their email addresses much more valuable for reselling to other spammers.

That's a long explanation for a simple feature: If you turn this option off, then Mail does not fetch "bug" image files at all. You're not flagged as a sucker by the spammers. You'll see empty squares in the email where the images ought to be. The actual pictures don't appear until you manually select the "Download all images in this message" link.

Note: Graphics sent by normal people and legitimate companies are generally pasted right into the email, so they'll still show up just fine.

- **Download email from.** How far back do you want your mail collection collected? (If you have a limited-storage device like a phone or tablet, you might not want your whole lifetime of mail stored on it. "The last 3 months" might be a good choice.)

- **Your name.** Whatever name you type here is what will show up in other people's inboxes when you write to them.

- **Sync options.** Some services, like Google and corporate Exchange servers, offer more than email; they also maintain online calendars and address books. Turn on the data types you want to display: Email, Contacts, and/or Calendar.

Note: Of course, Mail displays only email. If you turn on Contacts and Calendar for one of your accounts, then your lists of names and appointments show up elsewhere in Windows—namely, in the People and Calendar apps. Handily enough, Mail includes a Calendar button at lower left, for easy app hopping.

If you have a Microsoft account, such as a Live.com or Outlook.com account, then the Mail Account settings page offers another link: "Change account settings." It takes you into your Web browser, to a Web page that lets you manage your name, password, payment details, and so on.

Options

The main Settings panel also offers this enticing option: Options (Figure 11-7, right). Note that these, too, are account-specific; that is, you can set them up independently for each of your email accounts. Here's what you'll find:

Swipe actions

Swipe actions, a new feature in Windows 10 that's based on typical smartphone mail apps, let you operate on a message in the list by dragging your finger right or left across it. When you first use Mail on a touchscreen computer, swiping to the *right* across a message in the list marks the messages as flagged (page 405), and to the *left* archives it (moves it out of the Inbox and into the Archived folder).

But on this panel, you can redefine what that right swipe and left swipe do (or turn off the "Swipe actions" feature entirely). Your choices for swiping each direction include "Set flag/Clear flag," "Mark as read/Unread," Archive, Delete, or Move.

You might set things up so that a left swipe deletes a message and a right swipe moves it to a new folder, for example.

Signature

A *signature* is a bit of text that gets stamped at the bottom of your outgoing email messages. It can be your name, a postal address, or a pithy quote. Here's where you enter the signature you want to use for outgoing messages from this account. (Also turn on "Use an email signature," of course.)

Automatic replies

Not all email services offer this option; but if you have a Microsoft service, like Outlook or Exchange, you might get a kick out of it. You're supposed to use this option for

Figure 11-7:
Not everything on the Settings panel is, in fact, a panel of settings. (Trust Center, Feedback, and About just wound up here because they had nowhere else to go.)

But the Reading and Options panes, in particular, are worth your attention.

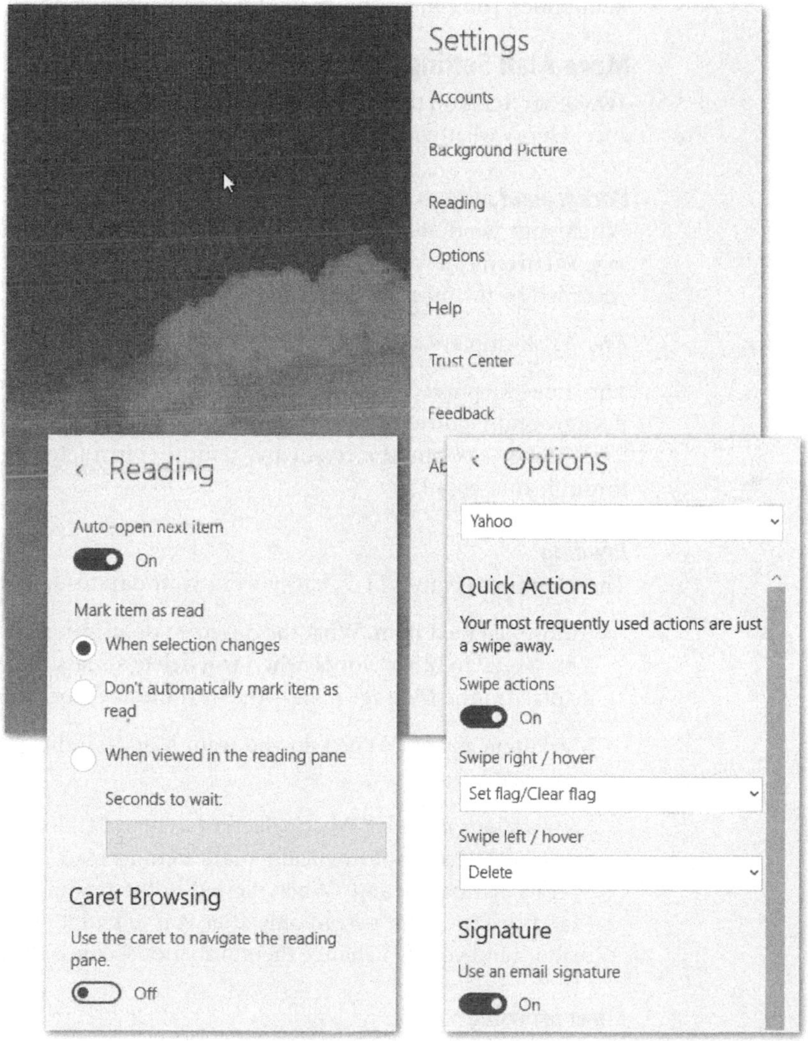

out-of-office automatic responses like, "I'm away on vacation until Monday, August 28." Turn this on when you leave, and specify the canned message.

Of course, then you run the risk of sending these auto-replies to *every* incoming message, including newsletters you've signed up for (and spam you haven't). That's why "Send replies only to my contacts" is usually worth turning on, too.

Notifications

Do you want Windows to let you know when new mail arrives from this account? If so, turn on "Show in action center," and then specify how you want to be notified. You can choose to "Play a sound," "Show a notification banner (page 111)," or both. Remember, you can set things up differently for each email account.

More Mail Settings

Two other items on the Settings panel affect other tweaky aspects of your Mail experience. Here's what you've got.

Background picture

When your window is wide enough to permit the three-column view, and no message is currently selected, what is Windows supposed to display in the area usually occupied by the message body?

Answer: It displays a photo.

The blue-sky photo that comes with Mail is nice (Figure 11-7, top), but using the Background Picture/Browse button, you can choose a photo of your own to install here. Maybe a photo of a couch and remote control, to suggest a reward for getting through your email.

Reading

These options (Figure 11-7, left) govern your day-to-day mail-reading experience:

- **Auto-open next item.** What the onscreen description leaves out is, "when I delete a message." In other words, when you delete a message, what do you want to take its place in the Message pane—the next message, or your background photo?

- **Mark item as read.** When do you want Mail to indicate that you've actually read a message?

  Your options include "When selection changes" (that is, when you choose another message); "Don't automatically mark item as read" (that is, you have to mark it as read manually); and "When viewed in the reading pane." That last one makes Mail flag a message as read only after you've had it open long enough to actually read it (and you can change the number of seconds that implies).

Caret browsing

Caret browsing isn't something you'd ever want to turn off. But this option must mean something to someone. See page 384.

CHAPTER 12

Security & Privacy

I f it weren't for that darned Internet, personal computing would be a lot of fun. After all, it's the Internet that lets all those socially stunted hackers enter our machines, unleashing their viruses, setting up remote hacking tools, feeding us spyware, trying to trick us out of our credit card numbers, and otherwise making our lives an endless troubleshooting session. It sure would be nice if they'd cultivate some other hobbies.

In the meantime, these lowlifes are doing astronomical damage to businesses and individuals around the world—along the lines of $100 billion a year (the cost to fight viruses, spyware, and spam).

In the days of Windows XP, these sorts of Internet attacks were far more common. Microsoft left open a number of back doors that were intended for convenience (for example, to let system administrators communicate with your PC from across the network) but wound up being exploited by hackers.

Microsoft wrote Windows Vista—and later Windows 7, 8, and 10—for a lot of reasons: to give Windows a cosmetic makeover, to give it up-to-date music and video features, to overhaul its networking plumbing—and, of course, to make money. But Job Number One was making Windows more secure. Evil strangers will still make every attempt to make your life miserable, but one thing is for sure: They'll have a much, much harder time of it.

Note: Most of Windows' self-protection features have to do with *Internet* threats—because, in fact, virtually all the infectious unpleasantness that can befall a PC these days comes from the Internet. A PC that never goes online probably won't get infected. So this chapter covers many features of Windows 10's browser, Edge (covered in more detail in Chapter 10).

Lots of Windows' security improvements are invisible to you. They're deep in the plumbing, with no buttons or controls to show you. If you're scoring at home, they include features with names like application isolation, service hardening, Protected Mode, Network Access Protection, PatchGuard, Data Execution Prevention, Code Integrity, and, of course, everybody's favorite, Address Space Layout Randomization. They're all technical barricades that stand between the bad guys and your PC.

The rest of this chapter describes features that *aren't* invisible and automatic—the ones you can control.

Note: And does it work? Do all these tools and patches actually reduce the number of virus and spyware outbreaks?

Apparently, yes. The years of annual front-page headlines about national virus outbreaks—called things like Melissa (1999), Blaster (2003), and Sasser (2004)—seem to be over. There will always be clever new attacks—but they'll be much less frequent and much harder to write.

Note, however, that built-in security tools can't do the whole job of keeping your PC safe; you play a role, too. So heed these tips before you or your family go online:

- **Don't trust a pretty face.** It doesn't take much expertise to build a snazzy-looking Web site. Just because a Web site *looks* trustworthy doesn't mean you can trust it. If you're visiting a little-known Web site, be careful what you do there.

- **Don't download from sites you don't know.** The Web is full of free software offers. But that free software may, in fact, be spyware or other *malware*. (Malware is a general term for viruses, spyware, and other Bad Software.) So be very careful when downloading anything online. Especially those free movies and songs.

- **Don't click pop-up ads.** Pop-up ads are more than mere annoyances; some of them, when clicked, download spyware to your PC.

With all that said, you're ready to find out how to keep yourself safe when you go online.

UP TO SPEED

Is It Spyware or Adware?

Spyware has a less-malignant cousin called *adware*, and the line between the two types is exceedingly thin.

Adware is free software that displays ads). In order to target those ads to your interests, it may transmit reports on your surfing habits to its authors. (Windows Defender doesn't protect against adware.)

So what's the difference between adware and spyware? If it performs malicious actions, like incapacitating your PC with pop-ups, it's spyware for sure. Adware, while annoying and disruptive, just displays ads.

Proponents of adware say, "Hey—we've gotta put bread on our tables, too! Those ads are how you pay for your free software. Our software doesn't identify you personally when it reports on your surfing habits, so it's not really spyware."

But other people insist that any software that reports on your activities is spyware, no matter what.

Windows Defender

It's historic. It's amazing. After all these decades, Microsoft finally built free antivirus software right into Windows. Thanks to Defender, you have no more excuses not to protect your PC.

Important: Most new PCs come with aggressive trial versions of commercial antivirus programs like Norton and McAfee—programs that require an annual fee forever. *You don't need them.* Windows Defender does a perfectly good job, and you already have it.

But to pacify the Nortons and McAfees of the world, Microsoft agreed to let PC companies ship new PCs with *Defender turned off.* So if you want Defender to defend you, you should (a) uninstall the Norton or McAfee trial version so it'll quit bugging you, and then promptly (b) turn Defender *on.* To do that, open Windows Defender as shown below; you'll see the big, red "Turn on" button staring you in the face on the Home tab.

Defender protects you from both major kinds of malware (software you don't know you have): viruses and spyware. You usually get it in one of two ways. First, a Web site may try to trick you into downloading it. You see what looks like an innocent button in what's actually a phony Windows dialog box, or maybe you get an empty dialog box—and clicking the Close button actually triggers the installation.

Second, you may get spyware or viruses by downloading a program you *do* want— "cracked" software (commercial programs whose copy protection has been removed) is a classic example—without realizing that a secret program is piggybacking on the download.

Once installed, the malware may make changes to important system files, install ads on your desktop, or send information about your surfing habits to a Web site that blitzes your PC with pop-up ads related in some way to your online behavior.

Spyware can do things like hijacking your home page or search page so that every time you open your browser, you wind up at a Web page that incapacitates your PC with a blizzard of pop-ups. *Keylogger* spyware can record your keystrokes, passwords and all, and send them to a snooper.

To open Defender, open Settings→"Update & security"→Windows Defender. At the bottom of that screen, hit "Use Windows Defender." You arrive at the screen shown in Figure 12-1, where you'll see that Defender has two functions: real-time scanning and on-demand scanning.

Real-Time Protection

Defender watches over your PC constantly, as a barrier against new infections of viruses and spyware. Each day, the program auto-downloads new *definitions files*—behind-the-scenes updates to its virus database, which keep it up to date with the latest new viruses that Microsoft has spotted in the wild.

Note: The Update tab shows you what definitions database you've got and offers a big fat Update button to download the latest one right now.

If it recognizes a virus or a piece of spyware on your PC, Defender generally zaps it automatically. Occasionally, it asks if you want to allow the questionable software to keep working, or instead remove it.

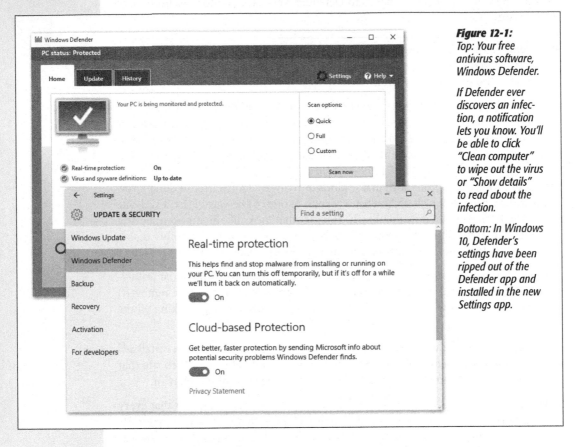

Figure 12-1:
Top: Your free antivirus software, Windows Defender.

If Defender ever discovers an infection, a notification lets you know. You'll be able to click "Clean computer" to wipe out the virus or "Show details" to read about the infection.

Bottom: In Windows 10, Defender's settings have been ripped out of the Defender app and installed in the new Settings app.

On-Demand Scanning

Defender also has a scanning function that's designed to clean out infections you already have (a feature that, thank heaven, you'll rarely need).

Ordinarily, the program scans your PC continuously. But if you're feeling a little antsy, you can also trigger a scan manually.

To do that, on the Home tab, specify what you want it to check out for you:

- **Quick.** Scans the most vulnerable parts of your system software, in an effort to save time.

- **Full.** A full scan of everything on your hard drive. As you'd guess, this can take a long time.

- **Custom.** This feature lets you scan one particular disk, folder, or file—something you just got as an email attachment, for example. When you click Custom and then "Scan now," you're shown a checkbox hierarchy of your entire computer. Expand the disks and folders until you can turn on the exact items you want scanned; then click OK to start the scan.

Tip: Similarly, you can exclude certain disks, folders, kinds of files, or open programs from the usual automated scanning—to shut Defender up, for example, when it keeps complaining about a certain item that you know is pristine. Click Settings to open the Settings app (Figure 12-1), which is where Defender's controls are now. Scroll down, click "Add an exclusion," and specify what you want omitted.

When Defender Strikes

When Defender finds spyware, it puts the offending software into a quarantined area where it can't do any more harm. On the History tab, you can see the quarantined software, delete it, or restore it (take it out of quarantine). In general, restoring spyware and viruses is a foolhardy move.

Here's what you see on the History tab:

- **Quarantined items.** Click this button and then "View details." You see each program Defender has taken action on, the alert level, and the date. You can use "Remove all" if you don't recognize any of it, or you can select just one, or a few, and then click Remove or Restore. (Restore means "It's fine. Put it back and let me run it.")

- **Allowed items.** If Defender announces that it's found a potential piece of malware, but you allow it to run anyway, it's considered an allowed item. From now on, Defender ignores it, meaning that you trust that program completely. Allowed programs' names appear when you click this button and then click "View details."

    If you highlight a program's name and then click Remove From List, it's *gone* from the Allowed list, and therefore Defender monitors it once again.

Now, Defender is certainly not the only antivirus program on the planet; it's not even the best one.

Several rival antivirus programs are free for personal use, like Avast (*www.avast.com*). These do have their downsides—some nag you to buy the Pro versions, for example, and there's nobody to call for tech support.

In any case, the bottom line is this: If your PC doesn't have antivirus software working for you right now, then getting some should be at the top of your to-do list.

Note: Get antivirus software written especially for Windows 10. Antivirus software from the old days won't work.

Action Center

One of the biggest annoyances in Windows of old was the nagginess. Windows was constantly bugging you, sending up balloons, popping up "Attention!" boxes, demanding your name and password at every turn. It's great that Microsoft tightened up security, but come on; it was like living with a needy 5-year-old.

Today, Windows harangues you much less. In fact, many not-that-urgent, security-related nags don't interrupt your work at all; instead, they quietly collect themselves into the Action Center (page 113): messages related to antivirus software, antispyware software, Windows Update settings, Internet security settings, your firewall software, and your backup settings.

You can poke in there from time to time to have a look.

Windows Firewall

If you have a broadband, always-on connection, you're connected to the Internet 24 hours a day. It's theoretically possible for some cretin to use automated hacking software to flood you with files or to take control of your machine. Fortunately, the Windows *Firewall* feature puts up a barrier to such mischief.

The firewall acts as a gatekeeper between you and the Internet. It examines all Internet traffic and lets through only communications that it knows are safe; all other traffic is turned away at the door.

How It Works

Every kind of electronic message sent to or from your PC—instant messaging, music sharing, file sharing, and so on—conducts its business on a specific communications channel, or *port*. Ports are numbered tunnels for certain kinds of Internet traffic.

The problem with Windows before Vista came along was that Microsoft left all your ports *open* for your convenience—and, as it turns out, for the bad guys'. Starting with Vista, all the ports on a new Windows PC arrive *closed*.

The firewall blocks or permits signals based on a predefined set of rules. They dictate, for example, which programs are permitted to use your network connection or which ports can be used for communications.

You don't need to do anything to turn on the Windows Firewall. When you turn on Windows, it's already at work. But you *can* turn the firewall off.

To do that, or to fiddle with any of its settings, there are plenty of ways to find it. It's an icon in the Control Panel, for example. Or you can find it from a search; type *firewall*. Select Windows Firewall in the results list.

As you can see in Figure 12-2, the Firewall screen is a close cousin to a space shuttle cockpit.

Tip: It's perfectly OK to use both the Windows Firewall and another company's firewall software–a first for Windows. If you're a supergeek, you can assign each to handle different technical firewall functions.

Firewall Settings

To see the ways you can adjust the Windows Firewall, click "Turn Windows Firewall on or off" in the left-side panel.

The resulting screen lets you tweak the settings for each location (Public, Private, and—if you're at a corporation—Domain) independently. You have these options:

- **Block all incoming connections, including those in the list of allowed apps.** When you're feeling especially creeped out by the threat of hackerishness—like when you're at the coffee shop of your local computer-science grad school—turn on this box. Now your computer is pretty much completely shut off from the Internet except for Web browsing, email, and instant messaging.

- **Notify me when Windows Firewall blocks a new app.** Windows will pop up a message that lets you know when a new program has attempted to get online, on the off chance that it's some evil app. Most of the time, of course, it's some perfectly innocent program that you happen to be using for the first time; just click Allow in the box and go on with your life.

Note: If you really are on a domain (Chapter 21), then you may not be allowed to make any changes to the firewall settings, because that's something the network nerds like to be in charge of.

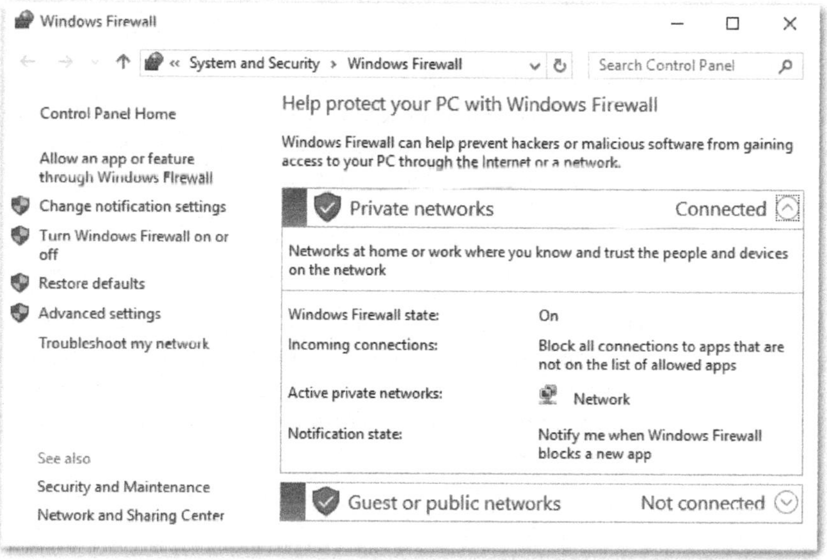

Figure 12-2:
The Windows Firewall window is basically a dashboard that tells you if your firewall is turned on, the name of your network, and what the settings are for each kind of network location– Domain (Work), Private, or Public. See page 603 for details on these network types.

- **Turn off Windows Firewall.** Yes, you can turn the firewall off entirely. There's very little reason to do that, though, even if you decide to install another company's firewall; its installer turns off the Windows Firewall if necessary.

You also might be tempted to turn off the firewall because you have a *router* that distributes your Internet signal through the house—and most routers have *hardware* firewalls built right in, protecting your entire network.

Still, there's no harm in having *both* a hardware and a software firewall in place. In fact, having the Windows Firewall turned on protects you from viruses you catch from other people on your own network (even though you're both "behind" the router's firewall). And if you have a laptop, this way you won't have to remember to turn the firewall on when you leave your home network.

Punching Through the Firewall

The firewall isn't always your friend. It can occasionally block a perfectly harmless program from communicating with the outside world—a chat program or a game that you can play across the Internet, for example.

Fortunately, whenever that happens, Windows lets you know with a message that says, "Windows Firewall has blocked some features of this program." Most of the time, you know exactly what program it's talking about, because it's a program you just opened *yourself*—a program you installed that might legitimately need Internet access. In other words, it's not some rogue spyware on your machine trying to talk to the mother ship. Click "Allow access" and get on with your life.

Alternatively, you can set up permissions for your apps in advance. At the left side of the firewall screen shown in Figure 12-2, click "Allow an app or feature through Windows Firewall." Then click "Change settings," and proceed as shown in Figure 12-3.

Advanced Firewall

The Windows Firewall screen gives you a good deal of control over how Windows Firewall works. But it doesn't offer nearly the amount of tweakiness that high-end geeks demand, like control over individual ports, IP addresses, programs, and so on. It also offers no way to create a log (a text-file record) of all attempts to contact your PC from the network or the Internet, which can be handy when you suspect that some nasty hacker has been visiting you in the middle of the night.

There is, however, an even more powerful firewall control panel. In an effort to avoid terrifying novices, Microsoft has hidden it, but if you're confident in your technical abilities, it's easy enough to open. It's called the Windows Firewall with Advanced Security. You get there by clicking "Advanced settings" at the left side of the Windows Firewall window.

In the resulting box, you can open a port for some app that needs access. Suppose, for example, some game needs a particular port to be opened in the firewall. Click Inbound Rules to see all the individual "rules" you've established. In the right-side pane, click New Rule. A wizard opens; it walks you through specifying the program and the port you want to open for it.

Then again, if you're really that much of an Advanced Security sort of person, you can find Microsoft's old-but-good guide for this console at *http://bit.ly/hxR0i*.

Figure 12-3:
Here you can specify when each program is allowed to connect to the Internet—independently for each kind of network you might be on (using the Private or Public checkboxes at far right). Turning off the checkbox at far left blocks the program completely. Click "Allow another app" to add a new program to this list so it won't bug you the first time you run it.

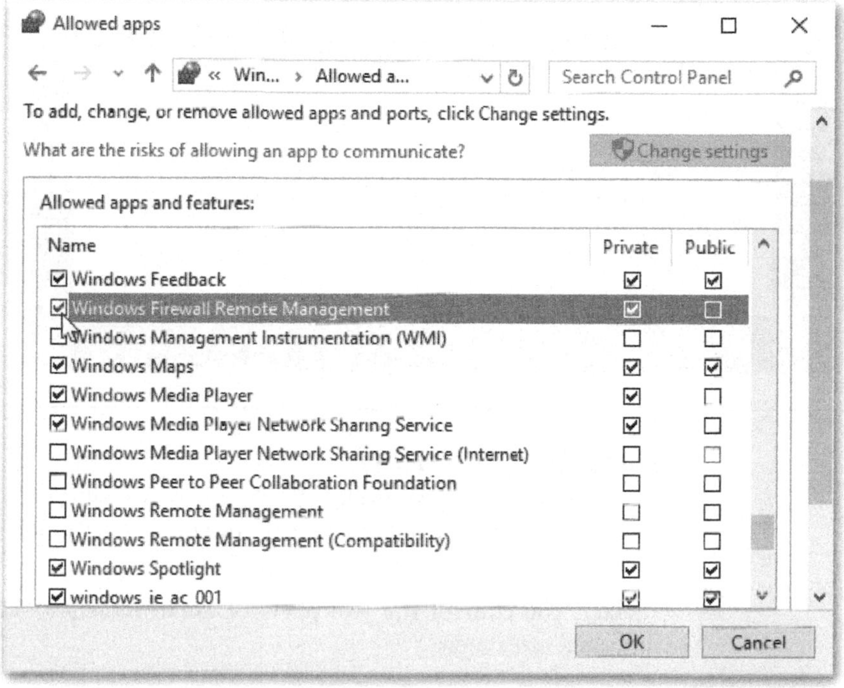

Windows SmartScreen

SmartScreen is an anti-phishing technology (see the box on the next page). If you try to visit a Web site that Microsoft knows is suspicious, it blocks your path with a warning banner (Figure 12-4).

In that situation, close the page, click "Close this tab," or go to another site. (If you know full well what trouble you're getting yourself into, and you really want to proceed, then click "More information" and then "Disregard and continue"; you'll go through to the phony site.)

SmartScreen also warns you when you try to open a downloaded *program* that might be fishy. One day, when you least expect it, you'll get a pop-up warning.

SmartScreen works by comparing the file's original Web site address against a massive list of Web sites and file downloads that have been reported to Microsoft as unsafe. If it blocks the program you're trying to open, just click "More information" and then (if you're sure it's OK) "Run anyway."

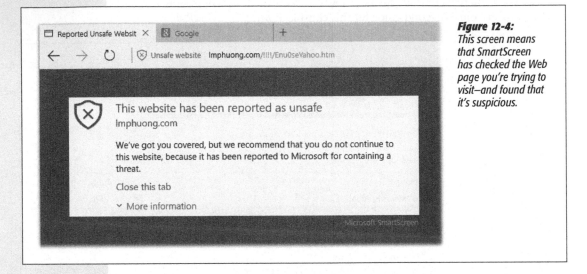

Figure 12-4:
This screen means that SmartScreen has checked the Web page you're trying to visit—and found that it's suspicious.

Phine-Tuning the Philter

There's not much to controlling SmartScreen; basically, you can turn it on or off. (And by golly, you should check right now; on many PCs, it comes from the factory turned off.)

In fact, you control the two parts of SmartScreen—Web blocking and app blocking—separately.

SmartScreen Web settings

In the Edge browser, click the ⋯ button (upper right), and then Settings. Scroll down to "View advanced settings." Scroll down and turn off "Help protect me from malicious sites and downloads with SmartScreen Filter."

UP TO SPEED

Phishing 101

What's phishing? That's when you're sent what appears to be legitimate email from a bank, eBay, PayPal, or some other financial Web site. The message tells you the site needs to confirm your account information, or warns that your account has been hacked and needs you to help keep it safe.

If you, responsible citizen that you are, click the provided link to clear up the supposed problem, you wind up on what looks like the bank/eBay/PayPal Web site. But it's a fake, carefully designed to look like the real thing; it's run by a scammer. If you type in your password and login information, as requested, then the next thing you know, you're getting credit-card bills for $10,000 charges at high-rolling Las Vegas hotels—the scammer has collected your login information. The fake sites look so much like the real ones that it can be extremely difficult to tell them apart.

SmartScreen app settings

In the taskbar search box, type enough of *smartscreen* until you can choose "Change SmartScreen settings" in the results. When the Control Panel opens, choose "Change Windows SmartScreen settings."

In the new dialog box, you have three options:

- **Get administrator approval before running an unrecognized app from the Internet.** In other words, you'll have to enter an administrator's password (page 580) before you can bypass the warning and open the fishy app.

- **Warn before running an unrecognized app, but don't require administrator approval.** Even your minions, those with standard accounts, can bypass the warning.

- **Don't do anything (turn off Windows SmartScreen).** You're flying without a net now, pal.

And why would you ever want to turn this feature off? Because maybe you're a privacy nut. SmartScreen works by sending the Web address of each page you visit, and the details of each program you download, back to Microsoft, where they're compared against the lists of evil sites and apps. It's all transmitted in encrypted form, and none of it, according to Microsoft, is stored anywhere. And no information associated with the site is sent, like search terms you've used, information you've entered into forms, or cookies.

Still. If that transmitting business creeps you out, you can turn the whole thing off.

Privacy and Cookies

Cookies are something like Web-page preference files. Certain Web sites—particularly commercial ones like Amazon.com—deposit them on your hard drive like little

---

FREQUENTLY ASKED QUESTION

Sherlock Edge

How does the Edge browser know what's a phishing site and what's not?

Edge uses three bits of information to figure out whether a site is legitimate or a phishing site.

Its first line of defense is a Microsoft-compiled, frequently updated database of known phishing sites that, believe it or not, sits right on your own hard drive. Whenever you head to a Web site, Edge consults that database. If the Web site appears in the list, you get a warning. (The database is compiled from several phish-tracking companies, including

Cyota, Internet Identity, and MarkMonitor, as well as from direct feedback.)

Second, Edge uses *heuristics,* a sort of low-level artificial intelligence. It compares characteristics of the site you're visiting against common phishing-site characteristics. The heuristics tool helps Edge recognize phishing sites that haven't yet made it into the database of known sites.

Finally, Edge quietly sends addresses of some of the sites you visit to Microsoft, which checks it against a frequently updated list of reported phishing sites (not the database on your PC).

---

bookmarks so they'll remember you the next time you visit. On Amazon, in fact, a greeting says, "Hello, Casey" (or whatever your name is), thanks to the cookie it uses to recognize you.

Most cookies are perfectly innocuous—and, in fact, are extremely helpful. They can let your PC log into a site automatically or let you customize what the site looks like and how you use it.

But fear is on the march, and the media fan the flames with tales of sinister cookies that track your movement on the Web. Some Web sites rely on cookies to record which pages you visit on a site, how long you spend on a site, what kind of information you like to find out, and so on.

If you're worried about invasions of privacy—and you're willing to trade away some of the conveniences of cookies—Edge is ready to protect you.

Cookie Options

In the Edge browser, click the ··· button (upper right), and then Settings. Scroll down to "View advanced settings." Scroll down to the Cookies pop-up menu. It offers three choices:

- **Block all cookies.** No cookies, no exceptions. Web sites can't read existing cookies, either.

- **Block only third-party cookies.** A first-party cookie is created by the site you're currently visiting. (These kinds of cookies generally aren't privacy invaders; they're the Amazon type described above, designed to log you in.)

  Third-party cookies, though, are deposited on your hard drive by a site other than the one you're currently visiting—often by an advertiser. Needless to say, this kind of cookie is more objectionable. It can track your browsing habits and create profiles about your interests and behaviors.

- **Don't block cookies.** All cookies are OK. Web sites can read existing cookies.

Choose the setting you want. You're ready to start browsing.

Note: Some sites don't function well (or at all) if you choose to reject all cookies. So if you choose "Block all cookies," and you run into trouble browsing your favorite sites, then return here and change the setting to "Block only third-party cookies."

History: Erasing Your Tracks

You'd be shocked to see the kinds of information your browser stores about you. Behind the scenes, it logs every Web site you ever visit. It stashes your cookies, of course, plus passwords and information you type into Web forms (your name and address, for example). Your hard drive also keeps cache files—graphics and text files that make up the Web pages themselves, stored to speed up their reappearance if you visit those sites again.

But the most visible tracks you leave when you surf the Web are on the History list. It's a menu, right there for anyone to see, that lists every Web site you've visited recently. In the Edge browser, you can view the History list by clicking the ☰ and then the ↻ tab. (Or just press Ctrl+H.)

Some people find that record-keeping unnerving. So:

- To delete just one particularly incriminating History listing, click the ✕ to its right.

  To delete your entire history from one day (or week), click the ✕ to *its* right.

  Actually, you can delete any of the history "folders" here—like Yesterday, Last Week, or Older—the same way.

- To erase the entire History menu, hit "Clear all history" at the top.

This is good information to know; after all, you might be nominated to the Supreme Court someday.

The Pop-Up Blocker

The ad banners at the top of every Web page are annoying enough—but nowadays, they're just the beginning. The world's smarmiest advertisers have begun inundating us with *pop-up* and *pop-under* ads: nasty little windows that appear in front of the browser window or, worse, behind it, waiting to jump out the moment you close your browser. They're often deceptive, masquerading as error messages or dialog boxes… and they'll do absolutely anything to get you to click inside them.

Pop-ups are more than just annoying; they're also potentially dangerous. They're a favorite trick that hackers use to deposit spyware on your PC. Clicking a pop-up can begin the silent downloading process. That's true even if the pop-up seems to serve a legitimate purpose—asking you to participate in a survey, for example.

Edge, fortunately, has a pop-up *blocker*. It comes automatically turned on; you don't have to do anything. You'll be browsing along, and then one day you'll see the "Pop-up blocked" message (Figure 12-5).

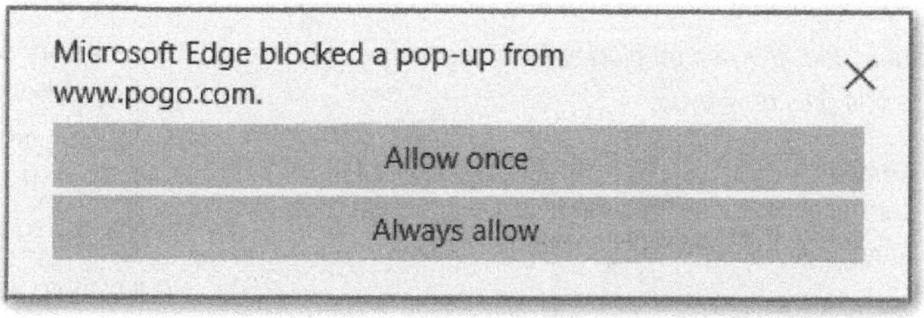

Figure 12-5:
Edge has just spared you from the spawn: a pop-up window that you haven't asked for.

Microsoft Edge blocked a pop-up from www.pogo.com.

Allow once

Always allow

Note that Edge blocks only pop-ups that are spawned *automatically,* not those that appear when you click something (like a seating diagram on a concert-tickets site). And it doesn't block pop-ups from your local network.

Overriding the Pop-Up Block

Sometimes, though, you *want* to see the pop-up. Some sites, for example, use pop-up windows as a way to deliver information—showing you a seating chart when you're buying plane tickets, for example.

In those situations, click one of the two buttons:

- **Allow once** lets this Web site's pop-ups through just for this browsing session. Next time, pop-ups will be blocked again.

- **Always allow** does what it says; pop-ups from this site will always appear.

Turning Off the Pop-Up Blocker

Many Internauts are partial to other companies' pop-up blockers, like AdBlock Plus or Pop Up Blocker. In that case, you'll want to turn off Edge's version.

To do that in the Edge browser, click the ⋯ button (upper right), and then Settings. Scroll down to "View advanced settings." Turn off "Block pop-ups."

InPrivate Browsing

If not everything you do on the Web is something you want your spouse/parents/boss/teacher to know about, then Microsoft has heard you.

History entries aren't the only tracks you leave as you browse the Web. Your hard drive collects cookies and temporary files; Edge collects passwords and other stuff you type into boxes; the address bar memorizes addresses you type so you'll have AutoFill working for you later; and so on.

A feature called InPrivate browsing lets you surf wherever you like within a single browser window. Then, when you close that window, all that stuff is wiped out. No History items, no cookies, no saved password list, no AutoFill entries, and so on. In other words, what happens in InPrivate browsing stays in InPrivate browsing.

FREQUENTLY ASKED QUESTION

The Wisdom of Edge

How does the pop-up blocker know a good pop-up from a bad one, anyway?

Edge generally tries to distinguish between pop-ups it considers necessary for a site to run and those it considers annoying or dangerous.

Although it doesn't always succeed, there is some logic behind its thinking.

At the factory setting, some pop-ups get through. For example, it allows pop-ups that contain "active content"—for example, important features that are integral to the proper functioning of a Web site: seating charts, flight-details screens, and so on.

Finally, if you already have a spyware infection, pop-ups may appear constantly; the pop-up blocker isn't designed to block spyware pop-ups.

To start InPrivate browsing, hit ⋯ and choose "New InPrivate window." A new window opens (Figure 12-6). Nothing you do in this window—or in the tabs within it—will leave tracks.

To stop InPrivate browsing, just close the window. Open a new Edge window to continue browsing "publicly."

Figure 12-6:
When you're brows-
ing InPrivate, a
special logo appears
at the left end of
the address bar to
remind you.

And if you're a
grammar curmud-
geon who feels that
the word "data" is
actually plural, well,
Microsoft apologizes.

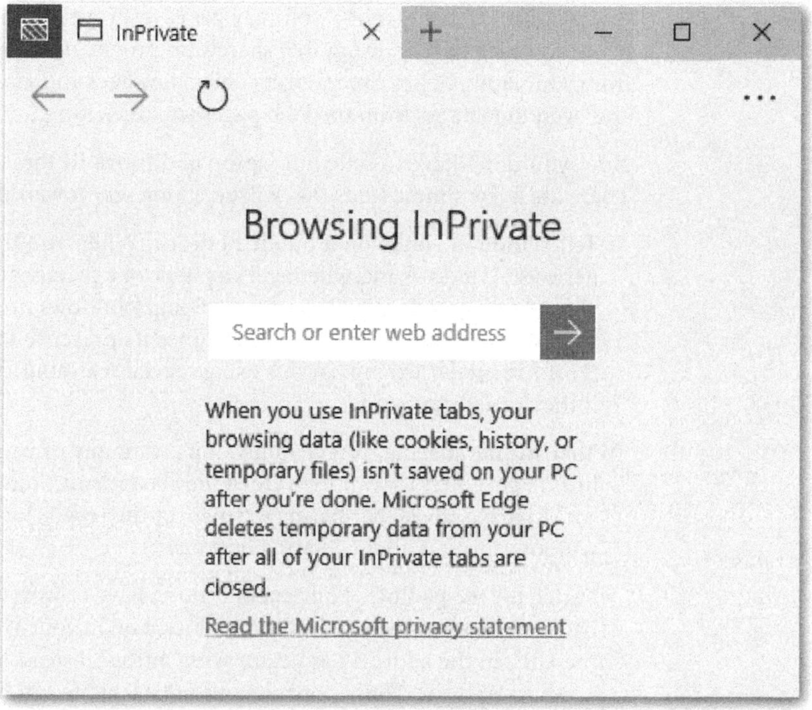

Browsing InPrivate

Search or enter web address →

When you use InPrivate tabs, your browsing data (like cookies, history, or temporary files) isn't saved on your PC after you're done. Microsoft Edge deletes temporary data from your PC after all of your InPrivate tabs are closed.

Read the Microsoft privacy statement

Do Not Track

You know how there's a "Do not call" list? If you register your phone number with this list, telemarketers are legally forbidden to call you.

Now there's a "Do not track" list, too. If you turn this feature on in your browser—like Edge—then Web advertisers are supposed to not track your Web activities, which they like to do in order to market to you better.

There's a difference, though. Advertisers' respect for your Do Not Track setting is *optional*. There's no law that says they *have* to obey it. As a result, it's essentially a useless feature.

If you care, you can find the Do Not Track setting like this: Click the ⋯ button (upper right), then Settings. Scroll down to "View advanced settings." Turn on "Send Do Not Track requests."

Hotspot Security

One of the greatest computing conveniences is the almighty public wireless hotspot, where you and your WiFi-enabled laptop can connect to the Internet at high speed, often for free. There are thousands of hotspots at cafés, hotels, airports, and other public locations.

But unless you're careful, you'll get more than a skinny latte from your local café if you connect to its hotspot—you may get eavesdropped on as well. It's possible for hackers sitting nearby, using free shareware programs, to "sniff" the transmissions from your laptop. They can intercept email messages you send, names and passwords, and even the images from the Web pages you're visiting.

Now, you don't have to sell your laptop and move to the Amish country over this. There are a few simple steps that will go a long way toward keeping you safe:

- **Tell Windows you're on a public network.** When you first connect to a wireless network, Windows asks whether it's a public or a private one. Choosing Public gives you extra protection. Technically speaking, Windows turns off *network discovery*, the feature that makes your PC announce its presence to others on the network. (Unfortunately, lurking hackers using special scanning software can still find you if they're determined.)

- **Turn off file sharing.** You certainly don't want any of your overcaffeinated neighbors to get access to your files. Open the Start menu. Start typing *sharing* until you see "Manage advanced sharing settings" in the results list; click it. In the resulting window, turn off all the Sharing options.

- **Watch for the padlock.** You generally don't have to worry about online stores and banks. Whenever you see the little padlock icon in your Web browser (or whenever the URL in the address bar begins with "https" instead of "http"), you're visiting a secure Web site. Your transmissions are encrypted in both directions and can't be snooped.

- **Look over your shoulder.** Hacking isn't always high-tech stuff; it can be as simple as "shoulder surfing," in which someone looks over your shoulder to see the password you're typing. Make sure no one can look at what you're typing.

- **Don't leave your laptop alone.** Coffee has a way of moving through your system fast, but if you have to leave for the restroom, don't leave your laptop unattended. Pack it up into its case and take it with you, or bring along a lock that you can use to lock it to a table.

- **Use a virtual private network (VPN).** If somebody intercepts your "Hi, Mom" email, it may not be the end of the world. If you're doing serious corporate work, though, and you want maximum safety, you can pay for wireless virtual private network (VPN) software that encrypts all the data you're sending and receiving. Nobody will be able to grab it out of the air using snooping software at a hotspot.

For example, HotSpotVPN (*www.hotspotvpn.com*) costs $3.88 per day or $8.88 per month. You get a password, user name, and the Internet address of a VPN server.

Open the Network and Sharing Center (quickest link to it: the Network icon on your system tray). Click "Set up a new connection or network." Select "Connect to workplace," and then follow the prompts for creating a new VPN connection with the information provided to you by HotSpotVPN.

Protect Your Home Wireless Network

Public wireless hotspots aren't the only ones that present a theoretical security risk; your wireless network at home harbors hacker potential, too. It's theoretically possible (barely) for so-called war drivers (people who drive around with laptops, looking for unprotected home WiFi networks) to piggyback onto home networks to download child pornography or to send out spam.

This one's easy to nip in the bud:

- **Use a password on your WiFi.** When you first set up your WiFi router (your base station or access point), you're offered the chance to create a password for your network. Take that chance. (Wireless routers have offered three different types of password-protected encryption over the years, called WEP, WPA, and WPA2. If it's available, choose the most modern, most secure one, which is WPA2.)

  You then have to enter the password when you first connect to that hotspot from each wireless PC on your network.

Note: You won't have to type this password every time you want to get onto your own network! Windows offers to memorize it for you.

- **Ban unwanted PCs.** Many routers include a feature that lets you limit network access to specific computers. Any PC that's not on the list won't be allowed in. The feature is called MAC address filtering, although it has nothing to do with Macintosh computers. (It stands for media access control, which is a serial number that uniquely identifies a piece of networking hardware.)

  Not all routers can do this, and how you do it varies from router to router, so check the documentation. In a typical Linksys router, for example, you log into the router's administrator screen using your Web browser and then select Wireless→Wireless Network Access. On the screen full of empty boxes, type the MAC address of the PC that you want to be allowed to get onto the network.

Note: To find out the MAC address of a PC, press ⊞+R to open the Run dialog box. Type *cmd* and press Enter. Type *ipconfig/all*, and press Enter. In the resulting info screen, look for the Physical Address entry. That's the MAC address.

Type all the MAC addresses into the boxes on the Linksys router, click Save Settings, and you're all done.

• **Place your router properly.** Placing your WiFi router centrally in the house minimizes the "leaking" of the signal into the surrounding neighborhood.

Family Safety (Parental Controls)

Many parents reasonably worry about the volatile mixture of kids+computers. They worry about kids spending too much time in front of the PC, rotting their brains instead of going outside to play stickball in the street like we did when we were their age, getting fresh air and sunshine. They worry that kids are playing disgusting, violent video games. They worry that kids are using programs they really shouldn't be using, corrupting themselves with apps like Skype and Quicken. (That's a joke.)

Above all, parents worry that their kids might encounter upsetting material on the Internet: violence, pornography, hate speech, illegal drug sites, and so on.

Fortunately, Windows comes with parental controls that give you a fighting chance at keeping this stuff off your PC: Family Safety. It's easy to use and fairly complete.

Specifically, Family Safety has four features to protect your youngsters:

• Blocking inappropriate Web sites from their impressionable eyes.

• Setting daily time limits on their computer use.

• Monitoring which programs they're using, and limiting games and apps they buy from the Windows Store.

• Sending you activity reports so you know what they're up to. Each week, you'll get emailed a report for each of your kids that summarizes which Web sites they've visited, what words they've searched for online, how much time they spent on the

---

NOSTALGIA CORNER

What Happened to the Old Parental Controls?

If you were a fan of the Family Safety feature in Windows 7 and 8, you may be about to crash hard. Microsoft has eliminated it in favor of a new system that requires you to administer the parental controls on a Web site.

Among other drawbacks, the new setup requires that each of your children has a Microsoft account. Which means having an email address. Which might seem a little silly for, say, a 5-year-old.

Also, those kids are going to have to log into your computer with that Microsoft account's password (unless you have a touchscreen, in which case maybe you could teach them the Picture Password as described on 567.)

On the other hand, there are two advantages to having a Web-based feature. First, you can make changes by remote control, without having to be in front of the PC you're adjusting. Second, your kid can log into any Windows 10 computer anywhere and find the same restrictions in place. And the activity report that Microsoft emails you will be able to track everything your kids have done online, even on different computers (assuming they used nothing but Windows 10 machines and sign in on each one).

---

computer each day, which programs and games they've used this week, and what apps they've downloaded from the Windows Store.

Turn on Family Safety

Before you can set up parental controls, some housekeeping is required. You, the parent, are presumably in charge of the computer and should therefore have an Administrator account (page 556). And it must be password-protected; if it's not, then the kid whose innocence you're trying to preserve can just log in as you and turn Parental Controls off.

Your child, on the other hand, must have what Microsoft calls a Child account (Figure 12-7). And it has to be a Microsoft account, meaning that it's stored online, not on your computer.

The process of creating that account gets pretty intrusive; you'll have to supply your phone number, provide a credit card number, agree to a 50-cent charge, decline Microsoft's intention to sell your kid's information to advertisers, and approve of an agreement that talks about what kinds of personal information about your kid will be exposed to online (especially in Xbox land).

In any case, the step-by-steps for creating a Child account begin on page 558.

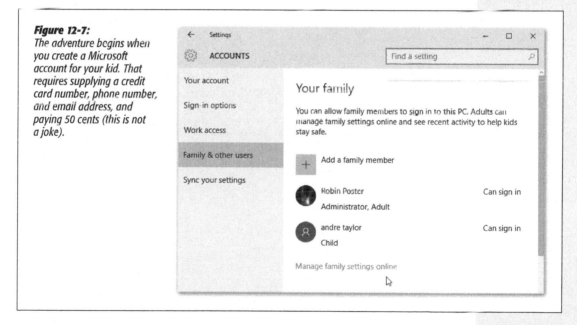

Figure 12-7:
The adventure begins when you create a Microsoft account for your kid. That requires supplying a credit card number, phone number, and email address, and paying 50 cents (this is not a joke).

Turning on Restrictions

Once you've created a Child account, you can turn on Family Safety in the same place. (That's the Settings→Accounts→"Family & other users" screen.)

The magic button is the "Manage family settings online" link.

It takes you to a special site on the Microsoft Web site where you can set up the guardrails for your youngster.

The main screen is a list of your family members (Figure 12-8, top).

Select a kid's name to open his main screen (Figure 12-8, bottom). You see his recent activity, and you can turn off those activity reports.

The good stuff, though, is below that. Scroll down and begin building your kid's padded room.

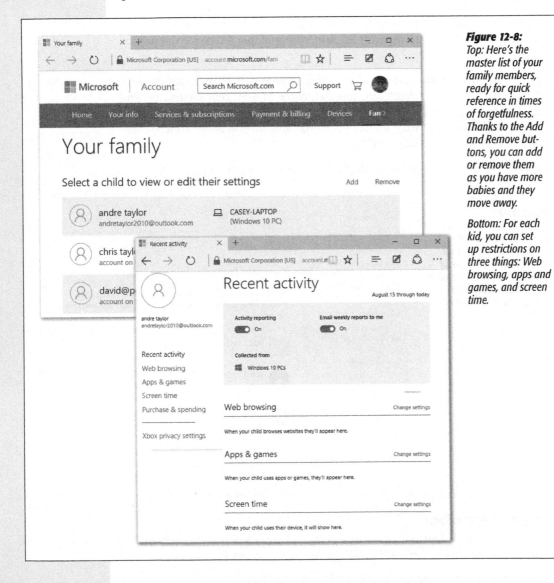

Figure 12-8:
Top: Here's the master list of your family members, ready for quick reference in times of forgetfulness. Thanks to the Add and Remove buttons, you can add or remove them as you have more babies and they move away.

Bottom: For each kid, you can set up restrictions on three things: Web browsing, apps and games, and screen time.

Web Browsing

Web filtering prevents your youngsters from opening inappropriate Web sites—dirty pictures, hate speech, and so on. You can either trust Microsoft's ever-evolving "blacklist" of known naughty sites, or you can add individual Web addresses to the blocked list.

To set it up, click "Change settings."

Here's where you can control what happens when your kid tries to surf the Web on a Windows 10 machine:

- **Block inappropriate websites.** This is the master on/off switch for filtering. (And who decides what's inappropriate? Microsoft.)

- **Always allow these.** Your little ragamuffin is allowed to use any sites whose addresses you add here.

- **Always block these.** And she's *not* allowed to visit any sites whose addresses you add *here.*

App, Game, and Movie Restrictions

This option offers some very simple protections from having your youngsters experience violent or sexy games or movies.

"Block inappropriate apps and games" is the on/off switch. When it's on, your kid can't play anything that Microsoft deems to be a mature game or movie.

You can also use the pop-up menu (under "Limit apps and games from the Windows Store") to limit apps by age— for example, if you choose "10 year olds," then your little darling can download and play anything intended for 10 and under.

Of course, all of this assumes that (a) you trust the age ratings the game and movie companies have given their own apps, and (b) your kid won't want to play any of the thousands of games that did *not* come from the Windows Store.

Fortunately, you have one final tool at your disposal: You can block an app or a game after your kid has played it. On the Recent Activity screen for your child, you see everything he's been doing on Windows 10 PCs. The beauty is that you, even sitting across town at your office, can monitor and stop stuff you don't believe in. Click Block to block an app or a Web site, on the spot.

And then hope that the damage hasn't been done.

Time Limits

This feature (Figure 12-9) lets you control when your little tyke can use the computer—a much more automated method than constant "Why don't you go out and play?" nagging.

You have two ways to limit this account holder's brain-rotting time: by total number of hours each day, or by specific times of the day (no computer on school nights, for example):

- **Curfew.** Use the pop-up menus to indicate the hours during which computer use is OK. You might want to block use during normal sleeping hours, for example.

- **Time Limits.** Use the "Limit per day" pop-up menu to specify a time allotment for each day of the week. No more than 3 hours on school days, for example (cumulatively). Of course, these limits apply only to this one computer.

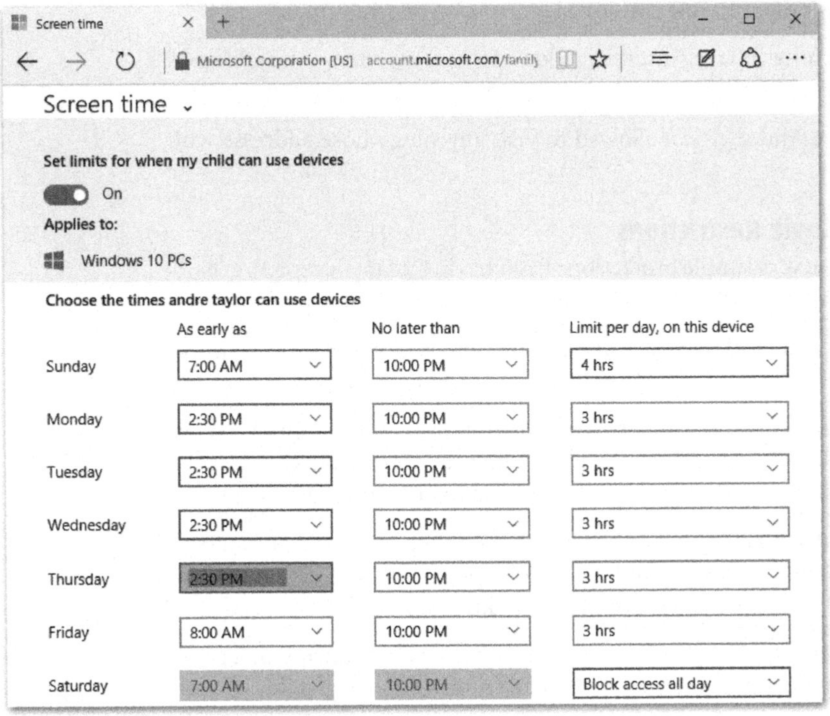

Figure 12-9:
If you set up time limits for your little rugrats, they won't be able to log in outside of the permitted hours. And if they're signed in when the time block ends, they get a "time remaining" warning or two, and then they're dumped off, with a message that they're out of time. (Their programs and windows remain open in the background, in suspended animation until the next approved time slot.)

Privacy from Your Apps

The miracle of the modern app is that it can help you in astounding ways. By analyzing your data, your movements, and your computer, it can make you more efficient and save you a lot of steps.

For example, a movie app can tell you which movies are playing nearby—because it has learned *where you are* by consulting your tablet's GPS. Or an email program can autocomplete somebody's email address, saving you time—because it has consulted your People app.

But plenty of people are creeped out by the notion of software following their movements around town, tracking the Web sites they visit, or even listening to their world through the built-in microphone.

Fortunately, the Settings→Privacy screen offers individual on/off switches that shut down your apps' access to every conceivable shred of useful data about you and your PC. Here's what the tabs do on that screen.

General

Here's a handful of important on/off switches that govern the kinds of information about you that's sent to other parties online.

- **Let apps use my advertising ID.** Ordinarily, you're identified (not by name, but by a serial number) to advertisers who pay Microsoft for this kind of data. As a result, if you download a lot of trout-fishing apps, you might begin to see more ads for fishing gear within apps. (This option has nothing to do with Web sites; it affects ads displayed *within apps*. There aren't many of those. Yet.)

  If you turn this option off, your app data won't be shared with advertisers—and you'll see random ads within your apps, rather than ads tailored to the sorts of interests you seem to have.

- **Turn on SmartScreen filter to check web content.** SmartScreen (page 423) is Microsoft's anti-malware service—the one that, when you're on the Web, blocks viruses and other nastiness. This option applies the same protection to Web sites requested by your apps. (Windows Store apps only, not traditional desktop apps.)

- **Send Microsoft info about how I write.** You know how the onscreen keyboard tries to predict the next word you'll type, to save you time and taps (page 448)? Now you know how it guesses what your next word is likely to be. Microsoft collects data on word frequency and word sequence from you and millions of other people—anonymously. Here's where you opt out.

- **Let websites provide locally relevant content by accessing my language list.** Web sites may tailor the kinds of information they show you, based on the languages you've enabled on your machine. For example, if you've turned on French, then some sites might display their articles in French, for your convenience, or they might show you news stories about French-speaking countries.

- **Manage my Microsoft advertising and other personalization info.** Takes you online to a Web page where you have some control over how much of your data Microsoft uses to advertise to you.

Location

This item is generally intended for tablets and laptops—computers that get moved around. It refers to apps that function best if they know where you are: a movie-listing app, for example, that can show you what's playing at local theaters.

Of course, letting such apps know where you are also means that your location might get transmitted to the software companies that wrote those apps. Here you can find on/off switches for each app's access to your location. You can delete the record of your locations that the computer is storing already.

And you can turn off location tracking altogether by turning off the "Let Windows and apps use my location" switch.

Camera, Microphone, Contacts, Calendar...

The rest of this Settings screen lists the various parts of your machine—both hardware features and apps like the Calendar and People apps—that various apps might want to access.

As always, these apps generally *require* that access to your stuff to do their jobs. (Furthermore, apps *ask your permission* before they access your built-in camera or microphone.)

But, now and then, you'll see an app listed on this screen that doesn't make immediate sense to you. ("Why does Super 3D Driving Simulator need access to my calendar?") In that case, you can shut down its access to that element of your computer.

You can also turn off the master switch at the top of each panel. "No app is going to use *my* camera!" you might declare, when you've had a particularly rough night.

Part Four:
Hardware and Peripherals

4

Chapter 13: Tablets, Laptops & Hybrids

Chapter 14: Printing, Fonts & PDFs

Chapter 15: Hardware & Drivers

Tablets, Laptops & Hybrids

If Microsoft's recent experiments with Windows show anything at all, it's that Microsoft is betting on the future of mobile. Fewer and fewer computers will be tethered to desks. More and more will be carried around—and most of them will have touchscreens. Microsoft believes that so strongly that it's designing all of its new apps to have big, fat, widely spaced buttons for finger touches.

But touchscreen friendliness isn't the only nod Windows 10 makes to easing the lives of road warriors. This chapter covers a motley collection of additional tools for anyone who travels.

Battery Saver

It's common for smartphones to have a battery-saver mode. That's where the phone, upon dropping to a low level of battery remaining, switches off a lot of nonessential background activities and features to save power. The screen dims, there are fewer animations, email and Facebook don't get checked in the background—all in the name of extending your phone's battery long enough to help you get through the day.

And now, the same feature comes to Windows laptops and tablets.

You can turn it on manually by opening the Action Center (■+A, or tap ▣ on the taskbar, or swipe in from the right on a touchscreen) and hitting "Battery saver."

Or you can do it the long way: Open Settings (■+ I)→System→"Battery saver."

Or you can wait until your battery hits 20 percent remaining, which is when Battery Saver kicks in automatically.

In Battery Saver, your screen dims (screen brightness is one of the biggest power drains). Apps running in the background go to sleep. You don't get notifications from apps. Things generally calm down and slow down, and your battery lasts a lot longer.

You can adjust or override most of those things, by the way. In Settings (⊞+I)→System→"Battery saver," hit "Battery saver settings." Now you can fiddle with these switches (Figure 13-1, right):

- **Turn battery saver on automatically.** If you turn off this switch, you can still use Battery Saver—but you'll have to turn it on yourself.

- **[percentage slider].** Battery Saver likes to kick in when your battery charge hits 20 percent. But using this slider, you can change that threshold. You can set it to anything from 5 percent to 100 percent. (100 percent would mean "on all the time.")

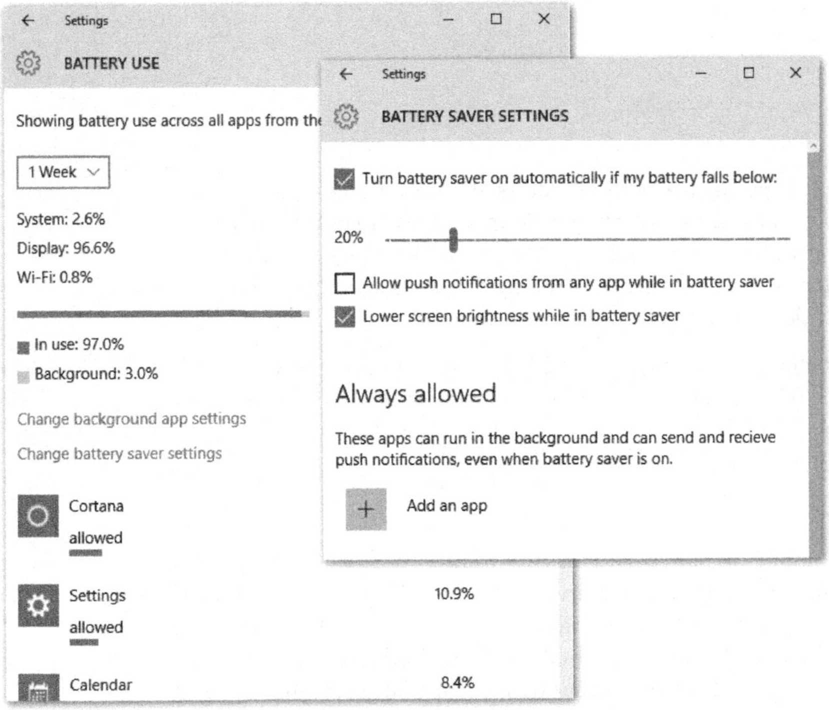

Figure 13-1:
Right: Battery Saver tries to save your battery. But if you insist, you can override its decisions to keep important functions still going.

Left: What can you do with the information on the "Battery use" screen? You can get a good idea of why your battery doesn't last as long as it should. Learn to recognize which apps are the battery hogs, and quit them when possible.

- **Allow push notifications from any app while in battery saver.** Those notification bubbles cost you some power. On the other hand, sometimes they alert you to important issues. Should they appear? You make the call.

- **Lower screen brightness while in battery saver.** What if you can't stand your screen dimming? You can turn off that aspect of Battery Saver here (but of course you won't get as much battery savings).

- **Always allowed.** What if you *mostly* want to reap the fruits of Battery Saver, but you really need one particular app to keep running in the background (and keep sending you notifications)? Here you can click "Add an app" to designate an app that *won't* be shut down in the background. Of course, here again, you won't save as much power, but at least your work won't grind to a halt.

Battery Detective Work

Battery Saver isn't the only help Windows 10 can give you with your battery. It also offers a new screen that sleuths out which apps have been eating up the most power in the last day, 2 days, or week. In Settings (⊞+I)→System→"Battery saver," hit "Battery use."

The screen shown in Figure 13-1, left, appears.

For Hybrid PCs Only: Tablet Mode (Continuum)

No matter how hard Microsoft's engineers pound their heads against the conference-room tables, they can't make one thing change: Touchscreen devices are not the same as regular PCs. Your finger and a mouse are not the same thing. They have radically different degrees of precision. One's on the screen all the time, and one taps it only occasionally.

But grafting together two completely different operating systems, as Microsoft did in Windows 8, was not the solution.

In Windows 10, Microsoft came up with a less drastic approach, designed for hybrid machines: tablets with detachable keyboards, like Microsoft's own Surface. The solution involves two parts:

- **Tablet mode.** In Tablet mode, you're pretty much back to Windows 8. The Start menu becomes the Start screen, filling the monitor. Every app runs in full-screen mode—no overlapping windows. The onscreen keyboard pops up automatically when you're in a place where you can type.

- **Continuum** simply means "Enters Tablet mode every time you detach the keyboard." Whenever you take your tablet out of its dock, or pull off its keyboard, or fold its keyboard behind the screen, the touch-friendly Tablet mode can kick in automatically.

Note: You can try out Tablet mode even if you don't have a touchscreen, although there's not much point to it. Tablet mode is designed to make Windows 10 more finger-friendly.

Here's what the two modes do.

Manual Tablet Mode

To turn on Tablet mode, hit the ▤ button on your taskbar (or press ⊞+A) to open the Action Center, and then hit "Tablet mode."

(There's a long way, too: Open Settings→System→"Tablet mode." Turn on "Make Windows more touch-friendly when using your device as a tablet.")

Here's what you'll see:

- **Start menu.** The most dramatic change in Tablet mode is that the Start menu goes full-screen, as shown in Figure 13-2. But you still have access to your "All apps" menu (hit the ☰ in the lower-left corner), and you still have access to the left side of the Start menu (hit the ☰ at the top-left corner).

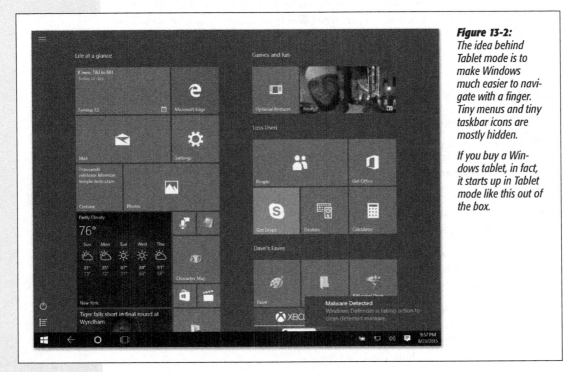

Figure 13-2:
The idea behind Tablet mode is to make Windows much easier to navigate with a finger. Tiny menus and tiny taskbar icons are mostly hidden.

If you buy a Windows tablet, in fact, it starts up in Tablet mode like this out of the box.

- **Taskbar.** You'll notice that the taskbar is a bit simpler, too. On the left, only four icons remain: the ⊞ button, a ← button (returns you to the Start menu from whatever app you're using), Cortana, and Task View. On the right, all you get is the battery, network, volume, Action Center, and clock icons.

  In other words, the usual taskbar icons—for open programs, and the programs you use often—are hidden.

Tip: You can bring them back, however. In Settings→System→Tablet mode, turn off "Hide app icons on the taskbar in tablet mode."

- **Apps full screen.** In Tablet mode, every app fills the entire screen. You can still split the screen as described on page 52, though—drag the top edge of an app to the left or right side of your screen. You'll see the window pop into the space, filling only half the screen.

- **Exiting an app.** Since every app fills the screen, you won't have much use for the Minimize and Maximize buttons. All that remains in the upper-right corner of an app window is the ✕ button—and even that's hidden.

  If you have a mouse or trackpad, point to the top edge without clicking; you'll see a title bar slide into view, complete with the ✕ you need to close the app.

  On a touchscreen, drag your finger all the way down the screen, from above to below, in one smooth motion. You'll see the app follow, shrink, and disappear.

Auto-Tablet Mode

Now that you know about Tablet mode, Windows 10 has another offer: Would you like Tablet mode to start up *automatically* when you take away the keyboard?

(That question makes the most sense if you have a hybrid tablet—one whose keyboard comes off or flips around to the back. For best results, do not try ripping off the keyboard of a *regular* laptop.)

Yes, this is the feature that Microsoft marketing executives call Continuum, although that term does not actually appear in Windows.

In Settings→System→"Tablet mode," you have two sets of controls. The first set controls what happens when you sign into your account. (In other words, different people may see something different when they log in.)

This pop-up menu offers you a choice of "Automatically switch to tablet mode," "Go to the desktop," or "Remember what I used last."

The second pop-up menu wants to know what happens when you attach or detach your hybrid's keyboard:

- **Nothing.** Choose "Don't ask me and don't switch."

- **Automatically switch to or from Tablet mode.** "Don't ask me and always switch."

- **Ask before switching.** This is the factory setting: When you attach or detach the keyboard, Windows asks if you want to pop into or out of Tablet mode.

The Onscreen Keyboard

If your computer has a physical keyboard, or if your tablet has a removable one, great! But touchscreens generally don't have moving keys. That's why, whenever you tap in a spot where typing is required, you can summon the onscreen keyboard. Just hit the keyboard button on the system tray (lower right of your screen). Figure 13-3 shows the idea.

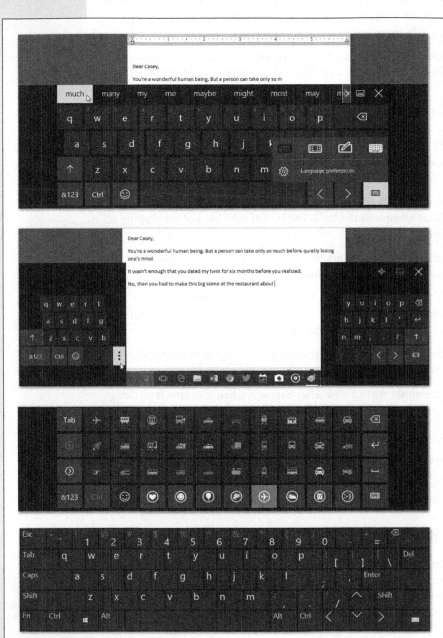

Figure 13-3:
*Top: The onscreen
keyboard has lots of
tricks up its sleeve.
When you hit the
lower-right key, you
get a pop-up menu
of different keyboard
styles.*

*Second from top:
The split keyboard
is for tablets—espe-
cially one you're
holding with fingers
beneath, so you
can tap with your
thumbs. You have
a choice of three
key sizes; to switch,
press the three-
vertical-dots button
identified by the
cursor.*

*Third from top: You
even get a rogue's
gallery of emoticons,
for when English just
isn't enough.*

*Bottom: If you miss
the full "101-key"
layout, complete
with symbols and
control keys, Win-
dows can accommo-
date you.*

In general, this keyboard works pretty much like any keyboard you've ever used, with a few exceptions:

- **The keys don't move.** Of course not—it's a piece of glass! The keys do everything they can, though, to tell you when they've been struck. They change color and make little sounds.

- **It has a symbol/number layout. Two, actually.** Tap the "&123" key to change all the letter keys into symbol keys: !, @, %, $, &, and so on. Tap the circled → key to view a second set of them—less common symbols like ©, <, >, and other currency symbols and brackets. And a numeric keypad appears at the right end of the keyboard.

To return to the regular alphabet keyboard, tap the "&123" key (which is now "lit up" in color) again.

Tip: You don't have to hit the "&123" twice—once to lock, once to unlock. Instead, you can treat it like a Shift key. That is, you can hold it down with one hand and type the symbol you want with the other hand.

- **It has a split, two-thumb version.** If you're holding a tablet, you might prefer the split keyboard shown in Figure 13-3, second from top. It lets you flail away with both thumbs, with the keys nicely arranged to hug the outer edges of the screen.

To split the keyboard in this way, tap the keyboard key in the lower-right corner. A tiny palette of keyboard options appears (Figure 13-3, top); tap the second one. Later, you can return to the full keyboard by tapping the *first* icon on this palette.

- **It has emoticons.** Tap the smiley-face key (☺) to change all the letters into a huge array of tiny smileys and other icons, also called emoticons or emoji (Figure 13-3, third from top). These are available wherever you type, but they're most appropriate when you're typing in a chat room or *maybe* an email message. (And even then, plenty of people would argue that they're *never* appropriate.)

The bottom row displays buttons for seven pages full of emoji, plus a heart button that displays symbols you've used recently for easier retrieval.

- **Its modifier keys are sticky.** If you want to press Shift+D, for example, or Ctrl+N, you don't have to *hold down* the Shift or Ctrl key. Just tap the modifier key (Shift, Ctrl, Alt) and *then* the letter that goes with it.

- **Caps Lock is there.** Just as on a phone, you can lock down the Shift key to type in ALL CAPITALS by *double*-tapping the Shift key. It lights up to show that it's locked down. (Tap it again to unlock it.)

- **Its letter keys are hiding numbers, punctuation, and accents.** To produce an accented character (like é, ë, è, ê, and so on), keep your finger pressed on that key for about a second.

The comma sprouts a semicolon (;) option, the period sprouts a colon (:), and the question mark—oh, baby. Its secret palette contains a wealth of other punctuation marks (parentheses, !, #, @, /, hyphen, and so on) that save you from having to call up the special-symbols layout.

Tip: Most keys on the symbol keyboard sprout variations, too; for example, the $ key offers an array of alternate currency symbols.

- **The double-space-bar trick is available.** If you press the space bar twice, you get a period, a space, and an automatically capitalized next letter—exactly what you want at the end of a sentence. (It's the same trick that saves you fussing with alternate keyboard layouts on the iPhone, Windows Phone, Android phones, BlackBerry, and so on.)

Note: The on/off switch for this feature is in Settings→Devices→Typing.

- **There are cursor keys.** See the ⟨ and ⟩ keys to the right of the space bar? Those don't mean "greater than" and "less than." They're cursor keys. They move your cursor left and right through the text.

- **There are typing suggestions.** When you've typed the beginning of a word that Windows can guess—*lun,* for example—three AutoComplete suggestions appear in a box just below what you've typed, proposing suggestions: in this case, *lung, lunch,* and *luncheon.*

    If one of those choices is indeed the word you wanted, tap or click it; Windows inserts it into whatever you were typing. Once you get used to this feature, you can save a lot of time and typos.

Tip: You can choose one of the autocomplete suggestions without lifting your hands. Swipe to the right *across the onscreen space bar* to highlight successive suggestions; when you've got the one you want, tap the space bar or the Enter key.

You can turn off the suggestions, if you like, as described on the facing page.

- **There's a full 101-key PC keyboard layout, too.** The standard Windows 10 keyboard layout was designed to make the letter keys big and easy to type. Microsoft chose to hide a lot of the other stuff you'd find on a real keyboard, including numbers, Tab, Esc, and so on.

    But if you'd prefer an onscreen version of the real thing, Windows can accommodate you. Open Settings→Devices→Typing, and turn on "Add the standard keyboard layout as a touch keyboard option." Now the standard pop-up menu of keyboard layouts (shown at top in Figure 13-3) offers the full 101-key PC keyboard (Figure 13-3, bottom).

When you're finished typing, tap anywhere outside the keyboard; it goes away, returning the full screen area to your command.

Keyboard Settings

In Settings→Devices→Typing, you'll find a raft of options that govern the onscreen keyboard. (Most of these don't appear if you don't have a touchscreen.) For example:

- **Show text suggestions as I type.** Here's the on/off switch for that row of "what word you'll probably type next" word suggestions above the keyboard.

- **Add a space after I choose a text suggestion.** When you hit one of the word suggestions, do you want Windows to add a space? (Yes, you do.)

- **Add a period after I double-tap the Spacebar.** As on smartphones: Hit the space bar twice when you get to the end of a sentence. Windows adds the period and the space for you automatically. (Doesn't work in all apps.)

- **Capitalize the first letter of each sentence.** You're spared having to hit the Shift key every time.

- **Use all uppercase letters when I double-tap Shift.** Usually called Caps Lock.

- **Add the standard keyboard layout as a touch keyboard option.** "Standard keyboard" actually means the *extended* layout shown at bottom in Figure 13-3. You get the superwide keyboard layout of a standard PC keyboard, complete with a row of number/symbol keys, cursor keys, and control keys (⊞, Fn, Ctrl, Alt). Maybe not as easy to type on as the regular, stripped-down keyboard. But far more complete.

- **Automatically show the touch keyboard in windowed apps when there's no keyboard attached to your device.** When there's no physical keyboard, would you like the onscreen keyboard to pop up automatically when you tap into a place where you can type? (If not, you'll have to open it manually by tapping ⌨ on the taskbar.)

Note: In Tablet mode, the keyboard appears automatically no matter what setting you make here.

Handwriting Recognition

The accuracy of Windows' handwriting recognition has come a very long way—which is great news if you have a tablet. Hey, if tablets can decipher doctors' handwriting, surely you can get your tablet to recognize yours.

In Windows 10, Microsoft has killed off the yellow two-line Input Panel of previous Windows versions. Instead, handwriting transcription is built right into the palette of available keyboards (Figure 13-4). It lets you handwrite text anywhere you can type: Microsoft Word, your email program, your Web browser, and so on.

To make Windows recognize your handwriting, open any program where you would otherwise type.

Now open the handwriting panel, which is one of the "keyboards" available from the Keyboards palette shown at top in Figure 13-3. It's a window that automatically converts anything you write into typed text. To view this panel, start by summoning the regular onscreen keyboard (tap the Keyboard icon on the taskbar).

Once the onscreen keyboard appears, tap the keyboard key (lower right); tap the Handwriting icon, third from left. Now the handwriting panel is ready to use (Figure 13-4).

Just write on the line.

The "digital ink" doesn't just sit there where you wrote it. A split second after you finish each word, Windows transcribes that word into typed text in your document, converted from your handwriting. After you write a phrase, press the space bar or tap the Insert button to clear out the panel, making it ready for new writing.

For your inking pleasure, buttons at the right end of the panel serve as space, Backspace, and Enter keys.

Tip: Ordinarily, the handwriting panel stretches across the entire bottom of your screen. But if you use the Detach button indicated in Figure 13-4, the panel becomes much smaller—and movable. You can drag it to any convenient position on the screen.

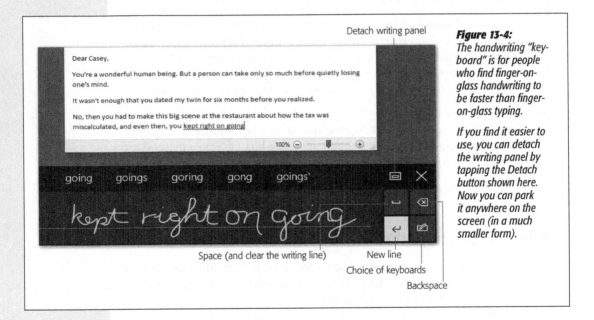

Detach writing panel

Dear Casey,

You're a wonderful human being. But a person can take only so much before quietly losing one's mind.

It wasn't enough that you dated my twin for six months before you realized.

No, then you had to make this big scene at the restaurant about how the tax was miscalculated, and even then, you kept right on going

100%

going   goings   goring   gong   goings'

kept right on going

Space (and clear the writing line)   New line   Choice of keyboards   Backspace

Figure 13-4:
The handwriting "keyboard" is for people who find finger-on-glass handwriting to be faster than finger-on-glass typing.

If you find it easier to use, you can detach the writing panel by tapping the Detach button shown here. Now you can park it anywhere on the screen (in a much smaller form).

Fixing mistakes

Windows' handwriting recognition is amazingly accurate. It is not, however, perfect. Fortunately, it's got some tools to help.

First, don't miss the row of alternative transcribed words above your handwriting (visible in Figure 13-4). Tap a word to insert it.

Second, if *you* make a mistake as you write, strike out the word (drag your finger or pen across it, right to left). Windows vaporizes just that word.

Finally, once the typed text appears in your document, you can use the Backspace button (identified in Figure 13-4) to delete something Windows got wrong.

Training Windows to Know Your Handwriting

Windows does amazingly well at understanding your handwriting right out of the box. But if you plan to use it a lot, you should also *train* it. You provide samples of your handwriting, and Windows studies your style.

Finding the training program is a little tricky, but it can be done if you have a really good computer book. Open the Control Panel (page 270); search for the *language* panel and open it. Proceed as shown in Figure 13-5.

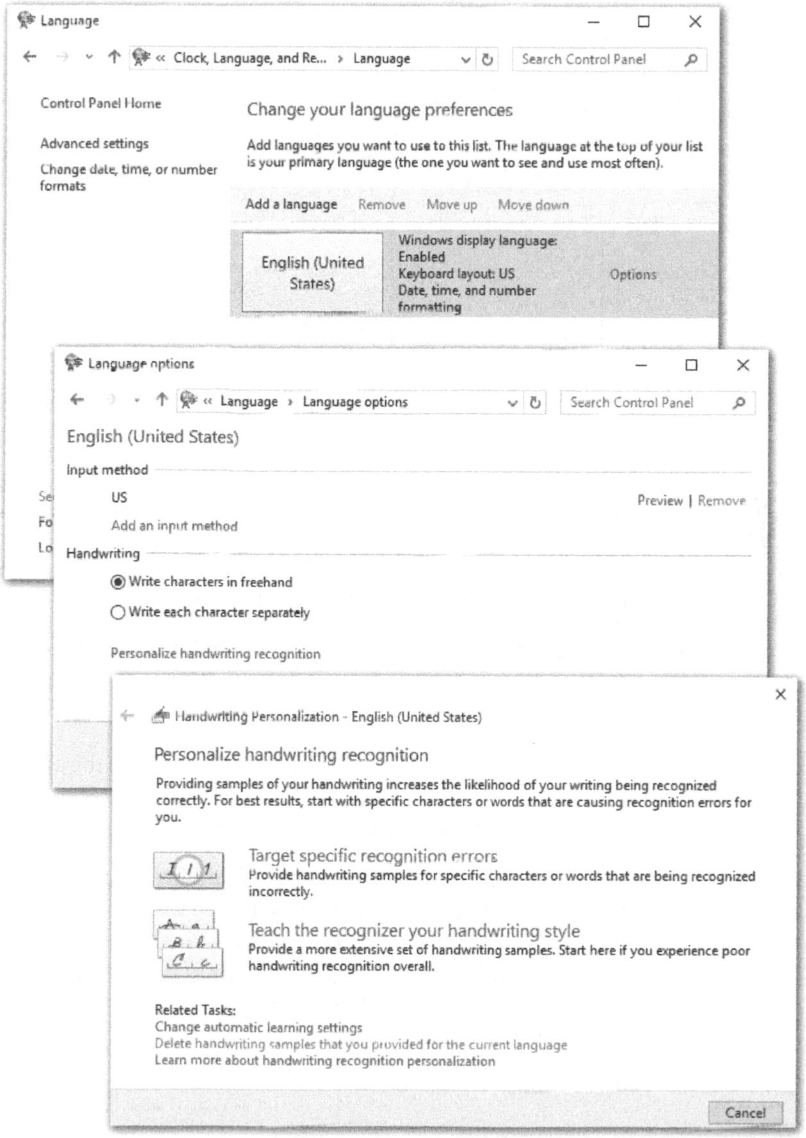

Figure 13-5:
Top: Once you've arrived at this screen in the Control Panel, next to your language, select Options.

Middle: In this dialog box, you can click "Write each character separately" if that's how you write; you'll get better recognition than "Write characters in freehand," which permits any kind of handwriting. But the star of this show is the "Personalize handwriting recognition" link. Click that.

Bottom: The handwriting training wizard offers you the chance to fix certain recognition errors (good if you've been at it awhile), or to teach it your general style (best if you're just starting out). You're offered the chance to write either sentences or numbers, symbols, and letters; for best accuracy, you should work through both. More than once, in fact. They're not brief exercises—the Sentences option involves about 50 screens—but it's all for a good cause.

After working through the exercises, you can start using handwriting recognition—with better accuracy.

Mobility Center

The Mobility Center is a handy, centralized hub for managing everything that makes a laptop a laptop (Figure 13-6): screen brightness, speaker volume, battery status, wireless networking, external projector connection, and so on. The quickest way to get there is to choose its name from the secret Utilities menu (press ⊞+X, or right-click the Start button).

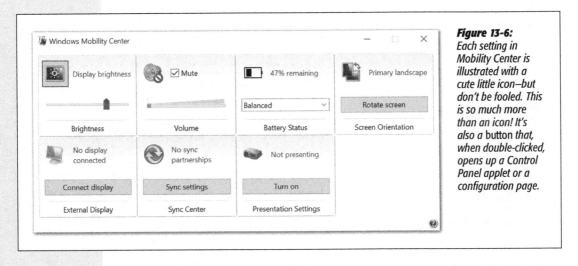

Figure 13-6:
Each setting in Mobility Center is illustrated with a cute little icon—but don't be fooled. This is so much more than an icon! It's also a button *that, when double-clicked, opens up a Control Panel applet or a configuration page.*

You can also open the Start menu, type *mobility*, and select Settings under the search box. In the search results, click Mobility Center.

Most of these tiles are now duplicated, in an easier-to-reach format, in the Quick Actions panel described on page 115. But the Mobility Center offers a little more control.

For example: **Presentation Settings.** This feature is the answer to a million PowerPoint pitchers' prayers. It makes sure that your laptop won't do anything embarrassing while you're in the middle of your boardroom presentation.

On the Presentation Settings tile of Mobility Center, click "Turn on." When the tile says "Presenting," your laptop won't go to sleep. No alarms or reminder dialog boxes appear. The screensaver doesn't kick in. You're free to give your pitch in peace. Click the icon to open the Presentation Settings dialog box shown in Figure 13-7.

Tip: Once the Mo' Center is open, you can also open its icons entirely from the keyboard. Try this: See the underlined letter beneath each panel, such as B̲attery Status or C̲onnect Display? (If not, tap the Alt key.) Press that letter key to highlight the icon, and then press Enter.

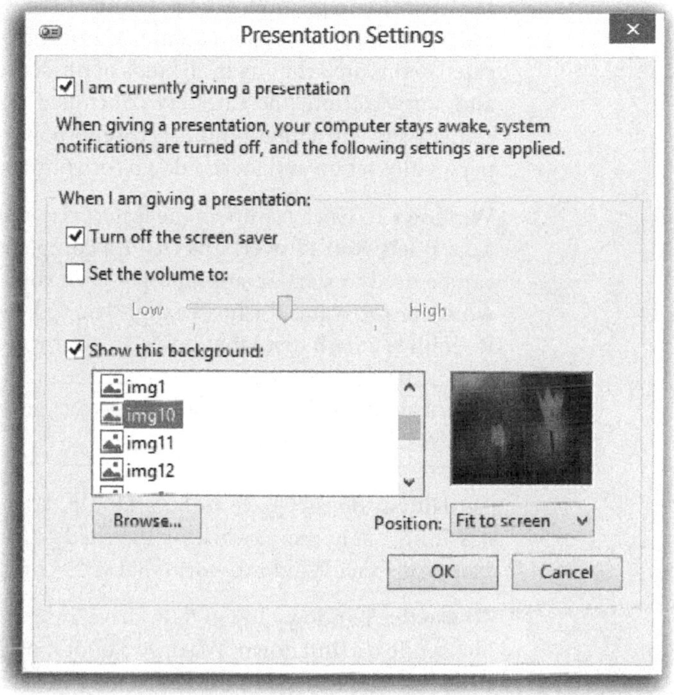

Figure 13-7:
When you're in Presentation mode, your screensaver and system notifications don't appear, and your laptop won't go to sleep. You might also want to specify a piece of uncontroversial artwork for your desktop wallpaper, so your bosses and potential employers won't accidentally spot the HotBikiniBabes.com JPEG you usually use.

Offline Files and Sync Center

The *offline files feature* is designed for laptop lovers. It lets you carry off files that generally live on your office network, so you can get some work done while you're away.

Then, when you return and connect your laptop to the office network, Windows automatically copies your edited, updated documents back to their original locations on the network, intelligently keeping straight which copies are the most recent.

Truth is, these days, the amount of time you're not actually online (and therefore able to connect to your work network) is probably very small. Connecting to your network via VPN (page 456) or using your OneDrive for documents are newer, much better ways to achieve the same effect.

But if you're interested in finding out about how Offline Files works, see the free downloadable PDF appendix "Offline Files" on this book's "Missing CD" page at *www.missingmanuals.com*.

Windows To Go

If you work in a corporation—especially if you're in charge of the computers there—you've heard of BYOD. It stands for "bring your own device," and it means "employees bringing their own tablets, laptops, and phones to work."

It sounds like a great idea; why shouldn't the worker bees enjoy the comfort of their own machines? But system administrators hate BYOD. It means that the unsophisticated peons are bringing in all kinds of unsecure, uninspected, unapproved hardware and software into the carefully controlled corporate environment. They'd much rather issue you a nine-pound, kerosene-powered Dell laptop from 2007 that they've personally set up and locked down for your use.

Windows To Go, a feature in the Enterprise edition of Windows, offers a clever solution. It lets your IT overlords create a complete Windows world *on a flash drive* that can be used to start up any laptop—even your own. It contains a copy of Windows, whatever programs the bosses want you to have, documents, the works. (That's why it requires a flash drive that holds 32 gigabytes or more!)

Note: If *you* are the IT overlord, here are the steps for creating a Windows To Go installation for use by your underlings: *http://j.mp/YetpTa*.

Actually, it doesn't have to be a laptop. You could start up *any* recent Windows machine—at home, at work, on the road—from this flash drive and find yourself in the same exact Windows world that your company set up for you.

To use the Windows To Go flash drive, insert it into the not-at-the-office PC's USB jack while it's shut down. When you boot it up again, it should start up from the USB drive automatically. If it doesn't, you may have to adjust your BIOS settings so that it does; ask your network geek or check the PC manufacturer's Web site. (Chances are pretty good that your system admin people turned on the BitLocker encryption feature described on page 549. You'll have to enter that password.)

At this point, you don't see any of your personal stuff. Your laptop's own hard drive doesn't even show up. Don't freak out; this is all in the name of keeping your work stuff and your personal stuff completely separate. When you're using Windows To Go, your laptop belongs to the corporation; everything else is hidden and offline. There's no possibility of cross-contamination.

When you shut down and yank out the flash drive, that same computer once again starts up from your own cluttered copy of Windows. The system administrators couldn't care less. (And if your flash-drive copy of Windows goes wrong somehow—maybe it gets a virus or something—who cares? The system admins can hit a couple of keys and spit out a fresh, virginal copy.)

The fine print goes like this:

- Only some flash-drive brands and models are officially compatible. (The list is here: *http://j.mp/YetAhl.*)

- Some features don't work when you've started up from the flash drive: hibernation, the Windows Recovery Environment, the Refresh and Reset PC commands, and the Windows App Store.

- If you knock the flash drive out of the USB jack—or if someone grabs it unthinkingly—Windows To Go simply freezes everything you were doing. Every document remains suspended; video or music playback pauses. If you reinsert the flash drive within 60 seconds, everything picks up exactly where you left off. If not, the system assumes you've gone home, and the PC shuts down. No trace of your activity remains on it.

Dialing In from the Road

Windows provides several avenues for accessing one PC from another across the Internet. If you're a road warrior armed with a laptop, you may be delighted by these features. If you're a corporate employee who used to think you could escape the office by going home, you may not.

In any case, each of these *remote access* features requires a good deal of setup and some scavenging through the technical underbrush, and each offers slightly different benefits and drawbacks. But when you're in Tulsa and a spreadsheet you need is on your PC in Tallahassee, you may be grateful to have at least one of these systems in place.

And besides—if you're connecting to PCs at your corporate office, your corporate IT people have probably already done all the hard work of getting the computers at work set up for you to connect to them from home or the road.

The two most common scenarios for using these remote access features are (a) controlling your home PC remotely using a laptop and (b) connecting to your office network from your PC at home. To help you keep the roles of these various computers straight, the computer industry has done you the favor of introducing specialized terminology:

- The *host computer* is the home-base computer—the unattended one that's waiting for you to connect.

- The *remote computer* is the one you'll be using: your laptop on the road, for example, or your home machine (or laptop) when you tap into the office network.

This chapter covers two systems of connecting:

- **Virtual private networking (VPN).** Using this system, you use the Internet as a secure link between the host and the remote machine. The remote computer behaves exactly as though it has joined the network of the host system—usually your company's network.

- **Remote Desktop.** This feature doesn't just make the remote PC join the network of the host; it actually turns your computer *into* the faraway host PC, filling your screen with its screen image. When you touch the trackpad on your laptop, you're actually moving the cursor on the home-base PC's screen, and so forth.

Tip: For added protection against snoopers, you should use Remote Desktop *with* a VPN connection.

To make Remote Desktop work, you have to connect *to* a computer running Windows 10, Windows 8 or 8.1, Windows 7 (Professional and above), Vista (Business and above), XP Pro, or Windows Server. But the machine you're connecting *from* can be any relatively recent Windows PC, a Macintosh (to get a free copy of Remote Desktop Connection for Mac, visit *www.microsoft.com/mac/*), or even a computer running Linux (you'll need the free *rdesktop client*, available from *www.rdesktop.org*).

Tip: The world is filled with more powerful, more flexible products that let you accomplish the same things as these Windows features, from software programs like Laplink and pcAnywhere to Web sites like *www.gotomypc.com*.

On the other hand, Remote Desktop is free.

Finally, note that these are all methods of connecting to an *unattended* machine. If somebody is sitting at the PC back home, you might find it far more convenient to connect using Remote Assistance. That's a screen-sharing feature that's easier to set up than Remote Desktop; it's described in the free downloadable PDF appendix "Remote Assistance.pdf" on this book's "Missing CD" page at *www.missingmanuals.com*.

Virtual Private Networking

All over the world, frequent travelers connect to distant homes or offices using *virtual private networking.* VPN is a fancy way of saying, "Your remote computer can become part of your host network over the Internet."

What corporations like most about VPN is that it's extremely secure. The information traveling between the two connected computers is encoded (encrypted) using a technology called *tunneling.* Your connection is like a reinforced steel pipe wending its way through the Internet to connect the two computers.

To create a VPN connection, the host computer has two important requirements. If you're VPNing into a corporation or a school, it's probably all set already. Otherwise:

- **It must be on the Internet** at the moment you try to connect. Usually that means it needs a full-time Internet connection, like cable modem or DSL.

- **It needs a fixed IP address.** (See the Note below.)

On the other hand, the remote computer—your laptop—doesn't have any such requirements. It just needs an Internet connection.

Note: Several of the remote-connection methods described in this chapter require that your home-base PC have a *fixed, public* IP address. (An IP address is a unique number that identifies a particular computer on the Internet. It's made up of four numbers separated by periods.)

If you're not immediately nodding in understanding, murmuring, "Ahhhhh, right," then download the bonus document available on this book's "Missing CD" page at *www.missingmanuals.com.* The free PDF supplement you'll find there is called "Getting a Fixed, Public IP Address."

Setting up your laptop

In general, the big network bosses who expect you to connect from the road have already set up the VPN software at *their* end. They may even have set up your laptop for you, so that dialing in from the road requires only one quick click.

But if not—if you want to set up your remote PC yourself—here are the steps:

1. **Open Settings→"Network & Internet"→VPN→"Add a VPN connection."**

   You wind up at the dialog box shown in Figure 13-8.

2. **Fill in the blanks.**

   You'll need to know the server name or registered IP address of the VPN host—that is, the computer you'll be tunneling into.

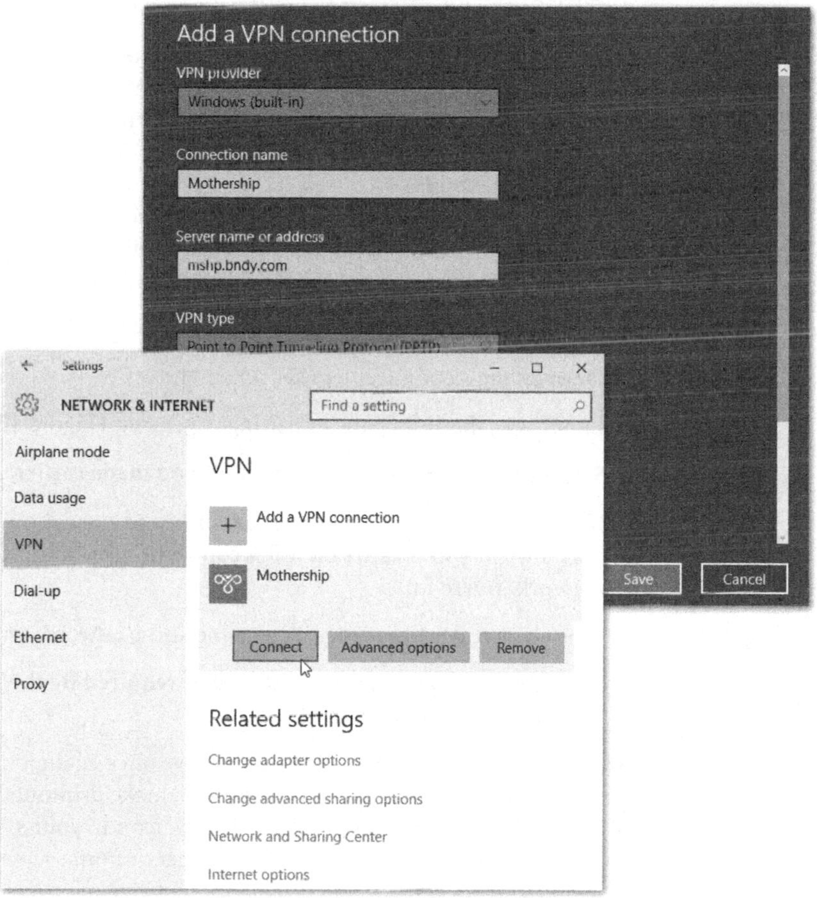

Figure 13-8:
Top: Here's where you set up your VPN connection, using the technical specs provided by the corporate IT person who takes care of you.

Bottom: Once you've set up the VPN, it shows up here, in Settings, ready for clicking and connecting.

If you fill in your user name and password now, and turn on "Remember my sign-in info," you won't have to retype it every time you connect. (Of course, don't set up a VPN this way on a public computer at the library or something.)

If you're connecting to a server at work or school, your system administrator can tell you what to type here. If you're connecting to a computer you set up yourself, specify its public IP address. (See the Note on page 456.)

This is *not* the private IP address on your home network, and definitely not its computer name (despite the fact that the New Incoming Connection wizard told you that you would need to use that name); neither of these work when you're logged into another network.

It doesn't matter what you type as the Connection name; this is just for your reference.

4. **Click Save.**

You might have noticed, if you're among the technically inclined, that you did not have to specify things like tunneling setups. Windows can figure that stuff out all by itself, saving you the technical bushwhacking.

Connecting to the VPN

Now, none of what you've achieved so far has actually gotten you online. All you've done is create a *VPN connection*—a stored, clickable icon for connecting to the mother ship. When the time comes to make the actual connection, read on.

1. **Open Settings→"Network & Internet"→VPN.**

Or open the Action Center (■+A) and hit VPN.

Either way, the VPN pane of Settings opens up (Figure 13-8, bottom).

2. **Select the icon of the VPN connection you made earlier, and then click Connect.**

If you entered your name and password (and turned on "Remember my sign-in info") when you created the VPN connection, you hop directly onto the distant network. You're in!

If not, you're asked to enter your name and password—take this final step:

3. **Type your user name, password, and, if required by the network administrator, the domain name. Then click OK.**

When you make the VPN connection, you've once again joined your home or office network. You should feel free to transfer files, make printouts, and even run programs on the distant PC. (If you open the Network icon in your system tray, you'll see that you're connected, and you'll see a Disconnect option.)

Changing your VPN settings

If the VPN connection doesn't work the first time—it hardly ever does—you can make some adjustments. Just reopen the panel of PC Settings where you created the

VPN connection in the first place, tap its name, and tap "Advanced options." Keep your company's highly trained network nerd nearby to help you.

Remote Desktop

Here's another remote-access option: Remote Desktop. When you use Remote Desktop, you're not just tapping into your home computer's network—you're actually bringing its screen onto your screen. You can run its programs, print on its printers, "type" on its keyboard, move its cursor, manage its files, and so on, all by remote control.

Remote Desktop isn't useful only when you're trying to connect to the office or reach your home computer from the road; it works even over an office network. You can actually take control of another computer in the office—to troubleshoot a novice's PC without having to run up or down a flight of stairs, perhaps, or just to run a program that isn't on your own machine.

If you do decide to use Remote Desktop over the Internet, consider setting up a VPN connection first; using Remote Desktop *over* a VPN connection adds a nice layer of security to the connection. It also means that you become part of your home or office network—and you can therefore connect to the distant computer using its private network address or even its computer name.

Tip: The computers on the *receiving* end of the connections require the fanciest versions of Windows Vista, 7, 8, or 10 (not the Home editions). But the laptop *you're* using can be running any edition. In fact, it can be running any version of Windows all the way back to 95, and even Mac OS X or Linux.

To install the Remote Desktop Connection client on OS X or an older version of Windows, visit the Microsoft Download Center (*www.microsoft.com/downloads/*) and search for "Remote Desktop Connection." For Linux, get the free rdesktop program at *www.rdesktop.org.*

Setting up the host machine

To get a PC ready for invasion—that is, to turn it into a host—proceed like this:

1. **Right-click the lower-left corner of the screen (or press ⊞+X). From the shortcut menu, choose System.**

   The System pane of the Control Panel appears.

2. **At the left side, click "Remote settings."**

   The System Properties dialog box opens to the Remote tab. Set things up as directed in Figure 13-9.

3. **Click OK twice to close the dialog boxes you opened.**

   The host computer is now ready for invasion. It's listening to the network for incoming connections from Remote Desktop clients.

Making the connection

When you're ready to try Remote Desktop, fire up your laptop, or whatever computer will be doing the remote connecting.

Note: *As a first step, you may be required (by your bosses) to connect to the VPN of the distant host computer, as described earlier in this chapter. If the host computer is elsewhere on your local network—in the same building, that is—you can skip this step.*

Figure 13-9:
Top: Here's the master switch for Remote Desktop (you're looking at the lower part of the box, not the Remote Assistance section).

Turn on "Allow remote connections to this computer."

A message may warn you that when this computer goes to sleep, people won't be able to connect to it. Click OK—or first click the Power Options link to turn off automatic sleep and hibernation.

For added protection against ruthless hackers, you can also turn on "Allow connections only from computers running Remote Desktop with Network Level Authentication (recommended)." What it means is, "Accept connections only from Windows 7 and higher machines." Turn this option off if any other kind of machine might want to hook up.

Now click Select Users.

Bottom: You certainly don't want teenage hackers to visit your precious PC from across the Internet, playing your games and reading your personal info. Fortunately, you can specify precisely who is allowed to connect.

Click Add. In the resulting dialog box, type the names of the people who are allowed to access your PC using Remote Desktop.

By default, local users with administrative privileges are automatically given access.

Choose your comrades carefully; remember that they'll be able to do anything to your system, by remote control, that you could do while sitting in front of it. (To ensure security, Windows insists that the accounts you're selecting here have passwords. Although you can add them to this list, password-free accounts can't connect.) Click OK.

1. **Open the Remote Desktop Connection program.**

   Here's one way. In the taskbar search box, type *remote* and then, when Remote Desktop Connections appears in the results list, click it or press Enter. The Remote Desktop Connection dialog box appears.

2. **Click Show Options to expand the dialog box (if necessary). Fill it out as shown in Figure 13-10.**

   The idea is to specify the IP address or DNS name of the computer you're trying to reach. If it's on the same network, or if you're connected via a VPN, you can use its computer name instead.

Figure 13-10:
Click Show Options (not shown) if you don't see these tabs.

Once you've made them appear, a few useful settings become available (and a lot of rarely useful ones).

On the General tab (top), you can enter (and tell Windows to remember) your name and password for the connection. If you're connecting to a network outside your building, you'll probably have to type in its IP address—something only the company's network nerds can tell you.

On the Display tab (bottom), for example, you can effectively reduce the size of the other computer's screen so that it fits within your laptop's. On the Experience tab, you can turn off special-effect animations to speed up the connection.

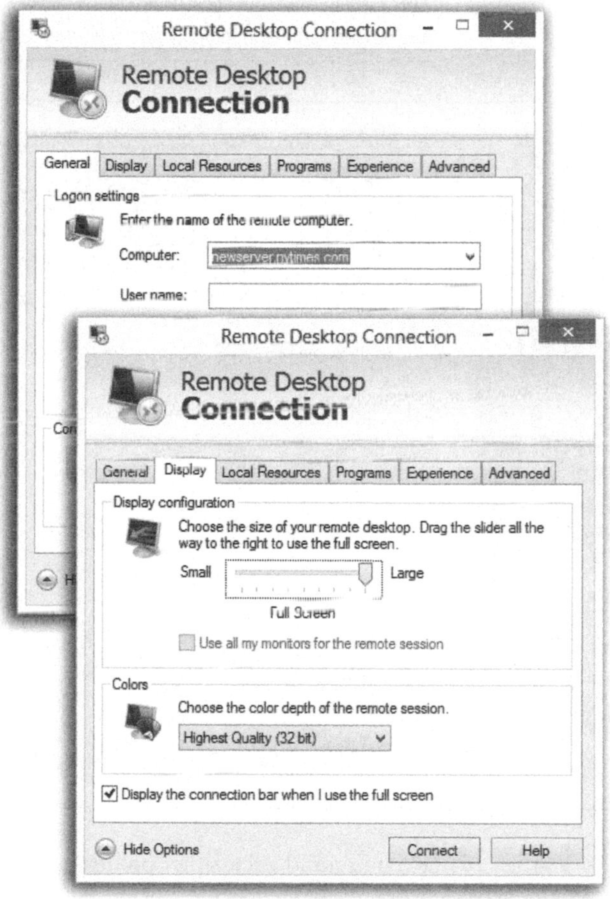

3. Click Connect.

Now a freaky thing happens: After a moment of pitch-blackness, the host computer's screen fills your own (Figure 13-11). Don't be confused by the fact that all the open windows on the computer you're using have now *disappeared*. (Actually, they won't if you click the Display tab and choose a smaller-than-full-screen remote desktop size before you connect.)

You can now operate the distant PC as though you were there in the flesh, using your own keyboard (or trackpad) and mouse. You can answer your email, make long-distance printouts, and so on. All the action—running programs, changing settings, and so on—is actually taking place on the faraway host computer.

Tip: You can even shut down or restart the faraway machine by remote control. Open a Command Prompt and run the command *shutdown /s*. The computer will shut down in less than a minute.

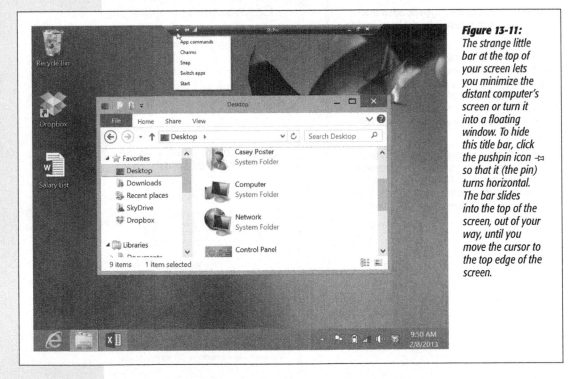

Figure 13-11:
The strange little bar at the top of your screen lets you minimize the distant computer's screen or turn it into a floating window. To hide this title bar, click the pushpin icon ⊷ so that it (the pin) turns horizontal. The bar slides into the top of the screen, out of your way, until you move the cursor to the top edge of the screen.

Keep in mind a few other points:

• You don't need to feel completely blocked out of your own machine. The little title bar at the top of the screen offers you the chance to put the remote computer's screen into a floating window of its own, permitting you to see both your own screen and the home-base computer's screen simultaneously (Figure 13-12). You can return to full-screen mode by pressing Ctrl+Alt+Break.

- If the host computer is running Windows 8, but you're on Windows 10, you might wonder: How can I open the App bar, Charms bar, Start screen, and so on? That's the purpose of the ▾ menu at the left end of the control bar, shown open in Figure 13-11. It lists "App commands" (meaning the App bar), Charms, Snap (meaning "Split the screen between two apps"), "Switch apps" (opens the app switcher at the left side), and Start (opens the Start screen).

- You can copy and paste highlighted text or graphics between the two machines (using regular Copy and Paste), and even transfer entire documents back and forth (using Copy and Paste on the desktop icons). Of course, if you've made both desktops visible simultaneously, you can move more quickly between local and remote.

- Even Windows can't keep its mind focused on two people at once. If somebody is trying to use the host machine in person, you'll see a message to the effect that you're about to bump that person off the PC.

  Similarly, if somebody logs on at the host computer, *you* get unceremoniously dumped off. (You just get a message that tells you, "Another user connected to the remote computer.") Fortunately, you don't lose work this way—your account remains logged on behind the scenes, just as in fast user switching. When you connect again later (after the interloper has signed off), you'll find all your programs and documents open exactly as you (or your interloper) left them.

- Back at the host computer, nobody can see what you're doing. The standard Welcome screen appears on the remote PC, masking your activities.

Keyboard shortcuts for the hopelessly confused

When the Remote Desktop Connection window is maximized (fills your entire screen), all the standard Windows keyboard shortcuts operate on the *host* computer, not the one you're actually using. When you press the ⊞ key, for example, you see the host computer's Start menu.

Note: There's one exception: When you press Ctrl+Alt+Delete, *your* computer processes the keystroke.

But in window-in-a-window mode (Figure 13-12), it's a different story. Now your current computer "hears" your keystrokes. Now, pressing ⊞ opens *your* Start menu. So how, with the remote PC's screen in a window, are you supposed to operate it by remote control?

One solution: On the Local Resources tab of the dialog box shown in Figure 13-10, you can specify which computer "hears" your keyboard shortcuts.

Another: Use Microsoft's alternatives for the key combinations. For example, when the Remote Desktop window isn't full screen, pressing Alt+Tab switches to the next open program on *your* computer—but pressing Alt+Page Up switches to the next program on the *host* computer.

Here's a summary of the special keys that operate the distant host computer—a table that can be useful if you're either an extreme power user or somebody who likes to win bar bets:

Standard Windows Key Combination	Remote Desktop Key Combination	Function
Alt+Tab	Alt+Page Up	Switches to the next open program
Alt+Shift+Tab	Alt+Page Down	Switches to the previous open program
Alt+Esc	Alt+Insert	Cycles through programs in the order in which you open them
Ctrl+Esc (or ⊞)	Alt+Home	Opens the Start menu
Ctrl+Alt+Delete	Ctrl+Alt+End	Displays the Windows Security dialog box

(Actually, you should use the alternative key combination for the Security dialog box whether the Remote Desktop window is maximized or not, because Ctrl+Alt+Delete is always interpreted by the computer you're currently using.)

Figure 13-12:
By putting the other computer's screen into a window of its own, you save yourself a little bit of confusion. You can even minimize the remote computer's screen entirely, reducing it to a tab on your taskbar until you need it again.

Disconnecting

To get out of Remote Desktop full-screen mode, click the Close box in the strange little bar at the top of your screen; if you're using the floating window, you can click the usual ✕ in the upper right.

Note, however, that this method leaves all your programs running and your documents open on the distant machine, exactly as though you had used fast user switching. If you log on again, either from the road or in person, you'll find all those programs and documents still on the screen, just as you left them.

If you'd rather log off in a more permanent way, open the Start menu on the other computer, click your account picture, and choose "Sign out."

Fine-tuning Remote Desktop connections

Windows offers all kinds of settings for tailoring the way this bizarre, schizophrenic connection method works. The trick is, however, that you have to change them *before* you connect, using the tabs on the dialog box shown in Figure 13-10.

Here's what you find:

- **General tab.** Here's where you can tell Windows to edit or delete credentials (user name and password) from your last login, or to save all the current settings as a shortcut icon, which makes it faster to reconnect later. (If you connect to a number of different distant computers, saving a setup for each one can be a huge timesaver.)

- **Display tab.** Use these options to specify the *size* (resolution) of the host computer's display.

- **Local Resources tab.** Using these controls, you can set up local peripherals and add-ons so they behave as though they were connected to the computer you're using. This is also where you tell Windows which PC should "hear" keystrokes like Alt+Tab, and whether or not you want to hear sound effects played by the distant machine.

- **Programs tab.** You can set up a certain program to run automatically as soon as you connect to the host machine.

POWER USERS' CLINIC

Remote Networking vs. Remote Control

When you connect to a PC using direct dial or virtual private networking (VPN), you're simply joining the host's network from far away. When you try to open a Word document that's actually sitting on the distant PC, your *laptop's* copy of Word opens and loads the file. Your laptop is doing the actual word processing; the host just sends and receives files as needed.

Windows' Remote Desktop feature is a different animal. In this case, you're using your laptop to *control* the host computer. If you double-click that Word file on the host computer, you open the copy of Word *on the host computer.* All the word processing takes place on the distant machine; all that passes over the connection between the two computers is a series of keystrokes, mouse movements, and screen displays. The host is doing all the work. Your laptop is just peeking at the results.

Once you understand the differences between these technologies, you can make a more informed decision about which to use when. For example, suppose your PC at the office has a folder containing 100 megabytes of images you need to incorporate into a PowerPoint document. Using a remote networking connection means you'll have to wait for the files to be transmitted to your laptop before you can begin working.

If you use a Remote Desktop connection, on the other hand, the files remain right where they are: on the host computer, which does all the processing. You see on your screen exactly what you would see if you were sitting at the office. When you drag and drop one of those images into your PowerPoint document, all the action is taking place on the PC at the other end.

Of course, if the computer doing the dialing is a brand-new Intel i35 zillion-megahertz screamer, and the host system is a 5-year-old rust bucket on its last legs, you might actually *prefer* a remote network connection, so the faster machine can do most of the heavy work.

- **Experience tab.** Tell Windows the speed of your connection, so it can limit fancy visual effects like menu animation, the desktop wallpaper, and so on, to avoid slowing down the connection.

- **Advanced.** You can control whether Remote Desktop Connection warns you if it can't verify the identity of a computer, and also whether to connect through a special gateway server (if you need to use one of these, your system administrator will tell you).

CHAPTER 14

Printing, Fonts & PDFs

Technologists got pretty excited about "the paperless office" in the 1980s, but the PC explosion had exactly the opposite effect. Thanks to the proliferation of inexpensive, high-quality PC printers, the world generates far more printouts than ever. Fortunately, there's not much to printing from Windows 10.

Since they seem like vaguely printing-related subjects, this chapter also covers Windows' font technologies, and one of the best new features in Windows 10: The ability to turn any document into a PDF document with one click. OK, two.

Installing a Printer

A printer is a peripheral device—something outside the PC—and as such, it won't work without a piece of *driver software* explaining the new hardware to Windows. In general, getting this driver installed is a simple process. It's described in more detail in Chapter 15.

The good news, though, is that Windows comes with the drivers for thousands of printers, all different brands, ready to be installed. Read on.

USB Printers

If the technology gods are smiling, then here's the entire set of instructions for installing a typical inkjet USB printer:

1. **Connect the printer to the computer.**

   That's it. Turn on the printer— you're ready to print. No driver operations, no setup. Next time you print something, you'll see the printer's name in the Print dialog box.

The backup plan

In certain situations, the printer doesn't "just work" when you plug it in. Maybe it's wireless. Maybe it's older.

In that case, here's your Plan B: Open Settings→Devices→Printers & Scanners (Figure 14-1). Choose "Add a printer or scanner." Now Windows shows you the printer's name; select it, hit "Add device," and off you go.

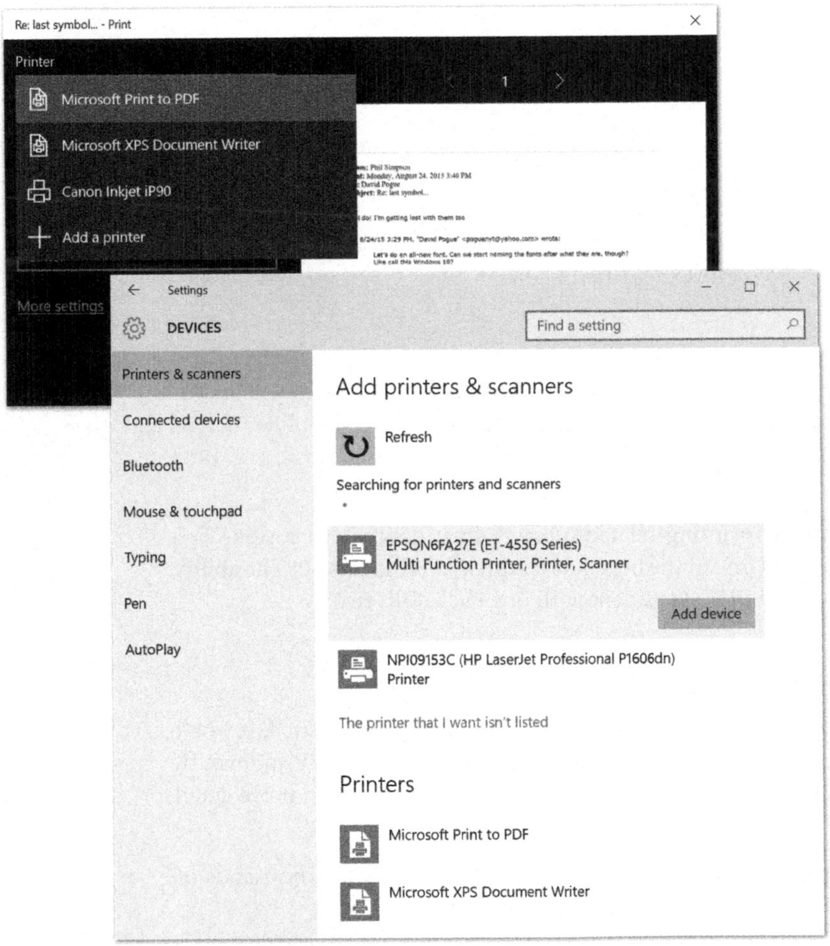

Figure 14-1:
Top: When you plug in a typical inkjet printer, its name shows up immediately in the Printer list (in the box that appears when you print). Mission accomplished.

Bottom: Now and then, you may have to visit the "Printers & scanners" page of Settings. At bottom are the printers your PC already knows about. At top are the controls to help you find a new wireless printer. If you still don't see the printer's name, yet it's turned on and connected (or on the network), hit "The printer that I want isn't listed."

The backup backup plan

If you have a *really* old printer, its drivers might not be compatible with Windows 10. Check the manufacturer's Web site, such as *www.epson.com* or *www.hp.com,* or a central driver repository like *www.windrivers.com* to see if there's anything newer.

In dire situations, you might have to call upon the mighty powers of the "Find a printer by other options" wizard. Open Settings→Devices→Printers & Scanners, hit "The printer that I want isn't listed," and walk through the friendly onscreen guidance.

Network Printers

If you work in an office where people on the network share a single printer (usually a laser printer), the printer usually isn't connected directly to your computer. Instead, it's elsewhere on the network; your PC's Ethernet cable or wireless antenna connects you to it indirectly.

In general, there's very little involved in ensuring that your PC "sees" this printer, either. Its icon simply shows up in your Print dialog box.

The Devices and Printers Window

The modern, Windows 10 resting place for printer and scanner icons is the Settings page shown in Figure 14-1.

The ancient, Windows 7–style resting place is still available, though. That would be the Devices and Printers window (Figure 14-2). It can still be useful, because it offers more commands and options than the Settings app does.

To get there, do a taskbar search for *printers*. In the search results, click Devices and Printers.

Figure 14-2:
At first, the toolbar in the Devices and Printers window offers few commands. But when you click a particular printer icon, other useful options appear, as shown here. Some of them duplicate the options that appear when you right-click a printer icon.

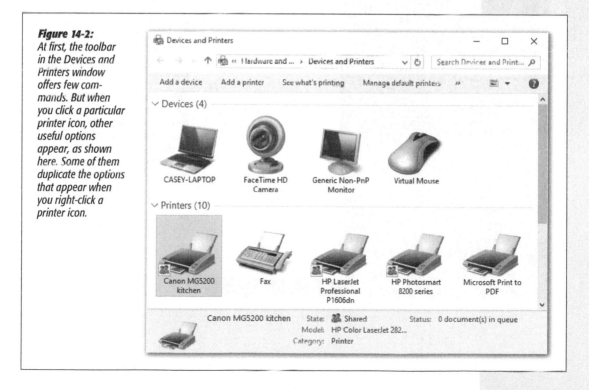

Printing

Once you've connected a printer or three, printing is little more than a one-click operation.

After you've created a document you want to see on paper, start the printout. The object is simply to find the Print command; it shouldn't be hard. For example, in Mail and the Edge browser, it's in the More (⋯) menu. In Microsoft Office programs Word and Excel, it's in the File menu. The steps differ depending on which kind of app you're using:

Printing from Windows Store Apps

If you're printing from a Windows Store app, like most of the built-in Windows 10 programs, you wind up at the Print dialog box (Figure 14-3).

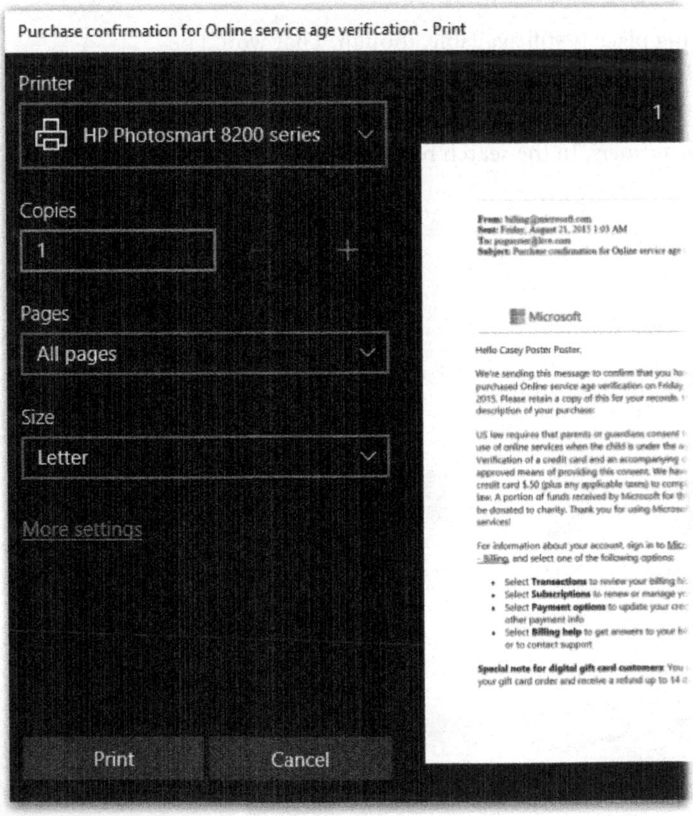

Figure 14-3:
Whereas the traditional Windows Print dialog box looks like a space shuttle cockpit, there's nothing to set up here except the printer you want to use, number of copies you want, which pages you want to print, and what paper size you're using.

If the printout is longer than one page, you can also use the number box below the page preview to have a glance at a different page of the preview.

And if you want to change any of the tweakier settings—page orientation, paper quality, color mode (for color printers), paper tray, and so on—hit "More settings." But that stuff is generally hidden until you need it, which is probably rarely.

Printing from Desktop Programs

In a desktop program—a non-Windows Store app—choose File→Print, click the Print button on the toolbar, or press Ctrl+P. The Print dialog box appears, as shown in Figure 14-4.

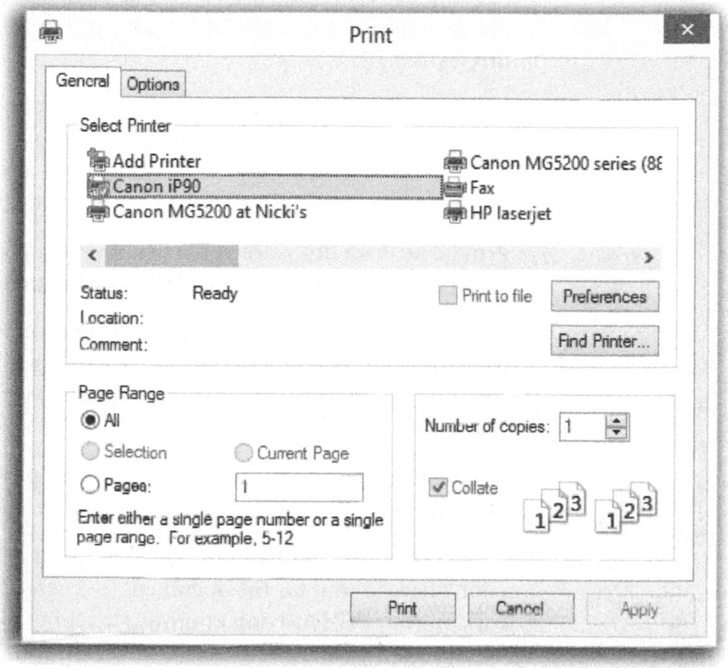

Figure 14-4:
The options in the Print dialog box are different for each printer model and each program, so your Print dialog box may look slightly different. Most of the time, the factory settings shown here are what you want (one copy, print all pages). Just click OK or Print (or press Enter) to close this dialog box and send the document to the printer.

This dialog box, too, changes depending on the program you're using—the Print dialog box in Microsoft Word looks a lot more intimidating than the WordPad version—and the printer model. But you'll usually find these basics here:

- **Select Printer.** If your PC is connected to several printers, choose the one you want from this list of printers.

- **Preferences/Properties.** Clicking this button opens a version of the printer's Properties dialog box, where you can change the paper size you're using, whether you want to print sideways on the page (landscape orientation), what kind of paper—or photo paper—you're using, and so on. Here you're making changes only for a particular printout; you're not changing any settings for the printer itself. (The specific features of this dialog box depend on the program you're using.)

- **Page Range** controls which pages of the document you want to print. If you want to print only some of the pages, click the Pages option and type in the page numbers you want (with a hyphen, like *3-6* to print pages 3 through 6).

Tip: You can also type in individual page numbers with commas, like *2, 4, 9,* to print only those three pages—or even add hyphens to the mix, like this: *1-3, 5-6, 13-18.*

Click Current Page to print only the page where you've placed the blinking insertion point. Click Selection to print only the text you selected (highlighted) before opening the Print dialog box. (If this option button is dimmed, it's because you didn't highlight any text—or because you're using a program that doesn't offer this feature.)

- **Number of copies.** To print out several copies of the same thing, use this box to specify the exact number. You get several copies of page 1, then several copies of page 2, and so on, in sequence—*unless* you also turn on the Collate checkbox, which produces complete sets of pages, in order.

- **Print.** The Print drop-down list that might appear in the lower-left section of the dialog box offers three options: "All pages in range," "Odd pages," and "Even pages."

  Use the Odd and Even pages options when you have to print on both sides of the paper but your printer has no special feature for this purpose. You'll have to print all the odd pages, turn the stack of printouts over, and then run the pages through the printer again to print the even pages.

- **Application-specific options.** The particular program you're using may add a few extra options of its own to an Options tab in this dialog box.

When you've finished making changes to the print job, click OK or Print, or press Enter. You don't have to wait for the document to emerge from the printer before returning to work on your PC. (Just don't put your machine to sleep until it's finished printing.)

Tip: During printing, the tiny icon of a printer appears in your system tray. Pointing to it without clicking produces a pop-up tooltip that reveals the background printing activity.

Printing from the Desktop

You don't necessarily have to print a document while it's open in front of you. You can, if you wish, print it directly from the desktop or from a File Explorer window in a couple of ways:

- Right-click the document icon, and then choose Print from the shortcut menu. Windows opens the program that created it—Word or Excel, for example. The document is then printed automatically to the default printer.

- If you've opened the printer's own print queue window (Figure 14-5) by right-clicking the Printers icon in your Devices and Printers window and choosing "See what's printing," then you can drag any document icon directly into the list of waiting printouts. Its name joins the others on the list.

These methods bypass the Print dialog box and therefore give you no way to specify which pages you want to print, or how many copies. You just get one copy of the entire document.

Controlling Printouts

Between the moment you click OK in the Print dialog box and the arrival of the first page in the printer's tray, there's a delay. Usually, it's brief, but when you're printing a complex document with lots of graphics, the delay can be considerable.

Fortunately, the waiting doesn't necessarily make you less productive, since you can return to work on your PC, or even quit the application and go watch TV. An invisible program called the *print spooler* supervises this background printing process. The spooler collects the document that's being sent to the printer, along with all the codes the printer expects to receive, and then sends this information, little by little, to the printer.

Note: The spooler program creates huge temporary printer files, so a hard drive that's nearly full can wreak havoc with background printing.

To see the list of documents waiting to be printed—the ones that have been stored by the spooler—open the Devices and Printers window, right-click your printer's icon, and then choose "See what's printing" to open its window.

Tip: While the printer is printing, a printer icon appears in the system tray. As a shortcut to opening the printer's window, just double-click that icon.

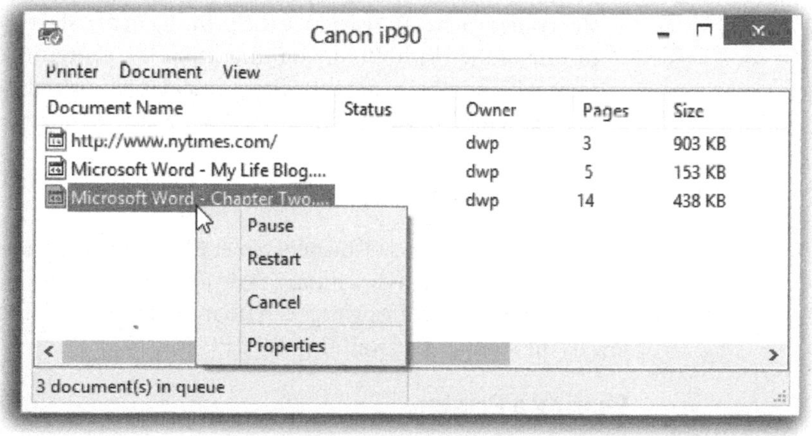

Figure 14-5:
By right-clicking documents in this list, you can pause or cancel any document in the queue— or all of them at once.

The printer's window lists the documents currently printing and waiting; this list is called the *print queue* (or just the *queue*), as shown in Figure 14-5. (Documents in the list print in top-to-bottom order.)

You can manipulate documents in a print queue in any of the following ways during printing:

- **Put one on hold.** To pause a document (put it on hold), right-click its name, and then choose Pause from the shortcut menu (Figure 14-5). When you're ready to let the paused document continue to print, right-click its listing and choose Resume.

- **Put them all on hold.** To pause the printer, choose Printer→Pause Printing from the window's menu bar. You might do this when, for example, you need to change the paper in the printer's tray. (Choose Printer→Pause Printing again when you want the printing to pick up from where it left off.)

- **Add another one.** As noted earlier, you can drag any document icon directly *from its disk or folder window* into the printer queue. Its name joins the list of printouts-in-waiting.

- **Cancel one.** To cancel a printout, click its name and then press the Delete key. If you click Yes in the confirmation box, the document disappears from the queue; it'll never print out. (Or right-click it and choose Cancel from the shortcut menu.)

- **Cancel all of them.** To cancel the printing of all the documents in the queue, choose Printer→Cancel All Documents.

Note: A page or so may still print after you've paused or canceled a printout. Your printer has its own memory (the *buffer*), which stores the printout as it's sent from your PC. If you pause or cancel printing, you're only stopping the spooler from sending *more* data to the printer.

- **Rearrange them.** To rearrange the printing order, start by right-clicking the name of one of the printouts-in-waiting; from the shortcut menu, choose Properties. On the General tab, drag the Priority slider left or right. Documents with higher priorities print first.

Fancy Printer Tricks

The masses of Windows owners generally slog through life choosing File→Print, clicking OK, and then drumming their fingers as they wait for the paper to slide out of the printer. But your printer can do more than that—much more. Here are just a few of the stunts that await the savvy PC fan.

Sharing a Printer

If you have more than one PC connected to a network, as described in Chapter 21, they all can use the same printer—even the cheapest little inkjet connected to a USB port.

To begin, sit down at the computer to which the printer is attached. Open the Devices and Printers window (Figure 14-2). Right-click the printer's icon; from the shortcut menu, choose "Printer properties." Continue as described in Figure 14-6.

Once you've *shared* the printer, its icon shows up in the Devices and Printers windows of all other computers on the same networking HomeGroup (Chapter 21). It's listed in their Print dialog boxes, their Printer windows, and so on.

Figure 14-6:
Open Devices and Printers. Right-click the printer you want to share, and then click "Printer properties." Click the Sharing tab. (If you see a "Change sharing options" button, click it.)

Finally, turn on "Share this printer." Click OK.

Now this printer is available to other computers on the same network.

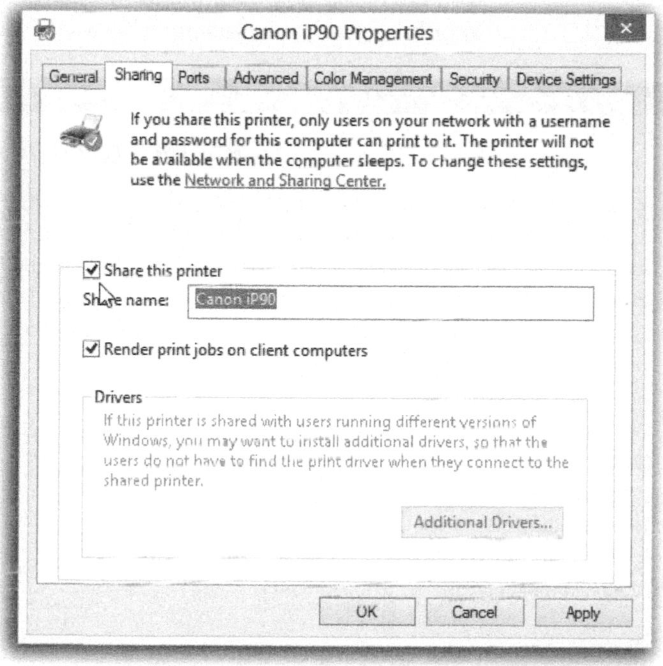

Limiting Hours of Access

If it's just you, your Dell, and a color inkjet, then you're entitled to feel baffled by this feature, which lets you declare your printer off-limits during certain hours of the day. But if you're the manager of some office whose expensive color laser printer makes printouts that cost a dollar apiece, you may welcome a feature that prevents employees from hanging around after hours in order to print out 500 copies of their headshots.

To specify such an access schedule for a certain printer, right-click your printer's icon in the Devices and Printers window. From the shortcut menu, choose Properties, and then click the Advanced tab. Select "Available from," and use the time-setting controls to specify when your underlings are allowed to use this printer from across the network. Clicking OK renders the printer inoperable during off hours.

Add a Separator Page

If your PC is on a network whose other members bombard a single laser printer with printouts, you might find *separator pages* useful—the printer version of fax cover sheets. A separator page is generated before each printout, identifying the document and its owner.

This option, too, is accessible from the Advanced tab of the printer's Properties dialog box. Click the Separator Page button at the bottom of the dialog box. In the Separator Page dialog box, click the Browse button to choose a *.sep* (separator page) file. Sysprint.sep is the one you probably want. Not only does this page include the name,

---

POWER USERS' CLINIC

Color Management

As you may have discovered through painful experience, computers aren't great with color. That's because each device you use to create and print digital images "sees" color a little bit differently, which explains why the deep amber captured by your scanner may be rendered as brownish on your monitor but come out as a bit orangey on your Epson inkjet printer. Since every gadget defines and renders color in its own way, colors are often inconsistent as a print job moves from design to proof to press.

The Windows *color management system* (CMS) attempts to sort out this mess, serving as a translator among all the different pieces of hardware in your workflow. For this to work, each device (scanner, monitor, printer, copier, and so on) must be calibrated with a unique *CMS profile*—a file that tells your PC exactly how your particular monitor (or scanner, or printer, or digital camera) defines colors. Armed with the knowledge contained within the profiles, the CMS software can make on-the-fly color corrections, compensating for the quirks of the various devices.

Most of the people who lose sleep over color fidelity do commercial color scanning and printing, where "off" colors

are a big deal—after all, a customer might return a product if the actual product color doesn't match the photo on a Web site. Furthermore, not every gadget comes with a CMS profile, and not every gadget can even accommodate one. (If yours does, you'll see a tab called Color Management in the Properties dialog box for your printer.)

If you're interested in this topic, open the Color Management applet of the Control Panel. (Do a taskbar search for *color management*.) From the Device pop-up menu, choose your printer's name.

The Automatic setting usually means that Windows came with its own profile for your printer, which it has automatically assigned. If you click Manual, you can override this decision and apply a new color profile (that you downloaded from the printer company's Web site, for example).

Remember to follow the same procedure for the other pieces of your color chain—monitors, scanners, and so on. Look for the Color Management tab or dialog box, accessible from their respective Properties dialog boxes.

---

date, time, and so on, but it also automatically switches the laser printer to PostScript mode—if it's not already in that mode, and if it's a PostScript printer.

Printer Troubleshooting

If you're having a problem printing, the first diagnosis you must make is whether the problem is related to *software* or *hardware*. A software problem may mean the driver files have become damaged. A hardware problem means there's something wrong with the printer, the port, the cable, the toner, the ink, or whatever.

If you're guessing it's a software problem—fairly likely—reinstall the printer driver. Open Settings→Devices→Printers & Scanners and hit "Add a printer or scanner," right-click the printer's icon, and then choose Remove Device from the shortcut menu. Then reinstall the printer as described at the beginning of this chapter.

If the problem seems to be hardware-related, try these steps in sequence:

- Check the lights or the LED panel readout on the printer. If you see anything other than the normal "Ready" indicator, then check the printer's manual to diagnose the problem.

- Turn the printer off and on to clear any memory problems.

- Check the printer's manual to learn how to print a test page.

- Check the cable to make sure both ends are firmly and securely plugged into the correct ports.

- Test the cable. Use another cable, or take your cable to another computer/printer combination.

If none of these steps leads to an accurate diagnosis, you may have a problem with the port, which is more complicated. Or, even worse, the problem may originate from your PC's motherboard (main circuit board), or the printer's. In that case, your computer (or printer) needs professional attention.

Fonts

Some extremely sophisticated programming has gone into the typefaces that are listed in the Fonts dialog boxes of your word processor and other programs. They use *OpenType* and *TrueType* technology, meaning that no matter what point size you select for these fonts, they look smooth and professional—both on the screen and when you print.

Managing Your Fonts

Windows comes with several dozen great-looking fonts: Arial, Book Antiqua, Garamond, Times New Roman, and so on. But the world is filled with additional fonts. You may find them on Web sites or in the catalogs of commercial typeface companies. Sometimes you'll find new fonts on your system after installing a new program, courtesy of its installer.

To review the files that represent your typefaces, do a search for *fonts*, and open the Control Panel result called Fonts. As Figure 14-7 illustrates, it's easy and enlightening to explore this folder.

Tip: The Fonts icon in your Control Panel window is only a shortcut to the *real* folder, which is in your Local Disk (C:)→Windows→Fonts folder.

To remove a font from your system, select its icon and then hit Delete on the toolbar. To install a new font, first download the font (from the Internet, for example) and then drag its file icon into this window (or right-click the font and then click Install). You can also choose to show or hide specific fonts in your programs. The Fonts window

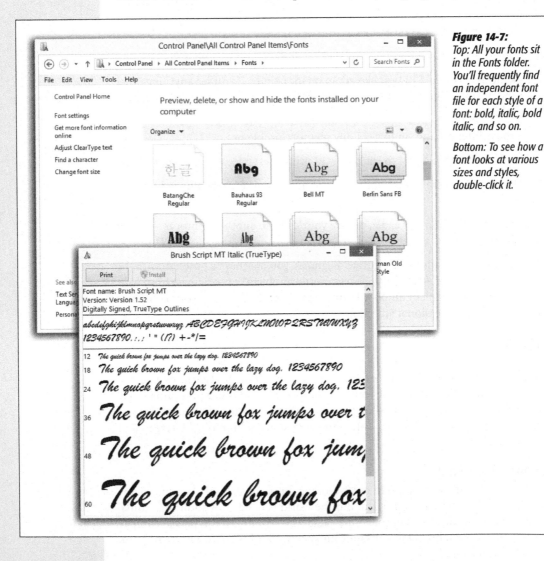

Figure 14-7:
Top: All your fonts sit in the Fonts folder. You'll frequently find an independent font file for each style of a font: bold, italic, bold italic, and so on.

Bottom: To see how a font looks at various sizes and styles, double-click it.

in Control Panel includes a column that shows the status of a font. Select a font, and then click Show or Hide to make this font available in the programs you use.

Whatever you do, you see the changes immediately reflected in your programs' Font dialog boxes; you don't even have to quit and reopen them.

PDF Files

Sooner or later, you'll encounter PDF (portable document format) files. Many a software manual, brochure, Read Me file, and downloadable "white paper" come in this format. Until recently, you needed the free program called Adobe Reader if you hoped to open or print these files. In Windows 10, they open up in the Edge browser, for your perusal pleasure.

In fact, in Windows 10, you can turn *any document* (in any program with a Print command) into a PDF file—a trick that once required a $250 program called Adobe Acrobat Distiller.

Note: All right, technically Windows alone creates *screen-optimized* PDF files: compact, easy-to-email files that look good onscreen but don't have high enough resolution for professional printing. For high-end purposes and more optimization for specific uses (Web, fancy press machines, and so on), you still need a program like Adobe Acrobat, Illustrator, or InDesign.

But why would you want to create PDFs? What's the big deal about them? Consider these advantages:

- **Other people see your layout.** When you distribute PDF files to other people, they see precisely the same fonts, colors, page design, and other elements you put in your original document. And here's the kicker: They get to see all of this even if they don't *have* the fonts or the software you used to create the document. (Contrast with the alternative: Say you're sending somebody a Microsoft Word document. If your correspondent doesn't have precisely the same fonts you have, then he'll see a screwy layout. And if he doesn't have Word or a program that can open Word files, he'll see nothing at all.)

- **It's universal.** PDF files are very common in the Windows, Mac, Unix/Linux, and even smartphone worlds. When you create a PDF file, you can distribute it (by email, for example) without worrying about what kinds of computers your correspondents are using.

- **It has very high resolution.** PDF files print at the maximum quality of any printer. A PDF file prints great both on cheapo inkjets and on high-quality image-setting gear at professional print shops. (Right now you're looking at a PDF file that was printed at a publishing plant.)

- **You can search it.** A PDF file may look like a captured graphic, but behind the scenes, its text is still text; Spotlight can find a word in a PDF haystack in a matter of seconds. That's an especially handy feature when you work with electronic software manuals in PDF format.

Opening PDF Files

There's nothing to opening up a PDF file: Just double-click it. Edge takes over from there and opens the PDF file on your screen. You can scroll through it, or zoom in and out (using the Zoom commands in the ⋯ menu).

Creating PDF Files

Opening, schmopening—what's really exciting in Windows 10 is the ability to create your *own* PDF files.

Just use the standard Print command as you always do—but in the spot where you'd specify which printer you want to use, choose Microsoft Print to PDF; see Figure 14-8).

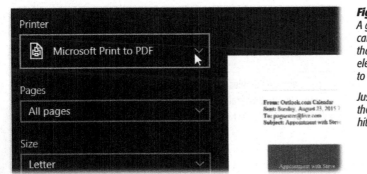

Figure 14-8:
A great new feature of Windows 10: You can now turn any document—anything that you can print to paper—into an electronic PDF file, for easy distribution to anyone with any kind of computer.

Just choose "Microsoft Print to PDF" as the printer, as shown here, and then hit Print.

Faxing

In the increasingly rare event that your PC has a built-in fax modem, and your PC is connected to a phone line, it can serve as a true-blue fax machine. This feature works like a charm, saves money on paper and fax cartridges, and may even spare you the expense of buying a physical fax machine.

You even get a dedicated program, Windows Fax and Scan, for the purpose of managing faxes. For step-by-step instructions, see the free downloadable PDF appendix, "Faxing from Windows 10," on this book's "Missing CD" page at *www.missingmanuals.com*.

Scanning Documents

Faxing isn't the only technology that turns paper into digital bits. Scanning is the other—and that, too, is a talent of Windows Fax and Scan.

First, install your scanner (and its driver) as described in Chapter 15.

Load it up with the page you want to scan. Open the Windows Fax and Scan program. (You can find it with a quick search.)

Click New Scan. The New Scan dialog box appears. Click Preview to trigger a quick, temporary scan so that you can see how the document will look after the scan (Figure 14-9). If it all looks good, click Scan.

Once the document has magically turned into a graphic in your Scan list, you can do all kinds of neat things with it: Forward it as a fax or an email attachment (click Forward as Fax or Forward as E-mail on the toolbar); export it as a JPEG, GIF, BMP, TIFF, or PNG document (click "Save as" on the toolbar); print it; or delete it.

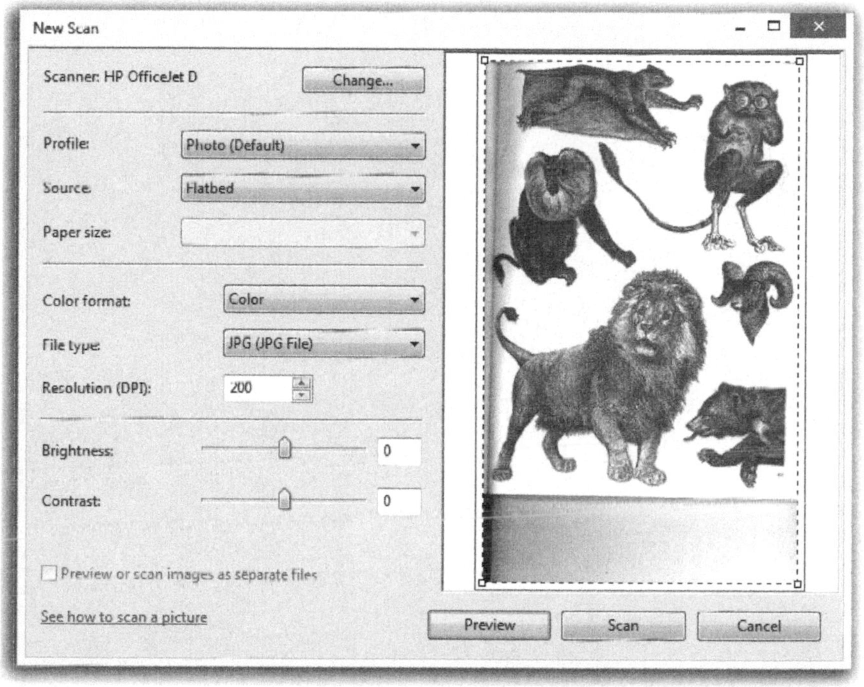
New Scan
Scanner: HP OfficeJet D
Change...
Profile:
Photo (Default)
Source:
Flatbed
Paper size:
Color format:
Color
File type:
JPG (JPG File)
Resolution (DPI):
200
Brightness:
0
Contrast:
0
Preview or scan images as separate files
See how to scan a picture
Preview
Scan
Cancel

Figure 14-9: *In this box, you have the chance to specify what sort of thing you want to scan–picture? document?–and specify its resolution and color settings.*

Choose 300 to 600 dots per inch resolution (dpi) for professional scans; for everyday scanning, 150 to 200 dpi is plenty. The more dots, the bigger the resulting file.

FREQUENTLY ASKED QUESTION

Scanning Text–and Then Editing It

I scanned an article from a magazine. How do I copy a couple of paragraphs from it into my word processor?

When you scan an article or a page of a book, you're not capturing text; you're just taking a *picture* of text. You can no more copy and paste a paragraph out of the resulting graphics file than you can copy text out of a photograph. Your PC sees everything on the scanned page as one gigantic graphic.

If you want to edit text you've scanned, then you need *optical character recognition (OCR)* software, which comes free with certain scanners. This kind of software analyzes the patterns of dots in a scanned graphics file and does a fairly good job of turning it into a word processor document that contains the original text. When businesses decide to convert old paper documents into computer files (insurance policies, research papers, and so on), OCR software is what they use.

Hardware & Drivers

If your Windows machine is a tablet, good for you. You probably won't have to spend much time mucking around with peripherals and their drivers. But if you have a regular PC, adding new gear is part of the fun. Hard drives, flash drives, cameras, phones, printers, scanners, network cards, video cards, keyboards, monitors, game controllers, and other accessories all make life worth living. When you introduce a new piece of equipment to the PC, you must hook it up and install its *driver*, the software that lets a new gadget talk to the rest of the PC.

The driver issue was once a chronic, nagging worry for the average Windows fan. Drivers conflicted; drivers went missing; drivers went bad; drivers went out of date.

Fortunately, Microsoft has made further strides in addressing the driver problem. Windows 10 comes with thousands upon thousands of drivers for common products already built in, and Microsoft deposits dozens more on your hard drive, behind the scenes, with every Windows update. Chances are good that you'll live a long and happy life without ever having to lose a Saturday manually configuring new gizmos, as your forefathers did.

Most of the time, you plug in some new USB gadget, and bam—it's ready to use. You don't have to install anything, walk through any wizards, or sacrifice any small animals.

This chapter counsels you on what to do when the built-in, autorecognized drivers don't do the trick.

Note: Chapter 14 contains additional hardware-installation details specific to printers.

External Gadgets

Over the years, various engineering organizations have devised an almost silly number of different connectors for printers, scanners, and other *peripherals*. The back panel—or front, or even side panel—of your PC may include any of these connector varieties.

USB Ports

Man, you gotta love USBs (Universal Serial Bus). The more of these jacks (also called connectors or ports) your PC has, the better.

The USB port itself is a compact, thin, rectangular connector that's easy to plug and unplug. It often provides power to the gadget, saving you one more cord and one more bit of clutter. And it's hot-pluggable, so you don't have to turn off the gadget (or the PC) before connecting or disconnecting it.

Tip: Be careful, though, not to yank a USB flash drive or hard drive out of the PC when it might be in the middle of copying files.

USB accommodates a huge variety of gadgets: USB hard drives, scanners, mice, phones, keyboards, printers, palmtop cradles, digital cameras, camcorders, and so on.

Most modern PCs come with at least two USB ports, often on both the front and back panels.

Note: Today's USB gadgets and PCs offer *USB 3.0* jacks—a faster, enhanced form of USB. You can still plug the older, slower USB 1.1 and 2 gadgets into USB 3.0 jacks, and vice versa—but you'll get the older, slower speed.

Other Jacks

At one time, the backs of PCs were pockmarked with all manner of crazy jacks: serial ports, PS/2 ports, SCSI ports, parallel ports, keyboard ports. Today, all these connectors are rapidly disappearing, thanks to the all-powerful superiority of the USB jack.

UP TO SPEED

Of Hubs and Power

If your PC doesn't have enough built-in USB jacks to handle all your USB devices, you can also attach a USB *hub* (with, for example, four or eight additional USB ports), in order to attach multiple USB devices simultaneously.

Whether the jacks are built in or on a hub, though, you have to be aware of whether or not they're *powered* or *unpowered* jacks.

Unpowered ones just transmit communication signals with the USB gadget. These kinds of USB gadgets work fine with unpowered jacks: mice, keyboards, flash drives, and anything with its own power cord (like printers).

Powered USB jacks also supply current to whatever's plugged in. You need that for scanners, Webcams, hard drives, and other gadgets that don't have their own power cords but transmit lots of data.

The bottom line? If a gadget isn't working, it may be because it requires a powered jack and you've given it an unpowered one.

Here's what else you may find on the modern PC, though:

- **Video (VGA), DVI, or DisplayPort.** These are all ways to connect a second monitor or a projector. The older but widely compatible VGA is a narrow female connector with 15 holes along three rows. The DVI (digital visual interface) jack has 24 pins and is designed for modern LCD screens. And DisplayPort, which is intended to replace VGA and DVI (but retain compatibility via adapters), looks like a USB jack with one diagonally clipped corner.

- **HDMI.** Handy! This kind of jack sends high-def video and audio to an HDTV set or an external monitor.

- **SD card reader.** Pop the SD memory card out of your camera and straight into this slot to import the photos. Sweet.

Connecting New Gadgets

In books, magazines, and online chatter about Windows, you'll frequently hear people talk about *installing* a new component. In many cases, they aren't talking about physically hooking it up to the PC—they're talking about installing its driver software.

But remember the insanely complete collection of drivers—especially for USB gadgets—that comes with Windows. When you plug the thing into the PC for the first time, Windows autodetects its presence, digs into its trunk for the driver, and installs it automatically. A flurry of balloons in the system tray may or may not appear.

If Windows can't find the driver, then a dialog box appears, suggesting that you insert whatever software-installation disc came with the gadget.

And now, the fine print:

- Usually plugging the device in is all it takes. Sometimes, though, you're supposed to install the driver before connecting the gizmo. (Check the manual.)

- Usually, the device should be turned off before you plug it in. Again, though, check the manual, because some devices are supposed to be switched on during the installation.

In either case, your gear is now completely installed—both its hardware and its software—and ready to use.

Troubleshooting Newly Installed Gear

If, when you connect a new component, Windows doesn't display a "successfully installed" message, then it probably can't "see" your new device.

- If you've installed an internal card, make sure that it's seated in the slot firmly (after shutting down your computer, of course).

- If you attached something external, make sure that it's turned on, has power (if it came with a power cord), and is correctly connected to the PC.

In either case, before panicking, try restarting the PC. If you still have no luck, try the Add Hardware wizard described in the box below. (And if even *that* doesn't work, then call the manufacturer.)

If your new gadget didn't come with a disc (or maybe just a disc with drivers, but no installer), then hooking it up may produce a "Found New Hardware" balloon in the system tray, but no message about happy success. In that case, click the balloon to make the Add Hardware wizard appear.

If you have the drivers from the manufacturer's Web site, then select the first option, "Locate and install driver software." Now Windows asks for the driver CD. If you do not, in fact, have the CD, then click "I don't have the disc." You're offered two final, fatalistic options: "Check for a solution" (Windows dials the mother ship on the off chance that a driver has miraculously cropped up since its last update) or "Browse my computer," designed for people who have downloaded a driver from the Web on their own.

The Add Hardware Wizard

Microsoft really, really hopes you'll never need the Add Hardware wizard. This little program is a holdover from Windows past, designed for very old, pre-Plug-and-Play gadgets (what Microsoft calls "legacy hardware") that Windows doesn't autorecognize when you plug them in.

Begin by connecting the new gear; turn off the computer first, if necessary. Turn the machine on again, and then open the Add Hardware wizard program, which takes a few steps. Right-click the Start menu; from the menu, choose Device Manager. Then, in the Device Manager window, choose "Add legacy hardware" from the Action menu.

The wizard makes another attempt to detect the new equipment and install its driver. If a happy little "Found new hardware" balloon appears in your system tray, then all is well; the wizard's work is done. If

not, you're walked through the process of specifying exactly *what* kind of gadget seems to have gone missing, choosing its manufacturer, inserting its driver disc, and so on.

If you choose "Install the hardware that I manually select from a list" and click Next (or if the previous option fails), the wizard displays a list of device types, as shown here. From that list, find and select the type of hardware you want to install—"Imaging devices" for a digital camera or a scanner, for example, or "PCMCIA adapters" for a PC card, and so on. (Click Show All Devices if you can't figure out which category to choose.)

Click Next to forge on through the wizard pages. You may be asked to select a port or to configure other settings. When you click the Finish button on the last screen, Windows transfers the drivers to your hard drive. As a final step, you may be asked to restart the PC.

Driver Signing

Every now and then, when you try to install the software for one new gadget or another, you see a warning box that says, "Windows can't verify the publisher of this driver software."

It's not really as scary as it sounds. It's just telling you that Microsoft has not tested this driver for Windows 10 compatibility and programming solidity. (Technically speaking, Microsoft has not put its digital signature on that driver; it's an *unsigned driver.*)

Note: In very rare circumstances, you may also see messages that say, "This driver software has been altered" or "Windows cannot install this driver software." In those cases, go directly to the hardware maker's Web site to download the official driver software; Windows is trying to warn you that hackers may have gotten their hands on the driver version you're trying to install.

In theory, you're supposed to drop everything and contact the manufacturer or its Web site to find out if a Windows 10–certified driver is now available.

In practice, just because a driver isn't signed doesn't mean it's no good; it may be that the manufacturer simply didn't pony up the testing fee required by Microsoft's Windows Hardware Quality Labs. After all, sometimes checking with the manufacturer isn't even possible—for example, it may have gone to that great dot-com in the sky.

So most people just plow ahead. If the installation winds up making your system slower or less stable, you can always uninstall the driver, or rewind your entire operating system to its condition before you installed the questionable driver. (Use System Restore, described on page 521, for that purpose. Windows automatically takes a snapshot of your working system just before you install any unsigned driver.)

The Device Manager

The Device Manager is an extremely powerful tool that lets you troubleshoot and update drivers for gear you've already installed. It's a master list of every component that makes up your PC: drives, keyboard, trackpad, screen, battery, and so on. It's also a status screen that lets you know which drivers are working properly and which ones need some attention.

The quickest way to open the Device Manager is to right-click the ⊞ button, which makes the secret Utilities menu appear; choose Device Manager.

You then arrive at the screen shown in Figure 15-1.

The Curse of the Yellow ! Badge

A yellow circled exclamation point next to the name indicates a problem with the device's driver. It could mean that either you or Windows installed the *wrong* driver, or that the device is fighting for resources being used by another component. It could also mean that a driver can't find the equipment it's supposed to control. That's what happens to your Webcam driver, for example, if you've detached the Webcam.

The yellow badge may also be the result of a serious incompatibility between the component and your computer, or the component and Windows. In that case, a call to the manufacturer's help line is almost certainly in your future.

Tip: To find out which company actually created a certain driver, double-click the component's name in the Device Manager. In the resulting Properties dialog box, click the General tab, where you see the name of the company, and the Driver tab, where you see the date the driver was created, the version of the driver, and so on.

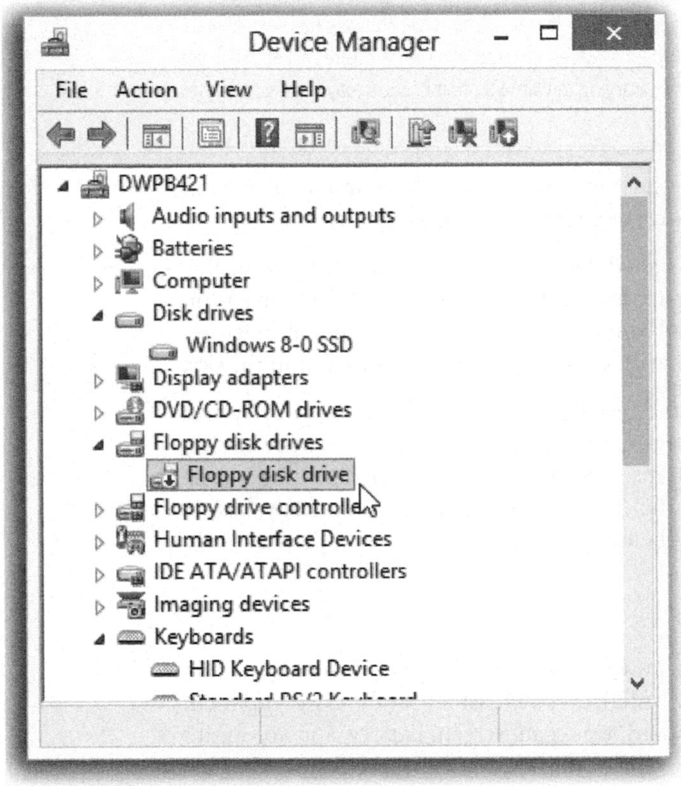

Figure 15-1:
The Device Manager lists types of equipment; to see the actual model(s) in each category, you must expand each sublist by clicking the flippy triangle.

A device that's having problems is easy to spot, thanks to the black down-arrows and yellow exclamation points.

You can see a disabled driver (⊕ logo) on the "Floppy disk drive" entry in this illustration.

Duplicate devices

If the Device Manager displays icons for duplicate devices (for example, two modems), then remove *both* of them. (To remove a device, click Uninstall in the dialog box shown in Figure 15-2.) If you remove only one, Windows will find it again the next time the PC starts up, and you'll have duplicate devices again.

If Windows asks if you want to restart your computer after you remove the first icon, click No, and then delete the second one. Windows won't ask again after you remove the second incarnation; you have to restart your computer manually.

When the PC starts up again, Windows finds the hardware device and installs it (only once this time). Open the Device Manager and make sure there's only one of everything. If not, contact the manufacturer's help line.

Resolving resource conflicts

If the yellow-! problem isn't caused by a duplicate component, then double-click the component's name to find an explanation of the problem.

Turning Components Off

The Driver tab shown in Figure 15-2 contains another useful tool: the Disable button. It makes your PC treat the component in question as though it's not even there.

You can use this function to test device conflicts. For example, if a yellow exclamation point indicates that there's a resource conflict, then you can disable one of the two gadgets, which may clear up a problem with its competitor.

When you disable a component, a circled arrow appears next to the component's listing in the Device Manager. To undo your action, click the device's name and click the Enable button in the toolbar (formerly the Disable button).

Figure 15-2:
To get here, double-click a component listed in your Device Manager and then click the Driver tab. Here you find four buttons and a lot of information. The Driver Provider information, for example, lets you know who's responsible for your current driver—Microsoft or the maker of the component.

Click the Driver Details button to find out where on your hard drive the actual driver file is. Or click Update Driver to install a newer version, the Roll Back Driver button to reinstate the earlier version, the Disable button to hide this component from Windows until you change your mind, or the Uninstall button to remove the driver from your system entirely—a drastic decision.

(If the buttons here are dimmed, click the General tab, click "Change settings," and then authenticate.)

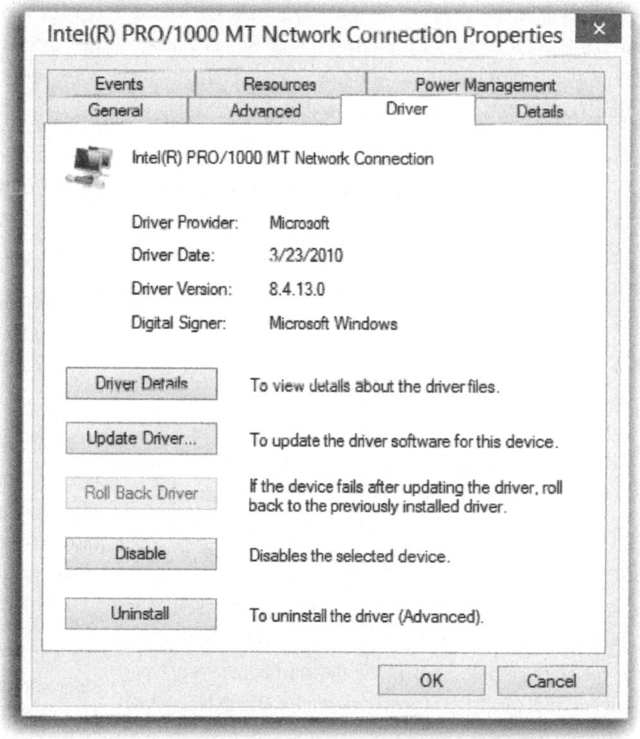

Intel(R) PRO/1000 MT Network Connection Properties

| Events | Resources | Power Management |
| General | Advanced | Driver | Details |

Intel(R) PRO/1000 MT Network Connection

Driver Provider: Microsoft
Driver Date: 3/23/2010
Driver Version: 8.4.13.0
Digital Signer: Microsoft Windows

Driver Details — To view details about the driver files.

Update Driver... — To update the driver software for this device.

Roll Back Driver — If the device fails after updating the driver, roll back to the previously installed driver.

Disable — Disables the selected device.

Uninstall — To uninstall the driver (Advanced).

OK   Cancel

Updating Drivers

If you get your hands on a new, more powerful (or more reliable) driver for a device, you can use the Device Manager to install it. (Newer isn't *always* better, however; in the world of Windows, the rule "If it ain't broke, don't fix it" contains a grain of truth the size of Texas.)

Open the dialog box shown in Figure 15-2, and then click the Update Driver button. The Update Device Driver wizard walks you through the process.

Along the way, the wizard offers to search for a better driver, or to display a list of drivers in a certain folder so you can make your own selection. In either case, you may have to restart the PC to put the newly installed driver into service.

Roll Back Driver

Suppose that you, the increasingly proficient PC fan, have indeed downloaded a new driver for some component—your scanner, say—and successfully installed it using

---

POWER USERS' CLINIC

Cards in Expansion Slots

Most people will never crack open their desktop PCs to install adapter cards. That hobbyist activity is fading away, now that PCs (or USB things you can plug into them) pretty much come with everything you need.

But expansion cards aren't completely gone. Adapter cards for video, TV, sound, network cabling, disk drives, and tape drives still come as circuit boards, or cards, that you install inside your PC's case. These slots are connected to your PC's *bus*, an electrical conduit that connects all the components of the machine to the brains of the outfit: the processor and memory.

The two common (and incompatible) kinds of slots are called PCI and PCI Express (PCIe). The PCI slot (Peripheral Component Interconnect) has been around since the dawn of the PC in the early 1990s. PCI Express is newer and offers much better speed but is typically used only for graphics cards. Most computers these days have both kinds of slots.

There's a third type of slot in some computers, called AGP (Accelerated Graphics Port). This slot is almost always occupied by a graphics card. PCIe is the most popular slot type for graphics cards, but you may encounter AGP in older PCs.

Knowing the characteristics of the different bus types isn't especially important. What is important is knowing what type of slots your computer has free, so you can purchase the correct type of expansion card. To do this, you'll have to open your PC's case to see which type of slots are empty:

PCIe slots come in different lengths, depending on their speed (from x1, the slowest, to x16, the fastest and most common). They have metal pins or teeth in the center and a small crossbar partway down the slot. There's also a slot on one end that the card uses to lock into place.

The plastic wall around a *PCI slot* is usually white or off-white, and shorter than an ISA slot. A PCI slot has a metal center and a crossbar about three-quarters of the way along its length.

Installing a card usually involves removing a narrow plate (the slot cover) from the back panel of your PC, which allows the card's connector to peek through to the outside world. After unplugging the PC and touching something metal to discharge static, unwrap the card, and then carefully push it into its slot until it's fully seated.

Note: Depending on the type of card, you may have to insert one end first, and then press the other end down with considerable force to get it into the slot. A friendly suggestion: Don't press so hard that you flex and crack the motherboard.

---

the instructions in the previous paragraphs. Life is sweet—until you discover that your scanner no longer scans in color.

In this situation, you'd probably give quite a bit for the chance to return to the previous driver, which, though older, seemed to work better. That's the beauty of the Roll Back Driver function. To find it, open the dialog box shown in Figure 15-2 and click Roll Back Driver.

Windows, forgiving as always, instantly undoes the installation of the newer driver and reinstates the previous driver.

Part Five:
PC Health

Chapter 16: Maintenance, Speed & Troubleshooting

Chapter 17: Backups & File History

Chapter 18: The Disk Chapter

5

Maintenance, Speed & Troubleshooting

Your computer requires periodic checkups and preventive maintenance—pretty much like you, its human sidekick. Fortunately, Microsoft has put quite a bit of effort into equipping Windows with special tools, all dedicated to keeping your system stable and fast. Here's a guide to keeping your PC—and its hard drive—humming.

The Action Center

If you're looking for the best place to go for at-a-glance information about the current state of your PC's maintenance and Internet security, open the Action Center. To open it, press ⊞+A, or click the tiny ▤ on your system tray.

Here, all in one place, are all the security and maintenance messages that Windows wants you to see. Be grateful; they *used* to pop up as individual nag balloons on the system tray all day. Now they accumulate here.

You can read the full scoop on the Action Center on page 113. For now, it's enough to remember that here's the place to check to see how your Windows Updates and PC backups are doing.

Windows Update

Microsoft emphasizes that Windows 10 isn't like other versions of Windows. There won't be annual "service packs." There won't be a Windows 10.1 or 10.2.

Instead, Microsoft intends to update your copy of Windows 10 continuously and automatically, over the Internet, as it develops new features and plugs new security holes, through a feature called Windows Update.

You may have noticed the word "automatically" casually slipped into that paragraph. This is the controversial part: For the first time in Windows history, *you can't decline Microsoft's Windows updates*. If your PC is connected to the Internet, you'll get each update, whether you like it or not.

You wouldn't think that'd be much of an issue. Microsoft wouldn't write one of these updates unless it made Windows *better*, right?

Unfortunately, updates sometimes backfire. In rare cases, the update itself has a bug that glitches up your computer. Or an update will "break" one of your drivers or printers. (This actually happened with one of the very first Windows 10 automatic updates—it introduced a bug in the Nvidia video-card driver.)

Online, PC veterans are up in arms about the automatic-updating business—partly because sometimes the updates introduce new glitches and partly because they don't like giving up control.

But there's a persuasive argument for leaving automatic updates turned on. Microsoft and other security researchers constantly find new security holes—and as soon as they're found, Microsoft rushes a patch out the door to fix it. But creating a patch is one thing; actually getting that patch installed on millions of copies of Windows around the world has been another thing entirely.

That's where Windows Update comes in. When Microsoft releases a security fix, it will be delivered straight to your PC and get automatically installed.

Note: In fact, it's Microsoft's *patches* that usually alert hackers to the presence of security holes in the first place! They used to exploit the fact that not everyone had the patch in place instantly.

What to Do If an Update Glitches Your Computer

For most people, most of the time, getting automatic Windows Updates is the safest, best way to go. It's fairly unlikely that an update will mess things up for you—and potentially dangerous to turn off Microsoft's ability to protect your machine from new viruses.

But what if it happens? What if that blue moon comes to pass, and an update makes your computer start crashing or acting weird?

In that case, you can uninstall it—and then prevent it from auto-reinstalling until you learn that a fixed driver or updated update is available.

The trick is to use the little-known View Installed Updates page of the Control Panel. (Easiest way to open it: In the search box, type *view installed updates* until you can select View Installed Updates in the results.)

Then proceed as shown in Figure 16-1.

Note: If the update in question messed up one of your drivers, you can surgically remove just that driver. Open the Device Manager (page 487), right-click the device with the bad driver, choose Uninstall from the shortcut menu, and confirm by clicking "Delete the driver software for this device if available."

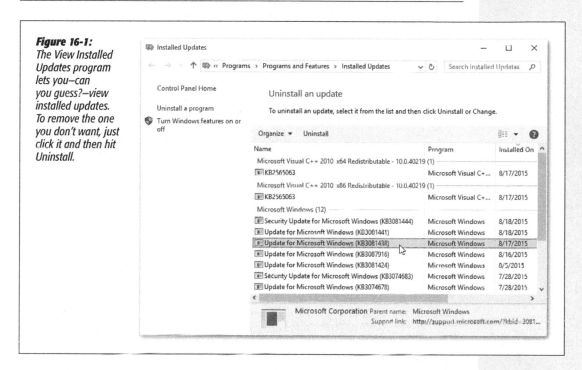

Figure 16-1:
The View Installed Updates program lets you—can you guess?—view installed updates. To remove the one you don't want, just click it and then hit Uninstall.

Prevent an Update from Reinstalling Itself

So you've successfully undone an update. Great! But if you just sit back on the couch now, Windows Update will just install it right back again.

To prevent that from happening, Microsoft offers a weird little program called the "Show or hide updates troubleshooter." You can grab it by Googling that name, or you can find it on this book's "Missing CD" page at *www.missingmanuals.com*.

When you download it, you come face to face with the screens shown in Figure 16-2.

Here's how to proceed. (These are the steps to take *after* uninstalling the balky update as described above.)

1. **On the opening screen (Figure 16-2, top), hit Next.**

   You arrive at the second box shown in Figure 16-2.

2. **Hit "Hide updates."**

   Windows shows you all the updates that you've uninstalled (or that have been downloaded but not yet installed), as shown in Figure 16-2, bottom.

3. **Turn on the update(s) that you want to block, and then hit Next.**

   After a moment of quiet contemplation, the app says, "Troubleshooting has completed."

Note: You should ignore the message in the box, which shows the glitchy update with a happy little green "Fixed!" checkmark. Nothing has been fixed.

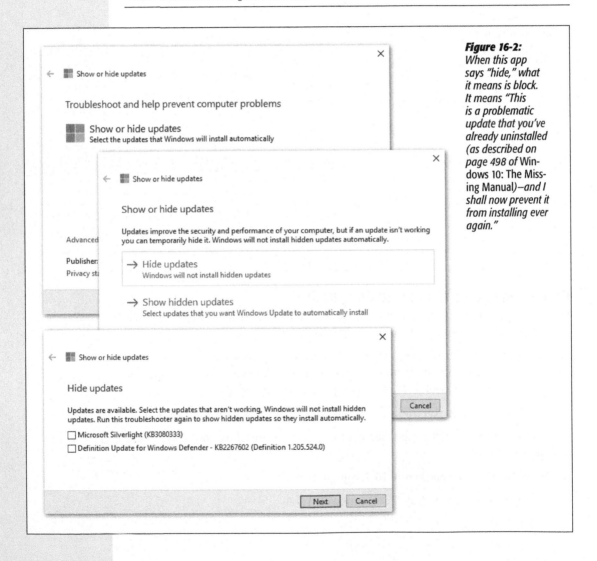

Figure 16-2:
When this app says "hide," what it means is block. It means "This is a problematic update that you've already uninstalled (as described on page 498 of Win-dows 10: The Miss-ing Manual*)—and I shall now prevent it from installing ever again."*

The update has been blocked. Microsoft won't try to install it again until you want it.

Later, when you decide that the update is now safe to install—maybe you've read online that it's been fixed—run this little app again. This time, in step 2, hit "Show updates." Turn on the update(s) you want to permit, and then hit Next.

At its next opportunity, Microsoft will send that update to you again—and install it automatically.

Delaying Updates (Pro Editions)

If you have the *Home* edition of Windows 10, the previous pages describe your only opportunity to prevent automatic-update disaster: Wait until it happens, and then remove the culprit.

If you have the *Pro or Enterprise* editions, though, you have another option: Defer all updates, meaning delay them for a few months.

Microsoft created this option for businesses that desperately need their computers to enjoy smooth, trouble-free, uninterrupted operation. When you defer Windows Updates, you're essentially letting the Home Edition masses be your beta testers. You're letting them enjoy/endure each new update for a while; you can install the updates only

---

POWER USERS' CLINIC

The "Metered Access" No-Updates Hack

It's worth repeating (over and over): In general, you *want* Microsoft's automatic updates. Almost always, they make your computer better and more secure.

All right. If you insist on resisting, here are the steps.

As noted in this chapter, if you have the Pro or Enterprise version of Windows, you can defer (delay) Microsoft's updates for a few months—long enough, one hopes, for the kinks to get worked out.

But if you have the Home edition, what then? It may seem as though you have no way at all to block the arrival of automatic updates.

Not true. If you really, truly mistrust Microsoft enough that you want to decline all automatic updates, there's a way to

do it. (This trick works only if you have a wireless connection; if you're wired to an Ethernet network, you're out of luck.)

Open Settings→Network & Internet→Wi-Fi→"Advanced options." Turn on "Metered connection."

> ### Metered connection
>
> If you have a limited data plan and want more control over data usage, make this connection a metered network. Some apps might work differently to reduce data usage when you're connected to this network.
>
> Set as metered connection
>
> ◉ On

You've just told Windows not to download any updates automatically—because you're on a metered connection (meaning a cellular connection, meaning that big downloads could cost you money).

Be careful with this, though. You've just turned off all Windows updates—even security updates that could make a big difference to the stability and safety of your machine.

(Turning off the "Metered connection" switch restores normal functioning of the Automatic Updates feature.)

---

when you're sure they've been battle-tested. (Of course, in the meantime, you're doing without whatever benefits and efficiencies those updates might have brought you.)

Note: You'll still get *security* updates instantly and automatically. What you're deferring is *other* kinds of Windows updates, like new Windows features.

If you decide that this kind of update delay is what you want, open Settings→System→ "Update & security"→"Advanced options." Turn on "Defer upgrades."

After "a few months" (Microsoft isn't saying anything more specific), those updates will arrive on your PC automatically. With luck, any kinks will have been reported by the early adopters—and fixed by Microsoft.

Installing Updates

The control center for Windows Update awaits at Settings→System→"Update & security."

Here you'll see what's going on with your updates. Most of the time, you'll see, "Your device is up to date." But sometimes, you'll see that an update has been downloaded, but hasn't yet been installed (see Figure 16-3).

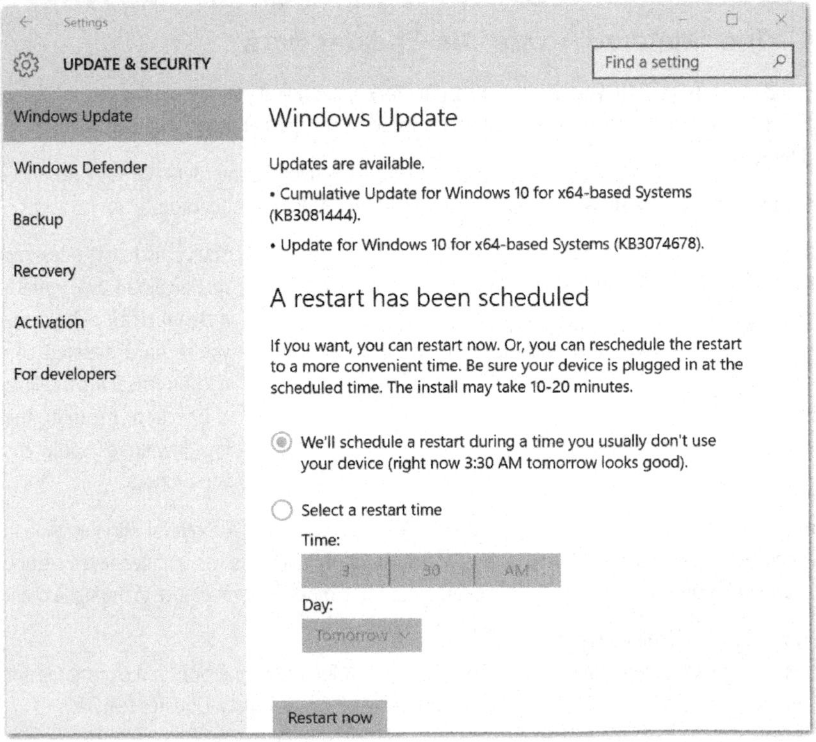

Figure 16-3:
Windows is thought-fully waiting until 3 a.m. (or some other time when you're not usually using the computer), because the installation will require restarting, and Windows doesn't want to interrupt your work.

In those situations, you can do nothing, content that Windows will quietly install the update and restart the PC when you're not using it. Or you can choose to interrupt your work *yourself*—and restart now. (Click "Restart now.") Or use the Time and Day controls to specify a more convenient time for the restart.

If, at this point, you click "Advanced options," you're treated to a few not-very-advanced options:

- **Notify to schedule restart.** If you change the first pop-up menu to say this, your PC will never restart automatically, even when you're not using it. Instead, once an update has finished downloading, Windows will pop up a notification, inviting you to schedule a time for the required restart.

- **Give me updates for other Microsoft products I use.** Ordinarily, Windows Update is about making changes to Windows. But what if there are updates to Office, Skype, Minecraft, or other Microsoft programs? Here's where you authorize automatic updates to those programs, too.

- **Defer updates.** This option (not available in Windows 10 Home Edition) is described earlier in this chapter.

- **View your update history.** Here's a complete list of all the updates your PC has received. Since updates, for most people, are automatic, you might not even realize that you've been upgraded until you consult this list. Click the final line of each entry (for example, "Successfully installed") to view a description. Most of them are probably security updates (antivirus, antispyware patches). For "Windows Update" items, you can click "Support info" to view a Web page that details exactly what was in the update.

- **Choose how updates are delivered.** This is the on/off switch for a new Windows 10 feature called Windows Update Delivery Optimization —and it requires some explanation.

  Every time Microsoft sends out an update, it has to send out *hundreds of millions of copies.* That's an unbelievable amount of data—all of it duplicated and identical—flooding out over the Internet airwaves. If you've got several PCs, each of them has to download that same data, redundantly, from Microsoft.

  In Windows 10, for the first time, your PC can join thousands of others in a peer-to-peer network, passing bits of update code to *one another.* In other words, all those Windows 10 machines become part of Microsoft's distribution system, passing along bits of Windows updates to other people. Now one of your computers can download an update and then pass pieces of it along to the others without having to download them again.

  Overall, the idea can save huge amounts of bandwidth and storage on the Internet. It can also get these updates to you faster, with a much lower consumption of Internet data if you're on an office network.

In other words, all of this is really kind of a cool idea. But if your Internet service has a monthly limit, you might worry that your computer sending out those bits of updates to other people online might eat up data unnecessarily.

Fortunately, this feature doesn't kick in at all if you're using a cellular connection. If you're on a WiFi network with monthly data limits, though, you should inform Windows so that it doesn't eat up your allotment on sending bits of update to strangers online. (To do that: Open Settings→Network & Internet→Wi-Fi→"Advanced options," and turn on "Set as metered connection.")

Finally, you have plenty of controls here. You can turn the whole thing off, using the master switch on this Settings page. Or leave it on and choose "PCs on my local network." That way, you get the benefit of bandwidth and data savings (by sharing update bits among your own computers), without worrying about becoming part of the larger Internet data-sharing network and running up your data bill.

Task Scheduler

The Task Scheduler, another power-user trick for techies, lets you set up programs and tasks (like disk defragmentation) so they run automatically according to a schedule you specify. Both mere mortals and power geeks may find it useful. For example:

- **Create an email message** that gets sent to your boss each morning, with yesterday's sales figures attached automatically.

- **Have the Recycle Bin emptied** automatically once a month.

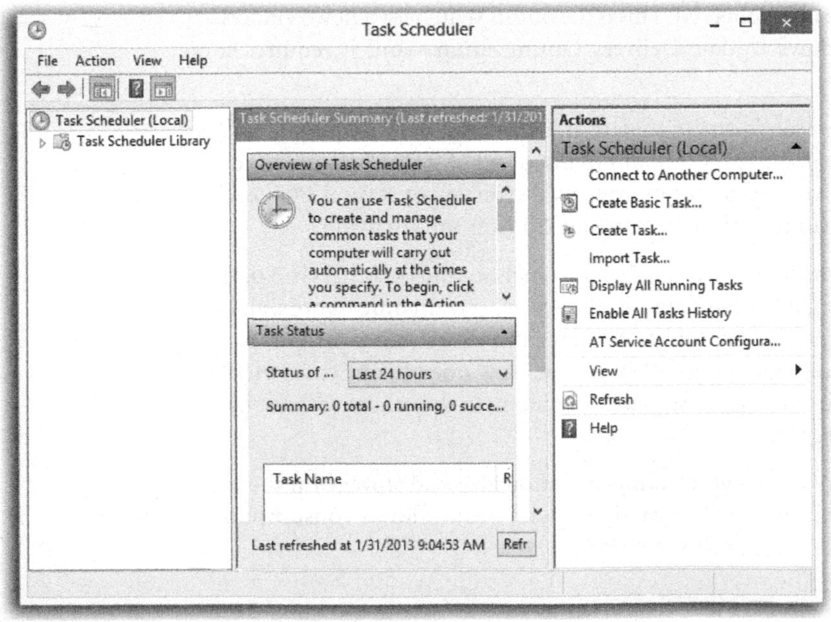

Figure 16-4:
It's easy to automate tasks using the Task Scheduler, but when you open it, don't be surprised to see many tasks there already. Windows does a lot of housekeeping work in the background, and it uses the Task Scheduler to run a lot of tasks without your having to know the details.

- **Create a phony dialog box** that appears every time the office know-it-all's PC starts up. Make it say: "The radiation shield on your PC has failed. Please keep back seven feet." You get the idea.

Adding a Task

Here's how you add a new task:

1. **Open the Task Scheduler.**

   To do that, do a search for *schedule*. In the search results, click "Schedule a task." The Task Scheduler window appears (Figure 16-4).

2. **In the right-side panel, click Create Basic Task.**

   A "wizard" dialog box appears.

3. **Type a name for the task and a description, and then click Next.**

   Now you're supposed to choose what Windows calls a "trigger"—in plain English, when to run the task (Figure 16-5). You can specify that it run daily, weekly, monthly, or just once; every time the computer starts or every time you log in; or when a specific event occurs—like when a program starts.

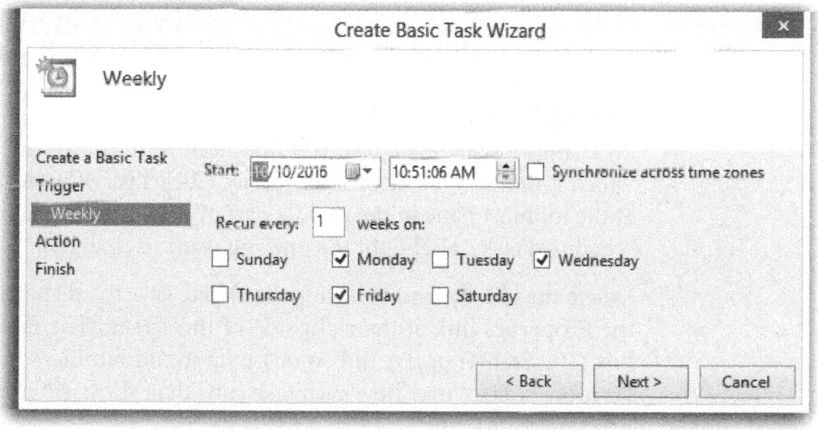

Figure 16-5:
This screen lets you set a schedule for your task. Depending on the trigger you set, you may see a completely different screen here, because the options are determined by the trigger you choose.

4. **Choose a trigger, and then click Next.**
   The next screen varies according to the trigger you chose. If you chose to run the task on a daily, weekly, or monthly basis, then you're now asked to specify *when* during that day, week, or month. Once that's done, click Next.

   You now wind up at the Action screen. This is where you say *what* you want to happen at the appointed time. Your choices are "Start a program," "Send an e-mail," or "Display a message."

5. **Choose an action; click Next.**

Now you're supposed to say *what* program, email, or message you want the PC to fire up.

If you choose the email option, you now fill out a form with the recipient's name, address, subject line, message body, and so on; you can even specify an attachment.

If you choose to run a program, you now browse to select the program. At this point, programmers can also add *arguments*, which are codes that customize how the program starts.

And if you opt to display a message, you get to type a name and text for the message. At the appointed time, an actual Windows dialog box will appear on the screen—except that it will contain text that *you* wrote.

6. **Complete the details about the email, program, or phony dialog box, and then click Next.**

Finally, a screen appears, summarizing the task, when it will run, and so on. To edit it, click the Back button.

7. **To confirm the automated task, click Finish.**

You return to the Task Scheduler window. Although you may have to scroll down to see it, your new task appears in the Active Tasks list at the bottom of the window. If all goes well, Windows will fire it up at the moment you specified.

Editing Scheduled Tasks

To change a scheduled task, you first need to find it in the Task Scheduler Library, which is on the left side of the window. Click Task Scheduler Library, and then look at the topmost pane in the middle part of your screen (Figure 16-6). You see a list of scheduled tasks. Highlight the one you want to change.

Delete the task by simply hitting the Delete key. To edit a task, click it and then click the Properties link at the right side of the screen. The tabs in the resulting dialog box (General, Triggers, and so on) may sound familiar, but they actually give you far more control over how each task runs than the basic controls you saw when you first set the task up.

Here are some examples of what you can do on each tab:

- **General.** Select which user account should run the task, and tell Windows whether or not to run when that person is logged in.

- **Triggers.** You can delay the task's execution by a few minutes or until a certain date; have it repeat automatically at regular intervals; stop it after a certain time period; and so on. The "Begin the task" pop-up menu offers a wealth of new triggers, like "On idle" and "On workstation unlock."

- **Actions.** Change the action.

- **Conditions.** Specify that the task will run only under certain conditions—for example, after the computer has been idle for a certain amount of time, when the computer is on AC power, or when it switches to battery power, and so on. You can even say you want to run the task if the PC is sleeping (by waking it first).

- **Settings.** Here's a miscellaneous batch of additional preferences: what actions to take if the task doesn't work, what to do if the computer was turned off at the appointed time, and so on.

- **History.** On this tab, you get to see the task's life story: when it ran and whether each attempt was successful.

Note: Lots of tasks are already present on your PC. Microsoft set them up to ensure the proper running of your computer. To see them all, expand the flippy triangle next to the words "Task Scheduler Library" and then expand Microsoft, and then Windows. You see dozens of tasks in many different categories. In other words, your PC is very busy even when you're not there.

Figure 16-6:
This screen lets you do more than just edit a task. Look at the right-hand pane; you see links that let you run the task right now, end the task if it's already started, and disable the task, among others.

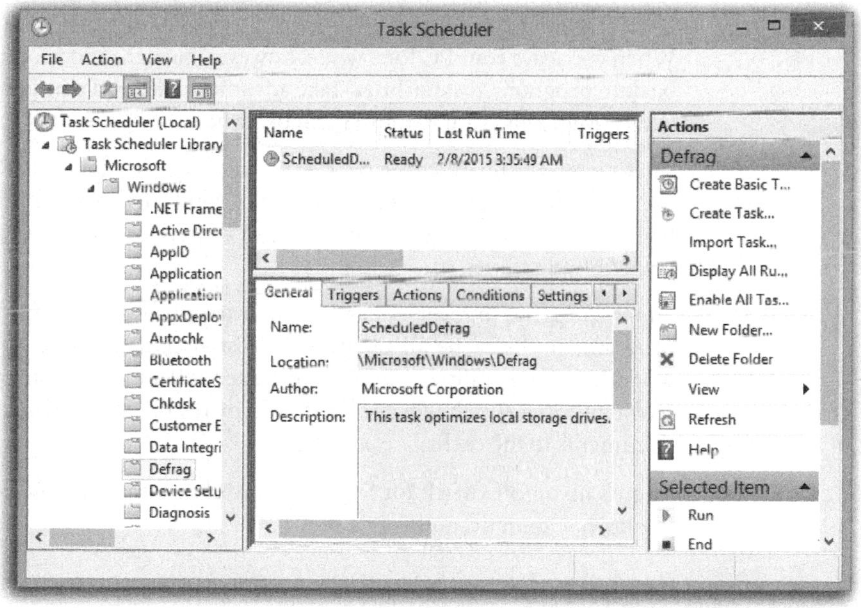

Two Speed Boosts

It's a fact of computing: Every PC seems to get slower the longer you own it. There are plenty of reasons. When the PC is new, consider that:

- The hard drive has loads of free space and zero fragmentation.

- The startup process hasn't yet been cluttered up by startup code deposited by your programs.

- Few background programs are constantly running, eating up your memory.

- You haven't yet drained away horsepower with antivirus and automatic backup programs.

Also, remember that every year, the programs you buy or download are more demanding than the previous year's software.

Some of the usual advice about speeding up your PC applies here, of course: Install more memory or a faster hard drive.

But in Windows 10, here and there, nestled among the 50 million lines of code, you'll find some *free* tricks and tips for giving your PC a speed boost. Read on.

SuperFetch

Your PC can grab data from RAM (memory) hundreds of times faster than from the hard drive. That's why it uses a *cache*, a portion of memory that holds bits of software code you've used recently. After all, if you've used some feature or command once, you may want to use it again soon—and this way, Windows is ready for you. It can deliver that bit of code nearly instantaneously the next time.

When you leave your PC for a while, however, background programs (virus checkers, backup programs, disk utilities) take advantage of the idle time. They run themselves when you're not around—and push out whatever was in the cache.

That's why, when you come back from lunch (or sit down first thing in the morning), your PC is especially sluggish. All the good stuff—*your* stuff—has been flushed from the cache and returned to the much slower hard drive, to make room for those background utilities.

SuperFetch tries to reverse that cycle. It attempts to keep your most frequently used programs in the cache all the time. In fact, it actually *tracks you* and your cycle of work. If you generally fire up the computer at 9 a.m., for example, or return to it at 1:30 p.m., SuperFetch will anticipate you by restoring frequently used programs and documents to the cache.

There's no on/off switch for SuperFetch, and nothing for you to configure. It's on all the time, automatic, and very sweet.

ReadyBoost

Your PC can get to data in RAM (memory) hundreds of times faster than it can fetch something from the hard drive. That's why it uses a *cache*, a portion of memory that holds bits of software code you've used recently. (Does this paragraph sound familiar?)

The more memory your machine has, the more that's available for the cache, and the faster things should feel to you. Truth is, though, you may have a bunch of memory sitting around your desk at this moment that's *completely wasted*—namely, USB flash drives. That's perfectly good RAM that your PC can't even touch if it's sitting in a drawer.

That's the whole point of ReadyBoost: to use a flash drive as additional cache storage.

You can achieve the same effect by installing more RAM, of course, but that job can be technical (especially on laptops), forbidden (by your corporate masters), or impossible (because you've used up all your PC's RAM slots already).

To take advantage of this speed-boosting feature, just plug a USB flash drive into your computer's USB jack.

Note: Both the flash drive *and* your PC must have USB 2.0 or later. USB 1.1 is too slow for this trick to work.

If the AutoPlay dialog box now opens, choose "Open folder to view files."

Whether the dialog box appears or not, open the flash device's window. On the Home tab of its Ribbon, click Properties. Click the ReadyBoost tab.

If you see a "Use this device" option, turn it on. That's all there is to it. Your PC will now use the flash drive as an annex to its own built-in RAM, and you will enjoy a tiny speed lift as a result.

Note: You won't run into problems if you yank out the flash drive; ReadyBoost stores a *copy* of the hard drive's data on the card/flash drive.

You also don't have to worry that somebody can steal your flash drive and, by snooping around the cache files, read about your top-secret plans for world domination. Windows encrypts the data using CIA-quality algorithms.

On the other hand, you may instead see a note that "This device cannot be used for ReadyBoost… This computer is fast enough that ReadyBoost is unlikely to provide additional benefit." In which case, well, no big deal.

And now, the fine print:

- ReadyBoost doesn't do anything for SSD (solid-state drives)—only traditional spinning hard drives.

- ReadyBoost doesn't give much of a boost if your computer has a lot of RAM to begin with. If you have 4 gigabytes installed and you're running Solitaire, it's not worth it. But if you're running a lot of big, memory-intensive programs simultaneously, you'll get a noticeable speed boost.

- Not all flash drives are equally fast, and therefore not all work with ReadyBoost. Look closely at the drive's packaging to see if there's a Windows ReadyBoost logo. (Technically speaking—very technically—its throughput must be capable of 2.5 MB per second for 4 KB random reads, and 1.75 MB per second for 512 KB random writes.)

- You can use one flash drive per PC, and one PC per flash drive.

Resetting (Erasing) Your Computer

For years, the most miserable moments of a PC owner's existence have been spent troubleshooting mysterious glitches. You have no idea exactly what went wrong, but something isn't behaving right. And off you go to a weekend of Googling, troubleshooting, and head-scratching. By the end of it, you may just be inclined to do a "nuke and pave"—erasing your hard drive completely and reinstalling everything from scratch.

In Windows 10, none of that is necessary. You have two incredibly powerful troubleshooting techniques that perform much the same purpose as a nuke and pave—that is, resetting everything to its original, virginal condition—but require far less work and effort. Both functions are part of a feature called Reset PC.

Reinstall Windows, Leave Your Files

This procedure gives your computer a fresh, clean copy of Windows 10 and all the programs that came with it. It leaves your files and your Windows Store apps in place, which is a huge improvement over the nuke-and-pave tradition. It's a powerful trick to remember when your computer just isn't behaving right.

But it erases all your *drivers, Windows settings, and programs you've installed* (the ones that didn't come with Windows itself). Any programs and drivers you've installed since getting Windows 10, you'll have to reinstall after the procedure.

(For your reconstructing convenience, Windows displays a thoughtful list of all the programs that are about to be deleted, as shown in Figure 16-7 at bottom. You'll find this same list on a text file on your desktop after the reset is over.)

1. **Open Settings→"Update & security"→Recovery. Under "Reset this PC," choose "Get started" (Figure 16-7, top).**

   Now you see the intriguing options shown in Figure 16-7.

2. **Choose "Keep my files" (Figure 16-7, middle).**

   After a moment, Windows shows you a list of the apps that you'll have to reinstall when this process is over (Figure 16-7, bottom).

3. **Click Next.**

   If you're now warned that you won't be able to restore an earlier version of Windows (if, indeed, you'd upgraded to Windows 10), click Next.

   You get one more warning, one final reminder that you're about to erase every program that you've installed on your PC (that didn't come with it).

4. **Click Reset.**

   After a minute or two, you get the "Choose an option" screen. It offers the Troubleshoot button shown on page 511. But for now, your troubleshooting is probably complete.

5. **Click Continue.**

After a moment, your freshly cleaned computer comes to. Your files and original programs are intact, but your settings, plus any programs and drivers you've installed, are gone.

And so, in most cases, are the glitches.

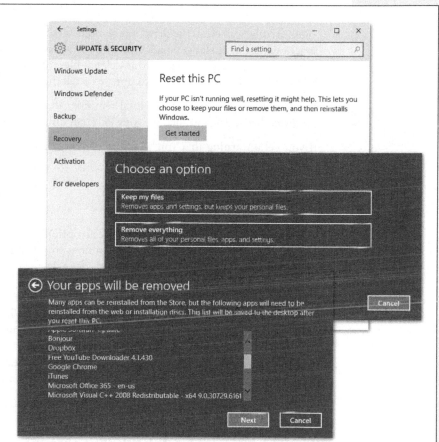

Figure 16-7:
Top: If you've made the proper sacrifices to the troubleshooting gods, you'll never have to visit this Recovery panel; it's for times of troubleshooting only.

Middle: Choose "Keep my files" if you're just troubleshooting. Choose "Remove everything" if you're planning to sell, donate, or recycle the computer, and you don't want to leave any trace of your own stuff on it.

Bottom: If you're just doing a Windows reinstall, you'll have some work to do after the surgery: reinstalling all of the programs listed here. These are the ones that didn't come with Windows.

Erase Your PC Down to Windows Itself

In more dramatic situations—for example, you're about to sell or donate your computer and want to make sure none of your stuff is going along for the ride to the new owner—you can also *reset* your PC. In other words, you're sending it back to its factory-fresh condition, with nothing on it except Windows and the software programs that came with it. All your files, settings, and software are completely wiped out.

1. **Open Settings→"Update & security"→Recovery. Under "Reset this PC," choose "Get started."**

Now you see the options shown in Figure 16-7, middle.

2. **Choose "Remove everything."**

   After a moment, Windows offers you another choice:

3. **Choose either "Just remove my files" or "Remove files and clean the drive."**

   "Just remove my files" quickly erases everything you've ever done to this PC, leaving it with a fresh copy of Windows and the apps that come with it. As the dialog box notes, this is a fine option if you intend to reinstall stuff and keep using the PC.

   "Remove files and clean the drive" erases your files and then scrubs those storage spaces with digital static, which will make it almost impossible for a sleuth or recovery company to resurrect your deleted files. (This takes longer, but it's the option to use if you're planning to donate or sell the computer.)

   You get one more warning, one final reminder that you're about to erase every program that you've installed on your PC (that didn't come with it).

   If you get a warning that you won't be able to reinstall your earlier version of Windows, just click Next.

   Finally, there's one more warning.

4. **Click Reset.**

   After a minute or two, you get the "Choose an option" screen. It offers the Trouble-shoot button shown in Figure 16-8. But for now, your troubleshooting is probably complete.

5. **Click Continue.**

   When it's all over, your computer is empty except for Windows and the apps it came with. It's shiny clean and ready to sell, donate, or reuse yourself.

Note: On some computers, there's a third option called "Restore factory settings." It's the same thing as "Remove everything," except that it also restores whatever version of Windows came on the PC from the store (assuming it wasn't Windows 10).

Windows Recovery Environment (WinRE)

You might play by all the rules. You might make regular backups, keep your antivirus software up to date, and floss twice a day. And then, one day, you get your reward: The PC won't even start up. You can't use any of Windows' software troubleshooting tools, because you can't even get to Windows.

In that most dire situation, Microsoft is pleased to offer what's known to techies as WinRE (Windows Recovery Environment), shown in Figure 16-8. It's a special recovery mode, loaded with emergency tools: System Reset, System Refresh, System Restore, System Image Recovery, Safe Mode, and on and on.

Windows Recovery Environment is a pure, protected mode that's separate from the normal workings of Windows—a place to do troubleshooting without worrying about changes that have been made by any software, good or bad.

If the problems you're having are caused by drivers that load just as the computer is starting up, for example, then turning them all off can be helpful. At the very least, WinRE allows you to get into your machine to begin your troubleshooting pursuit.

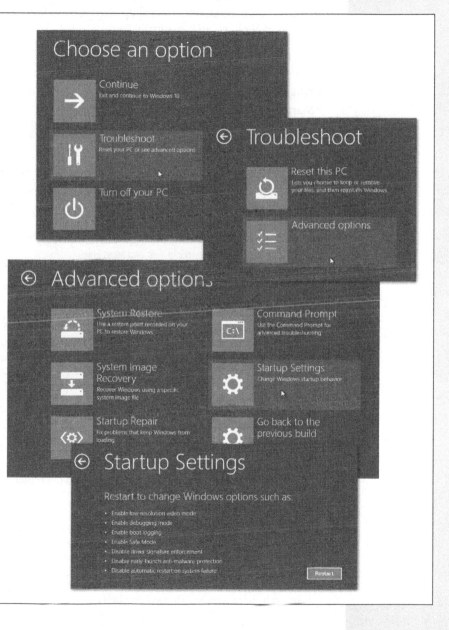

Figure 16-8:
Welcome to the Windows Recovery Environment. Somewhere in this series of screens, you'll encounter every conceivable troubleshooting tool.

The first one is the "Choose an option" screen. If you select the Troubleshoot option here, you get the Troubleshoot screen (second from top). Here, for your troubleshooting pleasure, are duplicates of the Refresh and Reset commands.

But if you click "Advanced options," you arrive at the "Advanced options" screen (third from top). This is a good place to recover data from a System Restore backup.

But if you choose Startup Settings, you open the actual, true-blue Startup Settings menu (bottom).

It's a menu most people never even know exists until they're initiated into its secret world by a technically savvy guru.

It used to be easy to open this screen; you just pressed the F8 key at the right moment during startup. But that trick doesn't work in Windows 10. Some machines start up so fast that you'd have only milliseconds to hit the F8 key at just the right time.

Instead, the Recovery Environment (Figure 16-8) appears *automatically* if the computer hasn't successfully started up after two attempts. If it doesn't, or if you're impatient, you can get to it manually.

The steps differ depending on how much trouble you're having getting the computer going. Choose *one* of these three techniques:

- Hold down the Shift key as you click Restart. (To find the Restart button, open the Start menu, select Power, and then select Restart.)

- In Settings→"Update & security"→Recovery, under "Advanced startup," click "Restart now."

- Start up from a Windows disc or a flash drive. At the Windows Setup screen, hit Next; then choose "Repair your computer." (This technique works even if the computer is too sick to start up normally.)

Tip: If you're a command-line kind of person, here's how you open the Recovery Environment from the command console: Type *shutdown.exe /r /o* and press Enter.

In each case, you arrive at the "Choose an option" screen. Follow the sequence shown in Figure 16-8 to find the Startup Settings screen.

The Startup Settings options include Safe Mode, Safe Mode with Networking, Safe Mode with Command Prompt, Enable Boot Logging, and so on. Use the arrow keys to walk through them, or type the corresponding number key or function key to choose one.

Here's what the Startup menu commands do:

1. **Enable debugging.**

   Here's an extremely obscure option, intended for very technical people who've connected one PC to another via a serial cable. They can then use the second computer to analyze the first, using specialized debugger software.

2. **Enable Boot Logging.**

   This startup method is the same as Normal, except that Windows records every technical event that takes place during the startup in a log file named *ntbtlog.txt* (located on the startup drive, in the Windows folder).

   Most of the time, you'll use the boot logging option only at the request of a support technician you've phoned for help. After confirming the operating system startup, the technician may ask you to open ntbtlog.txt in your Notepad program and search for particular words or phrases—usually the word "fail."

3. **Enable low-resolution video mode.**

In this mode, your PC uses a standard VGA video driver that works with all graphics cards, instead of the hideously ugly generic one usually seen in Safe Mode. Use this option when you're troubleshooting video-display problems—problems that you're confident have less to do with drivers than with your settings in the Display control panel (which you're now ready to fiddle with).

Of course, VGA means 640 × 480 pixels, which looks huge and crude on today's big monitors. Do not adjust your set.

4. **Enable Safe Mode.**

Safe Mode starts up Windows in a special, stripped-down, generic, somewhat frightening-looking startup mode—with the software for dozens of hardware and software features *turned off*. Only the very basic components work: your mouse, keyboard, screen, and disk drives. Everything else is shut down and cut off. In short, Safe Mode is the tack to take if your PC *won't* start up normally, thanks to some recalcitrant driver.

Once you select the Safe Mode option on the Startup menu, you see a list, filling your screen, of every driver Windows is loading. Eventually, you're asked to log in.

Your screen now looks like it was designed by drunken cavemen, with jagged, awful graphics and text. That's because in Safe Mode, Windows doesn't load the driver for your video card (on the assumption that it may be causing the very problem you're trying to troubleshoot). Instead, Windows loads a crude, generic driver that works with *any* video card.

The purpose of Safe Mode is to help you troubleshoot. If you discover that the problem you've been having is now gone, you've at least established that the culprit was one of the now-disabled startup items or drivers. If this procedure doesn't solve the problem, then contact a support technician.

5. **Enable Safe Mode with Networking.**

This option is exactly the same as Safe Mode, except that it also lets you load the driver software needed to tap into a network, if you're on one, or onto the Internet—an arrangement that offers a few additional troubleshooting possibilities, like being able to access files and drivers on another PC or from the Internet. (If you have a laptop that uses a PC Card networking card, however, this option may still not help you, since the PC Card driver itself is still turned off.)

6. **Enable Safe Mode with Command Prompt.**

Here's another variation of Safe Mode, this one intended for ultra–power users who are more comfortable typing out text commands at the command prompt than using icons, menus, and the mouse.

7. Disable driver signature enforcement.

As a way to protect your PC, Windows uses a technique called driver signature enforcement, which is designed to load only drivers that are verified to be valid. Of course, there are plenty of times when drivers aren't verified but are in fact usable. If you suspect that to be the case, choose this option; Windows will load all your drivers.

8. Disable early launch anti-malware protection.

It's an increasingly common trick by the bad guys: They release a *rootkit* (a virus-like bit of software) that installs a driver that loads into memory right when your computer starts up. Since it's there before your antivirus software has loaded, it's very difficult to detect and remove.

As revenge, Microsoft created Early Launch Anti-Malware Protection (ELAMP), a window of opportunity for certain antivirus programs to load before all other drivers. That way, the antivirus software can scan any other drivers that load and, if they're malware, block them from loading.

Ah—but what if one of these antivirus programs identifies a driver as evil but it's actually not? Then you won't be able to start up at all. In that situation, you'd want to turn ELAMP off using this option.

Once you've started up, update your virus software or remove the questionable driver. The next time you start up, ELAMP will be turned on again.

9. Disable automatic restart on system failure.

Under normal conditions, Windows automatically reboots after a system crash. Choose this option if you don't want it to reboot.

If you press F10, you go into the Windows Recovery Environment, described in Figure 16-8.

If you press Enter, you start the operating system in its usual fashion, exactly as though you'd never summoned the Startup menu to begin with. It lets you tell the PC, "Sorry to have interrupted you…go ahead."

Thanks to these powerful startup tools, there's less reason than ever to pay $35 for the privilege of talking to some technician named "Mike" who's actually in India, following a tech-support script that instructs you to first erase your hard drive and reinstall Windows from scratch.

Troubleshooting Tools

These days, a first-time Windows owner probably doesn't even know what you mean by the phrase "blue screen of death." PCs don't crash nearly as often as they used to.

But there are still a million things that can go wrong—and about a million trouble-shooting tools to help you, or somebody you've begged to help you, solve them. Here's the, ahem, crash course.

The Diary of Windows Crashes

Windows maintains a tidy list of all the problems you've been having with your machine. Needless to say, this little item isn't featured very prominently in Windows, but it's there.

To see it, type *reports* into the search box; hit "View all problem reports" in the results. You get the astonishing box shown in Figure 16-9 (top).

Tip: For techies, Windows includes an even more technical list of the goings-on on your PC: the Event Viewer. You can find it by searching for its name. Enjoy looking over eye-glazing lists of every log Windows keeps—lists of happenings concerning programs, setup, security, services, and more. You can sort, filter, and group these events. But if you can understand the significance of these obscure messages, you shouldn't be reading a Windows book—you should be writing one.

Figure 16-9:
Top: Diary of a typical Windows machine. It's a list of all the things that have gone wrong recently. Double-click one to open a screen of techie details that could be useful to a tech-support rep.

Bottom: Here's a mighty graph of your crashes stretching back one year, which explains why your PC has seemed so cranky lately. Each icon shows something that went wrong—a crash, a freeze, an error message. Click a column to see everything that happened that day.

If you see a lot of crashes following, for example, an installation or system change, you might have spotted yourself a cause-and-effect situation. You now have a clue to your PC's recent instability.

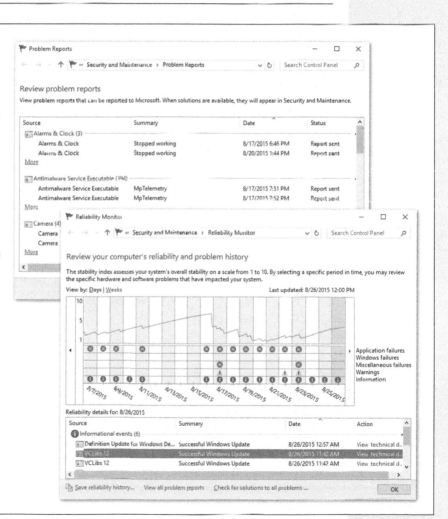

Reliability Monitor

If you prefer to get the bad news in visual form, try the Reliability Monitor (Figure 16-9, bottom). To see it, type *reliability* into the search box. Click "View reliability history."

Startup Items Revealed

Just say the words "startup items" to a Windows veteran, and you're sure to witness an involuntary shudder.

Startup items are programs that load automatically when you turn the computer on, without your invitation. Some of them are icons in the system tray. Some are designed to assist antivirus or iPod syncing apps. Some of them run in the background, invisibly.

But all of them use memory, and sometimes they can slow down your machine. And in older Windows versions, they were annoying and complex to manage.

Now, sometimes, there are on/off switches for the startup items in the programs themselves, in menus called Settings, Preferences, Options, or Tools. That's a clean, direct way to shut something up, but it won't help you with invisible startup items—those you didn't even know were running.

In Windows 10, the Task Manager has a tab called Startup Items. It's a startup/shutdowner's dream come true.

To open the Task Manager, right-click the Start menu and, from the shortcut menu, choose Task Manager. Now click its Startup tab, and proceed as shown in Figure 16-10.

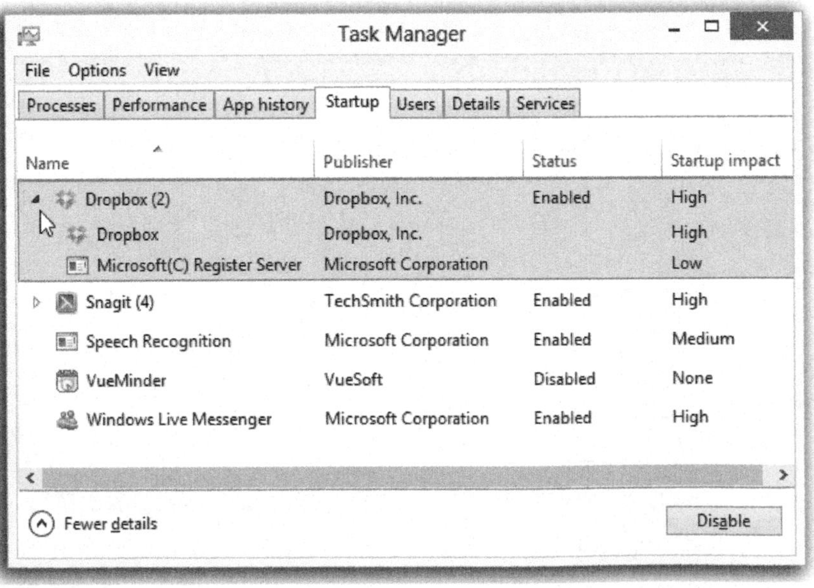

Figure 16-10:
To see what secret software is loading at startup time, open the Task Manager's Startup tab.

The "Startup impact" column shows you how much time and memory each item is sucking away from your computer's startup sequence.

The handy Disable button lets you turn off any selected item with one click.

Backups & File History

T here are two kinds of people in the world: those who have a regular backup system—and those who *will*.

You'll get that grisly joke immediately if you've deleted the wrong folder by accident, made changes that you regret, or worst of all, had your hard drive die. All those photos, all that music you've bought online, all your email—gone. It's painful

Yet the odds are overwhelming that, at this moment, you do not have a complete, current, automated backup of your computer. Despite about a thousand warnings, articles, and cautionary tales a year, guess how many people do? About *four percent*. Everybody else is flying without a net.

If you don't have much to back up—you don't have much in the way of photos, music, or movies—you can get by with copying stuff onto a flash drive or using a free online backup system like Dropbox or your OneDrive. But those methods leave most of your stuff unprotected: all your programs and settings.

What you really want, of course, is a backup that's rock-solid, complete, and *automatic*. You don't want to have to remember to do a backup, to insert a drive, and so on. You just want to know you're safe.

If you use Windows in a corporation, you probably don't even have to think about backing up your stuff. A network administrator generally does the backing up for you.

But if you use Windows at home, or in a smaller company that doesn't have network nerds running around to ensure your files' safety, you'll be happy to know about the various tools that come with Windows 10, all dedicated to the proposition of making safety copies. You have System Images and System Restore, for your entire system, and you have File History, for rewinding individual documents to earlier drafts—or recovering them if they've gotten deleted or damaged.

> *Note:* The dedicated backup program that used to come with Windows, Backup and Restore, has been "deprecated" by Microsoft. That's geek slang for "taken out behind the barn and shot." You'll have to rely on File History and Windows 10's other backup tools.
>
> But what if you used to have Windows 7, and you used Backup and Restore to back up your computer—and now you need those backups? Fortunately, the Backup and Restore program still comes with Windows (find it by searching for its name). You can use it to restore a backup from your old Windows 7 backups.

System Images

When your hard disk crashes, you lose more than just your personal files. You also lose your operating system—*and* all the programs you've installed, *and* all their updates and patches, *and* all your settings and options and tweaks. It can take you a very long time to restore your PC to that state.

A *system image* solves the problem easily. This feature (called Complete PC Backup in the Windows Vista days), creates a perfect snapshot of your entire hard drive at this moment: documents, email, pictures, and so on, *plus* Windows, *and* all your programs and settings. Someone could steal your entire hard drive, or your drive could die, and you'd be able to install a new, empty one and be back in business inside of an hour.

It's a good idea to make a fresh system image every few months, because you'll probably have installed new programs and changed your settings in the interim.

> *Note:* For the techies scoring at home, a system image is a .vhd file, the same kind that's created by Microsoft's Virtual PC software—and, therefore, you can mount it using Virtual PC, if you like.

Make the Image

To make a system image, do a search for *save backup*; in the results, choose "Save backup copies of your files with File History." Continue as shown in Figure 17-1.

No matter where you store the image, you'll need a *lot* of empty disk space. Not as much as your entire PC drive, because you won't be backing up empty space or temporary files. But a lot.

> *Note:* You can keep multiple system images around—representing your PC's world at different times—if you back up to discs or hard drives. If you save to a network location, though, you can keep only the most recent system image.

If you choose "On a hard disk," you're offered a list of all your computer's drives and informed how much storage space the backup will need. You may, if you wish, include other drives as part of the system image, so that they'll be restored, too, if the worst should come to pass. (Your Windows drive is automatically selected; you're not allowed to include the drive you're saving the image *onto*.)

Click "Next" and then "Start backup"; the backup begins. You'll be prompted if you need to insert new discs.

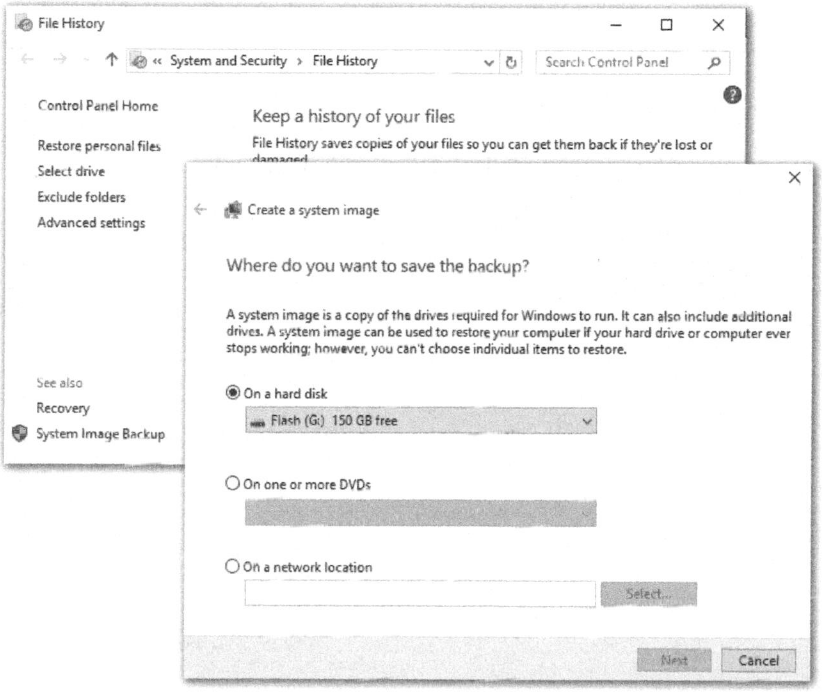

Figure 17-1:
Top: At the very lower-left side of this Control Panel screen, click System Image Backup.

On the next screen (not shown), choose "Create a system image."

Bottom: You're now asked where you want to store the backup image. Your options: a hard drive (must be NTFS formatted), a stack of CDs or DVDs, or (if you have the Pro or Enterprise editions of Windows) another computer on the network.

Restore the Image

Suppose disaster strikes: Your hard drive is trashed. Fortunately, restoring your entire system using a system image is very easy. You just have to open the Windows Recovery Environment, like this:

- **If your PC is running,** hold down the Shift key as you click Restart. (To find the Restart button, click the Start menu and select Power.)

- **If the PC won't even start up,** start up from a Windows DVD or flash drive. At the Windows Setup screen, hit Next; then choose "Repair your computer." (Alternatively, just boot up from the system repair disc you made when you created the system image.)

Once you see the "Choose an option" screen, click Troubleshoot, then "Advanced options" and then System Image Recovery. (You can see this sequence of screens illustrated in Figure 16-8 on page 511.)

In the System Recovery Options dialog box that appears, choose an administrator's account. Enter the appropriate password, and then click Continue.

On the next screen (Figure 17-2), choose "Use the latest available system image (recommended)," and click OK. (Of course, if you have some weird agenda, you can also choose an older system image using the other option here.)

When prompted, find the drive or disc that contains your system image.

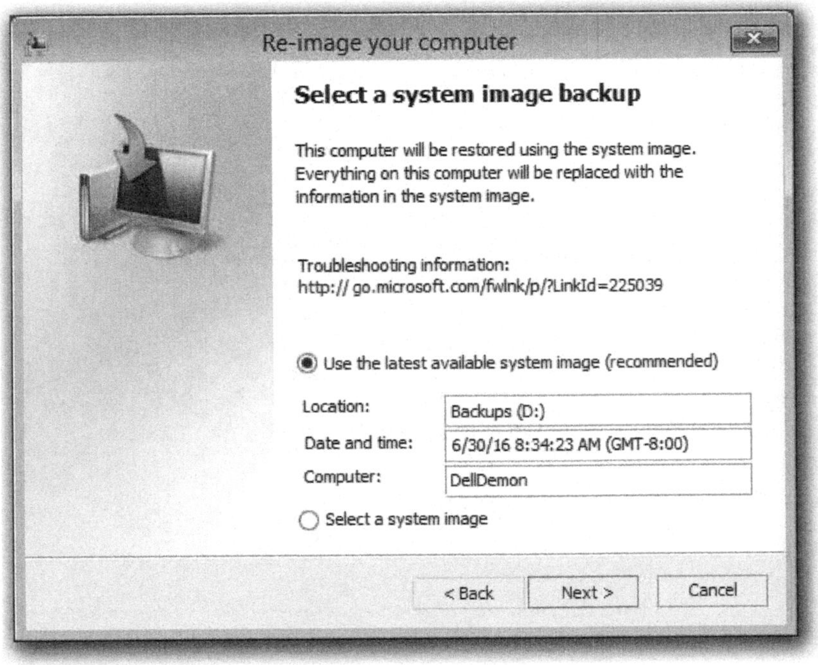

Figure 17-2:
Here's the payoff for your diligent system imaging. Windows is about to turn your current, messed-up computer back into the model of PC health that it was the day you made the image.

When you click Next, you're offered the "Choose additional restore options" dialog box, which offers some complicated options. The key element worth inspecting is the "Format and repartition disks" option:

- **If this option is turned on,** then every disk and partition will be formatted and partitioned to match the system image. (If this box is turned on and dimmed, then you have no choice; the disk will be formatted and partitioned to match the system image.)

- **If you can't turn on this checkbox**—it's dimmed and unchecked—then you're probably restoring a system image from one partition to another on the same disk. Clearly, Windows can't erase the disk it's operating from.

The "Only restore system drives" option does what it says: leaves your other drives alone.

When you click Finish and then Yes in the confirmation box, the long, slow restoration process begins. And the rest, as they say, is history recreated.

Just remember that this process *reformats your hard drive*, and in the process *wipes out all your data and files*. They'll be replaced with the most recent snapshot (system image) you've made. Of course, you may well have a *regular* backup that's more recent; you can restore that as the final step.

Note: If you were thinking of using a system image to turn a new PC into a replica of your old, crashed one, be warned: You can't restore a system image to a new PC's hard drive if it's smaller than the old one. (Yes, even if the data on the backup drive would easily fit on the target drive.)

System Restore

As you get more proficient on a PC, pressing Ctrl+Z—the keyboard shortcut for Undo—eventually becomes an unconscious reflex. In fact, you can sometimes spot veteran Windows fans twitching their Ctrl+Z fingers even when they're not near the computer—after knocking over a cup of coffee, locking the keys inside the car, or blurting out something inappropriate in a meeting.

Windows offers the mother of all Undo commands: System Restore. This feature alone can be worth hours of your time and hundreds of dollars in consultant fees.

The pattern of things going wrong in Windows usually works like this: The PC works fine for a while, and then suddenly—maybe for no apparent reason, but most often following an installation or configuration change—it goes on the fritz. At that point, wouldn't it be pleasant to be able to tell the computer, "Go back to the way you were yesterday, please"?

System Restore does exactly that. It "rewinds" your copy of Windows back to the condition it was in before you, or something you tried to install, messed it up. Best of all, System Restore *doesn't change your files*. Your email, pictures, music, documents, and other files are left up to date.

Tip: If your PC manages to catch a virus, System Restore can even rewind it to a time before the infection—*if* the virus hasn't gotten into your documents in such a way that you reinfect yourself after the system restore. An up-to-date antivirus program is a much more effective security blanket.

In fact, if you don't like your PC after restoring it, you can always restore it to the way it was *before* you restored it. Back to the future!

About Restore Points

System Restore works by taking snapshots of your operating system. Your copy of Windows has been creating these memorized snapshots, called *restore points*, ever since you've been running it. When the worst comes to pass, and your PC starts acting up, you can use System Restore to rewind your machine to its configuration the last time you remember it working well.

Windows is supposed to create landing points for your little PC time machine at the following times:

- Once a day.

- Every time you install a new program or a new device driver for a piece of hardware.

- When you install a Windows Update.

- Whenever you feel like it—for instance, just before you install a new component.

If you're new to all of this, it's probably worth visiting the System Properties dialog box shown in Figure 17-3—and ensuring that the System Restore feature is, in fact, turned on. If it's not, then Windows isn't protecting your computer with this awesome feature.

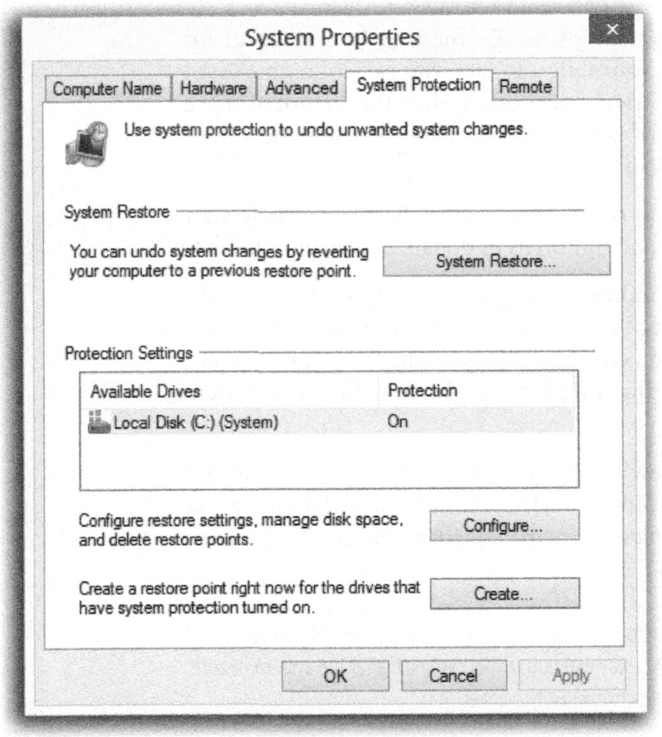

Figure 17-3:
Here's your command center for all System Restore functions. (One way to get here: Right-click the Start menu; from the shortcut menu, choose System. In the resulting dialog box, click "System protection.")

This box's layout is, more or less, upside-down.

For example, starting from the bottom of the box: Click the Create button to make a restore point right now, manually; click Configure to delete all restore points and limit disk space; click System Restore to perform the actual rewinding of your system.

It probably goes without saying, but System Restore works only if the master System Protection switch is turned on. It's hiding behind the Configure box shown here.

The System Protection Dialog Box

The central command center for the System Restore feature is the System Protection dialog box. Here are two good ways to open it:

- **Search for it.** Type *restore* into the search box. In the search results, click "Create a restore point" (yes, even though you're not creating one, you're using one).

- **Right-click the Start menu;** from the shortcut menu, choose System. In the resulting dialog box, click "System protection."

Either way, you now see the System Properties box shown in Figure 17-3.

Creating a Manual Restore Point

To create one of these checkpoints *manually*, open the System Protection tab on the System Properties dialog box (follow the steps above). At the bottom of that box, the Create button lets you create and name a new manual restore point. (Windows adds a date and time stamp automatically.)

Note: As you can imagine, storing all these copies of your Windows configuration consumes quite a bit of disk space. That's why System Restore lets you limit how much of your drive is allowed to fill up with restore points. Click Configure in the System Protection tab of the System Properties dialog box (Figure 17-3); you get a slider that lets you cap the percentage of the drive that can be swallowed up with restore-point data. When your drive gets full, System Restore starts *deleting* the oldest restore points as necessary.

Performing a System Restore

If something goes wrong with your PC, here's how to roll it back to the happy, bygone days of late last week:

1. **Open the System Protection tab on the System Properties dialog box (Figure 17-3).**

POWER USERS' CLINIC

System Restore vs. Your Hard Drive

Ever wonder where Windows stashes all these backup copies of your operating system? They're in a folder called System Volume Information, which is in your Local Disk (C:) window. Inside *that* are individual files for each restore point. (System Volume Information is generally an invisible folder, but you can make it visible by following the instructions on page 89. You still won't be allowed to move, rename, or delete it, however—thank goodness. In fact, you won't even be able to look inside it.)

You can turn off System Restore entirely, or you can limit it to eating up a certain percentage of your hard drive space.

Open a File Explorer window. Right-click This PC; from the shortcut menu, choose Properties.

In the resulting dialog box, click "System protection" in the left-side panel. Authenticate yourself if necessary. On the System Protection tab, click Configure. You get the dialog box shown here.

Use the Max Usage slider to put a cap on how much drive space all these restore points are allowed to eat up.

In times of strife, there's also a nuclear option here: the Delete button. Note, however, that this button deletes not just all your restore points, but also the backups of all your *documents* (those created by the File Histories feature described starting on page 526).

You've been warned. Be careful out there.

The steps are described on the previous pages.

2. Click System Restore.

The "Restore system files and settings" welcome screen appears (Figure 17-4, top).

Windows is suggesting that you rewind only as far as the most recent change you made to your machine—a software installation, for example. In Figure 17-4 at top, you can see that the most recent restore point was made when you installed

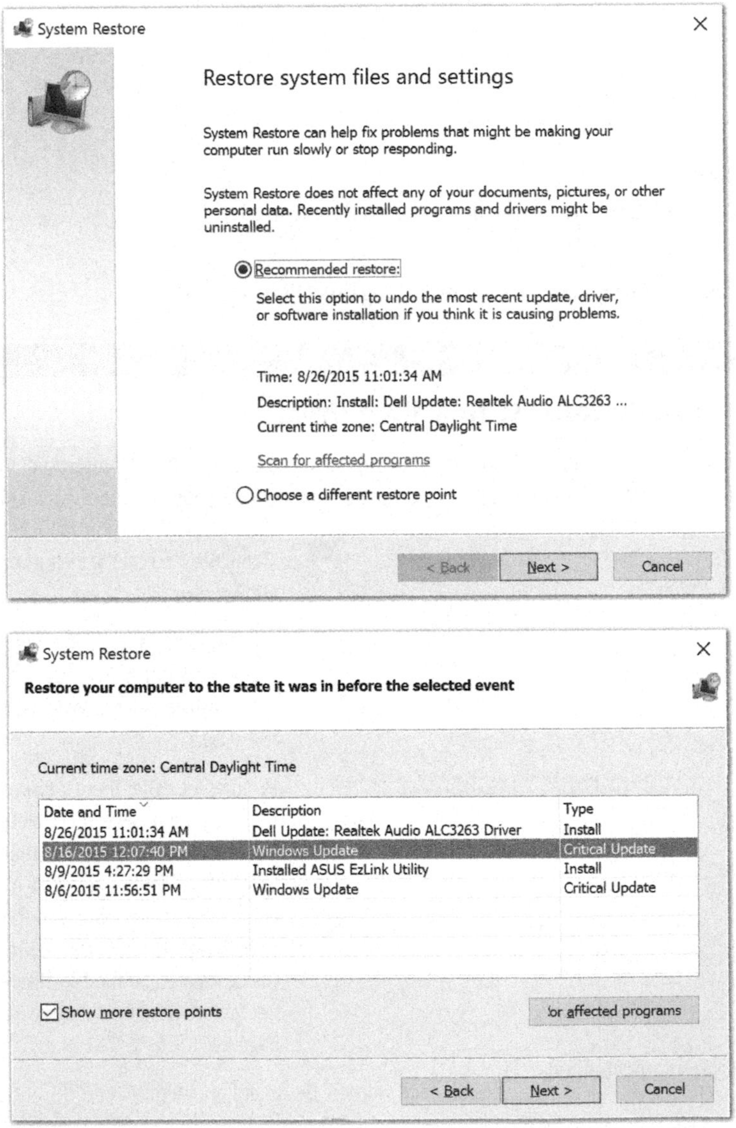

Figure 17-4:
Top: Windows suggests rewinding your computer to the most recent change you made to it. Most often, that's what you want.

Bottom: You can, however, also hit "Choose a different restore point" to view a list of older restore points Windows or you have made, anticipating just this moment. You're shown the date and time of each restore point, as well as why the restore point was created–for example, because you installed a new piece of software, or because you applied a Windows Update. That's a clue as to which restore point you should use.

Bottom: You can now see which programs will be affected by this system rewind.

a new device driver. If your computer suddenly started acting up, well, you've got your culprit.

If that seems like the right restore point, click Next, and then Finish; that's all there is to it. If it seems like you might want to rewind your computer to an even earlier point, though, read on:

3. **Choose "Choose a different restore point."**

   The list of all memorized restore points appears (Figure 17-4, bottom).

4. **Choose a restore point, and then select "Scan for affected programs."**

   Now Windows thoughtfully displays a list of which apps and drivers will be affected if you go through with the restore. Remember: Any apps and drivers you've *installed* since that point will be deleted; any apps and drivers you've *deleted* since then will be put back! You're literally rewinding your computer.

5. **If all looks good, choose Close, and then Next.**

   You have one more chance to back out: Windows displays the date and time of the restore point, shows you which drives will be affected, gives you another chance to create a password-reset disk, and asks if you *really* want to go back in time.

6. **Click Finish. In the confirmation box, click Yes.**

   Windows goes to town, reinstating your operating system to reflect its condition on the date you specified. Leave your PC alone while this occurs.

   When the process is complete, the computer restarts automatically. When you log in again, you're back to the past—and with any luck, your PC runs smoothly. (None of your emails or files are disturbed.)

If it didn't work—if you only made things worse—then repeat step 1. At the top of the System Restore welcome screen, you'll see an option called Undo System Restore. It lets you *undo* your undoing.

Or, of course, you can click "Choose a different restore point" if you think that maybe you didn't rewind your PC back far *enough* and want to try again with a different restore point.

Turning System Restore Off

You really shouldn't turn off System Restore. It's incredibly useful to hit rewind and get a smoothly running PC, even if you never do find out what the trouble was.

But if you're an advanced power user with no hard drive space to spare—is there such a person?—open the System Protection tab of the System Properties box (shown in Figure 17-3). Click Configure, click "Disable system protection," and click OK. (See the box on 523 for details.)

In the "Are you sure?" box, click Yes. That's it. You're flying without a net now, baby.

File History

System Restore is an amazing, powerful, career-saving feature—but it's awfully self-interested. It cares only about protecting *Windows*.

How can you rewind your *documents* to their earlier, healthier, or pre-edited conditions?

File History is a time machine for documents in the same way System Restore is a time machine for your system software. It's an incredible safety net against damage, accidental modification, or late-night bouts of ill-advised editing. It automatically backs up files in your libraries, on the desktop, in your address book, and on your OneDrive. If anything bad happens to the originals, you're covered. You can also rewind documents to specific dates—if, for example, you decide your novel was better before you tinkered with it last week. It's a lot like the Time Machine feature on the Mac.

> *Note:* There was a similar but less sophisticated feature in Windows 7 called either Previous Versions or Shadow Copy. They're gone now.

The beauty of File History is that it's automatic and invisible. And to save time and disk space, File History bothers copying only the files that have changed since the last restore point was created.

Set Up File History

The File History feature has its own dashboard in Settings→"Update & security"→ Backup (Figure 17-5, top).

> *Note:* If you're a nostalgia buff, you might be pleased to note that the older setup dashboard for File History—the one in the old Control Panel—is still around. To open it, search for *file history*. In the search results, click "File history." The newer Settings panel pretty much duplicates its features exactly, though.

File History works best if you direct it to create its backups on some other drive—not the one the files are on now. The whole point, after all, is to provide protection against something going wrong—and disk failure is a big something. So you're supposed to use an external drive—even a flash drive with decent capacity will do—or another computer on the network.

If there's already a second drive connected to your computer, Windows cheerfully begins using it to store the backups. If you've got more than one, hit "Add a drive" and choose it.

And that, dear reader, is it. If the "Automatically back up my files" button is on, then your computer is backing up your files automatically, once every hour. Isn't peace of mind wonderful?

File History Options

On the Settings→"Update & security"→Backup screen, the "More options" link takes you to a wonderland of additional settings (Figure 17-5, middle and bottom):

- **Back up now.** If you can't wait for the hourly backup, this button lets you trigger a backup now.

- **Back up my files [when].** Ordinarily, File History quietly checks your computer once an hour. If any file has changed, it gets backed up at the end of the hour. These follow-up backups are quick; Windows backs up only what's changed.

Figure 17-5:
Top: Here's the master panel for File History. It's where you turn the thing on or off.

Middle and bottom: Here's the "More options" screen (shown here in half because it's a very tall, scrolling screen). Here's where you add more folders to back up, or leave out folders of stuff you'll never need to rewind, to save disk space.

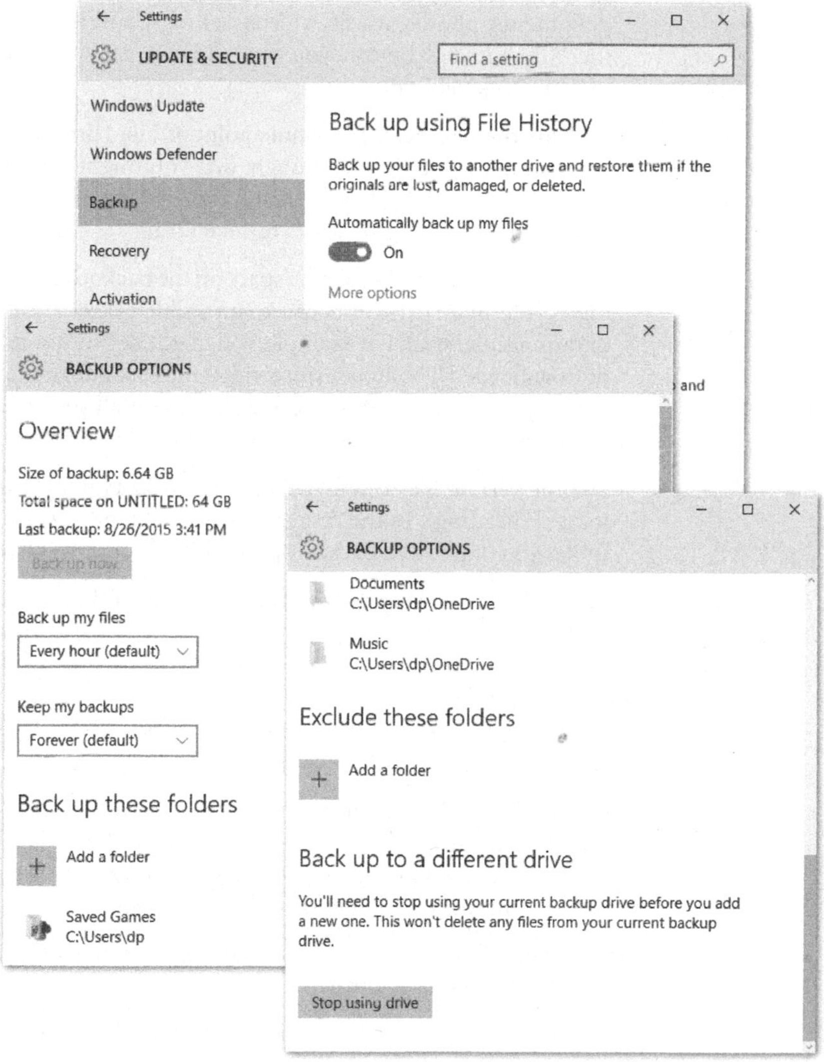

So, should disaster strike, the only files you can lose are those you've changed within the past 59 minutes.

With this pop-up menu, though, you can specify different backup intervals—anything from "Every 10 minutes" to "Every 12 hours" or just "Daily."

- **Keep my backups [how long].** This pop-up menu lets you specify how *long* you want Windows to hang on to the old versions of your documents. Maybe after a year, for example, it's OK for those old backups to start self-deleting, to save space on the backup drive.

- **Back up these folders.** Unless you start meddling, Windows automatically backs up your entire Personal folder—that is, everything in your own account folder: documents, photos, music, videos, settings, and so on (page 28). But by using the "Add a folder" button, you can tell File History to back up folders that *aren't* in your Personal folder.

- **Exclude these folders.** The whole point of File History is to have a backup of all your files. It's conceivable, though, that you might want to exclude some files or folders from the File History treatment. First, you might not want certain, ahem, private materials to be part of your data trail.

  Second, you might want to save space on the backup drive, either because it's not as big as your main drive or because you'd rather dedicate its space to more backups of the essential stuff. For example, you might decide not to back up your collection of downloaded TV shows, since video files are enormous. Or maybe you use an online photo-sharing Web site as a backup for all your photos, so you don't think it's necessary to include those in the File History backup.

  To omit certain files and folders, choose "Add a folder" (under the "Exclude these folders" heading). In the resulting dialog box, navigate your computer, choose a folder you don't need backed up, and hit "Choose this folder."

- **Switch backup drives.** If you want to choose a different drive for your backups, hit "Stop using drive."

Recovering Files

All right, you've got File History on the job. You sleep easy at night, confident that your life is in order—and your stuff is backed up.

Then, one day, it happens: Your hard drive crashes. Or you can't find a file or folder you know you had. Or you save a document and then wish you could go back to an earlier draft. Some kind of disaster—sunspots, clueless spouse, overtired self—has befallen your files. This is File History's big moment.

Open the File History pane of the Control Panel (search for *restore files*; choose "Restore personal files" in the results list).

Now you see the window shown in Figure 17-6 (top). Your job is to find the file in question, either because it's been deleted or because you want to rescue an older version of it. There are four ways to go about it: browsing, Ribboning, searching, or Properties-ing.

Browsing for the file

In the window shown in Figure 17-6, double-click folders as usual, looking for the file in its usual place.

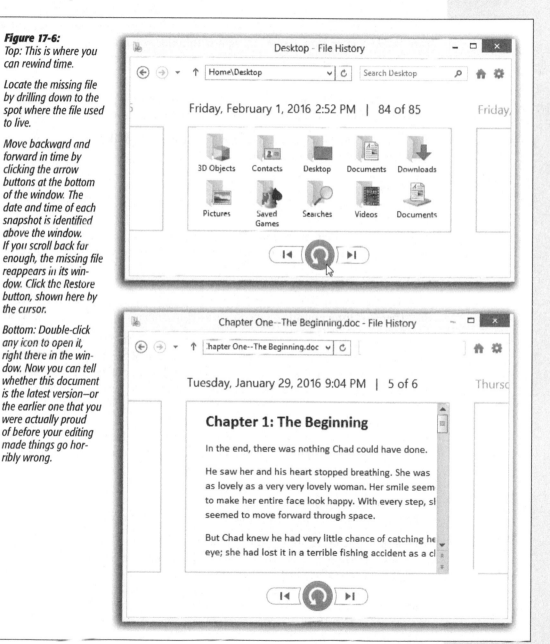

Figure 17-6:
Top: This is where you can rewind time.

Locate the missing file by drilling down to the spot where the file used to live.

Move backward and forward in time by clicking the arrow buttons at the bottom of the window. The date and time of each snapshot is identified above the window. If you scroll back far enough, the missing file reappears in its window. Click the Restore button, shown here by the cursor.

Bottom: Double-click any icon to open it, right there in the window. Now you can tell whether this document is the latest version—or the earlier one that you were actually proud of before your editing made things go horribly wrong.

If it's been deleted, of course, you won't find it—at least, not in *today's* listing. But if you click the ← button, the entire window slides to the right; you're viewing endlessly scrolling *versions* of the current window, going back in time.

If you scroll back far enough this way, you'll eventually see the missing file reappear. You've rewound time to a point before it went missing.

Scrolling back in time is also useful when you want to find an earlier *version*, or draft, of a document. And how will you know which version you're looking at? Because you can *double-click* an icon to open it, right within this window (Figure 17-6, bottom). You can keep clicking the ← button even when the document is open, so you can watch its contents change in real (backward) time.

Once you've found the file in question, click the big green Restore button. Magically enough, the lost file or folder (or outdated document) is brought back from the dead.

File History prides itself not just on recovering files and folders, but also on putting them back where they came from.

Tip: You can also tell File History to put the file or folder into a *new* location. To do that, right-click its icon; from the shortcut menu, choose "Restore to," and choose the recovered folder location.

If you recover a different version of something that's still there, then Windows asks if you want to replace it with the recovered version—or if you'd rather keep both versions.

Ribbon rewinding

You don't actually have to bother with the Control Panel when you want to restore a file. There's a History button on the Ribbon's Home tab in every File Explorer window.

In other words, you can start the recovery process by opening the folder that contains (or used to contain) the file you want. Or find the icon of the file you want to rewind. In either case, click that History button. You wind up in exactly the same spot illustrated in Figure 17-6; the recovery process is the same.

Searching for the file

Once you've opened the window shown in Figure 17-6, here's another way to find the missing or changed file: Type into the search box at the top of the window. That's handy if you can't remember what folder it was in. See Figure 17-7.

The Properties dialog box

The fourth way to rewind a file or folder is new in Windows 10.

Right-click its icon (or hold your finger down on it); from the shortcut menu, choose "Restore previous versions." The Properties dialog box opens for that item, where you can click the tab called Previous Versions.

Note: Question: If you have to click the Previous Versions tab anyway, why choose "Restore previous versions" from the shortcut menu instead of Properties? Answer: Who knows? Both commands do exactly the same thing.

Anyway, the result is a list of previous versions of your document. Each one is date-stamped. To inspect a version to see if it's the one you want, select it and then hit Open. (You can also use the button's pop-up menu to choose "Open in File History," which takes you to the box shown at the bottom of Figure 17-6.)

When you've found the one you want, click Restore; Windows cheerfully recovers the older version of that file or folder and puts it back where it used to be (or where the current version sits). Or you can save it into a different folder by using the Restore button's pop-up menu ("Restore to").

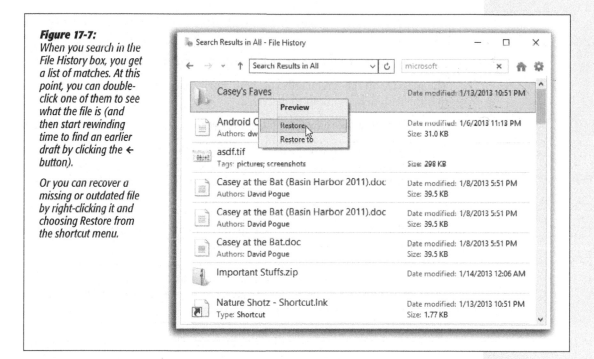

Figure 17-7:
When you search in the File History box, you get a list of matches. At this point, you can double-click one of them to see what the file is (and then start rewinding time to find an earlier draft by clicking the ← button).

Or you can recover a missing or outdated file by right-clicking it and choosing Restore from the shortcut menu.

The USB Recovery Drive

Here's the sneaky surprise: Your computer may have come with an invisible "hard drive" (a partition of your main drive). It's about 5 gigabytes in size.

When the day comes when your computer won't start up, you'll be glad you had this "separate" disk. On it, Microsoft has provided some emergency tools for fixing drive or software glitches, restoring files, and even reinstalling Windows.

Better yet, you can create a USB flash drive that does the same thing. That's handy if (a) your computer does not have a recovery partition, or (b) you wouldn't mind deleting the recovery partition from your drive, so you can use the space for your own files.

Note to techies: The *recimg* Command Prompt command is no longer in Windows 10.

---

1. **Do a search for** *recovery drive*; **in the results list, choose "Create a recovery drive."**

   Authenticate if necessary.

   Before you click the first Next button in the Recovery Drive wizard, note the checkbox called "Back up system files to the recovery drive." If that's turned on, then your flash drive will be able to reinstall a copy of Windows on your machine—a great safety net. (If you turn this box off, then your flash drive will contain troubleshooting tools only; you'll have to figure out some other way to reinstall Windows, if it comes to that.)

   Be sure that "Copy the recovery partition from the PC to the recovery drive" is selected.

2. **Hit Next. Insert a USB flash drive into your computer.**

   The message on the screen tells you how much space the flash drive needs—and that the flash drive is about to be *erased*.

3. **Select the USB drive's name; hit Next; hit Create.**

   Windows copies the recovery image and recovery tools to your flash drive. It takes awhile. At the end, you can choose Finish (to keep your PC's recovery partition) or "Delete the recovery partition from your PC" to free up the disk space.

Using Your Recovery Drive

Should trouble ever strike, you can start up the computer from that flash drive, even if (especially if) it can't start up normally on its own.

Note: Truth is, if your PC is having a problem, your first thought should be to use one of the reset options at this point (page 508); the recovery process will be faster and more convenient. Proceed with your recovery drive only if the Reset thing doesn't help get your PC going again.

Turn on the computer with the flash drive inserted. The "Choose an option" screen (page 511) appears. (Welcome to the Recovery Environment; hope you enjoy your stay.)

Select Troubleshoot and then "Recover from a drive."

Now the Windows virtual paramedics spin into action. They'll *delete all your files, programs, settings, and drivers*, leaving behind only a fresh, clean installation of Windows 10, as though it's Day One.

The Disk Chapter

To make life easier for you, the terminology of objects on your computer screen precisely mirrors the terminology of the real world. You use the computer to create *files*, just as in the real world. You put those files into *folders*, just as in the real world. And you put those folders into *filing cabinets*—

Well, OK. Maybe the metaphor doesn't hold up *that* well.

There is a term for the larger storage entity that holds all those files and folders, though: disks.

Lots of traditional disk types have faded out of fashion. Nobody uses floppy disks anymore, and even CDs and DVDs are rapidly disappearing.

But spinning hard drives are still cheap, big, reliable, and common, and SSDs (solid-state drives) are popular in laptops, despite their relatively high cost and small capacity.

In any case, this chapter is all about storage and disks: cleanups, defragmentation, compression, encryption, analysis, and management.

Note: Some of the features mentioned in this chapter—dynamic disks, disk compression, and EFS (encrypting file system)—all require the *NTFS file system* on your computer's disk drives. That's probably what you're using on your main hard drive, because Windows 10 requires it.

But many other kinds of disks—memory cards, flash drives, and so on—use the older FAT32 file system instead. You won't be able to use NTFS tricks on them.

Storage View

Microsoft may offer 10,000 different disk features, but there's always room for one more. Windows 10 introduces yet another feature that's surprisingly useful: Storage view.

The company noticed how many people were downloading apps that let them see what kinds of files were filling their hard drives: pictures, videos, music, documents, and so on. And now, that kind of analysis is built right in (see Figure 18-1).

The new Storage view makes it instantly clear what's using all your disk space. More important, it offers links that make it simple to *delete* files you don't need on your overstuffed drive. Keep Storage view in mind the next time your drive is full.

When you're viewing the graphs of file categories (Figure 18-1, bottom), you can select one of them (Pictures, say, or Videos) to open a summary window for that file

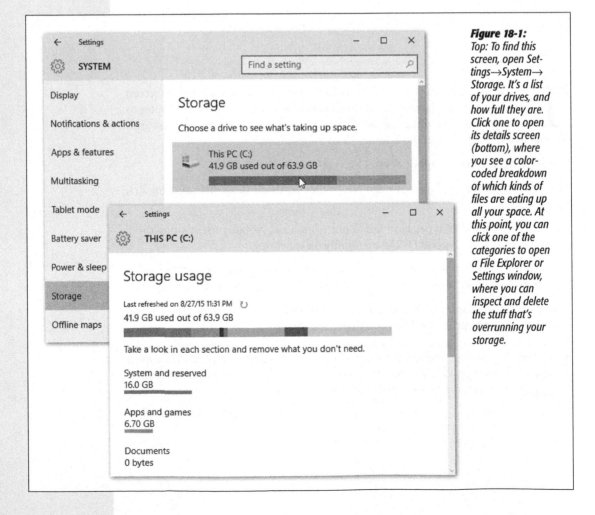

Figure 18-1:
Top: To find this screen, open Settings→System→ Storage. It's a list of your drives, and how full they are. Click one to open its details screen (bottom), where you see a color-coded breakdown of which kinds of files are eating up all your space. At this point, you can click one of the categories to open a File Explorer or Settings window, where you can inspect and delete the stuff that's overrunning your storage.

type. It always contains a View or Manage button that takes you to a tool for pruning your collection of those files.

- **System and reserved.** These are the files that make up Windows. Select this graph to see how much space Windows, virtual memory, and your hibernation file (page 38) are using up. (*Virtual memory* permits you to keep several large programs open at once—by laying down pieces of background apps on the disk.)

- **Apps and games.** Select this bar to open the "Apps & features" screen described on page 260, where it's easy to start deleting programs you don't need anymore.

- **Pictures, Music, Videos, Documents, Desktop.** Hit one of these graphs, and then the corresponding View button, to open a File Explorer window containing that file type for inspection and cleaning. (These tallies show what's in your Pictures, Music, Videos, and Documents *folders*. If you have pictures, music, video, and documents in other folders, they're not counted here.)

- **Mail.** "Manage mail" opens your Mail app, so you can delete some mail to save space.

- **OneDrive.** The Manage OneDrive button opens a list of checkboxes, representing all the folders on your OneDrive. You can turn off the ones you don't need synced to other computers (page 162), thus saving space on the computer you're using.

- **Maps** refers to offline maps (regions you've saved to your computer, so that you can view them without an Internet connection later; see page 261). Hit "Manage maps" to open a Settings page that lists your offline maps for easy purging.

- **Temporary files** may offer the most fruitful spring cleaning of all. Here are links to temporary files (cache files) that Windows doesn't really need; your Downloads folder; your Recycle Bin; and "Previous versions of Windows"—whatever copy of Windows you upgraded to Windows 10—which can eat up a huge amount of space (13 gigabytes per version). If you have no intention of going back, select "Delete previous versions" to reclaim a ton of space.

UP TO SPEED

Volumes Defined

You won't get far in this chapter, or at PC user group meetings, without understanding a key piece of Windows terminology: *volume*.

For most people, most of the time, volume means "disk." But technically, there's more to it than that—a distinction that becomes crucial if you explore the techniques described in this chapter.

If you open your This PC window, you see that each disk has its own icon and drive letter (C:, for example). But each icon isn't necessarily a separate disk. It's possible that you, or somebody in charge of your PC, has split a single drive into multiple *partitions* (Appendix A), each with a separate icon and drive letter. Clearly, the world needs a term for "an icon/drive letter in the This PC window, whether it's a whole disk or not." That term is *volume*.

Now it's easy to go on a cleaning binge, throwing out stuff you don't need and reclaiming some storage space.

Disk Cleanup

As you use your computer, Windows litters your hard drive with temporary files. Programs, utilities, and Web sites scatter disposable files everywhere. If you could see your hard drive's surface, it would eventually look like the floor of a minivan whose owners eat a lot of fast food.

If the problem is that your disk is running out of space, your first stop should be the new Storage view, described in the previous section. But an older, less comprehensive app, Disk Cleanup (Figure 18-2), is still available; its specialty is removing temporary files.

To run Windows' built-in housekeeper program, the quickest route is this: Do a search for *disk cleanup*; in the search results, click "Free up disk space by deleting unnecessary files." (Disk Cleanup is also available in the Control Panel. Somewhere.)

The Disk Cleanup program dives right in. If you have more than one drive, it lets you choose the one you want to work on; then it goes to work, inspecting your drive and reporting on files you can safely remove.

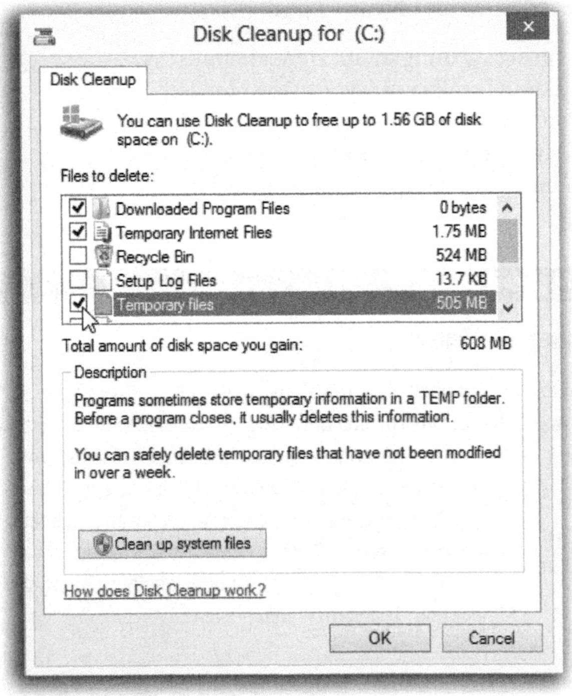

Figure 18-2:
Disk Cleanup announces how much free space you stand to gain. After you've been using your PC for a while, it's amazing how much crud you'll find there— and how much space you can recover.

If you're not sure what some of these categories are, a quick Google search will make all clear.

Left to its own devices, it will clean up only *your* files. But if you'd like to clean up all the files on the computer, including Microsoft's own detritus, click "Clean up system files." Authenticate if necessary.

The Disk Cleanup box shown in Figure 18-2 appears when the inspection is over. Turn on the checkboxes of the file categories you'd like to have cleaned out, and then click OK to send them to the digital landfill. It's like getting a bigger hard drive for free.

Disk Defragmenter

When you save a new file, Windows records its information onto the hard drive in small pieces called *blocks*. On a new PC, Windows lays the blocks end-to-end on the hard drive's surface. Later, when you type more data into a document (thus enlarging it), the file no longer fits in the same space. Windows puts as much of the file in the original location as can fit, but it may have to store a few of its blocks in the next empty spot on the hard drive.

Ordinarily, you'll never even notice that your files are getting chopped up in this way, since they open promptly and seamlessly. Windows keeps track of where it has stored the various pieces and reconstitutes them when necessary.

As your drive fills up, though, the free space that's left is made up of smaller and smaller groups of blocks. Eventually, a new file may not fit in a single "parking place" on the hard drive's surface, since there are no free spaces left large enough to hold it. Windows may have to store a file in several different areas of the disk, or even hundreds.

When you try to open such a *fragmented* file, the drive heads (which read the disk) must scamper all over the disk surface, rounding up each block in turn, which is slower than reading contiguous blocks one after the other. Over time, this *file fragmentation* gets worse and worse. Eventually, you wind up griping to your buddies or spouse that you need a new computer, because this one seems to have gotten *so slow*.

The solution: Disk Defragmenter, a program that puts together pieces of files that have become fragmented on your drive. The "defragger" also rearranges the files on your drives to make the operating system and programs load more quickly. A freshly defragged PC feels faster and more responsive than a heavily fragmented one.

POWER USERS' CLINIC

Beyond Disk Defragmenter

Disk Defragmenter isn't the only tool for the defrag job; the world is full of disk-defragmenting programs that offer additional features.

For example, some of them track how often you use the various files on your drive, so they can store the most frequently used files at the beginning of the disk for quicker access. In some programs, you can even *choose* which files go at the beginning of the disk.

Do these additional features actually produce a measurable improvement over Windows' built-in defragger? That's hard to say, especially when you remember the biggest advantage of Disk Defragmenter—it's free.

Windows' disk-defragging software runs *automatically* at regular intervals, in the tiny moments when you're not actually typing or clicking. It's like having someone take out your garbage for you whenever the can is full. Slow-PC syndrome should, therefore, be a much less frequent occurrence.

Tip: Fragmentation doesn't become noticeable except on hard drives that have been very full for quite a while. Don't bother defragmenting your drive unless you've actually noticed it slowing down. The time you'll spend waiting for Disk Defragmenter to do its job is much longer than the fractions of seconds caused by a little bit of file fragmentation.

And if you're the lucky owner of a solid-state drive (SSD)—fast, quiet, pricier—defragmenting is so irrelevant, Windows doesn't even do it. In fact, if Windows detects that you're using an SSD, the Optimize button shown in Figure 18-3 performs a different operation. It does a *trim*, a cleanup that helps the drive identify areas that are now empty and available for new storage.

Defragging Settings

Even though Windows defrags your hard drive automatically in the background, you can still exert some control. For example, you can change the schedule, and you can trigger a defragmentation manually when you're feeling like a control freak.

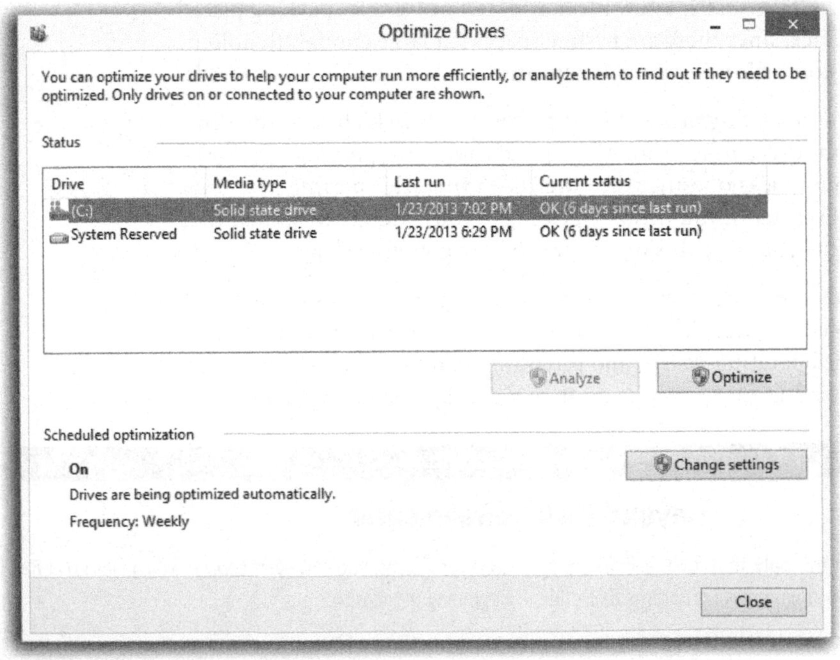

Figure 18-3:
Unless there's a good reason, you don't want to schedule defragmentation, it's a good idea to have Windows do it for you automatically—it's like getting someone else to take out your trash.

To reach the Optimize Drives main screen, do a search for *disk defrag* and select "Defragment and optimize your drives" in the results. (You can also find Disk Defragmenter in the Control Panel, if you dig deep enough.)

Tip: Throughout Windows, and throughout its book and magazine literature, disks are referred to as *volumes*. Usually, "volume" means disk. But technically, it refers to *anything with its own disk icon* in the This PC window—including disk partitions, flash drives, and so on.

The Optimize Drives window opens (Figure 18-3). From here, you can either adjust the schedule or trigger defragmentation manually:

- **Adjust the schedule.** Click "Change settings." Authenticate if necessary. A screen appears. You can use the pop-up menus here to specify a Weekly, Daily, or Monthly schedule. Click OK.

- **Manually.** Click Analyze to see how badly fragmented your disk is, or Optimize to start the defragging process. Depending on the size of your hard disk, your processor speed, and the amount of fragmentation, it will take anywhere from several minutes to several hours.

Tip: During the defragmentation process (on a traditional hard drive), Windows picks up pieces of your files and temporarily sets them down in a different spot, like somebody trying to solve a jigsaw puzzle. If your hard drive is very full, defragmenting will take a lot longer than if you have some empty space available—and if there's not enough free disk space, Windows can't do the job completely. Before you run Disk Defragmenter, use Storage view or Disk Cleanup and make as much free disk space as possible.

Hard Drive Checkups

It's true: Things can occasionally go wrong on the surface of your hard drive. Maybe there's a messed-up spot on its physical surface. Maybe, thanks to a system crash, power outage, or toddler playing with your surge suppressor, your computer gets turned off without warning, and some files are left open and stranded.

In the olden days, way back even before Windows XP, fixing your disk required running a program called ScanDisk, a utility designed to detect and, when possible, repair drive damage.

ScanDisk doesn't exist in Windows 10. But its functions, and many more, have been overhauled. Many disk problems are automatically detected and automatically fixed—and most of them don't require you to wait while the PC repairs itself. There's a lot less downtime.

You can also check your disk on command. (This is the old disk-checking procedure.)

Right-click the icon of the hard drive you want to check (in the This PC window). From the shortcut menu, choose Properties; click the Tools tab, and click Check.

Note: Geeks fondly refer to the feature described here as *chkdsk* (apparently named by someone with no vowels on his keyboard). You get to the geek-friendly, text-only version of it by typing *chkdsk* in a Command Prompt window. But the method described here is much better looking.

Disk Management

"Disk management" isn't just a cool, professional-sounding skill—it's the name of a built-in Windows maintenance program that lets you perform all kinds of operations on your hard disk. To open it, right-click the Start menu; from the shortcut menu, choose Disk Management. (Only Administrator account holders are welcome.)

In either case, you arrive at the window shown in Figure 18-4. At first glance, it appears to be nothing more than a table of every disk (and *partition* of every disk) currently connected to your PC. In truth, the Disk Management window is a software toolkit that lets you *operate* on these drives.

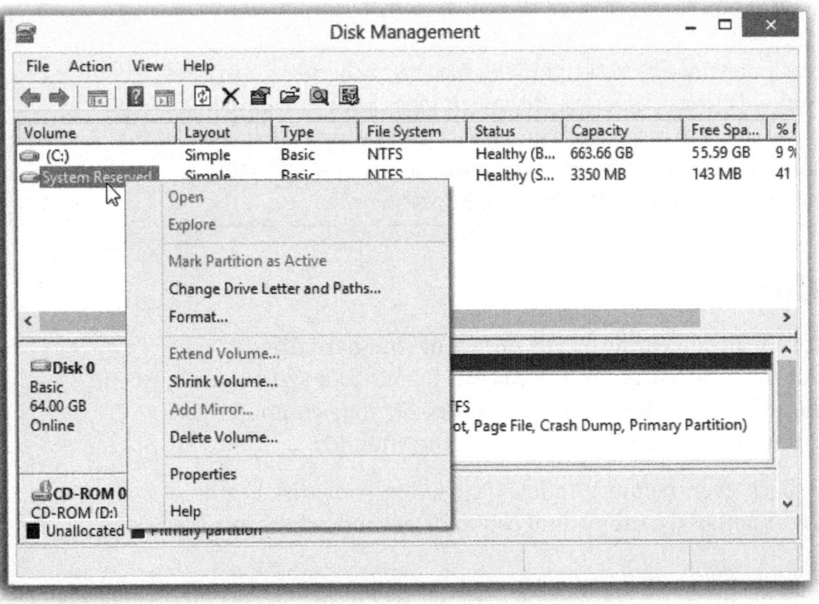

Figure 18-4:
The Disk Management window does more than just display your drives; you can also operate on them by right-clicking. Don't miss the View menu, by the way, which lets you change either the top or the bottom display. For example, you can make your PC display all your disks instead of your volumes. (There's a difference; see page 535.)

Change a Drive Letter

As you've probably noticed, Windows assigns a drive letter to each disk drive associated with your PC. In the age of floppy disks, the floppy drives were always A: and B:. The primary internal hard drive is generally C:; your CD/DVD drive may be D: or E:; and so on. Among other places, you see these letters in parentheses following the names of your drives in the This PC window.

Windows generally assigns these letters in the order that you install new drives to your system. You're not allowed to change the drive letter of any startup hard drive (the C: drive and, if you're set up for dual booting, any other boot drives).

You can, however, override the *other* drives' unimaginative Windows letter assignments easily enough, as shown in Figure 18-5. Your computer won't run any faster, but you may feel a tiny surge of pride at how much better organized you feel.

Note: If Windows is currently using files on the disk whose drive letter you're trying to change, Disk Management might create the new drive letter assignment but leave the old one intact until the next time you restart the computer. This is an effort to not pull the rug out from under any open files.

Figure 18-5:
Right-click a drive icon. From the shortcut menu, choose Change Drive Letter and Paths.

Top: In this dialog box, click Change.

Bottom: Next, choose a letter that hasn't already been assigned. Click OK, and then approve your action in the confirmation box.

Note that if you change a drive's letter, shortcut icons pointing to files on it no longer work. Programs that list Recently Used Documents on that drive get confused, too.

And although you can change the drive letter of a USB drive (like an external hard drive or a flash drive), it won't stick. Next time you attach it, Windows will give it the first available letter.

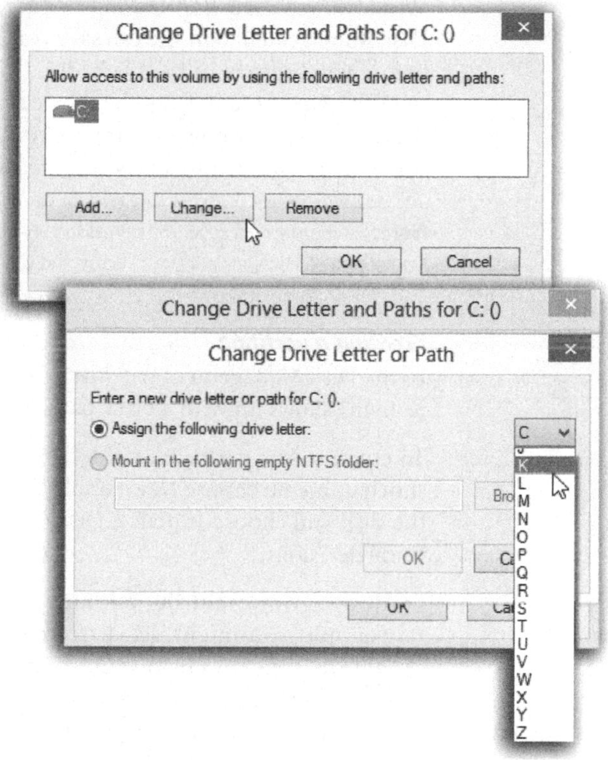

Partition a New Drive

The vast majority of Windows PCs have only one hard drive, represented in the This PC window as a single icon.

Plenty of power users, however, delight in *partitioning* the hard drive—dividing its surface so that it appears on the screen as two different icons with two different names.

At that point, you can live like a king, enjoying the following advantages (just like people who have two separate hard drives):

- **You can keep Windows 10 on one of them** and Windows 8.1 (for example) on the other, so you can switch between the two at startup. This feature, called *dual booting*, is described on page 630.

- **You can keep your operating system(s) separate from folders and files.** In this way, you can perform a clean install of Windows (page 631) onto one partition without having to worry about losing any of your important files or installation programs. Or you can keep your files safely on one partition while you install and reinstall different operating systems, or different versions of them, on the other.

Now, in earlier Windows days, partitioning a hard drive using the tools built into Windows required first erasing the hard drive completely. Fortunately, Windows' Disk Management console can save you from that hassle, although making a backup before you begin is still a smart idea. (The short version: Right-click the disk's icon in Disk Management; from the shortcut menu, choose Shrink Volume. In the Shrink dialog box, specify how much space you want to free up, and then click Shrink. Then turn the free space into a new volume, as described next.)

Note: Partitioning is an advanced kind of surgery that involves erasing disks and moving lots of files around. *Do not proceed* unless you have a backup and you're a technically confident soul.

Creating a partition

In the Disk Management window, free space (suitable for turning into a partition of its own) shows up with a black bar and the label "Unallocated."

To create a new partition, right-click one of these unallocated segments. From the shortcut menu, choose New Simple Volume (if this option isn't available, right-click the disk and choose Initialize Disk). A wizard appears; its screens ask you to make some decisions:

- **How big you want the volume to be.** If you're dividing up a 500 GB drive, for example, you might decide to make the first volume 300 GB and the second 200 GB. Begin by creating the 300 GB volume (right-clicking the big Unallocated bar). When that's done, you see a smaller Unallocated chunk still left in the Disk Management window. Right-click it and choose New Simple Volume *again*, this time accepting the size the wizard proposes (which is *all* the remaining free space).

- **What drive letter you want to assign to it.** Most of the alphabet is at your disposal.

- **What disk-formatting scheme you want to apply to it.** Windows 10 requires NTFS for the system drive. It's far safer and more flexible than the old FAT32 system.

  Consider FAT32 only if, for example, if you plan to dual-boot Windows 10 with Linux, Mac OS X, or an old version of Windows. (FAT32 might be the only file system all those operating systems can recognize simultaneously.)

When the wizard is through with you, it's safe to close the window. A quick look at your This PC window confirms that you now have new "disks" (actually partitions of the same disk), which you can use for different purposes.

Turn a Drive into a Folder

Talk about techie! Most people could go their entire lives without needing this feature, or even imagining that it exists. But it's there if you're a power user and you want it.

Using the Paths feature of Disk Management, you can actually turn a hard drive (or partition) into a *folder* on another hard drive (or partition). These disks-disguised-as-folders are technically known as *mounted drives, junction points*, or *drive paths*.

This arrangement affords the following possibilities:

- In effect, you can greatly expand the capacity of your main hard drive—by installing a second hard drive that masquerades as a folder on the first one.

- You can turn a burned CD or DVD into a folder on your main hard drive, too—a handy way to fool your programs into thinking the files they're looking for are still in

---

FREQUENTLY ASKED QUESTION

When Good Drives Go Bad

I was surprised when the Action Center found some problems with my hard drive. I don't understand what could have gone wrong. I treat my PC with respect, talk to it often, and never take it swimming. Why did my hard drive get flaky?

All kinds of things can cause problems with your hard drive, but the most common are low voltage, power outages, voltage spikes, and mechanical problems with the drive controller or the drive itself.

An inexpensive gadget called a *line conditioner* (sold at computer stores) can solve the low-voltage problem. A more expensive gizmo known as an *uninterruptible power supply* (UPS) maintains enough backup battery power to keep your computer going when the power goes out completely—for a few minutes, anyway, so you can shut it down properly. The more expensive models have line conditioning built in. A UPS is also the answer to power outages, if they're common in your area.

Voltage spikes are the most dangerous to your PC. They frequently occur during the first seconds when the power comes back on after a power failure. A surge suppressor is the logical defense here. But remember that the very

cheap devices often sold as surge suppressors are actually little more than extension cords. Furthermore, some of the models that do provide adequate protection are designed to sacrifice themselves in battle. After a spike, you may have to replace them.

If you care about your computer (or the money you spent on it), buy a good surge suppressor, at the very least. The best ones come with a guarantee that the company will replace your equipment (up to a certain dollar value) if the unit fails to provide adequate protection.

On the other hand, insufficient power is just as dangerous as a voltage spike. If you own a desktop PC, chances are good that the built-in power supply is strong enough for whatever components your PC was born with. But if you've upgraded—adding a faster hard drive or a beefier video card, for example—you may be pushing your PC's power supply to its limits.

If you're doing a bunch of upgrades to convert an entry-level office PC into a gaming powerhouse, then make sure you're including a newer, stronger power supply among those upgrades.

---

the same old place on your hard drive. (You could pull this stunt in a crisis—when the "real" folder has become corrupted or has been thrown away.)

- If you're a *power* power user with lots of partitions, disks, and drives, you may feel hemmed in by the limitation of only 26 assignable letters (A through Z). Turning one of your disks into a mounted volume bypasses that limitation, because a mounted volume doesn't need a drive letter at all.

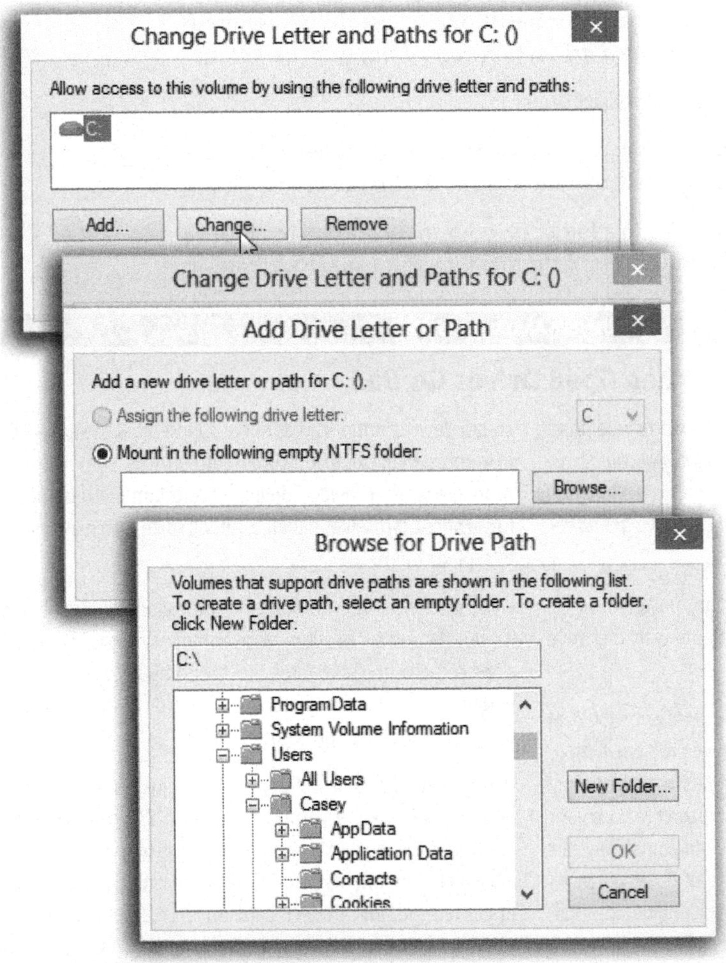

Figure 18-6:
Here's how to make a drive appear as a folder icon on any other drive: Designate an empty folder to be the receptacle—a metaphysical portal—for the drive's contents.

- A certain disk can be made to appear in more than one place at once. You could put all your MP3 files on a certain disk or a partition—and then make it show up as a folder in the Music folder of everyone who uses the computer.

Note: You can create a mounted volume only on an *NTFS-formatted* hard drive.

To bring about this arrangement, visit the Disk Management window, and then right-click the icon of the disk or partition you want to turn into a mounted volume. From the shortcut menu, choose Change Drive Letter and Paths.

In the Change Drive Letter and Paths dialog box (Figure 18-6, top), click Add; in the next dialog box (Figure 18-6, middle), click Browse. Navigate to and select an empty folder—the one that will represent the disk. (Click New Folder, shown at bottom in Figure 18-6, if you didn't create one in advance.) Finally, click OK.

Once the deed is done, take time to note a few special characteristics of a mounted volume:

- The mounted volume may behave just like a folder, but its icon is a dead giveaway, since it still looks like a hard drive (or a CD drive, or a DVD drive, or whatever).

  Still, if you're in doubt about what it is, you can right-click it and choose Properties from the shortcut menu. You see that the Type information says "Mounted Volume" and the Target line identifies the disk from which it was made.

- Avoid circular references, in which you turn two drives into folders on *each other*. Otherwise, you risk throwing programs into a spasm of infinite-loop thrashing.

- To undo your mounted-drive effect, return to the Disk Management program and choose View→Drive Paths. You're shown a list of all the drives you've turned into folders; click one and then click Remove.

  You've just turned that special, "I'm really a drive" folder into an ordinary folder.

Storage Spaces

For years, the data centers of big corporations have used RAID systems (Redundant Array of Independent Disks) for storage. A RAID array is a bunch of drives installed inside a single metal box; clever software makes them look to a computer like one big drive. Or three smaller ones, or fifty little ones—however the highly trained system administrator decides to chop them up.

And why bother? Because the files on a RAID system can be recovered even if one of the hard drives dies, thanks to a fancy encoding scheme. (Thus, the "redundant" in the name.)

But RAID systems are complicated to set up and incredibly inflexible; you generally have to install all drives of the same type and capacity simultaneously. And if you decide to expand your array, you have to erase all the existing drives and reformat them.

A technical Windows feature called Storage Spaces offers the same benefits as RAID systems—for example, data safety even if one of the drives croaks—without anywhere near the same complexity or inflexibility. Your setup doesn't require matching drives, and you can fiddle with the capacity at any time without having to reformat anything.

To get started, search for *storage spaces*, and open the Control Panel of that name. For step-by-step instructions, see the free downloadable PDF appendix "Storage Spaces.pdf" on this book's "Missing CD" page at *www.missingmanuals.com*.

Dynamic Disks

Before Storage Spaces came along, there were other ways to tell Windows to treat multiple drives as one. There was Drive Extender, a more technical version of what we know today as Storage Spaces.

That feature is gone now, but *dynamic disks, basic disks,* and *spanned volumes* are still around—other methods of slicing and dicing your actual disks in clever ways.

If this older, more complex, decidedly more advanced topic interests you, a free bonus appendix to this chapter awaits, called "Dynamic Disks.pdf." You can download it from this book's "Missing CD" page at *www.missingmanuals.com*.

Encrypting Files and Folders

If your Documents folder contains nothing but laundry lists and letters to your mom, data security is probably not a major concern for you. But if there's some stuff on your hard drive that you'd rather keep private, Windows can help you out. The Encrypting File System (EFS) is an NTFS feature, available in the Pro and Enterprise versions of Windows, that stores your data in a coded format that only you can read.

The beauty of EFS is that it's effortless and invisible to you, the authorized owner. Windows automatically encrypts your files before storing them on the drive, and decrypts them again when you want to read or modify them. Anyone else who logs onto your computer, however, will find these files locked and off-limits.

Figure 18-7:
To encrypt a file or folder using EFS, turn on the "Encrypt contents to secure data" checkbox (at the bottom of its Properties dialog box). If you've selected a folder, a Confirm Attribute Changes dialog box appears, asking if you want to encrypt just that folder or everything inside it, too.

If you've read ahead to Chapter 19, of course, you might be frowning in confusion at this point. Isn't keeping private files private the whole point of Windows' *accounts* feature? Don't Windows' *NTFS permissions* (page 583) keep busybodies out already?

Yes, but encryption provides additional security. If, for example, you're a top-level agent assigned to protect your government's most closely guarded egg salad recipe, you can use NTFS permissions to deny all other users access to the file containing the information. Nobody but you can open the file.

However, a determined intruder from a foreign nation could conceivably boot the computer using *another* operating system—one that doesn't recognize the NTFS permissions—and access the hard drive using a special program that reads the raw data stored there.

POWER USERS' CLINIC

Disk Quotas

Does one of your account holders have a tendency to become overzealous about downloading stuff, threatening to overrun your drive with shareware junk and MP3 files? Fortunately, it's easy enough for you, the wise administrator, to curb such behavior among holders of Standard accounts.

Choose This PC at the left side of any File Explorer window. Right-click the hard drive icon; from the shortcut menu, choose Properties. In the Properties dialog box, click the Quota tab. Click Show Quota Settings to bring up the Quota Settings dialog box, shown here, and then turn on "Enable quota management."

You might start by turning on "Deny disk space to users exceeding quota limit." This, of course, is exactly the kind of muzzle you were hoping to place on out-of-control downloaders. The instant they try to save or download a file that pushes their stuff over the limit, an "Insufficient disk space" message appears.

Use the "Limit disk space to ___" controls to specify the cap you want to put on each account holder. Using these controls, you can specify a certain number of kilobytes (KB), megabytes (MB), gigabytes (GB)—or even terabytes (TB), petabytes (PB), or exabytes (EB). (Then write a letter to *PCWorld* and tell the editors where you bought a multiexabyte hard drive.)

You can also set up a disk-space limit ("Set warning level to ___") that will make a *warning* appear—not to the mad downloader, but to you, the administrator. By clicking the Quota Entries button, you get a report that shows how much disk space each account holder has used up. (This is where you see the warning as a written notation.)

If you just want to track your underlings' disk usage without actually limiting them, then set the warning level to the desired value, but set the Limit Disk Space value to something impossibly high, like several exabytes.

When you click OK, Windows warns you that it's about to take some time to calculate just how much disk space each account holder has used so far.

But if you had encrypted the file using EFS, that raw data would appear as gibberish, foiling your crafty nemesis.

Using EFS

You use EFS to encrypt your folders and files in much the same way that you use NTFS compression. To encrypt a file or a folder, open its Properties dialog box, click the Advanced button, turn on the "Encrypt contents to secure data" checkbox, and then click OK (see Figure 18-7).

Depending on how much data you've selected, it may take some time for the encryption process to complete. Once the folders and files are encrypted, they appear in File Explorer in a different color from your compressed files (unless you've turned off the "Show encrypted or compressed NTFS files in color" option; see page 91).

Note: You can't encrypt certain files and folders, such as system files, or any files in the system *root folder* (usually the Windows folder). You can't encrypt files and folders on FAT32 drives, either.

Finally, note that you can't both encrypt *and* compress the same file or folder. If you attempt to encrypt a compressed file or folder, Windows needs to decompress it first. You can, however, encrypt files that have been compressed using another technology, such as .zip files or compressed image files.

After your files have been encrypted, you may be surprised to see that, other than their color, nothing seems to have changed. You can open them the same way you always did, change them, and save them as usual. Windows is just doing its job: protecting these files with the minimum inconvenience to you.

Still, if you're having difficulty believing that your files are now protected by an invisible force field, try logging off and back on again with a different user name and password. When you try to open an encrypted file now, a message cheerfully informs you that you don't have the proper permissions to access the file.

EFS Rules

Any files or folders you move *into* an EFS-encrypted folder get encrypted, too. But dragging a file *out* of one doesn't unprotect it; it remains encrypted as long as it's on an NTFS drive. A protected file loses its encryption only in these circumstances:

- **You manually decrypt the file** (by turning off the corresponding checkbox in its Properties dialog box).

- **You move it to a FAT32 or exFAT drive.**

- **You transmit it via a network or email.** When you attach the file to an email or send it across the network, Windows decrypts the file before sending it on its way.

By the way, EFS doesn't protect files from being deleted. Even if passing evildoers can't *open* your private file, they can still *delete* it—unless you've protected it using Windows' permissions feature (page 583). Here again, truly protecting important material involves using several security mechanisms in combination.

BitLocker Drive Encryption

EFS is a great way to keep prying eyes out of individual files. But Microsoft wouldn't be Microsoft if it didn't give you six variations on a theme. After all, when million-dollar corporate secrets are at stake, a determined, knowledgeable thief could swipe your laptop, nab your flash drive, or even steal the hard drive out of your desktop PC.

If security is that important for you, then you'll be happy to know about BitLocker Drive Encryption, a feature of the Pro and Enterprise versions of Windows. When you turn on this feature, your PC automatically encrypts (scrambles) everything on an *entire drive*, including all of Windows itself.

If the bad guy tries any industrial-strength tricks to get into the drive—trying to reprogram the startup routines, for example, or starting up from a different hard drive—BitLocker presents a steel-reinforced password screen. No password, no decryption.

In Windows 10, you also get BitLocker to Go—a disk-encryption feature especially for removable drives like USB flash drives. Even if you lose it or leave it behind, it's worthless to anyone without the password.

You don't notice much difference when BitLocker is turned on. You log in as usual, clicking your name and typing your password. But if a malefactor ever gets his hands on the actual disk, he'll be in for a disappointing surprise.

There are quite a few steps involved in setting up BitLocker, and it's not something most people would ever bother with. So the step-by-step instructions are on the free downloadable PDF "BitLocker.pdf" appendix on this book's "Missing CD" page at *www.missingmanuals.com*.

Part Six:
The Windows Network

Chapter 19: Accounts (and Logging On)

Chapter 20: Setting Up a Small Network

Chapter 21: Sharing Files on the Network

6

Accounts (and Logging On)

For years, teachers, parents, tech directors, and computer lab instructors struggled to answer two difficult questions: How do you rig one PC so several different people can use it throughout the day, without interfering with one another's files and settings? And how do you protect a PC from getting fouled up by mischievous (or bumbling) students and employees?

Easy: Use a multiple-user operating system like Windows. Anyone who uses the computer must *log on*—supply a name and password—when the computer turns on.

Since the day you installed Windows 10 or fired up a new Windows 10 machine, you've probably made a number of changes to your setup—fiddled with your Start menu, changed the desktop wallpaper, added some favorites to your Web browser, downloaded files onto your desktop, and so on—without realizing that you were actually making these changes only to *your account*.

Ditto with your Web history and cookies, Control Panel settings, email stash, and so on. It's all part of your account.

If you create an account for a second person, then when she turns on the computer and signs in, she'll find the desktop looking the way it was factory-installed by Microsoft: basic Start menu, standard desktop picture, default Web browser home page, and so on. She can make the same kinds of changes to the PC that you've made, but nothing she does will affect your environment the next time *you* log on.

In other words, the multiple-accounts feature has two benefits: first, the convenience of hiding everyone else's junk and, second, security that protects both the PC's system software and everyone's work.

Behind the scenes, Windows stores *all* these files and settings in a single folder—your Personal folder, the one that bears your name. (Technically, your Personal folder is in the This PC > Local Disk (C:) > Users folder.)

Tip: Even if you don't share your PC with anyone and don't create any other accounts, you might still appreciate this feature because it effectively password-protects the entire computer. Your PC is protected from unauthorized casual fiddling when you're away from your desk (or if your laptop is stolen)—especially if you tell Windows to require your logon password anytime the screensaver has kicked in (page 183).

If you're content simply to *use* Windows, that's really all you need to know about accounts. If, on the other hand, you have shouldered some of the responsibility for *administering* Windows machines—if it's your job to add and remove accounts, for example—read on.

Local Accounts vs. Microsoft Accounts

For most of Windows' history, any account you created on your PC was a *local* account, meaning *stored on the computer itself*. All your stuff—your files, email, settings, passwords—sat on the PC itself.

Seems obvious, right? Where else would you store all those details?

Today, there's an answer to that: online.

In Windows 10, you have the option to have your account details stored by Microsoft, online ("in the cloud," as the marketing people might say). You don't log in with a name like Fizzywinks; instead, you log in with an *email address* that you've registered with Microsoft. If your name and password are correct, you've just succeeded in logging in with your *Microsoft account* instead of with a local one.

And why is that a good thing? Because it means you can sign into *any Windows 8 or 10 computer anywhere*—your other laptop, a friend's PC, another company's—and find yourself instantly at home. You won't have your files, music collection, and movies, of course (unless you've stored them on your OneDrive). But you will find every possible account-related element ready and waiting, even on a computer you've never used before. Here's what you'll find:

- **Your email, Twitter, Facebook, LinkedIn, Hotmail, and other accounts.** You're supposed to link *these* to your Microsoft account. After that, no matter what computer you use, your People app, Skype program, and other address books will always be up to date and fully loaded.

- **Your online photos.** Once again, your Microsoft account can store your links to services like Flickr and Facebook, so their contents are automatically available when you sign into any Windows 8 or 10 machine.

- **Your OneDrive.** Any files you've stashed on the OneDrive (page 161) are available to you.

- **Your settings.** Your wallpaper, color scheme, Cortana settings, and many other settings. Many programs store their settings as part of your Microsoft account, too.

- **Your Xbox world.** As described on page 360, Windows 10 can show you all the details of your online Xbox universe; let you play an Xbox game on your computer; and let you play certain games against someone with an Xbox (while you're on a Windows 10 machine). All of that requires a Microsoft account.

- **Your Web world.** Your browser bookmarks (Favorites), browsing history, and even stored Web-site passwords will be there waiting for you in Edge or Internet Explorer.

Note: Your passwords don't get synced until you make each computer a "trusted PC." When you first log into a new Windows 8 or 10 computer, a message asks if you want to "Trust this PC." If you do, you're asked to confirm that this is your message account by replying to an email or text message.

- **Your Windows Store apps.** You can install a Windows Store app on up to 81 Windows machines. They don't show up automatically when you log into a brand-new computer, but you can open the Store app and click "Your apps" to re-download them.

A Microsoft account is also, of course, your Microsoft wallet; you can use your Microsoft ID to buy apps, music, videos, and games from Microsoft. It's also what you use to sign in if you have an Xbox (possible) or a Windows Phone (unlikely).

In fact, you can't download new Windows Store apps from the app store *at all* without a Microsoft account!

A Microsoft account still lets you into your PC when you don't have an Internet connection. You can turn off as many of the syncing features as you like, for privacy's sake. The company swears it won't send anything to the email address you use. And it's free. In general, it's the best way to log into Windows.

And what about the alternative—a local account? If you have only one computer (and therefore don't need the syncing business) and don't plan to buy anything online, it's fine, too. In fact, Windows 10 is much kinder to local accounts than Windows 8 was; for example, you can now use the built-in apps like Mail, Calendar, and People without having a Microsoft account.

You can always convert any account—from Microsoft to local or vice versa.

Accounts Central

To set up and survey your computer's accounts, open Settings→Accounts. You see the panel shown at top in Figure 19-1.

Here are all the accounts you've created so far. Here, too, is where you can create new accounts, edit the ones you've already made, or delete them, as described in the following pages.

First, though, it's important to understand the differences between the two account types you may see in the Control Panel: *Administrator* and *Standard.* Read on.

The Types of Accounts

On your own personal PC, the word "Administrator" probably appears under your name in the panel shown in Figure 19-1. As it turns out, that's one of two kinds of accounts you can create.

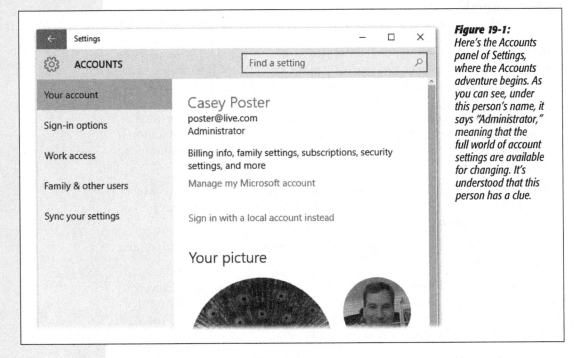

Figure 19-1:
Here's the Accounts panel of Settings, where the Accounts adventure begins. As you can see, under this person's name, it says "Administrator," meaning that the full world of account settings are available for changing. It's understood that this person has a clue.

Administrator accounts

Because you're the person who installed Windows, the PC assumes that you're one of its *administrators*—the technical wizards who will be in charge of it. You're the teacher, the parent, the resident guru. You're the one who will maintain this PC and who will be permitted to make system-wide changes to it.

You'll find settings all over Windows (and all over this book) that *only* people with Administrator accounts can change. For example, only an administrator is allowed to do the following:

- Create or delete accounts and passwords.
- Make changes to certain Control Panel programs.
- See and manipulate *any* file on the machine.
- Install new desktop programs (and certain hardware components).

Standard accounts

There's another kind of account, too, for people who *don't* have to make those kinds of changes: the Standard account.

Now, for years, people doled out Administrator accounts pretty freely. You know: The parents got Administrator accounts, the kids got Standard ones.

The trouble is, an Administrator account is a kind of security hole. Anytime you're logged in with this kind of account, any nasty software you may have caught from the Internet is *also,* in effect, logged in—and can make changes to important underlying settings on your PC, just the way a human administrator can.

Put another way: A virus you've downloaded while running a Standard account will have a much harder time infecting the rest of the machine than one you downloaded while using an Administrator account.

Today, therefore, Microsoft recommends that *everyone* use Standard accounts—even you, the wise master and owner of the computer!

So how are you supposed to make important Control Panel changes, install new programs, and so on?

That's gotten a lot easier. Using a Standard account no longer means you can't make important changes. In fact, you can do just about everything on the PC that an Administrator account can—if you know the *password* of a true Administrator account.

Note: Every Windows 10 PC can (and must) keep at least one Administrator account on hand, even if that account is rarely used.

Whenever you try to make a big change, you're asked to *authenticate yourself.* As described on page 580, that means supplying an Administrator account's password, even though you, the currently-logged-in person, are a lowly Standard account holder.

If you have a Standard account because you're a student, a child, or an employee, you're supposed to call an administrator over to your PC to approve the change you're making. (If you're the PC's owner, but you're using a Standard account for security purposes, you know an administrator password, so it's no big deal.)

Now, making broad changes to a PC when you're an administrator *still* presents you with those "prove yourself worthy" authentication dialog boxes. The only difference is that you, the administrator, can click Continue (or tap Enter) to bypass them, rather than having to type in a password.

You'll have to weigh this security/convenience tradeoff. But you've been warned: The least vulnerable PC is one on which everyone uses a Standard account.

Adding an Account

To create a new account, open Settings→Accounts. The top tab, "Your account," represents your account information—the account Windows created when you installed it (Figure 19-1).

Select "Family & other users." If you see some accounts listed here, then one of these situations probably applies:

- **You created them** when you installed Windows 10, as described in Appendix A.
- **You bought a new computer** with Windows preinstalled and created several accounts when asked to do so the first time you turned on the machine.
- **You upgraded from an earlier version** of Windows, and Windows 10 gracefully imported all your existing accounts.

The steps for adding another account depend on whether it's for a family member or not. What's the difference? Well, if it's a family member, then when you sign into any other Windows 10 computer, the rest of your family's accounts will appear on that machine, too, ready to use.

Also, if it's a family member who's a *kid*, you'll get periodic email reports on what he's been doing with his computer time, as described on page 432.

Finally, a family member *must* log in with a Microsoft account, as described on page 554. If you want to create a local account, you have to use the "Other users" option described below.

Adding a Family Member

Let's start with the steps for adding a family member. Assuming that you are, in fact, logged in with an Administrator account, start at Settings→Accounts→"Family & other users." Figure 19-2, top, shows you what this screen looks like.

Select "Add a family member." Now you see the screen shown at bottom in Figure 19-2.

Choose either "Add a child" or "Add an adult," and then enter the email address for this person's Microsoft account.

- **If this relative of yours has no email address:** Choose "The person I want to add doesn't have an email address." You'll be given the chance to create a free Outlook.com email address, which will become this person's Microsoft account.
- **If this person has an email address but it's not a Microsoft account:** When you click Next, a "sign up for a new one" link appears. Click it to enter your name, birthday, country, and a password, thus turning this person's existing email address into a Microsoft account.

In both cases, the "See what's most relevant to them" screen appears—it would be better named, "Please let us bombard you with junk email." The first checkbox asks permission to use this person's data to customize the ads she sees online; the second signs her up to get junk email from Microsoft. For most people, turning off both boxes is the smartest move.

You wind up on the "Your family" screen again (Figure 19-2, top), where your new family member's email address—a Microsoft account—appears in place. You've created the account! The new family member is now listed on the "Your accounts" screen and can log into this computer (or any other Windows 8 or 10 machine).

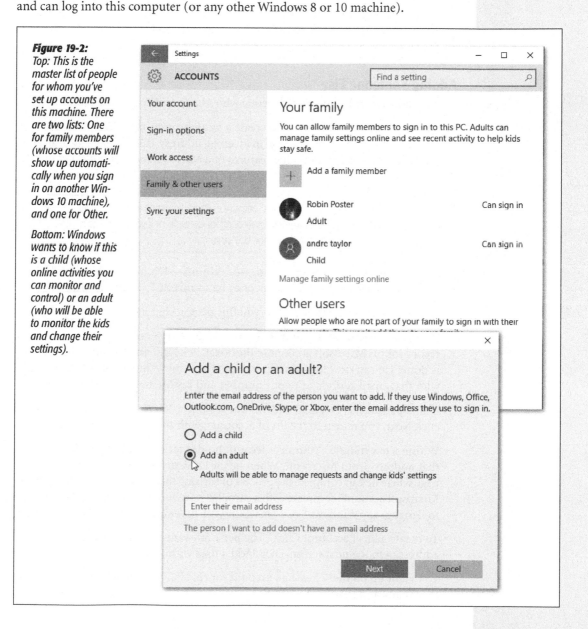

Figure 19-2:
Top: This is the master list of people for whom you've set up accounts on this machine. There are two lists: One for family members (whose accounts will show up automatically when you sign in on another Windows 10 machine), and one for Other.

Bottom: Windows wants to know if this is a child (whose online activities you can monitor and control) or an adult (who will be able to monitor the kids and change their settings).

Note: When you first sign into a new Windows machine, your family members' account names show up on the "Your family" screen. However, they can't immediately sign in and start computing. You, the administrator, must click each non-administrator person's name (where it says "Can't sign in") and then click Allow. It's a security thing.

Similarly, if *you* log in on a new PC and try to make some account changes, you'll find (on the Accounts page of Settings) a message that says, "You need to verify your identity on this PC." Microsoft will email you or text your phone with a confirmation code, which you must enter now to confirm that you really are who you say you are.

Adding Someone Else

You can add a new account for someone who's *not* a family member, too.

This time, you'll have the chance to create a *local account* (page 554), which lets the person sign in with his name instead of an email address. (Of course, a local account doesn't offer the syncing and other features of a Microsoft account; it exists only on *this* computer.)

Tip: It's perfectly OK to create an "Other users" account even for someone who *is* a family member. You'd do that if you wanted your relative to have a local account, for example, or if you wanted to create an account for a relative who does *not* need control over the kids' accounts.

The fun begins, as always, on the Settings→Accounts→"Family & other users" screen. Under "Other users," select "Add someone else to this PC" (Figure 19-3).

Windows now wants to know: "How will this person sign in?"

- **If he has a Microsoft account:** Enter the email address or cellphone number on record for his Microsoft account in the box. Click Next and then Finish. The deed is done: He can now log into this computer, or any Windows 8 or 10 computer, with that email address or phone number and his Microsoft account password.

- **If this person has an email address but it's not a Microsoft account:** When you click Next, you return to the list of accounts, with the new account in place.

  Within a few minutes, your new account holder receives a confirmation email, at that address, from Microsoft. When he clicks Verify, he's taken online to a Web page where he can complete the process of turning that email address into a proper Microsoft account (complete with a complex password). At that point, he'll be able to sign into any Windows 8 or 10 machine with his email address and that password.

- **To create a local account:** Click "The person I want to add doesn't have an email address." On the next screen, click "Add a user without a Microsoft account."

  You wind up on the "Create an account for this PC" screen, where you can make up a name and password.

Tip: Having a local account means that you can make up a very simple password, or no password at all—an attractive time-saver if this is your home computer and you don't have (or aren't worried about your) housemates. To set that up, just leave both password blanks empty. Later, whenever you're asked for your password, leave the Password box blank. You'll be able to log on and authenticate yourself that much faster each day.

Figure 19-3:
Top: You're about to create an account for a non-family member (or a family member who doesn't want a Microsoft account).

Bottom: This is where things get tricky. You're about to tell Windows that this person has a Microsoft account, doesn't have one but wants one, or doesn't have one but doesn't want one.

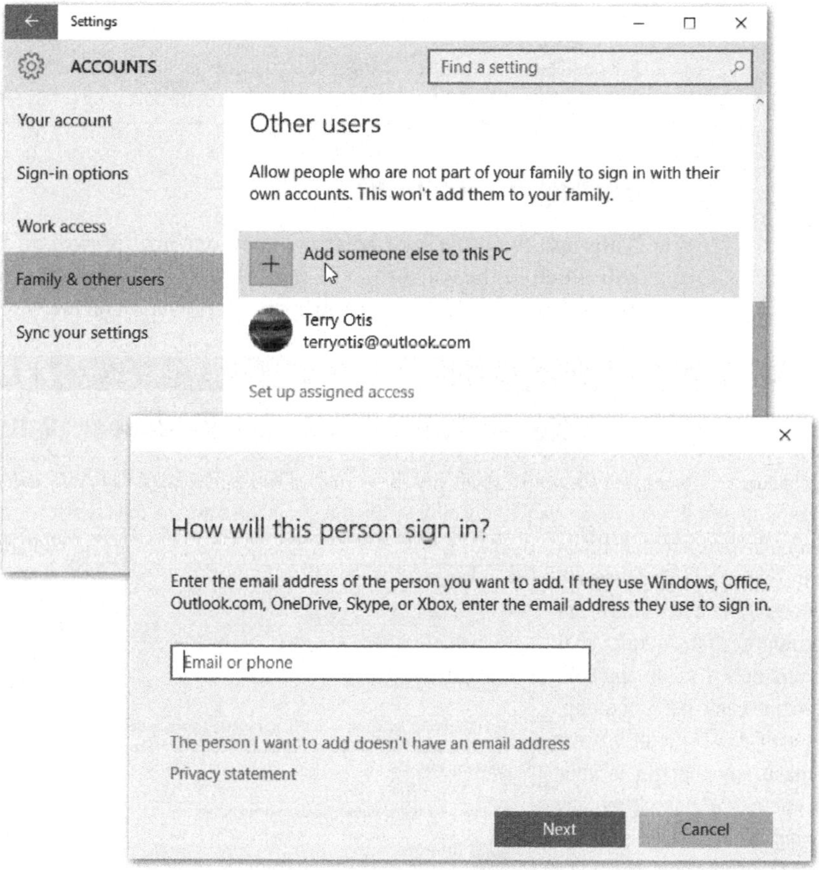

If you provide a password, you must also provide a *hint* (for yourself or for whichever coworker's account you're operating on). This is a hint that anybody can see (including bad guys trying to log on as you), so choose something meaningful only to you. If your password is the first person who ever kissed you plus your junior-year phone number, for example, your hint might be "first person who ever kissed me plus my junior-year phone number."

Later, when you log in and can't remember your password, leave the Password box empty and hit Enter. You wind up back at the Login screen to try again—but this time, your hint will appear just below the Password box to jog your memory.

After a moment, you return to the Accounts screen, where the new account holder's name joins whatever names were already there. You can continue adding new accounts forever or until your hard drive is full, whichever comes first.

Tip: If you never had the opportunity to set up a user account when installing Windows—if you bought a PC with Windows already on it, for example—you may see an account named Owner already in place. Nobody can use Windows at all unless there's at least *one* Administrator account on it, so Microsoft is doing you a favor here.

Just double-click it and click "Change the account name" to change the name "Owner" to one that suits you better. Make that account your own using the steps in the following paragraphs.

Editing an Account

Although the process of creating a new account is swift and simple, it doesn't offer you much in the way of flexibility. You don't even have a chance to specify the new person's account picture (rubber ducky, flower, or whatever).

POWER USERS' CLINIC

Assigned Access: Windows with Rubber Walls

Windows 10 comes with a feature that lets you shield your computer—or its very young, very fearful, or very mischievous operator—from confusion and harm. It's called Assigned Access, and it turns the entire computer into a kiosk that runs only a single app. The victim can't leave the app, can't get to the desktop, can't make any changes to your system, and doesn't see any notifications. This is a helpful feature for young children or easily intimidated adults, or for creating kiosks for display at stores or trade shows.

Before you begin, make sure there's at least one Admin account and one Standard account already set up. Open Settings→Accounts→"Family & other users." Scroll down to the master switch (visible in Figure 19-3, top): "Set up assigned access."

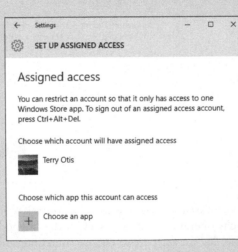

You're now asked which Standard account you want to limit in this way, and then which one app this person is allowed to use. (It must be a Windows Store app—no traditional Windows desktop programs, alas.)

When you log into that account, you'll discover a weird world. That one app fills the screen. There's no taskbar, no Start menu, no way out.

Actually, there is a way out: If you have a keyboard, press Ctrl+Alt+Delete. If you have a tablet, press the ■■ button five times. The machine gives you the opportunity to log in with a different account, so that you can do real work—or so that you can turn Assigned Access off the same way you turned it on.

By the way: In the first Windows 10 release, Assigned Access was too flaky to use. Once Microsoft fixes it, though, it will come in very handy indeed.

That's why the next step in creating an account is usually *editing* the one you just set up. You make these sorts of changes in two places: in Settings, and (for Microsoft accounts) online.

Note: The controls here are duplicated, with a different layout, in the old Control Panel. (Do a search for accounts; in the results, choose User Accounts.) In general, the Settings screen is far easier to use. But the old Control Panel is there for old-timers whose habits die hard.

Changing the Account Type

If you're logged in with an Administrator account, you have the power to change other people's account types (your choices: Administrator or Standard). To do that, open Settings→Accounts→"Family & other users."

Select the account name, choose "Change account type," and use the pop-up menu to choose Administrator or Standard User. Hit OK.

Changing Picture, Password, or Microsoft Account

On the "Your account" tab of Settings→Accounts (Figure 19-1), you can make changes *only to your own account.* So if you've just created a new account for somebody, she'll have to log in, open this panel, and make the following changes herself:

- **Change your picture.** The usual sign-in screen displays each account holder's name, accompanied by a little picture. When you first create the account, however, it assigns you a generic silhouette, meaning that everybody is identical—not exactly the sort of "I'm a PC" message Microsoft probably hopes to spread.

  To choose something more personal, hit Browse (to choose an existing picture from your hard drive) or "Create your picture" (meaning "Take a picture of your head right now, using the computer's camera").

Note: You may see other photos here. They represent account pictures you've used in the past, for easy re-selection.

- **Switch to a Microsoft or local account.** If you have a local account, you can switch to a Microsoft account, or vice versa; either way, the button to click is right there at the top of your Accounts panel.

  To change a local account to a Microsoft account: Click "Sign in with a Microsoft account instead." You're led through creating a Microsoft account to call your own. *To change a Microsoft account to a local account:* Click "Sign in with a local account instead." After you enter your password, you'll be asked to make up a name and password for a local account.

- **Change your login credentials.** Windows lets you log in with many different kinds of "password": a regular typed password, a four-digit number, a picture password (you draw lines on a photo you've selected), face or fingerprint recognition (on specially equipped machines), and so on. On the "Sign-in options" panel, you can create or change whatever you've set up. Page 566 has the details.

• **Change the wallpaper, color scheme, notifications, and other settings.** All the settings you make in PC Settings apply *only to your account.*

And if you've created a Microsoft account, guess what? Most of these settings are stored online—and if you sign into another Windows 8 or 10 computer somewhere, you'll find all your settings instantly recreated on that machine.

Settings You Change Online

Remember—a Microsoft account is stored on the Internet. It should come as no surprise, then, that Microsoft offers a Web site where you can make a lot of additional changes to your account.

On the Settings→Accounts→"Your account" screen (Figure 19-1), click "Manage my Microsoft account." Off you go into your Web browser, where you arrive at the peculiar page shown in Figure 19-4, where the tabs at top let you change things like these:

• **Home.** Edit your name and password (Figure 19-4, top). See a summary of all the stuff you've bought from Microsoft's various online stores. Enjoy a list of all the computers you've signed into with this account. Buy or redeem Microsoft gift cards.

POWER USERS' CLINIC

Sync Settings

It's one of the best parts of the Microsoft account system: Whenever you log into a Windows 8 or 10 computer, all your settings are in place. Your desktop picture, your color scheme, your Web bookmarks—the works. If you have a desktop PC at home and a laptop on the road, well, you're all set; everything is consistent as you move from computer to computer.

There are two reasons you may not love this idea, however.

First, maybe there's some reason that you don't want a certain setting synced. Maybe you use your laptop exclusively when you're in France and don't want your English-language preference synced. Maybe you want independent bookmarks on each machine.

Second, maybe the privacy implications just freak you out. Maybe you don't want your laptop browsing History showing up on the family PC in the living room. Or maybe you just don't want Microsoft knowing about your activity.

> ### Sync your settings
>
> Sync Windows settings to other devices using poguester@live.com.
>
> How does syncing work?
> **Sync settings**
> ⬤ On
>
> ### Individual sync settings
>
> Theme
> ⬤ On
>
> Web browser settings
> ⬤ On
>
> Passwords
> ⬤ On
>
> Language preferences
> ⬤ On

In any case, there are on/off switches for most of the synced settings. To find them, open Settings→Accounts→ "Sync your settings."

At the top: a master switch for the whole concept of syncing your settings. That's the one to flip if the whole idea just feels creepy. Below that: individual switches for various categories of settings.

In most cases, the descriptions tell you what gets synced for each switch. But some additional settings you might not guess: "Theme" governs your choice of theme, yes, but also your screensaver setting and taskbar configuration. And "Language settings" also stores your preferences for the Windows spell checker.

- **Your info.** Edit your name (again). Change your account photo. Change the email or phone number associated with your Microsoft account.

Tip: Using the "Manage your sign-in email or phone number" link, you can not only change the address or phone number associated with your Microsoft account, but you can also set up additional ones. If you have three email addresses, for example, you can register all three, so you don't have to remember which one you've hooked up to your Microsoft account. Or when you log into a Windows 10 machine, you can use whichever involves the least typing.

Figure 19-4:
Here's the central storage locker for all the information in your Microsoft account. If your computer gets broken or stolen, who cares? Your settings will be restored instantly the next time you log in with a Microsoft account. The tabs here range from the very basics, like your account name and email address (top left), to the list of devices you've ever signed into with this account (lower right).

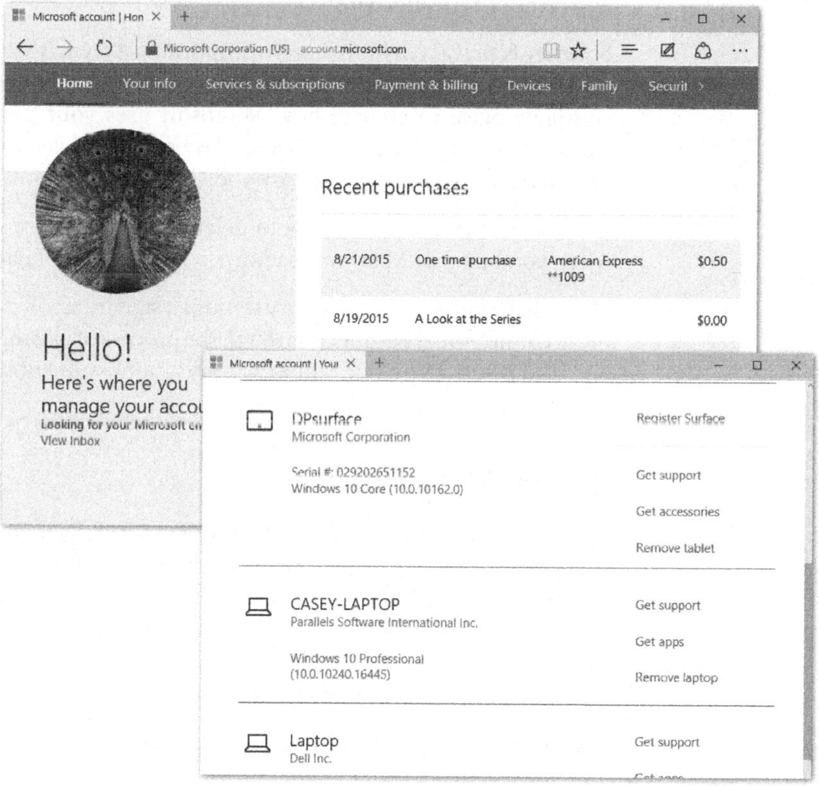

- **Subscriptions.** Here's the master dashboard for all the monthly payments you're making to Microsoft: for Office 365, Groove Music, Xbox Live, extra OneDrive storage, and so on. Here, too, is where you cancel one of these accounts, change credit cards, and see when the next renewal and payment dates are.

- **Payment & billing.** Here's the master list of stuff you've bought online from Microsoft: music, movies, apps, and so on. You can see your purchase history, change your credit card info, redeem gift cards, and so on.

- **Devices** is the list of computers you've logged into using your Microsoft account (Figure 19-4, bottom). Interesting, but not all that useful. There are links to get help with one, buy accessories for it, or remove it from the list.

Tip: Note the sub-toolbar, which lets you view sublists of devices on which you've installed apps, music, and movies/TV from Microsoft's stores.

- **Family.** Here's the master list of family-member accounts you've set up, as described earlier in this chapter. Tap the round icon to open up a child account's "Recent activity" screen and adjust the little tyke's account restrictions. You can also add and remove accounts here.

- **Security & privacy.** This is a pretty important screen. It's got links to places you've seen before, like permissions for your kid accounts. But it also gives you a fairly complete place to control how Microsoft uses your personal information for advertising and marketing purposes. You can also delete some personal information here, like your search history and Cortana Notebook information.

  Here, too, is your opportunity to delete your Microsoft account—for example, when you buy that Mac you've always wanted. (Joke! That's a joke.)

  To do that, choose "More security settings"; sign in; scroll down; and choose "Close my account." You'll be guided through the process of closing down your association with Microsoft. (What do you want to do about your subscriptions? Your leftover account balance? Your kid accounts?)

Seven Ways to Log In

As you now know from Chapter 1, which you've carefully memorized, you can log into your account using any of several methods. Typing out a password is one of them, yes, but everybody hates passwords. They're especially frustrating on touchscreens.

So now, in Windows 10, you have all these ways to prove that you're you:

- **Draw three lines, dots, or circles** on a photo you've selected.
- **Type in a four-digit number** you've memorized.
- **Type a traditional password.**
- **Use your fingerprint,** if your computer has a built-in fingerprint scanner.
- **Just look into the computer's camera.** If it recognizes your face, it logs you in.
- **Look into your computer's eye scanner** until it recognizes the iris of your eye.

Note: Those last three ways require specialized equipment; most computers don't offer them. They're part of a new Windows 10 feature called Windows Hello, described below.

- **Skip the security altogether.** Jump directly to the desktop when you turn on the machine.

So how do you specify which method you want? It all happens on the "Sign-in options" screen shown in Figure 19-5. Just follow the admirably simple steps in the sections that follow.

Note: Every account still requires a regular text password; you'll need it when, for example, installing new software or making system-wide Control Panel changes. The drawing-lines thing, the four-digit thing, the no-password-at-all thing, and Windows Hello are all *additional* ways to log in.

Figure 19-5:
Windows 10 gives you a wide variety of ways to sign in—ways that don't involve having to type in a password. Here in Settings→Accounts→ "Sign-in options," you can scroll down, and down, and down, to see all of them. Most people won't see the Windows Hello section here—it appears only if your computer has special login hardware—but the ones who do see it will have a blast logging in.

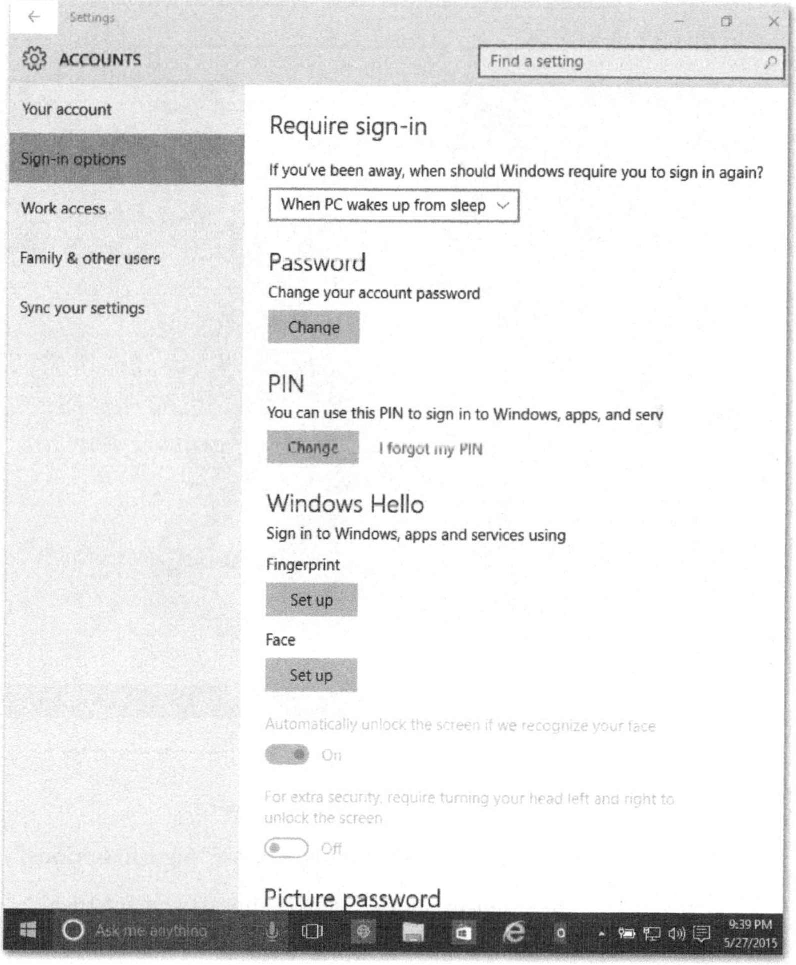

← Settings

⚙ ACCOUNTS — Find a setting

Your account

Sign-in options

Work access

Family & other users

Sync your settings

Require sign-in

If you've been away, when should Windows require you to sign in again?

When PC wakes up from sleep ⌄

Password

Change your account password

Change

PIN

You can use this PIN to sign in to Windows, apps, and serv

Change   I forgot my PIN

Windows Hello

Sign in to Windows, apps and services using

Fingerprint

Set up

Face

Set up

Automatically unlock the screen if we recognize your face

On

For extra security, require turning your head left and right to unlock the screen

Off

Picture password

Creating a Picture Password

This little stunt is perfect for touchscreens, especially tablets that lack physical keyboards, because it's so much easier than typing a password.

The password screen will show a photograph you've chosen. You draw three lines or taps on top of it, something like what's in Figure 19-6. The idea is that only you know how and where to draw these lines and taps. That's your security.

Note: Truth is, picture passwords aren't as secure as typed passwords. One reason is that bad guys might be able to learn your photo fingerstrokes by watching you from across the room.

But the even greater security hole is the finger grease you leave behind on your touchscreen. If you drag the same lines over and over, an evildoer can learn your fingerstrokes just by studying the finger-grease marks when the screen is turned off. You've been warned.

Figure 19-6:
The rules are simple: Choose a photo from your Pictures folder. Draw three lines on it—circles, curves, or lines. Don't forget them! (Although if you do, the world won't end; you can always use your regular typed password instead.)

Later, you'll recreate those gestures to unlock the tablet, which is easier than having to type some password. (The lines don't appear when you actually log in. Wouldn't want some bad dude sitting next to you to catch on!)

Here's how to set up a picture password.

1. **Open Settings→Accounts. Choose "Sign-in options."**

   The "Sign-in options" screen appears (Figure 19-5).

2. **Under "Picture password," click Add. Enter your current typed password to prove that you're not a criminal, and hit OK.**

   Now a screen appears where Windows explains the rules. Time to choose your photo!

3. **Hit "Choose picture."**

You're now shown the contents of your Pictures folder. Choose the one you want to draw on top of, and then hit Open (lower-right corner).

You now arrive at a "How's this look?" screen, showing how the picture will appear on the login screen. If the photo isn't perfectly suited to your screen dimensions, you can drag it around to fit the screen better.

4. **Pick "Use this picture."**

Now, on the "Set up your gestures" screen, you're supposed to draw on the photo—three taps, lines, or circles in any combination (Figure 19-6). On a baby photo, for example, you might circle the baby's mouth, tap her nose, and then draw an invisible antenna line right out of her head. Just don't forget what you did.

You're asked to repeat the three gestures in the same order to make sure you've got it.

If all went well, Windows says, "Congratulations!" If not—if your two tries weren't similar enough—it prompts you to perform this step again.

5. **Hit Finish.**

Now test your picture password. In the Start menu, click your account photo (upper left); from the shortcut menu, choose "Sign out." You arrive back at the Lock screen.

Dismiss it with a swipe up or a keypress (and, if you see the names of more than one account, tap yours). You arrive at the Picture Password screen, with your photo magnificently displayed.

POWER USERS' CLINIC

The Other Administrator Account

This will sound confusing. But there's another kind of Administrator account: *The* Administrator account.

This is an emergency backup account with full administrator powers and *no password*. Even if you delete all your other accounts, this one still remains, if only to give you some way to get into your machine. It's called Administrator, and it's ordinarily hidden.

Most people see it only in times of troubleshooting, when they start up their PCs in Safe Mode (page 510). It's the ideal account to use in those situations. Not only does it come with no password assigned, but it's also unlimited. It gives you free powers over every file, which is just what you may need to troubleshoot your computer.

In Windows XP, the problem was, of course, that anyone who knew about it could get into Windows with full administrator privileges—and no need to know a password. Your kid, for example, could blow right past your carefully established Parental Controls—and let's not even consider what a virus could do.

So in the more security-minded Windows 10, the secret Administrator account is still there. But it's ordinarily disabled. It comes to life *only* if you're starting your PC in Safe Mode.

(That's on a standard home or small-office PC. On a corporate domain network, only a networking geek who's got a Domain Admins account can start up in Safe Mode. You know who you are.)

Draw your three lines or taps, as you've set them up. If you do a good enough job, Windows logs you into your account.

If you give up, you can always tap "Switch to password" and just type the darned thing.

The Four-Digit Passcode (PIN)

You might not think that a four-digit passcode, or PIN (personal identification number), is as secure as a full-blown, "f8sh^eir23h*$$%23"-style password. But in one way, it's actually more secure—because it's local. It's stored only on this computer. It's useless to your enemies or faraway hackers, even if they guess it, because it works only when you're physically sitting in front of your machine.

Note: *Here again, you still have to create a regular text password for your account—as a backup method, if nothing else.*

---

1. **Open Settings→Accounts. Choose "Sign-in options."**

   You see the screen shown in Figure 19-5.

2. **Under PIN, select Add. Enter your current typed password to prove that you're you, and hit OK.**

   Now make up a four-digit PIN (personal identification number): the last four digits of your mom's phone number, the month and year of your birthday—whatever.

UP TO SPEED

Passwords Within Passwords

The primary password that you or your administrator sets up in the User Accounts program has two functions. You already know that it lets you log on each day so you can enter your Windows world of desktop clutter, Start-menu tailoring, Web bookmarks, and so on.

But what you may not realize is that it's also the master key that unlocks all the other passwords associated with your account: the passwords that Edge memorizes for certain Web sites, the passwords that get you into shared disks and folders on the network, the password that protects your encrypted files, and so on. The simple act of logging onto your account also unlocks all these other secure areas of your PC life.

But remember that anyone with an Administrator account can change your password at any time. Does that mean that whoever has an Administrator account—your teacher, boss, or teenager, for example—has full access to your private stuff? After you leave the school, company, or household, what's

to stop an administrator from changing your password, thereby gaining access to your electronic-brokerage account (courtesy of its memorized Edge password), and so on?

Fortunately, Microsoft is way ahead of you on this one. The instant an administrator changes somebody else's password, Windows wipes out all secondary passwords associated with the account. That administrator can log onto your account and see your everyday files, but he can't see Web sites with memorized passwords and so on. (The bad news is that he'll also wipe out your stored passwords for EFS-encrypted files, if any.)

Note that if you change your *own* password—or if you use a Password Reset Disk, described starting on page 575—none of this applies. Your secondary passwords survive intact. It's only when *somebody else* changes your password that this little-known Windows security feature kicks in, sanitizing the account for your protection.

---

3. Enter your chosen PIN into both boxes, and then hit Finish.

Next time you log in, you'll be able to use your PIN instead of a password (Figure 19-7). You don't even have to press Enter; after you type the fourth digit, bam—you're signed in.

Note: You'll also be offered a link that says "Sign-in options" (Figure 19-7). When you choose that, you're offered icons that represent all of the sign-in options you've created so far: picture password, PIN, Windows Hello biometric, and regular typed password. So if you can't get in one way, you can try a different method.

Figure 19-7:
Once you've set up a picture password and/ or a PIN password, your login choices become more plentiful. If you click "Sign-in options," you can choose a different way to sign in. In this example, the icons represent the picture password, the four-digit PIN, and the traditional password.

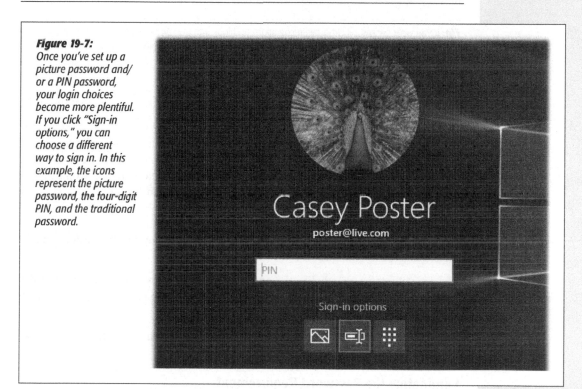

Face Recognition

Here's an absolutely brilliant feature, new in Windows 10: instant face recognition. When you sit down in front of your computer, it recognizes your face and unlocks the computer instantly. You can't fool it with a photograph, a 3D model of your head, or even an identical twin!

Here's the bummer: This stunt requires an Intel RealSense camera, a fairly sophisticated device that actually uses *three* cameras—infrared, color, and 3D—in combination. You can buy this camera as a USB peripheral; some computer companies are building the RealSense camera into their laptops, too.

If you're one of the lucky ones, you'll know it, because in Settings→Accounts→"Sign-in options," you'll see a heading for Windows Hello (Figure 19-5)—and below it, a "Set up" button for Face.

In the welcome screen, hit "Get started." Enter your PIN. (Yes, Windows Hello requires you to set up both a password and a PIN, so you'll be able to get into your machine if something goes wrong with either your RealSense camera or your face.)

Now you're asked to look into the camera. After just a couple of seconds, an "All set!" message appears; Windows now knows what you look like.

Tip: If you wear glasses, hit "Improve recognition" and look into the camera again, this time without them (or with them, if you didn't wear them the first time). Now Windows Hello will recognize you either way.

At this point, two more options await:

- **Automatically unlock the screen if we recognize your face.** Um, isn't that the entire point of this exercise? Turn it on.

- **Require turning your head left and right to unlock the screen.** If you're concerned that your PC might unlock accidentally, when it spots your face as you sit down or talk on the phone, turn on this extra-security option. Now the PC won't unlock unless you look at the camera *and* turn your head left and right.

Fingerprint, Iris

If your PC has a fingerprint reader, you'll see other Windows Hello options in Settings: Fingerprint and Iris.

The procedures are exactly like the one described above, except this time when you hit "Set up," you're asked to touch your finger to the reader a few times, or hold your eye up to the eye scanner.

When it's over, you'll be able to log in just by touching your fingertip to the reader, or peeking into the eye reader—fast and secure.

Eliminating the Password Requirement

The usual computer book takes this opportunity to stress the importance of a long, complex password. This is excellent advice if you create sensitive documents and work in a big corporation.

But if you share the computer only with a spouse, or with nobody, you may have nothing to hide. You may see the multiple-users feature more as a convenience (keeping your settings and files separate) than a protector of secrecy and security. In these situations, there's no particular urgency to the mission of thwarting the world's hackers with a password.

That is, you may prefer to blow *past* the password screen, so you can get right down to work. You may wish you could *turn off* the requirement to log in with a password.

No password required when waking

Fortunately, with one click or tap, you can eliminate the requirement for entering a password when you *wake* the computer. (You still need it when you turn it on or restart it.)

Open Settings→Accounts→"Sign-in options." Right there at the top, under "Require sign-in," you can change the usual setting ("When PC wakes up from sleep") to the much more convenient one, "Never."

Now you won't be asked for your password when you just wake the machine after it's gone to sleep.

No password required, ever

With a little more work, you can eliminate the requirement to enter your password even when you're starting up or restarting the machine:

1. **Open the Run dialog box (press ⊞+R.) In the Run box, type *netplwiz*. Hit OK.**

   You now find yourself in the little-seen User Accounts dialog box (Figure 19-8, top). Most of the functions are the same as what you'd find in the Settings panel

Figure 19-8:
Top: Here's the little-known User Accounts box. It's where you find the master switch for the requirement to enter a password when you log in.

Bottom: In this box, enter your user name and your text password. You're telling Windows to log you in automatically from now on.

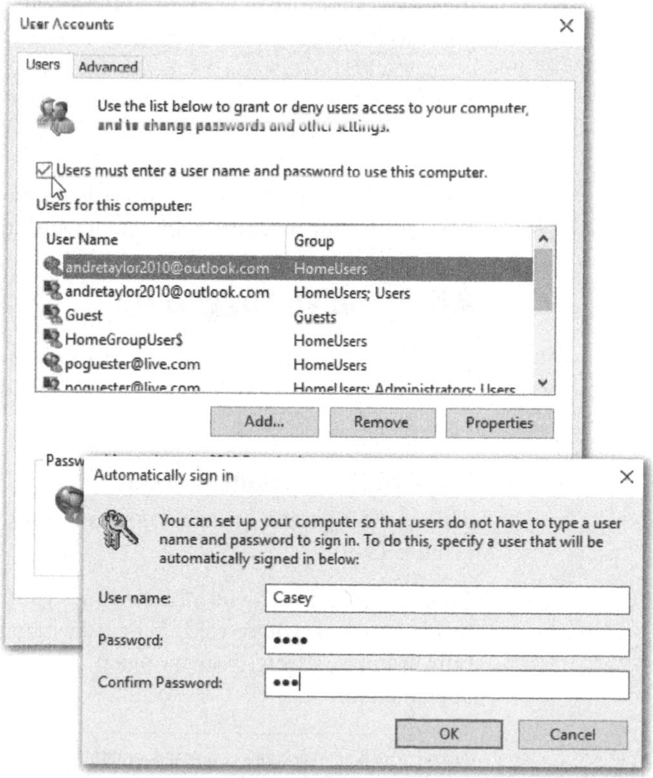

for accounts—it's just that you don't have to slog through several screens to get things done. Here you can add, remove, or edit accounts, all in a single screen.

But this older Control Panel program also offers a few features that you don't get at all in the new one. For example:

2. **Turn off "Users must enter a user name and password to use this computer." Click OK.**

You've told Windows that you want to sign in automatically. Now you have to tell it *who* gets to sign in automatically (Figure 19-8, bottom).

This lucky individual won't have to specify any name and password at logon time and can instead turn on the PC and cruise directly to the desktop. (This feature works only at startup time. If you choose "Sign out" from the Start menu, the standard Logon dialog box appears so that other people have the opportunity to sign in.)

3. **Enter your account name and password (and the password again); then hit OK.**

This is your real text password, not some measly four-digit PIN.

The next time you restart your computer, you'll gasp in amazement as it takes you all the way to the desktop without bothering to ask for your password. It's a great setup, provided you recognize the security hole it leaves open.

Note: To restore the password requirement, repeat these steps—but turn *on* "Users must enter a user name and password to use this computer" in step 2.

If you multiply the 5 seconds you've just saved by the thousands of times you'll wake or start up your machine, why, you'll wind up with literally *minutes* of free time!

After You've Logged On

When it comes to the screens you encounter when you log onto a Windows computer, your mileage may vary. What you see depends on how your PC has been set up. For example:

You Get the Accounts Screen

This is what people on standalone or workgroup computers see most of the time (Figure 19-9).

There's no limit to the number of times you can try to type in a password. With each incorrect guess, you're told, "The user name or password is incorrect," and an OK button appears to let you try again. The second time you try, your password hint appears, too.

Tip: If your Caps Lock key is pressed, another balloon lets you know. Otherwise, because you can't see anything on the screen as you type except dots, you might be trying to type a lowercase password with all capital letters.

You Zoom Straight to the Desktop

If you're the *only* account holder, and you've set up no password for yourself, you can cruise all the way to the desktop without any stops. The setup steps appear on page 573.

This password-free scenario, of course, is not very secure; any evildoer who walks by your machine when you're in the bathroom has complete access to all your files (and protected Web sites). But if you work in a home office, for example, where the threat of privacy invasion isn't very great, it's by far the most convenient arrangement.

You Get the "Press Ctrl+Alt+Delete to Begin" Message

You or your friendly network geek has added your PC to a domain while installing Windows and activated the "Require Users to Press Ctrl+Alt+Delete" option. This is the most secure configuration, and also the least convenient.

Figure 19-9:
To sign in, click your account name or icon. If no password is required for your account, then you proceed to your desktop with no further interruption.

If there is a password associated with your account, you see a place for it. Type your password and then press Enter.

The Forgotten Password Disk

As described on page 561, Windows contains a handy *hint* mechanism for helping you recall your password if you've forgotten it.

But what if, having walked into a low-hanging branch, you've forgotten both your password *and* the correct interpretation of your hint? In that disastrous situation, you don't have to fling your worthless PC into the freezing river quite yet. You have a few more options:

- If you've forgotten your Microsoft account password, you can reset it at *https:// account.live.com/password/reset*.

- On a corporate network, the system administrator can reset your password.

- Someone with an Administrator account can sign in and change your password for you. Even *you* can do that, if you remember the password for another Administrator account.

- If you've forgotten your *local* account password, you can use a Password Reset Disk.

This disk is a clever solution-in-advance. It's a USB flash drive that you can use like a physical key to unlock your account in the event of a forgotten password. The catch: You have to make this disk *now*, while you still remember your password.

To create this disk, insert a USB flash drive. Then search for *password reset;* in the results, select "Create a password reset disk." (If it doesn't open, open the Control Panel manually by right-clicking the Start menu and choosing its name; then search for *password reset,* and select "Create a password reset disk.")

The Forgotten Password Wizard appears. Click through it, supplying your current password when asked. When you click Finish, remove the disk or flash drive. Label it, and don't lose it!

Don't leave it in plain sight, though; anyone with that drive can now get into your stuff.

Tip: Behind the scenes, Windows saves a file onto the flash drive called *userkey.psw.* You can guess what that is.

When the day comes when you can't remember your password, leave the Password box empty and hit Enter. You wind up back at the Login screen; this time, in addition to your password hint, you see a link called "Reset password." Insert your Password Reset flash drive and then click that link.

A Password Reset Wizard now helps you create a new password (and a new hint to remind you of it). You're in.

Even though you now have a new password, your existing Password Reset Disk is still good. Keep it in a drawer somewhere for use the next time you experience a temporarily blank brain.

Deleting Accounts

It happens—somebody graduates, somebody gets fired, somebody dumps you. Sooner or later, you may need to delete an account from your PC.

If you're logged in with an Administrator account, you have the power to kill off other people's accounts. To do that, open Settings→Accounts→"Family & other users."

Select the account name, choose "Change account type," and hit either Remove (to remove a local account) or Block (to prevent a Microsoft account holder from logging in). Use the pop-up menu to choose Administrator or Standard User. Confirm by choosing "Delete account and data" or "Block."

A few more points about deleting accounts:

- You can't delete the account you're logged into.

- You can't delete the last Administrator account. One must remain.

- You can create a new account with the same name and password as one you deleted earlier, but in Windows' head, it's still not the same account. As described in the box on page 570, it won't have any of the original *secondary* passwords (for Web sites, encrypted files, and so on).

- Don't manipulate accounts manually (by fooling around in the Users folder). Create, delete, and rename them only using Settings or the Control Panel. Otherwise, you'll wind up with duplicate or triplicate folders in the Users folder, with the PC name tacked onto the end of the original account name (Bob, Bob.DELL, and so on)—a sure recipe for confusion.

Tip: If you're an administrator, don't miss the Users tab of the Task Manager dialog box. (Press Ctrl+Shift+Esc to get to the Task Manager.) It offers a handy, centralized list of all the people logged into your machine and contains buttons that let you log them off or disconnect them. This can be handy whenever you need some information, a troubleshooting session, or a power trip.

Disabling Accounts

If you *do* expect that your colleague may one day return to your life, you might consider *disabling* the account instead of deleting it. A disabled account doesn't show up on the Login screen or in the User Accounts program, but it's still there on the hard drive, and you can bring it back when necessary.

There's no pretty Control Panel link for disabling an account; you'll have to get your hands greasy in the power-user underpinnings of Windows. Open the lusrmgr.msc console, as described below—but instead of turning on "Account is disabled" for the Guest account, as shown in Figure 19-10, turn it on for whoever's taking the sabbatical.

The Guest Account

Believe it or not, Administrator and Standard aren't the only kinds of accounts you can set up on your PC.

A third kind, called the Guest account, is ideal for situations when somebody is just visiting you for the week. Rather than create an entire account for this person, complete with password, hint, little picture, and so on, you can just switch on the Guest account.

Guest accounts are pretty standard in computers these days, but you wouldn't think so if you just poked around Windows 10; Microsoft has buried the feature under mounds of dust and rubble, and you can get to it only if you have Windows 10 *Pro*.

To turn on the Guest account, in the search box, type *lusrmgr.msc*. In the results, choose "lusrmgr.msc."

The crazy window shown in Figure 19-10 appears; proceed as shown in the figure. (You can read more about this window on page 582.)

Tip: If you're a typing-out-commands sort of advanced person, you can also use the Command Prompt (running as Administrator) for this purpose. Just type *net user guest /active:yes* and hit Enter.

Now, when the visitor tries to log in, she can choose Guest as the account. She can use the computer but can't see anyone else's files or make any changes to your settings.

When the visitor is finally out of your hair, healthy paranoia suggests that you turn off the Guest account once again. (To do so, follow precisely the same steps, except turn "Account is disabled" on again.)

Tip: Don't get all excited just yet. In the initial versions of Windows 10, the Guest feature is broken. Even after you turn it on as shown in Figure 19-10, the Guest account doesn't show up on the Login screen for you to choose! (It does if you use the Command Prompt method, but after you log in, the account keeps crashing.) Microsoft says that a fix is on its to-do list.

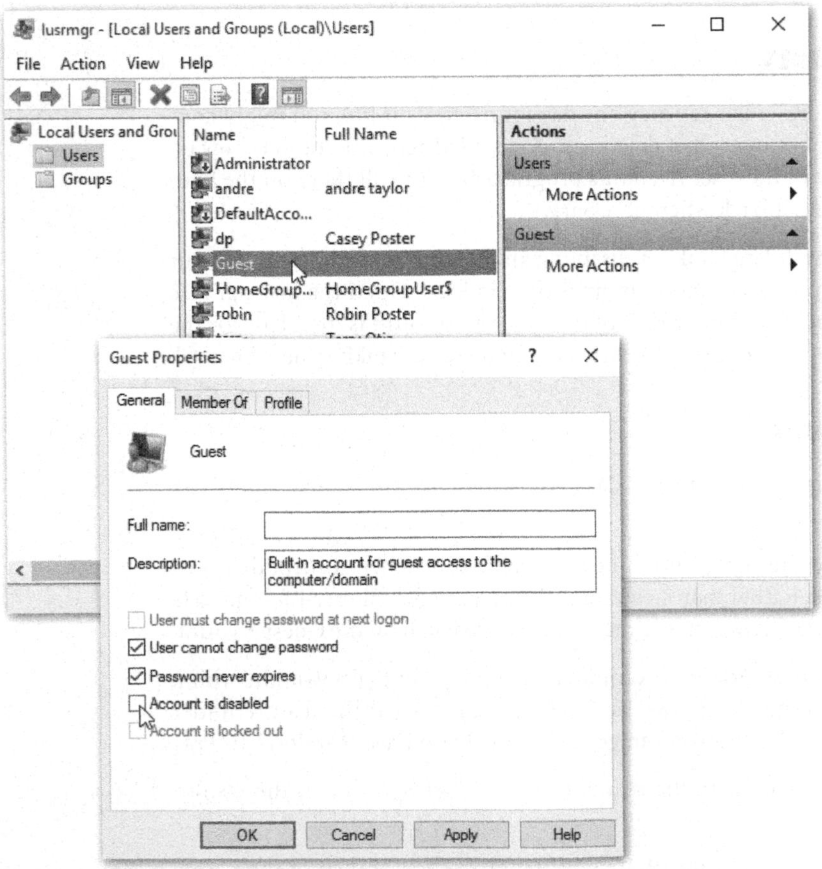

Figure 19-10:
To turn on the secret Guest account, choose Users (left column). Double-click Guest (middle column). In the resulting dialog box (bottom), type a name ("Guest" works fine), turn off "Account is disabled," and click OK.

Fast User Switching

Suppose you're signed in and you've got things just the way you like them. You have 11 programs open in carefully arranged windows, your Web browser is downloading some gigantic file, and you're composing an important speech in Microsoft Word. Now Robin, a coworker/family member/fellow student, wants to duck in to do a quick email check.

In the old days, you might have rewarded Robin with eye-rolling and heavy sighs, or worse. To accommodate the request, you would have had to shut down your whole ecosystem—interrupting the download, closing your windows, saving your work, and exiting your programs. You would have had to log off completely.

Thanks to Fast User Switching, however, none of that is necessary. See Figure 19-11.

Figure 19-11:
To log in while someone else is logged in, just press the magic keystroke ⊞ (to open the Start menu), and then click the current person's account photo. Boom: There's the list of people with accounts on this machine, including you.

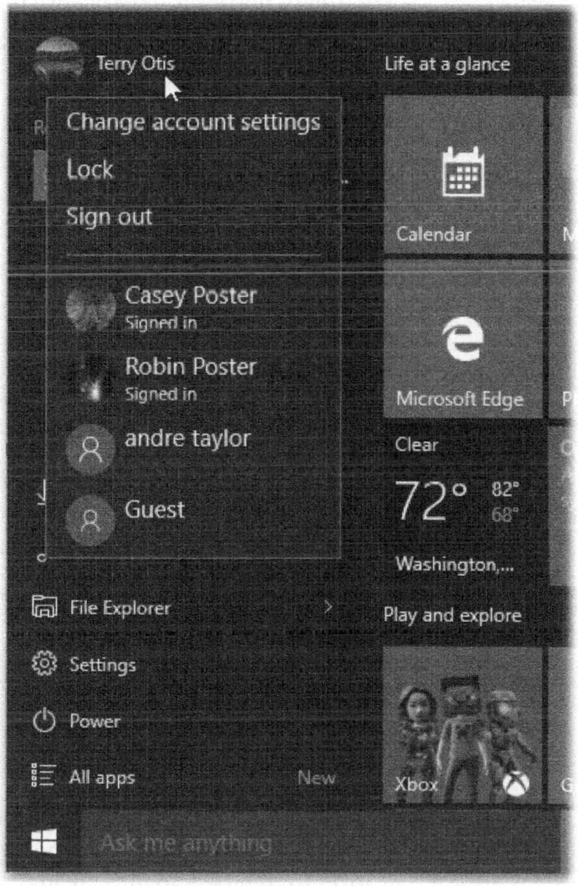

The words "Signed in" beneath your name indicate that you haven't actually logged off. Instead, Windows has *memorized* the state of affairs in your account—complete with all open windows, documents, and programs—and shoved it into the background.

Robin can now click the Robin button to sign in normally, do a little work, or look something up. When Robin signs out, the Accounts screen comes back once again, at which point *you* can log back on. Without having to wait more than a couple of seconds, you find yourself exactly where you began, with all your programs and documents still open and running—an enormous timesaver.

Authenticate Yourself: User Account Control

You can't work in Windows very long before encountering the dialog box shown in Figure 19-12 at top. It appears anytime you install a new program or try to change an important setting on your PC. (Throughout Windows, a colorful ♥ icon next to a button or link indicates a change that will produce this message box.)

Clearly, Microsoft chose the name User Account Control (UAC) to put a positive spin on a fairly intrusive security feature; calling it the IYW (Interrupt Your Work) box probably wouldn't have sounded like so much fun.

Why do these boxes pop up? In the olden days, nasties like spyware and viruses could install themselves invisibly, behind your back. That's because Windows ran in *Administrative mode* all the time, meaning it left the door open for anyone and anything to make important changes to your PC. Unfortunately, that included viruses.

Windows 10, on the other hand, runs in *Standard* mode all the time. Whenever somebody or some program wants to make a big change to your system—something that ought to have the permission of an *administrator* (page 556)—the UAC box alerts you. If you click Continue, Windows elevates (opens) the program's permissions settings just long enough to make the change.

Most of the time, *you* are the one making the changes, which can make the UAC box a bit annoying. But if that UAC dialog box ever appears by *itself,* you'll know something evil is afoot on your PC, and you'll have the chance to shut it down.

How you get past the UAC box—how you *authenticate yourself*—depends on the kind of account you have:

- **If you're an administrator,** the UAC box generally doesn't appear at all. Even when you click a link marked with a ♥ icon, you generally blow right past it. (That's a welcome change from the Vista version, when you'd see the UAC box for no good reason—you'd hit Enter to dismiss it.)

- **If you're a Standard account holder,** the UAC dialog box requires the password (or login PIN number) of an administrator. You're supposed to call an administrator over to your desk to indicate his permission to proceed by entering his own name and password.

Questions? Yes, you in the back?

- **Why does the screen go dark around the dialog box?**

That's another security measure. It's designed to prevent evil software from tricking you by displaying a *fake* Windows dialog box. Windows darkens and freezes everything on the screen except the one, true Windows dialog box: the UAC box.

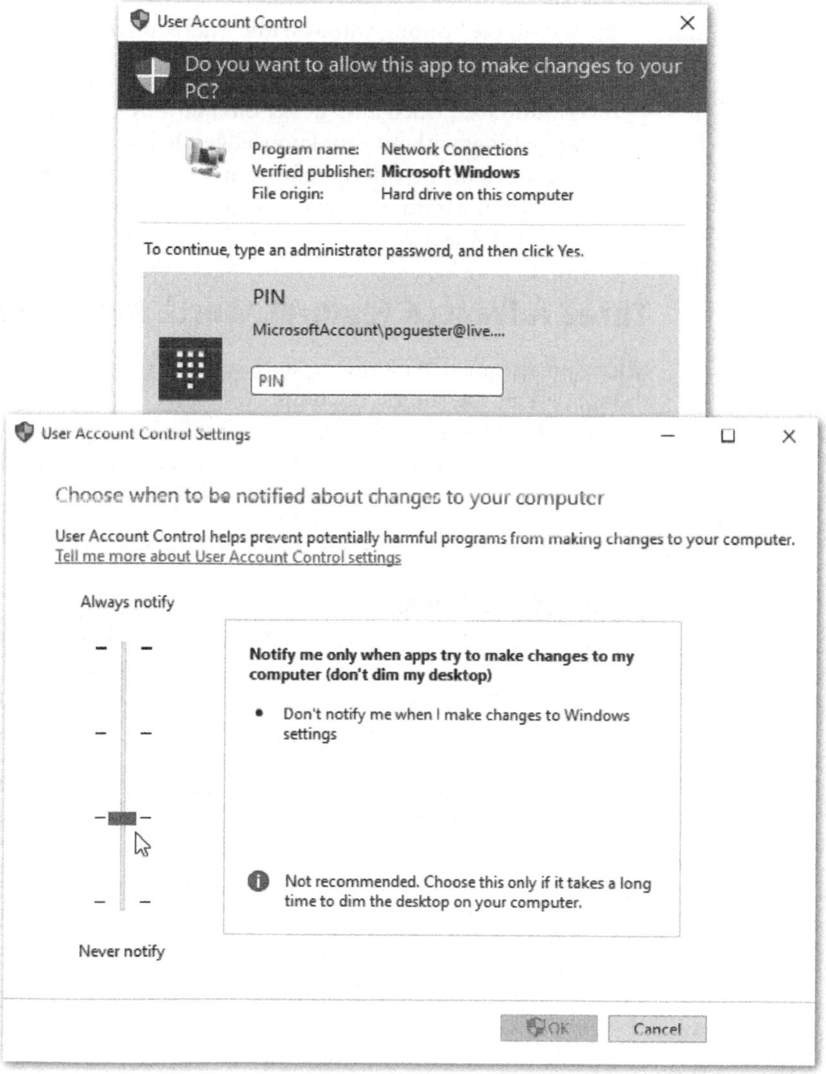

Figure 19-12:
Top: When you try to make a major change to Windows, like deleting an account or installing a new program, Windows wants to make absolutely sure that it's you and not some virus doing the changing. So it stops the show to ask for confirmation that it's you, an administrator, out there.

Bottom: This dialog box offers what amounts to a nuisance slider; you control where Windows stands on the security/interruption continuum by dragging it up (more alarmist) or down (no interruptions at all).

User Account Control ✕

Do you want to allow this app to make changes to your PC?

Program name: Network Connections
Verified publisher: **Microsoft Windows**
File origin: Hard drive on this computer

To continue, type an administrator password, and then click Yes.

PIN

MicrosoftAccount\poguester@live....

PIN

User Account Control Settings — ☐ ✕

Choose when to be notified about changes to your computer

User Account Control helps prevent potentially harmful programs from making changes to your computer. Tell me more about User Account Control settings

Always notify

Notify me only when apps try to make changes to my computer (don't dim my desktop)

- Don't notify me when I make changes to Windows settings

ⓘ Not recommended. Choose this only if it takes a long time to dim the desktop on your computer.

Never notify

OK Cancel

• **Can I turn off the UAC interruptions?**

Well, yes. But listen: You should be grateful that they don't appear *nearly* as often as they used to, when they became a profound nuisance.

But if even the few remaining interruptions are too much for you, you can turn them off altogether. Open the Start menu. Type *uac;* select Settings, and then hit "Change User Account Control settings."

You get the dialog box shown at bottom in Figure 19-12. If you drag the slider all the way to the bottom, you won't be interrupted by UAC boxes at all.

This truly isn't a good idea, though. You're sending your PC right back to the days of Windows XP, when any sneaky old malware could install itself or change your system settings without your knowledge. Do this only on a PC that's not connected to a network or the Internet, for example, or maybe when you, the all-knowing system administrator, are trying to troubleshoot and the UAC interruptions are slowing you down.

Three Advanced Features Worth Mentioning (Maybe)

Microsoft designed Windows in an era when only techies used computers. Lately, though, eyeing the success of companies like Apple, whose products are designed to appeal to the masses, Microsoft has been taking huge strides to hide the underlying complexity of Windows and make it appear simpler and cleaner.

But the old techie features are still there, hiding. Here are three advanced topics you can read about in free online appendixes to this book.

Local Users & Groups

The control panels you've read about so far in this chapter are designed for simplicity and convenience, but not for power. Windows offers a second way to create, edit, and delete accounts: an alternative window that, depending on your taste for technical sophistication, is either intimidating and technical or liberating and flexible.

It's called the Local Users and Groups console. Mostly, it offers the same options as the Settings→Accounts page described in this chapter—but for the technically proficient, it offers a few extra options. One of them is the ability to create account *groups*—named collections of account holders, all of whom have the same access to certain shared files and folders. They might be called, for example, Executives or Minimum-Wage Minions.

The quickest way to open up the Local Users and Groups window is to press ⊞+R to open the Run dialog box, type out *lusrmgr.msc,* and authenticate yourself if necessary. (Microsoft swears that "lusrmgr.msc" is *not* short for "loser manager," even though network administrators might hear that in their heads.)

For instructions from here, see the free downloadable PDF appendix "Local Users Console.pdf" on this book's "Missing CD" page at *www.missingmanuals.com*.

Profiles

As you read earlier in this chapter, every document, icon, and preference setting related to your account resides in a single folder: the one bearing your name in the Local Disk (C:) > Users folder. This folder's friendly name is your Personal folder, but to network geeks, it's known as your *user profile*.

Each account holder has a user profile. But your PC also has a couple of profiles that aren't linked to human beings' accounts.

Have you ever noticed, for example, that not everything you actually see on your desktop is, in fact, in *your* user profile folder?

Part of the solution to this mystery is the Public profile, which also lurks in the Users folder. It stores many of the same kinds of settings your profile folder does—except that anything in (C:) > Users > Public > Desktop appears on *everybody's* desktop.

All this is a long-winded way of suggesting another way to make some icon available to everybody with an account on your machine. Drag it into the Desktop folder inside the Public folder. (This folder is ordinarily hidden; it appears only when you un-hide Windows' protected files and folders; see page 89.)

For more on profiles, see the free downloadable PDF appendix "Profiles.pdf" on this book's "Missing CD" page at *www.missingmanuals.com*.

NTFS Permissions: Protecting Your Stuff

There's one final aspect of user accounts that's worth mentioning: *NTFS permissions,* a technology that's a core part of Windows' security system. Using this feature, you can specify exactly which coworkers are allowed to open which files and folders on your machine. In fact, you can also specify *how much* access each person has. You can dictate, for example, that Gomez and Morticia aren't allowed to open your Fourth-Quarter Projections spreadsheet at all, that Fred and Ginger can open it but not make changes, and that George and Gracie can both open it and make changes.

Your colleagues will encounter the permissions you've set up like this in two different situations: when tapping into your machine from across the network or when sitting down at it and logging in using their own names and passwords. In either case, the NTFS permissions you set up protect your files and folders equally well.

Tip: In Chapter 21, you can read about a very similar form of access privileges called *sharing permissions.* There's a big difference between share permissions and the NTFS permissions described here, though: Share permissions keep people out of your stuff only when they try to access your PC from *over the network*.

Actually, there are other differences, too. NTFS permissions offer more gradations of access. And using NTFS permissions, you can declare individual *files*—not just folders—accessible or inaccessible to specific coworkers.

Using NTFS permissions is most decidedly a power-user technique because of the added complexity it introduces. Entire books have been written on the topic of NTFS permissions alone.

An entire appendix to this chapter, too. Read the free PDF appendix "NTFS Permissions.pdf" on this book's "Missing CD" page at *www.missingmanuals.com*.

CHAPTER 20

Setting Up a Small Network

Almost every Windows machine on earth is connected to the Mother of All Networks, the one we call the Internet. But most PCs also get connected, sooner or later, to a smaller network—some kind of home or office network (known to nerds as a *local area network,* or *LAN*).

The payoff is considerable. Once you've created a network, you can copy files from one machine to another just as you'd drag files between folders on your own PC. You can store your music or photo files on one computer and play them on any other. Everyone on the network can consult the same database, phone book, or calendar. When the workday's done, you can play games over the network.

Most importantly, you can share a single printer or high-speed Internet connection among all the PCs in the house.

If you work at a biggish company, you probably work on a *domain network*—the big, centrally managed type found in corporations. In that case, you won't have to fool around with building or designing a network; your job, and your PC, presumably came with a fully functioning network (and a fully functioning geek responsible for running it).

But if you work at home, or if you're responsible for setting up a network in a smaller office, this chapter is for you. It guides you through the construction of a less formal *workgroup* network, which ordinary mortals can put together.

Setting up a network has never approached the simplicity of, say, setting up a desk lamp. But Windows offers a feature called *HomeGroups* that makes the setup incredibly fast and easy—*if* all your PCs are running Windows 7 or later, and *if* you have no particular need to keep your music, photo, and video collections private from the rest of your family members.

If you don't meet those requirements, you can still use the older, more complex Windows networking methods. They'll take you an afternoon to set up and understand—but this chapter will hold your hand.

Kinds of Networks

You can connect your PCs using any of several different kinds of gear. Many of the world's offices are wired with *Ethernet cable,* but as you probably know, WiFi (wireless) networks are very popular for small offices and homes. Here and there, a few renegades are even installing networking systems that rely on the phone or power lines already in the walls. Here's an overview of the most popular networking systems.

Note: Be sure that whatever networking gear you buy is compatible with Windows 10, either by checking logos on the package or by checking the maker's Web site. Networking is complicated enough without having to troubleshoot some gadget that's not designed for Win10.

Ethernet

Ethernet is the world's most popular networking protocol. It gives you fast, reliable, cheap, trouble-free communication. All you need are three components:

- **Network adapters.** An Ethernet jack is built into virtually every desktop PC and many laptops. That's your *network adapter*—the circuitry that provides the Ethernet jack (Figure 20-1).

  If your machine doesn't have an Ethernet jack—tablets don't, and slim laptops usually don't—you can add one. Adapters are available as internal cards, external USB attachments, or laptop cards.

UP TO SPEED

Network Devices Have Speed Limits

Ethernet cards and hubs are available in different speeds. The most common are *100BaseT* (100 Mbps, sometimes cleverly called *Fast Ethernet*) and *Gigabit Ethernet* (1,000 Mbps).

Note, however, that the speed of the network has no effect on your computers' *Internet* speed—Web surfing, email downloading, and so on. The reason: Even the slowest network operates far faster than your Internet connection. Remember, the top speed of a typical broadband Internet connection is around 5 or 10 megabits per second—still many times slower than the *slowest* home network.

So why does a faster network matter? Primarily to save time when you're transferring big files between the PCs on the network. For example, you can play MP3 music files stored on another computer over a 10BaseT connection with no problems at all. However, if you plan to install video cameras all around your palatial estate and want to watch all the video feeds simultaneously, opt for Fast Ethernet—or even Gigabit Ethernet, the current Ethernet speed champ at 1,000 Mbps.

The bottom line? As you shop for gear, you may as well go for the higher speeds so you'll be ready for any high-bandwidth application that comes down the pike.

- **A router.** If you have a cable modem or DSL connection to the Internet, a *router* (about $60) distributes that Internet signal to all the computers on your network. (The dialog boxes in Windows call these devices *gateways*, although almost no one else does.)

Routers with four or eight ports (that is, Ethernet jacks where you can plug in computers) are popular in homes and small offices.

It's worth noting that you can inexpensively expand your network by plugging a *hub* or *switch* into one of the router's jacks. Hubs and switches are similar-looking little boxes that offer *another* five or eight Ethernet jacks, connecting all your computers together. (A switch is more intelligent than a hub. It's more selective

Figure 20-1:
Top: The Ethernet cable is connected to a computer at one end, and the router (shown here) at the other end. The computers communicate through the router; there's no direct connection between any two computers. The front of the router has little lights for each connector port, which light up only on the ports in use. You can watch the lights flash as the computers communicate with one another.

Bottom: Here's what a typical "I've got three PCs in the house, and I'd like them to share my cable modem" setup might look like.

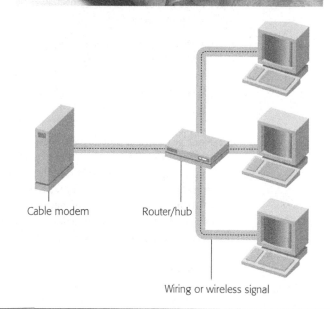

Cable modem   Router/hub

Wiring or wireless signal

when sending data to the right PCs on your network; as a result, the bits and bytes move a little faster.)

Tip: There's also such a thing as a router with both physical Ethernet jacks *and* wireless antennas that broadcast the signal throughout your place.

To set up a router, plug it into your cable or DSL modem using an Ethernet cable. Restart the cable modem. Now use whatever software came with the router to set up its security features. Often, the software is actually built into the router; you're supposed to view it by opening up a special page in your Web browser, of all things.

The router then logs onto your Internet service and stands ready to transmit Internet data to and from all the computers on your network.

As a bonus, the router provides excellent security, serving as a firewall that isolates your network computers from the Internet and keeps out hackers. (See Chapter 12 for much more on firewalls.)

- **Ethernet cables.** The cables used for most Ethernet networks look something like telephone cables, but they're not the same thing—and they're definitely not interchangeable. Both the cable itself (called *10BaseT, 100BaseT,* or *Cat 5*) and the little clips at each end (*RJ-45 connectors*) are slightly fatter than those on a phone cable. You can buy Ethernet cables in a variety of lengths and colors. Each computer must be connected to the hub, switch, or router with a cable that's no longer than about 100 yards.

Tip: If you've got a computer that sits in one place, like a desktop PC, then you should use an Ethernet cable even if you have a wireless network.

One reason is security (wired networks are harder for the baddies to "sniff"). Another is speed. Yes, wireless technologies like 802.11n promise speeds of 300 megabits per second, which is very, very fast. But, first of all, the real-world speed is about a third of that; second, that speed is shared among all computers on the network. As a result, if you're copying a big file across the network, it will probably go twice as fast if it's going between one wireless and one wired PC than between two wireless PCs.

Ethernet gear can be shockingly inexpensive; a search at Newegg.com, for example, reveals five-port Ethernet switches for $9 from no-name companies. If you're willing to pay slightly more—$20 for the card, $50 for the hub, for example—you can get brand-name gear (like D-Link, Netgear, 3Com, or Linksys) whose support with installation, phone help, and driver updates through the years may reward you many times over. Setting up an Ethernet network generally goes very smoothly, but in the few cases where trouble arises, cheapo equipment is often the problem.

Network hookups

On paper, the hardware part of setting up the network is simple: Just connect each computer to the router or hub using an Ethernet cable.

It's that "using an Ethernet cable" part that sometimes gets sticky. Depending on where your PCs are and how concerned you are about the network's appearance, this wiring process may involve drilling holes in floors or walls, stapling cables to baseboard trim, or calling in an electrician to do the job.

When all your computers are in the same room, you can run the cables along the walls and behind the furniture. If you have to run cables between rooms, you can secure the cables to the floor or baseboards using staples—use the round kind that won't crush the cables—or plastic "raceways" with adhesive backing.

Of course, you might not be thrilled about having *any* exposed cables in your home or office. In that case, the installation process can be much more complicated. You should probably hire a professional cable installer to do the job—or don't use cables at all. Read on.

Wireless Networks (WiFi or 802.11)

So far, this discussion has focused on using wired Ethernet to hook up your computers. Millions of people, however, have embraced the flexibility of *WiFi* (802.11), a *wireless* networking system.

Every computer sold today has a WiFi antenna built in. Your PCs can all communicate with one another without wires.

To get onto an *existing* wireless network, follow the steps on page 370.

But if you want your *own* wireless network, right there in your own home or office, you also need a *wireless router* (about $50)—a box that connects to your router or

---

UP TO SPEED

802 dot Whatever: Better Every Year

Over the years, networking gear has come in several flavors, each offering different degrees of speed, distance, and compatibility. They have such appetizing-sounding names as 802.11b, 802.11a, 802.11g, 802.11n, and 802.11ac.

In general, each generation of WiFi gear improves the speed and range of your hotspot. (Note that you never get the "up to" speed on the box; in fact, you'll usually get around half that speed, since a wireless network uses a lot of the bandwidth for such network housekeeping chores as correcting transmission errors.)

The current standard is 802.11ac, which offers better speed *and* better range than its predecessors (thanks to multiple antennas). Remember, though, you won't get the better speed unless *both* your base station *and* your networking cards speak "ac."

Meanwhile, keep in mind that faster equipment doesn't speed up your email and Web activity. A cable modem or a DSL box delivers Internet information at a fraction of the speed of your home or office network. The bottleneck is the Internet connection, not your network.

Instead, the speed boost you get with newer WiFi gear is useful only for transferring files *among computers on your network*, streaming video or audio *between computers* (or PCs and your TV), and playing networked games.

Finally, the great thing about wireless networking is that it all works together, no matter what kind of computer you have. There's no such thing as an "Apple" wireless network or a "Windows" wireless network. All computers work with any kind of access point.

---

hub and broadcasts the Internet signal to the whole building. The usual suspects—Linksys, Netgear, D-Link, and others—sell these routers. They're also called base stations or access points.

Now, WiFi equipment has a range of about 150 feet, sometimes even through walls. In concept, this setup works much like a cordless phone, where the base station is plugged into the wall phone jack and a wireless handset can talk to it from anywhere in the house.

Wireless networking is not without its downsides, however. You may get intermittent service interruptions from 2.4-gigahertz cordless phones, microwave ovens (when they're cooking), and other machinery, or even the weather. Furthermore, big metal things, or walls *containing* big metal things (like pipes) can interfere with communication among the PCs, much to the disappointment of people who work in subways and meat lockers.

A wireless network isn't as secure as a cabled network, either. It's theoretically possible for some hacker, sitting nearby, armed with "sniffing" software, to intercept the email you're sending or the Web page you're downloading. (Except secure Web sites, those marked by a little padlock in your Web browser.)

Still, nothing beats the freedom of wireless networking, particularly if you're a laptop lover; you can set up shop almost anywhere in the house or yard, slumped into any kind of rubbery posture. No matter where you go within your home, you're online at full speed, without hooking up a single wire.

Other Kinds of Networks

There are a couple of other network types that are worth looking into. Both are wired networks, but they use the wires you already have.

UP TO SPEED

Ad Hoc: PC-to-PC Micronetworks

If your network has modest ambitions—that is, if you have only two computers you want to connect—you can ignore all this business about hubs, routers, and wiring. Instead, you can create a tiny, two-computer wireless network between them.

These so-called ad hoc networks are great when you want to grab a folder full of files from a friend on a plane, for example. (You can also create a wired ad-hoc network, using an Ethernet crossover cable, instead of going wireless.)

Unfortunately, back in Windows 8, Microsoft removed the "Create ad hoc network" option from the Network and Sharing Center. Now creating one requires one of two tools.

First, you can follow along with a guided tour through the necessary command-line typed commands, like this tutorial here: *http://j.mp/YEIsrd*

Second, you can use a piece of free software to do the job for you, like Wi-MAN. You can download it from this book's "Missing CD" page at *www.missingmanuals.com*.

Phone line networks

Instead of going to the trouble of wiring your home with Ethernet cables, you might consider using the wiring that's already *in* your house—telephone wiring. That's the idea behind a kind of networking gear called HomePNA. With this system, you can use the network even when using the modem or talking on the phone, although you can't make a modem and a voice call simultaneously.

Unfortunately, the average American household has only two or three phone jacks in the *entire house,* meaning you don't have much flexibility in positioning your PCs. If you're trying to avoid the plaster-dust experience of installing additional wiring, consider WiFi or Powerline networking.

Power outlet networks

Here's another way to connect your computers without rewiring the building: Use the electrical wiring that's already in your walls. Unlike phone jacks, electrical outlets are usually available in every room in the house.

If you buy *Powerline adapters* (also called HomePlug adapters), you get very fast speeds (from 14 Mbps up to 100 Mbps), very good range (1,000 feet), and the ultimate in installation simplicity. You just plug the Powerline adapter from your PC's Ethernet or USB jack into any wall power outlet. Presto—all the PCs are connected.

Powerline adapters are inexpensive (about $40 apiece) and extremely convenient.

The Network and Sharing Center

Several times in this book, you'll read about the Network and Sharing Center. It used to be the master control center for creating, managing, and connecting to networks of all kinds (Figure 20-2). Now that you can do most network tasks right in the Settings app, the NaSC isn't quite as essential.

But it's still where you set up the sharing of files, folders, printers, and multimedia files over the network, as you'll discover in Chapter 21.

There are all kinds of ways to get there, but the quickest is to right-click the ▥ or ▤ icon on your taskbar system tray. From the shortcut menu, choose Open Network and Sharing Center.

You can also get there with a search for *network and*; select Open Network and Sharing Center.

To *do* anything with your network, you need to click one of the links in blue. They include these:

Change adapter settings

Click this link to view a list of all your network adapters—Ethernet cards and WiFi adapters, mainly—as well as any VPNs or dial-up connections you've set up on your computer (Figure 20-2).

Double-click a listing to see its connection status, which leads to several other dialog boxes where you can reconfigure the connection or see more information. The toolbar offers buttons that let you rename, troubleshoot, disable, or connect to one of these network doodads.

Note: If you right-click one of these icons and then choose Properties, you get a list of protocols that your network connection uses. Double-click "Internet Protocol Version 4" to tell Windows whether to get its IP and DNS server addresses automatically, or whether to use addresses you've specified. Ninety-nine times out of 100, the right choice is to get those addresses automatically. Every once in a while, though, you'll come across a network that requires manually entered addresses.

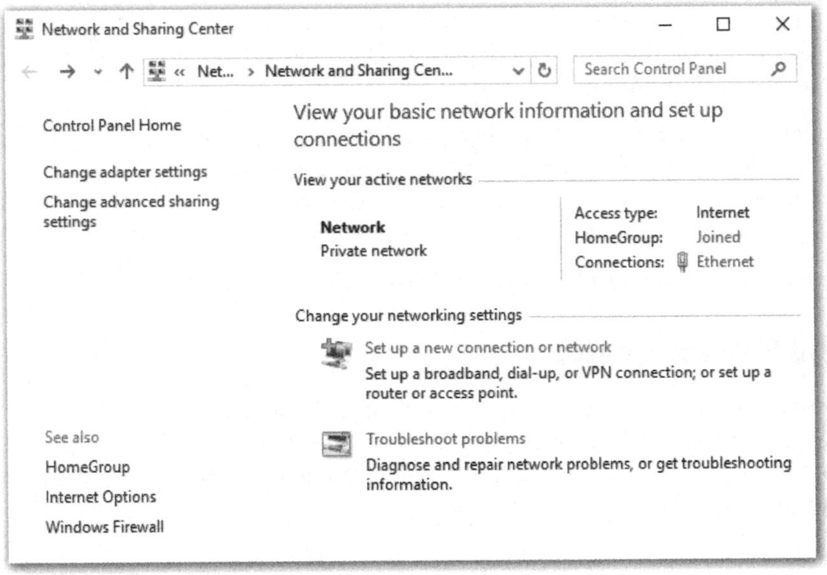

Figure 20-2:
Once it's open, the Network and Sharing Center offers links that let you connect to a network, create a new network, troubleshoot your connection, fiddle with your network or network adapter card settings, and so on.

Change advanced sharing settings

This section is the master control panel of on/off switches for Windows' *network sharing* features. (Most of these have on/off switches in other, more scattered places, too.) Here's a rundown.

Note: The options here are actually listed three times: once for Private networks (your own home or office networks), once for Public ones (coffee shops and so on), and once for All networks.

- **Network discovery** makes your computer visible to others and allows your computer to see other computers on the network.

- **File and printer sharing** lets you share files and printers over the network. (See Chapter 21.)

- **Homegroup connections.** Here's the master on/off switch for the delightful Homegroup feature described in Chapter 21.

- **Public folder sharing** lets you share whatever files you've put in the Users→Public folder. (See page 597.)

- **Media streaming** is where you listen to one PC's music playing back over the network while seated at another. (See Chapter 21.) It appears here only if you've turned this feature on.

- **File sharing connections** lets you turn off the super-strong security features of Windows file sharing, to accommodate older gadgets that don't recognize it.

- **Password protected sharing** is an on/off switch. When it's on, the only people who can access your shared folders and printers are those who have accounts on your PC. When it's off, anybody can access them. Details are in Chapter 21.

Links in the Main Window

In the main part of the Network and Sharing Center window, the "View your basic network information and set up connections" page offers a few more handy tools:

Set up a new connection or network

Most of the time, Windows does the right thing when it encounters a new network. For example, if you plug in an Ethernet cable, it assumes you want to use the wired network and automatically hops on. If you come within range of a wireless network, Windows offers to connect to it.

Some kinds of networks, however, require special setup:

- **Connect to the Internet.** Use this option when Windows fails to figure out how to connect to the Internet on its own. You can set up a WiFi, PPPoE broadband connection (required by certain DSL services that require you to sign in with a user name and password), or even a dial-up networking connection.

- **Set up a new network.** You can use this option to configure a new wireless router that's not set up yet, although only some routers can "speak" to Windows in this way. You're better off using the configuration software that came in the box with the router.

- **Manually connect to a wireless network.** Some wireless networks don't announce (broadcast) their presence. That is, you won't see a message popping up on the screen, inviting you to join the network, just by wandering into it. Instead, the very name and existence of such networks are kept secret to keep the riffraff out. If you're told the name of such a network, use this option to type it in and connect.

- **Connect to a workplace.** That is, set up a secure VPN connection to the corporation that employs you, as described on page 456.

Troubleshoot problems

Very few problems are as annoying or difficult to troubleshoot as flaky network connections. With this option, Microsoft is giving you a tiny head start.

When you click "Troubleshoot problems," Windows asks what, exactly, you're having trouble with. Click the topic in question: Internet Connections, Shared Folders, Homegroup, and so on. Invisibly and automatically, Windows performs several geek tweaks that were once the realm of highly paid networking professionals: It renews the DHCP address, reinitializes the connection, and, if nothing else works, turns the networking card off and on again.

If the troubleshooter doesn't pinpoint the problem, check that all the following are in place:

• **Your cables are properly seated** in the network adapter card and hub jacks.

• **Your router, Ethernet hub, or wireless access point** is plugged into a working power outlet.

• **Your networking card is working.** To check, open the Device Manager (type its name at the Start menu). Look for an error icon next to your networking card's name. See Chapter 15 for more on the Device Manager.

If that doesn't fix things, you'll have to call Microsoft, your PC maker, or your local teenage PC guru for help.

CHAPTER 21

Sharing Files on the Network

Whether you built the network yourself or work in an office where somebody has done that work for you, all kinds of fun can come from having a network. You're now ready to share all kinds of stuff among the various PCs that are connected:

- **Files, folders, and disks.** No matter what PC you're using on the network, you can open the files and folders on any *other* networked PC, as long as the other PCs' owners have made these files available for public inspection. That's where *file sharing* comes in, and that's what this chapter is all about.

  The uses for file sharing are almost endless. It means you can finish writing a letter in the bedroom, even if you started it downstairs at the kitchen table—without having to carry a flash drive around. It means you can watch a slideshow drawn from photos on your spouse's PC somewhere else in the house. It means your underlings can turn in articles for your small-company newsletter by depositing them directly into a folder on your laptop.

Tip: File sharing also lets you access your files and folders from the road, using a laptop. See Chapter 13 for more information on this road-warrior trick.

- **Music and video playback.** Windows Media Player can *stream* music and videos from one PC to another one on the same network—that is, play in real time across the network, without your having to copy any files. In a family situation, it's super-convenient to have Dad's Mondo Upstairs PC serve as the master holding tank for the family's entire music collection—and be able to play it using any PC in the house.

- **Printers.** All PCs on the network can share a printer. If several printers are on your network—say, a high-speed laser printer for one computer and a color printer on another—everyone on the network can use whichever printer is appropriate for a particular document. Step-by-step instructions start on page 474.

Note: Your network might include a Windows 10 PC, a couple of Windows 7, 8, XP, or Vista machines, older PCs, and even Macs. That's perfectly OK; all of these computers can participate as equals in this party. This chapter points out whatever differences you may find in the procedures.

Two Ways to Share Files

It's not easy to write an operating system that's supposed to please *everyone,* from a husband and wife at home, to a small-business owner, to a network administrator for the federal government. Clearly, these people might have slightly different attitudes on the tradeoff between convenience and security.

That's why Windows offers *two ways* to share files. Each falls at a different spot on the security/convenience spectrum:

- **HomeGroups.** The HomeGroup feature was invented for places where people don't have a lot to hide from one another, like families or very small businesses. This kind of network is *really* easy to set up and use; nobody has to enter names and passwords to use files on other computers in the house or the office.

  Setup is a one-time deal: You type a code into each computer, and presto—everyone can see everyone else's Music, Photos, Videos, and Documents folders. Everyone can send printouts to everyone else's printers. Everyone can listen to everyone else's music collections, too.

  Downsides: A PC can join a HomeGroup only if it's running Windows 7 or later. And HomeGroups don't offer the level of security, passwords, and networky red tape that bigger companies require. The idea is to give everyone in the house free access to everyone else's stuff with one click.

- **Any folder.** At the far end of the security/convenience spectrum, you have the "any folder" method. In this scheme, you can make any folder or disk available for inspection by other people on the network.

  This method gives you elaborate control over who's allowed to do what to your files. You might want to permit your company's executives to see and edit your documents but allow the peons in accounting only to see them. And Andy, that unreliable goofball in sales? You don't want him even *seeing* what's in your shared folder.

  Downsides: More complex and inconvenient than a HomeGroup.

These networking types can coexist, by the way. You can have a HomeGroup for the benefit of the other Windows 7/8/10 computers in your house, but still share with

Windows Vista or XP machines using the other method. (Nobody said this was going to be simple.)

The following pages walk you through both kinds of file sharing.

Note: Technically, there's a third kind of sharing: *Public-folder* sharing. Every PC has a Public folder. It's free for anyone on the network to use, like a grocery store bulletin board. Super-convenient, super-easy.

Yet you should probably skip this method, for two reasons. First, you have to move files *into* the Public folder before anyone else can see them; you can't leave them where they're sitting, as you can with the other sharing methods.

Second, in Windows 7 and 8, the Public folders containing your shared files sit inside the *libraries* described on page 72—but in Windows 10, Microsoft has hidden away the whole libraries feature. (The main Public folder still exists—but it's in your C: **>** Users folder.) The bottom line is that even if you share files by putting them into one of the Public folders, nobody on your network will be able to find them!

HomeGroups

Let's suppose there are two PCs in your house. Setting up a HomeGroup is incredibly easy. In fact, it's as easy as 1, 2, 3, 4, 5.

Creating a HomeGroup

Fingers ready? Make sure you're signed in with an Administrator account. It doesn't matter which PC you start with.

1. **On the first PC, open the HomeGroup page of the Control Panel (Figure 21-1, top).**

   The quickest way is to do a search for *homegroup*; choose HomeGroup in the results.

Tip: Here's another method. On the first PC, open any File Explorer window. On the Ribbon's Share tab, choose "Create or join a homegroup."

Now then. What you see here could be any of three things, depending on how kind you've been to others in your life:

"Libraries and devices you're sharing from this computer." A HomeGroup already exists, probably because you set one up the day you turned on Windows. Skip to page 599.

"There is currently no homegroup on the network." The HomeGroup hasn't been created yet. You've come to the right place. Proceed to step 2.

"This computer can't connect to a homegroup." Windows believes that you're on a public network, like a WiFi hotspot at a coffee shop (see the box on page 603).

If you're actually not on a public network (and instead, you're at home or at your office), choose "Change network location." In the panel at right, where a message asks if you want your PC to be "discoverable," choose Yes.

Now return to the HomeGroup pane and proceed to step 2.

2. **Click "Create a homegroup" (Figure 21-1, top).**

Windows explains what's about to happen.

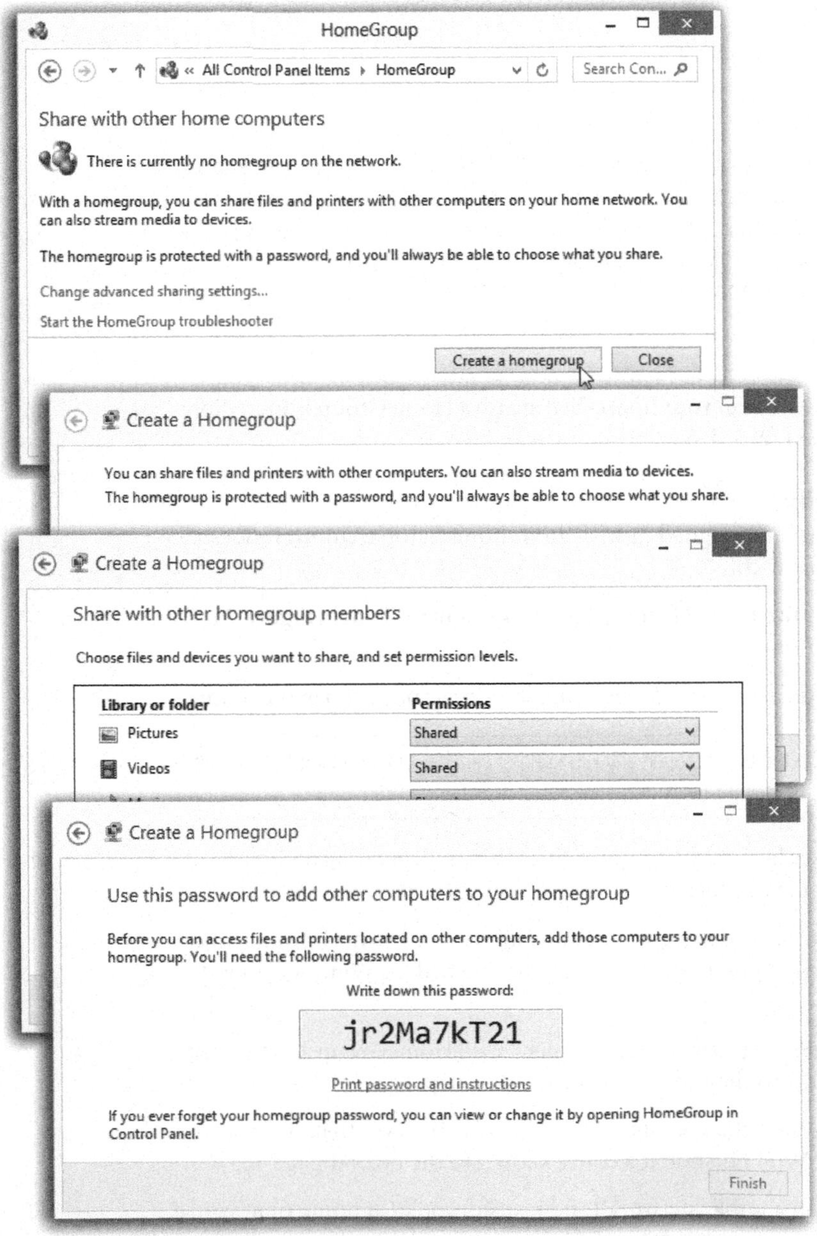

Figure 21-1:
Here's how to use the Control Panel to set up a HomeGroup.

(It doesn't matter which PC you start with, as long as it's using Windows 7 or later.)

Top: Click "Create a homegroup."

Second from top: Here's your complimentary explanation of what a HomeGroup is. Click Next.

Third from top: Specify which folders you want to share. Click Next.

Bottom: Here's the password other computers will need to join this HomeGroup.

3. **Click Next. Turn on the switches for the stuff you want to share.**

This is your opportunity to specify which stuff in *your* account, on *this* computer, you want to share with everybody else (Figure 21-1, third from top).

You can make your Pictures, Videos, Music, and Documents folders available for the other PCs in your house to use. (Windows proposes turning on Pictures, Videos, and Music but leaving Documents unshared, for privacy.) And you can share whatever printer is connected to your PC—an inkjet, for example.

Note: You can always change these settings later, as described below.

---

4. **Hit Next.**

Windows now displays a ridiculously unmemorable password, like E6fQ9UX3uR (Figure 21-1, bottom). Write it down or print it. (You can also change it to something less dorky.)

5. **Hit Finish.**

Joining a HomeGroup

Now walk to the second PC. Here's how it can join the HomeGroup:

1. **Open the HomeGroup panel just as you did in step 1 above.**

This time, the wording is different. It sees the *first* PC on the network, with a HomeGroup initiative already under way.

2. **Choose "Join now," and turn on the switches for the stuff you want to share on this computer.**

Pictures, Music, whatever.

UP TO SPEED

The Fine Print of HomeGroups

HomeGroups work quickly and well. But as with anything that seems too good to be true, there are a few footnotes:

1. If your PC is on a corporate domain network, you can join a HomeGroup but you can't create one. You'll be able to access libraries and printers on other computers in the HomeGroup, but you can't share your own.

2. If you have the Starter, Home Basic, or RT version of Windows, you can join a HomeGroup, but you can't create one.

3. HomeGroups don't work unless you declare your network to be private (see the box on page 603).

4. When you share a folder in the HomeGroup, all folders inside are also shared.

You've been warned. Sign here, please.

---

3. **Hit Next, enter the homegroup password you wrote down in step 4, and hit Next again.**

The setup is complete—for *this* computer. If you have a third PC, or a fourth or a fifth, repeat these three steps. If you buy another PC a year from now, repeat these three steps.

Tweaking a HomeGroup

Once your HomeGroup is chugging along, the Control Panel page you started with offers you some useful links; see Figure 21-2.

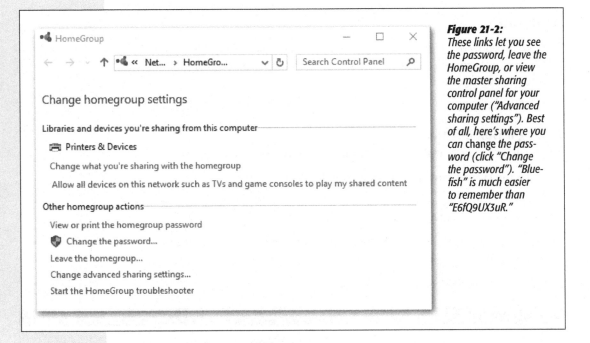

Figure 21-2:
These links let you see the password, leave the HomeGroup, or view the master sharing control panel for your computer ("Advanced sharing settings"). Best of all, here's where you can change the password (click "Change the password"). "Blue-fish" is much easier to remember than "E6fQ9UX3uR."

How to Use Your HomeGroup

Once a HomeGroup is set up, using it is a piece of cake.

- **Root through other people's folders.** On PC #2, click HomeGroup at the left side of any File Explorer window. Voilà! There are the icons for every PC—in fact, every *account* on every PC (Figure 21-3).

  And if you open one of them, you can see the pictures, music, videos, documents, and whatever else they've made available for sharing.

- **Share each other's printers.** When you go to print, you'll see that *all* the printers in the house are now available to *all* the PCs in the house. For example, if there's a color inkjet plugged into the USB jack of Computer #1, you can send printouts to it from the Print dialog box of Computer #2. (The other computers' shared printers even have their own icons in the Devices and Printers folder, as described in Chapter 14.)

Note: If the printer is a relatively recent, brand-name model, it should "just work"; Windows installs the printer automatically. If not, the HomeGroup feature notifies you that a printer is available, but you have to click Install to OK the driver installation.

- **Play each other's music and video.** When you're in Windows Media Player, same thing: You'll see the names of all the other computers listed for your browsing pleasure and, inside, all their music, photos, and videos, ready to play. (The other machines are listed in the navigation pane at left, in a category called "Other libraries.")

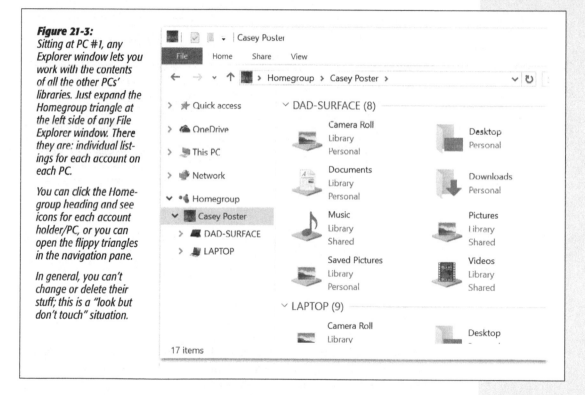

Figure 21-3:
Sitting at PC #1, any Explorer window lets you work with the contents of all the other PCs' libraries. Just expand the Homegroup triangle at the left side of any File Explorer window. There they are: individual listings for each account on each PC.

You can click the Home-group heading and see icons for each account holder/PC, or you can open the flippy triangles in the navigation pane.

In general, you can't change or delete their stuff; this is a "look but don't touch" situation.

How to Share More Files and Folders

Microsoft starts you off by sharing your main libraries—Photos, Videos, Music, Documents. Anything you put in them becomes available immediately.

But that doesn't mean you're limited to sharing those folders. You can share any folder you like, making it available for ransacking by everyone else in the HomeGroup.

To do that, open whatever Explorer window it's in. On the Ribbon's Share tab, the tiny scrolling list offers every conceivable way to share the contents of this window (Figure 21-4):

- **Homegroup (view).** Everybody else in the group can see and open these files and folders but can't delete, change, or add anything.

- **Homegroup (view and edit).** Everybody else in the group can do whatever they like to these files and folders—add, change, delete, whatever. This is a good choice if "everybody" means *you*, moving between computers, or maybe "you and your perfectly trustworthy partner."

- **Robin, Casey, Lee, Dana...** You can also share this window's contents with just *one* person. Select his name here.

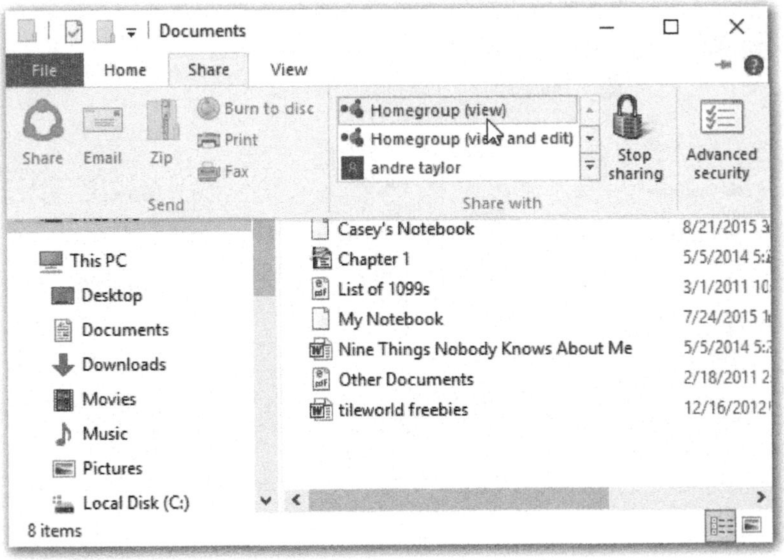

Figure 21-4:
This tiny scrolling list answers the question: "With whom would you like to share the contents of this folder, master?"

There's also a "Stop sharing" button on this tab. You probably don't need to be told what it does.

- **Specific people.** This option opens a dialog box that lets you add several people to the lucky-invitees list quickly. It's a lot less clunky than adding them one at a time as described in the previous paragraph. See Figure 21-5.

- **Advanced sharing.** When you've opened the window for a drive or a system folder, the Ribbon doesn't show all of those options. Instead, it shows only one option: Advanced sharing. It opens the Properties dialog box for that drive or folder, open to the Sharing tab, where you can fiddle with the more complex passwords and permissions described later in this chapter.

Leaving a HomeGroup

If you're feeling a little private, you can remove your PC from the big happy network family, either temporarily or permanently. Just use the "Leave the homegroup" link shown in Figure 21-2.

You can rejoin at any time—you'll see a Join button on the HomeGroup panel—but you'll need the password. (You can find out the password by opening the HomeGroup panel on any *other* PC.)

Tip: If you're not using the HomeGroup feature at all, you can also disable it completely. The advantage is that the HomeGroup heading won't take up space in your navigation bar anymore.

To do that, switch your network to the Public type (see the box below). The next time you start the PC, HomeGroup will have vanished from your Explorer windows.

Editing the Shared HomeGroup Libraries

If you ever decide to adjust which folders you're sharing—to turn off your Music, turn on your Documents, or whatever—no biggie. Open the HomeGroup panel shown in Figure 21-1 again, and just change the switches.

UP TO SPEED

Public Networks, Private Networks, and How to Switch

Throughout this chapter, throughout this book, and throughout your life with Windows, you'll encounter references to your network being "discoverable" or "not discoverable" or Public or Private. Microsoft introduced this terminology out of concern for you, the public but it's still complicated.

The problem is this:

When you're on a *public* WiFi hotspot—at a coffee shop, for example—bad guys with the right hacker software can, in theory, get into your computer. You wouldn't want that.

So when you've told Windows that you're on a public network, things attached to your machine, like printers and HomeGroups, are not discoverable. The bad guys can't see them on the network. *Nobody* can see them on the network.

When you're at home or at the office, though, your network is private. Bad guys couldn't get in if they tried. So it's OK

to share printers and files with other computers within your home or office.

That's the explanation, but here's the punch line: You can share files and printers only if Windows thinks you're on a private network—your own network.

Here's how you change Windows' mind about what kind of network yours is.

Open Settings→Network & Internet. On the left, choose how you're connected (WiFi or Ethernet). If you're on WiFi, hit "Advanced options"; if you're on Ethernet, choose the name of your Ethernet connection.

On the next screen, the master switch is right here: "Find devices and content." *On* means your network is private, and it's OK to share files and printers. *Off* means you're on a public network and you'd rather lock things down.

Sharing Any Folder

In what Microsoft cleverly calls the "share any folder" method, you can make *any* folder available to other people on the network. This time, you can set up elaborate *sharing permissions* that grant individuals different amounts of access to your files.

Better yet, files you share this way are available to other people on the network *and* other people with accounts on the *same computer*.

Here's how to share a file or folder on your PC:

1. **In a File Explorer window, open the window that contains the files or folders you want to share. On the Ribbon's Share tab, choose the names of the people you want to share with.**

   The names of this PC's other account holders all appear here, in this cramped scrolling list (Figure 21-5, top). You can click to share with one person.

   Or, to share with more than one person, click "Specific people" to open the "Choose people to share with" dialog box (Figure 21-5, bottom). You wanted individual control over each account holder's access? You got it.

Note: The steps for sharing a *disk* are different. See page 606.

---

2. **Choose a person's name from the upper pop-up menu, and then click Add.**

   This is the list of account holders (Chapter 19)—or account-holder *groups,* if someone has created them.

   If the person who'll be connecting across the network doesn't yet have an account on your machine, choose "Create a new user" from this pop-up menu. (This option is available if the PC is *not* part of a HomeGroup. Also, "Create a new user" isn't some kind of sci-fi breakthrough. You are not, in fact, going to create a human being—only an account for an *existing* person.)

   The name appears in the list.

   Now your job is to work through this list of people, specifying *how much* control each person has over the file or folder you're sharing.

3. **Click a name in the list. Click the ▼ in the Permission Level column and choose Read or Read/Write.**

   Read is that "look but don't touch" business. This person can see what's in the folder (or file) and can copy it, but can't delete or change the original.

   Contributors (available for folders only—not files) have much broader access. These people can add, change, or delete files in the shared folder—but only files *that they put there.* Stuff placed there by other people (Owners or Co-owners) appears as "look but don't touch" to a Contributor.

Read/Write means that this person, like you, can add, change, or delete any file in the shared folder.

Note: Your name shows up here as Owner. You have the most power of all—after all, it's your stuff.

This stuff may sound technical and confusing, but you have no idea how much simpler it is than it was in older Windows versions.

4. **Click Share.**

The "Your folder [or file] is shared" dialog box appears. This is more than a simple message, however; it contains the *network address* of the files or folders you shared. Without this address, your colleagues won't know that you've shared stuff and will have a tough time finding it.

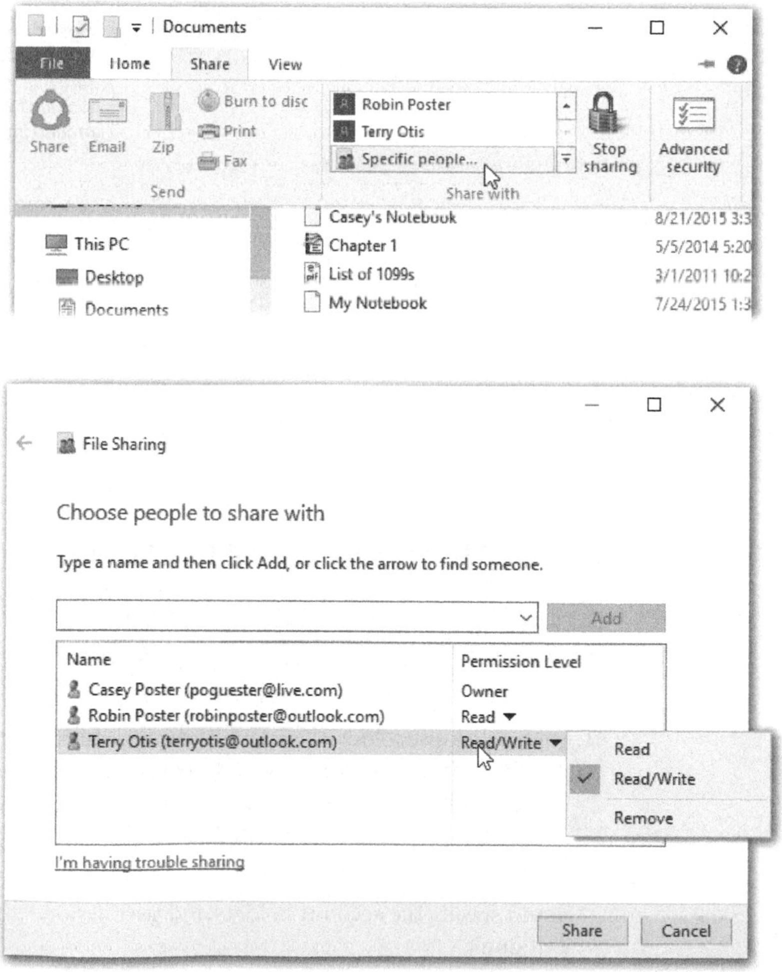

Figure 21-5:
Top: The Ribbon offers insta-sharing with any individual. Or, if you want more than one person to get in on the fun, choose "Specific people" to open...

Bottom: ...this box.

Use the pop-up menu at the top to choose an account holder's name. Or type it out, if you prefer.

After each name, click Add. Then use the Permission Level pop-up menu to specify either Read ("look but don't touch") or Read/Write ("you can edit and even delete stuff") permissions. Click Share when you're finished.

Note: If you've shared some files, you may see an interim message that appears before the "Your files are shared" box, warning you that Windows is about to adjust the access permissions to the folder that encloses them. That's normal.

5. **Click "e-mail" or "copy" (Figure 21-6).**

The "e-mail" link opens a new, outgoing message in your email program, letting the gang know that you've shared something and offering them a link to it. The "copy" link copies the address to the Clipboard so you can paste it into another program—which is your best bet if Mail isn't your email program of choice.

Tip: To stop sharing a folder or file, click it. Then, from the Share tab of the Ribbon of whatever window contains it, choose "Stop sharing."

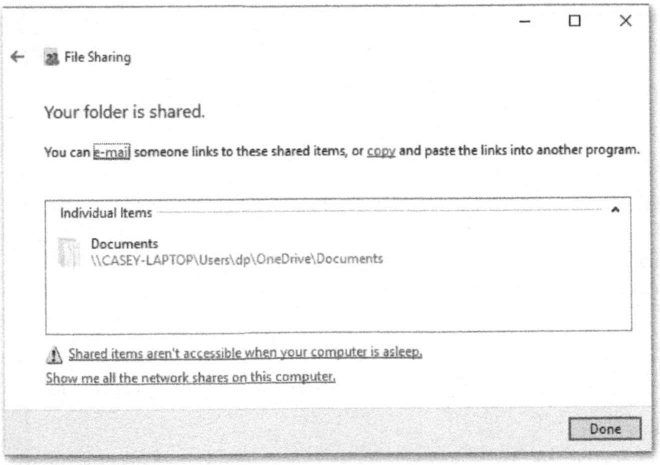

Figure 21-6:
Windows wants to make absolutely sure that you know what you've done. Wouldn't want the wrong people sniffing around the wrong personal files, now.

Advanced Folder Sharing—and Disk Sharing

Microsoft made a noble step forward in simplicity with the "share any folder" wizard described in the previous pages. But the older, more complicated—yet more flexible—method is still available. Here's a quick review of this alternate route (which is, by the way, the *only* route for sharing entire *disks):*

1. **Right-click the folder or disk you want to share. If it's a folder, choose Properties from the shortcut menu, and then click the Sharing tab. If it's a disk, choose "Share with"→"Advanced sharing."**

At this point, you *could* click the Share button (if you're operating on a folder, anyway). You'd arrive at the dialog box shown in Figure 21-5 (bottom) where you could specify the account holders and permission levels, just as described earlier. But don't.

2. **Click Advanced Sharing. Authenticate, if necessary.**

   The Advanced Sharing dialog box appears.

3. **Turn on "Share this folder." (See Figure 21-7, top.) Next, set up the power-user sharing options.**

   For example, you can limit the number of people who are browsing this folder at once. You can click Permissions to fine-tune who can do what (Figure 21-7, bottom). And you can edit the "Share name"—in fact, you can create *more than one* name for the same shared folder—to make it more recognizable on the network when people are browsing your PC.

Figure 21-7:
Top: Much finer-tuned sharing features are available in this more advanced box.

Bottom: For example, you can specify personalized permissions for different individuals.

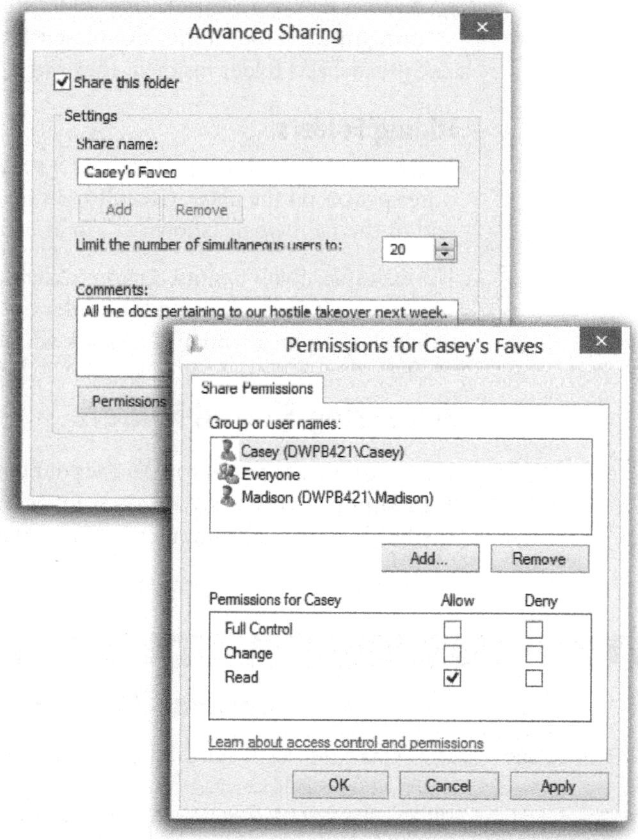

Notes on File Sharing

And now, the fine print on sharing files:

- Sharing a folder also shares all the folders inside it, including new ones you create later.

On the other hand, it's OK to *change* the sharing settings of a subfolder. For example, if you've shared a folder called America, you can make the Minnesota folder inside it off-limits by making it private. To do this, right-click the inner folder, choose Properties, click Sharing, click Advanced Sharing, and use the dialog box shown in Figure 21-7.

- **Be careful with nested folders.** Suppose, for example, that you share your Documents folder, and you permit other people to change the files inside it. Now suppose that you share a folder that's *inside* Documents—called Spreadsheets, for example—but you turn *off* the ability for other people to change its files.

  You wind up with a strange situation. Both folders—Documents and Spreadsheets—show up in other people's Network windows, as described below. If they double-click the Spreadsheets folder directly, they won't be able to change anything inside it. But if they double-click the Documents folder and then open the Spreadsheets folder inside *it*, they *can* modify the files.

Hiding Folders

If a certain folder on your hard drive is really private, you can hide the folder so that other people on the network can't even *see* it. The secret is to type a $ symbol at the end of the *share name* (shown at top in Figure 21-7).

For example, if you name a certain folder My Novel, anyone else on the network can see it (even if they can't read the contents). But if you name the folder *My Novel$*, it won't show up in anybody's Network window. They won't even know it exists.

Accessing Shared Folders

Now suppose you're not you. You're your coworker, spouse, or employee. You're using your laptop downstairs, and you want access to the stuff that's in a shared folder on the Beefy Main Dell computer upstairs. Here's what to do:

1. **Open any File Explorer window.**

Unhiding Hidden Folders

As sneaky and delightful as the hidden-folder trick is, it has a distinct drawback—*you* can't see your hidden folder from across the network, either. Suppose you went to the upstairs PC on the network to open something in your hidden My Novel folder (which is downstairs in the kitchen). Fortunately, you can do so—if you know the secret.

On the upstairs computer, press ⊞+R. In the Run dialog box, type the path of the hidden folder, using the format \\ *Computer Name\Folder Name*.

For example, enter *kitchen\my novel$* to get to the hidden folder called "My Novel$" on the PC called "Kitchen." (Capitalization doesn't matter.) Then click OK to open a window showing the contents of your hidden folder.

The navigation pane at left shows a Network heading. Click its > button, if necessary, to see icons for all the computers on the network (Figure 21-8, top). The same navigation pane is available in the Save and Open dialog boxes of your programs, too, making the entire network available to you for opening and saving files.

If you *don't* see a certain computer's icon here, it might be turned off, or off the network. It also might have *network discovery* turned off; that's the feature that lets a PC announce its presence to the network (see the box on page 603).

And if you don't see any computers at *all* in the Network window, then network discovery might be turned off on *your* computer.

2. **Double-click the computer whose files you want to open.**

If you're on a corporate domain, you may first have to double-click your way through some other icons, representing the networks in other buildings or floors, before you get to the actual PC icons.

Figure 21-8:
Top: The computers on your network are arrayed before you! Double-click the one you want to visit.

Bottom: Supply your account name and password as it exists on the distant PC, the one you're trying to access.

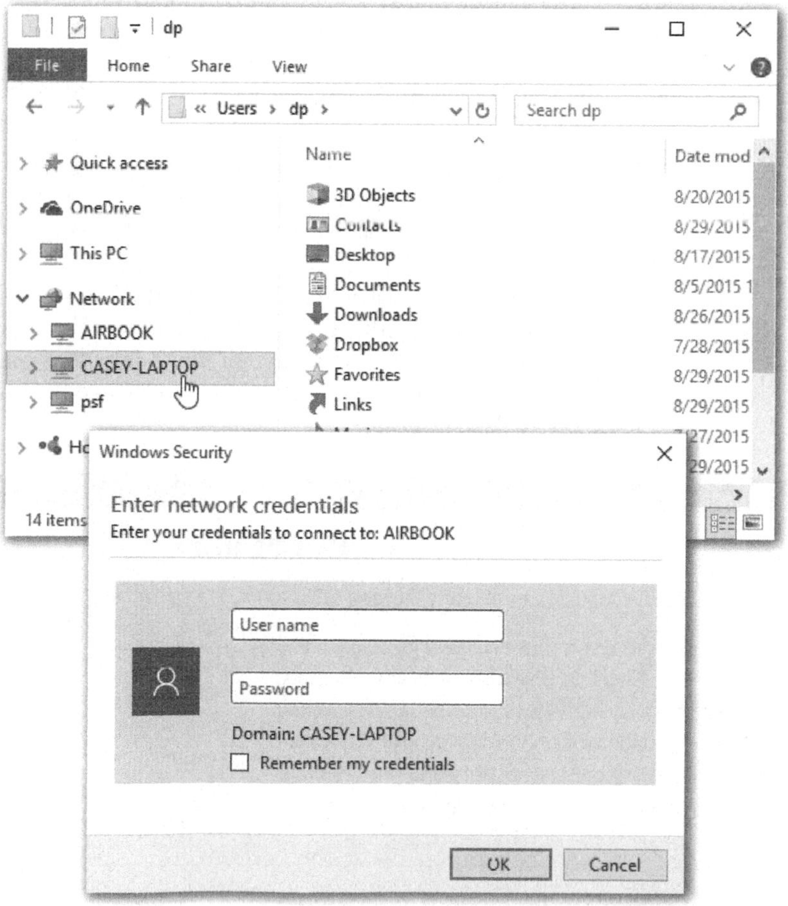

If you don't have an account on the PC you're invading—an account with the same name and password as you have on your own PC—then the Connect To box now appears (Figure 21-8, bottom).

Here you have to fill in the name and password of an account on the *other* computer. This, of course, is a real drag, especially if you access other people's files frequently. Fortunately, if you turn on "Remember my credentials," then you'll never see this box again. The next time you want to visit the other PC, you'll be able to double-click its icon for instant access.

Tip: In the unlikely event that you want Windows to *stop* memorizing your password, search for *credential* and select Credential Manager in the results. You see a list of every name/password Windows has memorized for you. You can use the options here to add a new memorized name/password, or expand one of the existing items in the list to remove it ("Remove from vault") or edit it.

---

3. **Click OK.**

If all went well, the other computer's window opens, presenting you with the icons of its shared folders and disks.

Tip: Working with the same shared folders often? Save yourself a lot of time and burrowing—make a desktop shortcut of it right now!

Once you've opened the window that contains the shared folder, grab your mouse. Right-click the shared item and drag it to the desktop. When you release the mouse, choose "Create shortcuts here" from the shortcut menu. From now on, you can double-click that shortcut to open the shared item directly.

Once you've brought a networked folder onto your screen, you can double-click icons to open them, drag them to the Recycle Bin, make copies of them, and otherwise manipulate them exactly as though they were icons on your own hard drive. (Of course, if you weren't given permission to change the contents of the shared folder, you have less freedom.)

GEM IN THE ROUGH

Sharing Disks

You can share files and folders, of course, but also *disks.*

Sharing an entire disk means that every folder on it, and therefore every file, is available to everyone on the network. If security isn't a big deal at your place (because it's just you and a couple of family members, for example), this feature can be a timesaving convenience that spares you the trouble of sharing every new folder you create.

On the other hand, people with privacy concerns generally prefer to share individual *folders.* By sharing only a folder or two, you can keep *most* of the stuff on your hard drive private, out of view of curious network comrades. For that matter, sharing only a folder or two does *them* a favor, too, by making it easier for them to find the files you've made available. This way, they don't have to root through your entire drive looking for the folder they actually need.

Tip: There's one significant difference between working with "local" icons and working with those that sit elsewhere on the network. When you delete a file from another computer on the network (if you're allowed to do so), either by pressing the Delete key or by dragging it to the Recycle Bin, it disappears instantly and permanently, without ever appearing in the Recycle Bin.

You can even use Windows' Search feature to find files elsewhere on the network. This kind of searching can be very slow, however.

Extra Credit: Universal Naming Convention (UNC)

For hard-core nerds, that business of double-clicking icons in the Network folder is for sissies. When they want to call up a shared folder from the network, or even a particular document *in* a shared folder, they just type a special address into the address bar of any folder window, or even the Edge browser—and then press the Enter key. You can also type such addresses into the Run dialog box (press ⊞+R).

It might look like this: *laptop\shared documents\salaries 2016.docx.*

Tip: Actually, you don't have to type nearly that much. The AutoComplete feature may propose the full expression as soon as you type just a few letters of it.

This path format (including the double-backslash before the PC name and a single backslash before a folder name) is called the *Universal Naming Convention (UNC)*. It was devised to create a method of denoting the exact location of a particular file or folder on a network. It also lets network geeks open various folders and files on networked machines without having to use the Network window.

You can use this system in all kinds of interesting ways:

- Open a particular folder like this: *computer name\folder name.*

- You can also substitute the IP address for the computer instead of using its name, like this: *192.168.1.44\my documents.*

- You can even substitute the name of a shared *printer* for the folder name.

- As described later in this chapter, Windows can even access shared folders that sit elsewhere on the Internet (offline backup services, for example). You can call these items onto your screen (once you're online) just by adding *http:* before the UNC code and using regular forward slashes instead of backward slashes, like this: *http://Computer Name/Folder Name.*

Tip: A great place to type UNC addresses is in the address bar at the top of any File Explorer window.

Mapping Shares to Drive Letters

If you access network shares on a regular basis, you may want to consider another access technique, called *mapping shares*. Using this trick, you can assign a *letter* to a particular shared disk or folder on the network. Just as your hard drive is called C: and your floppy drive is A:, you can give your Family Stuff folder the letter F: and the backup drive in the kitchen the letter J:.

Doing so confers several benefits. First, these disks and folders now appear directly in the My PC window. Getting to them this way can be faster than navigating to the Network window.

Second, when you choose File→Open from within one of your applications, you'll be able to jump directly to a particular shared folder instead of having to double-click, ever deeper, through the icons in the Open File dialog box. You can also use the mapped drive letter in pathnames anywhere you would use a path on a local drive, such as the Run dialog box, a File→Save As dialog box, or the Command Line.

FREQUENTLY ASKED QUESTION

Accessing Windows 10 Machines from XP, Vista, Mac...

How do I access my Windows 10 PC from my non–Windows 10 machines?

Piece of cake. All versions of Windows use the same networking scheme, so you can share files freely among PCs using different Windows versions.

Once some files are shared (on any PC), here's how to find them:

In Windows 7 or Windows Vista: Choose Start→Network.

In Windows XP or Windows Me: Choose Start→My Network Places.

On the Mac: Just look in the Sidebar of any Finder window in the Shared category. Open the Workgroup icon, if you see it, and then double-click the name of the computer you want. Enter your PC account's name and password. (You'll probably have trouble if your PC account doesn't have a password.)

Now you see icons that correspond to the computers on your network (including your own machine). That should be all there is to it.

If you don't see the Windows computers, it may be because all the machines don't have the same *workgroup* name. (A workgroup is a cluster of networked machines.) To change your Windows XP computer's workgroup name to match, choose Start→Control Panel, click "Performance and Maintenance," and then open System. Click the Computer Name tab, and then select Change.

To change a Vista PC's workgroup name, choose Start→Control Panel; click System and Maintenance; open System. Under the "Computer Name, Domain, and Workgroup Settings" heading, click Change Settings.

To change a Mac's workgroup name, open ⌘→System Preferences→Network. Click Advanced→WINS, and type right into the Workgroup box.

And to change your Windows 7/8/10 machine's name, type *rename* into the Start menu or search box; click "Change workgroup name" under Settings. Click Change, and enjoy the box shown here.

[Dialog box: Computer Name/Domain Changes. You can change the name and the membership of this computer. Changes might affect access to network resources. Computer name: Casey-PC. Full computer name: Casey-PC. More... Member of: Domain: / Workgroup: WORKGROUP. OK / Cancel]

To map a drive letter to a disk or folder, open the Computer window. (In any File Explorer window, click This PC in the navigation pane at left.) Then, on the Ribbon's Computer tab, click "Map network drive."

The Map Network Drive dialog box appears, as shown in Figure 21-9.

2. **Using the drop-down list, choose a drive letter.**

   You can select any unused letter you like (except B, which is still reserved for the second floppy disk drive that PCs don't have anymore).

Figure 21-9:
Top: Choose a letter, any letter. Then choose a folder, any folder.

Bottom: You've just turned a folder into a drive, complete with its own drive letter—and added instant access to the navigation pane.

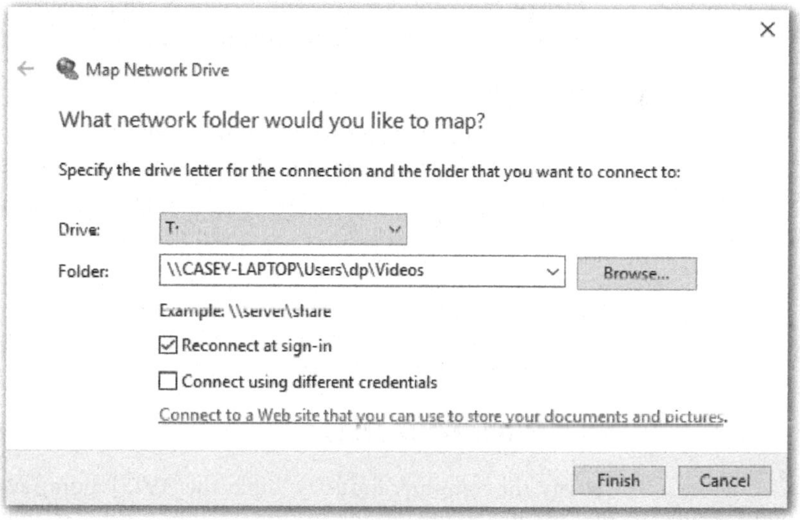

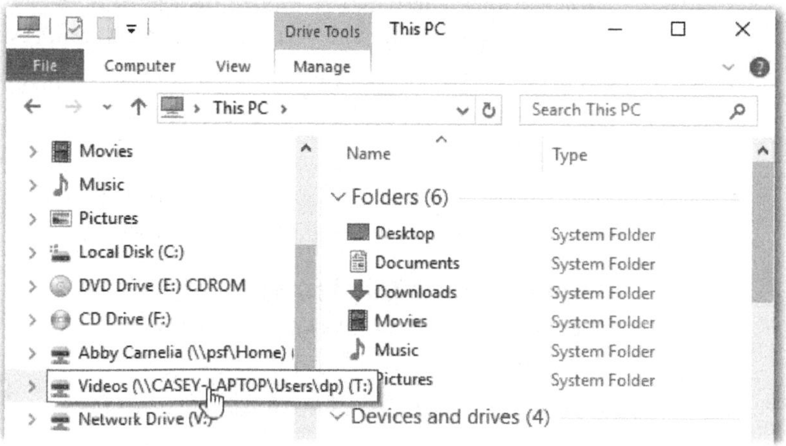

3. **Indicate which folder or disk you want this letter to represent.**

   You can type its UNC code into the Folder box, choose from the drop-down list of recently accessed folders, or click Browse.

Tip: Most people use the mapping function for disks and drives elsewhere on the network, but there's nothing to stop you from mapping a folder that's sitting right there on your own PC.

---

4. **To make this letter assignment stick, turn on "Reconnect at sign-in."**

   If you don't use this option, Windows forgets this assignment the next time you turn on the computer. (Use the "Connect using different credentials" option if your account name on the shared folder's machine isn't the same as it is on this one.)

5. **Click Finish.**

   A window opens to display the contents of the folder or disk. If you don't want to work with any files at the moment, just close the window.

From now on (depending on your setting in step 4), that shared disk or folder shows up in your navigation pane, as shown at bottom in Figure 21-9.

Tip: If you see a red X on one of these mapped icons, it means that the PC on which one of the shared folders or disks resides is either off the network or is turned off completely.

Sharing a DVD Drive

Clearly, the computer industry thinks the DVD is going away. More and more people rent movies by streaming them from the Internet instead of renting a disc. More and more software comes as a download instead of on a CD or a DVD. And more and more new laptop models (not to mention tablets) don't even come with DVD drives.

But discs aren't completely dead. Sooner or later, you might wind up wishing you had a DVD drive in your tablet or superthin laptop.

Fortunately, there's a workaround. If another Windows PC on your network has a DVD drive, you can share it over the network so that it appears on the screen of your laptop or tablet. Figure 21-10 shows how to set it up.

On the Tablet or Thin Laptop

Once you've shared the DVD drive, here's how to access it from another machine on the network:

1. **Open the This PC window. At the left side, click Network.**

   Icons for all the shared computers appear.

2. Double-click the name of the computer with the shared drive.

Its window opens.

3. Double-click the shared drive; now you can work with whatever disc is inside it.

As a final step, consider *mapping* this drive, as described earlier. That way, it will always show up on your tablet or laptop as though it were built right in.

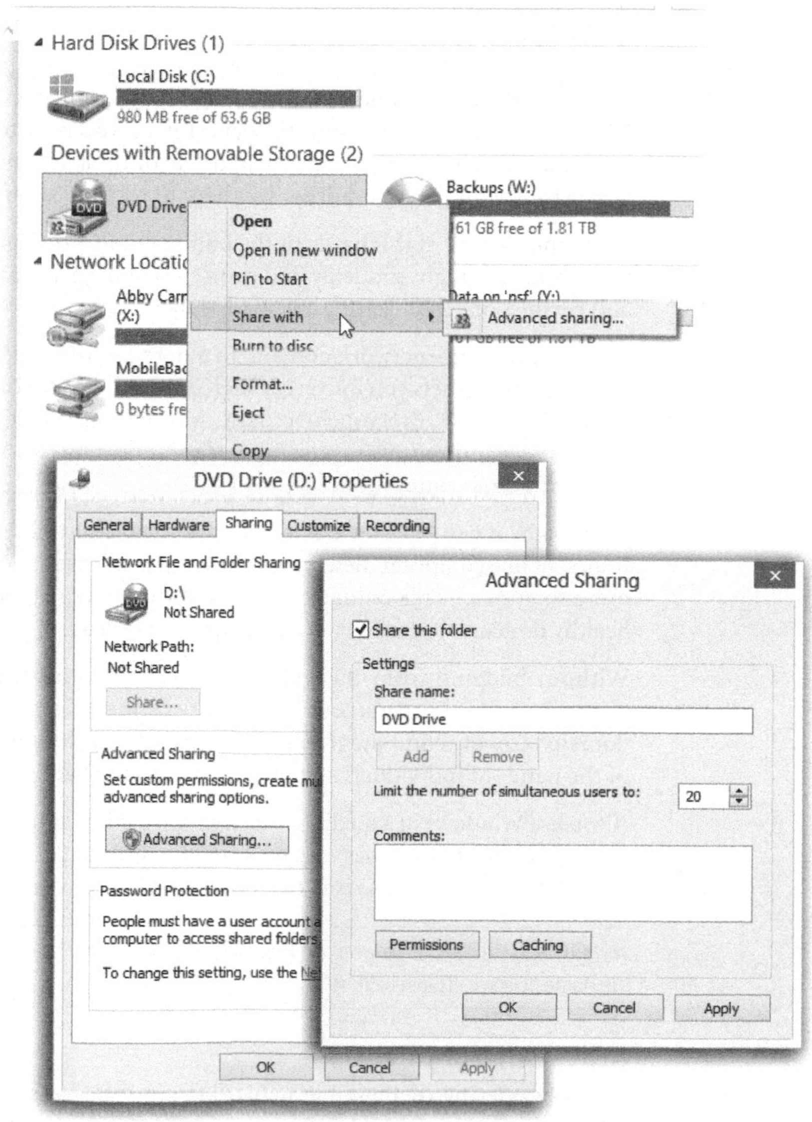

Figure 21-10:
Here's the procedure for sharing your DVD drive so that it appears in the Computer windows of other machines on the network.

Top: In the This PC window, right-click the DVD drive and share it.

Bottom left: Click Advanced Sharing.

Bottom right: Share the drive and name it.

Corporate Networks

Connecting to other machines in your house or small office is one thing. In huge companies, though, the ones that are Microsoft's bread and butter, networking is a full-time job—for a whole staff of people. These are the network administrators, who have studied the complexities of corporate networking for years. And their work—the sprawling, building-wide (or even worldwide) company networks—are called *domain* networks.

The Domain

On a regular small-office network, nobody else on a workgroup network can access the files on your PC unless you've created an account for them on your machine. Whenever somebody new joins the department, you have to create another new account; when people leave, you have to delete or disable their accounts. If something goes wrong with your hard drive, you have to recreate all of the accounts.

If you multiply all of this hassle by the number of PCs on a growing network, it's easy to see how you might suddenly find yourself spending more time managing accounts and permissions than getting any work done.

The solution is the network domain. In a domain, you only have a single name and password, which gets you into every shared PC and printer on the network that you're authorized to use. Everyone's account information resides on a central computer called a *domain controller*—a computer so important, it's usually locked away in a closet or a data-center room.

Most domain networks have at least two domain controllers with identical information, so if one computer dies, the other one can take over. (Some networks have many more than two.) This redundancy is a critical safety net, because without a happy, healthy domain controller, the entire network is dead.

Without budging from their chairs, network administrators can use a domain controller to create new accounts, manage existing ones, and assign permissions. The domain takes the equipment-management and security concerns of the network out of the hands of individuals and puts them into the hands of trained professionals.

If you use Windows in a medium- to large-sized company, you probably use a domain every day. You may not have been aware of it, but that's no big deal; knowing what's going on under your nose isn't especially important to your ability to get work done.

Note: One key difference between the Home and Pro versions of Windows 10 is that computers running the Home edition can't join a domain.

Active Directory

One key offering of these big networks—and the Windows Server software that runs them—is an elaborate program called *Active Directory*. It's a single, centralized database that stores every scrap of information about the hardware, software, and people on the network.

Active Directory lets network administrators maintain an enormous hierarchy of computers. A multinational corporation with tens of thousands of employees in offices worldwide can all be part of one Active Directory domain, with servers distributed in hundreds of locations, all connected by wide-area networking links. (A group of domains is known as a *tree*. Huge networks might even have more than one tree; if so, they're called—yes, you guessed it—a *forest*.)

Unless you've decided to take up the rewarding career of network administration, you'll never have to install an Active Directory domain controller, design a directory tree, or create domain objects. However, you very well may encounter the Active Directory at your company. You can use it to search for the mailing address of somebody else on the network, for example, or locate a printer that can print on both sides of the page at once. Having some idea of the directory's structure can help in these cases.

Three Ways Life Is Different on a Domain

The domain and workgroup personalities of Windows are quite different. Here are some of the most important differences.

GEM IN THE ROUGH

Accessing Macs Across the Network

When it comes to networking, Macs are people, too.

Windows is perfectly capable of letting you rifle through a Mac's contents from across the network. Here's how to set that up.

On the Mac, choose → System Preferences. Click Sharing, and then turn on File Sharing. Click Options.

Now you see the dialog box shown here. Turn on "Share files and folders using SMB." Then specify *which* Mac user accounts you want to be able to access; enter their passwords as necessary, and then click Done.

(Before you close System Preferences, you might notice that a line in the middle of the dialog box says "Windows users can access your computer at smb://192.168.1.203." Those numbers are the Mac's IP address. You'd need it only if you decided to access the Mac by typing its UNC

code [page 611] into your Windows address bar, like this: \\102.168.1.203.)

On the PC, proceed exactly as though you were trying to connect to another Windows PC. The Mac's name shows up in the Network section of the navigation pane (left side of any File Explorer window).

When you click the Mac's name, you see the dialog box shown at bottom in Figure 21-8. Enter your Mac account name and password, and turn on "Remember my credentials" (so that you won't be bothered for a name or password the next time you perform this amazing act). Click OK.

Now your Mac home folder opens on the screen before you. Feel free to work with those files exactly as though they were in a folder on your PC. Détente has never been so easy.

Logging on

What you see when you log onto your PC is somewhat different when you're part of a domain. The Lock screen instructs you to press Ctrl+Alt+Delete to log on. (This step is a security precaution, described in the box below.)

You can now type your user name and password. To save you time, Windows fills in the User Name box with whatever name was used the last time somebody logged in.

Browsing the domain

When your PC is part of the domain, all of its resources—printers, shared files, and so on—magically appear in your desktop windows, the Network window, and so on).

Searching the domain

You can read all about the search box in Chapter 3. But when you're on a domain, this tool becomes far more powerful—and more interesting.

When you open the Network window as described above, the Ribbon changes to include an option to Search Active Directory. Click it to open a special dialog box that can search the entire corporation at once.

GEM IN THE ROUGH

The Double-Thick Security Trick

If you use Windows in a corporation, the Lock screen probably bears a message when you first turn on the machine. You don't proceed to the regular Login screen until you first press Ctrl+Alt+Delete.

This somewhat inconvenient setup is intended as a security feature. By forcing you to press Ctrl+Alt+Delete to bypass the initial Welcome box, Windows rules out the possibility that some sneaky program (such as a Trojan-horse program), designed to *look* like the regular Login screen, is posing as the regular Login screen—in order to "capture" the name and password you type there.

Press Ctrl+Alt+Delete to sign in

This two-layer login system is what you get when you add your PC to a network domain during the Windows installation. If you want to use it on a workgroup machine, you can, but you have to do a little digging to find it. Press ⊞+R to open the Run dialog box; type *control Userpasswords2,* and then press Enter. Authenticate yourself. You see the program shown on page 573—the old-style User Accounts box. Click the Advanced tab.

At the bottom of the Advanced tab, turn on "Require users to press Ctrl+Alt+Delete," and then click OK. From now on, turning on the PC greets you not with a Login screen, but with the unfakeable Lock screen shown here.

Using this box, you can search for things like:

- **Users, Contacts, and Groups.** Use this option to search the network for a particular person or network group. You can find out someone's telephone number or mailing address, or see what users belong to a particular group.

- **Computers.** This option helps you find a certain PC in the domain. It's of interest primarily to network administrators, because it lets them manage many of the PCs' functions by remote control.

- **Printers.** In a large office, it's possible that you might not know where you can find a printer with certain features—tabloid-size paper, for example, or double-sided printing. That's where this option comes in handy; it lets you find the printing features you need.

FREQUENTLY ASKED QUESTION

FTP Sites and Other Online Disks

How do I bring an FTP server, or one of those Web-based backup drives, onto my PC?

The trick to bringing these servers online is to open the Computer window. On the Ribbon's Computer tab, click "Add a network location."

When the wizard appears, click Next. Then, on the second screen, click "Choose a custom network location." Click Next.

Finally you arrive at the critical screen, where you can type in the address of the Web site, FTP site, or other network location that you want your new shortcut to open.

Into the first text box, you can type any of these network addresses:

The UNC code. As described earlier in this chapter, a UNC code pinpoints a particular shared folder on the network. For example, if you want to open the shared folder named FamilyBiz on the computer named Dad, enter \\dad\family-biz. Capitalization doesn't matter. Or, to open a specific file, you could enter something like \\dad\finances\budget.xls.

http://website/folder. To see what's in a folder called Customers on a company Web site called BigBiz.com, enter

http://bigbiz.com/customers. (You can't just type in any old Web address. It has to be a Web site that's been specifically designed to serve as a "folder" containing files.)

ftp://ftp.website/folder. This is the address format for FTP sites. For example, if you want to use a file in a folder named Bids on a company site named WeBuyStuff.com, enter *ftp://ftp.wcbuystuff.com/bids*.

What happens when you click Next depends on the kind of address you specified. If it was an FTP site, you're offered the chance to specify your user name. (Access to every FTP site requires a user name and password. You won't be asked for the password until you actually try to open the newly created folder shortcut.)

Click Finish. Your network shortcut now appears in the Network Location area in the Computer window. The wizard also offers to connect to and open the corresponding folder.

You can work with these remote folders exactly as though they were sitting on your own hard drive. The only difference is that because you're actually communicating with a hard drive via the Internet, the slower speed may make it feel as if your PC has been drugged.

Part Seven: Appendixes

7

Appendix A: Installing & Upgrading to Windows 10

Appendix B: Where'd It Go?

Appendix C: Master List of Keyboard Shortcuts & Gestures

Installing & Upgrading to Windows 10

I f your computer came with Windows 10 already on it, you can skip this appendix—for now. But if you're running an earlier version of Windows and want to savor the Win10 experience, this appendix describes how to install the new operating system on your computer.

Before You Begin

Most of the work involved in installing Windows 10 takes place well before the installation software even approaches your computer. You have some research and planning to do, especially if you want to avoid a weekend in Upgrade Hell.

For example, you must ensure that your PC is beefy enough to handle Windows 10. You also have to decide which of two types of installation you want to perform: an *upgrade* or a *clean install.* (More on this in a moment.)

If you opt for the clean install (a process that involves *erasing your drive completely*), you must back up your data. Finally, you have to gather all the software bits and pieces you need in order to perform the installation.

Hardware Requirements

Windows 10 runs on all the same computers as Windows 7 and 8 did; its system requirements are no steeper. Your machine needs a 1-gigahertz processor (or faster), 2 gigabytes of memory (or more), and 20 gigabytes of free hard drive space (or more).

Microsoft also points out, helpfully, that the touchscreen features require a touchscreen.

What You Have to Lose

Upgrading to Windows 10 from an earlier version doesn't necessarily mean that all your stuff will survive the journey. Here's how the transition might go, depending on the version you have now:

- **Upgrading from Windows 8.1.** Your files, settings, and programs all survive. You will, however, lose Windows Media Center, Hearts, and Solitaire.

- **Upgrading from Windows 8.0.** Actually, don't bother. If your machine has Windows 8, it's infinitely smarter to upgrade it to 8.1 before the Windows 10 adventure. It's a free, easy upgrade that you should have done a long time ago.

- **Upgrading from Windows 7.** Almost everything survives the transition: files, settings, and programs. Windows 7's desktop gadgets go away, though.

- **Windows XP, Windows Vista.** You have to start up from an external drive and perform a clean install; none of your files, settings, or programs are preserved.

The Free Upgrade

If your computer is starting out with Windows 7, Windows 8, or Windows 8.1, get psyched: For the first time in Windows history, Windows 10 is a *free upgrade*. This company *really* wants the world to get with its program.

There is some fine print, of course:

- Windows 10 is free only if you're *upgrading from Windows 7, 8, or 8.1*. If you have some older version, it's not free. If you intend to install Windows 10 onto a PC you've just built yourself, it's not free.

Tip: If you're not eligible for the free upgrade, Microsoft charges $120 for Windows 10 Home or $200 for Windows 10 Pro. But here's something worth considering: For $200, you could get a *whole new computer*—with Windows 10 already on it.

- The RT and Enterprise versions of Windows aren't eligible for the free upgrade.

- Microsoft says that the free-upgrade offer is good at least until the beginning of August 2016. At that point, nobody knows if the deal will continue.

- The free upgrade gives you the same flavor of Windows as what you have. If you have Windows 7/8 Home, you'll get Windows 10 Home. If you have Windows 7/8 Pro, you'll get Windows 10 Pro. See the pattern there?

How to Upgrade to Windows 10

Suppose you're sitting in front of your computer—one that's currently running Windows 7 or 8.1.

The Taskbar Method (The Get Windows 10 App)

If you're running Windows 7 or 8.1, then you probably woke one morning to see a strange sight: a ⊞ logo near the right end of your taskbar. When you click it, you see something like Figure A-1.

Figure A-1:
This little balloon means that Windows 10 is ready to download—for free. Click to open the Get Windows 10 app, whose instructions guide you through the download and install process.

If you don't see that balloon, it's probably because:

- **You don't have a legal, activated copy** of Windows 7 or 8.1.

- **You don't have the *latest* versions of those.** That is, you need Windows 7 with Service Pack 1, or Windows 8.1 (not plain Windows 8).

- **You don't have automatic Windows Update turned on.**

- **You're connected to a corporate network domain.**

The balloon invites you to "reserve" your copy of Windows 10. It leads you to the Get Windows 10 app, which inspects your PC to make sure it's compatible and then auto-downloads the Windows 10 installer.

Tip: If you select "View report" in the Get Windows 10 app, it lets you know how many of your apps and drivers won't be compatible with Windows 10. Good to know.

Eventually, a happy screen appears, announcing: "Your free Windows 10 upgrade is here!"

Click "OK, let's continue." After a moment, you're shown some legalese; click Accept.

Now you have a choice: "Schedule it for later," or "Start the upgrade now." If you choose to proceed now, the rest is automatic—almost. You encounter only a few screens:

- **Welcome back.** Click Next.

- **Get going fast.** Do you want to accept Microsoft's "Express settings," which pertain to privacy, advertising, and auto-connecting to WiFi hotspots? (If not, click "Customize settings.")

- **New apps for the new Windows.** Here's a little blurb, alerting you to the Photos, Music, Edge, and Movies & TV apps. Hit Next.

- **Setup screens.** Sit it out while a few colorful setup screens entertain you with quippy messages about the joys of Windows.

And then you arrive at the desktop. All of your files, folders, programs, and settings are still in place. Welcome to Windows 10!

The Flash-Drive Method

If that taskbar thing never popped up for you, or you ignored it, you're not out of luck. You can go get Windows 10 yourself. But here's the thing: The days of buying Windows in a box are over. Nowadays, you download it. In fact, Microsoft offers a little program that automatically downloads Windows 10 and copies the installer to a flash drive (or DVD) that you supply.

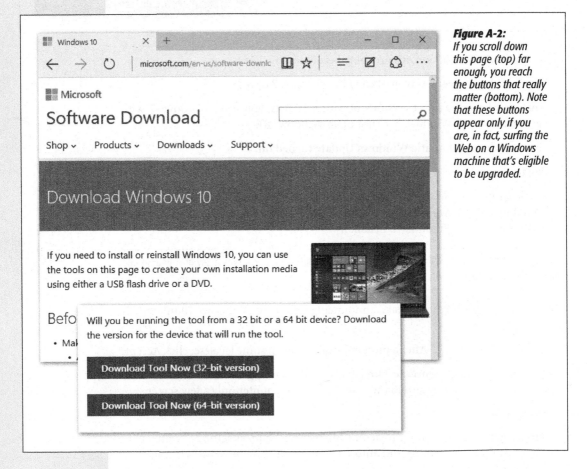

Figure A-2:
If you scroll down this page (top) far enough, you reach the buttons that really matter (bottom). Note that these buttons appear only if you are, in fact, surfing the Web on a Windows machine that's eligible to be upgraded.

Create the flash drive

The routine goes like this:

1. **On your PC, go to the Windows 10 download page (Figure A-2).**

   For the U.S. edition of Windows, that address is *www.microsoft.com/en-us/ software-download/windows10.*

   Now you need to know which *architecture* of Windows you want: 32-bit or 64-bit (Figure A-2, bottom). Choose the one that corresponds to the kind of computer you have.

Tip: If you're not sure, open your Control Panel. Choose "System and security." Under System, you'll see what kind of machine you've got.

---

2. **Click either "Download Tool Now (32-bit version)" or "Download Tool Now (64-bit version)."**

   The download process begins immediately. Click Run when your browser offers it.

   After a moment, you're asked: Do you want to upgrade your computer right now? Or make an installation flash drive (or disc) that you can use to upgrade other machines?

   If you choose "Upgrade this PC now" (and then hit Next), the installer springs into action, as described in the next section.

   For the sake of argument, though, suppose your intention here has been to create an installation flash drive or DVD.

4. **Choose "Create installation media for another PC"; click Next.**

   The little app begins downloading Windows 10 from the Internet. It's about 3 gigabytes, so it may take a while.

   When that's over, you see the screen in Figure A-3.

5. **Use the pop-up menus to specify your language, Windows 10 edition (Home or Pro), and architecture (32-bit or 64-bit).**

   For the architecture question, see step 1 above.

6. **Hit Next.**

   Now you're asked what kind of installation drive you want to create: A flash drive or a DVD.

7. **Choose "USB flash drive" or "ISO file."**

   Insert a blank flash drive that's at least 4 gigabytes in size. Windows goes to town, building you an installer on that drive.

If you don't have a flash drive, you can opt for the ISO option. It creates a disk image of the type described on page 171. You can install directly from this file, or you can burn it onto a blank DVD, if that's how you prefer to go.

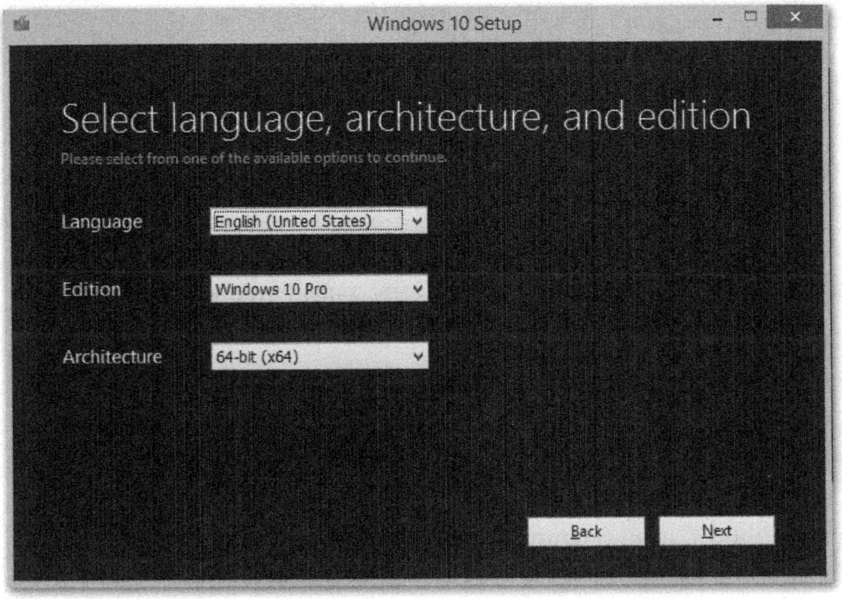

Figure A-3:
For the edition question, "Windows 10 Pro" is the correct answer if you'll be upgrading from any Pro or Ultimate version of Windows. If you'll be upgrading from any other version (Home, Basic, Starter), then choose "Windows 10 Home."

The Upgrade, Screen by Screen

Whether you start the upgrade cycle straight from the upgrade tool or from a flash drive, ISO, or DVD, the actual process is pretty much the same.

Preparing for the Installation

You have only a short checklist left to follow:

- **Update your virus program and scan for viruses—then turn it off.** If you're updating an existing copy of Windows, *turn off* your virus checker. Also turn off auto-loading programs like non-Microsoft firewall software and Web ad blockers.

- **Gather updated, Windows 10–compatible drivers** for all your computer's components. Graphics and audio cards are particularly likely to need updates, so be sure to check the manufacturers' Web sites—and driver-information sites like *www.windrivers.com* and *www.driverguide.com*—and download any new drivers you find there.

- **Plug in.** If it's a laptop or tablet you're upgrading, keep it plugged in to power during the upgrade; if its battery dies midway through, you're in trouble.

- **Back up your world.** Use File History (page 526). Upgrades that go wrong are very rare. But you don't want to be that one in a million who loses files.

If you've gone to all this trouble and preparation, the Windows installation process can be surprisingly smooth. The Windows 10 installer is much less painful than the ones for previous versions of Windows.

You're about to experience a series of instruction screens, with a Next button to click at the bottom of each one. The whole process takes about an hour.

Phase 1: Run the installer

Double-click the installer, called Setup.exe, whether it's on your hard drive, a flash drive, a DVD, or the downloaded ISO image that you've extracted from its .zip file.

Note: If the installer is on a DVD or a flash drive, insert it while running your *old* copy of Windows and then shut down your PC. When you restart it, it should start up from the disc or flash drive. (If it doesn't, go online to read up about how to make your PC start up from a DVD or a flash drive.)

These are some of the screens you'll encounter:

- **Check for updates.** By all means, let the installer see if there are even newer pieces of Windows 10 to download.

- **License terms.** Review the work of Microsoft's lawyers, and then accept it.

- **Language.** You're asked to specify your preferred language, currency, time, and keyboard formats right up front—this language, after all, is the one the installer will use to communicate with you.

- **Install now.** Click it.

Note: In some countries, a huge percentage of all copies of Windows are illegal duplicates. To fight that problem, Microsoft invented *activation*—a serial-number system that prevents you from installing one copy of Windows on even *two* computers. That's right: If you have a desktop PC as well as a laptop, you have to have a second product key. (Of course, the Windows 10 free upgrade is available to as many computers as you own.)

- **Which type of installation?** Here's where you choose between Upgrade and Custom installations.

  Upgrade means converting your existing, older Windows version to Windows 10, preserving as much of your stuff (files, settings, and programs) as possible. This is the choice you want if you're taking advantage of the free upgrade offer; you won't be required to type in a serial number (product key).

Tip: Even if you intend to do a clean install, start by doing the Upgrade. That's the only way to get the clean install for free, too, as described on page 632.

  Custom gives you the chance to partition your hard drive and create a dual-booting installation, as described previously. Custom is also the only option if your hard drive has no copy of Windows, or has a really old one like Windows XP.

Custom, however, requires a product key (purchased serial number), so you won't get Windows 10 for free.

Now the installer itself runs, chugging away quietly. The computer may restart a couple of times along the way.

Phase 2: Establish settings

When the installation is nearly complete, a few more screens ask you to choose the following:

- **A name for this computer (no spaces or punctuation allowed).**

- **Which WiFi network you want to join.**

- **If you want to accept "Express settings."** These are settings that concern privacy, automatic downloads of Windows patches, security, and local network connections. They're actually fine for most people, but if you'd like to review these factory settings and adjust them, then click Customize.

POWER USERS' CLINIC

Dual Booting

In the advanced setup know as dual booting, you install Windows 10 onto the *same* PC that contains an older version of Windows, maintaining both of them side by side. Then, each time you turn on the machine, it asks you which operating system you want to run for this computing session.

Dual booting comes in handy when you have some program or hardware gadget that works with one operating system but not the other. For example, if you have a scanner with software that runs on Windows 7 but not Windows 10, you can start up in 7 only when you want to use the scanner.

Choose an operating system
Windows 10
Windows 7

If you intend to dual boot, keep this in mind: You can't install both operating systems onto the same hard drive partition. If you did, your programs would become horribly confused.

Instead, keep your two Windows versions separate using one of these avenues:

- **Buy a second hard drive.** Use it for one of the two operating systems.

- **Back up your hard drive,** erase it completely, and then *partition* it, which means dividing it so that each chunk shows up with its own icon, name, and drive letter. Then install each operating system on a separate disk partition, using the "clean install" instructions in this appendix.

If you're less technically inclined, you might prefer to buy a program like Acronis Disk Director. Not only does it let you create a new partition on your hard drive without erasing it first, but it's also flexible and easy.

There's just one wrinkle with dual booting: If you install Windows 10 onto a separate partition (or a different drive), as you must, you won't find any of your existing programs listed in the Start menu, and your desktop won't be configured the way it is in your original operating system. You'll generally wind up having to reinstall every program into your new Windows world, and to reestablish all your settings, exactly as though the Windows 10 "side" were a brand-new PC.

Phase 3: Sign in

Next, you're asked to sign in with your Microsoft account name and password—and if you don't have one, you can create one on the spot. See page 558 for a walk-through of the account-creation process.

Phase 4: Set up OneDrive

At this point, Windows tells you about how cool it is that Windows is integrated with your OneDrive (page 161). It suggests that you accept these settings:

- **Photos** you take with this computer's camera will be copied automatically to your OneDrive (in lower-resolution versions), for ease in sharing.

- Windows will propose storing **new documents you create** on your OneDrive. (You'll be able to override that setting each time you save a particular document—to store it on your actual computer.)

- **Your Windows settings** will be backed up on the OneDrive, too. If you ever get a new computer, they'll be auto-set for you.

If you like the sound of those settings, hit Next. If not, choose "Turn off these OneDrive settings (not recommended)." (Either way, you can always change your mind later.)

Phase 5: A soft landing

Finally, against a color-changing background, Windows keeps you posted on its progress, saying things like, "Creating your account," "Finalizing your settings," "Installing apps," "Your PC will be ready in just a moment"—and then boom! There you are at the desktop, and you're ready to begin.

The Clean Install

Upgrading, as described above, retains all your existing settings and data files. Sounds great, right? Who wouldn't want to avoid having to redo all those settings?

There are two situations when you might prefer a clean install:

- **When you're working with an** *empty* **PC or hard drive**—one that doesn't already have Windows on it.

- **When you have a copy of Windows already**—but as a troubleshooting or speed step, you want to reformat your disk, wiping out everything on it. You wind up with a fresh system, 100 percent free of any little glitches and inconsistencies that have built up over the years. (Of course, you'll also have to take the time to reinstall all your programs, reconfigure your personalized settings, recreate your network connections, and so on.)

Note: You must also do a clean install if you're upgrading from Windows Vista or Windows XP, or if you're going from a 32-bit version of Windows to the 64-bit version.

Here's how to go about it. Note that if the PC *isn't* new and empty, there's a step 0 before step 1:

0. If your computer already has Windows 7 or 8.1 on it, *upgrade* it to Windows 10.

That may sound like strange advice. Why would you do the upgrade, if the whole point is to wipe out the disk and start from scratch?

Simple: So you can get Windows 10 for free.

If you perform the upgrade, as described on the previous pages, Microsoft will remember your PC and its free Windows 10 serial number (product key). *Then* you can erase it and do a clean install.

If you *don't* upgrade first, then attempting a clean install will require a product key—and you'll have to pay for it!

All right. Now here's the real clean-install ritual. It assumes that you've made yourself a Windows 10 installation flash drive or DVD, as described on page 627.

1. Turn on your PC, insert the DVD or flash drive containing the Windows 10 installer, and then shut down the PC.

The goal here is to start up from the flash drive/DVD.

2. Start the computer. Just after it chimes, hold down any key.

That's usually the trick for starting up from a DVD or a flash drive.

If it doesn't work, and the computer starts up into your existing Windows version, you probably have to fool around with the machine's BIOS or UEFI settings. To find out how you do that, visit your computer maker's Web site.

Eventually, the Install Windows page appears.

3. Specify your language, regional preferences, and keyboard language; hit Next.

Now the Install Windows screen appears.

4. Select Install Windows.

Now the setup program wants you to enter your product key (serial number).

If, in step 0, you wisely performed the Windows 10 upgrade before doing all of this, all you have to do here is hit Skip. The installer checks with Microsoft, confirms that you're not some software pirate, and proceeds.

If you didn't perform step 0 (because, for example, you weren't starting with Windows 7 or 8 to begin with), you'll have to enter an actual product key at this point—one that you bought from Microsoft. It's in a confirmation email that Microsoft sent you.

5. Choose Skip, or enter the product key. Hit Next.

A page of legalese appears.

6. Hit "I accept the license terms." Hit Next.

Now comes the important part: The "Which type of installation do you want?" screen (Figure A-4, top).

7. **Choose Custom, and set up your partition.**

Windows wants to know, "Where do you want to install Windows?"

It shows you a list of the *partitions* on your hard drive (Figure A-4, bottom). Unless you've set up your hard drive for dual booting as described earlier, you probably have only one.

Select the name of the partition (or choose some unallocated space) on which you want to install Windows, and then hit Next. Use the "Drive options (advanced)" link at the bottom of this window to delete, create, or format partitions. To create a dual-boot situation, you have to *erase a partition completely* to make it ready for Windows 10.

Figure A-4:
Top: Use the buttons on this screen to indicate whether you want a clean installation or an upgrade installation.

Bottom: You have to install Windows onto its own partition.

This window displays all your drives and partitions; the "Drive options" link gives you tools to erase partitions or delete them (thus merging their space together). Just remember that deleting a partition involves losing everything on it.

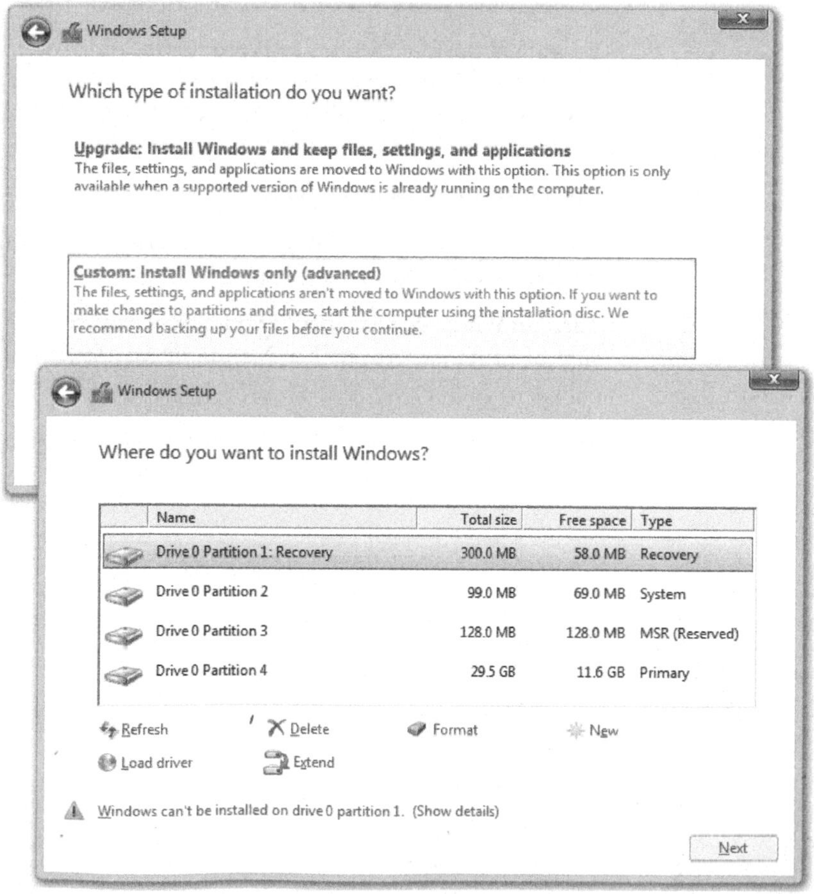

Name	Total size	Free space	Type
Drive 0 Partition 1: Recovery	300.0 MB	58.0 MB	Recovery
Drive 0 Partition 2	99.0 MB	69.0 MB	System
Drive 0 Partition 3	128.0 MB	128.0 MB	MSR (Reserved)
Drive 0 Partition 4	29.5 GB	11.6 GB	Primary

8. **After the formatting process is complete, click Next.**

The Setup program begins copying files to the partition you selected and, eventually, restarts the computer a time or two.

The regular installation process concludes the same way an upgrade does; see "Phase 2: Establish settings" on page 630.

Jobs Number 1, 2, 3...

Once you've installed Windows 10, you can start using the computer however you like. But if you're smart, you'll make these tasks your first order of business:

- **Transfer files from your old computer, if necessary.** The old Windows Easy Transfer program no longer comes with Windows, so you'll have to use file sharing, an external hard drive, or something like your OneDrive to bring all your stuff over.

Tip: If it's worth money to do the job right, programs like LapLink PCmover or Todo PCTrans can bring over not just your files and programs, but also your settings and every last shred of your old PC's account.

- **Download the free versions of Word, Excel, and PowerPoint.** The Windows app store offers Word Mobile, Excel Mobile, and PowerPoint Mobile. These are clean, basic, touchscreen-friendly versions of Microsoft's famous software suite. (Of course, if you have the real desktop versions of these, all the better.)

- **Customize the Start menu (page 22).**

- **Add users.** That means adding *accounts* to a PC that will be used by more than one person, as described in Chapter 19.

- **Turn on Windows Defender.** If you have a new PC, and it came with a trial version of antivirus software like Norton or McAfee, you'd be wise to mutter, "But Windows comes with its own antivirus software!"

Well done! Now uninstall the trialware and turn on Windows Defender (page 417).

The adventure begins!

Where'd It Go?

As the saying goes, you can't make an omelette without breaking a few eggs. And on the road to Windows 10, Microsoft broke enough eggs to make a Texan soufflé. Features got moved, renamed, and ripped out completely.

If you're fresh from Windows 7, Windows Vista, Windows XP, or even Windows 8, you might spend your first few days with Windows 10 wondering where things went. Here's a handy cheat sheet of features that aren't in Windows 10 (or aren't where you think they should be).

- **Ad hoc networking.** Microsoft removed the link that lets you set up this PC-to-PC wireless network. The feature is still available, though; page 590 has details.

- **Add or Remove Programs control panel.** The Settings page called "Apps and features" performs the software-removal function now. No Control Panel applet remains to *add* software, because every program these days comes with its *own* installer.

- **Aero.** Amazing. Microsoft must have spent tens of millions of dollars advertising the animated eye candy known as Aero in Windows 7: see-through window edges, flippy window switching, and so on. It's all gone now.

- **AutoRun.** There's no longer an option for a software installer to run as soon as you insert a flash drive. The bad guys were using it as an evil backdoor to install viruses and other nasties on your PC.

- **Briefcase.** This handy tool for syncing files between two computers has, after several decades, finally been taken out behind the barn and shot. It's gone, replaced by more modern alternatives like OneDrive syncing.

- **CardSpace.** This app was supposed to store your online identities, but Microsoft has abandoned it now.

- **Chess Titans.** No longer one of the included games.

- **Clipbook Viewer.** This handy multi-Clipboard feature is no longer in Windows.

- **Complete PC Backups** (from Vista) have been renamed "system images," and they're alive and well in Windows 10.

- **Contacts.** This Vista address-book entity is gone, replaced by the People app.

- **Desktop cleanup wizard** has gone away. You can't actually pretend that you'll miss it, can you?

- **Desktop gadgets.** Gadgets, and the old Sidebar, went away in Windows 8.

- **Discuss pane.** This Windows XP panel did nothing unless some technically proficient administrator set up something called a SharePoint Portal Server—a corporate software kit that permits chat sessions among employees. Anyway, it's no longer in Windows.

- **Documents & Settings folder.** Now called the Users folder.

- **DVD Maker.** Its full name is Windows Live DVD Maker, and it was part of the downloadable Windows Essentials—which Microsoft has now abandoned.

- **DVD playback.** In Windows 10, Microsoft demoted Windows Media Center but says that it plans to offer a free, basic DVD playback program for Windows 10. In the meantime, you can download a free DVD movie-playback program like VLC. You can download it from this book's "Missing CD" page at *www.missingmanuals.com*.

- **Explorer bar.** Gone.

- **Facebook and Flickr integration in Photos.** The Photos app no longer displays your photos from Flickr and Facebook. Pity.

- **Favorites toolbar.** Favorites are still around, in the sense of Web bookmarks. But the Favorites *toolbar* at the desktop is back in Windows 10, now called the "Quick access" list (page 68).

- **File Recovery.** It's been renamed System Image Recovery (page 519).

- **File types.** In Windows XP, you could define new file types and associate them with programs yourself, using the File Types tab in the Folder Options dialog box. In Windows 10, the File Types tab is gone. There's a similar dialog box now (page 240), but it doesn't let you make up your own file types and associations. It doesn't let you define custom secondary actions, either, or ask Explorer to reveal filename extensions for only specific file types.

- **Files & Settings Transfer Wizard.** Renamed Windows Easy Transfer in Windows 8, and then killed off in Windows 10.

- **Filmstrip view (Explorer windows).** Replaced by the any-size-you-like icon view.

- **Flip 3D.** This animated effect in Windows 7 displayed all open windows as 3D stacked "cards" floating in space. It really wasn't that useful. It's gone now.

- **Folder Options.** Still there, but renamed File Explorer Options.

- **FreeCell.** Windows 10 offers the new, improved Solitaire Collection

- **Gadgets.** Gadgets, of course, were what Mac or Android fans know as widgets: small floating windows that convey useful Internet information, like current stock, news, or weather reports. They were there in Windows 7, but now they've been retired.

- **Games.** There's no longer a Games folder—but the Solitaire collection and the Xbox app ought to see you through.

- **Hardware profiles.** Removed.

- **High performance power plan,** for laptops, is no longer listed in the Power icon on the taskbar. It's available, though, if you open the Power control panel.

- **InkBall.** InkBall is gone (but see "Games," above).

- **IP over FireWire.** Removed.

- **iSCSI Initiator.** Gone for good. Does anybody use iSCSI anymore?

- **Libraries.** They're hidden in Windows 10, but you can make them reappear; see page 72.

- **Mahjong Titans.** Gone, but see "Games," above.

- **Meeting Space.** This was Vista's replacement for NetMeeting, but now Meeting Space is gone, too. If you want to share someone's screen, use Remote Assistance or Remote Desktop. If you want to have audio or video calls, use Skype.

- **Messaging.** The original Windows 8 came with this bare-bones chat and texting app. But since Windows 10 comes with Skype, Messaging no longer exists.

- **Minesweeper.** Gone, but see "Games," above.

- **Movie Maker.** Windows Movie Maker, a basic video-editing app, was part of the downloadable Windows Essentials—meaning that it's gone now.

- **My Computer.** After 20 years, Microsoft has finally changed the name of your machine. In Windows 10, it's now called This PC.

- **My Network Places.** You no longer have to open a special window to see the other computers on your network. They're listed right there in the navigation pane at the left side of every File Explorer window.

- **NetMeeting.** Removed. Well, there's always Skype.

- **Network map.** The Network & Sharing Center used to offer a charming visual map, showing the various connections between your computer, your router, and the Internet itself. In Windows 10, the Network & Sharing Center is still there, but the map is gone.

- **Offline browsing/Offline favorites (Internet Explorer).** In Windows XP, you could right-click a Web page's name in your Favorites menu and store it for later perusal when you were no longer online—complete with whatever pages were linked to it. Internet Explorer would even update such pages automatically each time you got back online. This feature has been reborn as the Reading List in the Edge browser.

- **Outlook Express.** Gone. But there's a new Mail app, described in Chapter 11.

- **"Parent folder" button.** In Windows XP, you could click this button to go up one folder (that is, to see the folder that enclosed the current one). In Windows 10, it's back—it's the ↑ button next to the address bar in any Explorer window.

- **Parental controls.** Now called Family Safety, and expanded quite a bit (page 432).

- **Password protecting a .zip archive.** Removed. In the window of any open .zip file, there's still a column that indicates whether or not each file is password-protected—but there's no way to add such a password yourself.

- **Phishing filter,** the Internet Explorer feature that shields you from phony banking sites, has been renamed SmartScreen filter (page 423).

- **Photo Gallery.** Its full name is Windows Photo Gallery. It was part of Windows Essentials, which is gone now.

- **Pinball.** Gone.

- **Pointer themes.** You can make your cursor bigger or smaller in Windows 10, but the fun cursor designs like 3D-Bronze, 3D-White, Conductor, Dinosaur, Hands 1, Hands 2, Variations, and Windows Animated have been killed off by the No-Fun Committee.

- **PowerToys.** Microsoft seems to have lost its enthusiasm for these freebie software goodie-bag items; they disappeared back in Windows Vista.

- **Previous Versions.** It's now called File Histories, and it's even better.

- **Purble Place.** Nope.

- **Quick Launch toolbar.** Since the entire *taskbar* is pretty much a giant Quick Launch toolbar now, Microsoft took out all visible evidence of the Quick Launch toolbar.

- **Reversi.** Gone.

- **Run command.** It may seem to be missing from the Start menu, but you can find it by *right*-clicking the Start menu. Or you can just press ⊞+R to call it up.

- **Search pane.** Gone. But the new search box (Chapter 3) is infinitely superior.

- **Sidebar.** In Vista, the small, floating, single-purpose apps known as *gadgets* hung out in a panel called the Sidebar. Both it and its gadgets are gone now.

- **SkyDrive program.** You no longer need the desktop program called SkyDrive—its successor, OneDrive, is built right into Windows (page 161).

- **Solitaire.** It's back—now with ads!—as part of the Microsoft Solitaire Collection.

- **Sortable column headings** in File Explorer windows have gone away, except in Details view. That is, there's no longer a row of column headings (Name, Date, Size, Kind...) across the top of every window that you can click to sort the window—except, as noted, in Details view.

- **Spades.** Gone.

- **Stacking,** as an activity for organizing similar files in any Explorer window, arrived in Vista and then departed in Windows 7. (You can clump the contents of library windows only, and only by a few criteria.)

- **Startup Hardware Profiles.** Removed.

- **Taskbar dragging.** You can no longer drag the taskbar's top edge off the screen to hide it manually. You can't drag the taskbar to the middle of the screen anymore, either. And you can't drag a folder to the edge of the screen to turn it into a toolbar. (A guess: Too many people were doing this stuff *accidentally* and then getting frustrated.)

- **Telnet.** Removed.

- **Tip of the Day.** No longer part of Windows. Microsoft must expect you to get your tips from computer books now.

- **TweakUI.** Not available for Windows 10. But there are several billion freeware and shareware programs available to make tweaky little changes to the look of Windows.

- **Users.** This PC Settings pane is now called Accounts, to avoid implying that Microsoft customers are addicts.

- **Wallpaper.** Now called Desktop Background. (Right-click the desktop; from the shortcut menu, choose Personalize.)

- **Web Publishing Wizard.** Gone.

- **What's This? button in dialog boxes.** This little link is gone from Windows dialog boxes, probably because it didn't work in most of them. Now, if help is available in a dialog box, it lurks behind the ? button.

- **Windows 7 File Recovery.** It's been renamed System Image Recovery (page 519).

- **Windows Address Book.** Gone. The only address book left in Windows now is the People app.

- **Windows CardSpace.** This was Microsoft's attempt to save you the repetition of typing out your name and address on every Web form. Unfortunately, it worked only with Web sites that are, ahem, CardSpace-compatible—and there weren't many of them. Now, autofill serves the same purpose much more universally.

- **Windows DVD Maker.** Gone. Apparently nobody uses DVDs anymore.

- **Windows Live Mesh.** Replaced by OneDrive.

- **Windows Experience Index.** It used a weird scale for measuring the horsepower of your PC. It's gone now.

- **Windows Media Center.** This TV-recording program is no longer part of Windows—in fact, if you had it when you installed Windows 10, you may have noticed that it got deleted. Microsoft says that it will offer a free new app, called Windows DVD Player, just for Windows 10.

- **Windows Messenger.** Microsoft's chat program no longer comes preinstalled in Windows, thanks to antitrust legal trouble the company encountered.

- **Windows Movie Maker.** It was part of the downloadable Windows Essentials suite, now discontinued.

- **Windows Picture and Fax Viewer.** This old program's functions have been split. Now you view pictures in the Photos app and faxes in Windows Fax and Scan.

- **Windows Ultimate Extras.** There's no Ultimate version of Windows anymore.

- **Windows XP Mode.** Gone.

- **Xbox Music.** In Windows 10, this app has a much less confusing name: Groove Music.

- **Xbox Video.** In Windows 10, it's been renamed Movies & TV.

Master List of Keyboard Shortcuts & Gestures

H ere it is, by popular, frustrated demand: The master list of every secret (or not-so-secret) keystroke in Windows 10. Clip and post to your monitor (unless, of course, you got this book from the library).

General Windows shortcuts

Help Web site	F1
Open or close the Start menu	⊞
Open or close the Action Center	⊞+A
Speak to Cortana	⊞+C
Search	⊞+Q, ⊞+S
Open the Share panel	⊞+H
Open the Devices panel	⊞+K
Open Settings	⊞+I
Open the System Properties dialog box	⊞+Pause (or +Break)
Display the desktop	⊞+D
(At the desktop:) Highlight notification area	⊞+B
Lock the screen in current orientation	⊞+O
Open File Explorer to the "Quick access" list	⊞+E
Search a File Explorer window	⊞+F
Search for computers (if you're on a network)	Ctrl+⊞+F
Lock your computer or switch accounts	⊞+L
Open the Run dialog box	⊞+R

Choose an external-monitor/projector mode
(Duplicate, Extend, and so on) — ⊞+P

Cycle through notifications — ⊞+V (add Shift to go backward)

Switch to the app that just displayed a notification — Ctrl+⊞+B

Open Ease of Access Center — ⊞+U

Open Narrator — ⊞+Enter

Open secret Utilities menu — ⊞+X

Select all items in a document or window — Ctrl+A

Display properties for the selected item — Alt+Enter

Open a menu (some apps) — Alt+underlined letter

"Click" a menu command
(or other underlined command) — Alt+underlined letter

Open Task Manager — Ctrl+Shift+Esc

Take a screenshot (copied to Clipboard) — Alt+PrtScn

Take a screenshot (saved to Screenshots folder) — ⊞+PrtScn

Prevent the CD from automatically playing — Shift when you insert a CD

File Explorer

Open a new window — Ctrl+N, ⊞+E

Close the current window — Ctrl+W

Create a new folder — Shift+Ctrl+N

Display the bottom/top of the active window — End/Home

Display all subfolders under the selected folder — Num Lock+* on numeric keypad

Show/hide Preview pane — Alt+P

Display the contents of the selected folder — Num Lock+plus (+) on
numeric keypad

Collapse the selected folder — Num Lock+minus (-) on
numeric keypad

Collapse the current selection (if expanded),
or select parent folder — ←

Open the Properties dialog box for selected item — Alt+Enter

Back to the previous folder — Alt+←, Backspace

Next folder — Alt+→

Display the current selection (if it's collapsed),
or select the first subfolder — →

Open the parent folder — Alt+↑

Display all folders above the selected folder — Ctrl+Shift+E

Enlarge/shrink file and folder icons — Ctrl+mouse scroll wheel, or
pinch/spread two fingers
on the laptop trackpad

Select the address bar — Alt+D, Ctrl+L

Display the address bar Recents list	F4
Select the search box	Ctrl+E, Ctrl+F
Delete the selected item and move it to the Recycle Bin	Delete (or Ctrl+D)
Delete the selected item without moving it to the Recycle Bin first	Shift+Delete
Rename the selected item	F2
Scroll to top, bottom of window	Home, End

Taskbar

Cycle through programs on the taskbar	⊞+T
Open another window in a program	Shift-click a taskbar button
Open a program as an administrator	Ctrl+Shift-click a taskbar button
Show the window menu for the program	Shift+right-click a taskbar button
Show the window menu for the group	Shift+right-click a grouped taskbar button
Cycle through the windows of the group	Ctrl-click a grouped taskbar button
Open the first, second (etc.) program pinned to the taskbar	⊞+1, ⊞+2, etc.
Open another window in the first, second (etc.) pinned taskbar program	Shift+⊞+1, Shift+⊞+2, etc.
Switch to the last window in first, second (etc.) program pinned to the taskbar	Ctrl+⊞+1, Ctrl+⊞+2, etc.
Open a jump list for the first, second (etc.) program pinned to the taskbar	Alt+⊞+1, Alt+⊞+2, etc.

Virtual desktops

Task view	⊞+Tab, swipe up with three fingers on trackpad
New virtual desktop	Ctrl+⊞+D
Switch between virtual desktops	Ctrl+⊞+←, Ctrl+⊞+→
Close the current desktop	Ctrl+⊞+F4

Managing windows

Close the window	Alt+F4
Close the document (in apps that let you have multiple documents open)	Ctrl+F4
Open the shortcut menu for the active window	Alt+space bar
Switch among open programs	Alt+Tab
Use the arrow keys to switch among open programs	Ctrl+Alt+Tab
Task View	⊞+Tab

Cycle through screen elements in a window or on the desktop	F6
Display the shortcut menu for the selected item	Shift+F10
Refresh the active window	F5 (or Ctrl+R)
Maximize the window	⊞+↑
Maximize the window, maintain width	⊞+Shift+↑
Restore window, maintain width	⊞+Shift+↓
Minimize all windows	⊞+M
Restore minimized windows to the desktop	⊞+Shift+M
Snap window to the side of the screen	⊞+←, ⊞+→ (or drag window against the edge of the screen)
Move window to the previous/next monitor	⊞+Shift+←, ⊞+Shift+→
Restore/Minimize the window	⊞+↓
Maximize the window, maintain width	⊞+Shift+↓
Minimize all but the active window	⊞+Home
Peek at desktop	⊞+comma (,)

Languages and keyboard layouts

Next language and keyboard layout	⊞+space bar
Previous language and keyboard layout	⊞+Ctrl+space bar
Switch the input language when multiple input languages are enabled	Left Alt+Shift
Switch the keyboard layout when multiple keyboard layouts are enabled	Ctrl+Shift
Turn Chinese input method editor on/off	Ctrl+space bar
Change the reading direction of text in right-to-left reading languages	Ctrl+right Shift or Ctrl+left Shift
Zoom in or out (Magnifier)	⊞+plus, ⊞+minus
Zoom in or out (Web, mail, etc.)	Ctrl+turn mouse's scroll wheel

Inside apps

Go back a screen (most Windows Store apps)	Alt+←
Make the menu bar appear (some apps)	Alt or F10
Open the next menu to the right, or open a submenu	→
Open the next menu to the left, or close a submenu	←
Cancel the current task	Esc
Copy the selected item	Ctrl+C (or Ctrl+Insert)
Cut the selected item	Ctrl+X

Paste the selected item	Ctrl+V (or Shift+Insert)
Undo an action	Ctrl+Z
Redo an action	Ctrl+Y
Move the cursor to the beginning of the next word	Ctrl+→
Move the cursor to the beginning of the previous word	Ctrl+←
Move the cursor to the beginning of the next paragraph	Ctrl+↓
Move the cursor to the beginning of the previous paragraph	Ctrl+↑
Select a block of text	Shift+Ctrl with an arrow key
Select more than one item in a window, or select text within a document	Shift+any arrow key
Select multiple individual items in a window or on the desktop	Ctrl + any arrow key + space bar
Open Game bar (to record screen, for example)	⊞+G

Edge browser

Highlight address bar	Ctrl+L, Alt+D, F4
Add http://www. and .com to the text in address bar	Ctrl+Enter
New window	Ctrl+N
New InPrivate window	Shift+Ctrl+P
Refresh page	F5, Ctrl+R
Stop loading page	Esc
Scroll down a screenful	space bar (or Page Down)
Scroll up a screenful	Shift+space bar (or Page Up)
Zoom in/out	Ctrl+plus, Ctrl+minus
Return to 100 percent zoom	Ctrl+0 (that's a zero)
Close window	Alt+F4
View Reading List	Ctrl+G
View History list	Ctrl+H
View Favorites	Ctrl+ I
View Downloads	Ctrl+J
Hide or show Favorites bar	Ctrl+Shift+B
Open Cortana info for highlighted text	Alt+C
Open Home page	Alt+Home
Reader view on/off	Shift+Ctrl+R
Previous page (Back)	Backspace, Alt+←
Forward a page	Alt+→

Bookmark this page	Ctrl+B
Highlight address bar	Ctrl+L
Find text on this page	Ctrl+F
Find copied text on this page	Shift+Ctrl+L
Print	Ctrl+P
Open a new tab	Ctrl+T
Next tab	Ctrl+Tab
Previous tab	Shift+Ctrl+Tab
Open link in a new window	Shift+click
Open link in new tab	Ctrl+click
Open link in new background tab	Ctrl-click (or scroll wheel–click, or middle button–click)
Open link in new foreground tab	Shift+Ctrl+click (left or middle button)
Open URL in the address bar in a new tab	Alt+Enter
Duplicate this tab	Ctrl+K
Switch to tab 1, 2, 3, etc.	Ctrl+1, Ctrl+2, Ctrl+3, etc.
Switch to last tab	Ctrl+9
Cycle through tabs	Ctrl+Tab
Cycle backward through tabs	Shift+Ctrl+Tab
Close tab	Ctrl+F4, Ctrl+W
Reopen last closed tab	Shift+Ctrl+T
Turn on caret browsing	F7

Photos app

Open Share panel	⊞+H
Select thumbnail (and enter Selection mode)	Space
Select another thumbnail (in Selection mode)	Enter
Show/hide toolbar (on an open photo)	Space
Scroll thumbnails	arrow keys
Previous/next open photo	←, →
Zoom in /out	⊞+plus, ⊞+minus
Back to actual size	⊞+0
Previous screen	Esc
Save	Ctrl+S
Print	Ctrl+P
Rotate	Ctrl+R
Enhance the open photo	E
Compare edited photo with original	Ctrl+/
Resize the cropping area	Shift+arrow keys

Move the cropping area   Ctrl+arrow keys

Begin slideshow from open photo   F5

View photo details   Alt+Enter

Save this photo as your Lock screen image   Ctrl+L

Dialog boxes

Open the selected pop-up menu   F4

Move forward through tabs   Ctrl+Tab

Move back through tabs   Ctrl+Shift+Tab

Move forward through options   Tab

Move back through options   Shift+Tab

Perform the command (or select the option) that goes with that letter   Alt+underlined letter

Checkbox on/off   Space

Select highlighted command   Enter

In Save/Open dialog boxes, go up one folder level   Backspace

Game bar

Open Game bar (to record screen, for example)   ⊞+G

Save the last 30 seconds as a video   Alt+⊞+G

Start/stop video recording   Alt+⊞+R

Take a screenshot of current window   Alt+⊞+PrtScn

Show/hide recording timer   Alt+⊞+T

Ease of Access

Turn Filter Keys on and off   Right Shift for 8 seconds

Turn High Contrast on or off   Left Alt+Left Shift+PrtScn (or PrtScn)

Turn Mouse Keys on or off   Left Alt+Left Shift+Num Lock

Turn Sticky Keys on or off   Shift five times

Turn Toggle Keys on or off   Num Lock for 5 seconds

Open the Ease of Access Center   ⊞+U

Magnifier

Zoom in or out   ⊞+plus or +minus

Preview the desktop in full-screen mode   Ctrl+Alt+space bar

Switch to full-screen mode   Ctrl+Alt+F

Switch to lens mode   Ctrl+Alt+L

Switch to docked mode   Ctrl+Alt+D

Invert colors   Ctrl+Alt+I

Pan in the direction of the arrow keys   Ctrl+Alt+arrow keys

Resize the lens	Ctrl+Alt+R
Exit Magnifier	⊞+Esc

Remote Desktop Connection

Move among programs, left to right	Alt+Page Up
Move among programs, right to left	Alt+Page Down
Cycle through programs in the order they were started in	Alt+Insert
Open Start menu	Alt+Home
Switch between a window and full screen	Ctrl+Alt+Break
Display the Windows Security dialog box	Ctrl+Alt+End
Display the system menu	Alt+Delete
Place a copy of the active window, within the client, on the Terminal server clipboard (same as pressing Alt+PrtScn on a local computer)	Ctrl+Alt+minus (-) on the numeric keypad
Place a copy of the entire client window area on the Terminal server clipboard (same as pressing PrtScn on a local computer)	Ctrl+Alt+plus (+) on the numeric keypad
"Tab" out of the Remote Desktop controls to a control in the host program (for example, a button or a text box)	Ctrl+Alt+→ or ←

Touchscreen gestures

Right-click	Hold finger down 1 second
Open Apps list (from Start menu)	Swipe up
Task View	Swipe in from left edge
Action Center	Swipe in from right edge
Scroll	Slide across screen
Zoom in/zoom out (Maps, Photos, and so on)	Spread or pinch two fingers
Select next AutoComplete suggestion	Swipe across onscreen space bar
Close app	Drag from the top of the screen to the bottom
Open app into a split screen	Drag its title bar against the right or left edge of the screen

Tablet mode gestures

Switch apps	Swipe in from left edge
Close app	Drag from the top of the screen to the bottom
Open current app into a split screen	Drag from above the screen to middle, then veer to the right or the left

Index

Index

3D builder 293
3D Cities feature 318–319
64-bit
    vs. 32-bit 255

A

about your computer 262
accessibility. *See* **Ease of Access**
    closed captioning 266
    enlarging type and graphics 188
    magnifying the screen 187–189
    Narrator 325–326
    speech recognition 239–240
accessories
    Command Prompt 305–306
    Math Input Panel 320–321
    Narrator 325–326
    Notepad 328
    Paint 331–332
    Snipping Tool 346–349
    Steps Recorder 349–350
    Sticky Notes 350–351
    Windows Journal 355–357
    Windows PowerShell 358
    WordPad 358–360
    XPS Viewer 364–365
accounts 553–584. *See also* **logging in,**
    Microsoft accounts, passwords
    adding a family member 558–560
    adding new 558–562
    Administrator 556–557
    authentication 580
    basics 553
    changing local to Microsoft 563–564
    changing picture or password 563–564
    changing type 563
    deleting 576–577
    disabling 577
    emergency Administrator account 569
    Fast User Switching 579–580
    Guest 577–578
    in Mail app 411–412
    limiting to kiosk mode 562
    Local Users and Groups console 582–583
    logging into 574–575
    NTFS permissions 583–584
    personal folder 28
    Public profile 583
    searching other accounts 128
    Standard accounts 557
    switching in Start menu 24–25
    types of 556–557
    User Account Control (UAC) 580–582
    wallpaper and other settings 564
Action Center 113–117, 420
    notifications list 114–115
    Quick Action tiles 115–117
activation 270
Active Directory 616–617
Add Hardware wizard 486
Add or Remove Programs 635
address bar
    AutoComplete 385–386
    in File Explorer windows 63–66
    in taskbar 108
    navigating File Explorer from 66
    pop-up menus 65–66
    shortcuts 385–386
address book. *See* **People app**
ad hoc networks 590, 635
Administrator accounts 556–557
    authentication 557, 580–582
    security problems 557
    useful controls 577

ads
  in Start menu 38
advanced startup 270
adware 416
Aero 635
Aero Peek 51
airplane mode
  settings 264
alarms 293–294
  presentation mode 452–453
  setting with Cortana 203
Alarms & Clock app 293–296
  alarms 293–294
  stopwatch 296
  timer 295–296
  world clocks 294–295
alerts. *See* **notifications**
"All apps" list 29–30
  folders in it 30
  navigating 29
  opening 29
  uninstalling a program 31
Alt key
  sticky in onscreen keyboard 447
Alt+Tab 226
animations
  on/off switch 268
  turning off 185–186
"any folder" sharing 604–608
  defined 596
AppData 142
appearance. *See* **personalization**
apps. *See* **programs**
  opening with Cortana 200
app switcher 226
arrow keys
  in the Start menu 41–43
arrow notation 10–11
attachments
  opening 405
  sending 410–411
audio
  Cast to Device 62
authentication 580–582
AutoComplete 385–386
  erasing browsing history 426–427
  in onscreen keyboard 448
automatic updates 250–251
AutoPlay 139
  settings 274–275

B

Back button 386
  Explorer address bar 64–65
background 174–175
  across multiple monitors 175
  adding photo to 345
  in Mail app 414
  pictures 174
  sizing photos 175
  slideshows 175
  solid colors 174
backups 517–532
  recovering files 526–531
  Recovery HD 531–532
  system images 518–521
  System Protection dialog box 522–523
  System Restore 521–525
  Windows Backup and Restore 518
battery
  system tray 103
Battery Saver 441–443
  "Battery use" screen 443
  defined 441
  settings 442–443
  turning on 441
Bing search
  switching to Google 385
BitLocker Drive Encryption 549
Boolean searches 129–130
booting
  boot logging 512
  from a recovery drive 531–532
  Safe Mode 513
  Windows Recovery Environment 510–514
boot logging 512
Briefcase 635
burning
  "Burn to disc" Ribbon button 61
  CDs and DVDs 171–172
bus
  defined 490
buttons
  settings 281–282
BYOD 454

C

cable modems 373–374
cache
  defined 506
calculator
  using Cortana as 209
Calculator app 296

Calendar app
advantages 297
appointment details 301
day/week/month views 297–299
deleting events 302
editing events 302
filtering events 302
invitations 300–301
making an appointment 299–301
operating with Cortana 202–203
reminders 301
rescheduling events 302
settings 302–303
calling
Phone Companion app 337
Camera app 303–304
Camera Roll 304
self-timer 304
Camera Roll
defined 304
cameras
face recognition 571–572
"Can't sign in" message 560
Caps Lock
in onscreen keyboards 447
CardSpace 636
caret browsing 384
Cast to Device 62
Cc 410
C: drive 138–140
Desktop folder 140
PerfLogs 138
Personal folder 140–142
Program Files 138
Program Files (x86) 138
Users 138–140
Windows folder 140
CDs and DVDs
AutoPlay 139
burning 171–172
Password Reset Disk 575–576
sharing a drive 614–615
Character Map 304–305
character recognition 481
checkboxes
selecting with 143
Chess Titans 636
clean installs of Windows 10 631–634
the upgrade before the upgrade 632
ClearType 190
clicking
double-click speed 281

ClickLock 281–282
Clipboard 237–238
ClipBook Viewer 636
clock 104
adding more clocks 276–277
Internet time 277
operating with Cortana 203–204
setting the time 265, 276
stopwatch 296
timer 295–296
world clocks 294–295
closed captions 266
closing
desktop programs 228
programs 228
programs in Tablet mode 445
windows 49
colors
for desktop background 176
high contrast 176
in photos 343–344
managing between devices 476
monitor settings 189–190
reduced color mode 254
command prompt 305–306
in Safe Mode 513
opening 58
compatibility 253–256
64- and 32-bit versions 255
Compatibility mode 253–256
compatibility wizard 253–254
hardware 487–488
manual settings 254–256
of programs 253–256
reduced color mode 254
with really old apps 248
Complete PC Backup 636
Compressed Folder Tools/Extract tab 171
compression
data compression 169
files and folders 167–171
NTFS compression 167–168
show in color 91
connecting
hardware 485
contacts. *See* **People app**
Contact Support app 306
Content view 83
Continuum. *See* **Tablet Mode**
Control menu 46

Control Panel 270–289. *See also* **settings**
  add or remove programs 283
  AutoPlay 139, 274–275
  button controls 281–282
  date and time 275–277
  keyboard settings 279–280
  language settings 280–281
  opening 271
  Personalization 173–183
  power settings 282–283
  region settings 283–285
  RemoteApp and Desktop Connections 285
  security shield 270
  sounds 286–287
  System Properties 287–289
  views 271–274
conversions
  using Cortana for 209
cookies 425–426
  blocking 426
  defined 425–426
Copy and Paste 156–157
  speed graphs 154
  using Ribbon buttons 156
copying
  by dragging icons 154–156
  folders and files 154–157
  with the Navigation pane 155–156
  with the right mouse button 155
"Copy to" command 156
corporate networking
  Active Directory 616–617
  Windows To Go 454–455
corporate networks 616–619
  Ctrl+Alt+Delete requirement 618
  domains 616
Cortana 195–220
  and the Edge browser 390–391
  as a clipping service 216–219
  changing settings with 200
  checking stocks with 204
  checking the weather with 204
  Cortana Home panel 216
  differences from Siri 196
  email integrations 207–208
  fun things to ask 211–216
  getting definitions with 209–210
  getting movie times with 206–207
  getting sports info with 204–205
  Halo references 216
  "Hey, Cortana" 198
  how to use 198–199
  Maps integrations 208
  math and conversions with 209
  microphone button 198

  opening apps 200
  opening music with 208–209
  operating the clock with 203–204
  placing calls with 210
  scheduling appointments with 202–203
  searching the Web with 211
  setting reminders with 200–202
  settings 219–220
  setting up 196–197
  texting with 210
  tracking flights with 205–206
  tracking news with 206
  tracking packages with 206
  typing to 199
  using for reference 210
  using to set alarms 203
Credential Manager 275
Ctrl+Alt+Delete
  required at login 618
Ctrl key
  for locating cursor 183
  sticky in onscreen keyboard 447
  to select nonconsecutive items 142
Ctrl+Shift+Esc 228–231
cursor
  changing shape 181–183
  thickness setting 268
cursor keys
  in onscreen keyboard 448
customizing
  Search 133–137
  Start menu 30–31
Cut, Copy, Paste 236–238
  preserving formatting 237

D

data. *See also* **backups**
data compression 169
data usage 264
date and time
  settings 275–277
default programs 247
defragmenting 537–539
  settings 538–539
  with third-party software 537
deleting. *See also* **Recycle Bin**
  accounts 576–577
  email 405
  email accounts 401
  files 157–161
  folders 157–161
  fonts 478
  from removable drives 157
  live tiles 35
  Microsoft accounts 566

permanently 158
personalized themes 178
shortcut icons 152
Sticky Notes 351
tiles 35
virtual screens 194
Delivery Optimization 501
desktop
Aero Peek 51
appearance of icons 180
background 174–183
defined 22
Desktop folder 140
Desktop toolbar 110
keyboard shortcut to access 52
personalizing 173–183
printing from 472–473
Show Desktop button 52
virtual screens 193–194
Desktop cleanup wizard 636
Desktop gadgets 636
Details pane 68
Properties 79–80
Details view 81–83
edit columns 82
filtering with calendar 89
sorting files 84
Device Manager 487–491
opening 487
removing duplicate devices 488–489
resolving conflicts 487–489
resolving resource conflicts 489
rolling back drivers 490–491
turning components off 489
updating drivers 490
diacritical marks
in searches 136
dialog boxes
basics 234
keyboard shortcuts 647
navigating with the keyboard 234
presentation mode 452–453
Print 471–472
dial-up modems 375
dictionary
using Cortana as 209–210
directions 317–318
directories. *See* **folders**
disabling accounts 577
Discuss pane 636
Disk Cleanup 536–537
Disk Defragmenter. *See* **defragmenting**
disk images 171–172
disk management 540–545

disks 533–549
BitLocker Drive Encryption 549
dynamic disks 546
RAID 545
sharing 606–607
Storage view analysis tool 534–536
total disk space used 91
vs. volumes 535
Disks icon
properties 148
documents. *See* **files**
Documents folder 233–234
customizing icon 150
moving to a removable drive 141
Documents & Settings folder 636
domains 616
browsing 618
domain controller 616
logging in 618
searching 618–619
Do Not Track feature 429
double-click speed 281
download protection 423–425
Downloads folder 141
drag and drop 238–239
drawing
in OneNote 330
Paint app 331–332
Web page markup 391–393
drive letters
hiding/showing 91
drive paths 543–545
drivers
defined 15, 483
driver signature enforcement 514
Roll Back Driver feature 490–491
signing 487
updating 490
dual booting 630
DVD Maker 636
DVDs
AutoPlay 139
burning 171–172
DVI ports 485

E

early launch anti-malware protection 514
Ease of Access 266–269
high-contrast setting 266
keyboard help 266–267
keyboard shortcuts 647
Magnifier 312–313
mouse and pointer help 267–268
Narrator 325–326
visual notifications 268–269

Easy access shortcut menu 60
Edge browser 381–397
    address/search bar 384–387
    and Cortana 390–391
    AutoComplete 385–386
    Back and Forward buttons 386
    bookmarks 388–389
    cookies 425–426
    downloads 395
    Favorites 388–389
    History list 390, 426–427
    Home button 387
    keyboard shortcuts 397
    memorized passwords 394
    parental controls 432–436
    phishing 425
    photos online 394–395
    pop-up blocker 427–428
    printing pages 397
    Reader 395–396
    Reading List 395
    Refresh button 386
    scroll bars 386
    setting default search engine 385
    sharing pages 396–397
    start page 382–384
    Stop button 386
    tabs 387–388
    text size 393
    tips for Web surfing 393–397
    Web page markup 391–393
editing
    metadata 77–79
    photos 340–344
    scheduled tasks 504–505
    voice recordings 353
editions of Windows 10 8
email. See also Mail app
    adding a signature 413
    automatic replies 413–414
    composing with Cortana 207–208
    Exchange servers 401
    Gmail accounts 401
    Hotmail accounts 401
    IMAP accounts 401
    Outlook 401
    POP accounts 401
    Yahoo accounts 401
emoji/emoticons 447
emptying the Recycle Bin 159–161
encrypted files
    in searches 135
    show in color 91

Encrypting File System (EFS) 546–548
    rules 548
    using 548
encryption 546–549
    BitLocker Drive Encryption 549
    Encrypting File System (EFS) 546–548
Ethernet 586–589
    cables 588
    configuring 373–374
    equipment 586–588
    speed variation 586
Exchange servers 401
Explorer. See File Explorer
Explorer bar 636
exporting
    data 239

F

face recognition 571–572
Family Safety 432–436
    app, game, and movie restrictions 435
    setting restrictions 433–434
    setting up 433
    time limits 435–436
    updates to 432
    Web filtering 435
Fast User Switching 579–580
favorites 388–389
    folder 141
    in Maps app 318
    organizing 389
    toolbar 389
Favorites folder 636
faxing 480
Fetch 165–166
file associations 240–247
File Explorer 137–142. See also folders,
        windows
    address bar 63–66
    applying changes to all folders 83
    capture with Snipping Tool 348
    Content view 83
    controls 63–66
    Details pane 68
    Details view 81
    filtering icons 85–86
    filtering with calendar 89
    flippy arrows 72
    Folder Options 86–92
    grouping 84–85
    item checkboxes 143
    keyboard shortcuts 65, 642
    List view 81
    Navigation pane 68–72
    optional window panes 67–72

Preview pane 67–68
Properties 79–80
Ribbon 56–63
scroll bars 47
searching 124–130
similarities to Internet Explorer 143–145
sorting with column headings 84
status bar 91
tags and metadata 77–80
tiles view 82
uni-window vs. multi-window 87–88
views 80–83

File Explorer searches 124–130
filters 127–129
searching other accounts 128
search options 125–127
search syntax 129–130
tips 130

File History 526–531
recovering files 528–531
settings 527–528
setting up 526

filename extensions 240–247
defined 240
displaying 240–241
hidden 146
Ribbon on/off switch 90
unknown file types 241–242

filenames
forbidden symbols 146
maximum length 146

files
adding to OneDrive 162
attaching 410–411
backups 517–532
closing 235
compression 167–171
copying and moving 154–157
"Copy to" command 156
deleting 157–161
documents 235
encryption 91, 546–549
filename extensions 240–247
filtering with calendar 89
grouping 84–85
hide filename extensions 90
icon properties 148–149
"Move to" command 156
moving data between 236
moving with "Send to" 144
NTFS 91
offline files feature 453
opening 236
"Open with" command 243–244

overwriting 232
printing 470–473
privacy 78
Properties 79–80
protecting during refresh 508–509
read-only 148
recovering 526–531
saving 232–235
setting program defaults 242–247
sharing on a network 595–619
Sharing Wizard 91
single-click instead of double-click 88
tags and metadata 77–80
total disk space used 91
turning off document previews 91
unknown file types 241–242
views 80–83

file sharing 595–619. *See also* **HomeGroups**
accessing shared files and folders 608–611
across Windows versions 612
any folder 604–608
file transfer protocol (FTP) 619
HomeGroups 597–603
mapping folders to drive letters 611–614
nested folders 608
sharing a DVD drive 614–615
Universal Naming Convention (UNC) 611
with Macs 612, 617

Files & Settings Transfer Wizard 636
File tab
in File Explorer 57–59
file transfer protocol (FTP) 619
Filmstrip view 636
filtering
File Explorer searches 127–129
icons 85–86
filters 342
fingerprint recognition 572
flash drives
AutoPlay 139
estimating disk space 91
Password Reset Disk 575–576
ReadyBoost 506–508
using for system recovery 531–532
flights
tracking with Cortana 205–206
Flip 3D 637
flippy arrows 72
folder icons
properties 149
Folder Options 86–92
General tab 87–88
Search 133–135
View tab 88–92

folders 137–142. *See also* **File Explorer, windows**
    adding to a library 74–76
    always show menu bar 88
    applying changes to all folders 83
    automatically expanding 72
    compression 167–171
    Contacts 140
    copying and moving 154–157
    deleting 157–161
    Desktop 140
    Documents folder 233–234
    Downloads 141
    encryption 546–549
    Favorites 141
    flippy arrows 72
    folder path notation 611
    hide empty drives 90
    hiding on a network 608
    in Mail app 408
    in Start menu 30
    Links 141
    opening from address bar 66
    organizing 86–92
    personalizing icons 150–151
    read-only 148
    removing from a library 76
    Saved Games 141
    saving into 232–235
    searches 141
    sharing on a network 595–619
    Sharing Wizard 91
    show all 72
    show file icons on thumbnails 88
    show file path in title bar 89
    show file size information 88–89
    show hidden files and folders 89
    show icons, not thumbnails 88
    templates 149
    use checkboxes for selection 91
    vs. directories 141
fonts 477–479
    deleting 478
    Internet Explorer text size 393
    managing 477–479
    smooth edges onscreen 186
formatting
    in pasted text 237
    Sticky Notes 350–351
Forward button 386
    Explorer address bar 64–65
FreeCell 637

Frequent places list 59
frozen desktop programs 228–231

G

gadgets 637. *See also* **hardware**
games
    Games folder 637
    Microsoft Solitaire Collection 321–322
    parental controls 435
    Xbox app 360–364
    Xbox streaming 362–363
gestures
    delete a Start screen tile 35
    delete a tile 35
    dismiss Lock screen 20
    for Narrator 326
    in Mail app 412
    move a tile 33
    open "All apps" menu 29
    open Camera app 20
    opening jump lists 99
    picture passwords 567–570
    resize a tile 34
    right-click 31
Get Started app 307–308
Get Windows 10 app 625
Gmail accounts 401
Google
    switching to 385
Groove Music app 308–312
    controlling with keyboard 311
    display options 309–310
    Explore screen 311
    Now Playing 311
    playlists 312
    radio 310
    searching 309
    settings 311–312
Guest accounts 577–578

H

Halo
    references in Cortana 216
"hamburger button" 292
handwriting recognition 356–357, 449–452
    fixing mistakes 450–451
    training 451–452
hard drives
    (C:) drive 138–140
    changing a drive letter 540–541
    checkups 539–540
    compression 167–171

Disk Cleanup tool 536–537
Disk Defragmenter 537–539
disk management 540–545
disk quotas 547
line conditioner 543
naming conventions 138
partitioning 541–543
recovery partition 531
Storage Spaces feature 545–546
Storage view analysis tool 534–536
surge suppressors 543
turning a drive into a folder 543–545
Uninterruptible Power Supply (UPS) 543
hardware
Add Hardware wizard 486
compatibility 487–488
connecting new 485
Device Manager 487–491
Ethernet 586–589
networking equipment 589
printers 467–469
surge suppressors 543
troubleshooting 485–486
Hardware profiles 637
HDMI 485
help
Contact Support app 306
Get Started 307–308
Ribbon button 59
"Hey, Cortana" 198
Hibernate mode
defined 38
restoring 38
hidden files and folders 89–90
high performance power plan 637
History list 390, 426–427
erasing 427
Home button 387
HomeGroups
creating 597–599
defined 596
Explorer-window listings 72
joining 599–600
leaving 603
limitations 599
pros and cons 596
settings 600
sharing music and videos 601
sharing printers 600–601
using 600–602
home page 382–384

Home tab
in File Explorer 59–61
Hotmail accounts 401
hotspots. *See also* **WiFi**
sharing with WiFi Sense 378–379
hub
defined 587–588
Hub (Edge browser)
defined 386
freezing open 389
hybrid PCs 441–466
handwriting recognition 449–452
Mobility Center 452–453
split-screen apps 444–445
Tablet Mode 443–445

I

icon properties
Computer 146–147
custom 148–149
Disks 148
documents 148–149
keyboard shortcuts 146
program files 150
icons 145–151
appearance on desktop 180
changing illustrations 150–151
creating custom properties 148–149
filtering with calendar 89
grouping 84–85
hidden 148
opening with a single click 143–145
personalizing 150–151
properties 146–150
renaming 145–146
selecting 142–145
shortcuts 151–153
single-click instead of double-click 88
turning off document previews 91
IMAP accounts 401
"Important places" list 26–28
adding to 26–28
importing
data 239
index. *See* **search index**
InkBall 637
InPrivate browsing 428–429
installing hardware
printers 467–469
installing Windows 10 623–634
first steps after installation 634

Internet
better surfing in Edge 393–397
cellular modems 374–375
connection management 375–376
dial-up 375
Do Not Track feature 429
Edge browser 381–397
Ethernet connections 373–374
getting connected 369–379
InPrivate browsing 428–429
memorized passwords 394
parental controls 432–436
Reading List 395
searching 384
security and privacy 415–438
switching between modem types 377
WiFi Sense 376–379
Windows SmartScreen 423–425
Internet Explorer 381
Internet service providers (ISPs) 375
invitations (Calendar app) 300–301
IP addresses 374, 456
ipconfig command 306
IP over FireWire 637
iris recognition 572
iSCSI Initiator 637
ISO disk images 171–172

J

jump lists 98–102
clearing 102
downsides 101
in Start menu 42
opening 98–99
pinning to 99–101
settings 101–102
turning off 101
junction points 543–545

K

keyboard. *See also* **onscreen keyboard**
autocomplete 448
Mouse Keys 267
navigating dialog boxes 234
selecting icons 142
Toggle Keys 266
keyboard shortcuts
address bar 65
Alt+Tab 226
basics 12–13
closing a window 49
creating a new desktop 193
dialog boxes 647
dismiss Lock screen 20
Ease of Access 647

Edge browser 397
File Explorer windows 65
hide/show Ribbon 56
icon properties 146
in Photos 340
in Remote Desktop Connection 463–464, 648
in search box 41
in Start menu 41
log out 40
minimize, maximize, restore 48–49
on Lock screen 25
open secret Start menu 43
open Task Manager 25
Ribbon 58
shortcut icons 153
show desktop 52
Shut Down 40
sign out 25
Start menu 41
switch user 25
system tray 105
taskbar 94, 643
word processing 645
kiosk mode 562

L

language
settings 266, 280–281
laptop PCs 441–466
Battery Saver 441–443
data usage 264
dialing in from the road 455–466
location privacy settings 437–438
Mobility Center 452–453
offline files feature 453
presentation mode 452–453
Quick Action tiles 115–117
what happens when you close the lid 40–41
layering windows 51–52
libraries 72–77
adding folders to 74–76
advantages 73–74
creating 77
defined 72–73
hiding and showing 73, 74
limitations 76
removing folders from 76
saving into 76
working with contents 74
line conditioners 543
Links folder 141
links toolbar 108–110
List view 81
search box behavior 91–92
live tiles. *See* **tiles**

Local Disk (C:) window 138–140
Local Users and Groups 582–583
Lock screen 19–20
  accessing from Start menu 25
  defined 19
  dismissing 20
  making notifications appear 111
  wallpaper from Photos 344
logging in 566–574
  Ctrl+Alt+Delete required 618
  different techniques 21–22
  local vs. Microsoft accounts 554–555
  on a domain 618–619
  the Login screen 20–22
  what happens next 574–575
  with four-digit passcode 570–571
  without a password 572–574
logging out 25. *See also* shutting down
Login screen 20–22. *See also* logging in

M

MAC address filtering 431
Macs
  accessing on a network 612, 617
Magnifier app 312–313
Mahjong Titans 637
Mail app 399–414
  accounts 411–412
  adaptable layout 402–403
  adding a signature 413
  attaching files 410–411
  automatic replies 413–414
  avoiding spam 408
  background picture 414
  Cc and Bcc 410
  checking email 403–404
  deleting email 405
  flagging email 405–406
  forwarding email 405
  marking email as read 414
  marking email as unread 406
  message folders 408
  moving messages 408
  notifications 414
  opening attachments 405
  organizing email 405
  package tracking with Cortana 206–220
  reading options 414
  replying to email 405
  searching email 408
  settings 411–414
  setting up 400–401
  subject line 410
  swipe actions 412
  working with batches of messages 406–408
  working with email 404–411
  writing messages 409–411
maintenance 495–516. *See also* troubleshooting
  Disk Cleanup 536–537
  Disk Defragmenter 537–539
  hard drive checkups 539–540
  hard drive problems 543
  security patches 496
  Storage View 534–536
  Task Scheduler 502–505
  Windows Update 495–502
malware 416
Maps app 314–319
  3D Cities feature 318–319
  adding favorites 318
  getting directions 317–318
  searching for addresses 316–317
  settings 261
  Streetside feature 315–316
  using with Cortana 208
Markup feature 391–393
  exporting Web Notes 393
  sharing Web Notes 393
  using 392
Math Input Panel app 320–321
Maximize button 48
Meeting Space 637
memory
  SuperFetch 506
memory cards
  AutoPlay 139
metadata 77–80
  defined 77
  editing 77–79
  privacy 78
  removing 78
metered connections. *See* cellular modems
microphone
  settings 286–287
microphone button 198
Microsoft accounts 554–555. *See also* accounts
  billing page 565
  changing settings online 564–566
  defined 554
  deleting 566
  linked accounts 554
  synced bookmarks 555
  synced settings 555
  sync settings 564
Microsoft Edge. *See* Edge browser
Microsoft Solitaire Collection app 321–322
Microsoft Surface. *See* hybrid PCs
MiFi 374
Minesweeper 637

Minimize button 48–49
minimizing
    with mouse shake 50–51
Miracast 324
Mobility Center 452–453
modems
    cable 373–374
    cellular 369, 374–375
    connection settings 373–374
    dial-up 375
    switching between types 377
    types 369
Money app 322–323
monitors
    changing resolution 187–188
    ClearType 190
    color 189–191
    color management 476
    enlarging type and graphics 188
    Magnifier 189
    magnify screen 187–189
    multiple 190–192
    orientation 188
    reduced color mode 254
    screensavers 183–185
    settings 187–190
    virtual screens 193–194
"Most used" list 25–26
    getting rid of 25
mounted drives 543–545
mounting ISO disk images 171–172
mouse. *See also* **pointers**
    ClickLock 281–282
    cursor thickness 268
    double-click speed 281
    pointer settings 180–183, 267
    scroll wheel settings 282
    selecting icons 142
    settings 263
    speed 182
    swapping button functions 281
    switching left and right buttons 12
Mouse Keys 267
"Move to" command 156
Movie Maker 637
movies
    getting showtimes from Cortana 206–207
    parental controls 435
Movies & TV app 323–325
moving
    files 154–157
    folders 154–157
    "Send to" command 144
    taskbar 107–108

MSCONFIG 231
multiple monitors 190–192
    customizing 191–192
    wallpaper that spans 175
music. *See also* **Groove Music app**
    playing/identifying with Cortana 208–209
    sharing via HomeGroups 601
    tags and metadata 77–80
Music folder 141
My Computer 637. *See also* **This PC**
My Network Places 637

N

Narrator 325–326
    text to speech 239
    touchscreen basics 326
Navigation pane 68–72
    dragging icons to 155–156
    This PC 71
NetMeeting 637
Network and Sharing Center 591–594
    changing adapter settings 591–592
    changing advanced sharing settings 592–593
    setting up a new network 593
    troubleshooting 594
networking. *See also* **workgroup networks**
    accessing Macs 612, 617
    accessing shared files and folders 608–611
    adapters 591–592
    ad hoc 590
    corporate networks 616–619
    Ethernet 586–589
    file sharing 595–619
    hiding folders 608
    HomeGroups 597–603
    map 637
    Network and Sharing Center 591–594
    public vs. private 603
    Remote Desktop 459–466
    security 431–432
    setting up a small network 585–594
    shared printers 474–475
    sharing a DVD drive 614–615
    showing hidden folders 608
    system tray 103
    virtual private networks 456–459
network map 637
network printers
    installing 469
News app 326–328
    customizing 327–328
    videos 328

Notepad app 328–329
  basics 328–329
  defined 328
  Word Wrap 329
notification area. *See* system tray
notifications
  defined 111
  in Mail app 414
  silencing 112–113
NTFS compression 167–168, 169, 533
NTFS permissions 583–584

O

offline browsing 638
offline files 453
OneDrive 161–167
  adding files 162
  Fetch feature 165–166
  offline files 162–163
  sharing files 166–167
  syncing files 162–163
  Web site 164–165
OneNote 329–331
onscreen keyboard 445–449
  101-key PC keyboard layout 448
  accented characters 447
  autocapitalize next sentence 448
  autocomplete 448
  Caps Lock 447
  cursor keys 448
  numbers and symbols 447
  settings and shortcuts 449
  split, two-thumb version 447
  sticky Alt, Ctrl, Shift keys 447
  typing suggestions 448
Open dialog box 236
opening
  command prompt 58
  Control Panel 271
  documents 236
  files with different programs 242–247
  "Open with" command 243–244
  programs 223–224
  programs from taskbar 97–98
  setting file type defaults 242–247
optical character recognition 481
organizing
  live tiles 35–36
Outlook 401
Outlook Express 638
overwriting
  files 232

P

Paint 331–332
parental controls. *See* Family Safety
partitioning 541–543
passcode 570–571
passwords 566–574
  Credential Manager 610
  eliminating 572–574
  face recognition 571–572
  fingerprint and iris recognition 572
  four-digit passcode 570–571
  hints 561–562
  online 394
  Password Reset Disk 575–576
  picture passwords 21
  primary and secondary 570
Paste shortcut command 152
patches 496
path notation 611
PCI and PCI Express slots 490
PDF files 479–480
  creating 480
  defined 479
  opening 480
People app 332–337
  Contacts folder 140
  creating address cards 335–336
  editing entries 336
  finding people 336
  importing addresses 332–334
PerfLogs 138
performance
  Performance Options 185
  ReadyBoost 506–507
  speed tricks 505–507
  SuperFetch 506
permissions. *See* NTFS permissions, privileges
Personal folder 28, 140–142
  AppData 142
  basics of 28
  contacts 140
  defined 140
  Downloads 141
  Favorites 141
  Links 141
  Music, Pictures, Videos 141
  Saved Games 141
  Searches 141
personalization
  mouse pointers 180–183
  screensavers 183–185
  themes 176–183
  turning off the new look 185–187

phishing 425–426
  defined 424
  Edge's defenses 425
  filter 638
  filter options 424–425
  Windows SmartScreen 423–425
phone calls
  using Cortana for 210
Phone Companion app 337
photos
  adding a Mail background 414
  adding filters 342
  adjusting color 343–344
  adjusting light 343
  attaching in Mail 410
  auto-enhance 341
  Camera app 303–304
  cropping 341–342
  desktop backgrounds 174–183
  fixing red eye 342
  in Edge 394–395
  Photos app 337–345
  picture passwords 567–570
  retouching 342
  Rotate button (Ribbon) 62
  rotating 341
  saving changes 344
  selecting 345
  sharing 345
  sizing for wallpaper 175
  special effects 344
  straightening 342
Photos app 337–345
  automatic albums 338–339
  browsing photos 340
  changing wallpaper 344
  choosing photo for Start menu tile 345
  editing photos 340–344
  emailing photos 340
  importing from a camera 338
  keyboard shortcuts 340
  navigating 337
  Pictures folder 338
  selecting photos 345
  zooming in and out 340
picture passwords 21, 567–570
Pictures folder 141, 338
Pinball 638
ping command 306
pinning
  to jump lists 99–101
  to taskbar 97–98
playlists 312

pointers
  changing 182
  changing speed 182–183
  cursor thickness 268
  hide while typing 183
  options 182–183
  pointer trails 183
  scheme 182
  settings 267–268
  show location 183
  Snap To option 183
Pointer themes 638
POP accounts 401
pop-up blocker 427–428
  overriding 428
  turning off 428
power
  and hard drives 543
  Battery Saver 441–443
  "Battery use" screen 443
  settings 260–261
power button
  sleep vs. shut down 40
PowerPoint
  presentation mode 452–453
  silencing alerts 113
PowerShell 58–59, 358
PowerToys 638
presentation mode 452–453
Preview pane 67–68
Previous Versions 638
printers
  installing 467–469
  limiting hours of access 475
  networked 474–475
  settings 469
  sharing via HomeGroups 600–601
  troubleshooting 477
printing
  adding a separator page 476–477
  background 472
  bypassing Print dialog box 472–473
  canceling 474
  change print order 474
  color management 476
  from desktop programs 471–472
  from the desktop 472–473
  from Windows Store apps 470
  multiple copies 472
  on a network 474–475
  page ranges 471–472
  pausing 474

Print dialog box 471–472
print queue 473–474
spooler 473
Web pages 397
Print Screen key 346
privacy
cookies 425–426
Do Not Track feature 429
InPrivate browsing 428–429
removing metadata 78
settings 436–438
privileges. *See also* **NTFS permissions**
Program Files folder 138
programs 223–231
3D builder 293
access to your machine 438
Alarms & Clock 293–296
automatic updates 250–251
Calculator 296
Calendar 297–303
Camera 303–304
closing 228–230
closing in Tablet Mode 445
Command Prompt 305–306
compatibility with really old apps 248
Contact Support 306
default 247
desktop vs. Windows Store 224–225
Get Office 307
Get Skype 307
Get Started 307–308
Groove Music 308–312
installing 171–172, 248–251
jump lists 42
Magnifier 312–313
Mail 399–414
Maps 314–319
Math Input Panel 320–321
Microsoft Edge 381–397
Microsoft Solitaire Collection 321–322
Money (financial news) 322–323
Movies & TV 323–325
Narrator 325–326
News 326–328
Notepad 328–329
OneDrive 161–167
OneNote 329–331
Onscreen Keyboard 445–449
opening 223–224
Paint 331–332
parental controls 435
People 332–337
Phone Companion 337

Photos 337–345
preinstalled 291–366
privacy settings 436–438
RemoteApp and Desktop Connections 285
Remote Desktop Connection 459–466
Skype 346
Snipping Tool 346–349
Sports 349
Steps Recorder 349–350
Sticky Notes 350–351
switching between 226–228
Task Manager 228–231
Task View 226–228
unified design 291–293
uninstalling 252
universal 224
Voice Recorder 351–353
Weather 353–355
Windows 8 types 224–225
Windows 10 compatibility 253–256
Windows Defender 417–419
Windows Journal 355–357
Windows Media Player 358
Windows Store 249–251
Xbox 360–364
projectors. *See* **multiple monitors**
Properties
Details pane 79–80
folder icons 149
Ribbon button 60
system 147
System Properties 146
proxy server 265
Public folders 140
Purble Place 638

Q

Quick access 68–71
customizing 70
hiding 69
pinning to 69
removing items 69–70
turning off automation 70–71
Quick Action tiles 115–117
Quiet Hours 112–113

R

radio 310
RAID 545
Reader 395–396
Reading List 395
adding new page 395

read-only
 defined 148
ReadyBoost 506–507
"Recently added" list 26
recovering files 526–531
 by browsing 529–530
 by searching 530
 from the Ribbon 530
 using the Properties dialog box 530–531
recovery mode
 startup environment 510–514
Recycle Bin 157–161
 auto-emptying 160–161
 customizing icon 150
 eliminating warning windows 157–159
 emptying 159–161
 Permanently delete 158
 restoring deleted items 159
 Show recycle confirmation 158
red eye 342
Reduced color mode 254
Refresh button 386
Reliability Monitor 516
reminders 301
 operating with Cortana 200–202
RemoteApp and Desktop Connections 285
Remote Desktop Connection 459–466
 connecting 460–463
 disconnecting 464
 fine-tuning connections 465–466
 keyboard shortcuts 463–464, 648
 setting up host 459
 troubleshooting 463
 vs. remote control 465
renaming
 icons 145–146
 Rename button 60
Reset this PC command 269
resetting the computer 508–510
 to original condition 509–510
 without erasing files 508–509
Restart command 40
restore points 521–522
 creating 523
restoring folder windows on login 90
Reversi 638
Ribbon 56–63
 Compressed Folder Tools/Extract tab 171
 Copy, Move, Paste buttons 156
 "Copy to" command 156

 defined 56
 eliminating completely (shareware) 56
 filename extensions 90
 file recover tools 530
 File tab 57–59
 Frequent places 59
 Hidden files button 90
 hiding and showing 56
 Home tab 59–61
 Item check boxes 143
 keyboard controls 56, 58
 Library Tools/Manage tab 62
 "Move to" command 156
 Music Tools/Play tab 62
 "Paste shortcut" command 152
 Permanently delete 158
 Picture Tools/Manage tab 62
 Share tab 61
 Show recycle confirmation 158
 View tab 61
right-clicking 11–12
 Start menu 43
 taskbar icons 99
right-dragging 155
routers
 defined 587
 placement 432
 settings 431–432
 setting up 588
 wireless 589–590

S

Safe Mode 513
 with command prompt 513
 with networking 513
Saved Games folder 141
Save dialog box
 file formats drop-down menu 235
 navigating by keyboard 235
 shortcut for replacing documents 232
saving
 change default location 235
 changes to photos 344
 documents 232–235
 File Explorer changes 83
 file formats 235
 into Documents folder 233–234
 into libraries 76
 Save dialog box 232
 save locations 232
scanning 480–482

color management 476
for viruses 418–419
optical character recognition 481
scrap files 238
screen resolution 187–188
screensavers 183–185
choosing 184–185
need for 183
password protecting 184
presentation mode 452–453
previews 184
settings 184–185
screenshots
of Xbox games 363
scroll bars 328
in Edge browser 386
in File Explorer 47
SD card readers 485
search box 41
keyboard shortcuts 41
using 13–14
search engines
switching to Google 385
Searches folder 141
search index 130–133
adding new places 132–133
include encrypted files 135
moving 136
options 135–137
rebuilding 136
what's indexed 131
where Windows looks 131
searching 119–124
at the desktop 119–124
Boolean search terms 129–130
by file type 136–137
contacts in People app 336
customizing 133–137
diacritical marks 136
domains 618–619
File Explorer windows 124–130
Folder Options 133–135
from the taskbar 120–122
Groove Music 309
indexing options 135–137
in Mail app 408
maps 316–317
"More Results" window 122–125
other accounts 128
search index 130–133
search without clicking 91–92

settings 133
taskbar search box 120–122
tips 130
troubleshooting 136
Web 384
Web with Cortana 211
secret Start menu 43
security
Action Center 420
administrator accounts 557
backups 517–532
cookies 425–426
creating a password reset disk 575–576
Credential Manager 610
disk quotas 547
Encrypting File System (EFS) 546–548
face recognition 571–572
general good advice 416
Internet 415–438
limiting printer access 475
MAC address filtering 431
NTFS permissions 583–584
parental controls 432–436
patches 496
phishing 424–425
pop-up blocker 427–428
quarantining software 419
router placement 432
scanning for viruses 418–419
settings 269–270
spyware vs. adware 416
system images 518–521
User Account Control (UAC) 580–582
virtual private network (VPN) 430–431
WiFi hotspots 430–431
Windows Defender 417–419
Windows Firewall 420–423
Windows SmartScreen 423–425
Windows Update 495–502
security shield 270
selecting
by dragging 142
icons 142–145
nonconsecutive items 142
photos 345
text 359
with checkboxes 143
with the keyboard 142
with the mouse 142
"Send to" command 144

settings 257–289. *See also* **Control Panel**
  about your computer 262
  accessibility 266–269
  airplane mode 264
  apps 260
  Battery Saver 442–443
  calendar 302–303
  Cortana 219–220
  Devices page 262–264
  Disk Defragmenter 538–539
  Ease of Access page 266–269
  Ethernet 265
  external drives 261
  File Explorer searches 125–127
  File History 527–528
  Groove Music 311–312
  HomeGroups 600
  in Start menu 26
  jump lists 101–102
  Mail app 411–414
  mouse 180–183
  mouse and touchpad 263
  Network & Internet page 264–265
  offline maps 261
  online keyboard 449
  opening 258–259
  opening with Cortana 200
  Personalization page 173–183
  pointer 267
  power consumption 260–261
  printers 469
  privacy 436–438
  screensavers 184–185
  search index 135–137
  Settings app 257–259
  spell-checking 263–264
  syncing with Microsoft accounts 564
  System page 259–262
  Time & Language page 265–266
  Update & Security page 269–270
  Virtual Screens 260
  VPN 458–459
  Windows Firewall 421–422
  Windows SmartScreen 424–425
setting the clock 265
shaking
  turning off 54
sharing. *See also* **file sharing**
  disks 606–607, 610
  DVD drives 614–615
  File Explorer Share tab 61
  hotspots with WiFi Sense 376–379
  OneDrive files 166–167
  photos 345
  printers 474–475

  Share panel 61
  Sharing Wizard 91
  Web notes 393
  Web pages 396–397
Shift key
  sticky in onscreen keyboard 447
shortcut icons 151–153
  creating 152
  defined 151–152
  deleting 152
  finding original icon 151, 153
  keyboard triggers 153
  Paste shortcut command 152
  personalizing icons 150–151
Show Desktop button 52
Show recycle confirmation 158
Show status bar 91
shutting down 38–41
  defined 38
  hibernation 38
  keyboard shortcut 40
  showing the Hibernate option 38
  sleep mode 39–42
Sidebar 638
signature 413
"Sign out" command 25
single click
  to open icons 143–145
SkyDrive. *See* **OneDrive**
Skype 346
slash notation (paths) 611
Sleep mode 39–40
  advantages of 39–40
  closing the laptop 40
  desktop PC power button 40
  triggers 40–41
slideshows
  setting as desktop picture 175
SmartScreen. *See* **Windows SmartScreen**
Snap feature 52–55
  four windows 54–55
  turning off 54
  two windows 52–53
snap to OK button 183
Snipping Tool 346–349
  capturing menus 348
  capturing windows 348
  URL identification feature 349
software. *See* **programs, Windows Store**
solitaire 321–322
sound
  changing themes 178–180
  settings 286
  volume 103

Spaces. *See* virtual screens
Spades 639
spam
    tips for avoiding 408
speakers
    settings 286–287
speech. *See* Cortana
speech recognition 239–240
    text to speech 239
speed boosts 505–507
    ReadyBoost 506–507
    SuperFetch 506
spell-checking 263–264
sports
    information from Cortana 204–205
Sports app 349
spyware
    defined 417
    vs. adware 416
    Windows Defender 417–419
stacking 639
Standard accounts 557
Start menu 22–38. *See also* tiles
    account picture 24–25
    "All apps" list 29–30
    customizing 30–31, 33–38
    defined 23
    folders 30
    "Important places" list 26–28
    in Tablet Mode 444
    jump lists 42, 98–102
    keyboard navigation 41
    left side 24–31
    most-used programs 25–26
    opening 23
    "Recently added" list 26
    right side 31–38
    secret utility menu 43
    tiles 31–38
    turning off ads 38
Startup Hardware Profiles 639
startup items 231, 516
    defined 516
    disabling 516
startup problems 510–514
status bar 91
Steps Recorder 349–350
Sticky Keys 266
Sticky Notes 350–351
    creating 350
    deleting 351, 351–356
    formatting 350–351
stocks
    checking with Cortana 204

Stop button 386
stopwatch 296
Storage Spaces feature 545–546
Storage view 534–536
streaming
    Xbox games 362–363
Streetside maps feature 315–316
subtitles 266
SuperFetch 506
surge suppressors 543
switch (networking)
    defined 587–588
symbols
    in filenames 146
syncing
    offline files feature 453
    OneDrive 162–163
    settings 564
system
    settings 287–288
system files
    hiding/showing 90
system images 518–521
    creating 518–519
    restoring system 519–521
System Properties 146, 146–147, 147
System Restore 521–525
    limiting space on hard drive 523
    performing a restore 523, 525
    restore points 521–522
    turning off 525
    with low drive space 523
system tray 102–105. *See also* notifications
    clock 104
    defined 102
    hiding and showing icons 104–105
    keyboard shortcuts 105
    network 103
    onscreen keyboard 103
    power level 103
    rearranging icons 104
    volume 103

T

tabbed browsing 387–388
    shortcuts 387–388
Tablet Mode 443–445
    "Continuum" defined 443
    defined 443
    exiting apps 445
    turning on 443–444
    turning on automatically 445

tablet PCs 441–466
    Battery Saver 441–443
    handwriting recognition 449–452
    location privacy settings 437–438
    onscreen keyboard 445–449
    split-screen apps 444–445
    Tablet mode 443–445
tablets
    built-in cellular 375
tags 77–80
Tap and Do
    AutoPlay 139
taskbar 92–98
    as app switcher 93
    auto-hiding 106
    button groups 94–96
    customizing 110–111
    defined 92
    functions 92–93
    in Tablet mode 444
    jump lists 98–102
    keyboard shortcuts 94, 643
    launching programs 97–99
    limits on dragging 639
    moving 107–108
    pinning apps to 97–99
    resizing 106
    restoring classic look 107
    search box 120–122
    system tray 102–105
    Task View button 226–228
    thumbnails 94
    toolbars 108–111
    use small taskbar buttons 107
    window previews 94
Task Manager 228–231
    App history 231
    Details tab 231
    heat map 230
    Performance tab 231
    Processes tab 231
    Services tab 231
    startup items 516
    Startup tab 231
    Users tab 231
Task Scheduler 502–505
    adding a task 503–504
    editing a task 504–505
    library 505
Task View 226–228
Telnet 639
tethering 369, 374
text
    changing size online 393
    ClearType 190

    enlarging on monitor 187–189
    selecting 359
texting
    using Cortana for 210
text to speech 239
themes 176–183
    deleting 178
    desktop icon settings 180
    sound 178–180
This PC 71, 137, 637–640
    folders 137–142
    hiding devices 138
    properties 146–147
three-fingered salute 229
thumbnails
    in taskbar 94
tiles 31–38. *See also* **Start menu**
    adding 34
    changing the size of the menu 33
    choosing photo for Photos app tile 345
    deleting 35, 37
    grouping 35–36
    live tiles 31–33
    making them fill the screen 33
    moving 33
    rearranging 33
    resizing 34
    turning off animation 35
Tiles view 82
time and date
    formatting 265
timer 295–296
time zone 265
Tip of the Day 639
title bar 47
toast. *See* **notifications**
toolbars
    Address toolbar 108
    building your own 111–118
    Desktop toolbar 110
    Favorites 389
    Links toolbar 108–110
    on taskbar 108–111
    redesigning 110–111
tooltips
    hiding/showing 91
touchpad
    settings 263
touchscreen gestures. *See* **gestures**
touchscreens. *See also* **hybrid PCs, laptops**
    gestures for Narrator 326
    onscreen keyboard 445–449
    Tablet mode 443–445
    Windows Journal 355–357

troubleshooting
    Contact Support app 306
    disabling driver signature enforcement 514
    Disk Cleanup tool 536–537
    driver rollback 490–491
    emergency Administrator account 569
    hard drives 543
    in Device Manager 487–489
    interview screens 288
    Network and Sharing Center 594
    new hardware 485–486
    printers 477
    problem reports 515
    recovering files 526–531
    Reliability Monitor 516
    "Reset this PC" command 508–510
    Safe Mode 513
    Search 136
    starting up from a recovery drive 531–532
    startup 510–514
    startup items 516
    Steps Recorder 349–350
    Storage view analysis tool 534–536
    System Restore 521–525
    Task Manager 228–231
    three-fingered salute 229
    tools 514–516
    version compatibility 253–256
    WiFi connections 370–372
    Windows Recovery Environment 510–514
TweakUI 639
typing
    onscreen 445–449
    spell-checking 263–264
    to Cortana 199

U

unified app design 291–293
uninstalling programs 252
    from "All apps" list 31
Uninterruptible Power Supply (UPS) 543
universal apps 224
Universal Naming Convention (UNC) 611
Update Delivery Optimization 501
updates
    dealing with glitchy ones 496–499
    delaying 499–500
    installing 500–502
    preventing automatic updates 499
    Windows 10 system 495–502
upgrading to Windows 10 623–634
    clean installs 631–634
    two methods 624–634

USB
    hubs 484
    jacks 484
USB printers
    installing 467–469
User Account Control (UAC) 580–582
    turning off 582
user accounts. *See* **accounts**
Users folder 138–140

V

versions
    dual booting 630
    that qualify for free upgrades 624
VGA ports 485
video
    Cast to Device 62
videos
    attaching in Mail 410–411
    in News app 328
    Movies & TV app 323–325
    of Xbox games 363–364
Videos folder 141
views
    Content view 83
    Details view 81–82
    List view 81
    sorting files 84
    Tiles view 82
View tab
    in File Explorer 61
virtual private networks 456–459
    connecting to 458
    security 430–431
    settings 458–459
    setting up 457–458
virtual screens 193–194
    creating 193
    deleting 194
    settings 260
    switching among 194
viruses. *See also* **security**
    scanning for 418–419
Voice Recorder app 351–353
    controls 353
    finding recordings on computer 353
    trimming ends of recording 353
volume 103
volumes
    defined 535

W

wallpaper. *See* **background**
weather
    checking with Cortana 204

Weather app 353, 353–366
Web. *See also* Edge browser, Internet
 searching with Cortana 211
Web Notes. *See* Markup feature
Web pages
 parental controls 432–436
 printing 397
 sharing 396–397
 viewing with Reader 395–396
Web Publishing Wizard 639
what's new in Windows 10 1–8
 3D Cities feature 318–319
 Action Center 113–117
 Assigned Access (kiosk mode) 562
 automatic photo albums 338–339
 Battery Saver feature 441–443
 better handwriting recognition 449
 continuous updates 495–502
 Cortana 195–220
 Cortana Search 119–124
 face recognition 571–572
 fingerprint and iris recognition 572
 Money app 322–323
 Movies & TV app 323–325
 new file recovery tool 530–531
 new Settings app 257–259
 OneNote 329–331
 Phone Companion app 337
 Photos app 337–345
 print to PDF 479–480
 Quick access list 68–71
 Quiet Hours 112–113
 return of the system tray 102
 save locations 232
 Security and Maintenance applet 285
 settings for external drives 261
 Sleep/Shut Down/Restart commands 39–40
 snap windows into four panels 54–55
 Start menu 22–37
 Storage view 534–536
 swipe actions in Mail 412
 taskbar search box 41
 Task View 226–228
 unified app design 291–293
 universal apps 224
 virtual screens 193–194
 Web-based parental controls 432
 Web page markup 391–393
 WiFi Sense 376–379
 Windows SmartScreen 423–425
 Xbox app 360–364
WiDi (wireless display) 190
WiFi
 commercial hotspots 372
 connecting to a network 370–373

 downsides 590
 hotspot security 430–431
 MAC address filtering 431
 memorized hotspots 372–373
 networking equipment 589
 networks 589–590
 router placement 432
 router settings 431–432
 secret hotspots 372
 troubleshooting 370–372
 WiFi Sense 376–379
WiFi Sense 376–379
 defined 376–377
 sharing a hotspot 378–379
 turning on and off 378
windows. *See also* File Explorer, folders
 address bar 63–66
 button groups 94–96
 cascading 96
 closing 49
 Control menu 46
 controls 63–66
 Details pane 68
 edges 47
 elements of 45–47
 hiding 96
 layering 51–52
 maximizing 47, 48
 minimizing 48–49
 minimizing by shaking 50–51
 moving 49
 parts of 46–47
 Quick Access toolbar 46–47
 restored 49
 searching 124–130
 Show window contents while dragging 186
 side by side 53
 Snap 52–55
 snapping to full height 56
 title bar 47
Windows 7
 dual booting with Windows 10 630
Windows 8
 dual booting with Windows 10 630
 mistakes were made 1
 two types of programs 224–225
Windows 10
 accounts 553
 activation 270
 Control Panel 270–289
 Cortana 195–220
 defined 11
 discontinued features 635–640
 editions 8
 folders 137–142

free upgrades 624
hardware requirements 623
icons 145–151
installing and upgrading to 623–634
laptops 441–466
maintenance 495–516
preinstalled apps 291–365
searching 119–137
tablets 441–466
taskbar 92–98
turning off the new look 185–187
unified app design 291–293
Windows To Go 454–455
Windows Backup and Restore 518
Windows CardSpace 636
Windows Defender 417–419
definitions files 417–418
on-demand scanning 418–419
quarantining software 419
rival programs 419
spyware vs. adware 416
Windows DVD Maker 639
Windows Explorer. *See* **File Explorer**
Windows Firewall 420–423
allowing programs through 422
defined 420
how it works 420–421
use with other firewalls 422
with Advanced Security 422–423
Windows folder 140
Windows Hello 571–572
face recognition 571–572
fingerprint and iris recognition 572
Windows Journal app 355–357
exporting files 357
handwriting recognition 356–357
sketching 357
Windows Live Mesh 639, 640
Windows Media Player 358–365
alternatives 358
Windows Mobility Center 289
Windows Picture and Fax Viewer 640
Windows PowerShell 58–59, 358
Windows Recovery Environment 510–514
Windows SmartScreen 423–425
settings 424–425
Windows Store 249–251
advantages of 249
apps vs. desktop programs 224–225
automatic updates 250–251
downloading apps 249–250
navigating 250
Windows To Go 454–455
compatible flash drives 454
Windows Ultimate Extras 640

Windows Update 495–502
delaying updates 499–500
fixing glitchy updates 496–499
patches 496
preventing automatic updates 499
Windows Update Delivery Optimization 501
Windows XP Mode 256
wizards
Add Hardware 486
compatibility 253–254
Update Device Driver 490
WordPad 358–360
defined 358
find and replace 359
formatting text 359–360
word processing
keyboard shortcuts 645
WordPad 358–360
workgroup networks
Ethernet 586–589
Ethernet cables 588
hooking up 588–589
kinds 586–591
phone line networks 591
power outlet networks 591
WiFi 589–590

X

Xbox app 360–364
Cast to Device command 62–63
game streaming 362–363
recording gameplay video 363–364
screenshots and game DVR 363–364
Xbox Music 640
Xbox Video 640
XP Mode 640
XPS Viewer 364–365

Y

Yahoo accounts 401

Z

zipped files and folders
creating 169–172
defined 169
passwords 638
working with 170–171
zipping
Zip button on Ribbon 61
zooming in and out
Magnifier app 312–313
photos 340

Colophon

The book was written and edited in Microsoft Word, whose revision-tracking feature made life far easier as drafts were circulated from author to technical and copy editors. The steps in this book were tested on machines from HP, Toshiba, and Apple. (That's right: Apple. You can't believe how fast Windows 10 runs under the Parallels emulator [virtual machine], on a MacBook Air.)

Snagit (*www.techsmith.com*) captured the illustrations; Adobe Photoshop CC and Illustrator CC were called in as required for touching them up.

The book was designed and laid out in Adobe InDesign CC 2015 on a homemade PC. The fonts used include Formata (as the sans-serif family) and Minion (as the serif body face). To provide symbols like ■, Phil Simpson designed several custom fonts using FontLab Fontographer.

The book was generated as an Adobe Acrobat PDF file for proofreading and indexing, and final transmission to the printing plant.

Windows 10

THE MISSING CD

There's no
CD with this book;
you just saved $5.00.

Instead, every single Web address, practice file, and
piece of downloadable software mentioned in this
book is available at *missingmanuals.com*
(click the Missing CD icon).
There you'll find a tidy list of links,
organized by chapter.

CPSIA information can be obtained at www.ICGtesting.com
Printed in the USA
BVOW11s0150241215

430942BV00003B/3/P

31901056587126